lonely planet

New England

Maine
p364

Vermont
p276

New
Hampshire
p322

Central Massachusetts
& the Berkshires
p178

Around Boston p100
Boston p48

Connecticut
p240

Rhode
Island
p209

Cape Cod, Nantucket
& Martha's Vineyard
p132

Benedict Walker,

Isabel Albiston, Amy C Balfour, Robert Balkovich, Gregor Clark,

Adam Karlin, Brian Kluepfel, Regis St Louis, Mara Vorhees

Contents

PLAN YOUR TRIP

Welcome to
New England 6

New England Map 8

New England's Top
Experiences 10

Need to Know 24

Accommodations 26

Month by Month 28

Itineraries 32

Outdoor Activities 40

Regions at a Glance 44

ON THE ROAD

BOSTON 48

AROUND BOSTON . . 100
West of Boston 103
Lexington 103
Concord 104
Lowell 108
North Shore 110
Salem 110
Gloucester 115
Rockport 119
Ipswich & Essex 120
Newburyport 122
South Shore 124
Quincy 124

Plymouth 125
New Bedford 130

**CAPE COD, NANTUCKET
& MARTHA'S
VINEYARD 132**
Cape Cod 134
Sandwich 134
Falmouth 135
Hyannis 138
Yarmouth 141
Dennis 142
Brewster 144
Harwich 145
Chatham 146

LOBSTER ROLL, MAINE

FREEDOM TRAIL, BOSTON
P57

Contents

Orleans.................148
Eastham................149
Wellfleet...............151
Truro..................153
Provincetown..........154
Nantucket & Around .. 160
Nantucket Town........161
Siasconset............167
South Shore...........168
Martha's Vineyard 169
Vineyard Haven........169
Oak Bluffs.............172
Edgartown.............174
West Tisbury..........175
Aquinnah..............176

**CENTRAL
MASSACHUSETTS &
THE BERKSHIRES...178**
**Central
Massachusetts.......180**
Worcester.............180
Sturbridge............181
Pioneer Valley........183
Springfield............183
Northampton..........187
Amherst...............190
Shelburne Falls........192
The Berkshires.......193
Great Barrington
& Around..............194
Stockbridge...........197
Lee...................198
Lenox.................199
Pittsfield..............202
Williamstown..........203
North Adams..........205
Mt Greylock State
Reservation...........207

RHODE ISLAND ... 209
Providence...........212
**Blackstone
River Valley..........219**
Woonsocket...........219
East Bay.............221
Bristol................221
Tiverton..............222
Little Compton........223
Newport.............223
**Jamestown
& Conanicut Island ... 232**
**Southern
Rhode Island........233**
Narragansett
& Point Judith.........233
Westerly & Watch Hill ...234
Block Island.........235

CONNECTICUT 240
Hartford.............241
**Connecticut
River Valley..........249**
East Haddam..........249
Chester...............251
Essex.................251
Old Lyme.............252
**Southeastern
Connecticut..........253**
New London...........253
Mystic................255
Stonington............259
The Quiet Corner.....260
New Haven...........261
Gold Coast...........267
Westport..............268
Ridgefield.............269
Housatonic Valley.....270
Candlewood Lake......270
Litchfield Hills.........271

VERMONT 276
Southern Vermont 278
Brattleboro............278
Wilmington............281
Bennington............282
Manchester...........285
Dorset................289
Central Vermont......289
Woodstock
& Quechee Village......289
Killington Mountain.....293
Middlebury............295
Mad River Valley.......298
Northern Vermont 300
Burlington.............301
Stowe &
Smugglers Notch.......310
Montpelier............316
Northeast Kingdom.....318

PORTSMOUTH P324

ON THE ROAD

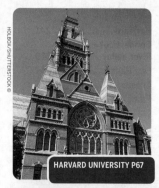

HARVARD UNIVERSITY P67

NEW HAMPSHIRE 322

New Hampshire Coast............... 324
Portsmouth............324
Rye &
Hampton Beach 330
Merrimack Valley 331
Concord...............331
Manchester...........332
Monadnock Region....334
Peterborough 334

Jaffrey Center..........336
Keene.................337
Upper Connecticut River Valley 338
Hanover...............338
Lakes Region.........340
Meredith 341
Squam Lake 342
Wolfeboro 343
Weirs Beach &
Laconia 345
White Mountains 346

APPALACHIAN TRAIL, VERMONT P41

Contents

North Woodstock
& Lincoln 347
Kancamagus Highway . . . 350
Franconia Notch
State Park 351
Littleton & Franconia 353
Mt Washington Valley . . . 354

MAINE 364

**Southern
Maine Coast** 367
The Yorks 367
Ogunquit 369
The Kennebunks 370
Saco Bay &
Old Orchard Beach 372
Portland 373
Midcoast Maine 380
Brunswick 380
Boothbay Harbor 382
Damariscotta 383
Pemaquid Point 384
Monhegan Island 385

Rockland 386
Camden 387
Rockport 388
Belfast 389
Inland Maine 390
Bangor 390
Augusta 391
Sabbathday Lake
& Poland Spring 392
Down East 393
Deer Isle &
Stonington 394
Mount Desert Island . . 395
Bar Harbor 395
Acadia National Park 397
Cranberry Isles 400
Machias Bay Area 401
Western Maine 402
Bethel 402
Rangeley Lake 403
North Maine Woods . . . 404
Baxter State Park 404
Moosehead Lake 405

History 408
New England
Literature 417
Universities
& Colleges 421

Directory A–Z 426
Transportation 431
Index 438
Map Legend 446

COVID-19

We have re-checked every business in this book before publication to ensure that it is still open after the COVID-19 outbreak. However, the economic and social impacts of COVID-19 will continue to be felt long after the outbreak has been contained, and many businesses, services and events referenced in this guide may experience ongoing restrictions. Some businesses may be temporarily closed, have changed their opening hours and services, or require bookings; some unfortunately could have closed permanently. We suggest you check with venues before visiting for the latest information.

Accommodations 26
Outdoor
Activities 40
New England
Literature 417
Universities
& Colleges 421

Right: Acadia
National Park
(p397)

BLUESKY2U/SHUTTERSTOCK ©

WELCOME TO

New England

My fondness for New England is deeply rooted in childhood memories – skating on frozen Connecticut ponds and seeing my first shooting star in Vermont's Green Mountains. Decades later, New England's natural beauty still moves me: fireflies on a June evening; the brilliance of maples, birches and cranberry bogs in fall; fresh snow clinging to February branches; and the sudden explosion of greenery after each long winter. I also love New England's cultural vibrancy: its arts scene, historical treasures, organic farms, dynamic cities, progressive politics and Red Sox games at Fenway Park.

By Gregor Clark, Writer

For more about our writers, see p448

New England

Acadia National Park
Where the mountains meet the sea (p397)

Mt Katahdin
Northern terminus of the Appalachian Trail (p405)

Burlington
Lively university town on Lake Champlain (p301)

White Mountains
Outdoor adventure and inspiring landscape (p346)

ROAD DISTANCES (miles)
Note: Distances are approximate

	Bar Harbor, ME	Boston, MA	Burlington, VT	Hartford, CT	Portsmouth, NH	Providence, RI
Boston, MA	285					
Burlington, VT	335	215				
Hartford, CT	375	100	235			
Portsmouth, NH	230	60	210	150		
Providence, RI	335	50	265	90	110	
Provincetown, MA	400	115	330	205	175	120

Map labels

QUÉBEC

St Lawrence River

Montmagny

Québec City

CANADA
USA

Montréal

ONTARIO

Massena

Malone

Saranac Lake

Lake Placid

Lake Champlain

Montpelier

St Albans

Burlington

Middlebury

Stowe

Mt Mansfield (4393ft)

VERMONT

Berlin

North Conway

White Mountain National Forest

Franconia Notch State Park

Sherbrooke

Drummondville

Victoriaville

NEW BRUNSWICK

Edmundston

Grand Falls

St John River

Fort Kent

Van Buren

Caribou

Presque Isle

Florenceville

Woodstock

Fredericton

St Stephen

Eastport

Grand Manan Island

Houlton

Lincoln

Bangor

Ellsworth

Bar Harbor

Acadia National Park

Belfast

Penobscot Bay

Camden

Rockland

Waterville

Pittsfield

Augusta

Kennebec River

MAINE

Chamberlain Lake

Allagash River

Mt Katahdin (5267ft)

Millinocket

Moosehead Lake

West Grand Lake

Flagstaff Lake

Rangeley Lake

Appalachian Trail

45°N

44°N

100 miles
200 km

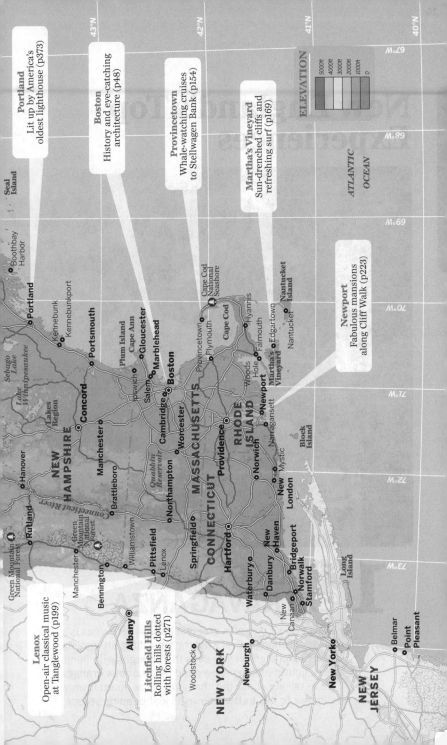

New England's Top Experiences

Portland
Lit up by America's oldest lighthouse (p373)

Boston
History and eye-catching architecture (p48)

Provincetown
Whale-watching cruises to Stellwagen Bank (p154)

Martha's Vineyard
Sun-drenched cliffs and refreshing surf (p169)

Newport
Fabulous mansions along Cliff Walk (p223)

Lenox
Open-air classical music at Tanglewood (p199)

Litchfield Hills
Rolling hills dotted with forests (p271)

ELEVATION

5000ft
4000ft
3000ft
2000ft
1000ft
0

ATLANTIC OCEAN

Seal Island

Boothbay Harbor

Portland

Kennebunk
Kennebunkport

Sebago Lake

Lake Winnipesaukee

Lakes Region

Concord

NEW HAMPSHIRE

Manchester

Hanover

Rutland

Brattleboro

Green Mountain National Forest

Manchester

Bennington

Williamstown

Pittsfield
Lenox

Northampton

Springfield

MASSACHUSETTS

Quabbin Reservoir

Worcester

Cambridge
Boston

Marblehead
Gloucester
Cape Ann
Plum Island
Ipswich
Salem

Portsmouth

Portland

Provincetown

Cape Cod National Seashore

Plymouth

Hyannis

Cape Cod

Falmouth
Woods Hole

Martha's Vineyard
Edgartown

Nantucket

Nantucket Island

CONNECTICUT

Hartford

Waterbury

Danbury

New Haven
Bridgeport
Norwalk
Stamford
New Canaan

RHODE ISLAND

Providence

Norwich

Narragansett
Newport

New London

Mystic

Block Island

Long Island

Albany

Woodstock

NEW YORK

Newburgh

New York

NEW JERSEY

Belmar
Point Pleasant

Connecticut River

Green Mountain National Forest

New England's Top Experiences

1 FALL FOLIAGE EXTRAVAGANZA

One of New England's greatest natural resources is seasonal change. Every fall the trees fling off that staid New England green and deck their boughs with flaming reds, light-bending yellows and ostentatious oranges. We're talking about the changing of the guard from summer to fall, better known as leaf-peeping season.

VT 100

Vermont is the star of the fall foliage show. Drive north on historic Rte 100 to ogle the array of colors on the slopes of Killington Peak and Mt Mansfield, and among the bucolic hills of the Mad River Valley. p294

Left: Mt Mansfield (p294); Right: Stowe (p310)

Kancamagus Highway

Rivers and forests hug the road on this scenic cruise through New Hampshire's White Mountains (fondly known as 'the Kanc'). Along the way are opportunities galore to pull over for a hike, a picnic or a panoramic view. p350

Above: Covered bridge, Kancamagus Highway

Mohawk Trail

Massachusetts' top fall foliage route is MA 2, winding ever upward from Central Massachusetts west through the beautiful Berkshires. The 63-mile scenic byway shows off raging rivers, idyllic farms and forest-covered hillsides. Drivers beware: it's practically impossible to keep your eyes on the road. p193

Above: Mohawk Trail, near Williamstown (p203)

11

2 NEW ENGLAND'S CORNUCOPIA

As a rule, when in New England, one should eat as much lobster as possible. But there's more to life than seafood. New England is also the home of the first Thanksgiving and of bountiful autumnal harvests, of organic growers and creative culinary artisans. Eat and drink your way across the region and sample the thriving 'locavore' movement, which highlights the bounty of local waters and New England farms.

Lobster Trap

The mighty lobster was once so plentiful it was fed to prisoners; now the Maine state symbol is rightfully esteemed as a delicacy. Crack the shell of a freshly steamed lobster with drawn butter at one of the many summertime lobster pounds.  p368

Below: Lobsters, Maine

Cheers to Craft Beer

The craft brewing revolution is sweeping New England, from Trillium Brewing Co on a buzzing roof-deck in downtown Boston to Hill Farmstead Brewery on a lonely dirt road in rural Vermont. Sample dozens of the local elixirs at the annual Vermont Brewers Festival in Burlington. p304

Top left: Flight of craft beers

Farm Fresh

Relish the bounty. Buy (or pick!) apples, berries and pumpkins straight from the farm; indulge in the sweet flavor of maple syrup from the local 'sugarbush'; or sample the creamy delights from Vermont's artisanal cheese producers. p282

Top right: Apple picking, Great Barrington (p194)

MATXDAVEY/SHUTTERSTOCK ©

NICOLAS EMERY/GETTY IMAGES ©

DANIEL GRILL/GETTY IMAGES ©

3 APPALACHIAN MOUNTAIN MAJESTY

Nothing defines New England's landscape like the Appalachian Mountains, an ancient range of rounded peaks, blanketed with forest, sprinkled with idyllic towns and busting with rural charm. With tree-covered hills in the lower states, and higher, rocky crests up north, the diversity of landscapes offers a multitude of mountain adventures.

Appalachian Trail

The Appalachian Trail runs more than 2100 miles from Georgia to Maine, passing through 14 states en route. If anyone is counting, 730 of those miles are in New England, creating ample opportunities for hikers to tackle a piece of it. p41

Left: Appalachian Trail, Maine

White Mountains

These are New England's ultimate destination for outdoor adventures, with 1200 miles of hiking trails and 48 peaks over 4000ft. Franconia Notch is a perfect starting point, with hiking routes, an aerial tramway, and the spectacular Flume Gorge. p350

Top right: Flume Gorge

Litchfield Hills

Here's an unheralded destination with scenery to rival the prettiest mountain range, pre-Colonial villages worthy of a movie set, and the finest food, culture and music in Connecticut. p271

Bottom right: Litchfield Hills

4 HISTORY LESSON

With 400 years of recorded history, New England is rich with stories of action, adventure and intellectual advancement. The region's living museums and historic sites allow travelers to experience firsthand what it was like in the olden days – from the earliest settlers who (might have) landed at Plymouth Rock, to revolutionary heroes who fought for American Independence, to the glamorous capitalists of the Gilded Age.

Plimoth Patuxet Museums

Five fantastic museums exhibit various aspects of life in 17th-century New England, starting with the Pilgrims' journey to the New World on the *Mayflower*. The English Village is a historically accurate re-creation of their early settlement, while Historic Patuxet teaches about the region's native Wampanoag peoples. p126

Above: 1627 English Village re-creation

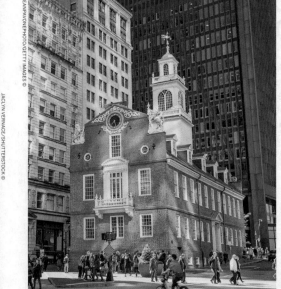

SEANPAVONEPHOTO/GETTY IMAGES ©

JACLYN VERNACE/SHUTTERSTOCK ©

Freedom Trail

Get an introduction to revolutionary Boston on the Freedom Trail. This walking trail winds its way past 16 sites that earned the town its status as the cradle of liberty. Follow the red-brick road through American revolutionary history, from the Boston Common to Bunker Hill. p57

Left: Old State House (p54); Bottom left: Sailor dressed in 1812 uniform, USS *Constitution* (p58)

Mansions of Newport

Offering a glimpse into a world of unabashed wealth, Newport's fabulous mansions are vestiges of the 19th-century capitalist boom, when the region's bankers and businesspeople built summer homes overlooking the Atlantic. See them all from the Cliff Walk, a footpath that snakes along the ocean's edge. p229

Below: The Breakers (p224), Newport

JOSEPH SOHM/SHUTTERSTOCK ©

BODHICHITA/SHUTTERSTOCK ©

5 OCEAN ADVENTURES

With 569 miles of coastline, New England offers countless opportunities to get out on the open ocean. Feel the breeze through your hair and the spray on your face as you sail the high seas, or climb aboard a cruise ship to spot some of the amazing marine mammals and birds that inhabit these waters.

Sailing Penobscot Bay

Explore the rugged coast of Maine the old-fashioned way – on board one of the grand, multi-masted windjammers that fill the harbors of Camden and Rockport. These majestic sailing ships offer cruises around the islands and coves of Penobscot Bay, all under the power of the wind. p387

Below: Windjammer, Penobscot Bay

BRYCE FLYNN/GETTY IMAGES ©

Whale Watching

Nothing matches the thrill of spotting a breaching humpback or watching a pod of dolphins play in a boat's wake. Catch them off the coast of Massachusetts at Stellwagen Bank, a national marine sanctuary that's rich in marine life. Educational and informative whale-watching cruises embark from Boston, Plymouth, Provincetown and Gloucester. p116

Above: Breaching humpback whale, Stellwagen Bank National Marine Sanctuary; Right: short-beaked common dolphin

6 EXPLORE ACADIA NATIONAL PARK

MANDRITOIU/SHUTTERSTOCK ©

WARREN PRICE PHOTOGRAPHY/SHUTTERSTOCK ©

ETHAN DANIELS/SHUTTERSTOCK ©

Acadia National Park is where the mountains meet the sea. Miles of rocky coastline and even more miles of hiking and biking trails make this wonderland Maine's most popular destination, and deservedly so. Acadia has something for everyone – challenging climbing trails for hardcore adventurers and civilized tea houses for the more epicurean traveler. Even the imposing Cadillac Mountain is accessible to all.

Cadillac Mountain

The high point of Acadia (literally) is Cadillac Mountain, a 1530ft peak that can be accessed by foot, bike or vehicle. Early risers can catch the country's first sunrise from this celebrated summit. p398
Above: Cadillac Mountain

Jordan Pond House

Stroll around scenic Jordan Pond, then stop for tea at the eponymous Pond House. Steaming pots of Earl Grey come with hot popovers and jam. Eat on the lawn overlooking the lake. p399

Ladder Trails

To get a bird's-eye view of Acadia, climb up to where the birds are. Precipice Trail and Beehive Loop are two 'ladder trails' that cling to the sides of exposed cliffs. p398

7 BEACHY KEEN

Summer in New England is hot and humid, so it's no surprise that the region's entire population flocks to the coast for cool breezes and brisk waters. Fortunately it's a long coast, with enticing beaches in every state, whether you're into surfing or sunbathing, beachcombing or birdwatching. Just be warned: this is the North Atlantic we are talking about and the water is super chill.

FRANKVANDENBERGH/GETTY IMAGES ©

KATKAMI/SHUTTERSTOCK ©

Cape Cod National Seashore

The outer Cape is lined with 40 miles of pristine seashore, backed by sand dunes and criss-crossed by hiking and biking trails. p150

Top left: Salt marsh, Cape Cod National Seashore

Martha's Vineyard

Ringed by vast stretches of sand, the Vineyard is pure beachy bliss. Head to Katama for surfing and swimming; or stop to soak in the dramatic view of the multi-hued Aquinnah Cliffs. p169

Bottom left: Aquinnah Cliffs (p176)

Southern Maine Coast

This coast offers family-friendly beaches with soft sand and gentle surf. Walk at Old Orchard Beach or relish the nature at Ogunquit Beach. p367

Above: Marginal Way, Ogunquit (p369)

8 SUMMER FESTIVALS

T PHOTOGRAPHY/SHUTTERSTOCK ©

JON DAVISON/LONELY PLANET ©

CARL BEUST/SHUTTERSTOCK ©

The Berkshires

Come summer, culture beckons in the Berkshires. Hear great musicians of every stripe at the Tanglewood Music Festival in Lenox. Nearby, the Williamstown Theatre Festival and Jacob's Pillow offer equally compelling summer celebrations of theater and dance. p193
Top: Tanglewood Music Festival (p201)

Newport Music Festivals

Newport's summer cultural calendar is packed, with three renowned music festivals that bring together top-notch classical, folk and jazz performances. p228
Bottom: Kamasi Washington performs at the Newport Jazz Festival

Bread & Puppets

The beloved Bread & Puppet theater summers in the Northeast Kingdom of Vermont. See the summer circus extravaganza on weekends in July and August. p318

New Englanders know how to make the most of their (short) summers. One seasonal highlight is the summer festivals that take place throughout the region, offering top-notch music, theater and dance in delightful outdoor settings. Spread a blanket on the lawn, uncork a bottle of wine and enjoy the show under New England summer skies.

9 COLLEGE TOWNS, USA

From the Five Colleges to the Seven Sisters (well, four of them), New England is crowded with colleges and overrun with universities, making for a dynamic, diverse student scene. Every college – and college town – has a different vibe: some are urban, while others are rural; some have period architecture, while others are modern. But they all benefit from a youthful population, myriad entertainment options and an indefinable creative energy.

Pioneer Valley

Five schools populate three quaint college towns along the Connecticut River. Each has its own particular charm, from distinguished Amherst, to bustling Northampton, to picture-perfect South Hadley. p187
Below: Mount Holyoke College (p188)

WANGKUN JIA/SHUTTERSTOCK ©

Harvard Square

Harvard Sq is overflowing with bookstores and boutiques, coffee shops and record shops, street performers and street dwellers – with the Harvard Yard as its centerpiece. p67
Above: Harvard Square

New Haven

The USA's third oldest university is Gothic Yale University, with surrounding streets filled with affordable eateries and cool music cafes, as well as excellent art museums. p261
Right: Decorative iron gate at Yale, crafted by Samuel Yellin

10 LAKESIDE LIVING

KONOPLYTSKA/SHUTTERSTOCK ©

FENG CHENG/SHUTTERSTOCK ©

SANDRA LEIDHOLDT/GETTY IMAGES ©

Freshwater lakes are oft overlooked among New England's many attractions. Sparkling crystalline blue and nestled into tree-lined shores, these are the region's unheralded gems. Flat waters and warm temperatures are perfect for swimming, sailing and kayaking, while lakeside trails invite hiking, biking and more. Lose the crowds and find your bliss at one of Mother Nature's swimming pools.

Lake Champlain

Burlington offers a very civilized way to enjoy the delights of Lake Champlain. Right downtown, its inviting waterfront is a convenient launching pad for swimming or sailing, biking or boating. p301

Lake Winnipesaukee

In summer, families flock to Lake Winnipesaukee in New Hampshire for warm-weather fun – swimming, sailing, playing miniature golf, watching for local wildlife or catching a drive-in movie at Weirs Beach. p340

Above: Lake Winnipesaukee

Rangeley Lakes

Forest-cloaked mountains surround six lakes in western Maine, offering spectacular scenery and epic adventures in every season. Relish the great outdoors as you hike or bike, snowshoe or ski on 40 miles of lakeside trails at Rangely Lakes Trails Center. p404

Need to Know

For more information, see Survival Guide (p425)

Currency
US dollar ($)

Language
English

Visas
Citizens of many countries are eligible for the Visa Waiver Program, which requires prior approval via the Electronic System for Travel Authorization (ESTA).

Money
ATMs are widely available, except in the smallest towns and most remote wilderness. Credit cards are accepted at most hotels and restaurants.

Cell Phones
Most modern quad-band smartphones are compatible with US cell networks, but international roaming charges can cause nasty surprises when you receive your next bill. If your phone is unlocked, buy a pre-paid SIM in the USA.

Time
Eastern Standard Time (GMT/UTC minus five hours)

When to Go

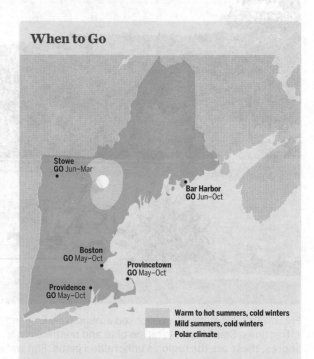

Stowe
GO Jun–Mar

Bar Harbor
GO Jun–Oct

Boston
GO May–Oct

Provincetown
GO May–Oct

Providence
GO May–Oct

Warm to hot summers, cold winters
Mild summers, cold winters
Polar climate

High Season
(May–Oct)

➡ Accommodation prices increase by 50% to 100%; book in advance.

➡ May has temperate spring weather and blooming fruit trees. July and August are hot and humid.

➡ September and October bring harvest season and cooler weather.

Shoulder
(Mar–Apr)

➡ Weather remains wintry throughout March; April sees some sunshine and spring buds.

➡ Less demand for accommodations; negotiate lower prices (also applies to beach areas in May and early June).

Low Season
(Nov–Feb)

➡ With snow comes ski season (usually from December onward), meaning higher prices in mountain resorts.

➡ Significantly lower prices for accommodations elsewhere.

➡ Some sights in seasonal destinations close.

Useful Websites

Appalachian Mountain Club (www.outdoors.org) Fantastic resource for hiking, biking, camping, climbing and paddling in New England's great outdoors.

Boston.com (www.boston.com/tags/new-england-travel) Travel news, tips and itineraries from the *Boston Globe*.

Lonely Planet (www.lonely planet.com/usa/new-england) Destination information, hotel reviews and more.

New England Network (www.newengland.com) New England travel resources from *Yankee Magazine*.

Important Numbers

USA country code	☑1
International access code from the USA	☑011 + country code
Emergency	☑911
Local directory	☑411

Exchange Rates

Australia	A$1	$0.72
Canada	C$1	$0.78
Euro zone	€1	$1.12
Japan	¥100	$0.87
New Zealand	NZ$1	$0.67
UK	UK£1	$1.34

For current exchange rates see www.xe.com.

Daily Costs

Budget: Less than $150

➡ Camping, dorm bed or budget hotel: $30–100

➡ Bus ticket: $10–20

➡ Street food: mains $8–12

➡ NPS walking tours and free-admission days at museums: free

Midrange: $150–300

➡ Double room in a midrange hotel: $100–250

➡ Car rental for a portion of the trip: from $30 per day

➡ Admission to museums and parks: $10–20

Top End: More than $300

➡ Double room in a high-end hotel: from $250

➡ Meal at the region's finest restaurants: mains from $25

➡ Tickets to concerts, events and tours: $30–100

Opening Hours

The following is a general guideline for opening hours. Shorter hours may apply during low seasons, when some venues close completely. Seasonal variations are noted in the listings.

Banks and offices 9am–5pm or 6pm Monday to Friday; sometimes 9am–noon Saturday

Bars and pubs 5pm–midnight, some until 2am

Restaurants Breakfast 6am–10am, lunch 11:30am–2:30pm, dinner 5pm–10pm daily

Shops 9am–7pm Monday to Saturday; some open noon–5pm Sunday, or until evening in tourist areas

Arriving in New England

Logan International Airport (Boston, MA; p431) The T (subway, $2.75) and the free silver line bus connect Logan airport to the city center from 5:30am to 2:30am; a taxi costs $25 to $35 and takes about 20 minutes.

Bradley International Airport (Hartford, CT; p431) The Bradley Flyer bus runs to the city center ($1.75, 30 to 40 minutes) roughly hourly from 4:45am to midnight; a taxi costs $45 and takes about 20 minutes.

Getting Around

Simply put, the best way to get around New England is by car. The region is relatively small, the highways are good and public transportation is not as frequent or as widespread as it could be.

Car The most convenient option for seeing rural New England, exploring small towns and partaking of outdoor adventure. Driving and parking can be a challenge in Boston.

Train Amtrak's main line travels up and down the Northeast Corridor, connecting Boston to Portland, ME, Providence, RI, New Haven, CT and other coastal destinations. Two other inland routes serve Connecticut and Vermont.

Bus Regional bus lines connect bigger towns throughout New England. While less comfortable and scenic than trains, buses serve more destinations and are almost always the most economical form of public transportation.

For much more on **getting around**, see p433

Accommodations

Find more reviews of accommodations throughout the On the Road chapters (from p48)

New England provides an array of accommodations, but truly inexpensive options are rare. Reservations are recommended, especially in high season.

Accommodation Types

B&Bs Intimate, family-run guesthouses often in historic or architecturally interesting homes.

Campgrounds The most basic have bathing facilities and electricity/water hookups, while others offer more extensive recreational facilities.

Hotels Includes run-of-the-mill chains, historic properties and stylish boutique options.

Roadside motels What they lack in style, they make up for in convenience and cost.

Hostels Typically feature a mix of dorms and private rooms and budget-friendly pricing.

Best Places to Stay

Hostels

The Notch Hostel (p349) Welcoming, hiker-friendly hostel with a world of outdoor adventure right out the front door.

Black Elephant Hostel (p377) Artfully decorated, community-focused hostel in a perfect Portland, ME setting.

HI-Boston (p79) Smack in the heart of Boston, with tours and activities galore.

Old Schoolhouse of Isle La Motte (p304) Cyclist-friendly converted schoolhouse on a Lake Champlain island.

Campgrounds

Jamaica State Park (p291) Fall asleep to the sound of rushing water at this southern Vermont beauty.

Hancock Campground (p351) The boulder-strewn Pemigewasset River is your backdrop at this campground on New Hampshire's scenic Kancamagus Hwy.

October Mountain State Forest Campground (p199) Tree-shaded sites and yurts near the banks of the Housatonic River.

Historic Inns

Inn at Shelburne Farms (p305) A 1400-acre estate and National Historic Landmark featuring afternoon tea and gorgeous carriage roads.

PRICE RANGES

The following price ranges refer to a double room with bathroom in high season. Unless otherwise indicated, breakfast is not included. Rates do not include taxes, which cost 5.7% to 15% depending on the state. Note that prices are higher in Boston.

CATEGORY	COST
$	less than $150 ($200 in Boston)
$$	$150–250 ($200–350 in Boston)
$$$	more than $250 ($350 in Boston)

Pentagöet Inn (p401) A Castine, ME, jewel, with a great restaurant and one of the most intriguingly decorated bars on the planet.

Castle Hill Inn (p230) Victorian mansion on 40 acres overlooking Narragansett Bay, RI, with cottages at the water's edge.

Goodwin (p246) A 19th-century gem in downtown Hartford, CT.

Luxury Lodgings

Guest House at Field Farm (p204) Gaze out over the Berkshires from this Bauhaus-style beauty on 300 bucolic acres.

Snowflake Inn (p357) Luxuriate with in-room fireplaces and an on-site spa after a day in the White Mountains.

Grafton Inn (p286) Watch the world from a front-porch rocker in one of Vermont's prettiest villages.

Gryphon House (p80) A Richardson Romanesque-style brownstone replete with 19th-century period details, overlooking Boston's Charles River.

The Chanler at Cliff Walk (p230) A true upper-class destination hotel, at the start of Newport's famous Cliff Walk.

Ocean House (p235) Perched high on Watch Hill, overlooking the mighty Atlantic.

JON LOVETTE/GETTY IMAGES ©

Pentagöet Inn (p401), Castine

Tips for...

Budget Travelers

Hosteling isn't as well developed in New England as it is in other parts of the world. But some prime destinations – including Boston, Portland, Burlington, Cape Cod, Bar Harbor, Martha's Vineyard, Nantucket and the mountains of New Hampshire and Vermont – have hostels from as little as $30 per night.

Happy Campers

With few exceptions, you'll have to camp in established campgrounds (there's no bivouacking on the side of the road). Make reservations well in advance (especially in July and August) for the best chance of getting a site. Most campgrounds are open from mid-May to mid-October. Rough camping is occasionally permitted in the Green Mountain National Forest or the White Mountain National Forest, but it must be at established sites.

Families

Children are not welcome at many smaller B&Bs and inns (even if they do not say so outright); make sure you inquire before booking. In motels and hotels, children under 17 or 18 years are usually free when sharing a room with their parents. Cots and roll-away beds are often available (sometimes for an additional fee) in hotels and resorts. Campgrounds are fantastic choices for families with kids – many are situated on waterways or lakes and offer family activities (tube rental, swimming, kayaking etc) and simple cabins.

Booking

It always pays to shop room rates online using sites such as kayak.com and expedia.com or booking.com.

Lonely Planet (lonelyplanet.com) Find independent reviews, as well as recommendations on the best places to stay.

B&B Agency of Boston (www.boston-bnbagency.com) Fully furnished vacation rentals.

Month by Month

TOP EVENTS

Boston Calling, May

Newport Folk Festival, July

Maine Lobster Festival, August

Foliage Season, October

Harvest on the Harbor, November

January

Most of New England is snowed in by January. That's good news for skiers, who are well into their season at this time.

February

The deepest, darkest part of winter; snow and cold temperatures continue. Many New Englanders retreat to warmer climes, making this an ideal time to enjoy the region's museums, restaurants, theaters and other indoor attractions.

🏃 Ski Season

Though the ski season extends from mid-December until the end of March, its peak is President's Day weekend (third weekend in February), when schools are closed for winter break. Book your accommodations well in advance if you plan to hit the slopes during this time.

March

New England is officially sick of winter. In Vermont and New Hampshire, ski season continues through to the end of the month.

🍴 Maple Syrup Tasting

Vermont's maple-sugar producers open the doors for two days in late March during Maple Open House Weekend (www.vermont maple.org/maple-open -house-weekend). Maine maple-syrup producers do the same on the fourth Sunday in March (www.maine mapleproducers.com/about -maine-maple-sunday).

April

Spring arrives, signaled by the emerging of crocuses and the blooming of forsythia. Baseball fans await Opening Day at Fenway Park. Temperatures range from 40°F (4°C) to 55°F (13°C), although the occasional snowstorm also occurs.

🏃 Boston Marathon

At the country's 'longest running' marathon, tens of thousands of spectators watch runners cross the finish line at Copley Sq in Boston on the third Monday in April. (p74)

May

The sun comes out on a semi-permanent basis, while lilac and magnolia trees bloom all around the region. Memorial Day, the last Monday in May, officially kicks off beach season.

☆ Boston Calling

Independent-music lovers take over a large outdoor Boston venue for three days of rock-out music. The festival (www.bostoncalling. com) occurs during the last weekend in May.

June

Temperatures range from 60°F (16°C) to 75°F (24°C), with lots of rain. After graduation, students leave

New Hampshire Pumpkin Festival (p31)

town, causing a noticeable decline in traffic and noise.

🎊 Celebration of Lupine

This little-known floral festival (www.facebook.com/LupineCelebration) in early June in Franconia, NH, celebrates the annual bloom of delicious lupine with garden tours, art exhibits and concerts.

☆ International Festival of Arts & Ideas

New Haven dedicates 15 days in June to dance, music, film and art. Besides the ticketed concerts and performances, there are free events, plus special programming for kids and families. (p264)

July

July is the region's hottest month and public beaches are invariably crowded. Temperatures usually range from 70°F (21°C) to 85°F (29°C), but there's always a week or two when the mercury shoots above 90°F (32°C).

🎊 Berkshires Arts Festivals

The Berkshires are alive with the arts throughout July and August. Hear world-class music in the open air at Tanglewood (p201) in Lenox, take in mesmerizing dance performances at Jacob's Pillow (p198) in Lee, or see top-notch theater productions at the Williamstown Theatre Festival (p204).

🎊 Mashpee Wampanoag Pow Wow

On the weekend nearest July 4, Native Americans from around the country join the Mashpee Wampanoag (www.mashpeewampanoagtribe-nsn.gov/powwow) for a big three-day heritage celebration in Mashpee, MA, that includes Native American dancing, crafts, competitions and an after-dark 'fireball' (a traditional healing ceremony).

🍷 Vermont Brewers Festival

The third weekend in July is dedicated to discussing beer, brewing beer and, of course, drinking beer, including Vermont's finest craft brews. (p304)

☆ North Atlantic Blues Festival

If you're feeling blue, go to Rockland, ME, in mid-July for the region's biggest blues festival (www.northatlanticbluesfestival.com). Nationally known performers and local-brewed beers guarantee a good time.

☆ Newport Folk Festival

One of the region's most exciting music events, this folk festival at Newport, RI, in late July attracts national stars, as well as new names, to perform all weekend long. (p228)

August

Summer continues unabated, with beaches packed to the gills. Only at the end of August do we begin to feel fall coming back on.

🍴 Maine Lobster Festival

If you love lobster like Maine loves lobster, come for the week-long Lobster Festival held in the first week in August in Rockland. King Neptune and the Sea Goddess oversee a week full of events and – of course – as much lobster as you can eat. (p387)

☆ Rhode Island International Film Festival

The region's largest public film festival, held in the second week of August in Providence, RI, attracts interesting independent films and sophisticated, film-savvy audiences. (p215)

🎊 Provincetown Carnival

Carnival in P-town, held in the third week in August, is a week of crazy dance parties and streets filled with beautiful boys in colorful costumes. (p428)

🍴 Machias Wild Blueberry Festival

Well into its fifth decade, this festival (www.machiasblueberry.com) includes pie-eating contests, cook-offs and hundreds of artisans hawking everything from blueberry jam to blueberry-themed artwork. Held on the third weekend in August.

September

The humidity disappears, leaving cooler temperatures and crisp air. Students return and streets are filled with

U-Hauls during the first week. The first Monday in September is Labor Day, the official end of summer.

☆ Big E

Officially known as the Eastern States Exposition, this fair in West Springfield, MA, in mid-September features animal shows, carnival rides, parades, concerts and more. (p185)

October

New England's best month. The academic year is rolling; the weather is crisp and cool; and the trees take on shades of red, gold and amber.

◉ Foliage Season

Witness Mother Nature at her most ostentatious. The colors all around the region are dazzling, but especially as they blanket the mountainsides in the Berkshires in Western Massachusetts, the Green Mountains in Vermont, and the White Mountains in New Hampshire and Maine.

☆ Fryeburg Fair

There's something for everyone at this old-fashioned agricultural fair (www.fryeburgfair.org) in Maine, from live animals to live music, and from fun rides to fireworks. Held in the first week in October.

Head of the Charles

The world's largest rowing event (www.hocr.org) takes place in Boston on the Charles River on the third weekend in October, attracting thousands of rowers and thousands more spectators.

☆ New Hampshire Pumpkin Festival

This annual event in Laconia, NH, draws big crowds to see the construction of a tower of jack-o'-lanterns as high as the sky. Held on the third or fourth weekend in October, there's also a craft fair, a costume parade, seed-spitting contests and fireworks. (p345)

November

Winter is coming and you may even feel it in the air. You may even see snow flurries. Thanksgiving Day – the fourth Thursday in November – kicks off the holiday season.

✕ Harvest on the Harbor

Maine's premier food and wine festival is a five-day feast for the senses, with events such as the Lobster Chef of the Year competition. (p376)

✲ America's Hometown Thanksgiving Celebration

Plymouth, MA, is the birthplace of Thanksgiving, so it's appropriate that the town celebrates its heritage with a parade, concerts, crafts and – of course – food. Held the weekend before Thanksgiving. (p128)

December

Winter sets in, with at least one big snowstorm in December to prove it. Christmas lights and holiday fairs make the region festive.

✲ Nantucket Christmas Stroll

Over a weekend in early December, carol singers, Santas and markets flood Nantucket's cobbled streets for a blast of holiday cheer.

✲ Boston Tea Party Reenactment

New Englanders take their reenactments seriously. In the case of the Tea Party, on December 16, they dress up like Mohawk warriors and dump tea into the Boston Harbor, just like their forebears in 1773. (p75)

☆ First Night

It actually starts on the 'last night,' New Year's Eve, and continues into the wee hours of the New Year. Activities, performances and other events are held at venues all around Boston. Buy a button and attend as many as you can. (p75)

Plan Your Trip
Itineraries

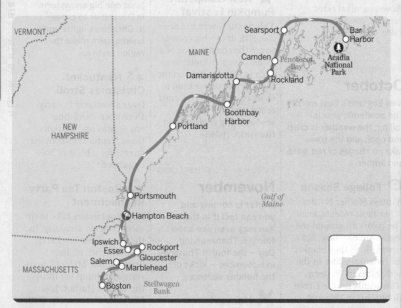

VERMONT

MAINE

Searsport

Bar Harbor

Camden · Penobscot Bay

Acadia National Park

Damariscotta

Rockland

NEW HAMPSHIRE

Boothbay Harbor

Portland

Portsmouth

Gulf of Maine

Hampton Beach

Ipswich
Essex

Rockport
Gloucester

Salem

Marblehead

MASSACHUSETTS

Boston

Stellwagen Bank

2 WEEKS Coastal New England

New England is intrinsically tied to the sea – historically, commercially and emotionally. To see this connection firsthand, follow the coastline.

Start in **Boston**, whose long-standing connection to the sea is reflected in a host of waterfront attractions. Follow the Harbor-Walk along the water's edge from Christopher Columbus Park, stopping at the New England Aquarium and the Institute for Contemporary Art. The following day, board a ferry to the Harbor Islands.

Continue northward to **Marblehead** and **Salem**, both rich in maritime history. Don't miss the Peabody Essex Museum and its wonderful maritime exhibit. To glimpse New England's fishing industry at work – and to sample its culinary treats – journey to **Gloucester**. This is also your jumping-off point for a whale-watching cruise to Stellwagen Bank.

Circle around Cape Ann to discover the charms of **Rockport** and the mysteries of Dogtown. Then continue up the coast to frolic in the waves at Crane Beach in **Ipswich** and feast on fried clams in **Essex**.

Portland Head Light (p373)

The New Hampshire coast is scant, but not without merit: walk **Hampton Beach's** boardwalk and admire the Colonial-era homes in historic **Portsmouth**.

Continuing into Maine, spend a day or two exploring **Portland**. Eat, drink and shop in the Old Port District and check out the Portland Museum of Art. Don't leave town without snapping a photo of the Portland Head Light on Cape Elizabeth. Continuing northeast, stop for a seafood lunch and a stroll around lovely (but crowded) **Boothbay Harbor**, or opt for oysters and bookstore browsing in **Damariscotta**.

Don't miss a stop in pretty **Camden** or artsy **Rockland**, where you can take a windjammer cruise up the rocky coast. When you return to dry land, clamber to the top of Mt Battie in Camden Hills State Park for sweeping Penobscot Bay views, or continue north to **Searsport**, home of the wonderful Penobscot Marine Museum.

End in **Bar Harbor** and **Acadia National Park**: highlights of the New England coast. You'll have no problem occupying yourself for a weekend or a week, exploring Mount Desert Island's scenery while hiking, biking, kayaking and camping. For a delicious detour, head to Thurston's Lobster Pound overlooking Bass Harbor.

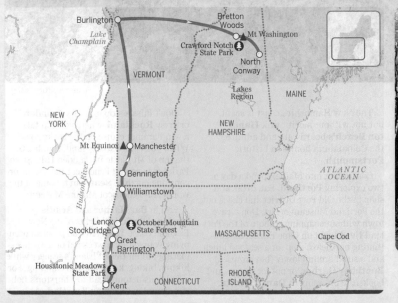

10 DAYS
Fall Foliage

The brilliance of fall in New England is legendary. Scarlet and sugar maples, ash, birch, beech, dogwood, tulip tree, oak and sassafras all contribute to the carnival of autumn color.

Start in Connecticut's **Kent**. Hike up Cobble Mountain in Macedonia Brook State Park for views of the forested hills against a backdrop of the Taconic and Catskill mountain ranges. Heading north on Rte 7, stop at **Housatonic Meadows State Park** to snap a photo of the Cornwall Bridge, then continue into Massachusetts.

Blanketing the westernmost part of the state, the rounded mountains of the Berkshires start turning crimson and gold as early as mid-September. Set up camp in **Great Barrington**, a formerly industrial town now populated with art galleries and upscale restaurants. It's a good base for exploring **October Mountain State Forest**, a multicolored tapestry of hemlocks, birches and oaks. This reserve's name – attributed to Herman Melville – gives a good indication of when this park is at its loveliest.

Cruising north from Great Barrington, you'll pass through the Berkshires' most charming towns: **Stockbridge**, **Lenox** and **Williamstown**. Stop for a few hours or a few days for fine dining, shopping and cultural offerings. Dedicate at least one day to exploring Mt Greylock State Reservation: the summit offers a panorama stretching up to 100 miles across more than five states.

Cross into Vermont and continue north through the historic villages of **Bennington** and **Manchester**. For fall foliage views head to the top of **Mt Equinox**, where the 360-degree panorama includes the Adirondacks and the lush Battenkill Valley. Continue north to **Burlington**, your base for frolicking on Lake Champlain, and sail away on a schooner for offshore foliage views.

Head southeast through Montpelier and continue into New Hampshire. Your destination is **Bretton Woods**, where you can admire the foliage from the porch of the historic hotel or from a hanging sky bridge. Then make your way to the summit of **Mt Washington**, whether by car, by train or on foot. When you're ready to descend from the clouds, follow the headwaters of the Saco River down through the forests of **Crawford Notch State Park** into **North Conway**.

Top: Williamstown (p203), The Berkshires
Bottom: North Conway (p354), New Hampshire

Mountain Meander

1 WEEK

If you're longing to breathe mountain air and gaze at majestic scenery, follow this route through New England's high country.

Enter the White Mountains' embrace amid the waterfalls and gorges of Maine's little-visited **Grafton Notch State Park**, then wind your way south into New Hampshire's awe-inspiring Presidential Range. Pause near **Pinkham Notch** to admire, photograph and perhaps climb New England's highest peak, Mt Washington, then continue south through the pretty village of **Jackson** to **North Conway**, which offers a plethora of lodging and dining options.

From here, drive west across the White Mountain National Forest on the supremely scenic **Kancamagus Hwy**. This route offers countless opportunities for hiking, camping and other outdoor adventuring. Turn north on I-93 to **Franconia Notch State Park**, where you can hike down the Flume, ride a tramway up Cannon Mountain and see what little remains of the Old Man of the Mountain. Spend a few nights at one of many welcoming inns in **Franconia**, or detour for dinner at Bethlehem's creative Cold Mountain Cafe. From here, enjoy the scenery as you motor west to I-91, heading southwest into Vermont. Expansive vistas unfold with abandon as you approach the Green Mountains on US 4. Continue on to **Killington** for a day of wintertime skiing or summertime mountain biking.

Turn north on VT 100, often called the spine of the state. Snaking north through the mountains, this classic route feels like a backcountry road, littered with cow-strewn meadows and white-steepled churches. Spend a few hours or a few days exploring, turning off on the gap roads and stopping in any number of tiny towns along the way. Don't miss Warren and Waitsfield in the **Mad River Valley** – a prime spot for browsing art galleries and antique shops, or horseback riding, swimming, tubing and skiing in the surrounding countryside.

Continuing north, make a beeline for the Ben & Jerry's factory in **Waterbury**, where you can tour the premises and sample Vermont's famous ice cream right at the source – not to mention mourn the loss of bygone flavors in the Flavor Graveyard out back. Finally, sidle on up to **Stowe**, Vermont's quintessential ski village, and end your trip with more four-season fun in Smugglers Notch, at the foot of **Mt Mansfield**.

Top: Views across Tuckerman Ravine (p360), Pinkham Notch

Bottom: Ben & Jerry's Ice Cream Factory (p315), Waterbury

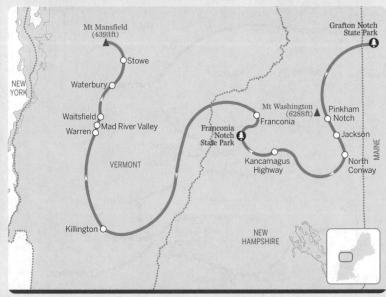

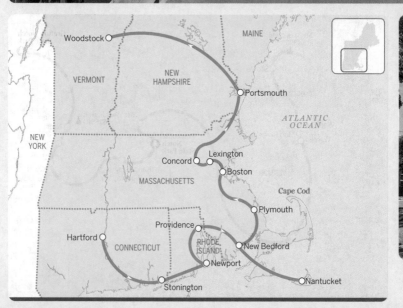

2 WEEKS Historical New England

History lurks round every corner in New England. This itinerary takes you on a journey through some of the region's prettiest early settlements and most significant historical sites.

Fly into **Hartford, CT**, and begin your trip at the Gothic Revival–style Wadsworth Atheneum, America's oldest public art museum, packed with nearly 50,000 artworks. Afterward, visit the gabled and turreted Victorian mansion where Mark Twain spent 17 years in the late 1800s.

Next, it's off to Connecticut's oldest village, **Stonington** – a lovely spot to stroll among the 18th- and 19th-century sea captains' homes arrayed on a peninsula jutting into Block Island Sound. Follow the coast east into Rhode Island and cross Narragansett Bay to **Newport**. Linger here a day or two to explore the Cliff Walk and tour the city's impressive 19th-century mansions built by wealthy American industrialists.

Next stop is **Providence**, where you can soak up the charms of College Hill's tree-shaded red-brick lanes and wander the beautiful campus of Brown University, founded in 1764.

Hop over to **New Bedford, MA**, and catch a ferry to **Nantucket**. In the 19th century, this island was the world's whaling capital. Today, you can step back in time at the Nantucket Whaling Museum and the Nantucket Atheneum, where luminaries including Ralph Waldo Emerson and Frederick Douglass once held forth.

Ferry back to the mainland and travel on to **Plymouth** to learn about the trials and triumphs of the Pilgrims. Next continue to **Boston**, reliving America's revolutionary days on a walk along the Freedom Trail and a visit to the Boston Tea Party Ships, or discovering the history of the city's 19th-century African American community on the Black Heritage Trail. From here, detour northwest to **Lexington** and **Concord** to follow the Battle Road and see where the War of Independence began.

Just up the coast, **Portsmouth, NH**, has one of New England's most attractive historical centers. The highlight is Strawbery Banke, a 10-acre waterfront parcel preserving some of Portsmouth's many fine 17th- and 18th-century buildings. End your journey in **Woodstock**, a quintessential Vermont village of brick-and-clapboard homes surrounding a village green.

Top: Wadsworth Atheneum (p241), Hartford
Bottom: Brown University (p213), Providence

Plan Your Trip

Outdoor Activities

New England offers unlimited opportunities to enjoy the great outdoors. The White Mountains, the Green Mountains and the Berkshires are high points for skiing, hiking and mountain biking. Countless miles of coastline entice travelers with sailing, sea kayaking and whale-watching, while ponds and glacial lakes invite swimming, canoeing and fishing.

Best Hikes

Sunset Ridge Trail (p291) Traverse rocky shelves and alpine tundra, surrounded by stunning Green Mountain vistas.

Beehive Loop (p398) Scale Acadia's favorite oceanside cliff on metal ladders bolted into the granite.

Lincoln Woods Trail (p350) Experience the White Mountains' wild beauty on this gorgeous stroll along an old railway bed.

Jones Nose Trail (p207) Follow a section of the legendary Appalachian Trail to the summit of Massachusetts' Mt Greylock.

Dune Shacks Trail (p155) Lose yourself in the dunes near the tip of Cape Cod.

Hiking

New England's plethora of peaks offers ample enticement to don a knapsack and hit the trails. The White Mountains in New Hampshire throw back some of the foulest weather on record, but offer New England's most spectacular hiking, with adventures for everyone from day-hikers to technical mountaineers. Pick a trail along the Kancamagus Hwy (p350) or around Crawford (p358) or Pinkham Notch (p360), plan a weeklong trek through the high country with overnights at Appalachian Mountain Club huts (www.outdoors.org), or climb to the summit of Mt Washington (p355), the highest peak in the Northeast.

New Hampshire's utterly accessible Mt Monadnock (p334) is a 'beginners' mountain,' a relatively easy climb up a bald granite batholith. Much less visited, Moosilauke Ravine Lodge (p340) offers great views, few crowds and miles of trails.

Maine's sublime Mt Katahdin (p405) remains practically untouched by tourism. Those who make it across the infamous Knife Edge will remember the experience for life. Acadia National Park (p397) and Grafton Notch State Park (p403) have miles of well-maintained trails for all skill levels.

Vermont's Green Mountains are also seamed with trails for all levels. Some of the finest hikes radiate out from Stowe

APPALACHIAN TRAIL

Every year, thousands of ambitious souls endeavor to hike all 2179 miles of the Appalachian Trail (AT; http://www.appalachiantrail.org). Everyone has their own reasons for taking on this challenge, but almost all hikers are seeking a life-changing experience. And how could it not be? Half a year carrying your life on your back – facing the harshest weather conditions and the most grueling physical challenges – is bound to affect you profoundly.

Such extreme challenges are not for everybody. Indeed, when the AT was dreamed up, it was never intended to be hiked all in one go. Rather, it was meant to connect various mountain communities where people could go to refresh and rejuvenate. As for refreshing and rejuvenating, the trail has been a smashing success: it's estimated that two to three million visitors hike a portion of the trail every year, inhaling the fresh air, admiring the spectacular scenery and partaking of the great outdoors.

Even if you don't have five to seven months to spare to tackle the full distance, you can still challenge yourself: every New England state but Rhode Island offers access to the AT; New Hampshire and Maine contain portions that are considered among the most difficult of the entire AT. New England also offers some of the most amazing vistas and remote wilderness along the trail. So load up your backpack and take a hike – even if it's just for the day.

(p311), which sports world-class ice climbing too. The ultimate Green Mountain challenge is Vermont's own end-to-ender, the Long Trail (p296), which runs nearly 300 miles from the Vermont–Massachusetts line to the Canadian border.

The highest peak in Massachusetts, Mt Greylock (p207) makes an excellent goal in the Berkshires, but there are scores of lesser hiking trails in the region's many state parks.

Biking

Bicycle Touring

See Boston by bike from the Charles River Bike Path (p71) or follow part of Paul Revere's midnight ride from Boston to Lexington on the Minuteman Commuter Bikeway (p103).

On Cape Cod in Massachusetts, tool around the Cape Cod Canal (www.cape codcanal.us), the Shining Sea Bikeway (p136), the Cape Cod Rail Trail (p142) or the Cape Cod National Seashore (p150) bike paths. In the Pioneer Valley, the **Norwottuck Rail Trail** (☑413-586-8706; www. mass.gov/locations/norwottuck-rail-trail) connects Amherst and Northampton, while the **Ashuwillticook Rail Trail** (☑413-442-8928; www.mass.gov/locations/ashuwillticook -rail-trail; ⊙dawn-dusk) follows the Hoosic River from Pittsfield to Adams in the Berkshires.

In Rhode Island, take a spin on the beautiful 14.5-mile East Bay Bike Path, which follows the waterfront out of Providence and weaves past picnic-worthy state parks. New Hampshire's Lakes Region is another lovely place to cycle, with the newish and still-growing WOW rail trail (p345) eventually slated to extend 9 miles along the shores of lakes Winnipesaukee, Opechee and Winniequam.

In Vermont, the Burlington Greenway (p303) takes cyclists along Burlington's beautiful lakeshore for 7.5 miles of smooth riding, linking up with the Island Line Trail and continuing into the middle of Lake Champlain on the Colchester causeway. Two other Vermont bike paths, the Lamoille Valley Rail Trail (www.lvrt.org) and the West River Trail (p279), offer pretty riverside riding.

The region's islands are particularly well suited to cycling. Rent wheels for the quaint roads of Block Island (p235), RI; for the carriage roads of Mount Desert Island (p395), ME; for the beachy trails of Nantucket (p161) and Martha's Vineyard (p169), MA; and for the long loop around Isleboro (www.townofislesboro.com), ME.

Mountain Biking & Fat Biking

Fire roads, snowmobile trails and hairy drops at ski areas are fair game for mountain bikers – with an increasing number of fat bikers joining the fun in winter. New England embraces the sport more each year, as resorts add miles of single-track to their offerings. Springtime thaws in April and early May are recuperative times for the trails, freshly exposed after a long winter's snow, but most trails are accessible by late May or early June. Foliage season is prime time for gallivanting through psychedelic forests. Local bike shops will gladly reveal their favorite haunts.

In Killington, VT, the hills are alive with whoops and hollers as riders roam roam the slopes on some of the most challenging terrain around in the dedicated mountain bike park (p293). New Hampshire's Loon Mountain (p350) ski area zooms daredevils up the mountain in a handy gondola for a white-knuckle, tooth-rattling trip back down. Western Maine's **Sunday River** (www.sundayriver.com; 15 S Ridge Rd, Newry; 🖼) ski area is another great place to set your wheels in motion, with a bike park set in stunning countryside.

Up in Vermont's Northeastern Kingdom, Kingdom Trails (p319) maintains an awesome network of trails. It's long been a mecca for summertime mountain biking, and now also offers 25 miles of groomed single-track for fat bikers once the snow falls. The nearby Craftsbury Outdoor Center (p320) has also recently opened its extensive trail network to fat bikers.

Swimming

The ocean never really heats up in New England, but that doesn't stop hordes of hardy Yankees from spilling onto the beaches and into the sea on hot summer days. Protected from the Arctic currents, Rhode Island's beaches tend to be the warmest, particularly at Block Island (p237) and Newport (p224). Beaches on

Cape Cod (p134), Nantucket (p132) and Martha's Vineyard (p132) are stunningly beautiful and the water is tolerably cold.

On the North Shore of Massachusetts, Plum Island offers a nice combination of dunes, a wide beach and a wildlife refuge (p122) harboring more than 800 species of plants and wildlife. In Ipswich, Crane Beach (p121) is a wonderful, pristine stretch of sand in the heart of a wildlife refuge, with trails traversing its dunes. Bring your surfboard and hang ten at **Good Harbor Beach** (www.gloucester-ma. gov; Thatcher Rd/Rte 127A; parking weekdays/ weekends $25/30; ⊙8am-9pm) and Long Beach (p119) on Cape Ann.

New Hampshire's short coastline is hemmed in with condos, but Rye Beach (p330) is an old favorite. Maine has a scattering of coastal beaches with icy water, including Ogunquit (p369) and Acadia National Park's Sand Beach (p397). Rangeley Lake (p403) in Maine and Lake Winnipesaukee (p345) in New Hampshire, two of New England's largest inland lakes, are ideal for a dip: the former is quite isolated, but the latter is bursting with resorts, shops and services.

Sailing & Boating

For maritime jaunts, options are wonderfully varied. Pluck lobster from their traps on a boat out of **Portland** (☎207-761-0941; www.luckycatch.com; Long Wharf, 170 Commercial St; adult/child $35/20; ⊙May-Oct), **Boothbay Harbor** (☎800-636-3244; www.booth bayboattrips.com; 42 Commercial St; ⊙late May-Oct) or Bar Harbor (p395), ME. Hop aboard a research vessel out of Norwalk (p268), CT, and learn about the inhabitants of the sea. Inherit the wind aboard a

Skier at Sunday River ski resort

windjammer out of Camden (p387), ME, or a 19th-century-style schooner in Mystic (p255), CT.

Trained sailors can take out their own boat on the Boston Harbor (p70) or in the Charles River Basin (p70), MA. The sailing capital of New England is undoubtedly Newport (p223), RI, where there are endless opportunities to sail – whether you want to do the work or have somebody else do it for you! Sailing is also superb on Vermont's Lake Champlain (p303), especially in late afternoon when you can watch sunset over the Adirondack Mountains.

Skiing & Snowboarding

New England has no shortage of snow. And there is no better way to enjoy it than to hit the slopes. Downhill skiing takes all forms, including free-heeling, telemarking and snowboarding. Vermont is ski central in New England. Killington Resort (p293) is known throughout the East for its extensive snowmaking apparatus and its steep mogul field. Mad River Glen (p298) is a rough-and-ready spot that re-

fuses admittance to boarders and proudly operates America's last remaining single chairlift. For beginner and intermediate skiers, Abenaki Ski Area (p344) in New Hampshire is a sweet, family-friendly spot with prices that hark back to its 1930s origins, while Jiminy Peak (p203) is the best resort in Massachusetts' Berkshires. Maine is home to the massive **Sunday River Ski Resort** (☑800-543-2754; www.sundayriver.com; 15 S Ridge Rd, Newry; lift ticket adult/teen/child $105/79/69; ⊕), with slopes on eight peaks, as well as Sugarloaf (p404) resort, sitting on the slopes of the state's second-highest mountain (4237ft).

If the gravity of the situation makes you nervous, you might prefer Nordic skiing. Stowe, VT (p313) hosts the largest cross-country ski trail network in the East, with connections to the Catamount Trail (www.catamounttrail.org), a 300-mile route running the full length of Vermont's Green Mountains. In the nearby Northeast Kingdom, Craftsbury Outdoor Center (p320) and Kingdom Trails (p320) collectively sport over 200 miles of groomed and ungroomed trails for your exploration, while New Hampshire's Jackson XC (p357) is famous for its 96 miles of trails and well-informed staff.

Regions at a Glance

Boston

History
Academia
Sports

Freedom Trail

For a sampler of Boston's American Revolution sights, follow the redbrick road. It leads 2.4 miles through the center of Boston, from the Boston Common to the Bunker Hill Monument, tracing the events leading up to and following the War of Independence.

College Town, USA

Boston is a college town: there's no doubt about it. No other element of the population is quite as influential as the students, who take over the city from September to May.

Sports Fanatics

'Fanatic' is no idle word here. Boston fans are passionate about sports, whether they are waking up at 5am to scull on the Charles River, running countless miles through the city streets or joining the raucous chorus of 35,000 fans singing 'Sweet Caroline' in the eighth inning of a Boston Red Sox game.

p48

Around Boston

History
Seafaring
Literature

Pilgrims & Presidents

From the Pilgrims' landing at Plymouth to witch hysteria in Salem, and from the first Revolutionary battle at Lexington to the presidents who were born and buried in Quincy, this region has shaped US history.

Ocean Economy

The fate of eastern Massachusetts has always been linked to the sea, especially for the whaling capital at New Bedford, the former sea-trade center at Salem and the fading fishing center at Gloucester.

Read a Book

Nineteenth-century Concord was central to the golden age of American literature, being home to literary greats including Emerson, Thoreau and Hawthorne.

p100

Cape Cod, Nantucket & Martha's Vineyard

Beaches
Wildlife
Cycling

Seashore

It's hard to imagine a place with a more world-class seashore: from tidal flats to gnarly open-ocean surf, and from soft sandy dunes to eons-old clay cliffs.

Marine Life

Humpback whales find the region ideal for summering. See them up close on a whale-watching tour. Seals and migratory birds are wildly abundant as well.

Bike Trails

The Cape's bike paths skirt marshes and beaches, cut through woods and soar up and down undulating dunes. When you've had your fill there, take your bike on the ferry to Nantucket and the Vineyard.

p132

Central Mass & the Berkshires

Culture
Food
Hiking

Summer Performances

Each summer a major symphony orchestra, top-notch dance troupes and renowned theater performers land in the hills of the Berkshires, transforming this rural region into a prime cultural destination.

Locavore Heaven

Apple orchards and farm fields are more than just scenery here. Their harvest is yours for the picking: menus are ripe with farm-to-table dishes.

Trails Galore

From the river valleys to the mountaintops, you're never far from a trailhead. Parks, forests and nature preserves offer everything from good birding to sweaty outings along the Appalachian Trail.

p178

Rhode Island

Nightlife
History
Beaches

Pumping Providence

Providence is positively hopping: from punk dives and hip art bars to loungy neighborhood joints with an art-nouveau aesthetic, there's something for everyone.

History Writ Small

From Providence's drawing-room radicals and Bristol's slave-trading profiteers to the Colonial clapboards of Little Compton and the mansions of Newport's capitalist kings, the East Bay tells the American story in microcosm.

Ocean State

The 'Ocean State' has some of the most beautiful beaches in the northeast – from South County's stretches of white sand to the bluff-backed shores of Block Island – perfect for swimming, surfing or building sandcastles.

p209

Connecticut

Art
Wine
Hiking

Artistic Gems

Connecticut's reputation as a culturally barren NYC suburb is belied by its wonderful galleries and museums. See avant-garde installations at the Aldrich, American masterpieces in New Britain, and esteemed collections in Hartford and New Haven.

Wine Tasting

Connecticut's hills may not be the most famous wine country, but among the state's two dozen or so wineries there are some real gems, including Hopkins Vineyard in New Preston.

Ponds & Peaks

With rolling hills and picturesque ponds, Connecticut is wonderful walking country. Hike to Caleb's Peak, amble along Squantz Pond or wander the trails of the Quiet Corner for the perfect antidote to big-city life.

p240

Vermont

Outdoors
Food & Drink
Villages

Outdoor Fun

Mountain bike the Kingdom Trails' 200-plus miles of paths in summer, survey Mt Mansfield's kaleidoscopic colors on a fall hike, or ski the best slopes in the East all winter long.

Local Produce

Vermont's classic patchwork of small farms is replete with organic producers, sugar shacks, cheese-makers and microbreweries, whose products appear on restaurant menus, in food co-ops and at farmers markets statewide.

Vintage Villages

Vermont celebrates small towns like few states in America. Billboards are prohibited and big-box stores are rare, allowing villages to show off their charms. Among the most picturesque are Newfane, Grafton and Woodstock.

p276

New Hampshire

Lakes
Leaf-Peeping
Winter Sports

Lake Life

On Golden Pond didn't do it justice. Something about paddling in a kayak, cruising on a boat, taking a sunset dip or gazing out at the bobbing loons from a deck makes time stand still in the Lakes Region.

Scenic Drives

Enjoy Kancamagus Hwy's winding turns through state parks and past gushing gorges, or village-hop along back roads in the Monadnock region. During the fall foliage season, almost every road qualifies as a scenic byway.

Let it Snow

When winter lasts as long as it does in New Hampshire, you find something to do. Ski the magnificent slopes at White Mountain ski resorts, or cruise cross-country at Jackson XC.

p322

Maine

Boating
Lobsters
Shopping

Take to the Sea

From the multi-masted windjammers of Camden and Rockport to whale-watching cruises of Bar Harbor and kayak trips amid the islands of Penobscot Bay, Maine is paradise for those who feel at home on the water.

Lobster by the Pound

Maine's famous crustaceans come fresh from the ocean at its many lobster pounds and seafood shacks. Tie on a bib, grab a metal cracker and go to town on these succulent beasties.

Antiques Road Show

Trolling the antiques stores of Maine's pretty fishing villages and mountain towns is a summer visitors' tradition.

p364

On the Road

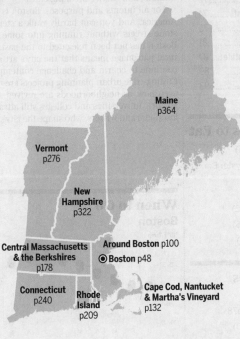

Maine
p364

Vermont
p276

New Hampshire
p322

Central Massachusetts & the Berkshires
p178

Around Boston p100
⊙ **Boston** p48

Connecticut
p240

Rhode Island
p209

Cape Cod, Nantucket & Martha's Vineyard
p132

Boston

📞 617 / POP 685,000

Includes ➡
Sights............................50
Activities......................70
Tours 72
Festivals & Events.........74
Sleeping......................75
Eating...........................81
Drinking & Nightlife.....87
Entertainment 89
Shopping......................93

Best Places to Eat

➡ Saltie Girl (p85)

➡ Island Creek Oyster Bar (p86)

➡ O Ya (p85)

➡ Pomodoro (p82)

➡ Courtyard (p86)

➡ jm Curley (p82)

Best Places to Stay

➡ Liberty Hotel (p78)

➡ Verb Hotel (p80)

➡ No 284 (p80)

➡ HI-Boston (p79)

➡ Gryphon House (p80)

Why Go?

Boston's history recalls revolution and transformation, and today the city is still among the country's most forward-thinking and barrier-breaking cities.

For all intents and purposes, Boston is the oldest city in America. And you can hardly walk a step over its cobblestone streets without running into some historic site. But Boston has not been relegated to the past. A history of cultural patronage means that the city's art and music scenes continue to charm and challenge contemporary audiences. Cutting-edge urban planning projects are reshaping the city even now, as neighborhoods are revived and rediscovered. Historic universities and colleges still attract scientists, philosophers and writers, who shape the city's evolving culture.

When to Go
Boston

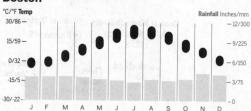

Apr On Patriots' Day, hordes of sports fans attend the world's oldest marathon.

Jul Hot and humid; many locals make for the beach.

Oct The city comes alive in fall, when students fill the streets.

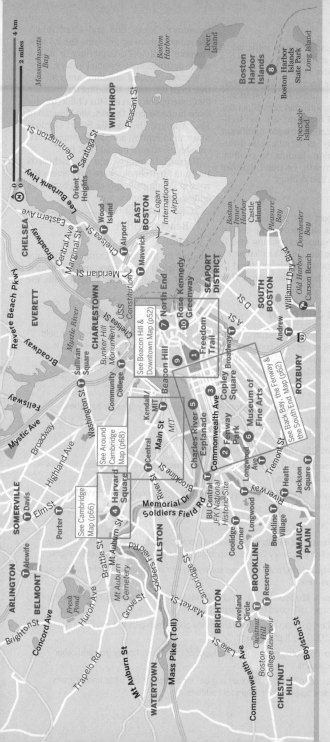

Boston Highlights

1 Freedom Trail (p57)
Following in the footsteps of patriots.

2 Fenway Park (p65)
Watching the Red Sox spank the Yankees.

3 Copley Square (p64)
Admiring the architecture of Boston's best-loved plaza.

4 Harvard Square (p95)
Rubbing shoulders with the top minds of tomorrow.

5 Charles River Esplanade (p61) Cycling along this scenic riverside pathway.

6 Museum of Fine Arts (p65) Admiring the Art of the Americas collection.

7 North End (p56) Drinking vino and dining on pasta, with cannoli for dessert.

8 Boston Harbor Islands (p69) Re-imagining Robinson Crusoe.

9 Beacon Hill (p50)
Contemplating the past in this history-rich neighborhood.

10 Rose Kennedy Greenway (p51) Celebrating Boston's urban renewal success story.

History

As one of the earliest European settlements in the New World and the birthplace of the American Revolution, Boston's ties to history are strong. A prosperous trading center, the city has long boasted fine educational and cultural institutions that are influential in philosophy and literature, art and technology. Industrialization brought significant changes, especially as immigrants diversified the population, leading to conflict, cooperation and growth – a trend that has continued into the 21st century.

◉ Sights

Boston is a compact city, so many sights are within walking distance of the central downtown area. Almost everything else is accessible by metro (or 'T' as it's called here). Most of the colonial sights are clustered in the oldest part of the city, ie Beacon Hill, Downtown, North End and Charlestown. See many of them by following the 2.5-mile Freedom Trail (p57). Cambridge is also a prime destination for colonial history.

Boston's excellent museums are a bit further from the center, including the Institute for Contemporary Art and the Children's Museum in the Seaport District, the Museum of Fine Arts and the Isabella Stuart Gardner Museum in Fenway, and the Museum of Science on the edge of the old West End.

Harvard University and Massachusetts Institute for Technology are both across the river in Cambridge, with enticing campuses and on-site museums.

◉ Beacon Hill & Boston Common

Abutted by the Boston Common – the nation's original public park and the centerpiece of the city – and topped with the

---

BOSTON FOR CHILDREN

Boston is one giant history museum, and the setting for many lively and informative field trips. Cobblestone streets and costume-clad tour guides can bring to life the events that kids read about in history books, while hands-on experimentation and interactive exhibits fuse education and entertainment.

Need to Know

Resources Boston Central (www.bostoncentral.com) for family-friendly activities, outings, shops and playgrounds.

Restaurants High chairs and kids' menus widely available.

Changing tables Often available in museums and public buildings.

Transport Kids aged 11 and under ride the T for free; older kids pay half-price. Reserve child seats in taxis in advance.

Babysitting Boston's Best Babysitters (www.bbbabysitters.com) or Summer Sitters (www.summersitters.com).

Sights & Activities

Museum of Science (p56) More opportunities to combine fun and learning than anywhere in the city. The Discovery Center is specially designed for kids aged under eight.

New England Aquarium (p55) Kids can see eye to eye with thousands of sea species in the Giant Ocean Tank.

Boston Children's Museum (p60) Hours of fun climbing, constructing and creating. The museum is especially good for kids aged three to eight.

Franklin Park Zoo (p59) In addition to the many animal exhibits, the zoo has a wild and wonderful 10,000-sq-ft playground.

MIT Museum (p70) Teenagers will get a kick out of the robots, holograms and other interesting science stuff.

Urban AdvenTours (p73) This bike tour is great for all ages. Kids' bikes and helmets are available for hire, as are bike trailers for toddlers.

gold-domed Massachusetts State House, Beacon Hill is the neighborhood most often featured on Boston postcards. The retail and residential streets on Beacon Hill are delightfully, quintessentially Boston.

★ **Boston Common**   PARK

(Map p52; btwn Tremont, Charles, Beacon & Park Sts; ⊙6am-midnight; Ⓟ⊛; ⓉPark St) America's oldest public park, Boston Common has a long and storied history, serving as a campground for British troops during the Revolutionary War and as green grass for cattle grazing until the 1830s. Nowadays, the Common is a place for picnicking and people-watching. In winter, the Frog Pond (p71) attracts ice-skaters, while summer draws theater lovers for Shakespeare on the Common (p91). This is also the starting point for the Freedom Trail.

**Massachusetts
State House**   NOTABLE BUILDING

(Map p52; ☑617-727-7030; www.sec.state.ma.us; cnr Beacon & Bowdoin Sts; ⊙8:45am-5pm Mon-Fri, tours 10am-3:30pm Mon-Fri; ⓉPark St) FREE High atop Beacon Hill, Massachusetts' leaders and legislators attempt to turn their ideas into concrete policies and practices within the State House. John Hancock provided the land (previously part of his cow pasture) and Charles Bulfinch designed the commanding state capitol, but it was Oliver Wendell Holmes who called it 'the hub of the solar system' (thus earning Boston the nickname 'the Hub'). Free 40-minute tours cover the history, artwork, architecture and political personalities of the State House.

Granary Burying Ground   CEMETERY

(Map p52; Tremont St; ⊙9am-5pm; ⓉPark St) Dating from 1660, this atmospheric atoll is crammed with historic headstones, many with evocative (and creepy) carvings. This is the final resting place of favorite revolutionary heroes, including Paul Revere, Samuel Adams, John Hancock and James Otis. Benjamin Franklin is buried in Philadelphia, but the Franklin family plot contains his parents.

Louisburg Square   STREET

(Map p52; ⓉCharles/MGH) There is no more prestigious address in Boston than Louisburg Square, a cluster of stately brick row houses facing a private park. Louisa May Alcott lived at No 10 after she gained literary success. At the northern corner of the

PUBLIC GARDEN

Adjoining Boston Common, the **Public Garden** (Map p52; ☑617-723-8144; www.friendsofthepublicgarden.org; Arlington St; ⊙dawn-dusk; ⊛; ⓉArlington) is a 24-acre botanical oasis of Victorian flower beds, verdant grass and weeping willow trees shading a tranquil lagoon. The old-fashioned pedal-powered Swan Boats (p71) have been delighting children for generations. The most endearing spot in the Public Garden is the **Make Way for Ducklings Statue**, depicting Mrs Mallard and her eight ducklings, the main characters in the beloved book by Robert McCloskey.

square is the home of former Secretary of State John Kerry and his wife Teresa Heinz.

**Museum of African
American History**   MUSEUM

(Map p52; ☑617-725-0022; www.maah.org; 46 Joy St; adult/child $10/free; ⊙10am-4pm Mon-Sat; ⓉPark St, Bowdoin) The Museum of African American History occupies two adjacent historic buildings: the African Meeting House, the country's oldest Black church and meeting house; and Abiel Smith School, the country's first school for blacks. The museum offers rotating exhibits about the historic events that took place here, and is also a source of information about – and the final destination of – the Black Heritage Trail (p74).

⦿ Downtown & Waterfront

Much of Boston's business and tourist activity takes place in this central neighborhood, which includes the Financial District. Downtown is not the thriving shopping area that it once was, especially since the closure of Filene's Department Store. But it is a bustling district crammed with modern complexes and colonial buildings, including Faneuil Hall and Quincy Market. The Waterfront is home to the Harbor Islands ferries and the New England Aquarium.

Rose Kennedy Greenway   PARK

(Map p52; ☑617-292-0020; www.rosekennedygreenway.org; ⊛; ⓉAquarium, Haymarket) Where once there was a hulking overhead highway, now winds a 27-acre strip of landscaped gardens, fountain-lined greens and public art

Beacon Hill & Downtown

N

0 — 500 m
0 — 0.25 miles

Cambridge Antique Market (0.5mi)

Science Park

2 Museum of Science

Science Park

Charles River

The Esplanade

40

Zakim Bridge

Charlestown Bridge

Nashua St

Charles St

Martha Rd

Lomasney Way

31

Lovejoy Wharf

Beverly St

96

North Station

North Station

92

Causeway St

John F Fitzgerald Expwy

Canal St

Haverhill St

Friend St

49

Stanford St

WEST END

Blossom St

Massachusetts General Hospital

Fruit St

Grove St

Parkman St

52

Charles/MGH

100 102

37

Phillips St

Revere St

Anderson St

Garden St

Irving St

S Russell St

Joy St 20

Hancock St

Temple St

Bowdoin St

Bowdoin

Cambridge St

Merrimac St

N Charden St

New Sudbury St

New Sudbury St

Somerset St

Cambridge St

Center Plaza

John F Kennedy Federal Building

10

Boston City Hall

Haymarket

N Washington St

Endicott St

N Margin St

Thacher St

Prince St

N Bennet St

Salem St

68

71

103

42

11

21

Hull St

Charter St

Commercial St

North End Playground

US Coast Guard Piers

Constitution Wharf

Battery Wharf

Boston Inner Harbor

Callahan Tunnel

Sumner Tunnel (toll)

Union Wharf

Battery Wharf

Sargents Wharf

Lewis Wharf

Commercial Wharf

Atlantic Ave

Christopher Columbus Park

Cross St

Boston Harbor Cruises

35

38 43 36

46

30

16

14

i

National Park Service Visitors Center

12

48

79

23

94

Congress St

Hanover St

NORTH END

3 Old North Church

Tileston St

Charter St

Hanover St

Clark St

Battery St

North St

Fleet St

75

62

28

Richmond St

101

70

63

60

77

Commercial St

Fulton St

North St

Richmond St

Charlestown (0.25mi); USS Constitution (0.4mi); Bunker Hill Monument (0.5mi)

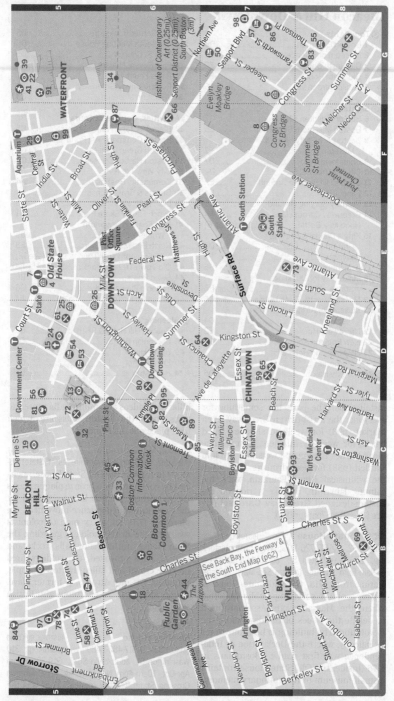

Beacon Hill & Downtown

◎ **Top Sights**

1 Boston Common	B6
2 Museum of Science	A1
3 Old North Church	F2
4 Old State House	E5
5 Public Garden	A6

◎ **Sights**

6 Boston Children's Museum	G7
7 Boston Massacre Site	E5
8 Boston Tea Party Ships & Museum	F7
9 Chinatown Gate	D7
10 City Hall Plaza	D4
11 Copp's Hill Burying Ground	E2
12 Faneuil Hall	E4
13 Granary Burying Ground	D5
14 Greenway Carousel	F4
Hood Milk Bottle	(see 6)
15 King's Chapel & Burying Ground	D5
16 Labyrinth	F4
17 Louisburg Square	B5
18 Make Way for Ducklings Statue	B6
19 Massachusetts State House	C5
20 Museum of African American History	C4
21 Narrowest House	E2
22 New England Aquarium	G5
23 New England Holocaust Memorial	E4
24 Old City Hall	D5

25 Old Corner Bookstore	D5
26 Old South Meeting House	D5
27 Park St Church	D5
28 Paul Revere House	F3
29 Rings Fountain	F5
30 Rose Kennedy Greenway	F4
31 West End Museum	C3

◎ **Activities, Courses & Tours**

32 Black Heritage Trail	C5
33 Boston Common Frog Pond	C6
34 Boston Green Cruises	G6
35 Boston Harbor Cruises	G4
36 City View Trolleys	F4
37 Community Boating	A4
38 Ghosts & Gravestones	F4
39 Liberty Fleet	G5
40 Lynch Family Skate Park	B1
41 New England Aquarium Whale Watch	G5
42 North End Market Tour	E3
NPS Freedom Trail Tour	(see 12)
43 Old Town Trolley Tours	F4
44 Swan Boats	B6
45 Tadpole Playground	C6
46 Urban AdvenTours	F4

◎ **Sleeping**

47 Beacon Hill Hotel & Bistro	B5
48 Bostonian Boston	E4
49 Boxer Hotel	C3
50 Envoy Hotel	G7
51 HI-Boston	C7

installations. The park has something for everyone: the artist-driven Greenway Open Market (p93) for weekend shoppers, food trucks for weekday lunchers, summertime block parties for music lovers and Trillium Garden (p88) for beer drinkers. Cool off in the whimsical Rings Fountain, walk the calming labyrinth, or take a ride on the custom-designed **Greenway Carousel** (per ride $3; ⊙11am-7pm Apr-Dec).

★**Old State House**   HISTORIC BUILDING
(Map p52; ☑617-720-1713; www.bostonhistory. org; 206 Washington St; adult/child $10/free; ⊙9am-6pm Jun-Aug, to 5pm Sep-May; ⊤State) Dating from 1713, the Old State House is Boston's oldest surviving public building, where the Massachusetts Assembly used to debate the issues of the day before the Revolution. The building is best known for its balcony, where the Declaration of Independence was first read to Bostonians in 1776. Inside, the Old State House contains a small museum of revolutionary memora-

bilia, with videos and multimedia presentations about the Boston Massacre, which took place out the front.

Boston Massacre Site   MONUMENT
(Map p52; cnr State & Devonshire Sts; ⊤State) Directly in front of the Old State House, encircled by cobblestones, a bronze plaque marks the spot where the first blood was shed for the American independence movement. On March 5, 1770, an angry mob of colonists swarmed the British soldiers guarding the State House, hurling snowballs, rocks and insults. Thus provoked, the soldiers fired into the crowd and killed five townspeople, including Crispus Attucks, a former slave. The incident sparked enormous anti-British sentiment.

**Old South
Meeting House**   HISTORIC BUILDING
(Map p52; ☑617-482-6439; www.osmh.org; 310 Washington St; adult/child $6/1; ⊙9:30am-5pm Apr-Oct, 10am-4pm Nov-Mar; ♿; ⊤Downtown Crossing, State) 'No tax on tea!' That was the

52	Liberty Hotel	A4
53	Nine Zero	D5
54	Omni Parker House	D5
55	Residence Inn Marriott	G8
56	XV Beacon	D5
57	Yotel	G7

🍴 Eating

58	75 Chestnut	A5
59	Avana Sushi	D7
60	Carmelina's	F3
61	Clover DTX	D5
62	Daily Catch	F3
63	Galleria Umberto	F3
64	Gene's Chinese Flatbread	D7
65	Gourmet Dumpling House	D7
66	James Hook & Co	F6
67	jm Curley	C6
68	Maria's Pastry	E3
69	Mike & Patty's	B8
70	Modern Pastry Shop	E3
71	Neptune Oyster	E3
72	No 9 Park	C5
73	O Ya	E7
74	Paramount	A5
75	Pomodoro	F3
76	Row 34	G8
77	Scopa	F3
78	Tatte	A5
79	Union Oyster House	E4
80	Yvonne's	D6

🍷 Drinking & Nightlife

81	21st Amendment	C5
82	Democracy Brewing	C6
83	Drink	G8
	Lookout Rooftop Bar	(see 50)
84	Pressed	A5
85	Thinking Cup	C6
86	Trillium Fort Point	G7
87	Trillium Garden	F6
88	Tunnel	C7

🎭 Entertainment

	Boston Ballet	(see 89)
89	Opera House	C6
90	Shakespeare on the Common	B6
91	Simons IMAX Theatre	G5
92	TD Garden	D2
93	Wilbur Theatre	C7

🛍 Shopping

	Artists for Humanity	(see 12)
94	Boston Public Market	E4
95	Brattle Book Shop	C6
96	Converse at Lovejoy Wharf	D2
97	Eugene Galleries	A5
98	For Now	G7
99	Greenway Open Market	F5
100	Marika's Antique Shop	A4
101	North Bennet Street School	F3
102	Paridaez	A4
103	Salmagundi	E3

decision on December 16, 1773, when 5000 angry colonists gathered here to protest British taxes, leading to the Boston Tea Party. Download an audio of the historic pre–Tea Party meeting from the museum website, then visit the graceful meeting house to check out the exhibit on the history of the building and the protest.

New England Aquarium   AQUARIUM
(Map p52; ☎617-973-5200; www.neaq.org; Central Wharf; adult/child $27/19; ⊙9am-5pm Mon-Fri, to 6pm Sat & Sun, 1hr later Jul & Aug; 🅿🚼; 🚇Aquarium) 🏊 Teeming with sea creatures of all sizes, shapes and colors, this giant fishbowl is the centerpiece of downtown Boston's waterfront. The main attraction is the three-story Giant Ocean Tank, which swirls with thousands of creatures great and small, including turtles, sharks and eels. Countless side exhibits explore the lives and habitats of other underwater oddities, as well as penguins and marine mammals.

New England Holocaust Memorial   MEMORIAL
(Map p52; www.nehm.org; btwn Union & Congress Sts; 🚇Haymarket) Constructed in 1995, the six luminescent glass columns of the New England Holocaust Memorial are engraved with six million numbers, representing those killed in the Holocaust. Each tower – with smoldering coals sending plumes of steam up through the glass corridors – represents a different Nazi death camp. The memorial sits along the Freedom Trail, a sobering reminder of its larger meaning.

Faneuil Hall   HISTORIC BUILDING
(Map p52; ☎617-242-5642; www.nps.gov/bost; Congress St; ⊙9am-5pm; 🚇State, Haymarket, Government Center) **FREE** 'Those who cannot bear free speech had best go home,' said Wendell Phillips. 'Faneuil Hall is no place for slavish hearts.' Indeed, this public meeting place was the site of so much rabble-rousing that it earned the nickname the 'Cradle of Liberty.' After the revolution, Faneuil Hall

WORTH A TRIP

ARNOLD ARBORETUM

Under a public-private partnership with Harvard University, the 265-acre **Arnold Arboretum** (☏617-524-1718; www.arboretum.harvard.edu; 125 Arborway; ⊙dawn-dusk; ♿; Ⓣ Forest Hills) is planted with over 15,000 exotic trees and flowering shrubs. This gem is pleasant year-round, but it's particularly beautiful in the bloom of spring. Dog walking, Frisbee throwing, bicycling, sledding and general contemplation are encouraged (but picnicking is not allowed). The southern Forest Hills gate is located on the Arborway just west of the metro station.

A **visitor center** (⊙10am-5pm Thu-Tue) is at the main gate, just south of the rotary at Rte 1 and Rte 203. Free one-hour walking tours are offered several times a week from April to November.

was a forum for meetings about abolition, women's suffrage and war. You can hear about the building's history from National Park Service rangers in the historic hall on the 2nd floor.

King's Chapel & Burying Ground
CHURCH, CEMETERY

(Map p52; ☏ 617-523-1749; www.kings-chapel.org; 58 Tremont St; donation $3, tours adult/child $7/3; ⊙ church 10am-4:30pm Mon-Sat, 1:30-5pm Sun, hourly tours 10am-3pm; Ⓣ Government Center) Puritan Bostonians were not pleased when the original Anglican church was erected on this site in 1688. The granite chapel standing today – built in 1754 – houses the largest bell ever made by Paul Revere, as well as a historic organ. The adjacent burying ground is the oldest in the city. Besides the biweekly services, recitals are held here every week (12:15pm Tuesday).

Design Museum Boston
MUSEUM

(☏888-287-0167; www.designmuseumboston.org; ⊙hours vary) Redefining what it means to be a 'museum,' Design Museum Boston brings the goods to you. This 'pop-up' museum launches exhibits in public spaces all around town, from shopping malls to public parks to airports. Keep your eyes open: design is all around you.

◉ West End & North End

Although the West End and North End are physically adjacent, they are worlds apart atmospherically. The West End is an institutional area without much zest. By contrast, the North End is delightfully spicy, thanks to the many Italian ristoranti and *salumerie* (delis) that line the streets.

★Old North Church
CHURCH

(Christ Church; Map p52; ☏ 617-858-8231; www.oldnorth.com; 193 Salem St; adult/child $8/4, plus $2 for tour; ⊙10am-4pm Nov-March, 9am-6pm April-Oct; Ⓣ Haymarket, North Station) Longfellow's poem 'Paul Revere's Ride' has immortalized this graceful church. It was here, on the night of April 18, 1775, that the sexton hung two lanterns from the steeple as a signal that the British would advance on Lexington and Concord via the sea route. Also called Christ Church, this 1723 Anglican place of worship is Boston's oldest church.

Copp's Hill Burying Ground
CEMETERY

(Map p52; Hull St; ⊙8am-5pm; Ⓣ North Station) The city's second-oldest cemetery – dating from 1660 – is the final resting place for an estimated 10,000 souls. It is named for William Copp, who originally owned this land. While the oldest graves belong to Copp's children, there are several other noteworthy residents.

★Museum of Science
MUSEUM

(Map p52; ☏617-723-2500; www.mos.org; Charles River Dam; museum adult/child $28/23, planetarium adult/child $10/8, theater adult/child $10/8; ⊙9am-7pm Sat-Thu Jul & Aug, to 5pm Sep-Jun, to 9pm Fri year-round; Ⓟ♿; Ⓣ Science Park/West End) This educational playground has more than 600 interactive exhibits. Favorites include the world's largest lightning-bolt generator, a full-scale space capsule, a world population meter and an impressive dinosaur exhibit. Kids go wild exploring computers and technology, maps and models, birds and bees, and human evolution. Don't miss the Hall of Human Life, where visitors can witness the hatching of baby chicks. The Discovery Center is a hands-on play area for kids under the age of eight.

Paul Revere House
HISTORIC SITE

(Map p52; ☏617-523-2338; www.paulreverehouse.org; 19 North Sq; adult/child $4.50/1; ⊙9:30am-5:15pm mid-Apr–Oct, to 4:15pm Nov–mid-Apr, closed Mon Jan-Mar; Ⓣ Haymarket) When

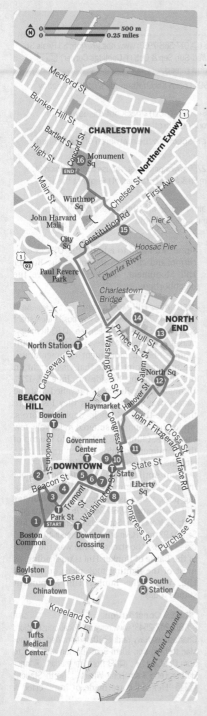

City Walk
Freedom Trail

START BOSTON COMMON
END BUNKER HILL MONUMENT
LENGTH 2.5 MILES; THREE HOURS

Start at ❶ **Boston Common** (p51), America's oldest public park, now dotted with monuments and public art. On the northern side, you can't miss the ❷ **Massachusetts State House** (p51) sitting atop Beacon Hill. Walk north on Tremont St, passing the soaring steeple of ❸ **Park St Church** (Map p52; www.parkstreet.org; 1 Park St; ⏰ 9:30am-3pm Tue-Sat mid-Jun–Aug, Sun year-round) and the Egyptian Revival gates of the ❹ **Granary Burying Ground** (p51), final resting place of many patriots.

At School St, the ❺ **King's Chapel** overlooks the adjacent burying ground. Turn east on School St, and take note of the plaque outside the ❻ **Old City Hall** (Map p52; www.oldcityhall.com; 45 School St) commemorating this spot as the site of the first public school. Continue past the ❼ **Old Corner Bookstore** (Map p52; cnr School & Washington Sts). Diagonally opposite, the ❽ **Old South Meeting House** (p54) saw the beginnings of the Boston Tea Party. Further north on Washington St, the ❾ **Old State House** (p54) was the seat of the colonial government. Later, it was the scene of the city's first public reading of the Declaration of Independence. Outside the Old State House a ring of cobblestones marks the ❿ **Boston Massacre site** (p54). Across the intersection, ⓫ **Faneuil Hall** (p55) has served as a public meeting place and marketplace for over 250 years.

From Faneuil Hall, follow Hanover St across the Rose Kennedy Greenway. One block east, North Sq is the site of the ⓬ **Paul Revere House**, the city's oldest wooden house. Back on Hanover St, the Paul Revere Mall offers a lovely vantage point to view the ⓭ **Old North Church**, where two lanterns were hung to signal the British soldiers' route. From the church, head west on Hull St to ⓮ **Copp's Hill Burying Ground**, with views across to Charlestown.

Across the Charlestown Bridge, Constitution Rd brings you to the Charlestown Navy Yard, home of the ⓯ **USS Constitution** (p58). Finally, wind your way through the historic streets of Charlestown center to the ⓰ **Bunker Hill Monument** (p58), site of the turning-point American Revolution battle.

KENNEDY FAMILY SITES

John F Kennedy National Historic Site (✆617-566-7937; www.nps.gov/jofi; 83 Beals St, Brookline; ⏰9:30am-5pm daily mid-May–Aug, Wed-Sun Sep & Oct; Ⓣ Coolidge Corner) **FREE** See where the 35th US president was born and raised.

John F Kennedy Library & Museum (p60) Learn about Kennedy's political legacy at the official presidential library.

Edward Kennedy Institute for the US Senate (p60) Check out the newest Kennedy venue, this one a tribute to JFK's youngest brother.

Rose Kennedy Greenway (p51) Pay your respects to the matriarch of the Kennedy clan.

Union Oyster House (Map p52; ✆617-227-2750; www.unionoysterhouse.com; 41 Union St; mains $24-32; ⏰11am-9:30pm Sun-Thu, to 10pm Fri & Sat; Ⓣ Haymarket) Request the JFK booth and order the lobster bisque.

Harvard University (p67) This was JFK's alma mater, and the university now has a public policy institute and a riverside park that bear his name.

silversmith Paul Revere rode to warn patriots of the British march to Lexington and Concord, he set out from this home on North Sq. This small clapboard house was built in 1680, making it the oldest house in Boston. A self-guided tour through the house and courtyard gives a glimpse of what life was like for the Revere family (which included 16 children!).

West End Museum MUSEUM
(Map p52; ✆617-723-2125; www.thewestendmuseum.org; 150 Staniford St; ⏰noon-5pm Tue-Fri, 11am-4pm Sat; Ⓣ North Station) **FREE** This gem of a neighborhood museum is dedicated to preserving the memory of the West End and educating the public about the ramifications of unchecked urban development. The main exhibit, the Last Tenement, traces the history of the neighborhood from 1850 to 1958, highlighting its immigrant populations, economic evolution and eventual destruction.

Narrowest House HISTORIC SITE
(Map p52; 44 Hull St; Ⓣ North Station) Across the street from Copp's Hill Burying Ground, this is Boston's narrowest house, measuring a whopping 9.5ft wide. Sometimes called a 'spite house,' the four-story, c 1800 edifice was reportedly built to block light from the neighbor's house and to obliterate the view of the house behind it.

◉ Charlestown

The site of the original settlement of the Massachusetts Bay Colony, Charlestown is the terminus for the Freedom Trail. Many tourists tramp across these historic cobble-stone sidewalks to admire the USS *Constitution* and climb to the top of the Bunker Hill Monument, which towers above the neighborhood.

★**Bunker Hill Monument** MONUMENT
(✆617-242-7275; www.nps.gov/bost; Monument Sq; ⏰9am-5pm, to 6pm Jun-Sep; ⛟93 from Haymarket, Ⓣ Community College) **FREE** This 220ft granite obelisk monument commemorates the turning-point battle that was fought on the surrounding hillside on June 17, 1775. Ultimately, the Redcoats prevailed, but the victory was bittersweet, as they lost more than one-third of their deployed forces, while the colonists suffered relatively few casualties. Climb the 294 steps to the top of the monument to enjoy the panorama of the city, the harbor and the North Shore.

From April to June – due to the seasonal influx of school groups – you'll need a climbing pass, which is available at the **Bunker Hill Museum** (✆617-242-7275; www.nps.gov/bost; 43 Monument Sq; ⏰9am-5pm, to 6pm Jun-Sep; ⛟93 from Haymarket, Ⓣ Community College) **FREE** across the street. By the way, the name of the Battle of Bunker Hill is misleading, as most of the fighting took place on Breed's Hill, where the Bunker Hill Monument stands today.

★**USS Constitution** SHIP
(✆617-242-2543; www.navy.mil/local/constitution; Charlestown Navy Yard; ⏰10am-4pm Wed-Sun Jan-Mar, to 6pm Apr, 10am-6pm Tue-Sun May-Sep, to 5pm Oct-Dec; ♿; ⛟93 from Haymarket, ⛴ Inner Harbor Ferry from Long Wharf, Ⓣ North Station) **FREE** 'Her sides are made of iron!' cried a

crewman upon watching a shot bounce off the thick oak hull of the USS *Constitution* during the War of 1812. This bit of irony earned the legendary ship its nickname. Indeed, it has never gone down in a battle. The USS *Constitution* remains the oldest commissioned US Navy ship, dating from 1797, and it is normally taken out onto Boston Harbor every July 4 in order to maintain its commissioned status.

Make sure you bring a photo ID to go aboard. You'll learn lots, like how the captain's son died on the ship's maiden voyage (an inauspicious start).

Charlestown Navy Yard HISTORIC SITE
(☏617-242-5601; www.nps.gov/bost; ☺visitor center 10am-5pm Wed-Sun Jan-Apr, 9am-5pm May-Sep, 10am-5pm Oct-Dec; ☐93 from Haymarket, ☒Inner Harbor Ferry from Long Wharf, Ⓣ North Station) FREE Besides the historic ships docked here and the museum dedicated to them, the Charlestown Navy Yard is a living monument to its own history of shipbuilding and naval command. Visit the National Park Service Visitor Center here for a free film, guided tours and other info about the Navy Yard and Freedom Trail sites.

◉ Seaport District & South Boston

The Seaport District is a section of South Boston that is fast developing as an attractive waterside destination, thanks to a dynamic contemporary-art museum and the explosion of new dining and entertainment options. Travel deeper into 'Southie' for seaside breezes, a little history and a lot of beer.

★**Institute of Contemporary Art** MUSEUM
(ICA; ☏617-478-3100; www.icaboston.org; 25 Harbor Shore Dr; adult/child $15/free, Thu 5-9pm free; ☺10am-5pm Tue, Wed, Sat & Sun, to 9pm Thu & Fri; ♿; ☐SL1, SL2, Ⓣ South Station) Boston has become a focal point for contemporary art in the 21st century, with the Institute of Contemporary Art leading the way. The building is a work of art in itself: a glass structure cantilevered over a waterside plaza. The vast light-filled interior allows for multimedia presentations, educational programs and studio space, as well as the development of the permanent collection.

BOSTON SIGHTS

BOSTON'S GLORIOUS GREENWAYS

The Emerald Necklace (www.emeraldnecklace.org) is an evocative name for a series of parks and green spaces that weave some 7 miles through Boston, from the Boston Common to Franklin Park. Designed by Frederick Law Olmsted in the late 19th century, the Emerald Necklace treats city residents to fresh air, green grass and flowing water, right within the city limits. It's well suited for cycling, so hop on a bike and go for the green.

At its northern end, the Boston Common (p51) and the Public Garden (p51) anchor the green chain. From here, the **Commonwealth Ave mall** stretches west to Fenway. The Back Bay Fens (p65) follows the muddy river as it winds its way south.

Olmsted Park (Jamaica Plain; Ⓣ Riverway) features a paved path that hugs the banks of Leverett Pond and Ward's Pond in Jamaica Plain. The idyllic spring-fed **Jamaica Pond** (☏617-522-5061; www.jamaicapond.com; 507 Jamaica Way, Jamaica Plain; boat rental per hour $15-20; ☺boathouse noon-sunset Mon-Thu, from 10am Fri-Sun Apr-Oct; ♿; Ⓣ Green St), on the west side of the Jamaicaway, is more than 50ft deep and great for boating, fishing, jogging and picnicking. Beautifully landscaped and wonderfully serene, the Arnold Arboretum (p56) will appeal not only to green thumbs and plant lovers, but also to anyone who can take time to smell the roses. Check the website to see what's blooming when you're visiting.

Franklin Park (Ⓣ Stony Brook, Green St, Forest Hills), at 500-plus acres, is an underutilized resource, partly because it is so huge. Still, on weekend afternoons the park is full of families from the nearby neighborhoods of Jamaica Plain, Dorchester and Roxbury. Take the orange line to Stony Brook, Green St or Forest Hills and walk about a half-mile east to the park's edge. **Franklin Park Zoo** (☏617-541-5466; www.zoonewengland.com; 1 Franklin Park Rd; adult/child $20/14; ☺10am-5pm Mon-Fri, to 6pm Sat & Sun Apr-Sep, 10am-4pm daily Oct-Mar; Ⓟ♿; Ⓣ Ruggles) is also contained within the park.

WORTH A TRIP

FOREST HILLS CEMETERY

Dating from 1848, **Forest Hills** (☑ 617-524-0128; www.foresthillstrust.org; 95 Forest Hills Ave; ☉ 8:30am-dusk; P; T Forest Hills) is a gorgeous, green cemetery that is filled with art and whimsy. It is still an active burial ground, but it also plays the role of open-air museum. The walking paths are lined with sculptures paying tribute to individuals and causes from times past, while a contemporary sculpture path winds its way around the historic gravestones, connecting then and now.

Gravestones are dedicated to such famous figures as Revolutionary War heroes William Dawes and Joseph Warren, abolitionist William Lloyd Garrison and suffragette Lucy Stone, poets ee cummings and Anne Sexton, sculptors Daniel Chester French and Martin Milmore, and playwright Eugene O'Neill. The on-site Forsyth Chapel, in the midst of the greenery, is a spot for peaceful contemplation surrounded by vaulted wood ceilings and stained-glass windows. Concerts, poetry readings and other events are often held in this exquisite space. Walk east along the Arborway a half-mile from Forest Hills station.

Boston Tea Party
Ships & Museum   MUSEUM
(Map p52; ☑ 866-955-0667; www.bostonteaparty ship.com; Congress St Bridge; adult/child $30/18; ☉ 10am-5pm; ♠; T South Station) 'Boston Harbor a teapot tonight!' To protest against unfair taxes, a gang of rebellious colonists dumped 342 chests of tea into the water. The 1773 protest – the Boston Tea Party – set into motion the events leading to the Revolutionary War. Nowadays, replica Tea Party Ships are moored at Griffin's Wharf, alongside an excellent experiential museum dedicated to the catalytic event. Using re-enactments, multimedia and fun exhibits, the museum addresses all aspects of the Boston Tea Party and subsequent events.

John F Kennedy
Presidential Library & Museum   MUSEUM
(☑ 617-514-1600; www.jfklibrary.org; Columbia Point; adult/child $14/10; ☉ 9am-5pm; T JFK/ UMass) The legacy of JFK is ubiquitous in Boston, but the official memorial to the 35th president is the presidential library and museum – a striking, modern, marble building designed by IM Pei. The architectural centerpiece is the glass pavilion, with soaring 115ft ceilings and floor-to-ceiling windows overlooking Boston Harbor. The museum is a fitting tribute to JFK's life and legacy. The effective use of video re-creates history for visitors who may or may not remember the early 1960s.

Edward M Kennedy Institute
for the United States Senate   MUSEUM
(EMK Institute; ☑ 617-740-7000; www.emkinstitute. org; Columbia Point; adult/child $16/8; ☉ 10am-5pm Tue-Sun; T JFK/UMass) Ted Kennedy served in the US Senate for nearly half a century. It is fitting, therefore, that his legacy should include an institute and museum designed to teach the public about the inner workings of democracy. Opened in 2015, this state-of-the-art facility uses advanced technology, multimedia exhibits and interactive designs to engage visitors and demonstrate the functioning (and sometimes nonfunctioning) of the legislative process. The museum centerpiece is a full-scale replica of the Senate chamber.

Castle Island & Fort Independence   PARK
(Marine Park; ☉ dawn-dusk May-Sep; ♠; ☐ 11, T Broadway) FREE The 19th-century Fort Independence sits on 22 acres of parkland called Castle Island (a misnomer, as it's connected to the mainland). A paved pathway follows the perimeter of the peninsula – good for strolling or cycling – and there is a small swimming beach. Kids get a kick out of watching the low-flying planes heading in and out of Logan Airport.

Boston Children's Museum   MUSEUM
(Map p52; ☑ 617-426-6500; www.bostonchildrens museum.org; 308 Congress St; $17, 5-9pm Fri $1; ☉ 10am-5pm Sat-Thu, to 9pm Fri; ♠; T South Station) 🌊 The interactive, educational exhibits at the delightful Boston Children's Museum keep kids entertained for hours. Highlights include a bubble exhibit, rock-climbing walls, a hands-on construction site and intercultural immersion experiences. The light-filled atrium features an amazing three-story climbing maze. In nice weather kids can enjoy outdoor eating and playing in the waterside park. Look for the iconic **Hood Milk Bottle** (Map p52) on Fort Point Channel.

☉ South End & Chinatown

Chinatown, the Theater District and the Leather District are overlapping areas, filled with glitzy theaters, Chinese restaurants and the remnants of Boston's shoe and leather industry (now converted lofts and clubs). Nearby, the Victorian manses in the South End have been reclaimed by artists and the LGBTIQ+ community, who have created a vibrant restaurant and gallery scene.

★Underground at Ink Block   PUBLIC ART
(www.undergroundinkblock.com; 90 Traveler St; ⊘24hr; Ⓣ Tufts Medical Center) What used to be an abandoned parking lot beneath the interstate is now an 8-acre playground and art space. The main draw is the fantastic mural project, which turned 150,000 sq ft of concrete wall space into a fabulous outdoor gallery for street art, with bold colorful pieces by a dozen local and national artists. To say the mural brightens the place up is an understatement. There's also a dog park, walking paths and fitness classes to get you moving.

SoWa Artists Guild   GALLERY
(Map p62; ☑857-362-7692; www.sowaartistsguild. com; 450 Harrison Ave; ⊘5-9pm 1st Fri of month; 🚇SL4, SL5, Ⓣ Tufts Medical Center) FREE The brick-and-beam buildings along Harrison Ave were originally used to manufacture goods ranging from canned food to pianos. Now these factories turn out paintings and sculptures instead. Housing about 70 artist studios and more than a dozen galleries, the SoWa Artists Guild is the epicenter of the South End art district. There is a SoWa Open Studios event on the first Friday of every month, while many artists also welcome visitors on Sundays.

Chinatown Gate   LANDMARK
(Map p52; Beach St; Ⓣ Chinatown) The official entrance to Chinatown is the decorative gate *(paifong)*, a gift from the city of Taipei. It is symbolic – not only as an entryway for guests visiting Chinatown, but also as an entryway for immigrants who are still settling here, as they come to establish relationships and put down roots in their new home.

Surrounding the gate and anchoring the southern end of the Rose Kennedy Greenway is **Chinatown Park**. A bamboo-lined walkway runs through the modern gardens. The plaza is often populated by local residents engaged in *Xiangqi* (Chinese chess) and Falun Gong (a Chinese spiritual practice).

☉ Back Bay

Boston's best architecture – including the Boston Public Library and Trinity Church – is clustered around Copley Square, while the art galleries are lined up along Newbury St. The Charles River Esplanade is not exactly a destination in and of itself, but it's a fantastic place for a bike ride or a stroll.

★Boston Public Library   LIBRARY
(Map p62; ☑617-536-5400; www.bpl.org; 700 Boylston St; ⊘9am-9pm Mon-Thu, to 5pm Fri & Sat year-round, plus 1-5pm Sun Oct-May; Ⓣ Copley) FREE Founded in 1852, the esteemed Boston Public Library lends credence to Boston's reputation as the 'Athens of America.' The old McKim building is notable for its magnificent facade and exquisite interior art. Pick up a free brochure and take a self-guided tour; alternatively, free guided tours depart from the entrance hall (times vary; see the website for the current schedule).

★Charles River Esplanade   PARK
(Map p62; www.esplanadeassociation.org; 🖝; Ⓣ Charles/MGH, Kenmore) The southern bank of the Charles River Basin is an enticing urban escape, with grassy knolls and cooling waterways, all designed by Frederick Law Olmsted. It stretches almost 3 miles along the Boston shore of the Charles River, from the Museum of Science to Boston University Bridge. The park is dotted with public art, including an oversized bust of Arthur Fiedler, longtime conductor of the Boston Pops. Paths along the river are ideal for bicycling, jogging or walking.

★Trinity Church   CHURCH
(Map p62; ☑617-536-0944, ext 206; www.trinitychurchboston.org; 206 Clarendon St; adult/child $10/free; ⊘10am-4:30pm Tue-Sat, 12:15-4:30pm Sun Easter-Oct, reduced hours rest of year; Ⓣ Copley) A masterpiece of American architecture, Trinity Church is the country's ultimate example of Richardsonian Romanesque. The granite exterior, with a massive portico and side cloister, uses sandstone in colorful patterns. The interior is an awe-striking array of murals and stained glass, most by artist John LaFarge, who cooperated closely with architect Henry Hobson Richardson to create an integrated composition of shapes, colors and textures. Free architectural tours are offered

Back Bay, the Fenway & the South End

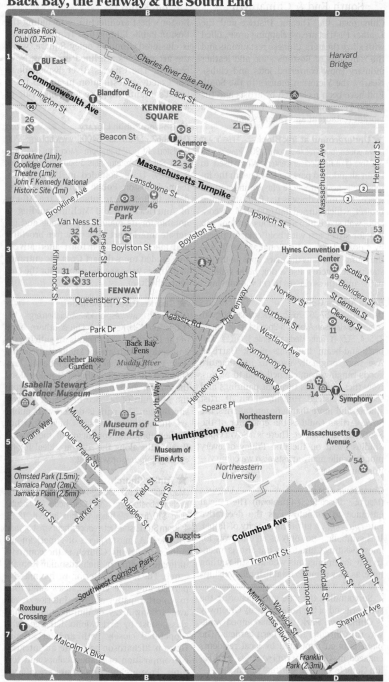

Paradise Rock Club (0.75mi)

BU East

Commonwealth Ave

Cummington St

Bay State Rd

Charles River Bike Path

Back St

Harvard Bridge

Blandford

KENMORE SQUARE

26

Beacon St

8

Kenmore

21

Massachusetts Ave

Hereford St

Brookline (1mi);
Coolidge Corner
Theatre (1mi);
John F Kennedy National
Historic Site (1mi)

22 34

Massachusetts Turnpike

Lansdowne St

2

2

Fenway
Park

3

46

Ipswich St

Van Ness St

32 44

Jersey St

25

Boylston St

Boylston St

Hynes Convention
Center

61

53

49

Scotia St

31

33

Peterborough St

7

Belvidere St

St Germain St

FENWAY

Queensberry St

Norway St

Burbank St

Clearway St

11

Agassiz Rd

The Fenway

Westland Ave

Park Dr

Back Bay
Fens

Muddy River

Symphony Rd

Gainsborough St

Kelleher Rose
Garden

Hemenway St

51

14

Symphony

Isabella Stewart
Gardner Museum

4

Forsyth Way

Speare Pl

Evans Way

Museum Rd

5

Northeastern

Massachusetts
Avenue

Louis Prang St

Museum of
Fine Arts

Huntington Ave

54

Olmsted Park (1.5mi);
Jamaica Pond (2mi);
Jamaica Plain (2.5mi)

Museum of
Fine Arts

Northeastern
University

Ward St

Parker St

Field St

Leon St

Ruggles St

Ruggles

Columbus Ave

Tremont St

Lenox St

Camden St

Southwest Corridor Park

Melnea Cass Blvd

Warwick St

Hammond St

Kendall St

Shawmut Ave

Roxbury
Crossing

Malcolm X Blvd

Franklin
Park (2.3mi)

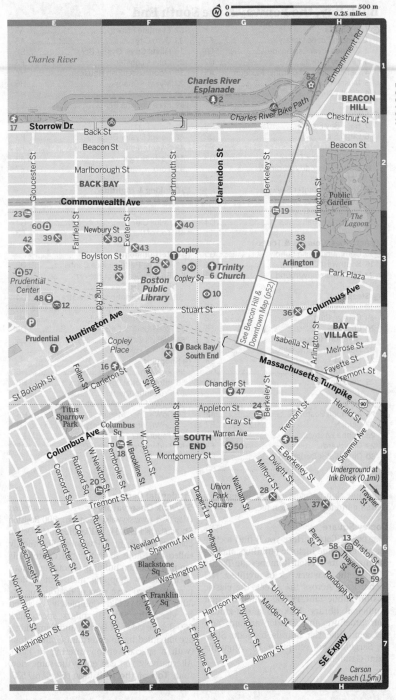

0   500 m
0   0.25 miles

Charles River

Charles River
Esplanade

⭐ 2

Charles River Bike Path

BEACON
HILL

🚻 17   **Storraw Dr**

Back St

Chestnut St

Beacon St

Beacon St

Marlborough St

BACK BAY

Gloucester St

Dartmouth St

Clarendon St

Berkeley St

Arlington St

Public
Garden

Commonwealth Ave

23 🏛

60 🔒

42   39 ✖

Fairfield St

Newbury St

Exeter St

✖ 40

🍴 19

The
Lagoon

✖ 30

43

Copley

29

🔒 57
Prudential
Center

48 🚇 12

🅿
Prudential
Ⓣ

35

1 ◎

**Boston
Public
Library**

9 ◎

Copley Sq

◎ 10

Stuart St

Ring Rd

Huntington Ave

Copley
Place

✝ Trinity
6 Church

Arlington
Ⓣ

38 ✖

Park Plaza

36 ✖ **Columbus Ave**

Isabella St

**BAY
VILLAGE**

Melrose St

41 Ⓣ Back Bay/
South End

See Beacon Hill &
Downtown Map (p52)

Fayette St
Tremont St

Massachusetts Turnpike

16 ✖

Follen St

St Botolph St

Carleton St

Yarmouth St

Chandler St
🍴 47

Berkeley St

24

90

Herald St

Titus
Sparrow
Park

Columbus
Sq

W Newton St

Pembroke St

18

Columbus Ave

W Canton St

W Brookline St

Dartmouth St

Appleton St

Gray St

**SOUTH
END**

Warren Ave

Montgomery St

Tremont St

🏛 15

Tremont St

E Berkeley St

Shawmut Ave

Underground at
Ink Block (0.1mi)

Traveler St

Concord Sq

Rutland Sq

20

W Newton St

Rutland St

Tremont St

Union Park
Square

Drapers La

Waltham St

Milford St

Dwight St

28 ✖

37 ✖

Massachusetts Ave

W Springfield St

Worcester St

W Concord St

Newland St

Shawmut Ave

Pelham St

Blackstone
Sq

Washington St

Union Park St

Perry
St

58

55 🔒

13 🛏 Bristol St

Thayer
St

56   59

Randolph St

Franklin
Sq

Northampton St

Washington St

✖ 45

E Newton St

E Concord St

E Brookline St

Harrison Ave

E Canton St

Plympton St

Malden St

Albany St

SE Expwy

27 ✖

Carson
Beach (1.5mi)

Back Bay, the Fenway & the South End

◉ Top Sights
1 Boston Public Library F3
2 Charles River Esplanade G1
3 Fenway Park B2
4 Isabella Stewart Gardner Museum A5
5 Museum of Fine Arts B5
6 Trinity Church G3

◉ Sights
7 Back Bay Fens C3
8 Citgo Sign B2
9 Copley Square F3
10 John Hancock Tower G3
11 Mary Baker Eddy Library &
    Mapparium D4
12 Prudential Center Skywalk
    Observatory E3
13 SoWa Artists Guild H6
14 Symphony Hall D4

◐ Activities, Courses & Tours
15 Community Bike Supply G5
16 Southwest Corridor F4
17 Stoneman Playground E2

◑ Sleeping
18 Clarendon Square Inn F5
19 College Club G2
20 Encore E5
21 Gryphon House C2
22 Hotel Commonwealth B2
23 No 284 .... E3
24 Revolution Hotel G5
25 Verb Hotel B3

◉ Eating
26 Audubon Boston A2
27 Blunch E7
28 Coppa Enoteca G5
29 Courtyard F3
30 Dirty Water Dough Co F3
31 El Pelon A3

32 Eventide Fenway A3
33 Gyro City A3
34 Island Creek Oyster Bar B2
35 Luke's Lobster F3
36 Mooncusser Fish House H4
37 Myers + Chang H6
38 Parish Café H3
39 Puro Ceviche Bar E3
40 Saltie Girl F3
41 Salty Pig F4
42 Select Oyster Bar E3
43 Sweetgreen F3
44 Tasty Burger A3
45 Toro E7

◉ Drinking & Nightlife
Beehive .... (see 50)
46 Bleacher Bar B2
47 Delux Café G4
48 Top of the Hub E3

◉ Entertainment
49 Berklee Performance Center D3
50 Boston Center for the Arts G5
   Boston Red Sox .... (see 3)
51 Boston Symphony Orchestra D4
   Company One .... (see 50)
52 Hatch Memorial Shell H1
53 Red Room @ Cafe 939 .... D3
54 Wally's Café D5

◉ Shopping
55 Ars Libri H6
56 International Poster Gallery H6
57 Prudential Center E3
58 SoWa Farmers Market H6
59 SoWa Open Market H6
   SoWa Vintage Market .... (see 13)
60 Topdrawer E3
61 Trident Booksellers & Café D3

following Sunday service; on other days there's a modest admission fee.

Copley Square
PLAZA

(Map p62; T Copley) Here you'll find a cluster of handsome historic buildings, including the ornate French-Romanesque Trinity Church, the masterwork of architect HH Richardson. Across the street, the classic Boston Public Library was America's first municipal library. Pick up a self-guided tour brochure and wander around, noting gems like the murals by John Singer Sargent and sculpture by Augustus Saint-Gaudens.

Prudential Center Skywalk Observatory
VIEWPOINT

(Map p62; www.skywalkboston.com; 800 Boylston St; adult/child $20/14; ⊙10am-10pm Mar-Oct, to 8pm Nov-Feb; P ♿; T Prudential) Technically called the Shops at Prudential Center, this landmark Boston building is not much more than a fancy shopping mall. But it does provide a bird's-eye view of Boston from its 50th-floor Skywalk. Completely enclosed by glass, the Skywalk offers spectacular 360-degree views of Boston and Cambridge, accompanied by an entertaining audio tour (with a special version catering to kids). Alternatively, you can enjoy the same view from **Top of the Hub** (Map p62; ☑617-536-

1775; www.topofthehub.net; ⊙11:30am-1am; ⓣ; ⓣPrudential) for the price of a drink.

Mary Baker Eddy
Library & Mapparium   LIBRARY
(Map p62; ☑617-450-7000; www.marybakereddy library.org; 200 Massachusetts Ave; adult/child $6/4; ⊙10am-5pm; ⓗ; ⓣSymphony) The Mary Baker Eddy Library houses one of Boston's hidden treasures. The intriguing Mapparium is a room-sized, stained-glass globe that visitors walk through on a glass bridge. It was created in 1935, which is reflected in the globe's geopolitical boundaries. The acoustics, which surprised even the designer, allow everyone in the room to hear even the tiniest whisper.

John Hancock Tower   NOTABLE BUILDING
(Map p62; 200 Clarendon St; ⓣCopley) Constructed with more than 10,000 panels of mirrored glass, the 62-story John Hancock Tower was designed in 1976 by Henry Cobb. It is the tallest and most beloved skyscraper on the Boston skyline – despite the precarious falling panes of glass when it was first built. The Hancock offers an amazing perspective on Trinity Church (p61), reflected in its facade.

◉ Kenmore Square & Fenway

Art lovers should make a beeline for Kenmore Sq & Fenway, a neighborhood that's home to two fabulous art museums. (You'll need more than one day if you intend to see them both.) Sports fans, plan ahead if you are hoping to catch a Red Sox game or to take a tour of the baseball park, as the Hometown Team is Boston's hottest ticket.

★Fenway Park   STADIUM
(Map p62; ☑617-226-6666; www.redsox.com; 4 Jersey St; tours adult/child $20/14, pre-game $35-45; ⊙9am-5pm Apr-Oct, special schedule game days, 10am-5pm Nov-Mar; ⓣKenmore) Home of the Boston Red Sox since 1912, Fenway Park is the oldest operating baseball park in the country. As such, the park has many quirks that make for a unique experience. See them all on a ballpark tour, or come see the Sox playing in their natural habitat.

The most famous feature at Fenway Park is the **Green Monster**, the 37ft-high wall in left field. It is a popular target for right-handed hitters, who can score an easy home run with a high hit to left field. At the base of the Green Monster is the original

scoreboard, still updated manually from behind the wall.

★Museum of Fine Arts   MUSEUM
(MFA; Map p62; ☑617-267-9300; www.mfa.org; 465 Huntington Ave; adult/child $25/free; ⊙10am-5pm Sat-Tue, to 10pm Wed-Fri; ⓣMuseum of Fine Arts, Ruggles) Founded in 1876, the Museum of Fine Arts is Boston's foremost art museum. The museum covers all parts of the globe and all eras, from the ancient world to contemporary times. The collections are strong in Asian and European art, but the uncontested highlight is the gorgeous Art of the Americas wing.

★Isabella Stewart
Gardner Museum   MUSEUM
(Map p62; ☑617-566-1401; www.gardnermuseum. org; 25 Evans Way; adult/child $15/free; ⊙11am-5pm Wed-Mon, to 9pm Thu; ⓣMuseum of Fine Arts) Once home to Isabella Stewart Gardner, this splendid palazzo now houses her exquisite collection of art. The museum includes thousands of artistic objects, especially Italian Renaissance and Dutch Golden Age paintings. The interior courtyard, lush with seasonal plants and flowers, is an oasis of tranquility and beauty.

Citgo Sign   LANDMARK
(Map p62; ⓣKenmore) London has Big Ben, Paris has the Eiffel Tower and Boston has the Citgo sign. It's an unlikely landmark in this high-minded city, but Bostonians love the bright-blinking 'trimark' that has towered over Kenmore Sq since 1965. Every time the Red Sox hit a home run over the left-field wall at Fenway Park, Citgo's colorful logo is seen by thousands of fans. It also symbolizes the end of the Boston Marathon, as it falls at Mile 25 in the race.

Back Bay Fens   PARK
(Map p62; Park Dr; ⊙dawn-dusk; ⓣMuseum of Fine Arts) The Back Bay Fens, or the Fenway, follows the Muddy River, an aptly named creek that is choked with tall reeds. The Fens features well-cared-for community gardens, the elegant Kelleher Rose Garden, and plenty of space to toss a Frisbee, play pick-up basketball or lie in the sun.

◉ Cambridge

Stretched out along the north shore of the Charles River, Cambridge is a separate city with two distinguished universities, a host of historic sites, and artistic and cultural

Cambridge

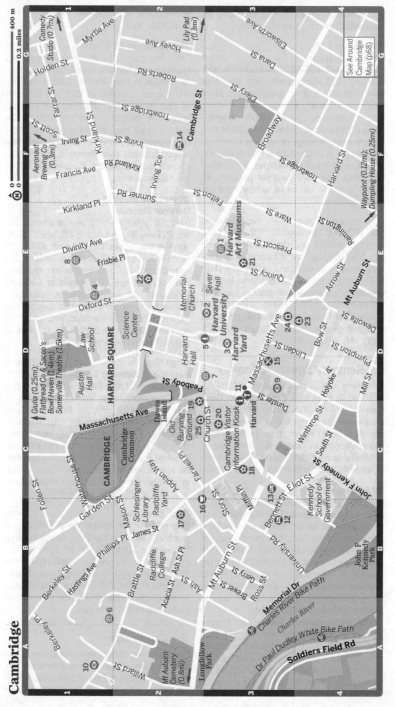

0.2 miles
400 m

See Around
Cambridge
Map (p63)

Cambridge

◎ Top Sights
1 Harvard Art Museums E3
2 Harvard University D3
3 Harvard Yard D3

◎ Sights
4 Harvard Museum of Natural History E1
5 John Harvard Statue D3
6 Longfellow House A1
7 Massachusetts Hall D3
8 Peabody Museum of Archaeology &
   Ethnology E1
9 Smith Campus Center D3
10 Tory Row A1

◎ Activities, Courses & Tours
11 Hahvahd Tour D3

◎ Sleeping
12 Charles Hotel B3
13 Harvard Square Hotel C3
14 Irving House at Harvard F2

◎ Eating
15 CloverHSQ D3

◎ Drinking & Nightlife
16 LA Burdick B2

◎ Entertainment
17 American Repertory Theater B2
18 Brattle Theatre C3
19 Cambridge Forum C2
20 Club Passim C3
21 Harvard Film Archive
   Cinematheque E3
22 Sanders Theatre at Memorial
   Hall E2

◎ Shopping
23 Grolier Poetry Bookshop D4
24 Harvard Bookstore D3
25 Raven Used Books C2

BOSTON SIGHTS

attractions galore. The streets around Harvard, Central Sq and Kendall Sq are home to restaurants, bars and clubs that rival their counterparts across the river.

★**Harvard University** UNIVERSITY
(Map p66; ☑617-495-1000; www.harvard.edu; Massachusetts Ave; tours free; ⓣHarvard) America's oldest college, Harvard University was founded in 1636 and remains one of the country's most prestigious universities. Alumni of the original Ivy League school include eight US presidents, and dozens of Nobel Laureates and Pulitzer Prize winners. For visitors, the university campus contains some historic buildings clustered around Harvard Yard, as well as impressive architecture and excellent museums. Free historical tours depart from the Smith Campus Center; self-guided tours are also available.

★**Harvard Yard** AREA
(Map p66; Harvard University; ⓣHarvard) Harvard Yard remains the historic and geographic heart of the university campus. Flanked by its oldest buildings, the yard's main entrance at Johnston Gate opens up to wide lawns, gracious architecture and a buzzy academic atmosphere.

★**Harvard Art Museums** MUSEUM
(Map p66; ☑617-495-9400; www.harvardart museums.org; 32 Quincy St; adult/child/student $15/free/free; ⓢ10am-5pm; ⓣHarvard) The 2014 renovation and expansion of Harvard's

art museums allowed the university's massive 250,000-piece collection to come together under one very stylish roof, designed by architect extraordinaire Renzo Piano. The artwork spans the globe, with separate collections devoted to Asian and Islamic cultures, northern European and Germanic cultures and other Western art, especially European modernism.

★**Mt Auburn Cemetery** CEMETERY
(☑617-547-7105; www.mountauburn.org; 580 Mt Auburn St; ⓢ8am-8pm May-Sep, to 5pm Oct-Apr; ⓟ71, 73, ⓣHarvard) This delightful spot at the end of Brattle St is worth the 30-minute walk west from Harvard Square. Developed in 1831, it was the first 'garden cemetery' in the USA. Maps pinpoint the rare botanical specimens and notable burial plots. Famous long-term residents include Mary Baker Eddy (founder of the Christian Science Church) and Henry Wadsworth Longfellow (19th-century writer).

Smith Campus Center UNIVERSITY
(Map p66; ☑617-495-6916; www.common spaces.harvard.edu/smith-campus-center/about; 30 Dunster St; ⓢ7am-midnight Sun-Fri, to 1am Sat; ⓣHarvard) After a massive overhaul, the Smith Campus Center has been transformed into a fabulous 'living room' for students and visitors to congregate, study, socialize, eat and drink. The two-story lobby is abloom with 12,000 plants, growing on the living walls and irrigated by rainwater collected

Around Cambridge

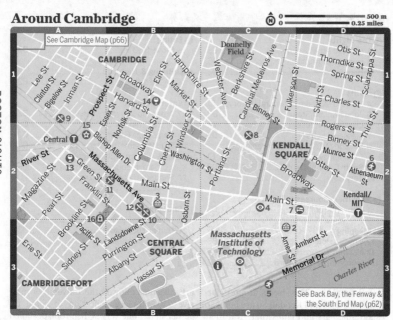

Around Cambridge

◎ Top Sights
1 Massachusetts Institute of Technology	C3

◎ Sights
2 List Visual Arts Center	C3
3 MIT Museum	B2
4 Ray & Maria Stata Center	C2

✪ Activities, Courses & Tours
5 Charles River Bike Path	C3
6 Community Ice Skating @ Kendall Square	D2

🛏 Sleeping
7 Kendall Hotel	D2

✪ Eating
8 Bon Me	C2
9 Life Alive	A1
10 Roxy's Grilled Cheese	B2
11 Veggie Galaxy	B2
12 Whole Heart Provisions	B2

🍸 Drinking & Nightlife
A4cade	(see 10)
13 Havana Club	A2
14 Lamplighter Brewing Co	B1

🎭 Entertainment
15 Improv Boston	A2

🛍 Shopping
16 Central Flea	A2

on the roof. Inviting outdoor spaces include street-side plazas and a rooftop terrace.

Tory Row STREET
(Map p66; Brattle St; 🇹 Harvard) Heading west out of Harvard Square, Brattle St is the epitome of colonial posh. Lined with mansions that were once home to royal sympathizers, the street earned the nickname Tory Row. Nowadays, it's a delightful place for a stroll to admire the gracious homes and glean some history from the environs.

Harvard Museum of Natural History MUSEUM
(Map p66; ☎ 617-495-3045; www.hmnh.harvard. edu; 26 Oxford St; adult/child/student $15/10/10; ⊗ 9am-5pm; 📷 86, 🇹 Harvard) This institution is famed for its botanical galleries, featuring some 3000 pieces of handblown, intricately crafted glass flowers and plants. There is a smaller, complementary exhibit of Sea Creatures in Glass by the same artists. Nearby, the zoological galleries house an enormous number of stuffed animals and

reassembled skeletons, as well as an impressive fossil collection.

Other cool exhibits feature climate change, sparkling gemstones and arthropods (yes, cockroaches). The price of admission includes entry into the Peabody Museum of Archaeology & Ethnology, which is in the same building.

Peabody Museum of Archaeology & Ethnology   MUSEUM

(Map p66; 617-496-1027; www.peabody.harvard.edu; 11 Divinity Ave; adult/child/student $15/10/10; 9am-5pm; 86, Harvard) The centerpiece of the Peabody is the impressive Hall of the North American Indian, which traces how these peoples responded to the arrival of Europeans from the 15th to 18th centuries. Other exhibits examine indigenous cultures throughout the Americas, including a fantastic comparison of cave paintings and murals of the Awatovi (New Mexico), the Maya (Guatemala) and the Moche (Peru). The price of admission includes entry to the neighboring Harvard Museum of Natural History.

Longfellow House   HISTORIC BUILDING

(Map p66; 617-876-4491; www.nps.gov/long; 105 Brattle St; tours 9:30am-5pm Wed-Sun late May-Oct, grounds dawn-dusk year-round; 71, 73, Harvard) FREE Brattle St's most famous resident was Henry Wadsworth Longfellow, whose stately manor is now a National Historic Site. The poet lived here from 1837 to 1882, writing many of his most famous poems, including 'Evangeline' and 'The Song of Hiawatha.' Accessible by guided tour, the Georgian mansion contains many of Longfellow's belongings and is surrounded by lush period gardens.

Massachusetts Hall   HISTORIC BUILDING

(Map p66; Harvard Yard; Harvard) On the south side of Johnston Gate, Massachusetts Hall is the oldest building on the Harvard campus, dating from 1720. Originally it was a dormitory building, home to 64 students. During the War of Independence, it was occupied (and much damaged) by revolutionary militiamen. Nowadays, it houses the offices of the President of the University and is not open to the public.

Boston Harbor Islands

Boston Harbor is sprinkled with 34 islands, many of which are open for trail walking, bird-watching, fishing, swimming and camping. You can't visit them all in one day, so consider the activities on offer and plan accordingly.

Hop on the first ferry to Georges Island, where you can spend the morning exploring Fort Warren. After lunch, take the shuttle to one of the other islands. Hit Spectacle Island for good walking trails and marvelous city views. Head to Lovells to catch some rays on the otherwise empty beach and cool off in the refreshing Atlantic waters. Or venture to Grape Island to hunt for wild berries.

Catch a shuttle (if necessary) and ferry back to the mainland from Spectacle or Georges Islands.

Georges Island   ISLAND, FORT

(early May–mid-Oct; ; from Long Wharf or Hingham) Georges Island is one of the transportation hubs for the Boston Harbor Islands. It is also the site of Fort Warren, a 19th-century fort and Civil War prison. While National Park Service rangers give guided tours of the fort and there is a small museum, it is largely abandoned, with many dark tunnels, creepy corners and magnificent lookouts to discover. Weekends on Georges are packed with kids programs, Civil War–era baseball games and jazz concerts.

This is one of the only islands with facilities such as a snack bar and restrooms.

LOCAL KNOWLEDGE

THE STATUE OF THREE LIES

The focal point of Harvard Yard (p67) is the **John Harvard Statue** (Map p66; Harvard), where every Harvard hopeful has a photo taken (and touches the statue's shiny shoe for good luck). Daniel Chester French's sculpture, inscribed 'John Harvard, Founder of Harvard College, 1638,' is known as the 'statue of three lies': it does not actually depict Harvard (since no image of him exists), but a random student; John Harvard was not the founder of the college, but its first benefactor in 1638; and the college was actually founded two years earlier in 1636. The Harvard symbol hardly lives up to the university's motto, Veritas, or 'truth.'

DON'T MISS

MIT: MASSACHUSETTS INSTITUTE OF TECHNOLOGY

The **Massachusetts Institute of Technology** (MIT; Map p68; ☑617-253-1000; www.mit.edu; 77 Massachusetts Ave; ⊙info session incl campus tour 10am & 2:30pm Mon-Fri; T Kendall/MIT) offers a different perspective on academia. MIT has a proud history of pushing the boundaries, from its innovative architecture and oddball art to its cutting-edge technology and playful pranks. Campus tours depart from the **MIT Information Center** (Map p68; ☑617-253-3400; www.web.mit.edu/visitmit; 77 Massachusetts Ave, No 7-121, Rogers Bldg; ⊙9am-5pm Mon-Fri).

Of all the eye-catching buildings on the MIT campus, none has received more attention than the **Ray & Maria Stata Center** (CSAIL; Map p68; ☑617-253-5851; www.csail.mit.edu; 32 Vassar St; T Kendall/MIT), an avant-garde edifice that was designed by architectural legend Frank Gehry. Other worthwhile stops on campus include the **MIT Museum** (Map p68; ☑617-253-5927; http://mitmuseum.mit.edu; 265 Massachusetts Ave; adult/child $10/5; ⊙10am-6pm Jul & Aug, to 5pm Sep-Jun; P; T Central) and the **List Visual Arts Center** (Map p68; ☑617-253-4680; http://listart.mit.edu; 20 Ames St, Weisner Bldg; donation $5; ⊙noon-6pm Tue, Wed & Fri-Sun, to 8pm Thu; T Kendall/MIT). You can also pick up or download a map of MIT's fantastic collection of public art.

Spectacle Island ISLAND
(⊙dawn-dusk early May–mid-Sep; 🛝; 🚢from Long Wharf) 🌿 A Harbor Islands hub, Spectacle Island has a large marina, a solar-powered visitor center, a healthy snack bar and sandy, supervised beaches. Five miles of walking trails provide access to a 157ft peak overlooking the harbor. Special events include Saturday morning yoga classes, Sunday afternoon jazz concerts and Thursday evening clam bakes. Spectacle Island is relatively close to the city and a ferry runs here directly from Long Wharf (hourly in July and August, less frequently in June and September).

World's End PARK
(www.thetrustees.org; 250 Martin's Lane, Hingham; adult/child $8/free; ⊙8am-dusk) This 251-acre peninsula was designed by Frederick Law Olmsted for residential development in 1889. Carriage paths were laid out and trees were planted, but the houses were never built. Instead, wide, grassy meadows attract butterflies and grass-nesting birds. Today, management by the Trustees of Reservations guarantees continued serenity and beauty. The 4 miles of tree-lined paths are perfect for walking, mountain biking or cross-country skiing – download a map from the website. World's End is accessible by car from Hingham.

Little Brewster Island ISLAND, LIGHTHOUSE
(☑617-223-8666; www.bostonharborislands.org/bostonlight; adult/child $35/25; ⊙9:30am & 1pm Fri-Sun Jun-Sep; 🚢from Long Wharf) Little Brewster is the country's oldest light station and site of the iconic **Boston Light**, dating from 1783. To visit Little Brewster, you must take an organized tour (reservations required). Learn about Boston's maritime history during a narrated sail around the harbor, passing Graves Light, Long Island Light and Boston Light.

Tours depart from the Boston Harbor Islands Pavilion on the Rose Kennedy Greenway. At the time of research, public access to Little Brewster Island was cut off due to storm damage. Check the website to discover whether travelers can once again climb the 76 steps to the top of the lighthouse for a close-up view of the rotating light and a far-off view of the city skyline.

Lovells Island ISLAND
(⊙late Jun-early Sep; 🚢from Long Wharf or Georges) With camping and picnicking facilities, Lovells is one of the most popular Harbor Islands destinations. Two deadly shipwrecks may bode badly for seafarers, but that doesn't seem to stop recreational boaters, swimmers and sunbathers from lounging on Lovells' long rocky beach. Some of the former uses of Lovells are evident: European settlers used the island as a rabbit run, and until recently descendant bunnies were still running this place; Fort Standish dates from WWI and is ripe for exploration.

🏃 Activities

Boating
Community Boating WATER SPORTS
(Map p52; ☑617-523-1038; www.community-boating.org; Charles River Esplanade; kayak/stand-up

paddleboard/sailboat per day from $45/45/89; ☺1pm-dusk Mon-Fri, 9am-dusk Sat & Sun Apr-Oct; ⓣCharles/MGH) Offers experienced sailors unlimited use of sailboats and kayaks on the Charles River, but you'll have to take a test to demonstrate your ability. A 30-day 'learn to sail' package costs $179, while a 30-day Wicked Basic, No-Frills sailing pass is $99.

Swan Boats   BOATING
(Map p52; ✍617-522-1966; www.swanboats.com; Public Garden; adult/child $4/2.50; ☺10am-4pm Apr-Jun, to 5pm Jul-Aug; ⓣArlington) A relic of Boston's bygone days, a ride on the swan boats on the tranquil lagoon of the Public Garden offers 15 minutes of serenity.

Courageous Sailing   BOATING
(✍617-242-3821; www.courageoussailing.org; Pier 4; 2hr sail $190; ☺noon-sunset Mon-Fri, from 10am Sat & Sun May-Oct; 🖭; 🚌93 from Haymarket, 🛳Inner Harbor Ferry from Long Wharf, ⓣNorth Station) Named after a two-time America's Cup winner, Courageous Sailing offers instruction and boat rental for sailors and would-be sailors. A unique public-private partnership, this outfit was established by the City of Boston with the support of private individuals, with the aim of making sailing accessible to kids and adults of all ages, incomes and abilities.

Cycling

★ **Minuteman Bikeway**   CYCLING
(www.minutemanbikeway.org; ⓣAlewife, Davis) The best of Boston's bicycle trails starts near Alewife station and leads 5 miles to historic Lexington Center, then traverses an additional 4 miles of idyllic scenery and terminates in the rural suburb of Bedford. The wide, straight, paved path gets crowded on weekends. Rent a bike at the **Bicycle Exchange** (✍617-864-1300; www.cambridgebicycleexchange. com; 2067 Massachusetts Ave; rental 1 day $25, additional days $10; ☺hours vary; ⓣPorter). The Minuteman Bikeway is also accessible from Davis Sq in Somerville (Davis T station) via the 2-mile Community Path to Alewife.

Charles River Bike Path   CYCLING
(Map p68; Storrow Dr & Memorial Dr; 🖭; ⓣHarvard, Kendall/MIT, Charles/MGH, Science Park) A popular cycling circuit runs along both sides of the Charles River between the Museum of Science and the Mt Auburn St Bridge in Watertown center (5 miles west of Cambridge). The round trip is 17 miles, but 10 bridges in between offer ample op-

portunities to shorten the trip. Rent a bike at **Cambridge Bicycle** (✍617-876-6555; www. cambridgebicycle.com; 259 Massachusetts Ave; per 24hr $35; ☺10am-7pm Mon-Sat, noon-6pm Sun; ⓣCentral) or Papa Wheelies. Ride carefully! This trail is not particularly well maintained (watch for roots and narrow passes) and is often crowded with pedestrians.

Community Bike Supply   CYCLING
(Map p62; ✍617-542-8623; www.communitybicy cle.com; 496 Tremont St; per day $25-35; ☺10am-7pm Mon-Sat year-round, noon-5pm Sun Apr-Sep; ⓣBack Bay) These friendly folks will rent a hybrid so you can explore the area on two wheels. Conveniently located for a ride along the Southwest Corridor.

Southwest Corridor   CYCLING
(Map p62; www.swcpc.org; ⓣBack Bay/South End) Extending for almost 5 miles, the Southwest Corridor is a paved walkway running between and parallel to Columbus and Huntington Aves. It's an ideal urban cycling route, leading from Back Bay, through the South End and Roxbury, to Forest Hills in Jamaica Plain. Borrow a bike from Blue Bikes or rent one at Community Bicycle Supply or **Papa Wheelies** (Back Bay Bicycles; ✍617-247-2336; www.papa-wheelies.com; 362 Commonwealth Ave; rental per day $55-65; ☺10am-7pm Mon-Fri, to 6pm Sat, noon-5pm Sun; ⓣHynes).

Skating

Lynch Family Skate Park   SKATING
(Map p52; Education St, Cambridge; ☺dawn-9pm; ⓣScience Park) FREE Local sculptor Nancy Schön had the brilliant idea of turning an under-highway urban wasteland into a playground for Boston's BMX riders, skateboarders and anybody that rolls. It's under the access ramp to the Zakim Bridge. Access the park from North Point Park in Cambridge or Paul Revere Park in Charlestown.

Boston Common Frog Pond   SKATING
(Map p52; ✍617-635-2120; www.bostonfrogpond. com; Boston Common; adult/child $6/free, skate rental $12/6; ☺10am-3:45pm Mon, to 9pm Tue-Thu & Sun, to 10pm Fri & Sat mid-Nov–mid-Mar; 🖭; ⓣPark St) When temperatures drop, the Boston Common becomes an urban winter wonderland, with slipping and sliding, swirling and twirling on the Frog Pond. Weekends are often crowded, as are weekdays around noon, as local skate fiends spend their lunch break on the ice. In warmer weather, the Frog Pond becomes a wet and wild spray pool where kids can cool off.

The nearby **Tadpole Playground** is another fun place for the kids to expend some extra energy.

Community Ice Skating
@ Kendall Square
ICE SKATING

(Map p68; ☑ 617-492-0941; www.skatekendall. com; 300 Athenaeum St; adult/child $5/1, rental $8/5; ☻ noon-8pm Mon-Thu, 11am-9pm Fri & Sat, to 6pm Sun Dec-Mar; 🚼; Ⓣ Kendall/MIT) Kendall Sq may not have the same charm as the Boston Common, but this smallish rink has many other benefits. There are usually fewer people, for a start, which means more room for your pirouettes (or whatever you do on the ice). The rental skates are in excellent condition and the staff are helpful if you're not an experienced skater.

Other Activities

★ New England
Aquarium Whale Watch
WHALE WATCHING

(Map p52; ☑ 617-227-4321; www.neaq.org/ex hibits/whale-watch; Central Wharf; adult/child/ infant $53/33/16; ☻ times vary late Mar–mid-Nov; Ⓣ Aquarium) ✦ Set off from Long Wharf for the journey to Stellwagen Bank, a rich feeding ground for whales, dolphins and marine birds. Keen-eyed boat captains and onboard naturalists can answer all your questions and have been trained by New England Aquarium experts to ensure that the tours do not interfere with the animals or harm them in any way.

★ Flatbread Co
& Sacco's Bowl Haven
BOWLING

(☑ 617-776-0552; www.flatbreadcompany.com; 45 Day St, Somerville; per lane per hour $30, shoe rental $3; ☻ 9am-midnight Mon-Sat, to 10:30pm Sun; 🚼; Ⓣ Davis) ✦ Founded in 1939, Sacco's Bowl Haven is a Somerville institution – old-time candlepin bowling lanes that managed to survive into the 21st century. When Flatbread Company took over they brightened the space and added clay ovens, but preserved most of the lanes and the good-time atmosphere. Now you can enjoy delicious organic pizzas and cold craft beers with your candlepins.

Carson Beach
SWIMMING

(☑ 617-727-8865; Day Blvd; ☻ dawn-dusk; 🚼; 🚌 11, Ⓣ Broadway) Heading west from Castle Island (p60), 3 miles of beaches offer opportunities for swimming in an urban setting. L and M St beaches are adjacent to each other along Day Blvd, while Carson Beach is further west. They all have smooth sand,

nice harbor views, decent facilities and frigid water.

The Lawn on D
PLAYGROUND

(☑ 877-393-3393; www.signatureboston.com/ lawn-on-d; 420 D St; ☻ 7am-10pm; 🚌 SL1, SL2) This open-air 'adult playground' is a fun summer destination. At the heart of the experience is SwingTime, a set of glow-in-the-dark swings (yes, for adults), lit by multicolored, solar-powered LEDs. The vast lawn and adjacent tented area host a variety of special events each summer, featuring food, drink, movie nights, games and live music.

Stoneman Playground
PLAYGROUND

(Map p62; Charles River Esplanade; 🚼; Ⓣ Hynes) Two gated play areas on the Charles River Esplanade get wonderful river breezes. The first is designed for toddlers, with baby swings and slides, while the second has a cool, challenging climbing structure for older kids.

🖝 Tours

Boat Tours

Boston Green Cruises
CRUISE

(Map p52; ☑ 617-261-6620; www.bostongreen cruises.com; 60 Rowes Wharf; adult/child from $28/24; 🚼; Ⓣ Aquarium, South Station) ✦ See the sights and hear the sounds of the city from Boston's first super-quiet, zero-emissions electric boat. Spend an hour floating in the Boston Harbor or cruising on the Charles River (or upgrade to a 90-minute combo trip for $39/35 per adult/child).

Boston Harbor Cruises
CRUISE

(BHC; Map p52; ☑ 617-227-4321; www.boston harborcruises.com; 1 Long Wharf; cruises adult/ child from $26/22, Codzilla $33/25; Ⓣ Aquarium) BHC claims to be America's oldest and largest operator of passenger boats. The options range from a basic Historic Sightseeing Tour around Boston's inner harbor to sunset cruises, weekend lighthouse cruises, whale-watching and more. Codzilla is a 2800HP speedboat that cruises through the waves at high speeds and guarantees that passengers will get wet.

Liberty Fleet
CRUISE

(Map p52; ☑ 617-742-0333; www.libertyfleet.com; Central Wharf; adult/child from $19/30; ☻ times vary Jun-Sep; Ⓣ Aquarium) The 125ft *Liberty Clipper* and the smaller *Liberty Star* take passengers out for a two-hour, 12-mile cruise around the harbor. The schooners sail sever-

LGBTIQ+ BOSTON

Out and active gay communities are visible all around Boston, especially in the South End and Jamaica Plain.

There is no shortage of entertainment options catering to LGBTIQ+ travelers. From drag shows to dyke nights, this sexually diverse community has something for everybody. There are excellent sources of information for the gay and lesbian community.

Bay Windows (www.baywindows.com) is a weekly newspaper for LGBTIQ+ readers. The print edition is distributed throughout New England, but the website is also an excellent source of news and information.

Edge Boston (www.edgeboston.com) is the Boston branch of the nationwide network of publications offering news and entertainment for LGBTIQ+ readers. Includes a nightlife section with culture and club reviews.

al times a day, sometimes offering historical re-enactments, brunch or sunsets. Purchase tickets online or from the office on Long Wharf.

Themed Tours

★**Urban AdvenTours** CYCLING
(Map p52; ☏617-670-0637; www.urbanadventours.com; 103 Atlantic Ave; tours from $55, rentals per 24hr $40-75; ⏱9am-8pm Apr-Oct, reduced hours rest of year; ⓣAquarium) This outfit was founded by avid cyclists who believe the best views of Boston are from a bicycle. And they're right! The City View Ride tour provides a great overview of how to get around by bike, including ride-bys of some of Boston's best sites. Other specialty tours include Bikes at Night and the Emerald Necklace tour. Bicycles, helmets and water are all provided.

Photo Walks WALKING
(☏617-851-2273; www.photowalks.com; adult/youth $40/20; ⓐ) A walking tour combined with a photography lesson. Different routes cover Boston's most photogenic neighborhoods.

Ghosts & Gravestones HISTORY
(Map p52; ☏866-754-9136; www.ghostsandgravestones.com; Long Wharf; adult/child $42/25; ⓣAquarium) A hair-raising tour telling tales of Boston's darker side, hosted by a cursed gravedigger. Tickets are discounted slightly if you buy them online.

Boston Foodie Tours FOOD
(☏617-461-5772; www.bostonfoodietours.com; $68-88; ⓣNorth Station) Make sure you start the tour hungry, is the advice from participants in these recommended walking tours. The most popular option is a three-

hour walking tour of the Boston Public Market and environs, including tastings of award-winning lobster rolls and clam chowder. Alternatively, the North End Neighborhood Tour focuses on pizza, mozzarella and Italian treats, ending with a pasta dinner.

Boston Duck Tours BOATING
(☏617-267-3825; www.bostonducktours.com; adult/child $42/28; ⓐ; ⓣAquarium, Science Park, Prudential) These ridiculously popular tours use WWII amphibious vehicles that cruise the downtown streets before splashing into the Charles River. The 80-minute tours depart from the Museum of Science (p56), the **Prudential Center** (Map p62; ☏800-746-7778; www.prudentialcenter.com; 800 Boylston St; ⏱10am-9pm Mon-Sat, 11am-7pm Sun; ⓐ; ⓣPrudential) or the New England Aquarium (p55). Reserve in advance.

North End
Market Tour WALKING
(Map p52; ☏617-523-6032; www.bostonfoodtours.com; tours $60; ⏱tours 10am & 2pm Wed & Sat, 10am & 3pm Fri) A three-hour tour around the North End that includes shopping in a *salumeria* (deli), sampling pastries at the local *pasticceria*, smelling the herbs and spices that flavor Italian cooking, and sampling spirits at an *enoteca* (wine bar). Guests have the opportunity to chat with local shopkeepers and other longtime North End residents to reminisce about living and eating in this food-rich neighborhood.

On Location Tours WALKING
(☏212-683-2027; www.onlocationtours.com; adult/child $27/19) It's not Hollywood, but Boston has hosted its share of famous movie scenes. More than 30 films were shot along

Boston's Movie Mile, which you will see on this 90-minute walking tour.

Trolley Tours

Beantown Trolley
BUS

(☑800-343-1328, 617-720-6342; www.brushhill-tours.com; adult/child $40/20; ⊙tours 10am, 12:30pm & 3pm May-Nov) Take a two-hour tour of the city on these red-colored trolleys, with 15-minute photo breaks at Copley Square and the USS Constitution (but no other hop-on, hop-off privileges). The price includes a harbor cruise from the New England Aquarium or admission to the Mapparium.

City View Trolleys
BUS TOUR

(Map p52; ☑617-363-7899; www.cityviewtrolleys.com; 296 State St; ⊙9:30am-5pm daily Apr-Nov, Fri-Mon Dec, Sat & Sun Jan-Mar) Stay on board and take a loop around Boston in one go, or hop off and back on at any of nine stops along the way. Tour guides are entertaining and informative.

Old Town Trolley Tours
TOURS

(Map p52; ☑855-396-7433; www.trolleytours.com/boston; 200 Atlantic Ave, Long Wharf; adult/child $79/21; ⊤Aquarium) Tour around the city, hopping on and off all day long. Save up to 50% when you book online. This ticket also includes admission to the Old State House, as well as a $10 discount at the Boston Tea Party Ships & Museum.

Walking Tours

NPS Freedom Trail Tour
WALKING

(National Park Service; Map p52; ☑617-242-5642; www.nps.gov/bost; Faneuil Hall; ⊙10am, 11am, 2pm & 3pm Jun-Sep; ⊤State) FREE Show up at the NPS Visitor Center in Faneuil Hall at least 30 minutes early to snag a spot on one of the free, ranger-led Freedom Trail tours. Each 60-minute tour follows a portion of the Freedom Trail and is limited to 30 people. Alternatively, take a self-guided tour with the NPS Freedom Trail app (www.nps.gov/bost/planyourvisit/app.htm).

Free Tours By Foot
WALKING

(☑617-299-0764; www.freetoursbyfoot.com/boston-tours) Take the tour then decide how much you think it's worth. Popular 90-minute walking tours cover the **Freedom Trail** (☑617-357-8300; www.thefreedomtrail.org; ⊤Park St) FREE, Harvard University, the North End and the Beacon Hill 'crime tour.' Tour guides are passionate and entertaining. Best of all, you'll never pay more than you think you should.

Boston by Foot
WALKING

(☑617-367-2345; www.bostonbyfoot.com; adult/child $15/10; 🚶) This fantastic nonprofit organization offers 90-minute walking tours, with neighborhood-specific walks and specialty theme tours such as the Hub of Literary America, the Dark Side of Boston and Boston by Little Feet – a kid-friendly version of the Freedom Trail.

Black Heritage Trail
WALKING

(Map p52; ☑617-742-5415; www.nps.gov/boaf; ⊙tours 1pm Mon-Sat, more frequently in summer; ⊤Park St) The NPS conducts excellent, informative 90-minute guided tours exploring the history of the abolitionist movement and African American settlement on Beacon Hill. Tours depart from the Robert Gould Shaw memorial on Boston Common. Alternatively, take a self-guided tour with the NPS Freedom Trail app (www.nps.gov/bost/planyourvisit/app.htm) or grab a route map from the Museum of African American History (p51).

Hahvahd Tour
WALKING

(Trademark Tours; Map p66; ☑855-455-8747; www.harvardtour.com; adult/child $12/10.50; ⊤Harvard) This company was founded by a couple of Harvard students who shared the inside scoop on history and student life at the university. Now the company offers a whole menu of Boston tours, but the funny, offbeat Hahvahd Tour is the trademark. Tour guides are students who are not afraid to ask for tips.

⚞ Festivals & Events

★ Boston Marathon
SPORTS

(www.baa.org; ⊙3rd Mon Apr) One of the country's most prestigious marathons takes runners on a 26.2-mile course ending at Copley Sq on Patriots' Day.

Patriots' Day
CULTURAL

(www.lexingtonma.gov/patriotsday; ⊙3rd Mon Apr) On the third Monday in April, history buffs commemorate the start of the American Revolution with a re-enactment of the battle on Lexington Green (11 miles west of Boston) and a commemoration ceremony at the North Bridge in Concord (17 miles west of Boston).

Hidden Gardens of Beacon Hill
CULTURAL

(www.beaconhillgardenclub.org; $50-60; ⊙9am-5pm on 3rd Thursday in May) Sponsored by the Beacon Hill Garden Club, here's your chance to get a peek at a dozen of the neighborhood's urban gardens. Hidden courtyards and secret passageways are opened up to visitors to marvel at the beautiful blooms and other lovely landscaping. The tour is self-guided.

Independence Day CULTURAL
(www.bostonpopsjuly4th.org; ☉ Jul 4) Boston hosts one of the biggest Independence Day bashes in the USA, with a free Boston Pops concert on the Esplanade and a fireworks display that's televised nationally.

Boston Tea Party Reenactment CULTURAL
(www.oldsouthmeetinghouse.org; $30; ☉ Dec) On the Sunday prior to December 16, costumed actors march from Old South Meeting House to the waterfront and toss crates of tea into the harbor. Nowadays, the ticketed event takes place on the rebuilt Griffin's Wharf, where the Tea Party ships are docked.

First Night NEW YEAR
(www.firstnightboston.org; ☉ Dec 31) New Year celebrations begin early and continue past midnight, culminating in fireworks over the harbor. The fun continues on New Year's Day, with more activities and exhibitions.

🛏 Sleeping

Boston is a relatively expensive place to stay, due to its busy conference and academic calendars and popular tourist appeal. Book in advance online for the best prices. The city offers a wide range of accommodations, from inviting guesthouses in historic quarters to swanky hotels with all the amenities. There is no shortage of stately homes that have been converted into B&Bs, offering an intimate atmosphere and personal service. Considering that this city is filled with students, there are surprisingly few accommodations targeting budget travelers and backpackers, so book your beds as early as possible.

A few welcoming guesthouses and smaller hotels welcome midrange travelers, while many hotels of all sizes cater to high-enders. Prices increase dramatically during peak travel times.

Massachusetts levies a 5.7% hotel tax, while Boston levies a 6% hotel tax and a 2.75% convention-center fee, bringing your total tax to 14.45%. Note that there's no room tax on B&Bs with fewer than three rooms.

🛏 Beacon Hill & Boston Common

Beacon Hill Hotel & Bistro BOUTIQUE HOTEL $$
(Map p52; ☎617-723-7575; www.beaconhillhotel. com; 25 Charles St; d/ste $269/369; P☀☎; T Charles/MGH) This upscale European-style inn blends into the neighborhood without flashiness or fanfare. Carved out of former residential buildings typical of Beacon Hill, the hotel has 12 very small but stylish rooms decorated with contemporary furniture, louvered shutters and a designer's subdued palette of paint choices. Added perks include the exclusive roof deck, and complimentary breakfast at the urbane, on-site bistro.

XV Beacon BOUTIQUE HOTEL $$$
(Map p52; ☎617-670-1500; www.xvbeacon.com; 15 Beacon St; d from $349; P☀☎☸; T Park St) Housed in a turn-of-the-20th-century beaux-arts building, XV Beacon sets the standard for Boston's boutique hotels. Guest-room decor is soothing, taking advantage of color schemes rich with taupe, espresso and cream. You'll find custom-made gas fireplaces and built-in mahogany entertainment units, alongside heated towel racks and rainforest shower heads in the bathrooms, and romantic canopy beds dressed in Frette linens.

🛏 Downtown & Waterfront

Bostonian Boston HOTEL $$
(Map p52; ☎617-523-3600; www.millenniumhotels. com; 26 North St; d from $279; P☀☎; THay-market) ✏ The Bostonian proudly touts its roots as part of the Blackstone Block, the city's oldest block. From the moment you enter the cool, contemporary lobby to the time you step out onto your balcony overlooking the bustle of Haymarket, you'll appreciate this hotel's singular position.

Nine Zero BOUTIQUE HOTEL $$$
(Map p52; ☎617-772-5810; www.ninezero.com; 90 Tremont St; d from $352; P☀☎☸; T Park St) ✏ This chic Kimpton hotel appeals to a broad audience, courting business travelers with complimentary shoe-shine service and ergonomic workspace; active visitors with complimentary bikes and in-room yoga mats; and animal lovers with Kimpton's signature pet service. All of the above enjoy excellent customer service and marvelous views of the gold-domed Massachusetts

Where to Stay in Boston

Cambridge
Harvard, history and the heart and soul of Boston are on the doorstep.

Best for Location and value

Transport A short ride on the T into town

Price Runs the gamut from budget to high end

Harvard University

Cambridge

Beacon Hill & Boston Common
Boston's most historic and charming enclave is appealing.

Best for Historic B&Bs, romantic escapes

Transport Short walk to the city center

Price Very expensive

Massachusetts Institute of Technology

Beacon Hill & Boston Common

Boston Common

Back Bay
Neighborhood charm. Close to major sights. Wide range of dining and shopping options.

Best for A good, all-round choice

Transport Easy to get everywhere

Price Mostly expensive

Back Bay

Copley Square

Fenway Park

Kenmore Square & Fenway

South End & Chinatown

Museum of Fine Arts

Kenmore Square & Fenway
Caters to both business travelers and sports fans.

Best for Broad selection, from boutique to high-end chains

Transport Easy to get everywhere on the T

Price Mostly expensive

South End & Chinatown
Close to major sights. Great dining, shopping and nightlife. Gritty city atmosphere: not the best choice for families.

Best for Getting among the action

Transport Convenient travel to most areas

Price Budget to midrange

Charlestown

A hip neighborhood with good vibes and views, but limited accommodations.

Best for Being by the water, living like a local

Transport Limited

Price Pricey, but not the priciest

Bunker Hill Monument

Charlestown

West End & North End

The North End has atmospheric dining but limited accommodations. The West End lacks soul, but has plenty of beds.

Best for Convenience and value

Transport Easy access to other areas

Price As affordable as Boston gets

West End & North End

Downtown & Waterfront

In the middle of the action: the perfect base for exploring Boston, but can be a bit 'big city generic.'

Best for Solo and time-poor travelers

Transport Convenient transport links everywhere

Price Expensive

Old State House

Downtown & Waterfront

Institute of Contemporary Art

Seaport District & South Boston

Seaport District & South Boston

Close to the airport and waterfront, with a city buzz and great people-watching.

Best for Dining and shopping

Transport Excellent airport and Downtown options

Price Generally expensive but deals can be found

BOSTON ACCOMMODATIONS BOOKING SERVICES

Lonely Planet (lonelyplanet.com/usa/boston/hotels) Independent reviews about the best places to stay.

B&B Agency of Boston (www.boston-bnbagency.com) Fully furnished vacation rentals.

Bed & Breakfast Associates Bay Colony (www.bnbboston.com) Huge database of unhosted, furnished rooms and apartments.

Inn Boston Reservations (www.innbostonreservations.com) Studio and apartment rentals in Boston's best neighborhoods.

Boston Green Tourism (www.bostongreentourism.org) Up-to-date listings of ecofriendly hotels.

Boston Luxury Hotels (www.bostonluxuryhotels.com) Individualized service for upscale travelers.

State House (p51) and the Granary Burying Ground (p51) from the upper floors.

Omni Parker House HISTORIC HOTEL $$$
(Map p52; ☑617-227-8600; www.omnihotels.com; 60 School St; d from $354; P✻🅿🛜☎; Ⓣ Park St) 🌿 History and the Parker House go hand in hand like JFK and Jackie O (who got engaged here). Malcolm X was a busboy here; Ho Chi Minh was a pastry chef; and Boston cream pie, the official state dessert, was created here. Rooms are comfortable and traditional, and the hotel's location, in the heart of the Freedom Trail, is incomparable.

🛏 West End & North End

Boxer Hotel BOUTIQUE HOTEL $$
(Map p52; ☑617-624-0202; www.theboxerboston.com; 107 Merrimac St; d from $209; P✻@🛜☎; Ⓣ North Station) 🌿 Exemplifying the up-and-coming character of this once-downtrodden district, this boutique hotel occupies a fully restored 19th-century flatiron building on the western edge of the Bulfinch Triangle. Design elements like open-frame wardrobes and plaid bedding exhibit a subtly masculine sophistication. Technology perks include Keurig coffee makers, iHomes and flat-screen TVs.

Due to the triangular shape of the building, the rooms vary by size and shape, and some of them are pretty cramped. If this is a concern, it's worth requesting a larger room when you make your reservation.

★ Liberty Hotel HOTEL $$$
(Map p52; ☑866-961-3778, 617-224-4000; www.libertyhotel.com; 215 Charles St; r from $375; P✻✻🛜; Ⓣ Charles/MGH) It is with intend-

ed irony that the notorious Charles St Jail has been converted into the classy Liberty Hotel. Today, the 90ft ceiling soars above a spectacular lobby. All 298 guest rooms come with luxurious linens and high-tech amenities, while the 18 in the original jail wing boast floor-to-ceiling windows with amazing views of the Charles River and Beacon Hill.

🛏 Charlestown

Constitution Inn HOTEL $
(☑617-241-8400; www.constitutioninn.org; 150 Third Ave; d $100-150; P✻🛜☎; 🚌93 from Haymarket, 🚢F4 from Long Wharf) Housed in a granite building in the historic Charlestown Navy Yard (p59), this excellent, affordable hotel accommodates active and retired military personnel, but you don't have to have a crew cut to stay. Somewhat institutional, the rooms are mostly clean, freshly painted, and furnished with cherrywood beds and desks. Some have kitchenettes. Guests gain free access to the Olympic-class fitness center (Charlestown YMCA).

Green Turtle B&B $$
(☑617-337-0202; www.greenturtlebb.com; Pier 8, 13th St; d $290; P✻🛜; 🚢F4 from Long Wharf) It's not just a B&B, but a floating B&B. If you want to be lulled to sleep by the sound of waves lapping and wake up to the cry of seagulls, maybe you should be sleeping on a houseboat.

The two contemporary guest rooms are surprisingly spacious, complete with kitchenettes. Hot coffee and fresh pastries are served in your room.

Seaport District & South Boston

Yotel
HOTEL $$

(Map p52; www.yotel.com; 65 Seaport Blvd; d from $226; ❄☎; ⛔SL3 to Courthouse, Ⓣ South Station) A new concept for Boston, Yotel offers accommodations, or 'cabins,' that are cool, comfortable and compact, complete with adjustable 'smart' beds, luxury linens, heated towel racks and rain showers. Every thing you need is here – it's very cozy. If you need to spread out, make yourself at home in the chic lobby or on the rooftop deck.

While service is pleasant across the hotel, the perennial favorite staff member is YO2D2, the house robot, who is trained in the art of guest services.

Envoy Hotel
DESIGN HOTEL $$$

(Map p52; ☑617-338-3030; www.theenvoyhotel. com; 70 Sleeper St; d $339-419; ❄☎❆; Ⓣ South Station) Here's a gorgeous boutique hotel perched at the corner where the Fort Point Channel meets the sea. In the rooms, floor-to-ceiling windows optimize the vantage point, offering wonderful water views. The interior design is sophisticated and stylish, keeping it simple with colors, but playing with textures, materials and even words. The rooftop bar (p88) is an obvious draw.

This is a Marriott property, so you'll get a better price if you book in advance.

Residence Inn Marriott
BOUTIQUE HOTEL $$$

(Map p52; ☑617-478-0840; www.marriott.com; 370 Congress St; d from $352; ℗❄☎❆; ⛔SL1, SL2, Ⓣ South Station) ✦ This is not your typical Marriott. Housed in a historic, brick warehouse, this boutique hotel now features an old-style atrium and glass elevators leading up to spectacular, spacious suites. Twelve-foot ceilings and enormous windows are in every room, as is a floor-to-ceiling cityscape mural. King-size beds, fully equipped kitchens and up-to-date gadgetry ensure optimal comfort and convenience.

As with every Marriott property, significant discounts are available if you book in advance.

Seaport Boston Hotel
HOTEL $$$

(☑617-385-4000; www.seaportboston.com; 1 Seaport Lane; d from $369; ℗❄☎❆❆; ⛔SL1, SL2, Ⓣ South Station) ✦ With glorious views of the Boston Harbor, this business hotel is up to snuff when it comes to high-tech amenities and creature comforts. Soothing tones, plush linens and robes, and a rare no-tipping policy guarantee a relaxing retreat.

South End & Chinatown

★ HI-Boston
HOSTEL $

(Map p52; ☑617-536-9455; www.bostonhostel.org; 19 Stuart St; dm from $47, d with bath from $230; ❄@☎; Ⓣ Chinatown, Boylston) ✦ HI-Boston sets the standard for urban hostels, with its modern, ecofriendly facility in the historic Dill Building. Purpose-built rooms are functional and clean, as are the shared bathrooms. Community spaces are numerous, from fully equipped kitchen to ground-floor cafe, and there's a whole calendar of activities on offer. The place is large, but it books out, so reserve in advance. Dorms vary in size and with guest gender; prices vary accordingly.

Revolution Hotel
HOTEL $

(Map p62; ☑617-848-9200; www.therevolution hotel.com; 40 Berkeley St; d/tr/q without bath $100/125/150, d/ste from $150/250; ❄☎; Ⓣ Back Bay) A beacon for budget travelers, the Revolution Hotel is a concept hotel with a cool, creative atmosphere. Rooms are compact, comfortable and affordable. The cheapest share bathrooms are spacious, private and well stocked with plush towels and high-end products. The place exudes innovation, especially thanks to the fantastic mural that adorns the lobby.

★ Encore
B&B $$

(Map p62; ☑617-247-3425; www.encorebandb. com; 116 W Newton St; r $230-260; ℗❄☎; Ⓣ Back Bay) If you love the theater, or if you love innovative contemporary design, or if you just love creature comforts and warm hospitality, you will love Encore. Co-owned by an architect and a set designer, this 19th-century South End town house sets a stage for both of their passions.

Clarendon Square Inn
B&B $$

(Map p62; ☑617-536-2229; www.clarendon square.com; 198 W Brookline St; d $258-358; ℗❄☎; Ⓣ Prudential) On a quiet residential street in the South End, this fabulous brownstone is a designer's dream. Guest room details might include Italian marble wainscoting, French limestone floors, a silver-leaf barrel-vaulted ceiling or a hand-forged iron-and-porcelain washbasin. Common areas are decadent (case in point: roof-deck hot tub); continental breakfast is served in the paneled dining room and butler's pantry.

Back Bay

College Club
B&B $$

(Map p62; ☑ 617-536-9510; www.thecollege clubofboston.com; 44 Commonwealth Ave; s without bath from $179, d $269-289; ❄ 🛜; 🚇 Arlington) Originally a private club for female college graduates, the College Club has 11 spacious rooms with high ceilings, now open to all genders. Period details – typical of the area's Victorian brownstones – include claw-foot tubs, ornamental fireplaces and bay windows. Local designers have lent their skills to decorate the various rooms, with delightful results. Prices include a continental breakfast.

★ No 284
BOUTIQUE HOTEL $$$

(Map p62; ☑ 617-603-0084; www.no284.com; 284 Commonwealth Ave; d from $349; ❄ 🛜; 🚇 Hynes) This gorgeous guesthouse invites you to make yourself at home in a luxurious Back Bay brownstone. The comfort starts in the delightful common areas – an elegant library and a serene urban courtyard – and extends to the guest rooms, which are equipped with many thoughtful touches, from corkscrews and wine glasses to professionally curated artwork. Prices include a continental breakfast.

Kenmore Square & Fenway

★ Gryphon House
B&B $$

(Map p62; ☑ 617-375-9003; www.innboston.com; 9 Bay State Rd; r $268-335; 🅿 ❄ 🛜; 🚇 Kenmore) A premier example of Richardson Romanesque, this beautiful five-story brownstone is a paragon of artistry and luxury overlooking the picturesque Charles River. Eight spacious suites have different styles, including Victorian, Gothic and arts and crafts, but they all have 19th-century period details. And they all have home-away-from-home perks such as entertainment centers, wet bars and gas fireplaces.

Prices include a continental breakfast. If you're planning to see a baseball game, inquire about the Red Sox special.

★ Verb Hotel
BOUTIQUE HOTEL $$$

(Map p62; ☑ 617-566-4500; www.theverbhotel. com; 1271 Boylston St; r $349-399; 🅿 ❄ 🛜 ♒ ❄; 🚇 Kenmore, Fenway) The Verb Hotel took a down-and-out HoJo property and turned it into Boston's most radical, retro, rock-and-roll hotel. The style is mid-century modern; the theme is music. Memorabilia is on display throughout the joint, with turntables in the guest rooms and a jukebox cranking out tunes in the lobby. Classy, clean-lined rooms face the swimming pool or Fenway Park.

Hotel Commonwealth
HOTEL $$$

(Map p62; ☑ 617-784-4000, 617-933-5000; www. hotelcommonwealth.com; 500 Commonwealth Ave; r/ste $349/379; 🅿 ❄ 🛜; 🚇 Kenmore) Set amid Commonwealth Ave's brownstones and just steps away from Fenway Park, this independent luxury hotel enjoys prime real estate. Spacious Commonwealth suites offer king-size beds and two LCD TVs. The rooms are slightly smaller, but some do offer a view onto the ballpark. All guests can enjoy the amazing amenities, which range from turndown service to iPods and PlayStations.

Cambridge

Irving House at Harvard
GUESTHOUSE $$

(Map p66; ☑ 617-547-4600; www.irvinghouse.com; 24 Irving St; r with/without bath from $245/185; 🅿 ❄ @ 🛜; 🚇 Harvard) 🌱 Call it a big inn or a homey hotel, Irving House welcomes the world-weariest of travelers. Rooms range in size, but every bed is quilt-covered, and big windows admit plenty of light. There is a bistro-style atmosphere in the brick-lined basement, where you can browse through books or munch on a complimentary continental breakfast. Free parking is a great bonus.

Kendall Hotel
BOUTIQUE HOTEL $$

(Map p68; ☑ 617-566-1300; www.kendallhotel.com; 350 Main St; r $248-317; 🅿 ❄ 🛜; 🚇 Kendall/MIT) Once the Engine 7 Firehouse, this city landmark is now a cool and classy all-American hotel. Its 65 guest rooms exhibit a firefighter riff, alongside the requisite creature comforts. The hotel excels with its service, style, and appetizing breakfast spread. The on-site Black Sheep restaurant is worth visiting for lunch or dinner, too.

Charles Hotel
HOTEL $$$

(Map p66; ☑ 617-864-1200; www.charleshotel.com; 1 Bennett St; r from $349; 🅿 ❄ 🛜 ♒ ❄; 🚇 Harvard) Calling itself 'the smart place to stay,' this institution has hosted the university's most esteemed guests, ranging from Bob Barker to the Dalai Lama. Guest rooms include sleek Shaker-style furnishings, Italian marble bathrooms with TV mirrors, and all the luxuries and facilities one would expect from a highly rated hotel. Prime location overlooking the Charles River.

Eating

The Boston area is the home of the first Thanksgiving and of bountiful autumnal harvests. It's also America's seafood capital. In this era of creative culinary discovery, many Bostonians are reclaiming their roots in one crucial way: through appreciation of local, seasonal and organic products. This thriving 'locavore' movement highlights the bounty of local waters and rich New England farms.

Reservations are recommended for most top-end restaurants, especially on Friday and Saturday evenings. Make reservations at www.opentable.com.

Beacon Hill & Boston Common

★Tatte BAKERY $
(Map p52; ☑617-723-5555; www.tattebakery.com; 70 Charles St; mains $10-14; ☺7am-8pm Mon-Fri, from 8am Sat, 8am-7pm Sun; ⊤Charles/MGH) The aroma of buttery goodness – and the lines stretching out the door – signal your arrival at this fabulous bakery on the lower floor of the historic Charles St Meeting House. Swoon-worthy pastries (divinely cinnamon-y buns, chocolate-hazelnut twists, avocado and mushroom tartines) from $3 taste even more amazing if you're lucky enough to score a table on the sunny front patio.

★Paramount CAFETERIA $$
(Map p52; ☑617-720-1152; www.paramountboston.com; 44 Charles St; mains $17-24; ☺7am-10pm Mon-Fri, from 8am Sat & Sun; ☑⚙; ⊤Charles/MGH) This old-fashioned cafeteria is a neighborhood favorite. A-plus diner fare includes pancakes, home fries, burgers and sandwiches, and big, hearty salads. Banana and caramel French toast is an obvious go-to for the brunch crowd. Don't sit down until you get your food! The wait may seem endless, but patrons swear it is worth it.

At dinner, add table service and candlelight, and the place goes upscale without losing its down-home charm.

75 Chestnut AMERICAN $$
(Map p52; ☑617-227-2175; www.75chestnut.com; 75 Chestnut St; mains $18-27; ☺10:30am-2:30pm Sat & Sun, 5-11pm daily; ⚙; ⊤Charles/MGH) You might not think to take a peek around the

corner, away from the well-trod sidewalks of Charles St. But locals know that Chestnut St is the place to go for tried-and-true steaks and seafood, and a genuine warm welcome. It's a perfect place to stop for a drink, complemented by cheese and crackers served at the bar. But you'll probably end up staying for dinner because the place is that comfy-cozy.

No 9 Park EUROPEAN $$$
(Map p52; ☑617-742-9991; www.no9park.com; 9 Park St; mains $37-47, 6-course tasting menu $125; ☺5-9pm Mon-Wed, to 10pm Thu-Sat, 4-8pm Sun; ⊤Park St) This swanky place has been around since 1998, but it still tops many fine-dining lists. Chef-owner Barbara Lynch has now cast her celebrity-chef spell all around town, but this is the place that made her famous. Delectable French and Italian culinary masterpieces and first-rate wine list. Reservations recommended.

Downtown & Waterfront

Gene's Chinese Flatbread CHINESE $
(Map p52; ☑617-482-1888; www.genescafe.com; 86 Bedford St; mains $6-11; ☺11am-6:30am Mon-Sat; ⊤Chinatown) It's not often that we recommend leaving Chinatown for Chinese food, but Gene's is only a few blocks away. And it's worth the detour to this unassuming storefront for chewy Xi'an-style noodles. No 9 (cumin lamb hand-pulled noodles) and No 3 (pork flatbread sandwich) are perennial fan favorites. Seating is limited and credit cards are not accepted.

Clover DTX VEGETARIAN $
(Map p52; www.cloverfoodlab.com; 27 School St; mains $8-12; ☺7am-9pm Mon-Fri, 8am-8pm Sat-Sun; ☑; ⊤State) Right on the Freedom Trail, the first Downtown branch of this socially conscious local success story serves veggie treats morning, noon and night, from breakfast sandwiches in the morning to

platters of BBQ seitan or chickpea fritters the rest of the day.

★ jm Curley
PUB FOOD $$

(Map p52; ☑ 617-338-5333; www.jmcurleyboston. com; 21 Temple Pl; mains $10-20; ◷ 11:30am-1am Mon-Sat, to 10pm Sunday; ☑; Ⓣ Downtown Crossing) This dim, inviting bar is a perfect place to settle in for a Dark & Stormy on a dark and stormy night. The fare is bar food like you've never had before: Curley's cracka jack (caramel corn with bacon); mac 'n' cheese (served in a cast-iron skillet); and fried pickles (yes, you read that right). That's why they call it a gastropub.

James Hook & Co
SEAFOOD $$

(Map p52; ☑ 617-423-5501; www.jameshook lobster.com; 15-17 Northern Ave; lobster rolls $20-24; ◷ 10am-5pm Mon-Thu & Sat, to 6pm Fri, to 4pm Sun) For a superlative lobster roll close to Downtown, look no further than this harborside seafood shack near the bridge to the Seaport district. Outdoor ta-

---

TOP PICKS FOR VEGETARIANS

Veggie Galaxy (Map p68; ☑ 617-497-1513; www.veggiegalaxy.com; 450 Massachusetts Ave; mains $8-14; ◷ 9am-10pm Sun-Thu, to 11pm Fri & Sat; ☑; Ⓣ Central) Your favorite diner fare – all animal-free.

Whole Heart Provisions (Map p68; ☑ 617-945-8991; www.wholeheart provisions.com; 298 Massachusetts Ave; mains $9-11; ◷ 10:30am-10pm; ☑; Ⓣ Central) Vegans delight! Dinner in a bowl.

Sweetgreen (Map p62; ☑ 617-936-3464; www.sweetgreen.com; 659 Boylston St; mains $10-12; ◷ 10:30am-10:30pm; ☑ ♿; Ⓣ Copley) Caters to every kind of special diet, as well as to people who enjoy fresh, delicious food.

Life Alive (p87) Smoothies, salads and sandwiches that are good for body and soul.

Clover DTX (p81) Clover's chickpea fritter is a thing of beauty.

Clover HSQ (Map p66; www.cloverfood lab.com; 1326 Massachusetts Ave; mains $8-11; ◷ 11am-11pm Mon-Sat, to 10pm Sun; ☎ ☑ ♿; Ⓣ Harvard) ✔ Ditto.

---

bles make it a perfect low-key lunch stop as you make your way between museums on a sunny afternoon.

Yvonne's
MODERN AMERICAN $$$

(Map p52; ☑ 617-267-0047; www.yvonnesbos ton.com; 2 Winter Pl; ◷ 5-11pm, bar to 2am; ☑; Ⓣ Park) Upon arrival at Yvonne's, staff will usher you discreetly through closed doors into a hidden 'modern supper club.' The spectacular space artfully blends old-school luxury with contemporary eclecticism. The menu of mostly small plates does the same, with items from tuna crudo to baked oysters to chicken and quinoa meatballs.

✕ West End & North End

Galleria Umberto
PIZZA $

(Map p52; ☑ 617-227-5709; www.galleriaumberto northend.com; 289 Hanover St; mains $2-5; ◷ 11am-3pm Mon-Sat; ☑; Ⓣ Haymarket) Paper plates, cans of soda, Sicilian pizza. This lunchtime legend (and 2018 James Beard Award winner!) closes as soon as the slices are gone. And considering their thick and chewy goodness, that's often before the official 3pm closing time. Loyal patrons line up early so they're sure to get theirs. Other snacking options include calzone, panini and arancini. Cash only.

★ Pomodoro
ITALIAN $$

(Map p52; ☑ 617-367-4348; 351 Hanover St; mains $22-26; ◷ 5:30-11pm; Ⓣ Haymarket) Seductive Pomodoro offers a super-intimate, romantic setting (reservations are essential). The food is simple but perfectly prepared: fresh pasta, spicy tomato sauce, grilled fish and meats, and wine by the glass. If you're lucky, you might be on the receiving end of a complimentary tiramisu for dessert. Cash only.

Daily Catch
SEAFOOD $$

(Map p52; ☑ 617-523-8567; http://thedailycatch. com; 323 Hanover St; mains $18-25; ◷ 11am-10pm; Ⓣ Haymarket) Although owner Paul Freddura long ago added a few tables and an open kitchen, this shoebox fish joint still retains the atmosphere of a retail fish market (complete with chalkboard menu and wine served in plastic cups). Fortunately, it also retains the freshness of the fish. The specialty is *tinta de calamari* (squid-ink pasta). Cash only.

SWEET NORTH END

It wouldn't be a night in the North End if you didn't end it with a cannoli or some other sweet thang. Here's where to get yours:

Maria's Pastry (Map p52; ☑617-523-1196; www.mariaspastry.com; 46 Cross St; pastries $3-5; ☉7am-7pm Mon-Sat, to 5pm Sun; ☑; ⊤Haymarket) Three generations of women from the Merola family are now working to bring you Boston's most authentic Italian pastries. Many claim that Maria makes the best cannoli in the North End, but you'll also find more-elaborate concoctions like *sfogliatelle* (layered, shell-shaped pastry filled with ricotta) and *aragosta* (cream-filled 'lobster tail' pastry). Note the early closing time: eat dessert first!

Modern Pastry Shop (Map p52; ☑617-523-3783; www.modernpastry.com; 257 Hanover St; sweets $2-4; ☉8am-10pm Sun-Thu, to 11pm Fri, to midnight Sat; ⊤Haymarket) The 'Modern' Pastry Shop feels anything but. This family-owned bakery has been making delectable cookies and cannoli for some 70 years. Always a contender in the ongoing 'best cannoli in Boston' feud. Cash only.

Scopa
ITALIAN $$

(Map p52; ☑857-317-2871; www.scopaboston.com; 319 Hanover St; mains $19-28; ☉11am-11pm; ⊤Haymarket) Every meal at Scopa starts with delectable, warm Italian flatbread, served with a selection of olive oils for dipping. This is just a teaser of the delights to come, which might include Venetian meatballs or porcini mushroom risotto. The atmosphere is intimate and service is consistently excellent.

Carmelina's
ITALIAN $$

(Map p52; ☑617-742-0020; www.carmelinasboston.com; 307 Hanover St; mains $18-29; ☉noon-10pm; ☑; ⊤Haymarket) There's a lot to look at when you sit down at Carmelina's, whether you face the busy, open kitchen or the massive windows overlooking Hanover St. This understated, contemporary space serves up Sicilian dishes with a modern American twist – customers are crazy about the Crazy Alfredo and the Sunday Macaroni (which is served every day, in case you're wondering).

★Neptune Oyster
SEAFOOD $$$

(Map p52; ☑617-742-3474; www.neptuneoyster.com; 63 Salem St; mains $19-39; ☉11:30am-9:30pm Sun-Thu, to 10:30pm Fri & Sat; ⊤Haymarket) Neptune's menu hints at Italian, but you'll also find elements of Mexican, French, Southern and old-fashioned New England. The impressive raw bar and daily seafood specials confirm that this is not your traditional North End eatery. Reservations are not accepted so come early and be prepared to wait.

Seaport District & South Boston

Yankee Lobster Co
SEAFOOD $

(☑617-345-9799; www.yankeelobstercompany.com; 300 Northern Ave; mains $11-26; ☉10am-9pm Mon-Sat, 11am-6pm Sun; ⬛SL1, SL2, ⊤South Station) The Zanti family has been fishing for three generations, so they definitely know their stuff. A relatively recent addition is this retail fish market, scattered with a few tables in case you want to dine in. And you do. Order something simple like clam chowder or a lobster roll, accompany it with a cold beer, and you won't be disappointed.

★Row 34
SEAFOOD $$

(Map p52; ☑617-553-5900; www.row34.com; 383 Congress St; oysters $2-3, mains $14-32; ☉11:30am-10pm Sun-Thu, to 11pm Fri & Sat; ⊤South Station) In the heart of the new Seaport District, set in a sharp, postindustrial space, this place offers a dozen types of raw oysters and clams, alongside an amazing selection of craft beers. There's also a full menu of cooked seafood, ranging from the traditional to the trendy.

Legal Harborside
SEAFOOD $$

(☑617-477-2900; www.legalseafoods.com; 270 Northern Ave; mains $18-30; ☉11am-10pm Sun-Thu, to 11pm Fri & Sat; ⬛SL1, SL2, ⊤South Station) This vast glass-fronted waterfront complex offers three different restaurant concepts on three floors. Our favorite is the 1st floor – a casual restaurant and fish market that is

FOOD TRUCKS

Boston has dozens of food trucks cruising its streets, serving up cheap, filling fare to hungry patrons who are short on time and/or money. There's a full range of meals on offer, from noodles and tacos to burgers, hot dogs, lobster rolls and vegetarian food.

You'll find food trucks on the Rose Kennedy Greenway and on the Boston Common, among other places. In Cambridge, look for trucks on the plaza in front of the Harvard Science Center or on Carleton St across from the Kendall Sq T station. And on summer weekends, head for the Food Truck Bazaar at the SoWa Open Market along Harrison Ave. Find out more at the Boston Food Truck Blog (www.bostonfoodtruckblog.com) or Hub Food Trucks (www.hubfoodtrucks.com).

a throwback to Legal's original outlet from 1904.

The updated menu includes a raw bar, small plates, seafood grills and plenty of international influences. There is outdoor seating in the summer months.

✕ South End & Chinatown

★ Mike & Patty's   SANDWICHES $

(Map p52; ☑617-423-3447; www.mikeandpattys. com; 12 Church St; sandwiches $9-12; ☺8am-2pm; ☑; ⓣTufts Medical Center, Arlington) Tucked away in Bay Village, this hole-in-the-wall gem of a corner sandwich shop does amazing things between two slices of bread. There are only eight options and they're all pretty perfect, but the hands-down favorite is the Breakfast Grilled Crack (fried egg, bacon and four kinds of cheese on sourdough). There's always a line but it moves quickly. No seating.

Gourmet Dumpling House   CHINESE $

(Map p52; ☑617-338-6223; www.gourmetdump linghouse.com; 52 Beach St; dumplings $5-8, mains $9-17; ☺11am-1am; ☑; ⓣChinatown) *Xiao long bao*. That's all the Chinese you need to know to take advantage of the specialty at the Gourmet Dumpling House (or GDH, as it is fondly called). They are Shanghai soup dumplings, and they are fresh, doughy and delicious. The menu offers plenty of other options, including scrumptious crispy scallion pancakes. Come early or be prepared to wait.

Avana Sushi   SUSHI $

(Map p52; ☑617-818-7782; www.avanasushi.com; 42 Beach St; sushi & sashimi $4-6; ☺11am-10pm; ⓣChinatown) This place is essentially unmarked from the street, tucked into a tiny, cramped food court, sharing the space with a few other takeout places. There's only a handful of seats, but the sushi is fresh and affordable, and service is personable. It's hard to beat. We also appreciate the Styrofoam artwork, offering a commentary on our disposable culture, perhaps?

Blunch   SANDWICHES $

(Map p62; ☑617-247-8100; www.eatblunch.com; 59 E Springfield St; sandwiches $5-10; ☺8am-3pm Mon-Fri, from 9am Sat; ☑; ⓣMassachusetts Ave) This is a tiny place with counter service, blackboard menu and a-MAZ-ing chocolate chip cookies. The sandwiches are also delish, especially the eggs-ellent fluffy breakfast sandwiches, which are available all day long. If you can't decide what to order, the Bird is the word, at least according to Guy Fieri of the Food Network.

★ Coppa Enoteca   ITALIAN $$

(Map p62; ☑617-391-0902; www.coppaboston. com; 253 Shawmut Ave; small plates $9-17, pizza & pasta $14-25; ☺noon-10pm Mon-Thu, to 11pm Fri, 11am-11pm Sat, to 10pm Sun; ⓢSL4, SL5, ⓣBack Bay) This South End *enoteca* (wine bar) recreates an Italian dining experience with authenticity and innovation, serving up *salumi* (cured meats), antipasti, pasta and other delicious small plates. Wash it all down with an Aperol spritz and you might be tricked into thinking you're in Venice.

★ Myers + Chang   ASIAN $$

(Map p62; ☑617-542-5200; www.myersandchang. com; 1145 Washington St; small plates $7-17, mains $16-25; ☺5-10pm Sun-Thu, to 11pm Fri & Sat; ☑; ⓢSL4, SL5, ⓣTufts Medical Center) This super-hip Asian spot blends Thai, Chinese and Vietnamese cuisines, which means delicious dumplings, spicy stir-fries and oodles of noodles. The kitchen staff do amazing things with a wok, and the menu of small plates allows you to sample a wide selection of dishes. Dim sum for dinner? This is your place.

Toro

TAPAS $$

(Map p62; 617-536-4300; www.toro-restau
rant.com; 1704 Washington St; tapas $9-16;
noon-10pm Mon-Thu, to 11pm Fri, 4-11pm Sat,
10:30am-2:30pm & 5-10pm Sun; ; SL4, SL5,
Massachusetts Ave) True to its Span-
ish spirit, Toro is bursting with energy,
from the open kitchen to the communal
butcher-block tables. The menu features
simple but sublime tapas – seared foie
gras with pistachio and sour cherries;
grilled corn on the cob dripping with aioli,
lime and cheese; and delectable, garlicky
shrimp. Wash it down with rioja, sangria
or spiced-up mojitos.

★ O Ya

SUSHI $$$

(Map p52; 617-654-9900; www.o-ya.restaurant;
9 East St; nigiri & sashimi pieces $14-30; 5-
10pm Tue-Sat; ; South Station) Who knew
that raw fish could be so exciting? Here,
each piece of nigiri or sashimi is dripped
with something unexpected but exquisite,
from burgundy truffle sauce to ginger
kimchee jus. A fried Kumamoto oyster is
topped with a Japanese citrus fruit and
squid ink bubbles. Foie gras is drizzled in
balsamic chocolate *kabayaki* (sweet, soy
glaze). And so on.

Back Bay

★ Luke's Lobster

SEAFOOD $

(Map p62; 857-350-4626; www.lukeslobster.
com; 75 Exeter St; mains $9-19; 11am-9pm Sun-
Wed, to 10pm Thu-Sat; Copley) Luke Hold-
en took a Maine seafood shack and put it in
the middle of Back Bay (and other places
around Boston), so that hungry shoppers
could get a classic lobster roll for lunch. The
place looks authentic, with weathered wood
interior and nautical decor, but more importantly, the lobster rolls are the real deal –
and affordable. The only thing lacking is sea
breezes.

Dirty Water Dough Co

PIZZA $

(Map p62; 617-262-0090; www.dirtywaterdough.
com; 222 Newbury St; slices $3-4, pizzas $11-15;
11am-10pm Sun-Thu, to 11pm Fri & Sat; ;
Copley) If there's anything that Bostonians
love more than the Standells, it's pizza. That
explains why the kids are lining up to get
theirs from Dirty Water Dough, where they
can get a big slice and a soda for $5. Other
perks: locally sourced ingredients, unusual
topping combos and gluten-free options, not
to mention the Dirty Water IPA.

Parish Café

SANDWICHES $

(Map p62; 617-247-4777; www.parishcafe.com;
361 Boylston St; sandwiches $12-20; 11:30am-
1am, bar to 2am; ; Arlington) Sample the
creations of Boston's most famous chefs
without exhausting your expense account.
The menu at Parish features a rotating
roster of salads and sandwiches, each designed by local celebrity chefs, including
Jamie Bissonnette, Barbara Lynch and
Tony Maws. The place feels more 'pub'
than 'cafe,' with a long bar backed by big
TVs and mirrors.

Salty Pig

ITALIAN $$

(Map p62; 617-536-6200; www.thesaltypig.
com; 130 Dartmouth St; charcuterie $7, mains
$12-19; 11:30am-midnight; Back Bay) With
prosciutto, pâté, *rillettes*, *testa* (head
cheese), *sanguinaccio* (blood sausage),
porchetta (pork shoulder) and more, you'll
feel like you're in one of those cultures that
eats every part of the animal. 'Salty Pig
Parts' get paired with stinky cheeses and
other accompaniments for amazing char-
cuterie plates. There's pizza and pasta for
the less adventurous, and cocktails and
craft beers too.

★ Puro Ceviche Bar

LATIN AMERICAN $$

(Map p62; 617-266-0707; www.puroceviche bar.
com; 264 Newbury St; small plates $10-16; 4-
11pm Mon-Thu, 11am-11pm Fri-Sun; Hynes)
Serves up delightfully modern yet still authentic Latin American fare in its funky
downstairs digs, where exposed brick walls
are covered with bold murals. Choose between six types of *ceviche*, six kinds of tacos
and a slew of Latin-inspired small plates.
Also on offer are classic cocktails and a
nicely curated wine list. Attention, budget-
minded travelers: $2 tacos on Tuesdays.

★ Saltie Girl

SEAFOOD $$$

(Map p62; 617-267-0691; www.saltiegirl.com;
281 Dartmouth St; small plates $12-18, mains $18-
40; 11:30am-10pm; Copley) Here's a new
concept in dining: the seafood bar. It's a
delightfully intimate place to feast on tan-
talizing dishes that blow away all precon-
ceived notions about seafood. From your
traditional Gloucester lobster roll to tinned
fish on toast to the irresistible torched
salmon belly, this place is full of delightful
surprises.

Reservations are not accepted and the
place is tiny, so expect to wait. (It's worth it.)

★ **Courtyard** AMERICAN $$$

(Map p62; ☑617-859-2251; www.thecatered affair.com/bpl; 700 Boylston St; afternoon tea adult/child $39/19; ⊙11:30am-5pm Mon-Sat, 1-5pm Sun; ⊺Copley) The perfect destination for an elegant afternoon tea is – believe it or not – the Boston Public Library (p61). Overlooking the beautiful Italianate courtyard, this grown-up restaurant serves an artfully prepared selection of sandwiches, scones and sweets, accompanied by a wide range of teas (black, green and herbal). Reserve ahead, especially on weekends.

Mooncusser Fish House SEAFOOD $$$

(Map p62; ☑617-917-5193; www.mooncusser fishhouse.com; 304 Stuart St; mains $32-45, 3-course prix-fixe $49; ⊙5-10pm Mon-Sat; ⊺Arlington) This elegant spot pairs an old-fashioned concept (the 'fish house') with thoroughly modern presentations of local seafood, from bluefish to swordfish and everything in between. The dishes are understated, showing off local flavors, but not lacking sophisticated embellishments. The menu is short but sweet, including a few divine appetizers and to-die-for desserts.

Select Oyster Bar SEAFOOD $$$

(Map p62; ☑857-233-0376; www.selectboston. com; 50 Gloucester St; mains $30-42; ⊙11:30am-9:30pm Sun-Thu, to 10:30pm Fri & Sat; ⊺Hynes) New England seafood meets Mediterranean flavors at this trendy little oyster bar off Newbury St. The space is delightfully compact and the menu is innovative and amazing. Unfortunately, it's too expensive to be the 'neighborhood spot' that Chef Michael Serpa is going for, but it's still a charmer. Note the 20% gratuity included on all tabs.

✗ Kenmore Square & Fenway

★ **Eventide Fenway** SEAFOOD $

(Map p62; ☑617-545-1060; www.eventideoysterco. com; 1321 Boylston St; mains $9-16; ⊙11am-11pm; ☂; ⊺Fenway) James Beard award winners Mike Wiley and Andrew Taylor opened this counter-service version of their beloved Maine seafood restaurant. Fast, fresh and fabulous, the menu features just-shucked oysters and brown-butter lobster rolls, along with some pretty sophisticated seafood specials. Wash it down with a craft beer or a glass of rosé and the whole experience feels (and tastes) gourmet.

El Pelon MEXICAN $

(Map p62; ☑617-262-9090; www.elpelon.com; 92 Peterborough St; mains $6-9; ⊙11am-11pm; ☑; ⊺Fenway) If your budget is tight, don't miss this chance to fill up on Boston's best burritos, tacos and tortas, made with the freshest ingredients. The *tacos de la casa* are highly recommended, especially the *pescado,* made with crispy cod and topped with chili mayo. Plates are paper and cutlery is plastic.

Tasty Burger BURGERS $

(Map p62; ☑617-425-4444; www.tastyburger. com; 1301 Boylston St; burgers $5-6; ⊙11am-2am; ⊺Fenway) Once a Mobil gas station, this place is now a retro burger joint, with picnic tables outside and a pool table inside. The name is a nod to *Pulp Fiction,* as is the wall-mounted poster of Samuel L Jackson, whose character would surely agree that 'this is a tasty burger.'

Gyro City GREEK $

(Map p62; ☑617-266-4976; www.gyrocityboston. com; 88 Peterborough St; mains $9-10; ⊙11am-11pm Mon-Sat, to 9pm Sun; ☑; ⊺Fenway) This authentic *gyrotico* fits right in on Peterborough St (aka Fenway's restaurant row), with cheap, scrumptious, filling food. There is a variety of gyros, each with a delightful twist (eg french fries on the traditional pork gyro) – as well as baklava made by a real live Greek mama. Counter seating inside, patio seating outside.

Audubon Boston PUB FOOD $$

(Map p62; ☑617-421-1910; www.audubonboston. com; 838 Beacon St; sandwiches $10-13, mains $16-19; ⊙11:30am-midnight, bar to 1am; ☑; ⊺St Mary's Street) Audubon is a long-standing Fenway favorite that mixes minimalist decor with a friendly neighborhood vibe. Stop in to sample the intriguing cocktail menu and interesting dishes like crispy salt and pepper shrimp and fantastic veggie burgers. Highly recommended for grabbing a bite before the Sox game.

★ **Island Creek Oyster Bar** SEAFOOD $$$

(Map p62; ☑617-532-5300; www.islandcreekoys terbar.com; 500 Commonwealth Ave; oysters $3, mains lunch $13-21, dinner $24-36; ⊙4-11pm Mon-Fri, 11:30am-11:30pm Sat, 10:30am-11pm Sun; ⊺Kenmore) Island Creek claims to unite farmer, chef and diner in one space – and what a space it is. It serves up the region's finest oysters, along with other local seafood, in an ethereal new-age setting. The specialty – lobster-roe noodles topped with braised short ribs and grilled lobster – lives up to the hype.

Cambridge

Bon Me
VIETNAMESE $

(Map p68; 617-945-2615; www.bonmetruck. com; 1 Kendall Sq; mains $7-10.50; 11am-8pm; Kendall/MIT) Bon Me started as a food truck that catered to the Kendall Sq crowd, and you'll still see the trucks tooling around town. This little storefront sells the same, simple, fresh, insanely good Vietnamese fare. Choose your dish (sandwich, rice or noodles), filling (chicken, pork or tofu) and extras (edamame, papaya, greens or deviled eggs), then eat up and enjoy.

Dumpling House
CHINESE $

(617-661-8066; www.dumplinghousecambridge ma.com; 950 Massachusetts Ave; lunch specials $9, mains $8-18; 11am-10pm; Central) Midway between Central and Harvard, this bustling spot is the sister restaurant to the Chinatown favorite Gourmet Dumpling House (p84). If you're a fan of soup dumplings, you'll love it here. There are more than a dozen variants of dumplings to try, in addition to many specialties from both northern and southern Chinese cuisine. Service is fast and furious.

Life Alive
VEGETARIAN $

(Map p68; 617-354-5433; www.lifealive.com; 765 Massachusetts Ave; mains $7-10; 8am-11pm Mon-Sat, 10am-10pm Sun; ; Central) Life Alive offers a joyful, healthful, purposeful approach to fast food. The unusual combinations of animal-free ingredients yield delicious results, most of which come in a bowl (like a salad) or in a wrap. There are also soups, sides and smoothies, all served in a colorful, light-filled space.

Roxy's Grilled Cheese
SANDWICHES $

(Map p68; 617-945-7244; www.roxysgrilled cheese.com; 292 Massachusetts Ave; sandwiches $5-9; 11am-11pm Sun-Thu, to midnight Fri & Sat; ; Central) What started as a food truck is now an actual restaurant, specializing in exotic combinations of bread and cheese (plus some other ingredients). There are still some food trucks roaming around town, but none of them has a games arcade in the back room (p89).

★ Waypoint
GASTRONOMY $$

(617-864-2300; www.waypointharvard.com; 1030 Massachusetts Ave; mains $16-25; 10am-2:30pm Sun, 5pm-1am daily; Harvard) Af-

ter his success at Alden & Harlow, chef Michael Scelfo turned his attention to seafood and other 'coastally inspired fare.' The wide-ranging menu includes a raw bar, original pizzas, decadent pasta dishes and whole roasts for the table. There is some pretty daring stuff here, so come with an open mind as well as an empty stomach.

★ Giulia
ITALIAN $$$

(617-441-2800; www.giuliarestaurant.com; 1682 Massachusetts Ave; mains $21-31; 5:30-10pm Mon-Thu, to 11pm Fri & Sat; Harvard, Porter) A half-mile north of Harvard Square, this intimate Italian restaurant opened in 2012 to universal acclaim. Chef Michael Pagliarini's sophisticated, locally sourced creations range from grilled veal with asparagus and wild greens to homemade tortelli stuffed with lamb, sorrel and pecorino cheese. Larger parties can sit family-style at the long oak table where the pasta is rolled out each day.

Drinking & Nightlife

Despite the city's Puritan roots, modern-day Bostonians like to drink. While Boston has its fair share of Irish pubs, it also has a dynamic craft-beer movement, with more and more microbreweries opening yearly; a knowledgeable population of wine drinkers (and pourers); and a red-hot cocktail scene, thanks to some talented local bartenders. So pick your poison...and drink up!

Beacon Hill & Boston Common

Pressed
JUICE BAR

(Map p52; 857-350-3103; www.pressedboston. com; 120 Charles St; 8am-6pm Mon-Fri, from 9am Sat & Sun; ; Charles/MGH) We'll call it a juice bar, since it does make its own juices (out of every fruit and vegetable imaginable) as well as delicious vegan 'superfood shakes' ($10). But the 'toasts' and 'greens' also deserve mention. Both your body and your taste buds will thank you for eating and drinking this tasty, healthy fare.

21st Amendment
PUB

(Map p52; 617-227-7100; www.21stboston.com; 150 Bowdoin St; 11:30am-2am; Park St) Named for one of the US Constitution's most important amendments – the one repealing Prohibition – this quintessential tavern is an ever-popular haunt for State House workers to meet up and talk about the wheels of government. The place feels especially cozy during winter, when you'll feel pretty good about yourself as you drink a stout near the copper-hooded fireplace.

Downtown & Waterfront

Democracy Brewing　　　　BREWERY
(Map p52; ☑857-263-8604; www.democracy brewing.com; 35 Temple Pl; ⊙11:30am-11pm Sun-Thu, to 1am Fri & Sat; ⊤Downtown Crossing) The beer is fresh, the fries are crispy perfection and the politics are 'woke.' Not only do they brew exceptional beer at Democracy Brewing, they also foment revolution – by supporting democratic businesses, organizing community events and showcasing the revolutionaries and rabble-rousers from Boston's past and present.

Trillium Garden　　　　BEER GARDEN
(Map p52; ☑857-449-0083; www.trilliumbrewing.com; cnr Atlantic Ave & High St; ⊙2-10pm Wed-Fri, from 11am Sat, 1-8pm Sun May-Oct; ☎; ⊤South Station, Aquarium) To say that this seasonal beer garden is a welcome addition to the Rose Kennedy Greenway is an understatement. When the weather is fine, Bostonians are flocking to this shady spot to sample the delicious beers that are brewed just across the canal in Fort Point. No food is served but there are food trucks parked nearby.

Thinking Cup　　　　CAFE
(Map p52; ☑617-482-5555; www.thinkingcup.com; 165 Tremont St; ⊙7am-10pm Mon-Wed, to 11pm Thu-Sun; ⊤Boylston) 🍴 There are a few things that make the Thinking Cup special. One is the French hot chocolate – *ooh la la*. Another is the Stumptown Coffee, the Portland brew that has earned accolades from coffee drinkers around the country. But the best thing? It's across from the Boston Common, making it a perfect stop for a post-Frog Pond warm-up.

Seaport District & South Boston

★**Drink**　　　　COCKTAIL BAR
(Map p52; ☑617-695-1806; www.drinkfortpoint.com; 348 Congress St; ⊙4pm-1am; ▣SL1, SL2, ⊤South Station) There is no cocktail menu at Drink. Instead you have a chat with the bartender, and he or she will whip something up according to your mood and taste. It takes seriously the art of mixology – and you will too, after you sample one of its concoctions. The subterranean space, with its low-lit, sexy ambience, makes a great date destination.

Trillium Fort Point　　　　MICROBREWERY
(Map p52; ☑857-449-0083; www.trilliumbrewing.com; 50 Thompson Pl; ⊙11am-11pm; ⊤South Station) Trillium has been brewing beer in the Fort Point area for years. But it was only in 2018 that they opened this fantastic taproom, complete with bar, dining room and rooftop deck. Enjoy the full range of Trillium favorites – not only India pale ales, but also American pale ales, gose ales, wild ales and stouts.

Lookout Rooftop Bar　　　　BAR
(Map p52; ☑617-338-3030; www.theenvoyhotel.com; Envoy Hotel, 70 Sleeper St; ⊙4-11pm Mon-Thu, to midnight Fri & Sat, from noon Sun; ▣SL1, SL2, ⊤South Station) This trendy bar starts filling up almost as soon as it opens, as hotel guests and local workers ascend to the rooftop to take in potent drinks and spectacular views. When temperatures drop, there are heaters and igloos to keep you warm. Note the dress code (no baseball caps, sleeveless shirts, swim or athletic wear).

South End & Chinatown

Beehive　　　　COCKTAIL BAR
(Map p62; ☑617-423-0069; www.beehiveboston.com; 541 Tremont St; ⊙5pm-midnight Mon-Wed, to 1am Thu, to 2am Fri, 9:30am-2am Sat, to midnight Sun; ⊤Back Bay) The Beehive has transformed the basement of the Boston Center for the Arts into a 1920s Paris jazz club. This place is more about the scene than the music, which is often provided by students from Berklee College of Music. But the food is good and the vibe is definitely hip. Reservations required if you want a table.

Delux Café　　　　BAR
(Map p62; ☑617-338-5258; 100 Chandler St; ⊙5pm-1am; ⊤Back Bay) The South End's best – and perhaps only – hipster dive bar. This long-standing favorite has Christmas-light decor and a totally laid-back atmosphere. The kitchen (open till 11pm nightly) turns out an incredible grilled cheese sandwich. No credit cards.

Tunnel　　　　CLUB
(Map p52; ☑617-357-5005; www.tunnelboston.com; 100 Stuart St; cover $10-20; ⊙11pm-2am Tue & Thu-Sat; ⊤Boylston) This is a slick lounge – albeit a tiny one – in the basement of the W

hotel. The 'tunnel' is the effect of the LED lights on the ceiling, which lead the way through the chic lounge and back to the dance floor. Tunnel is the rare nightclub where bouncers and bartenders are actually friendly to the patrons.

No cover before 11pm if you sign up on the online 'guest list' ahead of time.

Kenmore Square & Fenway

★ **Bleacher Bar** SPORTS BAR
(Map p62; ☑ 617-262-2424; www.bleacherbarboston.com; 82a Lansdowne St; ◉ 11am-1am Sun-Wed, to 2am Thu-Sat; ⊤ Kenmore) Tucked under the bleachers at Fenway Park, this classy bar offers a view onto center field. It's not the best place to watch the game, as it gets packed, but it's a fun way to experience America's oldest ballpark, even when the Sox are not playing.

If you want a seat in front of the window, get your name on the waiting list an hour or two before game time; once seated, diners have 45 minutes in the hot seat.

Cambridge

★ **Lamplighter Brewing Co** BREWERY
(Map p68; ☑ 617-945-0450; www.lamplighterbrewing.com; 284 Broadway; ◉ 11am-midnight Tue-Sat, to 10pm Sun; ⊤ Central) This East Cambridge brewery and taproom is a favorite Boston hangout. In addition to the flights and pints of frothy goodness, there are free beer snacks and board games, plus a front-row view of the beer-brewing process.

Aeronaut Brewing Co BREWERY
(☑ 617-987-4236; www.aeronautbrewing.com; 14 Tyler St, Somerville; ◉ 6-11pm Mon, 5pm-midnight Tue-Fri, noon-12:30am Sat, noon-9:30pm Sun; ☐ 86 from Harvard, ☐ 87 from Lechmere) Aeronaut Brewery is a bold experiment in beer, founded by a couple of MIT grads with a passion for local ingredients and scientific methods. Down a dark alley and tucked inside a courtyard, the hidden facility is usually filled with in-the-know and high-tech types, quaffing the seasonal creations and playing Jenga.

A4cade BAR
(Map p68; ☑ 617-714-3960; www.areafour.com; 292 Massachusetts Ave; ◉ 5pm-1am Mon-Fri, noon-1:30am Sat & noon-midnight Sun; ⊤ Central) Slipping through a barely marked door inside Roxy's Grilled Cheese, you know it's gonna be good. And it is... This retro bar will whisk you back to 1980 with

pinball, Pac-Man and other old-timey arcade games. They're made all the more fun thanks to the menu of local brews and creative cocktails (and, of course, grilled cheese sandwiches).

Havana Club CLUB
(Map p68; ☑ 617-312-5550; www.havanaclubsalsa.com; 288 Green St; admission $5-12; ◉ 8pm-midnight Mon & Thu, 9pm-2am Fri & Sat; ⊤ Central) Five nights a week, this old social club on a backstreet in Central Sq transforms into the Boston area's most happening salsa and *bachata* dance party. It's an international crowd – not just Latino – and the first hour is devoted to lessons.

LA Burdick CAFE
(Map p66; ☑ 617-491-4340; www.burdickchocolate.com; 52 Brattle St; ◉ 8am-9pm Sun-Wed, to 10pm Thu-Sat; ⊤ Harvard) This boutique chocolatier doubles as a cafe, usually packed full of happy patrons drinking hot cocoa. Whether you choose dark or milk, it's sure to be some of the best chocolate you'll drink in your lifetime. There are only a handful of tables, so it's hard to score a seat when temperatures are chilly.

☆ Entertainment

Cinema
Harvard Film Archive Cinematheque CINEMA
(Map p66; ☑ 617-495-4700; https://library.harvard.edu/film/index.html; 24 Quincy St; tickets $9-12; ◉ screenings Fri-Mon; ⊤ Harvard) Five nights a week, the Cinematheque presents retrospectives of distinguished actors, screenings of rare films, thematic groupings and special events featuring the filmmakers themselves. The screenings – which often sell out – take place in the 200-seat theater in the esteemed Carpenter Center for the Arts (designed by

MOVIE NIGHT

Catch a flick at one of Boston's historic theaters or academic institutions.

Coolidge Corner Theatre (☑617-734-2500; www.coolidge.org; 290 Harvard St, Brookline; tickets $9-13; Ⓣ Coolidge Corner) An art deco neighborhood palace, this old theater blazes with exterior neon. Inside, view select Hollywood hits, cult flicks, popular independent fare and special events. Fifty cents of every ticket sale goes to the upkeep of the building.

Brattle Theatre (Map p66; ☑617-876-6837; www.brattlefilm.org; 40 Brattle St; Ⓣ Harvard) The Brattle is a film lover's *cinema paradiso*. Film noir, independent films and series that celebrate directors or periods are shown regularly in this renovated 1890 repertory theater. Some famous (or infamous) special events include the annual Valentine's Day screening of *Casablanca* and occasional cartoon marathons.

Somerville Theatre (☑617-625-5700; www.somervilletheatreonline.com; 55 Davis Sq, Somerville; Ⓣ Davis) This classic neighborhood movie house dates from 1914 and features plenty of well-preserved gilding and pastel murals of muses. On offer are first- and second-run Hollywood hits, live performances by local and world musicians, and the Independent Film Festival of Boston screenings. The main theater is the biggest, best and oldest, and has the added treat of a balcony. This gem is in Davis Sq, just a hop and a skip north from Cambridge. Don't miss the amusing Museum of Bad Art in the basement (free with your movie ticket).

Le Corbusier). Tickets go on sale 45 minutes ahead of show times.

Simons IMAX Theatre   CINEMA
(Map p52; ☑617-973-5200; www.neaq.org; Central Wharf; adult/child $10/8; Ⓣ Aquarium) At the New England Aquarium (p55), this IMAX cinema plays mostly educational 3D films on a six-story screen (the largest in New England). Many shows have an underwater theme, so you might find yourself swimming with tropical penguins, breaching with whales or fleeing from hungry sharks. Aquarium/IMAX combo tickets offer a discounted film price ($5).

Comedy

Comedy Studio   COMEDY
(☑617-661-6507; www.thecomedystudio.com; 1 Bow Market Way #23, Somerville; shows $10-20; ☺ show 8pm; ☐ 86 from Harvard or Sullivan) This low-budget, cutting-edge comedy gem moved out of its Harvard Square noodle-house digs and settled into happening Union Sq, Somerville. Mondays are reserved for the Mystery Lounge, a weird (and hilarious) magic show. Tuesdays are called Comedy Hell (aka open mike night); and Wednesdays are for Fresh Faces.

The Comedy Studio has a reputation for discovering new talent, so pay attention. It's in Bow Market, which is tucked into a former industrial complex in Union Sq. There's no street front, but look for signs and enter from Somerville Ave.

Improv Boston   COMEDY
(Map p68; ☑617-576-1253; www.improvboston.com; 40 Prospect St; tickets $10-20; ☺ Wed-Sat; 🌢; Ⓣ Central) This group has been making things up and making people laugh for more than a quarter of a century. Nowadays, the troupe's funny shows feature not just improv, but also comedy competitions, musical comedy and nude stand-up. The early Saturday show (4pm) is family oriented. There's free stand-up every Friday at 11:30pm for night owls.

Laugh Boston   COMEDY
(☑617-725-2844; www.laughboston.com; 425 Summer St; tickets $20-30; ☺ times vary Wed-Sun; ☐ SL1, SL2, Ⓣ South Station) The funny guys over at Improv Asylum decided that Boston needed a few more laughs, so they opened this premier, stand-up comedy club in the Westin Hotel. The place has a swanky, happy atmosphere, and there's programming five nights a week. In addition to local and national acts, look out for The Moth, the legendary true-story slam.

Wilbur Theatre   COMEDY
(Map p52; ☑617-248-9700; www.thewilbur.com; 246 Tremont St; tickets $22-65; Ⓣ Boylston) The colonial-style Wilbur Theatre dates from 1914, and over the years has hosted many prominent theatrical productions. These days it is Boston's premier comedy club. The smallish house hosts nationally known cut-ups, as well as music acts and other kinds of

hard-to-categorize performances. The theater itself could do with a renovation, but the talent is good.

Live Music

★Boston

Symphony Orchestra CLASSICAL MUSIC
(BSO; Map p62; ☎617-266-1200, 617-266-1492; www.bso.org; 301 Massachusetts Ave; tickets $30-145; Ⓣ Symphony) Flawless acoustics match the ambitious programs of the world-renowned Boston Symphony Orchestra. From September to April, the BSO performs in the beauteous Symphony Hall, featuring an ornamental high-relief ceiling and attracting a well-dressed crowd. In summer months the BSO retreats to Tanglewood in Western Massachusetts.

★Red Room @ Cafe 939 LIVE MUSIC
(Map p62; ☎617-747-2261; www.berklee.edu/cafe939; 939 Boylston St; tickets free-$20; ☺box office 10am-6pm Mon-Sat; Ⓣ Hynes) Run by Berklee students, the Red Room @ Cafe 939 has emerged as one of Boston's least predictable and most enjoyable music venues. It has an excellent sound system and a baby grand piano; most importantly, it books interesting up-and-coming musicians. Buy tickets in advance at the **Berklee Performance Center** (Map p62; ☎617-747-2261; www.berklee.edu/bpc; 136 Massachusetts Ave; tickets $10-65; ☺box office 10am-6pm Mon-Sat; Ⓣ Hynes).

★Wally's Café JAZZ
(Map p62; ☎617-424-1408; www.wallyscafe.com; 427 Massachusetts Ave; ☺5pm-2am; Ⓣ Massachusetts Ave) When Wally's opened in 1947, Barbadian immigrant Joseph Walcott became the first African American to own a nightclub in New England. Old-school, gritty and small, it still attracts a racially diverse crowd to hear jammin' jazz music 365 days a year. Berklee students love this place, especially the nightly jam sessions (6pm to 9pm).

★Club Passim LIVE MUSIC
(Map p66; ☎617-492-7679; www.clubpassim.org; 47 Palmer St; tickets $10-32; Ⓣ Harvard) The legendary Club Passim is a holdout from the days when folk music was a staple in Cambridge (and around the country). The club continues to book top-notch acts, single-handedly sustaining the city's folk scene. The colorful, intimate room is hidden off a side street in Harvard Square, just as it has been since 1969.

Paradise Rock Club LIVE MUSIC
(☎617-562-8800; www.crossroadspresents.com; 967 Commonwealth Ave; tickets $20-40; Ⓣ Pleasant St) Top bands rock at this landmark club – like U2, whose first gig in the USA was on this stage. Nowadays, you're more likely to hear the likes of Lucinda Williams, the Floozies, and plenty of Boston bands that made good but still come home to play the 'Dise.

Sanders Theatre at Memorial Hall CONCERT VENUE
(Map p66; ☎617-495-8676; www.ofa.fas.harvard.edu; 45 Quincy St; Ⓣ Harvard) Set inside the magnificent Memorial Hall, this beautiful, 1166-seat, wood-paneled theater is known for its acoustics. It is frequently used for classical musical performances by local chorales and ensembles, as well as occasional concerts by jazz and world musicians. Buy tickets at the booth inside the Smith Campus Center (p67).

Performing Arts

★Shakespeare on the Common THEATER
(Map p52; ☎617-426-0863; www.commshakes.org; Boston Common; ☺Jul & Aug; Ⓣ Park St) Each summer, the Commonwealth Shakespeare Company stages a major production on the Boston Common, drawing crowds for (free) Shakespeare under the stars. Productions often appeal to the masses with a populist twist, thus *The Taming of the Shrew*, set in a North End restaurant.

★Lily Pad PERFORMING ARTS
(www.lilypadinman.com; 1353 Cambridge St; tickets $5-15; ☎91; Ⓣ Central) Lily Pad is a tiny space that fills up with music and performance art, whether it's tango dancing or narrated

THEATER DISCOUNTS

ArtsBoston (www.artsboston.org) offers discounted tickets to theater productions through BosTix Deals (up to 25% for advance purchases online; up to 50% for same-day purchase at ArtsBoston kiosks at Quincy Market and Prudential Center).

Visit the **BosTix** (www.artsboston.org; 650 Boylston St; ☺11am-5pm Thu & Fri, 10am-4pm Sat & Sun; Ⓣ Copley) booth run by ArtsBoston on Copley Square for same-day, discounted tickets to local theater, comedy and music events.

jazz storytelling. You might also hear indie, avant-garde, folk and even chamber music. The space is stripped down – basically benches in a room – which adds to the underground ambience. There's not much here, but there is beer and wine!

Opera House   LIVE PERFORMANCE
(Map p52; ☑ 800-982-2787; www.bostonopera house.com; 539 Washington St; Ⓣ Downtown Crossing) This lavish theater has been restored to its 1928 glory, complete with mural-painted ceiling, gilded molding and plush velvet curtains. The glitzy venue regularly hosts productions from the Broadway Across America series, and is also the main performance space for the Boston Ballet.

Boston Ballet   DANCE
(Map p52; ☑ 617-695-6955; www.bostonballet. org; Opera House, 539 Washington St; tickets $37-204) Boston's skillful ballet troupe performs modern and classic works at the Opera House. The program varies every year, but at Christmas they always put on a wildly popular performance of the *Nutcracker*. Student and child 'rush' tickets are available for $30 cash two hours before some performances; seniors get the same deal,

---

LOCAL KNOWLEDGE

CLASSICAL MUSIC ON THE CHEAP

The Boston Symphony Orchestra often offers various discounted ticket schemes, which might allow you to hear classical music on the cheap:

➡ Same-day 'rush' tickets ($10) are available for Tuesday and Thursday evening performances (on sale from 5pm) as well as Friday afternoon performances (on sale from 10am).

➡ Check the schedule for occasional Open Rehearsals, which usually take place in the afternoon midweek. General admission tickets are $18 to $30.

➡ Discounted tickets are offered for certain segments of the population (eg under 40 = $20).

➡ Tomorrow's BSO musicians are today's New England Conservatory musicians. NEC concerts and recitals are often free!

---

but only for select Saturday and Sunday matinees.

Hatch Memorial Shell   CONCERT VENUE
(Map p62; www.hatchshell.com; Charles River Esplanade; Ⓣ Charles/MGH, Arlington) Free summer concerts take place at this outdoor bandstand on the banks of the Charles River. Most famously, there's Boston's biggest annual music event, the Boston Pops' July 4 concert. But throughout the summer, there are also Friday-night movies, Wednesday-night orchestral ensembles and the occasional oldies concert.

Barbara Lee Family Foundation Theater   THEATER
(☑ 617-478-3100; www.icaboston.org; 25 Harbor Shore Dr; ▣ SL1, SL2, Ⓣ South Station) Against a gorgeous, blue-water backdrop, the glass theater at the ICA (p59) is one of its coolest features and a venue for dance, music and other performance art. The ICA also hosts occasional film festivals and screenings of offbeat and arty cinema.

Company One   THEATER
(C1; Map p62; ☑ 617-292-7110; www.companyone. org; 539 Tremont St; Ⓣ Back Bay) This radical theater company strives to be at the 'intersection of art and social change' by offering provocative performances and fostering socially engaged artists. Critics are crazy for C1, which has racked up a slew of awards and nominations for its innovative productions. Most shows are performed in the **Boston Center for the Arts** (BCA; Map p62; ☑ 617-426-5000; www.bcaonline.org; 539 Tremont St; Ⓣ Back Bay) theaters.

American Repertory Theater   PERFORMING ARTS
(ART; Map p66; ☑ 617-547-8300; www.american repertorytheater.org; 64 Brattle St; tickets from $45; Ⓣ Harvard) There isn't a bad seat in the house at the Loeb Drama Theater, where the prestigious ART stages new plays and experimental interpretations of classics. Artistic Director Diane Paulus encourages a broad interpretation of 'theater,' staging interactive murder mysteries, readings of novels in their entirety and robot operas. The ART's musical productions, in particular, have been racking up Tony awards.

Sports

★ **Boston Red Sox**   BASEBALL
(Map p62; ☑ 617-226-6666; www.redsox.com; 4 Jersey St; bleachers $10-45, grandstand $23-87,

box $38-189; ⓣKenmore) From April to September you can watch the Red Sox play at Fenway Park, the nation's oldest and most storied ballpark. Unfortunately it is also the most expensive – not that this stops the Fenway faithful from scooping up the tickets. There are sometimes game-day tickets on sale, starting 90 minutes before the opening pitch. Head to Gate E on Lansdowne St; arrive early (but no earlier than five hours before game time) and be prepared to enter the ballpark as soon as you purchase your tickets. Otherwise, you can always get tickets in advance from online vendors or on game-day from scalpers around Kenmore Sq. If the Sox are doing well, expect to pay twice the face value (less if you wait until after the game starts).

Gillette Stadium SPECTATOR SPORT
(New England Patriots; ☑508-543-8200; www. patriots.com; 1 Patriot Pl, Foxborough) The six-time Super Bowl champs play football in the state-of-the-art Gillette Stadium, which is just 50 minutes south of Boston, but it's hard to get a ticket (most seats are sold to season-ticket holders). From I-93, take I-95 south to Rte 1. Otherwise, direct trains go to Foxborough from South Station.

TD Garden STADIUM
(Map p52; ☑event info 617-624-1000; www.td garden.com; 150 Causeway St; ⓣNorth Station) TD Garden is home to the NHL Boston Bruins, who play hockey here from September to June, and the NBA Boston Celtics, who play basketball from October to April. It's the city's largest venue, so big-name musicians perform here, too.

🔒 Shopping

Boston is known for its intellectuals and its arts, so you can bet it's good for bookstores, art galleries and music shops. The streets are also sprinkled with offbeat boutiques – some carrying vintage treasures and local designers. Besides to-die-for duds, indie shops hawk handmade jewelry, exotic household decorations and arty, quirky gifts. Fun to browse, even if you don't buy.

🔒 Beacon Hill & Boston Common

Paridaez CLOTHING
(Map p52; ☑617-835-5396; www.paridaez.com; 127 Charles St; ⊙noon-6pm; ⓣCharles/MGH) Boston designer Allison Daroie knows wom-

en play many roles, and she believes their clothing should too. That's why her classy, minimalist pieces can transform from daytime to evening, from dressy to casual, from conservative to flirtatious. These styles are so versatile, it's sometimes hard to say exactly what they are (like the ingenious Albatross 3-in-1 skirt+dress+tank).

Eugene Galleries ANTIQUES
(Map p52; ☑617-227-3062; www.eugenegalleries. com; 76 Charles St; ⊙11am-6pm Mon-Sat, from noon Sun; ⓣCharles/MGH) This tiny shop has a remarkable selection of antique prints and maps, especially focusing on old Boston. Follow the history of the city's development by examining 18th- and 19th-century maps and witness the filling in of Back Bay and the greening of the city. Historic prints highlight Boston landmarks, making for excellent old-fashioned gifts.

🔒 Downtown & Waterfront

Brattle Book Shop BOOKS
(Map p52; ☑617-542-0210; www.brattlebook shop.com; 9 West St; ⊙9am-5:30pm Mon-Sat; ⓣPark St, Downtown Crossing) Since 1825, the Brattle Book Shop has catered to Boston's literati: it's a treasure trove crammed with out-of-print, rare and first edition books. Ken Gloss – whose family has owned this gem since 1949 – is an expert on antiquarian books, moonlighting as a consultant and appraiser (see him on *Antiques Roadshow*). Don't miss the bargains on the outside lot.

Artists for Humanity GIFTS & SOUVENIRS
(Map p52; ☑617-268-7620; www.afhboston.org; 1 Faneuil Hall; ⊙10am-9pm Mon-Sat & 11am-7pm Sun Apr-Oct, 10am-7pm Mon-Thu, to 9pm Fri & Sat, noon-6pm Sun Nov-Mar; ⓣState) Artists for Humanity is a local charity organization that encourages urban youth to get in touch with their creative sides. That means you're doing a good deed by shopping here, as if you needed an excuse to treat yourself to one of the cute, clever T-shirts or totes bags. (We're partial to the cycling lobster, aka 'Lobsta Roll.')

Greenway Open Market ARTS & CRAFTS
(Map p52; ☑800-401-6557; www.newengland openmarkets.com; Rose Kennedy Greenway; ⊙11am-5pm Sat, plus 1st & 3rd Sun May-Oct; 🛜; ⓣAquarium) This weekend artist market brings out dozens of vendors to display their wares in the open air. Look for unique,

handmade gifts, jewelry, bags, paintings, ceramics and other arts and crafts – most of which are locally and ethically made. Food trucks are always on hand to cater to the hungry.

Boston Public Market
MARKET
(BPM; Map p52; ☑617-973-4909; www.boston publicmarket.org; 136 Blackstone St; ⊗8am-8pm Mon-Sat, 10am-6pm Sun; ☎; ⊤Haymarket) A locavore's longtime dream come true, this daily farmers market – housed in a brick-and-mortar building – gives shoppers access to fresh foodstuffs, grown, harvested and produced right here in New England. Come for seasonal produce, fresh seafood, meats and poultry from local farms, artisanal cheeses and dairy products, maple syrup and other sweets. Don't miss the local brews found in Hopsters' Alley.

Reserve your spot for a free one-hour tour (10am and 11am, Thursday and Friday).

🅐 West End & North End

★ Salmagundi
HATS
(Map p52; ☑617-936-4015; www.salmagundi boston.com; 61 Salem St; ⊗11am-7pm Tue-Fri, to 8pm Sat, to 6pm Sun & Mon; ⊤Haymarket) While the flagship Salmagundi store in Jamaica Plain has a bigger selection, this second location in the North End still offers some 4000 hats for your head-topping pleasure. From functional caps and protective sun hats to flashy fedoras and gorgeous special-occasion toppers, you'll find something that meets your needs and fits your style. (The passionate, knowledgeable staff guarantee it.)

Converse at Lovejoy Wharf
SHOES
(Map p52; ☑617-377-1000; www.converse.com; 140 N Washington St; ⊗10am-7pm Mon-Sat, 11am-6pm Sun; ⊤North Station) Occupying the ground level of the Converse world headquarters, this flagship store has a sweet selection of its classic sneakers, including some true originals. Look for a handful of styles with Boston themes – 'Exclusive at Lovejoy Wharf' as they say. Or you can customize a pair with your own colors and images.

Converse started making shoes right up the road in Malden, MA, way back in 1908. Chuck Taylor joined the 'team' in the 1920s and the rest is history.

North Bennet Street School
ARTS & CRAFTS
(Map p52; ☑617-227-0155; www.nbss.edu; 150 North St; ⊗9:30am-5:30pm Mon-Fri; ⊤Haymarket) The North Bennet Street School has been training craftspeople for over 100 years. Established in 1885, the school offers programs in traditional skills like bookbinding, woodworking and locksmithing. The school's on-site gallery sells incredible handcrafted pieces made by students and alumni. Look for unique jewelry, handmade journals and exquisite wooden furniture and musical instruments.

🅐 Seaport District & South Boston

★ For Now
CONCEPT STORE
(Map p52; ☑857-233-4639; www.itsfornow.com; 68 Seaport Blvd; ⊗10am-7pm Mon-Fri, 10am-6pm Sat, 11am-5pm Sun; ⊤South Station) Calling itself a 'retail incubator' and a 'pop-up collective,' For Now showcases a constantly changing and growing collection of local and regional designers and brands. Come in to browse and you'll likely find fashion-forward clothing, shoes, jewelry, handbags, stationery, body-care products and homewares. Or something else completely unexpected, but totally unique.

🅐 South End & Chinatown

★ SoWa Open Market
MARKET
(Map p62; ☑857-362-7692; www.sowaboston. com; 460 Harrison Ave; ⊗10am-4pm Sun May-Oct; ᮀSL4, SL5, ⊤Tufts Medical Center) Boston's original art market, this outdoor event is a fabulous opportunity for strolling, shopping and people-watching. More than 100 vendors set up shop under white tents. It's never the same two weeks in a row, but there's always plenty of arts and crafts, as well as edgier art, jewelry, homewares, and homemade food and body products.

International Poster Gallery
ART
(Map p62; ☑617-375-0076; www.international poster.com; 460c Harrison Ave; ⊗10am-6pm Mon-Sat, from noon Sun; ᮀSL4, SL5, ⊤Tufts Medical Center) This niche gallery stocks thousands of vintage posters from around the world. Thousands. The posters span the globe, with themes ranging from food and drink to travel and political propaganda. They are all there for the browsing, though it's easier to scroll through the online archive, which also

BOSTON'S BEST ANTIQUE SHOPPING

Cambridge Antique Market (☑617-868-9655; www.marketantique.com; 201 Monsignor O'Brien Hwy; ⊙11am-6pm Tue-Sun; ⊤Lechmere) An old warehouse crowded with trash and treasures.

SoWa Vintage Market (Map p62; ☑617-286-6750; www.sowavintagemkt.com; 450 Harrison Ave; ⊙10am-4pm Sun year-round; ▣SL4, SL5, ⊤Tufts Medical Center) Intriguing indoor flea market, open on Sundays.

Marika's Antique Shop (Map p52; ☑617-523-4520; 130 Charles St; ⊙10am-5pm Tue-Sat; ⊤Charles/MGH) Beacon Hill classic, hawking antiques for more than 50 years.

Eugene Galleries (p93) Maps, magazines and other old printed matter.

Central Flea (Map p68; ☑800-401-6557; www.newenglandopenmarkets.com; 91 Sidney St; ⊙11am-5pm Sun May-Oct; ⊤Central) Find some treasures amid the...other stuff.

offers all kinds of useful information and tips for would-be collectors.

SoWa Farmers Market　　　MARKET
(Map p62; ☑857-362-7692; www.sowaboston. com; 500 Harrison Ave; ⊙10am-4pm Sun May-Oct; ▣SL4, SL5, ⊤Tufts Medical Center) With some 60 stands, this is the largest farmers market in New England, and features fresh produce, meats and poultry, dairy products, flowers and more. If all this fresh, local deliciousness is making you hungry, never fear. There are also more than a dozen food trucks serving hot and hearty fare.

Ars Libri　　　BOOKS
(Map p62; ☑617-357-5212; www.arslibri.com; 500 Harrison Ave; ⊙9am-6pm Mon-Fri, 11am-5pm Sat; ▣SL4, SL5, ⊤Tufts Medical Center) Ring the doorbell: it's worth it. Specializing in rare and out-of-print titles, Ars Libri is an art bookstore extraordinaire, filled from floor to ceiling with volumes on all aspects and eras of art, architecture and design. If you love books or art, and especially books about art, you'll love Ars Libri.

🔒 Back Bay

Topdrawer　　　GIFTS & SOUVENIRS
(Map p62; ☑857-305-3934; www.kolo.com; 273 Newbury St; ⊙11am-7pm; ⊤Hynes) Travelers! Here is a store full of things you need, even if you didn't realize you needed them. Everything from plush fold-up slippers (perfect for the chilly airplane) to fabulous, functional daypacks and travel pouches. The aesthetic is modern and minimalist, but you'll also find an appealingly old-fashioned selection of pen sets and travel journals to record all your memories.

Trident Booksellers & Café　　　BOOKS
(Map p62; ☑617-267-8688; www.tridentbooks cafe.com; 338 Newbury St; ⊙8am-midnight; 🛜; ⊤Hynes) Pick out a pile of books and retreat to a quiet corner of the cafe to decide which ones you really want to buy. There's a little bit of everything here, and the 'hippie turned back-to-the-lander, turned Buddhist, turned entrepreneur' owners really know how to keep their customers happy.

🔒 Cambridge

Harvard Square is home to upwards of 150 shops, all within a few blocks of the university campus. The area used to boast an avant-garde sensibility and dozens of independent stores, and vestiges of this free spirit remain. Certainly, there are still more bookstores in Harvard Square than anywhere else in the Boston area. However, many of the edgier shops have been replaced by chains, leading critics to complain that the square has become an outdoor shopping mall.

Harvard Bookstore　　　BOOKS
(Map p66; ☑617-661-1515; www.harvard.com; 1256 Massachusetts Ave; ⊙9am-11pm Mon-Sat, 10am-10pm Sun; ⊤Harvard) Family-owned and -operated since 1932, the Harvard Bookstore is not officially affiliated with Harvard University, but it is the university community's favorite place to come to browse. While the shop maintains an academic focus, there is plenty of fiction for less lofty reading, as well as used books and bargain books in the basement.

Harvard Bookstore hosts author talks and other interesting lectures, often in conjunction with **Cambridge Forum** (Map p66;

www.cambridgeforum.org; 3 Church St; ⏱7pm Wed; Ⓣ Harvard) **FREE**.

Grolier Poetry Bookshop

BOOKS

(Map p66; 📞617-547-4648; www.grolierpoetry bookshop.org; 6 Plympton St; ⏱11am-7pm Tue & Wed, to 6pm Thu-Sat; Ⓣ Harvard) Founded in 1927, Grolier is the oldest – and perhaps the most famous – poetry bookstore in the USA. Over the years, TS Eliot, ee cummings, Marianne Moore and Allen Ginsberg have all passed through these doors. Today, Grolier continues to foster young poets and poetry readers. Besides selling written poetry and recordings, the store hosts readings and festivals.

Raven Used Books

BOOKS

(Map p66; 📞617-441-6999; www.ravencambridge. com; 23 Church St; ⏱10am-9pm Mon-Sat, 11am-8pm Sun; Ⓣ Harvard) This cherished shop is one of the last used-books holdouts in Harvard Square. Its huge collection focuses on scholarly titles, especially in the liberal arts, with hundreds of new arrivals each week.

ⓘ Information

EMERGENCY

Ambulance, fire and police (📞911).

INTERNET ACCESS

Most hotels and hostels offer internet access in one way or another. Usually that means wi-fi access, though some hotels also have an on-site business center or internet corner that provides computers. Aside from at hotels, wi-fi is common in cafes, on buses and even in public spaces such as shopping malls and airports.

MEDIA

Boston Globe (www.bostonglobe.com) One of two major daily newspapers, the *Globe* has extensive lifestyle and arts coverage, with plenty of entertainment listings.

Boston Herald (www.bostonherald.com) A right-wing daily, competing with the *Globe*; has its own entertainment section.

Boston Magazine (www.bostonmagazine.com) The city's monthly glossy magazine.

Improper Bostonian (www.improper.com) A sassy biweekly distributed free from sidewalk dispenser boxes.

MEDICAL SERVICES

Massachusetts General Hospital (📞617-726-2000; www.massgeneral.org; 55 Fruit St; Ⓣ Charles/MGH) Boston's largest and most reputable hospital.

Mount Auburn Hospital (📞617-492-3500; www.mountauburnhospital.com; 330 Mount Auburn St; 🚌71, 73, Ⓣ Harvard) A respected private hospital in Cambridge.

TOURIST INFORMATION

Boston Common Information Kiosk (GBCVB Visitors Center; Map p52; 📞617-426-3115; www.bostonusa.com; Boston Common; ⏱8:30am-5pm Mon-Fri, from 9am Sat & Sun; Ⓣ Park St) Provides maps and all kinds of tourist information; starting point for the Freedom Trail and many other walking tours.

Boston Harbor Islands Pavilion (Map p52; 📞617-223-8666; www.bostonharborislands. org; cnr State St & Atlantic Ave; ⏱9am-4:30pm mid-May–Jun & Sep-early Oct, to 6pm Jul & Aug; 🚢; Ⓣ Aquarium) Ideally located on the Rose Kennedy Greenway. This information center will tell you everything you need to know to plan your visit to the Boston Harbor Islands. Don't miss the nearby *Harbor Fog* sculpture, which immerses passersby in the sounds and sensations of the harbor.

Cambridge Visitor Information Kiosk (Map p66; 📞617-441-2884; www.cambridge-usa.org; Harvard Sq; ⏱9am-5pm Mon-Fri, to 1pm Sat & Sun; Ⓣ Harvard) Has detailed information on current Cambridge happenings and self-guided walking tours.

Greater Boston Convention & Visitors Bureau (www.bostonusa.com) Has a website packed with information on hotels, restaurants and special events, as well as LGBTIQ+, family travel and more.

Massachusetts Office of Travel & Tourism (www.massvacation.com) Has information about events and activities throughout the state, including an excellent guide to green tourism.

National Park Service Visitors Center (NPS; Map p52; 📞617-242-5642; www.nps. gov/bost/planyourvisit/index.htm; Faneuil Hall; ⏱9am-6pm; Ⓣ State) It has loads of information about the Freedom Trail sights and is the starting point for the free NPS Freedom Trail Tour (p74). There is an additional NPS Visitors Center at the Charlestown Navy Yard (p59).

USEFUL WEBSITES

Boston.com (www.boston.com) The online presence of the *Boston Globe*, with event listings, restaurant reviews, local news, weather and more.

Universal Hub (www.universalhub.com) Bostonians talk to each other about whatever is on their mind (sometimes nothing).

ⓘ Getting There & Away

Most travelers arrive in Boston by plane, with many national and international flights in and out of **Logan International Airport** (BOS; 📞800-235-6426; www.massport.com/logan).

Two smaller regional airports – Manchester Airport in New Hampshire and Green Airport near Providence, RI – offer alternatives that are also accessible to Boston and are sometimes less expensive.

Most trains operated by Amtrak (www.amtrak.com) go in and out of South Station. Boston is the northern terminus of the Northeast Corridor, which sends frequent trains to New York City, NY (3½ to 4½ hours), Philadelphia, PA (five to six hours) and Washington, DC (6¾ to eight hours). *Lake Shore Limited* goes daily to Buffalo, NY (11 hours) and Chicago, IL (22 hours), while the *Downeaster* goes from North Station to Portland, ME (2½ hours).

Buses are most useful for regional destinations, although Greyhound (www.greyhound.com) operates services around the country. In recent years, there has been a spate of new companies offering cheap and efficient service to New York City (four to five hours).

Flights, cars and tours can be booked online at lonelyplanet.com/bookings.

AIR
On Massachusetts Route 1A in East Boston, Logan International Airport has four separate terminals (A, B, C and E) that are connected by frequent shuttle buses. Downtown Boston is just a few miles from the airport and is accessible by bus, subway, water shuttle and taxi.

BUS
The infamous 'Chinatown Buses' originated in the late 1990s as an affordable way for Chinese workers to travel to and from jobs. They offered supercheap tickets between Boston and New York, traveling from Chinatown to Chinatown. Young, savvy travelers caught wind of the bargain transportation, and the phenomenon began to spread. It was crowded and confusing and probably not that safe, but it sure was cheap.

In recent years, more and more companies are running buses on this route; however, they don't always start and end in Chinatown. With competition has come improved service and better safety records, and many offer free wi-fi service on board. But the prices remain blissfully low.

GO Buses (www.gobuses.com) Buses to New York City ($18 to $44) depart from Alewife station in Cambridge. Buses also go to Providence, RI; Hartford and New Haven, CT; and Washington, DC.

Lucky Star Bus (www.luckystarbus.com) Leaves from South Station 12 to 14 times daily. Tickets must be purchased at least one hour before departure time. Full fare one way costs $25 to $35, while nonrefundable last-minute tickets can go for as little as $8.

Megabus (www.megabus.com) Rates vary from $5 to $50 depending on the time of day of travel and how far in advance tickets are purchased. In addition to New York, buses go to Burlington and Montpelier, VT; Portland, ME; Philadelphia, PA; Baltimore, MD; and Washington, DC. Buses leave from South Station.

CAR & MOTORCYCLE
If you're driving into Boston, you'll likely enter from north or south via I-93 (aka, the Central Artery) or from the west I-90 (the Mass Pike).

In central Boston, from I-93, there are exits to Storrow Dr (to points west), Causeway St (near North Station), Callahan Tunnel (to the airport), Purchase St (to Government Center), Surface Rd and Kneeland St (near Chinatown), I-90 and South Station.

From I-90, there are exits to Allston-Brighton (and Cambridge), Prudential Tunnel (to Copley Sq), South Station and I-93, and the Ted Williams Tunnel (to the airport). The Mass Pike is a toll road, although you don't have to stop and pay. Bills are delivered through the mail, based on the address associated with the automobile's license plate. For rental cars, you'll want to investigate how the rental agency handles these charges.

TRAIN
Located in downtown Boston, **South Station** (Map p52; ☏ 617-523-1300; www.south-station.net; 700 Atlantic Ave; Ⓣ South Station) is the terminus for Amtrak trains to/from New York City, Philadelphia and Washington, DC. It's also a stop for silver-line buses and the red line of the T.

ⓘ Getting Around
Boston is geographically small and logistically manageable. The sights and activities of principal interest to travelers are contained within an area that's only about 1 mile wide by 3 miles long. This makes Boston a wonderful walking or cycling city. Otherwise, most of the main attractions are accessible by subway. Some outlying sites require a bus ride. And a few – namely the Boston Harbor Islands – require a boat ride or two.

Incidentally, Boston is a waterside city, and riding in boats is part of the fun. Water shuttles are a convenient transportation option for a few harborside destinations, including the airport.

Aside from two feet and a heartbeat, your best friends for getting around town are the following:

T (Subway) The quickest and easiest way to get to most destinations. Runs from 5:30am or 6am until 1:30am.

Blue Bikes Boston's bike-share program, with 1800 bikes available to borrow at 200 stations.

MBTA bus Supplements the subway system.

TO/FROM THE AIRPORT
Bus

The silver line is the MBTA's 'bus rapid transit service.' It travels between Logan International Airport and South Station, with stops in the Seaport District. This is the most convenient way to get into the city if you are staying in the Seaport District or anywhere along the red line (Downtown, Beacon Hill, Cambridge).

Silver-line buses are free for passengers embarking at the airport, and they connect directly to the red-line subway at South Station, so you don't have to buy a separate ticket for the T. Returning to the airport, silver-line prices and hours are the same as for subway lines.

Car & Motorcycle

Three tunnels connect Logan Airport to I-93 and downtown Boston. If you're driving from the airport into Boston or to points north of the city, the Sumner Tunnel will lead you to Storrow Dr or over the Zakim Bridge to I-93 North. To points south of Boston, use the Ted Williams Tunnel to I-93 South. To or from points west, the Mass Pike connects directly with the Ted Williams Tunnel.

To reach the airport from downtown Boston, take the Callahan Tunnel or the Ted Williams Tunnel.

The toll is the same for all three tunnels ($2.65). Automatic pay-by-plate billing has eliminated the need for toll booths; you'll receive a bill in the mail based on an electronic scan of your license plate. (Check with your car-rental agency about how they handle this.)

Subway

The T, or the MBTA subway (www.mbta.com), is a fast and cheap way to reach the city from the airport. From any terminal, take a free, well-marked shuttle bus (22, 33, 55 or 66) to the blue-line T station called Airport and you'll be downtown within 30 minutes. The one-way subway fare is $2.75; buy tickets at machines in the station.

Taxi

Taxi fares from Logan are approximately $25 to downtown Boston, $30 to Kenmore Square and $35 to Harvard Square.

BICYCLE

In recent years, Boston has made vast improvements in its infrastructure for cyclists, including painting miles of bicycle lanes, upgrading bike facilities on and around public transportation, and implementing an excellent bike-share program. Boston drivers are used to sharing the roads with their two-wheeled friends (and they are used to arriving *after* their two-wheeled friends, who are less impeded by traffic snarls). Cyclists should always obey traffic rules and ride defensively.

Boston's bike-share program is Blue Bikes (www.bluebikes.com). There are 200 Blue Bikes stations around Boston, Cambridge, Brookline and Somerville, stocked with 1800 bikes that are available for short-term loan.

→ Download the app or visit any bicycle kiosk to purchase your pass.
→ Pay $2.50 per half-hour for bike use or purchase a one-day Adventure Pass for an unlimited number of two-hour bike rides in 24 hours.
→ Return the bike(s) to any station in the vicinity of your destination.

Generally speaking, Blue Bikes pricing is designed so a Single Use ticket can substitute for a cab ride (eg to make a one-way trip or run an errand). The Adventure Pass might work for leisurely riding or long trips, as long as you keep track of your time. Check the website for a map of Blue Bikes stations.

Blue Bikes recommends that all riders wear helmets (and state law requires the same for children under age 16).

BUS

The MBTA (www.mbta.com) operates bus routes within the city. These can be difficult to figure out for the short-term visitor, but schedules are

---

CHEAPER TRAVEL WITH CHARLIE

The Charlie in question is a fictional character from the Kingston Trio hit *Charlie on the MTA*. Charlie's sad story was that he could not get off the Boston T (then known as the Metropolitan Transit Authority) because he did not have the exit fare.

Now Charlie has been immortalized – yet again – by the MBTA's fare system: the Charlie Card. The plastic cards are available from the attendant at designated T stations. Once you have a card, you can add money at the automated fare machines; at the turnstile you will be charged $2.25 per ride.

The system is designed to favor commuters and cardholders. If you do not request a Charlie Card, you can purchase a paper fare card from the machine, but the turnstile will charge you $2.75 per ride. Similarly, Charlie Card–holders pay $1.70 to ride the bus, but for those paying cash it's $2.

posted on the website and at some bus stops along the routes. The standard bus fare is $2, or $1.70 with a Charlie Card. If you're transferring from the T on a Charlie Card, the bus fare is free.

The silver line, a so-called 'rapid' bus, starts at Downtown Crossing and runs along Washington St in the South End to Roxbury's Dudley Sq. Another route goes from South Station to the Seaport District, then under the harbor to Logan International Airport. This waterfront route costs $2.75 ($2.25 with a Charlie Card), instead of the normal bus fare.

The silver line is different from the regular MBTA buses because it drives in a designated lane (supposedly reducing travel time). More importantly, the silver line starts/terminates inside the South Station or Downtown Crossing subway terminal, so you can transfer to/from the T without purchasing an additional ticket.

SUBWAY (THE T)

The MBTA (www.mbta.com) operates the USA's oldest subway, built in 1897 and known locally as the 'T.' There are four lines – red, blue, green and orange – that radiate from the principal down-town stations: Downtown Crossing, Government Center, Park St and State. When traveling away from any of these stations, you are heading 'outbound.'

Although the MBTA might like you to believe otherwise, the silver line is a bus line with a dedicated traffic lane – not a subway line.

Tourist passes with unlimited travel (on subway, bus or water shuttle) are available for periods of one day ($12) or one week ($21.25). Kids 11 and under ride for free. Passes may be purchased from vending machines in most T stations and at MBTA sales outlets citywide (see www.mbta.com for a full list). For longer stays, you can buy a monthly pass allowing unlimited use of the subway and local buses ($84.50). Otherwise, buy a paper fare card ($2.75 per ride) at any station or a Charlie Card ($2.25 per ride) at designated stations.

BRING YOUR BIKE ON THE T

You can bring bikes on the T (subway), the bus and the commuter rail for no additional fare. Bikes are not allowed on green-line trains or silver-line buses, nor are they allowed on any trains during rush hour (7am to 10am and 4pm to 7pm, Monday to Friday). Bikes are not permitted inside buses, but most MBTA buses have bicycle racks on the outside.

At night, the last red-line trains pass through Park St around 12:40am (depending on the direction), but all T stations and lines are different: check the posting at the station.

TAXI

Cabs are plentiful but expensive. Rates are determined by the meter, which calculates miles. Expect to pay about $15 to $20 between most tourist points within the city limits, without much traffic. If you have trouble hailing a cab, head to any nearby hotel, where they congregate.

Cabbie's Cab Offers $35 flat-fee airport transfers from Cambridge; call ☎ 617-547-2222 or visit www.cabbiescab.com.

Chill Out First Class Cab Offers flat-rate airport transfers from all parts of Boston and Cambridge; call ☎ 617-212-3763.

TRAIN

The MBTA (www.mbta.com) commuter rail services destinations in the metropolitan Boston area. Trains heading west and north of the city, including to Concord and Salem, leave from bustling North Station on Causeway St. Trains heading south, including to Plymouth and TF Green Airport in Providence, leave from South Station.

Around Boston

☎ 781, 339, 978, 617, 508 / POP 4.8 MILLION

Includes ➜

Lexington	103
Concord	104
Lowell	108
Salem	110
Gloucester	115
Rockport	119
Newburyport	122
Plymouth	125
New Bedford	130

Best Places to Eat

➜ Blue Blinds Bakery (p129)

➜ New England Soup Factory (p113)

➜ Glenn's Food & Libations (p124)

➜ JT Farnham's (p122)

➜ Roy Moore Lobster Company (p120)

Best Places to Stay

➜ Inn at Castle Hill (p122)

➜ Rocky Neck Accommodations (p117)

➜ Hotel Salem (p113)

➜ Bearskin Neck Motor Lodge (p119)

➜ Inn at Hastings Park (p104)

Why Go?

Boston may be the state capital, but it's not the only town in eastern Massachusetts with traveler appeal. Many nearby places with rich histories, vibrant cultural scenes and unique events merit a visit. Easily accessible from Boston, most of these are ideal day-trip destinations.

The towns surrounding Boston represent every aspect of New England history: Colonial, revolutionary, maritime, literary and industrial. Inspired by intriguing events of the past and spectacular seascapes in the present, writers, artists and filmmakers continue to enrich the region's cultural life. Miles of pristine coastline draw beachcombers and sunbathers. Hikers and cyclists, canoeists and kayakers, bird-watchers and whale-watchers have myriad opportunities to engage with the local active lifestyle.

When to Go
Gloucester

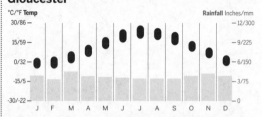

Apr Lexington and Concord re-create the battles that launched the American War of Independence.

Jul–Aug North Shore beaches become irresistible in July and August, thanks to hot sun and cold sea.

Oct–Nov Halloween is a hoot in Salem in October; Plymouth hosts Thanksgiving in November.

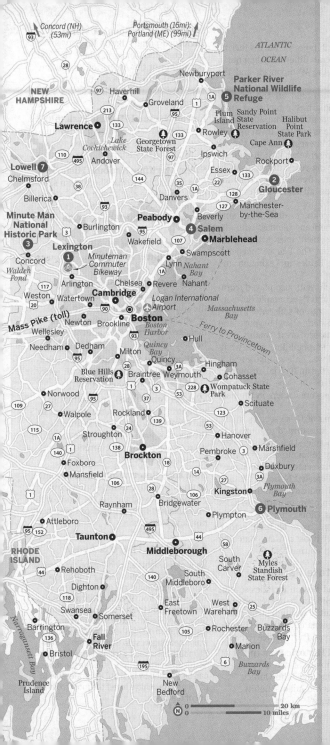

Around Boston Highlights

1 **Minuteman Commuter Bikeway** (p103) Cycling through history, from Cambridge to Lexington.

2 **Gloucester** (p115) Hitting the beaches, admiring the art and feasting on seafood.

3 **Minute Man National Historic Park** (p103) Traversing the park and recalling the beginnings of American independence.

4 **Peabody Essex Museum** (p110) Admiring the collection of treasures from around the world.

5 **Parker River National Wildlife Refuge** (p122) Spying on birds and frolicking in the waves at this island sanctuary.

6 **Plimoth Patuxet Museums** (p126) Witnessing the realities of Pilgrim life.

7 **Lowell Folk Festival** (p109) Enjoying the cultural diversity and lively music in this vibrant immigrant town.

History

The original inhabitants of Massachusetts belonged to several different Algonquian tribes, including the Wampanoag and the Pennacook.

After running aground off the coast of Cape Cod, the Pilgrims established their permanent settlement at Plymouth Colony in 1620. The Puritans followed them in 1628, establishing the Massachusetts Bay Colony on the sites of present-day Boston and Salem. In the following years, daring souls in search of religious freedom or economic opportunity settled all along the coast of Massachusetts.

In the 18th century, discontent simmered in the American colonies, with the independence movement most active in the area around Boston. The War of Independence started with battles in Lexington and Concord.

Eastern Massachusetts also played a crucial role in the country's economic development. During the age of sails and whales, towns such as Salem, Newburyport and New Bedford amassed great wealth from maritime trade, shipbuilding and whaling. Later, Lowell was an exemplary textile town, integral to the industrial revolution in the USA. Villages on Cape Ann – especially Gloucester – were leaders in the fishing industry.

With the decline of these sectors in the 20th century, the area turned to tourism to pick up the economic slack, with varying degrees of success. In an attempt to revitalize their aging city centers, Salem, Lowell and New Bedford created National Historic Sites, turning old industrial buildings into museums and opening restaurants and cafes to cater to tourists. Gloucester, too, touts its working waterfront as a heritage center, where visitors can book a whale-watching tour or learn about marine life.

National & State Parks

The region around Boston includes several diverse sites – significant to the region's revolutionary, mercantile and industrial past – that have been designated National Historic Parks by the National Park Service (NPS).

Adams National Historic Park (p125) Includes the birthplace of two US presidents (John Adams and John Quincy Adams), as well as the Adams' family homestead in Quincy.

Minute Man National Historic Park Incorporates Battle Rd between Lexington and Concord, where the first skirmishes of the American Revolution developed into full-blown fighting. This area remains much as it was 200 years ago.

Lowell National Historic Park (p108) A key player in the US industrial revolution, Lowell now hosts museums and tours dedicated to its history.

Salem Maritime National Historic Site (p110) This North Shore town shows off its maritime roots, with ships, docks, captains' homes and a customs house, all preserved from the 18th century.

State efforts to limit intrusive development and preserve ecosystems include the following:

Sandy Point State Reservation (p123) A delightfully pristine beach located at the southern tip of Plum Island, most of which is protected by the federally managed Parker River National Wildlife Refuge.

Halibut Point State Park (p119) A fantastic snapshot of Cape Ann, with rocky shores and an abandoned quarry.

Walden Pond (p108) An inspirational, wonderful natural resource managed by the Commonwealth of Massachusetts; the acres of undisturbed woods around it are protected by the efforts of private institutions.

Blue Hills Reservation Just a few miles south of Boston, this little-known but much-appreciated park is the work of the Massachusetts Department of Conservation and Recreation.

ⓘ Getting There & Away

Many of the sights around Boston are accessible by the Massachusetts Bay Transportation Authority commuter rail (www.mbta.com). Trains depart from Boston's North Station to destinations on the North Shore, including Gloucester, Rockport, Newburyport and Salem. North Station is also the departure point for trains heading west to Concord and Lowell. Plymouth is served by trains departing from South Station in Boston. Other destinations can be reached by bus, but it's preferable to use a private vehicle to get the most from a trip out of the city.

WEST OF BOSTON

Lexington

📐 781, 339 / POP 33,700

This upscale suburb, about 18 miles from Boston's center, is a bustling village of white churches and historic taverns, with tour buses surrounding the village green. Here, the skirmish between patriots and British troops jump-started the War of Independence. Each year on April 19, historians and patriots don their 18th-century costumes and grab their rifles for an elaborate re-enactment of the events of 1775.

While this history is celebrated and pre-served, it is in stark contrast to the peaceful, even staid, community that is Lexington today. If you stray more than a few blocks from the green, you could be in Anywhere, USA, with few reminders that this is where it all started. Nonetheless, it is a pleasant enough Anywhere, USA, with restaurants and shops lining the main drag, and im-pressive Georgian architecture anchoring either end.

⊙ Sights

★ Minute Man
National Historic Park   PARK

(www.nps.gov/mima; 3113 Marrett Rd; ⊘9am-5pm Apr-Oct; ♿) FREE The route that British troops followed to Concord has been des-ignated the Minute Man National Historic Park. The visitor center at the eastern end of the park shows an informative multi-media presentation depicting Paul Revere's ride and the ensuing battles. Within the park, Battle Rd is a 5-mile wooded trail that connects the historic sites related to the bat-tles – from Meriam's Corner, where gunfire erupted while British soldiers were retreat-ing, to the Paul Revere capture site.

Battle Green   HISTORIC SITE

(Lexington Common; Massachusetts Ave) The historic Battle Green is where the skir-mish between patriots and British troops jump-started the War of Independence. The **Lexington Minuteman Statue** (crafted by Henry Hudson Kitson in 1900) stands guard at the southeastern end of Battle Green, honoring the bravery of the 77 minutemen who met the British here in 1775, and the eight who died.

Buckman Tavern   MUSEUM

(www.lexingtonhistory.org; 1 Bedford Rd; adult/child $8/5; ⊘9:30am-4pm mid-Mar–Nov) Fac-ing the Battle Green, the 1709 Buckman Tavern was the headquarters of the minute-men. Here, they spent the tense hours be-tween the midnight call to arms and the dawn arrival of the Redcoats. Today, the tavern has been restored to its 18th-century appearance, complete with bar, fireplace and bullet holes resulting from British musket fire.

Munroe Tavern   HISTORIC SITE

(www.lexingtonhistory.com; 1332 Massachusetts Ave; adult/child $8/5; ⊘noon-4pm Jun-Oct) One mile east of the Battle Green, this his-toric tavern is named for the 18th-century proprietor, William Munroe, who was also an orderly sergeant in the minuteman bri-gade that fought on April 19, 1775. Later that day, the tavern was occupied by Brit-ish troops, who raided the provisions and used the dining room as a field hospital. Nowadays, many Munroe family heir-looms and other Revolution-era relics are on display.

Hancock-Clarke House   HISTORIC SITE

(www.lexingtonhistory.org; 36 Hancock St; adult/child $8/5; ⊘10am-4pm Jun-Oct) This 1737 house was the home of Reverend John Hancock (grandfather of *the* John Han-cock, the Declaration signer). On the night of April 18, 1775, the good Reverend hosted John Hancock and Samuel Adams in this parsonage. The house now has an exhibit of the personal items of Reverend Hancock and his successor, Reverend Jonas Clarke.

🏃 Activities

★ Minuteman
Commuter Bikeway   CYCLING

The Minuteman Commuter Bikeway follows an old railroad right of way from near the Alewife Red Line subway terminus in Cam-bridge through Arlington to Lexington and Bedford, a total distance of about 14 miles. From Lexington center, you can also ride along Massachusetts Ave to Rte 2A, which parallels the Battle Rd trail, and eventually leads into Concord center.

⌲ Tours

Liberty Ride   BUS

(www.libertyride.us; adult/child $28/12; ⊘10am-4pm daily Jun-Oct, 10am-4pm Sat & Sun Apr & May) If you don't have your own wheels, consider

PATRIOTS' DAY

The Patriots' Day (p74) celebration in Lexington starts early – really early. On the third Monday in April, as dawn breaks, local history buffs are assembled on the village green, some decked out in 'redcoats,' while others sport the scruffy attire of minutemen, fire-arms in hand, ready to re-enact the fateful battle that kicked off the American War of Independence. Later in the day, the conflict at Old North Bridge in Concord is re-enacted, as are skirmishes at Meriam's Corner and Hartwell Tavern in Minute Man National Historic Park. Spectators can witness the arrival of Paul Revere in Lexington, as well as his capture along Battle Rd.

Massachusetts is one of only two states in the USA that recognize Patriots' Day as a public holiday. See the website for a complete schedule of events.

catching the Liberty Ride, a hop-on, hop-off trolley, which includes all of the major sites in both Lexington and Concord. Buy tickets at the Lexington Visitors Center.

🛏 Sleeping

Inn at Hastings Park   BOUTIQUE HOTEL $$$
(☑781-301-6660; www.innathastingspark.com; 2027 Massachusetts Ave; r from $295) The Inn at Hastings Park is racking up all kinds of awards for its winning merger of historic architectural details with a sophisticated design aesthetic. Spread out across three buildings, the 22 guestrooms are individually decorated and delightfully plush, some with fireplaces, marble bathrooms and other special touches. The on-site restaurant, Artistry on the Green, also gets rave reviews.

✗ Eating & Drinking

Rancatore's Ice Cream   ICE CREAM $
(www.rancs.com; 1752 Massachusetts Ave; ⊙10am-11pm; ⊕) Cool off with a scoop of homemade ice cream or sorbet from this family-run place. Some of Ranc's flavors inspire worshipful devotion, such as bourbon butter pecan and classic coconut. The hot-fudge sundaes are also legendary.

ℹ Information

Lexington Visitors Center (Lexington Chamber of Commerce; www.lexingtonchamber.org; 1875 Massachusetts Ave; ⊙9am-5pm) Opposite Battle Green, next to Buckman Tavern.

ℹ Getting There & Away

MBTA (www.mbta.com) buses 62 (Bedford VA Hospital) and 76 (Hanscom Field) run from the Red Line Alewife subway terminus through Lexington center at least hourly on weekdays and less frequently on Saturday; there are no buses on Sunday.

Concord

☑978 / POP 19,200

On April 18, 1775, British troops marched out of Boston, searching for arms that colonists had hidden west of the city. The following morning, they skirmished with Colonial minutemen in Lexington, then continued on to Concord, where the rivals faced off at North Bridge, in the first battle of the War of Independence.

Today, tall white church steeples rise above ancient oaks, elms and maples, giving Concord a stateliness that belies the revolutionary drama that occurred centuries ago. Indeed, it's easy to see how writers such as Ralph Waldo Emerson, Nathaniel Hawthorne, Henry David Thoreau and Louisa May Alcott found their inspiration here. Concord was also the home of famed sculptor Daniel Chester French (who went on to create the Lincoln Memorial in Washington, DC).

These days travelers can relive history in Concord. **Patriots' Day** (www.lexingtonma.gov/patriotsday) is celebrated with gusto, and many significant literary sites are open for visitors.

⊙ Sights

★**DeCordova Sculpture Park & Museum**   MUSEUM
(www.decordova.org; 51 Sandy Pond Rd, Lincoln; adult/child $14/free; ⊙10am-5pm daily Jun-Aug, closed Mon & Tue Sep-May; ⊕) The magical DeCordova Sculpture Park encompasses 35 acres of green hills, providing a spectacular natural environment for a constantly changing exhibit of outdoor artwork. As many as 75 pieces are on display at any given time. Inside the complex, a museum hosts rotating exhibits of sculpture, painting, photography and mixed media.

★**Old North Bridge** HISTORIC SITE
(www.nps.gov/mima; Monument St; ⊙dawn-dusk) A half-mile north of Monument Sq in Concord center, the wooden span of Old North Bridge is the site of the 'shot heard around the world' (as Emerson wrote in his poem *Concord Hymn*). This is where enraged minutemen fired on British troops, forcing them to retreat to Boston. Daniel Chester French's first statue, *Minute Man*, presides over the park from the opposite side of the bridge.

Discovery Museum & Discovery Woods MUSEUM
(www.discoverymuseums.org; 177 Main St, Acton; $14.50; ⊙9am-4:30pm Sat-Thu, to 8pm Fri, closed Mon Sep-May; ⬥) This fabulous kids' spot offers a slew of newly imagined, immersive experiences focused on science. Even better, the new outdoor space offers many opportunities to climb, crawl, swing, spin and chill out in nature, including an amazing tree house. Free admission on Fridays after 4pm.

Concord Museum MUSEUM
(www.concordmuseum.org; 200 Lexington Rd; adult/child $10/5; ⬥) Southeast of Monument Sq, Concord Museum brings the town's diverse history under one roof. The museum's prized possession is one of the 'two if by sea' lanterns that hung in the steeple of the Old North Church in Boston as a signal to Paul Revere. It also has the world's largest collection of Henry David Thoreau artifacts, including his writing desk from Walden Pond.

Robbins House HOUSE
(www.robbinshouse.org; 320 Monument St; admission by donation; ⊙11am-4pm Wed-Mon Jun-Aug, 11am-4pm Fri-Sun Sep-Oct) **FREE** Just opposite the Old North Bridge, this modest 544-sq-ft clapboard farmhouse belonged to the family of Caesar Robbins, one of Concord's first freed African Americans. There's not much to see inside, save some old documents and photos, but the exhibits and staff recount the fascinating story of three generations of the Robbins family, as they worked for their own and others' freedom in the 18th and 19th centuries. Robbins House also hosts talks, tours and other events highlighting Concord's African American history.

Wayside HOUSE
(www.nps.gov/mima; 455 Lexington Rd; adult/child $7/5; ⊙9:30am-5:30pm Thu-Mon May-Oct) Also known as the 'Home of Authors,' this gracious Colonial mansion was home to three writers of note during the 19th century. Louisa May Alcott, Nathaniel Hawthorne and Harriett Lothrop (Margaret Sidney) all stayed here at different times. The house is part of the Minute Man National Historic Park (p103).

AROUND BOSTON CONCORD

WORTH A TRIP

FRUIT, VEGETABLES & TRANSCENDENTALS

Fruitlands Museums (www.fruitlands.org; 102 Prospect Hill Rd, Harvard; adult/child $15/6, grounds only $6/3; ⊙11am-4pm Mon & Wed-Fri, 10am-5pm Sat & Sun Apr-Oct) is a beautifully landscaped, 210-acre property that was the site of Bronson Alcott's short-lived experiment in communal living. The original hillside farmhouse was used by Alcott and his utopian 'Con-Sociate' family. Other museums have since been moved to the estate, including a 1794 Shaker House, a Native American museum and a gallery featuring paintings by 19th-century itinerant artists and Hudson River School landscape painters. There are also several miles of walking trails through picturesque woods and farmland.

In the early 19th century, Concordian thinkers were at the forefront of transcendentalism, a philosophical movement that espoused that God 'transcends' all people and things. Bronson Alcott (1799–1888), educational reformer and father of Louisa May Alcott, was a leader among this group pursuing transcendental ideals. Toward this end, he founded Fruitlands, an experimental vegetarian community (read: commune).

Nowadays, Fruitlands hosts all kinds of special events, including a summer concert series. One of the highlights is the Fruitlands Tearoom. Fruitlands is in Harvard, about 30 miles west of Boston. Take Rte 2 to exit 38A, Rte 111, then take the first right onto Old Shirley Rd.

Concord

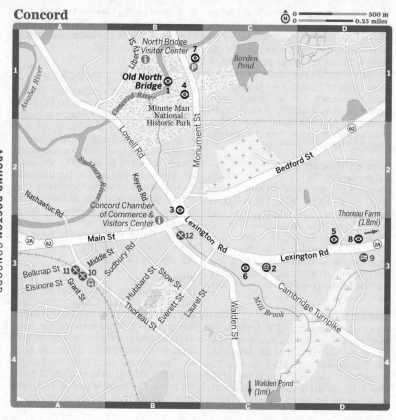

Concord

◉ Top Sights
1 Old North Bridge...................................B1

◉ Sights
2 Concord Museum.................................C3
3 Monument Square...............................B2
4 Old Manse...B1
5 Orchard House.....................................D3
6 Ralph Waldo Emerson Memorial
   House...C3
7 Robbins House.....................................B1
8 Wayside...D3

🛏 Sleeping
9 Hawthorne Inn.....................................D3

🍽 Eating
10 80 Thoreau...A3
11 Bedford Farms....................................A3
12 Concord Cheese Shop........................B3

Orchard House HISTORIC SITE
(www.louisamayalcott.org; 399 Lexington Rd; adult/child $10/5; ⏱10am-4:30pm Mon-Sat, from 11am Sun Apr-Oct, 11am-3pm Mon-Fri, 10am-4:30pm Sat & 1-4:30pm Sun Nov-Mar) Louisa May Alcott (1832–88) was a junior member of Concord's august literary crowd, but her work proved to be durable: *Little Women* is among the most popular young-adult books ever written. The mostly autobiographical novel is set in Concord. Take a tour of Alcott's childhood home, Orchard House, to see how the Alcotts lived and where the novel was actually written.

Ralph Waldo Emerson Memorial House HISTORIC SITE
(📞978-369-2236; www.facebook.com/emersonhouseconcord; 28 Cambridge Turnpike; adult/child $10/7; ⏱10am-4:30pm Thu-Sat, from 1pm Sun mid-Apr–Oct) This house is where the philosopher lived for almost 50 years until 1882.

Emerson was the paterfamilias of literary Concord, one of the great literary figures of his age and the founding thinker of the transcendentalist movement. The house often hosted his renowned circle of friends and still contains many original furnishings.

Old Manse
HISTORIC SITE

(www.thetrustees.org; 269 Monument St; adult/child $10/5; ☉ noon-4pm Wed-Sun Apr-Jun, 11am-5pm Wed-Mon Jul-Oct, Sat & Sun only Nov-Mar) Right next to Old North Bridge, the Old Manse was built in 1769 by Ralph Waldo's grandfather, Reverend William Emerson. Today, it's filled with mementos, including those of Nathaniel and Sophia Hawthorne, who lived here for a few years. The highlight of Old Manse is the gorgeously maintained grounds – the fabulous organic garden was planted by Henry David Thoreau as a wedding gift to the Hawthornes.

Monument Square
SQUARE

The grassy center of Monument Sq is a favorite resting and picnicking spot for cyclists touring Concord's scenic roads. At the southeastern end of the square is **Wright Tavern**, one of the first places the British troops searched in their hunt for arms on April 19, 1775. It became their headquarters for the operation.

Thoreau Farm
HISTORIC SITE

(www.thoreaufarm.org; 341 Virginia Rd; adult/child $6/free; ☉ tours 11am, 1pm & 3pm Sat & Sun May-Oct) Fans of Thoreau can travel off the beaten path to the house where he was born, which is about 2.4 miles east of Concord center. Henry David lived in his grandmother's farmhouse for only a few months after his birth, but the rural retreat would prove influential and inspirational throughout his life. The grounds are still an inviting place for exploration and reflection.

🕜 Tours

Concord Tour Company
WALKING

(www.concordtourcompany.com; per person $25) Fantastic, multitalented passionate tour guides bring Concord's history to life on 90-minute walking tours. There's a revolutionary tour, a literary tour and a spooky tour. Four-person minimum.

🛏 Sleeping & Eating

Longfellow's Wayside Inn
B&B $$

(☎ 978-443-1776; www.wayside.org; 76 Wayside Inn Rd, Sudbury; d $170-190; ❄ 🐾) Made famous by Longfellow's collection of poems *Tales of a Wayside Inn,* this hostelry offers 10 period rooms and lovely landscaped grounds. Also on-site is an extensive archive of the history of the inn, which has been operating since 1716, making it the country's oldest functioning inn. It's 13 miles south of Concord on US 20.

★ Hawthorne Inn
B&B $$$

(☎ 978-369-5610; www.hawthorneinnconcord.com; 462 Lexington Rd; r from $249; 🅿 ❄ 🐾) The aesthetic here is transcendental, incorporating elements of nature, splashes of color and an atmosphere of serenity. Some rooms have four-poster beds and fireplaces, but there's nothing cutesy going on here – just contemporary class. The complimentary breakfast is served on the delightful dining room porch.

Concord Cheese Shop
DELI $

(www.concordcheeseshop.com; 29 Walden St; sandwiches $8-12; ☉ 10am-5:30pm Tue-Sat; 🖉) This is a cheese shop, as it claims, with an excellent selection of imported and local cheese, as well as wine and other specialty food items. But the folks behind the counter can whip those ingredients into an amazing sandwich (or soup or salad) – perfect for a picnic on Memorial Sq. Want something fabulous? Try the Thursday/Saturday special sandwich.

Bedford Farms
ICE CREAM $

(www.bedfordfarmsicecream.com; 68 Thoreau St; ice cream from $4; ☉ 11am-9:30pm Mar-Nov, noon-7pm Dec-Feb; 🖈) Dating from the 19th century, this local dairy specializes in delectable ice cream, and frozen yogurt that tastes like delectable ice cream. If prices seem a tad high, it's because the scoops are gigantic. Its trademark flavor is Moosetracks (vanilla ice cream, chocolate swirl, peanut-butter cups). Conveniently located next to the train depot.

80 Thoreau
MODERN AMERICAN $$$

(☎ 978-318-0008; www.80thoreau.com; 80 Thoreau St; mains $26-30; ☉ 5:30-10:30pm Mon-Thu, 5-11:30pm Fri & Sat) Understated and elegant, this modern restaurant is an anomaly in historic Concord – but that's a good thing. The menu – short but sweet – features deliciously unexpected combinations of flavors, mostly using seasonal, local ingredients. There's also a busy bar area, which offers a concise selection of classic cocktails and long list of wines suitable for pairing.

AROUND BOSTON CONCORD

ON WALDEN POND

Henry David Thoreau took the naturalist beliefs of transcendentalism out of the realm of theory and into practice when he left the comforts of the town and built himself a rustic cabin on the shores of **Walden Pond** (☑ 978-369-3254; www. mass.gov/dcr; 915 Walden St; parking $15; ⊙ dawn-dusk). His famous memoir of his time spent there, *Walden; or, Life in the Woods* (1854), was full of praise for nature and disapproval of the stresses of civilized life – sentiments that have found an eager audience ever since. The glacial pond is now a state park, surrounded by acres of forest preserved by the Walden Woods project, a nonprofit organization.

ℹ Information

Concord Chamber of Commerce & Visitors Center (☑ 978-369-3120; www.concordcham berofcommerce.org; 58 Main St; ⊙ 10am-4pm Apr-Oct) Concord Chamber of Commerce has full details on sites, including opening hours for the homes, which vary with the season.

North Bridge Visitor Center (www.nps.gov/ mima; 174 Liberty St; ⊙ 9am-5pm Apr-Oct) On the west side of the Old North Bridge, the Buttrick mansion houses the NPS visitor center, where you can see a video about the Battle of Concord and admire the Revolutionary War brass cannon, the Hancock. Along with the skirmish at Lexington, the face-off at North Bridge was the first major clash between British regulars and Colonial minutemen.

ℹ Getting There & Away

MBTA commuter rail (www.mbta.com) trains run between Boston's North Station and Concord ('the Depot'; $9.25, 40 minutes, 12 daily) on the Fitchburg/South Acton line.

Lowell

☑ 978 / POP 111,300

In the early 19th century, textile mills in Lowell churned out cloth by the mile, driven by the abundant waterpower of Pawtucket Falls. Today, the city at the confluence of the Concord and Merrimack Rivers doesn't have such a robust economy, but its historic center recalls the industrial revolution glory days – a working textile mill, canal boat tours and trolley rides evoke the birth of America as an industrial giant.

In modern Lowell, 25 miles north of Boston, an influx of Southeast Asian immigrants has diversified the culture (and cuisine) of this classic New England mill town. A short walk from the historic center into the ethnic neighborhood known as the Acre reveals that Lowell has definitely changed from the city it was 150 years ago.

Lowell was also the birthplace of two American cultural icons: painter James Abbott McNeill Whistler and writer Jack Kerouac.

◉ Sights

Lowell National Historic Park   HISTORIC SITE
(🏛) The historic buildings in the city center – connected by the trolley and canal boats – constitute the national park, which gives a fascinating peek at the workings of a 19th-century industrial town. Stop first at the Market Mills Visitors Center to pick up a map and check out the general exhibits. An introductory multimedia video on historic Lowell is shown every half-hour.

Boott Cotton Mills Museum   MUSEUM
(☑ 978-970-5000; www.nps.gov/lowe; 115 John St; adult/child $6/3; ⊙ 9:30am-5pm May-Nov; 🏛) Five blocks northeast of the visitors center, the Boott Cotton Mills Museum has exhibits that chronicle the rise and fall of the industrial revolution in Lowell, including technological changes, labor movements and immigration. The highlight is a working weave room, with 88 power looms.

Whistler House Museum of Art   MUSEUM
(www.whistlerhouse.org; 243 Worthen St; adult/ child $12/7; ⊙ 11am-4pm Wed-Sun) James Abbott McNeill Whistler's birthplace, built in 1823, is the home of the Lowell Art Association. It houses a small collection of work by New England artists, including some etchings by Whistler himself. Outside, an 8ft bronze statue of the artist by sculptor Mico Kaufman is the centerpiece of the Whistler Park and Gardens.

New England Quilt Museum   MUSEUM
(www.nequiltmuseum.org; 18 Shattuck St; adult/ child $8/free; ⊙ 10am-4pm Tue-Sat, from noon Sun May-Oct, 10am-4pm Wed-Sat Nov-Apr) This little museum has found its niche. The friendly, knowledgeable staff members show off a collection of nearly 500 antique and contemporary quilts from around New England. Rotating exhibits highlight thematic work such as Japanese quilts, appliqué quilts and the Red Sox (of course). Great gift shop.

Edson Cemetery
CEMETERY

(1375 Gorham St) Two miles south of Lowell center, Kerouac is buried in the Sampas family plot at Edson Cemetery. His grave remains a pilgrimage site for devotees who were inspired by his free spirit.

✪ Festivals & Events

Lowell Folk Festival
MUSIC

(www.lowellfolkfestival.org; ⊙ Jul) Three days of food, music (on six stages!), art, parades and other festivities honor the diverse multicultural community that is Lowell.

Lowell Celebrates Kerouac
LITERATURE

(LCK; www.lowellcelebrateskerouac.org; ⊙ Oct) A local nonprofit organization hosts four days of events dedicated to Beat writer Jack Kerouac, featuring tours of many places in his novels, as well as panel discussions, readings, music and poetry. Literature buffs travel from around the world for this unique event, which takes place during the first weekend in October.

🛏 Sleeping & Eating

UMass Lowell Inn
& Conference Center
HOTEL $

(📞 978-934-6920; www.acc-umlinnandconference center.com; 50 Warren St; r from $139; ❋ 🛜 🐾) Located in the heart of downtown Lowell overlooking the canals. Some rooms have scenic views of the Merrimack, and all rooms are freshly renovated with standard amenities. The price includes a continental breakfast.

Heng Lay
CAMBODIAN, THAI $

(www.facebook.com/HengLayRestaurant; 153 Liberty St; mains $8-15; ⊙ 8am-8pm Thu-Tue) A half-mile west of the train station, this is one of Lowell's favorite family-run Cambodian restaurants, serving up spicy chicken wings, pad thai and big bowls of Phnom Penh noodles to satisfied customers. Accommodating service with a smile is a hallmark of this place.

Life Alive
VEGETARIAN $

(www.lifealive.com; 194 Middle St; meals $8-10; ⊙ 10am-8pm Mon-Sat, to 6pm Sun; 🍴) Scrumptious salads, fresh, fantastic food and jubilant juices fill out the menu at this funky cafe. The choices can be overwhelming, but you can't go wrong with the signature dish known as 'The Goddess': veggies and tofu served over rice with a zinger ginger nama shoyu sauce. The food is healthy and veg friendly; the setting is arty and appealing.

Arthur's Paradise Diner
DINER $

(112 Bridge St; meals $6-10; ⊙ 6am-noon Mon-Fri, from 7am Sat & Sun; 🍴) The epitome of 'old school,' this place is open only for breakfast and lunch and specializes in something called the Boot Mill sandwich (egg, bacon, cheese and home fries on a grilled roll). Housed in an authentic Worcester Diner Car #727. Cash only.

🍷 Drinking & Entertainment

Worthen House
PUB

(www.worthenhousecafe.com; 141 Worthen St; ⊙ 11am-2am) This brick tavern (Lowell's oldest, dating from 1834) is famed for its amazing pulley-driven fan system (which is still operational). The pressed-tin ceiling and wooden bar remain from the early days, giving this place an old-fashioned neighborhood feel. Stop by for a pint of Guinness and a burger. Cash only.

LeLacheur Park
BASEBALL

(www.lowellspinners.com; 450 Aiken St; tickets $12; 🍴) The Lowell Spinners, a Class A organization, is a Red Sox feeder team. Locally, it plays at this park, which is north of the center on the Merrimack River. If your kid's not into baseball, check out the Swampland Kids Area in the left-field corner of the ball park, featuring a giant slide, a bouncy house and lots more fun and games.

🛈 Information

Market Mills Visitors Center (📞 978-970-5000; www.nps.gov/lowe; 246 Market St; ⊙ 9am-5pm May-Nov) Starting place for the Lowell National Historic Park. Stop by to pick up a map and check out the general exhibits. An introductory multimedia video on historic Lowell is shown every half-hour.

🛈 Getting There & Around

MBTA commuter rail trains (www.mbta.com) depart Boston's North Station for Lowell ($10). Trains go in either direction 10 times a day during the week, and four times on weekends. Trains from Boston terminate at the Gallagher Transportation Terminal on Thorndike St, a 15-minute walk southwest of the city center (or take the shuttle).

The Lowell Regional Transit Authority (www. lrta.com) runs the Downtown Shuttle (route 18) that departs every 15 minutes from the Downtown Transit Center, stopping near the museums and visitor center. The fare is $1.25.

NORTH SHORE

The entire coast of Massachusetts claims a rich history, but no part offers more recreational, cultural and dining diversions than the North Shore. Salem was among America's wealthiest ports during the 19th century; Gloucester is the nation's most famous fishing port; and Marblehead remains one of the premier yachting centers. Trade and fishing have brought wealthy residents, sumptuous houses, and great collections of art and artifacts to the area. Explore the region's rich maritime history and spectacular coastal scenery, and don't miss the opportunity for a seafood feast.

Salem

☑ 978 / POP 43,400

This town's very name conjures up images of diabolical witchcraft and people being burned at the stake. The famous Salem witch trials of 1692 are ingrained in the national memory. Indeed, Salem goes all out at Halloween, when the town dresses up for parades and parties, and shops sell all manner of Wiccan accessories.

These incidents obscure Salem's true claim to fame: its glory days as a center for clipper-ship trade with the Far East. Elias Hasket Derby, America's first millionaire, built Derby Wharf, which is now the center of the Salem Maritime National Historic Site. The marvelous Peabody Essex Museum displays some of the treasures that were brought home from these merchant expeditions.

Today, Salem is a middle-class commuter suburb of Boston with an enviable location on the sea. Its rich history and culture, from witches to ships to art, continue to cast a spell on visitors.

◎ Sights & Activities

★ **Punto Urban Art Museum**   PUBLIC ART
(www.puntourbanartmuseum.org; Lafayette, Peabody & Ward Sts) **FREE** If you walk south on Lafayette from Derby St, you'll find yourself on the other side of the tracks (or river, in this case). Welcome to El Punto, or 'The Point,' a rough-and-tumble Dominican neighborhood that has been transformed into a vibrant, open-air art museum. A group of local and nationally renowned artists painted 50 murals on the brick walls and buildings, all within a three-block radius, creating a fantastical colorful cityscape.

★ **Peabody Essex Museum**   MUSEUM
(☑ 978-745-9500; www.pem.org; 161 Essex St; adult/child $20/free; ◎ 10am-5pm Tue-Sun; ♿) All of the art, artifacts and curiosities that Salem merchants brought back from the Far East were the foundation for this museum. Founded in 1799, it is the country's oldest museum in continuous operation. The building itself is impressive, with a light-filled atrium, and it's a wonderful setting for the vast collections, which focus on New England decorative arts and maritime history.

Salem Maritime
National Historic Site   HISTORIC SITE
(www.nps.gov/sama; 160 Derby St; ◎ 9am-5pm May-Oct, 10am-4pm Wed-Sun Nov-Apr) **FREE** This National Historic Site comprises the Custom House, the wharves and other buildings along Derby St that are remnants of the shipping industry that once thrived along this stretch of Salem. Of the 50 wharves that once lined Salem Harbor, only three remain, the longest of which is Derby Wharf. Check the website for a schedule of guided tours of the various buildings, or download an audio walking tour of the whole area.

Abbott Hall   HISTORIC BUILDING
(www.marblehead.org; Washington Sq, Marblehead; ◎ 8am-5pm Mon-Thu, to 12:30pm Fri) **FREE** Every American is familiar with *The Spirit of '76*, the patriotic painting (c 1876) by Archibald M Willard, depicting three American Revolution figures – a drummer, a fife player and a flag bearer. The painting hangs in the selectmen's meeting room in Abbott Hall, home of the Marblehead Historical Commission.

House of the Seven Gables   HISTORIC SITE
(www.7gables.org; 54 Turner St; adult/child $16/11; ◎ 10am-7pm Jul-Oct, to 5pm Nov-Jun) 'Halfway down a by-street of one of our New England towns stands a rusty wooden house, with seven acutely peaked gables facing towards various points of the compass, and a huge clustered chimney in their midst.' So wrote Nathaniel Hawthorne in his 1851 novel *The House of Seven Gables*. The house brings to life the gloomy Puritan atmosphere of early New England. Look for wonderful seaside gardens, many original furnishings and a mysterious secret staircase.

Witch House   HISTORIC SITE
(Jonathan Corwin House; ☑ 978-744-8815; www.the witchhouse.org; 310 Essex St; adult/child $8.25/4.25, guided tour $2; ◎ 10am-5pm mid-Mar–mid-Nov,

WITCHES, WITCHES, EVERYWHERE!

The city of Salem embraces its witchy past with a healthy dose of whimsy. But the history offers a valuable lesson about what can happen when fear and frenzy are allowed to trump common sense and compassion. By the time the witch hysteria of 1692 had finally died down, a total of 156 people had been accused, 55 people had pleaded guilty and implicated others to save their own lives, and 14 women and six men who would not confess had been executed. The **Witch Trials Memorial** (Charter St) is a simple but dramatic monument that honors the innocent victims who were persecuted and killed because of human hysteria.

Sadly, most of Salem's spooky sites are simply cashing in on the historic tragedy. But for some light-hearted whimsy, bypass the rest and head to the **TV Land Statue** (Lappin Park, cnr Washington & Essex Sts) to have your picture taken with Samantha Stephens, the spell-casting, nose-twitching beauty from the classic show *Bewitched*.

noon-4pm Thu-Sun mid-Nov–mid-Mar) Of more than a score of witchy attractions in town, this is the only actual historic site. The house was once the home of Jonathan Corwin, a local magistrate who was called on to investigate witchcraft claims. He examined several accused witches, possibly in the 1st-floor rooms of this house. The house demonstrates the family's daily life at the time of the witch hysteria, providing historical context for the episode. Open longer hours in October.

Witch Dungeon Museum MUSEUM
(www.witchdungeon.com; 16 Lynde St; adult/child $10/8; ⊙10am-5pm Apr-Nov, extended hours in Oct) This place offers a 15-minute live re-enactment of a witch trial, using historical transcripts for dialog (which is interesting, but it makes it difficult for kids to understand). Afterward, visitors descend into the gaol (dungeon), which is creepy and hokey, thanks to the mannequins chained up in the cells. There are no artifacts in this 'museum,' save the beam from the actual gaol that once existed nearby. Beware: the dungeon's final scene depicts a hanging on Gallows Hill.

Derby Lanes at Flatbread Salem BOWLING
(www.derbylanes.com; 311 Derby St; ⊙11am-10pm Sun-Thu, to 11am Fri & Sat; ▣) Nothing could be finer than pizza and bowling, especially when it's good old-fashioned candlepin bowling (small balls) and wood-fired flatbread pizza. This is a fabulous place for a night out with family or friends.

☞ Tours

Hocus Pocus Tours HISTORY
(☎781-248-2031; www.hocuspocustours.com; 176 Essex St; adult/child $17/10) It's called Hocus Pocus, but it's not hokey (or pokey). This is an informative, historically accurate over-view of Salem's sordid past, given by an enthusiastic and entertaining couple.

Spellbound Tours TOURS
(www.spellboundtours.com; adult/child $16/8; ⊙8pm daily, plus 2pm Fri-Sun) Guided by a professional paranormal investigator, this 75-minute nighttime tour covers the darkest and scariest episodes of Salem's history. Visit actual sites from the witch hysteria, but also learn about voodoo, haunted houses and modern-day vampires. Apparently, some visitors have reported seeing ghosts on this tour. Now *that's* scary.

Tours depart from in front of the NPS Regional Visitor Center (p114).

Salem Night Tour HISTORY
(www.salemghosttours.com; 127 Essex St; adult/child $15/10; ⊙tours 8pm daily, plus 3pm Sat & Sun) Lantern-led tours offer insights into Salem's haunted history. The tour covers a dozen historic sites, thus providing a pretty good overview of the witch hysteria of 1692. Guides are well informed and enthusiastic, although the tour groups are perhaps too big for comfort.

Salem Trolley BUS
(www.salemtrolley.com; adult/child $18/8; ⊙10am-5pm Apr-Oct) This one-hour tour starts at the NPS Regional Visitor Center and covers most of the town's places of interest. Tickets are good for the whole day, which means you can get on and off at will. Catch the courtesy shuttle from the MBTA commuter rail station.

☆ Festivals & Events

★ Haunted Happenings Halloween CULTURAL
(www.hauntedhappenings.org; ⊙Oct) Everyone in Salem celebrates Halloween, not just the

Salem

N

200 m
0.1 miles

Fort Ave
Webb St
English St
Becket St
Carlton St
Derby St
Turner St
3
16
24
22
Hardy St
Bentley St
Essex St
Webb St
Forester St
Emerton St
Boardman St
Briggs St
Daniels St
Kosciusko St
4
Orange St
Curtis St
Hodges Ct
Herbert St
Union St
Wharf St
18
Pickering Wharf
Derby Wharf
Salem Harbor

Boston Harbor Cruises

ATLANTIC OCEAN

Andrew St
Pleasant St
Washington Sq E
Salem Common
Washington Sq N
Washington Sq W

Winter St
Hawthorne Blvd
Congress St
14
17

Mall St
Williams St
Essex St
11
12
13
1
Peabody Essex Museum
Charter St
8
Derby St
Punto Urban Art Museum
2
9

St Peters St
Church St
New Liberty St
10
20
Central St
Lafayette St

Clipper Ship Inn (0.5mi)

MBTA Commuter Rail
Salem Depot

North River

Front St
15
Dodge St
23
Marblehead (4mi)

St Peters St
Washington St
21 **5**
Barton Sq
19
Canal St
Margin St
Essex St
Gedney St
High St

Federal St
Lynde St
6
Sewell St
Crombie St
Norman St

Bridge St
Franklin St
North St

Summer St
7
Cambridge St
Hamilton St
Essex St
Federal St
Chestnut St
Broad St
Mason St

114
107

Salem

◉ Top Sights
1 Peabody Essex Museum........................D3
2 Punto Urban Art Museum....................D4

◉ Sights
3 House of the Seven Gables..................G3
4 Salem Maritime National Historic
   Site...F3
5 TV Land Statue...................................C3
6 Witch Dungeon Museum.....................B2
7 Witch House.......................................B3
8 Witch Trials Memorial.........................D3

◎ Activities, Courses & Tours
9 Derby Lanes at Flatbread Salem.........D4
10 Hocus Pocus Tours.............................D3
11 Salem Night Tour.................................D3
12 Salem Trolley......................................D2
13 Spellbound Tours................................D3

◎ Sleeping
14 Hawthorne Hotel.................................E2
15 Hotel Salem..C3
16 Morning Glory.....................................G3

◎ Eating
17 Bella Verona..E2
18 Finz..E4
19 New England Soup Factory.................C3
20 Red's Sandwich Shop.........................D3

◎ Drinking & Nightlife
21 Gulu-Gulu Café...................................C3
22 Mercy Tavern......................................F2

◎ Shopping
23 Artists Row...C4
24 Ye Olde Pepper Candy Companie........G2

witches. And they celebrate for much of the month of October with special exhibits, parades, concerts, pumpkin carvings, costume parties and trick-or-treating. It all culminates on October 31 with the crowning of the King and Queen of Halloween. Book your lodging way in advance and expect to pay more.

⌂ Sleeping

Clipper Ship Inn
MOTEL $
(✆978-745-8022; www.clippershipinn.com; 40 Bridge St; r $135-150; P✻☎) Crisp, clean rooms and efficient service make this red-brick motel a comfortable place to lay your head, even if it's not in a historic home. The place is far from fancy, but staff are helpful, the rooms are clean, and you can walk to downtown Salem.

Morning Glory
B&B $$
(✆978-741-1703; www.morningglorybb.com; 22 Hardy St; d/ste $195/225; ⊗Mar-Nov; P✻@☎) Next to the House of Seven Gables, this glorious B&B is hard to beat. To make guests feel welcome, innkeeper and Salem native Bob Shea pulls out all the stops, not the least of which is a delectable breakfast of fresh fruit and homemade granola. Three frilly rooms and one sweet suite are named for Salem celebrities – that is, the witch victims of 1692.

Hawthorne Hotel
HOTEL $$
(✆978-744-4080; www.hawthornehotel.com; 18 Washington Sq W; r $189-259; P✻@☎) This historic Federalist-style hotel is at the heart of Salem. For years it was the only full-service hotel, with 84 updated rooms, a fancy restaurant and a cozy pub. Rooms are decked out with reproduction 18th-century furnishings, so you can feel like a wealthy merchant from Salem's glory days.

Hotel Salem
DESIGN HOTEL $$$
(✆978-451-4950; www.thehotelsalem.com; 209 Essex St; micro/d from $199/238; ✻☎) This swish new design hotel is nothing like the competition. The rooms are thoughtfully designed with plush beds, bold artwork and contemporary decor. New 'micro rooms' cater to more budget-minded travelers who are willing to give up some space. The common spaces include a delightful mid-century-modern lounge area and an inviting rooftop bar.

✕ Eating

★New England Soup Factory
SOUP $
(www.nesoupfactorysalem.com; 140 Washington St; soup $6.50-7.50, sandwiches $5-9; ⊗11am-8pm Mon-Fri, noon-7pm Sat & Sun; ☏🖶) When there's a chill in the air, nothing warms body and soul like a bowl of hot soup. It's not much to look at, but the New England Soup Factory offers 10 amazing, rotating options every day. Favorites include chicken-pot-pie soup (topped with puff pastry) and pumpkin lobster bisque. In summer it serves cold soups, of course.

Red's Sandwich Shop
DINER $
(www.redssandwichshop.com; 15 Central St; mains $6-10; ⊗5am-3pm Mon-Sat, 6am-1pm Sun) This Salem institution has been serving eggs and sandwiches to faithful customers for over

50 years. The food is hearty and basic, but the real attraction is Red's old-school decor, complete with counter service and friendly faces. It's housed in the old London Coffee House building (around since 1698).

Bella Verona
ITALIAN $$
(www.bellaverona.com; 107 Essex St; mains $14-24; ⊙4-10pm; ☑) The striped awning and overflowing flower boxes are the perfect gateway to this romantic trattoria in the heart of Salem. Owner Giorgio Manzana has brought the flavors from his home region (Verona, of course) and the results are delightful. Aside from the impeccable food and service, this place is cozy, ie crowded.

Finz
SEAFOOD $$
(www.hipfinz.com; 76 Wharf St; sandwiches $11-18, mains $18-33; ⊙11:30am-midnight) The highlight here is the gracious, spacious dining room with three walls of windows and a sweet patio overlooking Salem Harbor. The kitchen keeps customers sated, with a seductive raw bar and other fresh-out-of-the-water local seafood. The carefully chosen wine list is an added perk.

🍷 Drinking & Nightlife

★ Gulu-Gulu Café
CAFE
(www.gulugulucafe.com; 247 Essex St; ⊙8am-1am Tue-Sat, to 11pm Sun & Mon; 🛜) *Gulu-gulu* means 'gulp, gulp' in French, and this place is named after a now-defunct cafe in Prague. That's an indication of how eclectic it is, featuring (in no particular order) delicious coffee, art-adorned walls, live music, exotic liqueurs and board games.

WORLD-FAMOUS BEEF & CHOWDAH!
....

Only one vestige of the 'old' Revere Beach remains: the world-famous **Kelly's Roast Beef** (☑781-284-9129; www.kellysroastbeef.com; 410 Revere Beach Blvd, Revere; sandwiches $9-15, mains $13-25; ⊙10am-1am Sun-Thu, to 2:30am Fri & Sat; Ⓣ Wonderland), which has been around since 1951 and still serves up the best roast-beef sandwiches and clam chowder in town. There's no indoor seating, so pull up some sand and enjoy the view. Beware of the seagulls: they're crazy for roast beef.

Revere is just north of Boston.

★ Mercy Tavern
BAR
(www.mercysalem.com; 148 Derby St; ⊙11:30am-1am Mon-Sat, to 11pm Sun) A dark and cozy pub with exposed brick walls, this is the perfect place to sip a pint and listen to the blues. This happens every Friday (4pm to 7pm), with other live music acts throughout the week. The 'pub fare' here includes the typical burgers and tacos, but it's locally sourced and made with love.

🛍 Shopping

Artists Row
MARKET
(www.artistsrowsalem.com; 24 New Derby St; ⊙noon-6pm May-Oct) This little alleyway is lined with seasonal shacks where local artists create, display and sell their wares. The streets and sidewalks are painted and the environs are otherwise spruced up by the artists, who are usually on hand to chat to passersby.

Ye Olde Pepper Candy Companie
FOOD
(☑978-745-2744; www.oldepeppercandy.com; 122 Derby St; ⊙10am-6pm Jul-Oct, to 5pm Nov-Jun) For more than 200 years Ye Olde Pepper Candy Companie has been making sweets – you gotta believe that it knows what it's doing. The current owners (for *only* four generations) continue to use original 19th-century recipes for old-fashioned delights such as Black Jacks (flavored with blackstrap molasses) and Gibraltars (lemon and peppermint treats). Sweet!

ℹ Information

NPS Regional Visitor Center (☑978-740-1650; www.nps.gov/sama; 2 New Liberty St; ⊙9am-5pm May-Oct, from 10am Wed-Sun Nov-Apr) Offers information on Salem. For a good overview, catch a free screening of *Where Past Is Present,* a short film about Salem history. There's another longer film *Salem Witch Hunt* that screens three times a day (adult/child $5/3). You can also pick up a map and description of several self-guided walking tours and other area attractions.

ℹ Getting There & Around

The Rockport/Newburyport line of the MBTA commuter rail (www.mbta.com) runs from Boston's North Station to Salem Depot ($7.50, 30 minutes). Trains run every 30 minutes during the morning and evening rush hours, hourly during the rest of day, and less frequently at weekends.

Boston Harbor Cruises (Salem Ferry; ☑617-227-4320; www.bostonharborcruises.com; 10 Blaney St; ferry round trip adult/child $45/35; ⊙May-Oct) operates the Salem ferry between

WORTH A TRIP

MARBLEHEAD

First settled in 1629, Marblehead is a maritime village with winding streets, brightly painted Colonial and Federal houses, and 1000 sailing yachts bobbing at moorings in the harbor. As indicated by the number of boats, this is the Boston area's premier yachting port and one of New England's most prestigious addresses.

Meander down to the Old Town to admire the old houses, stop for a seafood lunch and pop into Abbott Hall (p110). The redbrick building with a lofty clock tower is the seat of the town government, and houses artifacts of Marblehead's history.

To reach Marblehead, drive south on MA 114, locally known as Pleasant St, which takes you through modern commercial Marblehead en route to the Marblehead Historic District (Old Town). Stop by the **Marblehead Chamber of Commerce Information Booth** (📞781-639-8469; www.marbleheadchamber.org; cnr Pleasant, Essex & Spring Sts, Marblehead; ☺noon-5pm Mon-Fri, from 10am Sat & Sun May-Oct) for information about local B&Bs, restaurants and a weekly gallery walk.

Long Wharf in Boston and the Salem Ferry Center. From June to August, the company also runs a harbor shuttle (adult/child $7/4) with five stops around the Salem waterfront: Blaney St, Winter Island, Village St, Maritime National Historic Park and Marblehead.

Gloucester

📞978 / POP 30,200

Founded in 1623 by English fisherfolk, Gloucester is one of New England's oldest towns. This port on Cape Ann has made its living from fishing for almost 400 years, and it has inspired books and films such as Rudyard Kipling's *Captains Courageous* and Sebastian Junger's *The Perfect Storm*. And despite some recent economic diversification, the town still smells of fish. You can't miss the fishing boats, festooned with nets, dredges and winches, tied to the wharves or motoring along into the harbor, with clouds of hungry seagulls hovering expectantly above. It's a perfect place to catch a whale-watching tour or observe the activity along the working waterfront. A vibrant artist community – Rocky Neck Art Colony – is across the harbor in East Gloucester.

☉ Sights

Maritime Gloucester   MUSEUM
(📞978-281-0470; www.maritimegloucester.org; 23 Harbor Loop; adult/child $10/7; ☺10am-5pm late May-early Oct, closed Tue-Thu mid-Oct–May; 🚶) Visit Gloucester's working waterfront and see the ongoing restoration of wooden boats, watch the operation of a marine railway that hauls ships out of the water and compare the different kinds of fishing boats that were

used over the years. Excellent exhibits showcase the local creatures of the sea.

The **Sea Pocket Aquarium** is a hands-on outdoor aquarium with exhibits on local marine habitats. It's a great chance for kids to get down and dirty with sea stars, sea urchins, snails, crabs and seaweed. The **Stellwagen Bank Marine Sanctuary Exhibit** provides an excellent introduction for whale-watchers heading out on an excursion.

From the Grant Circle rotary, take Washington St to its terminus, then turn left on Rogers St to Harbor Loop.

Beauport   HISTORIC SITE
(www.historicnewengland.org; 75 Eastern Point Blvd, Eastern Point; adult/student $15/8; ☺10am-4pm Tue-Sun Jun–mid-Oct) The lavish home of interior designer Henry Davis Sleeper is known as Beauport, or the Sleeper-McCann mansion. Sleeper scoured New England for houses that were about to be demolished and scavenged wood paneling, architectural elements and furniture. In place of unity, he created a wildly eclectic but artistically surprising – and satisfying – place to live.

Rocky Neck Art Colony   GALLERY
(www.rockyneckartcolony.org) The artistic legacy of Gloucester native Fitz Henry Lane endures, as Gloucester still boasts a vibrant artists community at Rocky Neck Art Colony. In addition to the cooperative **Gallery 53 on Rocky Neck** (53 Rocky Neck Ave; ☺10am-6pm Sun-Thu, to 8pm Fri & Sat Jun–mid-Oct), there are about a dozen galleries and studios that open to visitors, as well as a couple of restaurants. Follow Main St east and south around the harbor to East Gloucester.

DON'T MISS

STELLWAGEN BANK NATIONAL MARINE SANCTUARY

You will be forgiven for thinking that **Stellwagen Bank** (www.stellwagen.noaa.gov) is yet another New England establishment eager to get its hands on your precious travel money. On the contrary, this 'bank' really is all about savings and growth: it's an open ocean National Marine Sanctuary, covering a whopping 842 sq miles, which was dedicated in 1992 to protect the biological diversity at the mouth of Massachusetts Bay, and to facilitate research and other beneficial activity. The name, however, has nothing to do with banking or conservation, but refers to the submerged plateau on the ocean floor within the sanctuary bounds. Its waters teem with cod, haddock, flounder and even giant bluefin tuna, making it a hotspot for diving and managed fishing. But the best reason to visit is to see the whales – Stellwagen Bank is regarded as one of the top whale-watching sites in the world. Several companies operate regular whale-watching cruises from Boston, Gloucester, Plymouth and Provincetown.

Stage Fort Park BEACH
(www.gloucester-ma.gov; parking weekdays/ weekends $10/15; ⊙9am-5pm Jun-Aug) There are two lovely, small beaches at Stage Fort Park: the picturesque Half-Moon Beach and the more remote Cressy's Beach. The latter is a bit of a trek from the parking lot, but it's worth it to get away from the other bathing beauties. The park itself is an attractive, well-maintained recreation area with picnic tables, playgrounds, athletic fields and hiking trails.

Wingaersheek Beach BEACH
(www.gloucester-ma.gov; 232 Atlantic Rd; parking weekdays/weekends $25/30; ⊙8am-9pm) The biggest and best of Cape Ann's beaches is Wingaersheek Beach, a wide swath of sand surrounded by Ipswich Bay and guarded by Annisquam Lighthouse.

North Shore Arts Association GALLERY
(www.nsarts.org; 11 Pirates Lane; ⊙10am-5pm Mon-Sat, from noon Sun May-Oct) With some 600 members, this vibrant local arts association has been hosting exhibits and performances since 1922. Visit the lovely harborside setting to see one of the rotating exhibits, catch a lecture or workshop, or hobnob with local artists.

Cape Ann Museum MUSEUM
(www.capeannmuseum.org; 27 Pleasant St; adult/ child $12/free; ⊙10am-5pm Tue-Sat, 1-4pm Sun; ♿) This small museum is a gem – particularly for its paintings by Gloucester native Fitz Henry Lane. Exhibits also showcase the region's granite-quarrying industry and - of course - its maritime history. The museum is in the heart of downtown Gloucester, just north of Main St.

St Peter's Square SQUARE
Don't leave Gloucester without paying your respects at St Peter's Sq, where Leonard Craske's famous statue *Gloucester Fisherman* is dedicated to 'They That Go Down to the Sea in Ships, 1623–1923.'

Hammond Castle Museum MUSEUM
(www.hammondcastle.org; 80 Hesperus Ave; adult/ child $12/9; ⊙10am-4pm Tue-Sat Jun-Aug, Sat & Sun only May & Sep–mid-Oct) Dr John Hays Hammond Jr (1888–1965) was an electrical engineer and inventor who amassed a fortune fulfilling defense contracts. With this wealth, Hammond pursued his passion for collecting European art and architecture. His eccentric home is a medieval castle that he built to house all his treasures, dating from the Romanesque, medieval, Gothic and Renaissance periods.

Tours

Yankee Fleet FISHING
(www.yankeefleet.com; 1 Parker St; adult/child full day $68/59, half-day $49/38) Summon your inner Gloucester fisher and see what you can reel in. Boats go out to Stellwagen Bank, or to closer fishing grounds at Jeffreys Ledge or Tillies Bank (depending on whether you choose the half-day or full-day option). The crew is accommodating – yes, they will clean your catch!

Seven Seas Whale Watch BOATING
(☎978-283-1776, 888-283-1776; www.7seaswhale-watch.com; 63 Rogers St; adult/child $48/32; ♿) Three generations of sea captains have navigated the waters around Stellwagen Bank. Seven Seas vessels depart from Rogers St in the center of Gloucester, between St Peter's Sq and the Gloucester House Restaurant.

Ryan & Wood Distillery

DISTILLERY

(www.ryanandwood.com; 15 Great Republic Dr; ⊘ tours 10am & 1pm Mon, Wed, Fri & Sat, tasting room 10am-4pm Mon-Sat) As you learn about the process of distilling fine spirits here, you will feel, hear and taste the passion that goes into this operation. Admire the shiny old-fashioned alembic copper pot that is still in use. Try your hand at filling and labeling bottles. And of course, sample the goods – gin, rum, whisky and vodka – and buy a bottle too.

Schooner Thomas E Lannon

BOATING

(☑ 978-281-6634; www.schooner.org; Rogers St; adult/child $45/32.50; ⛵) This 65ft ship is the spitting image of the Gloucester fishing schooners. It leaves on two-hour sails from the Seven Seas wharf. Sunset cruises feature live music, ranging from Celtic to classical to bluegrass. Bonus for families: on Saturday mornings one kid sails for free with the purchase of one adult fare.

★ Festivals & Events

St Peter's Festival

RELIGIOUS

(www.stpetersfiesta.org) Honoring the patron saint of fisherfolk, this carnival at St Peter's Sq takes place over five days in late June. Besides rides and music, the main event is the procession through the streets of a statue of St Peter. Customarily, the cardinal of the Catholic Archdiocese of Boston attends to bless the fishing fleet.

One highlight of the festival is something called the Greasy Pole, where contestants try to make their way across a 200ft, greased-up pole that extends out over the water. Anyone who can grab the flag at the end of the pole wins bragging rights and probably a few beers.

🛏 Sleeping

Crow's Nest Inn

INN $

(☑ 978-281-2965; www.crowsnestgloucester.com; 334 Main St; r $90) If you want to wake to the sound of fisherfolk's cries and the smell of salt air, and you don't mind basic bunks, stay at the Crow's Nest, upstairs from the pub made famous by *The Perfect Storm*. Rooms are clean; the price is right.

★ Rocky Neck Accommodations

APARTMENT $$

(☑ 978-381-9848; www.rockyneckaccommodations. com; 43 Rocky Neck Ave; r $119-250, ste $175-235; P 🕸 🤶) You don't have to be an artist to live the bohemian life in Gloucester. The colony association offers light-filled efficiencies – all equipped with kitchenettes – at the Rocky Neck Art Colony. The rooms are sweet and simple, most with beautiful views of Smith Cove. Weekly rates also available.

Julietta House

GUESTHOUSE $$

(☑ 978-281-2300; www.juliettahouse.com; 84 Prospect St; r $175-255; P 🕸 🤶) Steps from Gloucester Harbor, this grand Georgian house has eight spacious and elegant rooms with period furnishings and private bathrooms. The environment is quite luxurious, while service is purposefully hands off. This

---

DON'T MISS

DOGTOWN

Much of the interior of Cape Ann is wild and undeveloped, partially protected by reservations, but mostly left to the whims of nature and history. This vast territory is known as Dogtown.

Those who venture into Dogtown might discover the mysterious glacial rock formations that inspired artist Marsden Hartley; the ruins of an abandoned Colonial settlement; or strange, stern rock inscriptions that date from the Great Depression. It's a beautiful but forbidding place, which has seen more than its fair share of mystery and tragedy, as detailed in Elyssa East's award-winning book *Dogtown: Death and Enchantment in a New England Ghost Town*.

Dogtown contains miles and miles of trails, but they're poorly maintained and mostly unmarked. Simply put, it's not easy to navigate. Let a local expert show you the way with **Walk the Words** (www.walkthewords.com; adult/child $20/10), a two-hour hike to Dogtown's most intriguing spots. If you want to go it alone, pick up a map from the **Bookstore of Gloucester** (www.facebook.com/thebookstoreofgloucester; 61 Main St; ⊘ 9am-6pm Mon-Sat, to 8pm Thu, 10am-5pm Sun). You can access Dogtown between Gloucester and Annisquam. From MA 127, take Reynaud St to Cherry St.

CAPE ANN FOR FOODIES

If you're the type of person who likes to discover a place by taste, **Cape Ann Foodie Tours** (☑617-902-8291; www. capeannfoodietours.com; walking tours $25-55, boat tours $75; ☉tours 11:30am) could be for you. Eat your way around Gloucester or Newburyport (or both!). Fresh-caught seafood, locally brewed beers and handcrafted sweets are all served with a side of history.

place promises privacy and comfort, without the overwrought frills and friendliness of some guesthouses.

Sea Lion Motel & Cottages MOTEL $$
(☑978-283-7300; www.sealionmotel.com; 138 Eastern Ave; r $139-559, ste $185-205; ❉ 🐾 ⊜) Less than a mile from Good Harbor Beach, this welcoming, woodsy spot offers excellent value. The accommodations are simple and spotless, whether you opt for a basic double or a more fitted-out suite. All suites and cottages have kitchenettes – ideal for families.

✖ Eating

Two Sisters Coffee Shop DINER $
(☑978-281-3378; www.facebook.com/TwoSisters CoffeeShop; 27 Washington St; mains $5-8; ☉6:30am-noon Mon-Fri, to 1pm Sat & Sun; ☑) This local place is where the fisherfolk go for breakfast when they come in from their catch. They're early risers, so you may have to wait for a table. Corned-beef hash, eggs in a hole and pancakes all get rave reviews. Service is a little salty.

Franklin Cape Ann AMERICAN $$
(www.franklincapeann.com; 118 Main St; mains $21-27; ☉5-10:30pm Sun-Thu, to midnight Fri & Sat; ☑) The North Shore branch of a South End favorite in Boston, this cool place has an urban atmosphere and an excellent, modern New American menu. More often than not, daily specials feature fresh seafood and seasonal vegetables, always accompanied by an appropriate wine. Regulars rave about the cocktails too.

Causeway Restaurant SEAFOOD $$
(www.thecausewayrestaurant.com; 78 Essex Ave; mains $12-25; ☉11am-8pm Sun-Thu, to 9pm Fri & Sat) Gloucester's favorite seafood shack is about a mile west of town, on the mainland. It's a convivial, crowded place serving irresistible clam chowder, heaped portions of fried clams and twin lobster specials. Expect to wait for a table and don't forget to BYOB.

Duckworth's Bistrot AMERICAN $$$
(☑978-282-4426; www.duckworthsbistrot.com; 197 E Main St; mains $22-34; ☉5-9:30 Tue-Sat; ☑) Half-portions and wines by the glass (or carafe) mean that Duckworth's won't break the bank. But the menu of fresh seafood and local produce means you will dine like a gourmand. Specialties include a hearty seafood stew and to-die-for lobster risotto. Reservations recommended.

🍷 Drinking & Entertainment

Crow's Nest PUB
(www.crowsnestgloucester.com; 334 Main St; ☉11am-1am) The down-and-dirty fisherfolk bar made famous in *The Perfect Storm*. But this is the real deal, not the set the movie folks threw up for a few weeks during filming. Come early if you want to drink with the fishing crews.

Gloucester Stage Company THEATER
(www.gloucesterstage.com; 267 E Main St; $20-40) This company stages excellent small-theater productions of classics and modern works. It's a small venue known for top-notch acting. Excellent summer theater.

🛍 Shopping

Liquor Locker ALCOHOL
(www.liquorlockergloucester.com; 287 Main St; ☉8am-10pm Mon-Sat, noon-6pm Sun) You can't purchase alcohol in Rockport or in the surrounding villages, as they are 'dry.' Many restaurants allow you to bring your own, so you can stock up at this local 'packie' (package store).

ℹ Information

Cape Ann Chamber of Commerce (www.capeannchamber.com; 33 Commercial St; ☉9am-5pm Mon-Fri, from 10am Sat, 11am-4pm Sun) South of St Peter's Sq.

Gloucester Visitor Information Center (www.discovergloucester.org; Stage Fort Park; ☉9am-6pm) The little house at Stage Fort Park is filled with information and has helpful staff.

ℹ Getting There & Around

Take the Rockport line of the MBTA commuter rail (www.mbta.com) from Boston's North Station to Gloucester ($10.50, one hour).

The Cape Ann Transportation Authority (www.canntran.com) runs five routes around Cape

Ann to destinations such as Good Harbor Beach, Rockport and other villages.

Gloucester Harbor Water Shuttle (www.capeannharbortours.com; adult/child $10/5; ◎noon-6pm daily Jun-Aug, to 4pm Sat & Sun Apr, May, Sep & Oct) The M/V *Lady Jillian* makes stops at the Heritage Center (Harbor Loop), in downtown Gloucester (Gloucester House Restaurant), on Rocky Neck and at St Peter's Landing. You can hop on and off to visit local sights, or stay on board for a tour.

Rockport

✏️978 / POP 7250

On the northern side of Cape Ann, Rockport is a quaint contrast to gritty Gloucester. The town takes its name from its 19th-century role as a shipping center for granite cut from the local quarries. The stone is still ubiquitous: monuments, building foundations, pavements and piers remain as testament to Rockport's past.

That's about all that remains of this industrial history, however. A century ago, Winslow Homer, Childe Hassam, Fitz Henry Lane and other acclaimed artists came to Rockport's rugged shores, inspired by the hearty fisherfolk who wrested a hard-won but satisfying living from the sea. Today, Rockport earns a crust from the tourists who come to look at the artists. The artists themselves have long since given up looking for hearty fisherfolk because the descendants of the fishers are all running boutiques and B&Bs.

◉ Sights & Activities

Long Beach BEACH
(Thatcher Rd) Some claim that Long Beach, which straddles the Rockport–Gloucester border, is the best beach on the North Shore. It is lovely indeed – ideal for swimming, surfing, snorkeling and sunbathing – with a unique view of the twin lighthouses on Thacher Island. Unfortunately, there's no parking for non-residents unless you buy a sticker from the Rockport website (www.rockportma.gov).

**Halibut Point State
Park & Reservation** WILDLIFE RESERVE
(www.thetrustees.org; parking $5-10; ◎8am-9pm; P) FREE Only a few miles north of Dock Sq along MA 127 is Halibut Point Reservation. A 10-minute walk through the forest brings you to yawning, abandoned granite quarries, huge hills of granite rubble, and a granite foreshore of tumbled, smoothed rock perfect for picnicking, sunbathing,

reading or painting. The surf can be strong here, making swimming unwise, but natural pools can be good for wading or cooling your feet. A map is available at the entrance.

Motif No 1 SQUARE
The red fishing shack decorated with colorful buoys is known as Motif No 1, since it has been captured by so many artists for so many years. (Actually, it should be called Motif No 1-B, as the original shack vanished during a great storm in 1978 and a replica was erected in its place.)

Paper House NOTABLE BUILDING
(www.paperhouserockport.com; 52 Pigeon Hill St; adult/child $2/1; ◎10am-5pm Apr-Oct) In 1922, long before there was any municipal recycling program, Elis F Stenman decided that something useful should be done with all those daily newspapers lying about. He and his family set to work folding, rolling and pasting the papers into suitable shapes as building materials. Twenty years and 100,000 newspapers later, they had built the Paper House.

**North Shore Kayak
Outdoor Center** KAYAKING
(✏️978-546-5050; www.northshorekayak.com; 9 Tuna Wharf; tours adult/child $48/28, per half-day bikes/kayaks/tandem kayaks $22/32/52, per hour stand-up paddleboards $20) Rockport is a perfect base for sea kayaking – a great way to explore the rocky coast of Cape Ann. Besides renting kayaks, this outfit offers kayak tours, ranging from a two-hour trip to Straitsmouth Island to an overnight camping trip on Thacher Island.

★ Festivals & Events

★**Rockport Chamber
Music Festival** MUSIC
(✏️978-546-7391; www.rockportmusic.org; 37 Main St; ◎Jun & Jul) This festival hosts concerts by internationally acclaimed performers. Concerts take place at the Shalin Liu Performance Center, a gorgeous hall overlooking the ocean. Most concerts sell out, so it's advisable to order tickets in advance.

🛏 Sleeping

★**Bearskin Neck
Motor Lodge** MOTEL $$
(✏️978-546-6677; www.bearskinneckmotorlodge.com; 64 Bearskin Neck; d $215-235; P🐾) The only lodging on Bearskin Neck is this seaside motel near the end of the strip. Needless to say, every room has a great view and a balcony from which you can enjoy it.

The rooms are quite spiffy, with traditional wooden furniture, striking light fixtures and intriguing sea-glass artwork on the walls.

Captain's Bounty on the Beach MOTEL **$$**
(📞978-546-9557; www.captainsbountymotorinn.com; 1 Beach St; r from $229, ste $269; 🅿❄🛜) The draw here is the prime location, right on Front Beach and a short stroll from Dock Sq. The 24 simple rooms all have lovely views of the beach, where lobster folk check their traps at dawn. All rooms have refrigerators and microwaves, and some are equipped with full kitchens.

Eden Pines Inn B&B **$$**
(📞978-546-2505; www.edenpinesinn.com; 48 Eden Rd; r $225; 🅿❄🛜) Eden Pines is all about the view: it's spectacular. Perched up on the rocks, the inn faces Loblolly Cove, the Thacher Island lighthouses and the big blue beyond. It's gorgeous no matter where you're standing – your private balcony, the breakfast nook or the wide, breezy front porch. Rooms are spacious and comfortable, and service is impeccable.

Sally Webster Inn B&B **$$**
(📞978-546-9251, 877-546-9251; www.sallywebster.com; 34 Mt Pleasant St; r $150-170; 🅿❄@🛜) This handsome brick Colonial place, built in 1832, offers six rooms with early-American decor. Many have working fireplaces, and all have authentic architectural details and period furniture. The owner is also an accomplished chef, and she puts out an impressive spread for breakfast.

✖ Eating

Red Skiff SEAFOOD **$**
(www.facebook.com/RedSkiffRestaurant; 15 Mount Pleasant St; breakfast $5-10, mains $8-18; ⊗7am-2pm Mon-Sat, 8am-noon Sun; 🖐) Be prepared to wait for a table at this old-fashioned seafood shack, in the heart of Rockport, close to the T Wharf. Come for pancakes and eggs for breakfast, or clam chowder and lobster rolls for lunch. It doesn't look like much, but the service is friendly and the fish is fresh.

Helmut's Strudel BAKERY **$**
(📞978-546-2825; 69 Bearskin Neck; desserts $5-8; ⊗7am-5:30pm Mon-Thu, to 7pm Fri-Sun; 🖋🖐) For dessert, try this Austrian bakery, near the outer end of the Neck. Helmut's serves various strudels, filled croissants, pastries, cider and coffee. Four shaded tables overlook the yacht-filled harbor.

★Roy Moore Lobster Company SEAFOOD **$$**
(www.facebook.com/Roy-Moore-Lobster-Co-125287641097; 39 Bearskin Neck; lobsters $15; ⊗9am-6pm Apr-Oct) This takeout kitchen has the cheapest lobster-in-the-rough on the Neck. Your beast comes on a tray with melted butter, a fork and a wet wipe for cleanup. The stuffed clams and fish cakes are also very tasty. Find a seat at a picnic table on the back patio and dig in. Don't forget to bring your own beer or wine.

❶ Information

Rockport Visitor Center (www.rockportusa.com; Upper Main St; ⊗9am-5pm Mon-Sat Apr-Oct) Located about 1 mile out of town on Rte 127.

❶ Getting There & Around

Take the MBTA commuter rail (www.mbta.com) from Boston's North Station to Rockport ($11.50, one hour).

If you're driving, MA 127/127A loops around Cape Ann, connecting Magnolia and Gloucester to Rockport, with some wonderful seaside vistas along the way. Street parking in Rockport in summer is in short supply, but you can park for free in the **Blue Gate Meadow Parking Lot** (5 Blue Gate Lane; ⊗11am-7pm mid-May–Sep), then take the trolley ($1) or walk the three-quarters of a mile to Dock Sq.

The Cape Ann Transportation Authority (www.canntran.com) operates bus routes between the towns of Cape Ann. Fares are $1 to $1.25.

Ipswich & Essex

📞978 / POP IPSWICH 14,000, ESSEX 3700

North of Cape Ann, Ipswich and Essex are pretty New England towns surrounded by rocky coast and sandy beaches, extensive marshland, forested hills and rural farmland.

Ipswich and Essex are examples of New England towns that are pretty today because they were poor in the past. There was no harbor, and no source of waterpower for factories, so commercial and industrial development went elsewhere in the 18th and 19th centuries. As a result, the 17th-century houses were not torn down to build grander residences, and you can still visit some of these old architectural gems. Today, the towns are famous for their ample antique shops and succulent clams. Formerly the home of novelist John Updike, Ipswich is also the setting for some of his novels and short stories such as *A&P*, which is based on the local market.

◉ Sights

Essex Shipbuilding Museum MUSEUM
(www.essexshipbuildingmuseum.org; 66 Main St, Essex; guided tours adult/child $10/5, self-guided tours $7; ☉ 10am-5pm Wed-Sun Jun-Oct, Sat & Sun Nov-May; ⊞) This museum was established in 1976 as a local repository for all of the shipbuilding artifacts of Essex residents. The fascinating collections of photos, tools and ship models came from local basements and attics, allowing the village to preserve its history. Guided tours (10:30am, 1pm and 3pm) are well worth the extra time and money, as docents (many former fishers and shipwrights) are well informed and passionate about local history.

Appleton Farms FARM
(www.thetrustees.org; 219 County Rd, Ipswich; $3; ☉ grounds 8am-dusk, visitor center 11am-6pm Mon-Fri, 10am-4pm Sat & Sun; ⊞) ⚲ Six miles of trails wind along old carriageways, past ancient stonewall property markers and through acres of grasslands. Farm friends dot the pastures, while wilder animals are spotted in the woodlands. Visitors can observe the milking of cows, the making of cheese and other farm activities – and partake of their goodness. The store sells fresh, organically grown produce, not to mention tantalizing jams, spreads and sauces made with said produce.

Crane Beach BEACH
(www.thetrustees.org; Argilla Rd, Ipswich; pedestrian & cyclist $2, car weekday/weekend $25/30; ☉ 8am-dusk; ⊞) One of the longest, widest, sandiest beaches in the region is Crane Beach, with 5.5 miles of fine-sand barrier beach on Ipswich Bay. It is set in the midst of the Crane Wildlife Refuge, so the entire surrounding area is pristine and beautiful. Five miles of trails traverse the dunes. The only downside is the pesky greenhead flies that buzz around (and bite) in late July and early August.

Cogswell's Grant HISTORIC BUILDING
(www.historicnewengland.org; 60 Spring St, Essex; adult/child $10/5; ☉ 11am-4pm Wed-Sat Jun–mid-Oct) This Colonial-era farmhouse dates from 1728, and is furnished and decorated with all manner of 'country arts' from the era. The home is the product of six decades of redecorating and refurbishing by Bertram and Nina Fletcher Little. In the early 20th century, the couple were renowned collectors and scholars of American folk art, and their home remains largely as it was when the family lived there. From Main St, Essex, take Rte 22, then turn right on Spring St.

Ipswich Museum MUSEUM
(www.ipswichmuseum.org; 54 S Main St, Ipswich; 1/3 houses $10/15; ☉ 10am-4pm Thu-Sat Apr & May, Wed-Sun Jun-Oct; ⊞) Three houses comprise this village historical museum, including the 'first period' Whipple House, which dates from 1677. The bulk of the collection is in the 1800 **Heard House**, which also contains historic furnishings, textiles and decorative arts, as well as an excellent collection of paintings by Ipswich artists from the 19th and 20th centuries.

Whipple House HISTORIC BUILDING
(www.ipswichmuseum.org; 1 South Village Green, Ipswich; adult/child $10/5; ☉ 10am-4pm Thu-Sat Apr & May, Wed-Sun Jun-Oct) Dating from 1677, this was the home of Captain John Whipple, a military officer and entrepreneur. Now maintained by the Ipswich Museum, it contains period furniture and many original architectural details. It is one of the best examples of 'first period' American architecture (1625–1725).

Castle Hill on the Crane Estate HISTORIC SITE
(www.thetrustees.org; Argilla Rd, Ipswich; house tours $15-20, grounds car/bike $15/2; ☉ house 10am-4pm Tue-Sun Jun-Oct, Sat & Sun Apr, May & Dec, grounds 8am-dusk year-round; P⊞) High atop Castle Hill sits the 1920s estate of Chicago plumbing-fixture magnate Richard T Crane. The 59-room Stuart-style **Great House** is open for guided tours and special events.

Check the website for a variety of thematic tours that show off the history, architecture and extensive grounds of the estate home. The lovely landscaped grounds, which are open daily, contain several miles of walking trails.

⌂ Sleeping

Shea's Riverside INN, MOTEL $$
(☏ 978-768-6800; www.sheasinn.com; 132 Main St, Essex; r motel $165-175, inn $199-259; P⊚) Shea's Riverside is a two-in-one accommodation in a picturesque spot on the Essex River. The inn is a 1760 Colonial home. It contains six gorgeous rooms furnished with antiques and artwork. The nearby motel has 15 wood-paneled rooms that are less elegant but still comfy. There are glorious views of the estuary all around.

★ **Inn at Castle Hill** INN $$$
(📞 978-412-2555; http://innatcastlehill.thetrus
tees.org; 280 Argilla Rd, Ipswich; r woodland view
$235-285, ocean view $395-515; 🅿❄🛜) 🌊 On
the beautiful grounds of the Crane Estate,
this inn is an example of understated luxu-
ry, its 10 rooms each individually decorated
with subtle elegance. Turndown service,
plush robes and afternoon tea are some of
the perks. Instead of TVs (of which there
are none), guests enjoy a wraparound ve-
randa and its magnificent views of sand
dunes and salt marshes.

🍴 Eating & Drinking

★ **JT Farnham's** SEAFOOD $$
(www.jtfarnhams.com; 88 Eastern Ave, Essex; mains
$16-32, sandwiches $8-12; ⊙11am-8pm Mar-Dec;
📶) When the Food Network came to Essex
to weigh in on the fried-clam debate for the
show *Food Feud,* the winner was JT Farnham, thanks to the crispiness of his clams.
Pull up a picnic table and enjoy the amazing
estuary view.

Clam Box SEAFOOD $$
(www.clamboxipswich.com; 246 High St/MA 133,
Ipswich; mains $15-32; ⊙11am-8pm) You can't
miss this classic clam shack, just north of Ip-
swich center. Built in 1938, it actually looks
like a clam box, spruced up with striped
awnings. Folks line up out the door for
crispy fried clams and onion rings – some
claim they're the best in the land.

Woodman's of Essex SEAFOOD $$$
(www.woodmans.com; 121 Main St/MA 133, Essex;
sandwiches $8-24, mains $15-32; ⊙11am-10pm
mid-Jun–Aug, to 8pm Sun-Thu & to 9pm Fri & Sat
Oct–mid-Jun) This roadhouse is the most famous spot in the area to come for clams, any
way you like them. The specialty is Chubby's
original fried clams and crispy onion rings,
but this place serves everything from boiled
lobsters and homemade clam cakes to a seasonal raw bar.

Ipswich Ale Brewery BREWERY
(www.ipswichalebrewery.com; 2 Brewery Pl;
⊙11am-11pm Mon-Sat, noon-9pm Sun) A long-
standing New England favorite, Ipswich
Ale started making craft beer before it was
cool (in 1991, to be precise). Now it has an
on-site tap-room and restaurant to show
off its stuff. Stop by to sample from the 15
tap lines, nosh eclectic eats and observe the
beer-brewing process firsthand.

ℹ️ Getting There & Away

Ipswich is on the Newburyport line of the MBTA
commuter rail (www.mbta.com). Trains leave
Boston's North Station for Ipswich ($10, 50
minutes) about 12 times each weekday and five
times on Saturday and Sunday.

Newburyport

📞 978 / POP 18,000

At the mouth of the Merrimack River, Newburyport prospered as a shipping port and
silversmith center during the late 18th century. Not too much has changed in the last
200 years, as Newburyport's brick buildings and graceful churches still show off
the Federal style that was popular back in
those days. Today the center of this town is
a model of historic preservation and gentri-
fication. Newburyport is also the gateway to
the barrier Plum Island, a national wildlife
refuge with some of the best bird-watching
in New England.

⊙ Sights & Activities

Parker River
National Wildlife Refuge WILDLIFE RESERVE
(www.fws.gov/refuge/parker_river; Plum Island;
car/bike & pedestrian $5/2; ⊙dawn-dusk) This
4662-acre sanctuary occupies the southern
three-quarters of Plum Island. More than 800
species of bird, plant and animal reside in its
many ecological habitats, including beaches,
sand dunes, salt pans, salt marshes, freshwater impoundments and maritime forests.
This is prime bird-watching territory, with
a few miles of foot trails and several observation areas set up specifically for spotting
shorebirds and waterfowl. Stop at the visitors
center (p124) for maps, bird lists and loads of
informative exhibits and programs.

The beaches are also pristine and lovely.
But much of the beachfront is closed in summer because it is an important habitat for
the endangered piping plover. During spring
and fall, you can observe migrating song-
birds, including magnificent wood warblers
in the forest. In winter the refuge is a good
place to see waterfowl, the rough-legged
hawk and the snowy owl.

Custom House
Maritime Museum MUSEUM
(www.customhousemaritimemuseum.org; 25 Water
St; adult/child $7/5; ⊙10am-4pm Tue-Sat, from
noon Sun May-Dec, 10am-4pm Sat & Sun Jan-Apr)
The 1835 granite Custom House, built by

Robert Mills (of Washington Monument fame), is an excellent example of Classical Revival architecture. It now houses the Maritime Museum, which exhibits artifacts from Newburyport's maritime history as a major shipbuilding center and seaport. Seafaring folk will have a field day in the Moseley Gallery with its collection of model clipper ships.

Cushing House Museum & Garden
HISTORIC SITE

(www.newburyhistory.com; 98 High St; adult/child $5/free; ⊙10am-4pm Tue-Fri, from noon Sat & Sun Jun-Oct) This 21-room Federal home is decked out with fine furnishings and decorative pieces from the region. Collections of portraits, silver, needlework, toys and clocks are all on display, not to mention the impressive Asian collection from Newburyport's early Chinese trade. The museum offers guided tours, exhibits, special events and lectures.

Sandy Point State Reservation
BEACH

(www.mass.gov/dcr; ⊙dawn-8pm; 🚻) **FREE** At the southern tip of Plum Island, Sandy Point is a 77-acre state park that is popular for swimming, sunning and tide-pooling. Walking trails and an observation tower also make for good bird-watching. Access Sandy Point through the Parker River National Wildlife Refuge, but note that parking is limited, so you'd best get an early start. Also, beware the blood-thirsty greenhead flies, which buzz and bite in July and August.

Plum Island Kayak
KAYAKING

(✆978-462-5510; www.plumislandkayak.com; 38 Merrimac St; tours $45-60, single/tandem kayaks per day $60/80; ⊙9am-5pm Mon-Thu, to 8pm Fri-Sun Jun-Sep, 9am-5pm Sat & Sun May & Oct) Rent a kayak and explore Plum Island on your own, or join one of several tours during the day (or night) exploring the islands, mud bars, salt marshes and shoreline. Expect to see lots of birds, or for a unique experience, paddle among the resident seals.

✯ Festivals & Events

Yankee Homecoming
FIREWORKS

(www.yankeehomecoming.com) This week-long celebration was founded to draw folks back to their roots to see where history happened. It's a week of art fairs, sidewalk sales, waterside concerts and food feasts, plus a road race, a parade and fireworks.

🛏 Sleeping

Clark Currier Inn
GUESTHOUSE $$

(✆978-465-8363; www.clarkcurrierinn.com; 45 Green St; r $185-210; 🅿✳@🛜) Travelers in search of a genteel experience can luxuriate in this 1803 Federal mansion, with its stately parlor and welcoming library. Details such as fireplaces and canopy beds make the seven guest rooms extra charming. A continental breakfast – fresh fruit and pastries – is served. Two-night minimum on weekends in summer.

Blue
INN $$$

(✆855-255-2583; www.blueinn.com; 20 Fordham Way, Plum Island; d from $490; 🅿✳🛜❄) In a drop-dead-gorgeous location on a beautiful beach, this sophisticated inn is quite a surprise on unassuming Plum Island. Rooms feature high ceilings, contemporary decor, fresh white linen and streaming sunlight. Private decks, shared hot tubs and in-room fireplaces are a few of the perks – all steps from the surf. Breakfast is delivered to your room. Three-night minimum in summer.

Garrison Inn
BOUTIQUE HOTEL $$$

(✆978-499-8500; www.garrisoninn.com; 11 Brown Sq; d $210-300, ste from $360; 🅿✳🛜❄) Once a private mansion, this gracious red-brick building is named for William Lloyd Garrison, the abolitionist who was born in Newburyport. Its 24 luxurious beige-and-black 'boudoirs' are done up in a stylish, eclectic mix of contemporary and classic. Original architectural features such as exposed-brick walls, cathedral ceilings and spiral staircases are highlighted. Made-to-order breakfast.

✗ Eating

Revitalive Cafe & Juice Bar
VEGAN $

(www.revitalive.com; Tannery Mall, 50 Water St; mains $8-10; ⊙10am-7pm Mon-Fri, 9am-5pm Sat & Sun; 🍽) Vegan, gluten-free, raw – whatever your dietary restriction, this sweet little cafe has got you covered. Even if you're an omnivore, you'll drool over the fresh salads, fresh-made soups and cold-pressed juices. Or feast on a deliciously healthy 'bowl,' built on quinoa or rice. Also: smoothies. It's located inside the Tannery shopping mall.

Loretta
AMERICAN $$

(✆978-463-0000; www.lorettarestaurant.com; 15 Pleasant St; sandwiches $8-17, mains $17-30; ⊙11am-11pm Sun-Thu, to midnight Fri & Sat) With memorabilia on the walls and ribs and burgers on

ULTIMATE ROMANCE: DINNER ATOP A LIGHTHOUSE

You'll have to climb five flights of stairs, plus a 6ft ladder. And you'll have to bring your own bottle of wine. At the top of **Rear Range Lighthouse** (☑800-727-2326; www.lighthousepreservation.org; 61½ Water St; reservation $350 plus meals), you'll dine in complete privacy, surrounded by views of city, sea and sky. The food comes from one of six local restaurants, but the lighthouse location is what makes this a unique and supremely romantic experience.

The reservation fee is a $350 tax-deductible donation to the Lighthouse Preservation Society. The cost of the meals is additional.

the menu, Loretta specializes in all-American goodness. This classic restaurant is a longtime favorite in Newburyport, but it has moved to a bigger, swankier space. More to love.

★ Glenn's Food & Libations
INTERNATIONAL, SEAFOOD $$$

(☑978-465-3811; www.glennsfoodandlibations.com; 50 Water St; mains $25-38; ☺5-10pm Tue-Sat, from noon Sun) Glenn is out to spice up your life. He's got the seafood you're looking for, but he's serving it in ways you never imagined. Oysters might come baked with chili and pumpkin-seed pesto. Blackened haddock is served with crab cake, sweet mashers and pineapple pepper relish. The menu changes frequently, but it's always exciting.

Plum Island Grille
SEAFOOD $$$

(☑978-463-2290; www.plumislandgrille.com; Sunset Blvd, Plum Island; mains lunch $14-28, dinner $25-36; ☺5-9pm Mon-Fri, noon-8pm Sat & Sun, closed Mon & Tue Oct-Apr) Cross the bridge to Plum Island to find this sophisticated seafood grill serving up grilled fish and a specialty oyster menu. The food can be inconsistent, but the setting is spectacular. Watch the sun set over the salt marsh and feast on the fruits of the sea. Sunday brunch comes with live music. Reservations are recommended in season.

ℹ️ Information

Greater Newburyport Chamber of Commerce (www.newburyportchamber.org; 38R Merrimac St; ☺9am-5pm Mon-Fri, 10am-4pm Sat,

noon-4pm Sun) Seasonal information booth in Newburyport center from June to October.

Parker River Visitors Center (www.fws.gov/refuge/parker_river; 6 Plum Island Turnpike; ☺9am-4pm) On the mainland, just east of the causeway. Stop by for maps, exhibits and other information about the refuge.

ℹ️ Getting There & Away

MBTA commuter rail (www.mbta.com) runs a line from North Station to Newburyport ($11.50, one hour). There are more than 10 trains daily on weekdays, and six on weekends.

C&J Trailways (www.ridecj.com; Storey Ave) runs hourly buses from Logan International Airport (adult/child $22/11) and Boston's South Station (adult/child $16/8).

SOUTH SHORE

As with much of the Massachusetts coast, the South Shore is blessed with historic sites and natural beauty. Seeing firsthand the challenges faced by the Pilgrims who first settled in Plymouth is a vivid reminder of the value of religious tolerance and stubborn endurance – both at the core of the nation's foundation. Generations later, these values were lived out by founding father John Adams and his son John Quincy Adams, who lived in nearby Quincy.

Quincy

☑617 / POP 94,200

Like all good New England towns, Quincy is not pronounced the obvious way: say '*Quin-zee*' if you want to talk like the locals.

What makes Quincy notable – and earns this town the nickname 'The City of Presidents' – is that it is the birthplace of the second and sixth presidents of the United States: John Adams and John Quincy Adams. The collection of houses where the Adams family lived now makes up the Adams National Historic Park. Visit the presidential homes on a bus tour that starts at the Adams National Historic Park Visitor Center.

In more recent history, Quincy is the birthplace of the Dropkick Murphys and Dunkin' Donuts.

History

Quincy was first settled in 1625 by a handful of raucous colonists who could not stand the strict and stoic ways in Plymouth. History has it that this group went so far as to dance around a maypole and engage in other festive Old English customs, which enraged the Pilgrims down the road. Nathaniel Hawthorne immortalized this history in his fictional account *The Maypole of Merrimount*. Eventually, Myles Standish arrived from Plymouth to restore order to the wayward colony.

Quincy was officially incorporated as its own entity in 1792, named after Colonel John Quincy, a respected local leader and ancestor of revolutionary Josiah Quincy and First Lady Abigail Adams.

◉ Sights

Adams National Historic Park HISTORIC SITE
(www.nps.gov/adam; 1250 Hancock St; adult/child $15/free; ◷ 9am-5pm mid-Apr–mid-Nov; Ⓣ Quincy Center) The Adams family sights are accessible by guided tours departing from the Adams National Historic Park Visitor Center. Every half-hour (until 3:15pm), trolleys travel to the **John Adams and John Quincy Adams Birthplaces**, the oldest presidential birthplaces in the USA. The half-hour film *Enduring Legacy* is also shown at the visitor center. Note that the admission fee is payable by credit card only.

Presidential Crypt CHURCH
(www.ufpc.org; 1306 Hancock St; donation adult/child $5/free; ◷ 11am-4pm Mon-Sat, from noon Sun mid-Apr–mid-Nov; Ⓣ Quincy Center) John and Abigail Adams and John Quincy and Louisa Catherine Adams are all interred in the basement of the handsome granite United First Parish Church, in the center of Quincy. The crypt is open by guided tour.

Hancock Cemetery CEMETERY
(1307 Hancock St; ◷ dawn-dusk; Ⓣ Quincy Center) Opposite the United First Parish Church, Hancock Cemetery is the final resting place of many notable Quincy residents, including most of the Quincy and Adams families. The Adams family vault, near the street, was the original site of the graves of the presidents and their wives, before they were interred in the Presidential Crypt in the church across the street. A map to Hancock Cemetery is available from the church.

🛏 Sleeping & Eating

Adams Inn MOTEL $$
(☏ 844-638-8715; www.bwadamsinn.com; 29 Hancock St; d $230; Ⓣ North Quincy) Overlooking the Neponsett River, this Best Western property offers comfortable rooms, decent service and a free shuttle to Logan airport. Otherwise, it's 3 miles to Quincy center and three-quarters of a mile to the nearest T-station, from where the red line is a straight shot into Boston.

Craig's Cafe CAFE $
(www.craigscafe.com; 1354 Hancock St; mains $8-13; ◷ 7am-3pm Mon-Fri, to 1pm Sat, to 2pm Sun, plus 5-9pm Wed-Sun; Ⓣ Quincy Center) This simple cafe serves soups, salads and sandwiches with a smile. Breakfast is a highlight, with half a dozen Benedicts and equal number of breakfast sandwiches. Daily specials guarantee a fresh and delicious lunch. This place is a local favorite.

Fat Cat AMERICAN $$
(www.fatcatrestaurant.com; 24 Chestnut St; sandwiches $8-12, mains $14-24; ◷ 11am-1am; Ⓣ Quincy Center) Quincy native Neil Kiley has transformed the city's old marketplace into a cool, contemporary restaurant and bar, complete with exposed-brick walls and painted pipes, lending a hip post-industrial vibe. The menu has been created to match, featuring traditional pub fare with a twist. The specialty is the Fat Cat Wings, served with a dipping sauce of your choice.

ℹ Information

Adams National Historic Park Visitor Center
(www.nps.gov/adam; 1250 Hancock St; ◷ 9am-5pm mid-Apr–mid-Nov, 10am-4pm Tue-Fri mid-Nov–mid-Apr; Ⓣ Quincy Center) Directly opposite the T station. Tours of the national park start here, and plenty of information about the surrounding area is also available.

ℹ Getting There & Away

The easiest way to reach the Adams National Historic Park from Boston is to take the Red Line to Quincy Center (Braintree line).

Plymouth

📞 508 / POP 59,900

Plymouth calls itself 'America's Home Town.' It was here that the Pilgrims first settled in the winter of 1620, seeking a place where they could practice their religion as they wished, without interference from government. An innocuous, weathered ball of granite – the famous Plymouth Rock – marks the spot where they supposedly first stepped ashore in this foreign land, but Plimoth Patuxet Museums provides a more informative and accurate account of their experiences. Many other museums and historic houses in the surrounding streets recall their struggles, sacrifices and triumphs.

◉ Sights

★ Plimoth Patuxet Museums MUSEUM
(☑ 508-746-1622; www.plimoth.org; 137 Warren Ave; adult/child $28/16; ⊙ 9am-5pm Apr-Nov; 🖫) Three miles south of Plymouth center, Plimoth Patuxet Museums authentically re-creates the Pilgrims' settlement in its primary exhibit, entitled **1627 English Village**. Everything in the village – costumes, implements, vocabulary, artistry, recipes and crops – has been painstakingly researched and remade. Costumed interpreters, acting in character, explain the details of daily life and answer your questions as you watch them work and play.

During the winter of 1620–21, half of the Pilgrims died of disease, privation and exposure to the elements. But new arrivals joined the survivors the following year, and by 1627 – just before an additional influx of settlers founded the colony of Massachusetts Bay – Plymouth Colony was on the road to prosperity. Plimoth Patuxet Museums provides excellent educational and entertaining insight into what was happening in Plymouth during that period.

In the **crafts center**, you can help artisans as they weave baskets and cloth, throw pottery and build fine furniture using the techniques and tools of the early 17th century. Exhibits explain how these manufactured goods were shipped across the Atlantic in exchange for Colonial necessities.

The **Wampanoag Homesite** replicates the life of a Native American community in the same area during that time. Homesite huts are made of wattle and daub (a framework of woven rods and twigs covered and plastered with clay); inhabitants engage in crafts while wearing traditional garb. Unlike the actors at the English Village, these individuals are not acting as historic characters but are indigenous people speaking from a modern perspective.

★ Mayflower II SHIP
(www.plimoth.org/what-see-do/mayflower-ii; State Pier, Water St; 🖫) If Plymouth Rock tells us little about the Pilgrims, *Mayflower II* speaks volumes. Climb aboard this replica of the small ship in which the Pilgrims made the fateful voyage, where 102 people lived together for 66 days as the ship passed through stormy North Atlantic waters. Actors in period costume are on board, recounting harrowing tales from the journey.

★ Pilgrim Hall Museum MUSEUM
(www.pilgrimhall.org; 75 Court St; adult/child $12/8; ⊙ 9:30am-4:30pm Feb-Dec; 🖫) Claiming to be the oldest continually operating public museum in the country, Pilgrim Hall Museum was founded in 1824. Its exhibits are not reproductions but real objects that the Pilgrims and their Wampanoag neighbors used in their daily lives – from Governor Bradford's chair to Constance Hopkins' beaver hat. The exhibits are dedicated to correcting the misrepresentations about the Pilgrims that have been passed down through history.

1667 Jabez Howland House HISTORIC SITE
(www.pilgrimjohnhowlandsociety.org; 33 Sandwich St; adult/child $6/2; ⊙ 10am-4:30pm late May–mid-Oct) This is the only house in Plymouth that was home to a known *Mayflower* passenger. John Howland lived here with his wife, Elizabeth Tilley, and their son Jabez and his family. The house has been restored to its original appearance, complete with period furnishings and many artifacts and documents from the family.

Plimoth Grist Mill MUSEUM
(☑ 508-746-1622; www.plimoth.org/mill; 6 Spring Lane; adult/child $7/5; ⊙ 9am-5pm Apr-Oct; 🖫) In 1636, local leaders constructed a gristmill on Town Brook so that the growing community could grind corn and produce cornmeal. Today, the replica mill is on the site of the original, still grinding corn the old-fashioned way. Take home a bag of freshly ground cornmeal as a souvenir.

Myles Standish State Forest FOREST
(www.mass.gov/dcr; Cranberry Rd, South Carver; parking $8-15; ⊙ dawn-dusk; 🖫) About 6 miles south of Plymouth, this 16,000-acre park is the largest public recreation area in southeastern Massachusetts. It contains 13 miles of biking and hiking trails and 16 ponds – two with beaches. It's a wonderful wilderness for picnicking, fishing, swimming and camping. From MA 3, take exit 5 to Long Pond Rd.

Richard Sparrow House HISTORIC SITE
(www.sparrowhouse.com; 42 Summer St; adult/child $2/1; ⊙ 10am-5pm) Plymouth's oldest house was built by one of the original Pilgrim settlers in 1640. Today, there is a small

art gallery in the more recent addition, while the oldest, original part of the house is maintained to 17th-century standards as a small museum.

1749 Spooner House
HISTORIC SITE

(www.plymouthantiquariansociety.org; 27 North St; adult/child $6/3; ⊘2-6pm Thu & Sun Jun-Aug) On pretty North St, this 18th-century house was the home of the Spooner family for more than two centuries. Nowadays, the two-story house still contains the original furnishings, china and paintings, showcasing 200 years of Plymouth domestic life.

Sacrifice Rock
MEMORIAL

(www.plymouthantiquariansociety.org; 394 Old Sandwich Rd) FREE 'The other rock' is an ancient landmark where Wampanoag travelers would place branches and stones as offerings in exchange for safe travels. It's about 6 miles south of Plymouth center, next to the Pinehills residential development.

1809 Hedge House
HISTORIC SITE

(www.plymouthantiquariansociety.org; 126 Water St; adult/child $6/3; ⊘2-6pm Wed-Sun Jun-Aug) You can't miss this grand, Federal edifice overlooking Plymouth Harbor. Originally built on Court St for a sea captain, it became the home of merchant Thomas Hedge, one of the town's early industrialists and entrepreneurs.

In the early 20th century, the house was purchased by the Antiquarian Society and moved to its current location. A 30-minute tour shows off the furniture, textiles and other treasures that would have been collected by a wealthy merchant family.

1677 Harlow
Old Fort House
HISTORIC SITE

(www.plymouthantiquariansociety.org; 119 Sandwich St; ⊘11am-3pm Tue Jun-Aug) FREE A half-mile east of Town Brook, this is one of the few remaining 17th-century structures in Plymouth. Furnished with early-American artifacts, it's open only occasionally.

Plymouth Rock
MONUMENT

(Water St) Thousands of visitors come each year to look at this weathered granite ball and consider what it was like for the Pilgrims who stepped ashore on a foreign land in the fall of 1620. In firsthand accounts of the fledgling colony there's no mention of a granite rock, but the story gained popularity during colonial times.

ⓘ HERITAGE PASS

If you intend to visit all of Plymouth's most significant historic sites, consider purchasing the **Heritage Pass** (adult/child $36/22), which includes admission to all the exhibits at Plimoth Patuxet Museums (two days), as well as the *Mayflower II* and Plimoth Grist Mill (one day each). Alternatively, a **Combination Ticket** (adult/child $31/20) includes Plimoth Patuxet Museums and one of the other sites. Both passes are good for one year after the date of purchase.

Mayflower
Society Museum
HISTORIC SITE

(www.themayflowersociety.com; 4 Winslow St; adult/child $7/5; ⊘11am-4pm May-Oct) The offices of the General Society of Mayflower Descendants are housed in the magnificent 1754 house of Edward Winslow, the great-grandson of Plymouth Colony's third governor. Guided tours show off antique furniture, family portraiture and stunning architectural details.

☞ Tours

Native Plymouth Tours
WALKING

(☑774-454-7792; www.facebook.com/native plymouthtours; adult/child $15/10) A two-hour walking tour with a Native American guide. You'll see many typical sights, but your guide Timothy Turner will debunk myths, give unusual insights and share a completely different perspective on Plymouth (and American) history. Four-person minimum.

Plymouth Cruises
Aboard Lobster Tails
BOATING

(☑508-746-5342; www.plymouthcruises.com; 9 Town Wharf; tickets $15-19) Fantastic boat tours for families, including a hands-on lobstering excursion and an fun, educational pirate cruise for mateys.

Dead of Night
Ghost Tours
HISTORY

(☑508-866-5111, 508-277-2371; www.deadofnight ghosttours.com; $15-20) Here's where you'll learn about the dark side of Plymouth history. As the sun sets, hoist a gas lantern and set out to explore the city's age-old streets and ancient burial grounds. You can choose to end by visiting two haunted houses. There is no guarantee that you'll witness paranormal activity on the tour, but there's no guarantee that you won't!

Capt John Boats BOATING

(☎ 508-927-5587; www.captjohn.com; Town Wharf; adult/child $53/30; ☺ tours Apr-Oct; ⊕) Offers loads of options to get you out on the water, including whale-watching cruises and fishing trips. The whale-watching is a four-hour journey out to Stellwagen Bank (p116), the primary feeding grounds for five species of whale, not to mention dolphins and seabirds.

★ Festivals & Events

America's Hometown
Thanksgiving Celebration CULTURAL

(www.usathanksgiving.com; ☺ Nov) The weekend before Thanksgiving, historic Plymouth comes to life as pilgrims, pioneers and patriots parade the streets of 'America's Hometown.' The event features a celebratory parade, a food festival, a concert series, a Wampanoag pavilion and a 'historic village.' Have some fun, then stop by Plimoth Patuxet Museums to see how the Pilgrims really celebrated (or rather, didn't celebrate) Thanksgiving.

🛏 Sleeping

By the Sea B&B B&B $$

(☎ 508-830-9643; www.bytheseabedandbreakfast. com; 22 Winslow St; ste $190-225; ☺ May-Nov; ℗✳☎) There are three suites in this Victorian home overlooking Plymouth Harbor. They all offer lovely ocean views, which you might even enjoy from bed. There is also a front porch, should you care to feel the breeze – or shoot the breeze with your friendly hosts. Breakfast is served at a nearby restaurant.

Seabreeze Inn B&B $$

(☎ 508-746-0282, 866-746-0282; 20 Chilton St; ste $150-175; ☺ Apr-Dec; ℗✳☎) A grand Victorian with ocean views, this beauty was built in

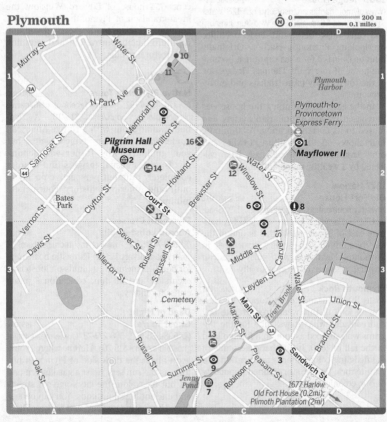

1885 as the home of a sea captain. Now it is a delightful place to stay. Three pastel-painted suites have ornamental fireplaces, hardwood floors and lacy curtains. Breakfast is made to order, featuring bacon and eggs and homemade breads and pastries.

John Carver Inn HOTEL **$$**
(☎888-906-6181; www.johncarverinn.com; 25 Summer St; d $219-297, ste $359; ⓟ❄🚭🛜🏊) This 80-room inn is a boon for families: special packages allow kids to stay for free and include entry to local sights. Best of all, the indoor Pilgrim-theme swimming pool (complete with a *Mayflower* replica!) will keep your little ones entertained for hours. All rooms feature traditional and tasteful decor, while the fancier ones boast four-poster beds and fireplaces.

✖ Eating & Drinking

★ Blue Blinds Bakery BAKERY **$**
(www.blueblindsbakery.com; 7 North St; mains $5-9; ⊙6am-9pm Sun-Thu, 7am-3pm Fri; 🅿🖶) Blue Blinds is a cozy house – it feels like a home, really – with plants in the windows, a fire in the fireplace, and folks sipping coffee on the shady front porch. The baked goods are out of this world, including fresh-baked

---

Plymouth

◉ **Top Sights**
| 1 Mayflower II | D2 |
| 2 Pilgrim Hall Museum | B2 |

◉ **Sights**
3 1667 Jabez Howland House	C4
4 1749 Spooner House	C3
5 1809 Hedge House	B1
6 Mayflower Society Museum	C2
7 Plimoth Grist Mill	C4
8 Plymouth Rock	D2
9 Richard Sparrow House	C4

⊕ **Activities, Courses & Tours**
10 Capt John Boats	B1
11 Plymouth Cruises Aboard	
Lobster Tails	B1

🛏 **Sleeping**
12 By the Sea B&B	C2
13 John Carver Inn	C4
14 Seabreeze Inn	B2

🍴 **Eating**
15 Blue Blinds Bakery	C3
16 Carmen's Café Nicole	C2
17 Tasty	B2

ⓘ **PLYMOUTH-TO-PROVINCETOWN FERRY**

The **Plymouth-to-Provincetown Express Ferry** (☎508-746-2643; www.captjohn.com; State Pier, 77 Water St; ⊙round-trip adult/child $53/32) deposits you on the tip of Cape Cod faster than a car would. From late June to early September, the 90-minute journey departs Plymouth at 10am and leaves Provincetown at 4:30pm.

---

organic breads, muffins and pastries. Breakfast is served all day, but the sandwiches and homemade soups are also divine.

Carmen's Café Nicole MEXICAN, SEAFOOD **$**
(www.carmenscafenicole.com; 114 Water St; breakfast $6-10, lunch $10-20; ⊙7am-2pm) Boasting a wonderful view of Plymouth Harbor and outdoor seating, this eclectic cafe pulls off a wide variety of delicious dishes including decadent breakfasts (featuring the signature 'Bananas Foster' French toast), traditional seafood and surprisingly satisfying Mexican combos (eg tacos del mar). The 'famous' Pilgrim wrap with turkey, stuffing and cranberry sauce is famous for a good reason.

Tasty GASTROPUB **$$**
(www.thetastyplymouth.com; 42 Court St; mains lunch $8-16, dinner $18-27; ⊙5-9pm Tue, 11:30am-9pm Wed & Thu, 11:30am-10pm Fri & Sat, 4-8pm Sun) Plymouth is loving this gastropub, located on the main drag. The space is modern yet cozy, while the food is locally sourced and inventively prepared. Look for delightfully surprising combinations, such as fried calamari in a pea shoot and snap pea salad, cod risotto with braised greens, or cranberry bread pudding for dessert. Tuesday is noodle night.

Mayflower Brewing Company MICROBREWERY
(www.mayflowerbrewing.com; 12 Resnik Rd; ⊙tasting room noon-8pm Wed-Sat, to 6pm Sun, tours 1pm, 3pm & 5pm Sat & Sun) History has it that the Pilgrims drank more beer than water (because the water contained unsafe bacteria, but whatever). So it stands to reason that Plymouth should be home to an excellent microbrewery, mixing up some excellent IPAs, a golden ale and a porter, as well as seasonal brews. Tour the

OFF THE BEATEN TRACK

BATTLESHIP COVE

'You sank my battleship!' This cry was ne'er heard aboard the mighty USS *Massachusetts*, a hulk of a craft that survived 35 battles in WWII, gunning down almost 40 aircraft and never losing a man in combat. Today, this heroic vessel sits in a quiet corner of Mt Hope Bay. This beaut – longer than two football fields and taller than a nine-story building – is one of eight historic ships that visitors can explore at **Battleship Cove** (www.battleshipcove.org; 5 Water St, Fall River; adult/child $25/15; ⊙ 9am-5pm Apr-Sep, to 4pm Oct, to 4pm Wed-Sun Nov-Mar).

The USS *Joseph P Kennedy Jr,* named for President John F Kennedy's older brother, did battle in the Korean and Vietnam Wars and is now a museum. The USS *Lionfish* is a WWII submarine still in full working condition. The Soviet-built *Hiddensee* is a fast attack craft that was obtained from Germany after the communist collapse. There are also two Patrol Torpedo (PT) boats, as well as some exhibits highlighting the personal stories of the sailors who served on the USS *Massachusetts*.

Battleship Cove is approximately 14 miles west of New Bedford, in Fall River, near the Massachusetts–Rhode Island state line.

brewery or just sample the goods in the tasting room.

ℹ Information

Destination Plymouth (www.seeplymouth.com; 130 Water St; ⊙ 9am-5pm Apr-Oct, to 8pm Jun-Aug) Located at the rotary across from Plymouth Harbor; provides loads of information about local attractions, as well as assistance with B&B reservations.

ℹ Getting There & Away

You can reach Plymouth from Boston by MBTA commuter rail trains (www.mbta.com), which depart from South Station three or four times a day ($11.50, 90 minutes). From the station at Cordage Park, GATRA buses connect to Plymouth center.

Buses operated by Plymouth & Brockton (www.p-b.com) travel hourly to South Station ($16, 50 minutes) or Logan International Airport ($22, 70 minutes) in Boston. The Plymouth P&B terminal is at the commuter parking lot, exit 5 off MA 3. Hop on a GATRA bus into Plymouth center.

ℹ Getting Around

GATRA (www.gatra.org) operates several shuttle buses. The Freedom Link runs from the train depot to Plymouth center, while the Mayflower Link runs from Plymouth center to Plimoth Patuxet Museums. A day pass costs $3.

New Bedford

🎣 508 / POP 95,100

During its heyday as a whaling port (1765–1860), New Bedford commanded as many as 400 whaling ships. This vast fleet brought home hundreds of thousands of barrels of whale oil for lighting America's lamps. Novelist Herman Melville worked on one of these ships for four years, and thus set his celebrated novel, *Moby-Dick; or, The Whale,* in New Bedford. Nowadays, the city center constitutes the New Bedford Whaling National Historic Park, which encompasses an excellent whaling museum, some other historic buildings and the gritty working waterfront. It's enough to occupy you for half a day (unless you're here for the marathon reading of *Moby-Dick,* in which case you'll be busy for at least 24 hours).

⊙ Sights

New Bedford Whaling Museum   MUSEUM
(www.whalingmuseum.org; 18 Johnny Cake Hill; adult/child $17/7; ⊙ 9am-5pm Apr-Dec, to 4pm Tue-Sat & 11am-4pm Sun Jan-Mar) The centerpiece of New Bedford, this excellent, hands-on museum remembers the town's heyday as a whaling port. The museum occupies seven buildings situated between William and Union Sts. A 66ft skeleton of a blue whale and a smaller skeleton of a sperm whale welcome you at the entrance. To learn what whaling was all about, you need only tramp the decks of the *Lagoda,* a fully rigged, half-size replica of an actual whaling bark.

Seamen's Bethel   CHURCH
(www.seamensbethel.org; 15 Johnny Cake Hill; admission by donation; ⊙ 8am-4pm Jun-Sep, 11am-3pm Mon-Fri & 11am-4pm Sat & Sun Oct-May, closed Mon Jan-Mar) Across from the Whaling Museum, this small chapel was a refuge from the rigors and stresses of maritime life. Melville immortalized it in *Moby-Dick,* where

he wrote: 'In this same New Bedford there stands a Whaleman's Chapel, and few are the moody fishermen...who fail to make a Sunday visit to the spot.'

✨ Festivals & Events

Moby-Dick Marathon   LITERATURE
(www.whalingmuseum.org; ⊘1st weekend in Jan) On or around the anniversary of Melville's embarkation from New Bedford harbor, literature buffs participate in a marathon, nonstop reading of the novel *Moby-Dick*. The event takes place at Seamen's Bethel, though many watch the live recording from the theater in the Whaling Museum.

🛏 Sleeping & Eating

New Bedford Harbor Hotel   HOTEL $$
(☑508-999-1292; www.newbedfordharborhotel. com; 222 Union St; d from $179) Central, stylish and up to snuff, this boutique hotel caters to travelers catching the ferry to Martha's Vineyard, as well as the occasional New Bedford weekender.

DNB Burgers   BURGERS $$
(www.dnbburgers.com; 22 Elm St; burgers $13-15; ⊘11:30am-9pm) Here's the requisite gourmet burger place, serving beef from grass-fed cows and topped with all manner of interesting ingredients. But DNB isn't just about the burgers; it's also about the addictive herbed fries, served with garlic aioli dipping sauce. Also: craft beer.

Quahog Republic Whaler's Tavern   SEAFOOD $$
(www.quahogrepublic.com; 24 North Water St; mains $10-25; ⊘11:30am-11pm) You're in Whaling City: why not grab lunch at this friendly whaler's tavern, where you can feast on a well-stocked raw bar, divine cod cakes or 'monsta lobsta' rolls? To complement the food (or not), there are a dozen mostly local beers on tap, enticing craft cocktails and dangerous rum flights. The bar is open until 1am Friday and Saturday.

ℹ Information

Park Visitor Center (www.nps.gpv/nebe; 33 William St; ⊘9am-5pm, closed Mon & Tue Jan-Mar) Pick up a map for a self-guided tour or activity books for kids.

ℹ Getting There & Away

Peter Pan Bus (www.peterpanbus.com) offers bus services to/from Providence ($18, 50 minutes, six daily) and Boston ($22, 2½ hours, six daily) from the New Bedford ferry dock.

Dattco (www.dattco.com) runs buses to Boston and Cambridge ($15, 1½ hours, six daily), departing from the Southeastern Regional Transit Authority (SRTA) station at the corner of Elm and Pleasant Sts.

Sea Streak fast ferry (www.seastreak.com) runs from New Bedford to Martha's Vineyard ($40, one hour, four to six daily) and Nantucket ($50, 1½ hours, four to six daily) from mid-May to mid-October.

Cape Cod, Nantucket & Martha's Vineyard

☏ 508, 774

Includes ➡

Cape Cod	134
Falmouth	135
Hyannis	138
Yarmouth	141
Chatham	146
Wellfleet	151
Truro	153
Provincetown	154
Nantucket Town	161
Martha's Vineyard	169
Vineyard Haven	169
Oak Bluffs	172

Best Places to Eat

➡ Chatham Fish Pier Market (p148)

➡ BlackFish (p154)

➡ Chilmark Tavern (p172)

➡ Joon (p159)

➡ Proprietors (p166)

Best Places to Stay

➡ Inn at the Oaks (p150)

➡ Wequassett Resort (p145)

➡ Summercamp (p173)

➡ Roux (p158)

➡ Greydon House (p165)

Why Go?

When summer comes around, New England's top seashore destination gets packed to the gills. Cars stream over the two bridges that connect Cape Cod to the mainland, ferries shuttle visitors to and from the islands, and sun-seeking bodies plop down on towels all along the shore.

This trio of destinations offers a beach for every mood. You can surf a wild Atlantic wave or dip a paddle into a quiet cove. Or just chill out and watch the kids build sandcastles.

But there's much more than sun, sand and surf. You'll find lighthouses to climb, clam shacks to frequent and beach parties to revel in. The Cape and Islands have scenic cycling paths and hiking trails, excellent art galleries and summer theater – and any one of them alone would be reason enough to come here. In combination, the appeal is undeniable.

When to Go
Barnstable

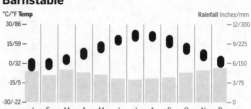

Jul & Aug In peak summer the ocean's warmest, the partying's hardest and the festivities maxed.	Jun & Sep The beaches still dazzle but crowds are thinner, hotel rates cheaper and traffic jams fewer.	Oct & Nov Ideal for cycling, hiking, kayaking – even a little swimming.

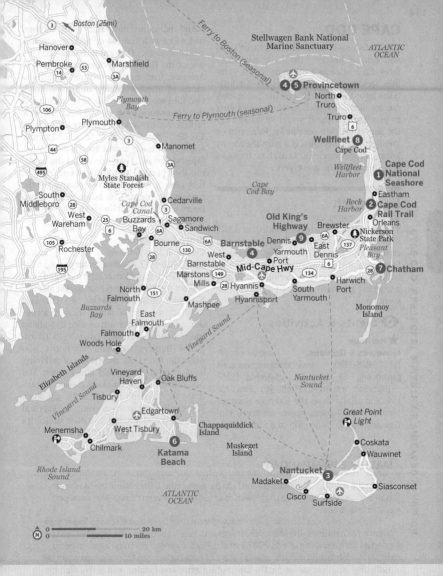

Cape Cod, Nantucket & Martha's Vineyard Highlights

❶ Cape Cod National Seashore (p150) Climbing dunes and bodysurfing waves.

❷ Cape Cod Rail Trail (p142) Cycling the bicycle trail and discovering your own swimming hole.

❸ Nantucket (p161) Wandering the cobbled, Moby Dick–era streets of this town.

❹ Whale-watching (p156) Ogling humpbacks from a boat out of Provincetown or Barnstable.

❺ Provincetown (p154) Dining superbly and reveling in the carnival street scene.

❻ Katama Beach (p174) Riding a wave on Martha's Vineyard's south coast.

❼ Chatham Pier Fish Market (p148) Eating fresh-off-the-boat seafood and scouting for seals.

❽ Beachcomber (p152) Joining the party scene at the Cape's hottest nightspot.

❾ Old King's Highway (p145) Admiring sea captains' mansions and antiquing.

CAPE COD

Quaint fishing villages, kitschy tourist traps and genteel towns – the Cape has many faces. Each attracts a different crowd. Families seeking calm waters perfect for little tykes favor Cape Cod Bay on the peninsula's quieter north side. College students looking to play hard in the day and let loose after the sun goes down set out for Falmouth or Wellfleet. Provincetown is a paradise for art lovers, whale-watchers, LGBTIQ+ travelers and...well, just about everyone.

Sandwich

🔲 508, 774 / POP 20,300

The Cape's oldest town (founded in 1637) makes a perfect first impression as you cross over the canal from the mainland. Head straight to the village center, where white-steepled churches, period homes and a working grist mill surround a picturesque swan pond.

◉ Sights & Activities

★ Heritage
Museums & Gardens   MUSEUM, GARDENS
(🔲508-888-3300; www.heritagemuseumsand gardens.org; 67 Grove St; adult/child $18/7; ◉10am-5pm mid-Apr–mid-Oct; 🖼) Fun for kids and adults alike, the 100-acre Heritage Museums & Gardens sports a superb vintage automobile collection in a Shaker-style round barn, an authentic 1908 carousel (rides free with admission) and unusual folk art collections. The grounds also contain one of the finest rhododendron gardens in America; from mid-May to mid-June thousands of 'rhodies' blaze with color. You'll also find ways to get your heart racing, via the **Adventure Park** (🔲508-866-0199; www. heritageadventurepark.org; 67 Grove St; 2hr ticket $38-49; ◉8am-8pm Jun & Jul, to 7:30pm mid-Aug, to 7pm late Aug, shorter hours mid-Apr–May & Sep–mid-Nov; 🖼). Here, you'll find five 'aerial trails' of planks, rope bridges and ziplines that offer a whole new perspective on the trees and gardens. Tickets are valid for two hours of climbing; online booking is strongly recommended.

Green Briar Nature
Center & Jam Kitchen   MUSEUM
(🔲508-888-6870; www.thorntonburgess.org; 6 Discovery Hill Rd; suggested donation adult/child $5/3; ◉10am-4pm Mon-Sat, from noon Sun late May-Dec, 10am-4pm Tue-Sat Jan–mid-May; 🖼) This is a lovely mixed bag of family-friendly attractions: a nature center surrounded by walking trails; a small museum dedicated to Thornton W Burgess, the Sandwich native who wrote the Peter Cottontail series of children's books; and a century-old jam kitchen. You can sign up for jam-making classes, or purchase the kitchen's output in the gift shop. There's also a program of events for kids and adults, from gardening to nature walks. It's east of town, signposted off Rte 6A.

MASHPEE WAMPANOAG

Before the arrival of European colonists to the area in the 17th century, the Mashpee Wampanoag tribe controlled huge swaths of territory between coastal Massachusetts and Rhode Island.

European colonization saw them removed from their lands and forced to forget their culture. For centuries, the Mashpee struggled to survive and were not federally recognized as a tribe until as late as 2007. In the 1970s they began pursuing legal action to regain lost lands, and in 2015, after 30 years of legal battles, the federal government set aside over 300 acres of land in the towns of Mashpee and Taunton as a reservation for the tribe. A small, but significant, victory for the tribesfolk.

In a cruel twist of fate, in 2018, that court ruling was overturned by the Department of the Interior under President Trump.

The tribe's land claim may currently be in limbo, but their presence in the small town of Mashpee is strong. Stop in to the **Mashpee Wampanoag Museum** (🔲508-477-9339; https://mashpeewampanoagtribe-nsn.gov; 414 Main St, Mashpee; adult/child $5/2; ◉10am-4pm Mon-Fri May-Nov) to learn more about the tribe's culture and history. If you are in the area around the 4th of July make sure to attend the **Mashpee Wampanoag Powwow** (www.mashpeewampanoagtribe.com/powwow; 483 Great Neck Rd South, Mashpee; tickets adult/child $12/10; ◉early Jul), for three days of dancing, drumming and invaluable cultural exchange.

Sandwich Glass Museum `MUSEUM`

(☑508-888-0251; www.sandwichglassmuseum.
org; 129 Main St; adult/child $10/2; ⊙9:30am-
5pm Apr-Dec, to 4pm Wed-Sun Feb & Mar, closed
Jan) Sandwich glass, now prized by collectors, had its heyday in the 19th century, and
this heritage is artfully displayed in this
excellent, sprawling museum. But it's not
just a period glass collection – there are also
glass-blowing demonstrations given hourly
throughout the day and a cool contemporary gallery.

🛏 Sleeping & Eating

Shawme-Crowell
State Forest `CAMPGROUND $`

(☑info 508-888-0351, reservations 877-422-6762;
www.reserveamerica.com; 42 Main St; tent sites
$27, yurts $60-70; ⊙mid-Apr–mid-Oct; 🐾) You'll
find 285 cool and shady campsites (none
with hookups) in this 760-acre pine and
oak woodland. It's just 1 mile from the Cape
Cod Canal and is popular with cyclists. If
you don't have a tent, there are a handful
of yurts on-site. Winter weekend camping is
available.

Belfry Inn & Bistro `B&B $$`

(☑508-888-8550; www.belfryinn.com; 6 Jarves St;
r $158-242; 🏵🐾) Ever fall asleep in church?
Then you'll love the rooms, some with
stained-glass windows, in this creatively
restored former church, now an upmarket
B&B. If, on the other hand, you're uneasy
about the angel Gabriel watching over you
in bed, Belfry also has two other nearby
inns that are home to more conventional,
high-quality rooms.

Brown Jug `DELI, CAFE $`

(☑508-888-0053; www.thebrownjug.com; 1 Jarves
St; large pizza $18-23; ⊙10am-8pm Tue-Thu, to
10pm Fri & Sat, noon-8pm Sun May-Nov, 10am-6pm
Tue-Sat, from noon Sun Dec-Apr) Prime picnic
supplies can be found at this specialty food
store that also serves as a wine purveyor and
a cafe. Wood-fired pizzas make for a perfect
pit stop.

❶ Information

Sandwich Visitor Center (☑508-833-9755;
www.sandwichchamber.com; 520 MA 130;
⊙10am-5pm Mon-Sat, to 4pm Sun mid-May–
mid-Oct, to 4pm Mon-Fri mid-Oct–mid-May)
Has local information. Operated by the local
chamber of commerce.

❶ Getting There & Away

If you arrive on the Cape via US 6, take exit 2
(MA 130). Water (MA 130), Main and Grove Sts
converge in the village center at Shawme Pond.
Tupper Rd, off MA 6A, leads to the Cape Cod
Canal.

Falmouth
☑508, 774 / POP 31,100

Crowd-pleasing beaches, a terrific bike trail
and one of the busiest downtowns outside of
Provincetown make this charmer of a town
worth checking out. There's also plenty for
history buffs to be found here: Falmouth
puffs with pride over its most cherished
daughter, Katharine Lee Bates, who wrote
the words to the nation's favorite patriotic
hymn, *America the Beautiful*.

◉ Sights

Old Silver Beach `BEACH`

(Quaker Rd, North Falmouth; 🐾) Of all Falmouth's beaches, none is finer than Old Silver Beach. This long, sandy stretch of beach
attracts scores of college students, families
and day-trippers from the city. A rock jetty,
sandbars and tidal pools provide lots of fun
diversions for kids. The parking lot often
fills up on hot days, so plan on getting there
early. Facilities include changing rooms and
a snack bar. Parking costs $20 in summer.

Highfield Hall & Gardens `HISTORIC BUILDING`

(☑508-495-1878; www.highfieldhallandgardens.
org; 56 Highfield Dr; adult/child $8/free; ⊙10am-
4pm Mon-Fri, to 2pm Sat & Sun mid-Apr–Oct, also
4-7pm Fri Jul & Aug) Saved from the wrecking
ball in the 1990s and lovingly restored by the
community, Highfield Hall dates from 1878
and was one of the early summer mansions
to grace Cape Cod. It's now open to the public as a museum and cultural center; check
the website for events and activities (art exhibitions, concerts on the lawn etc). **Beebe
Woods**, the lovely surrounding gardens and
trails, is open to visitors year-round.

Falmouth Museums
on the Green `MUSEUM`

(☑508-548-4857; http://museumsonthegreen.
org; 55 Palmer Ave; tours adult/child $10/free;
⊙10am-3pm Mon-Fri, to 1pm Sat Jun–mid-Oct)
Falmouth's quaint village green has an air
of history about it – it's where members of
the Colonial militia practiced in the 1700s
and 19th-century sea captains built their
homes. Today, two 18th-century houses are

Cape Cod

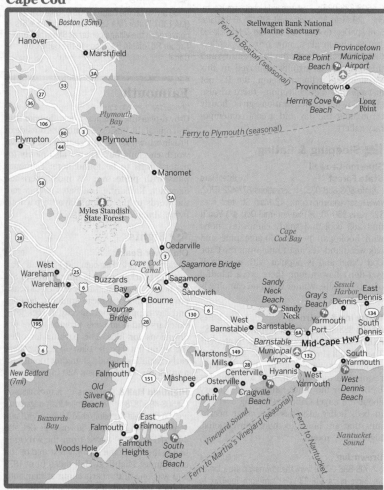

maintained here by the Falmouth Historical Society, and show period furniture and fine arts. Some of the grounds are open to stroll for free, but the society also conducts **guided tours** ($10) at 10am Tuesday and Thursday mornings, from June to mid-October.

Activities

★ Shining Sea Bikeway   CYCLING

(🚲) A bright star among the Cape's stellar bike trails, this 10.7-mile beaut runs along the entire west coast of Falmouth, from County Rd in North Falmouth to Woods Hole ferry terminal, offering unspoiled views of salt ponds, marsh and seascapes. Completed in 2009, the bikeway follows an abandoned railroad bed, taking you places you'd never get a glimpse of otherwise.

Bike Zone Rentals   CYCLING

(☏ 508-563-2333; www.bikezonecapecod.com; 13 County Rd, North Falmouth; bike rental per day from $20; ⊙10am-5pm Mon-Sat, to 4pm Sun) Rents kids', adult and tandem bicycles at the northern end of the Shining Sea Bikeway. Locks and helmets included. Winter hours may vary so call ahead before visiting.

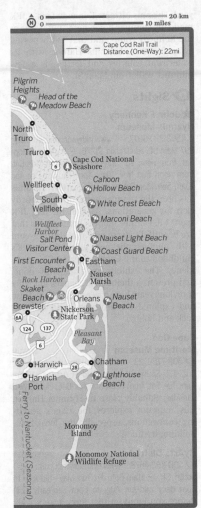

gourmet breakfast can be served to you on the beach, in the dining room or on your deck – it's your call.

Eating

Cupcake Charlie's
BAKERY $

(📞 508-540-2253; www.cupcakecharlies.com; 153 Main St; cupcakes from $3.29; ⊘11am-6pm Sun-Thu, to 9pm Fri & Sat) Cupcake nirvana can be found here, where pretty confections beckon from the cabinet: lemon drop, peanut butter pleasure, Oreo delight. There's also soft-serve ice cream mixed with your favorite cake flavor.

Pickle Jar Kitchen
MODERN AMERICAN $

(📞508-540-6760; www.picklejarkitchen.com; 170 Main St; mains $8-15; ⊘7am-3pm Thu-Mon; 🖉) Hearty, healthy comfort food, prepared with seasonal ingredients and lots of love. Look for satisfying hash for breakfast, lovingly prepared sandwiches, creative soups and lots of fresh fruit and veggies all around. And, of course, don't miss the house-made pickles.

★ Añejo
MEXICAN $$

(📞508-388-7631; www.anejomexicanbistro.com; 188 Main St; mains $13-26; ⊘11:30am-late Mon-Sat, from 10:30am Sun) This buzzing bistro and tequila bar brings a little year-round heat to the Main St scene, with a big selection of margaritas and tequilas, and a menu of fab street food – enchiladas, tacos, tostadas – that spins fresh Mexican flavors Cape Cod–style, with lots of fish and local seafood.

Glass Onion
MODERN AMERICAN $$$

(📞508-540-3730; www.theglassoniondining.com; 37 N Main St; mains $20-35; ⊘5-9pm Tue-Sat) The place to go in the area for a romantic dinner. The menu stars New American cuisine with French and Italian influences. Top billing goes to the butter-poached lobster, which is served with a creamy mushroom risotto. Service and wine selections are as top-shelf as the food. No bookings taken.

🍷 Drinking & Entertainment

Liam Maguire's Irish Pub & Restaurant
IRISH PUB

(📞508-548-0285; www.liammaguire.com; 273 Main St; ⊘11:30am-1am Mon-Sat, from noon Sun) The perfect Irish pub: good food (from beef and Guinness stew to fish tacos), good *craic*, a good selection of draft beers, Irish bartenders, live music nightly and boisterous Irish songfests.

🎆 Festivals & Events

Independence Day Celebration FIREWORKS
(www.falmouthfireworks.org; ⊘Jul 4) The Cape's largest fireworks display explodes over Falmouth Harbor on the 4th of July.

🛏 Sleeping

Inn on the Sound
B&B $$$

(📞508-457-9666; www.innonthesound.com; 313 Grand Ave; r $159-479; 🅿🀆) Falmouth's finest inn exudes a clean, contemporary elegance. It's across from the beach, and many of the 11 guest rooms have private decks with ocean views. Depending on your mood, a

LOBSTER ICE CREAM!

Lobster mania takes a new twist at **Ben & Bill's Chocolate Emporium** (☑508-548-7878; www.benandbills.com; 209 Main St; cones $6; ☺9am-11pm Jun-Aug, shorter hours rest of year), where the crustacean has crawled onto the summertime ice-cream menu. It's a butter-based ice cream with chunks of lobster meat mixed in. Too radical? There are plenty of traditional flavors as well, and lots of sweet fudge and chocolate, too.

Cape Cod Theatre Project THEATER
(☑508-457-4242; www.capecodtheatreproject. org; 7 Highfield Dr, Falmouth Academy; tickets $25; ☺Jul) The Theatre Project brings professional actors together with playwrights to perform staged readings of four new works during the month of July. Many of the past seasons' plays have gone on to open on and off Broadway in New York.

ℹ Information

Falmouth Chamber of Commerce (☑508-548-8500; www.falmouthchamber.com; 20 Academy Lane; ☺8:30am-4:30pm Mon-Fri, also 10am-2pm Sat late May-Aug) Stop by this helpful office in the town center, just off Main St.

ℹ Getting There & Away

Sitting at the southwest corner of the Cape, Falmouth is reached via MA 28, which becomes Main St in the town center. Buses connect the town with Boston and other Cape destinations.

Ferries to Martha's Vineyard (p169) leave from Falmouth Harbor in summer, and year-round from Woods Hole, 4.5 miles southwest of downtown.

Hyannis

☑508, 774 / POP 14,100

Ferries, buses and planes all converge on Hyannis, the Cape's commercial hub (and part of the larger Barnstable township). So there's a good chance you will, too. Although the downtown area lacks the charm of others on Cape, the village center and harborfront have been rejuvenated, making them a pleasant place to break a journey.

In addition to being a jumping-off point for boats to Nantucket and Martha's Vine-

yard, Hyannis attracts Kennedy fans – JFK made his summer home here, and it was at the Kennedy compound that Teddy passed away in 2009. Hyannis Harbor, with its waterfront eateries and ferries, is a few minutes' walk from Main St.

◉ Sights

★**John F Kennedy Hyannis Museum** MUSEUM
(☑508-790-3077; www.jfkhyannismuseum.org; 397 Main St; adult/child $12/6; ☺9am-5pm Mon-Sat, from noon Sun Jun-Oct, 10am-4pm Mon-Sat, from noon Sun Nov, 10am-4pm Thu-Sat Dec-Apr, 10am-5pm Mon-Sat, noon-5pm Sun May) Hyannis has been the summer home of the Kennedy clan for generations. Back in the day, JFK spent the warmer months here – times that are beautifully documented at this museum with photographs and video from JFK's childhood to the Camelot years of his presidency. The exhibits are poignantly done, and present a theme that changes annually (previous years have covered matriarch Rose and explored the brotherly bond between Jack and Bobby).

Cape Cod Maritime Museum MUSEUM
(☑508-775-1723; www.capecodmaritimemuseum. org; 135 South St; adult/child $6/free; ☺10am-4pm Tue-Sat, from noon Sun Apr-Dec, closed Wed Jan-Mar) Suitably close to Hyannis Harbor, this museum explores the Cape's seafaring connections, especially the local boat-building tradition.

HyArts District ARTS CENTER
(☑508-862-4678; www.hyartsdistrict.com; 250 South St; ☺11am-6pm Fri-Sun May-mid-Jun, to 8pm daily mid-Jun-Aug, to 6pm Sep-early Oct) Before you jump on that ferry, take a walk through the harborside HyArts District, which includes the Guyer Barn community art space and neighboring artist studios, the colorful artist shanties near the ferry docks, and the art-strewn Walkway to the Sea.

Kalmus Beach BEACH
(Ocean St) You'll find plenty of space in which to lay your towel on wide Kalmus Beach, at the south end of Ocean St in Hyannis. Thanks to its steady breezes, it's a haven for windsurfers. The warm summer waters also attract plenty of swimmers. Facilities include a snack bar, lifeguard and changing rooms. Parking costs $20 in summer.

✨ Festivals & Events

Pops by the Sea   MUSIC

(www.artsfoundation.org; 367 Main St, Hyannis Village Green; tickets from $25; ⊘mid-Aug) This concert on the village green on the second Sunday in August features the Boston Pops Orchestra and a celebrity guest conductor. It's the Cape's single largest cultural event.

🛏 Sleeping

HI Hyannis   HOSTEL $

(📞508-775-7990; www.hiusa.org; 111 Ocean St; dm/d from $40/119; ⊘mid-May–mid-Oct; 🅿@🛜) For a million-dollar view on a backpacker's budget, book yourself a bed at this hostel overlooking the harbor. It was built in 2010 by adding new wings to a period home and is within walking distance of the Main St scene, beaches and ferries. Now the caveat: there are only 42 beds, so book well in advance.

SeaCoast Inn   MOTEL $$

(📞508-775-3828; www.seacoastcapecod.com; 33 Ocean St; r $149-189; ⊘Apr-Oct; 🆒🛜) This small, two-story motel offers neat, clean rooms just a two-minute walk from the harbor in one direction and Main St restaurants in the other. OK, there's no view or pool, but the rooms are thoroughly comfy, most have kitchenettes and the rates are a pretty good deal.

⭐ Anchor-In   HOTEL $$$

(📞508-775-0357; www.anchorin.com; 1 South St; r $206-316; 🆒@🛜🏊) This family-run boutique hotel puts the chains to shame. The harbor-front location offers a fine sense of place, and the heated outdoor pool is a perfect perch from which to watch fishing boats unload their catch. The rooms are bright and smart, with water-view balconies. If you're planning a day trip to Nantucket, the ferry is just a stroll away.

🍴 Eating

Pizza Barbone   PIZZA $

(📞508-957-2377; www.pizzabarbone.com; 390 Main St; pizzas $11-15; ⊘11am-9pm Sun-Thu, to 10pm Fri & Sat) Take a break from seafood at this stylishly rustic pizza palace, doling out delicious Neapolitan-style thin-crust pizzas from its wood-fired oven. Toppings are high-quality, like mushroom with rosemary, smoked mozzarella and truffle oil. Gluten-free and vegan options available.

⭐ Pain D'Avignon   BAKERY, BISTRO $$

(📞508-778-8588; www.paindavignon.com; 15 Hinckley Rd; lunch $8-17, dinner mains $19-32; ⊘7am-4pm daily, plus 5-10pm Tue-Thu & Sun, to 11pm Fri & Sat Jun-Sep, also 5-9pm Tue-Thu, to 10pm Fri & Sat Oct-May) It's not in the likeliest of locations (out by the airport, off MA

WORTH A TRIP

OCEAN-GEEK HEAVEN: WOODS HOLE

All eyes are on the sea in this tiny, salty village with a huge reputation: ferries for Martha's Vineyard depart throughout the day, fishing boats chug in and out of the harbor and oceanographers ship off to distant lands.

Indeed, Woods Hole is home to one of the most prestigious marine research facilities in the world. Research at the private, nonprofit Woods Hole Oceanographic Institution (WHOI; pronounced 'hooey') has run the gamut, from exploring the sunken *Titanic* to studying global warming. With dozens of buildings and laboratories, and staff and students numbering about 1000 (including world-class scientists and engineers, and Nobel laureates), it's the largest independent oceanographic institution in the US. Learn about what goes on here at the **WHOI Ocean Science Exhibit Center** (📞508-289-2663; www.whoi.edu/visitus; 15 School St; suggested donation $3; ⊘10am-4:30pm Mon-Fri mid-Apr & May, also Sat Jun-Oct, Tue-Fri Nov-Dec; 🚼), or, if you're a true WHOI wanna-be, stick around for a free guided site tour. Suitable for teens to adults, the informative 75-minute tours visit a number of buildings, facilities and docks. They depart from the **WHOI information office** (📞508-289-2252; www.whoi.edu/visit; 93 Water St; ⊘8am-4pm Mon-Fri) at 10:30am and 1:30pm Monday to Friday in July and August; reservations are essential.

Parking in Woods Hole can be painful. Summer visitors are encouraged to ride the WHOOSH Trolley from Falmouth (originating at Falmouth Mall) operated by the **Cape Cod Regional Transit Authority** (📞800-352-7155; www.capecodrta.org; single ride/day pass $2/6).

SNACK ATTACK!

The much-admired chips of **Cape Cod Potato Chip Factory** (📞 888-881-2447; www.capecodchips.com; 100 Breed's Hill Rd; ⏰ 9am-5pm Mon-Fri) are of the potato, not the computer, variety, so although they won't work in your laptop, they'll taste good in your gateway. The factory has a self-guided tour; in effect, it's just observing the chips march across the production and packaging lines through windows. The whole visit might take you 10 minutes, and you get free samples.

132), but seek this place out for a delectable slice of Paris. Patisserie favorites beckon in the morning, but more leisurely options like omelets and galettes (savory crepes) can be ordered. At lunch and dinner, classic French bistro fare shines: croque monsieur, quiche Lorraine, steak *frites*.

Spanky's Clam Shack SEAFOOD $$
(📞 508-771-2770; www.spankysclamshack.com; 138 Ocean St; mains $11-30; ⏰ 11am-10pm mid-Apr–mid-Oct; 🚸) One of those fun, family-friendly, unstuffy waterfront places the Cape specializes in. The menu is big (including options for kids and land-food-only folks) and screams of local seafood: chowder, whole-belly fried clams, lobster rolls, oysters on the half-shell, a full lobster dinner. It's not far from the ferry docks.

⭐ **Naked Oyster** SEAFOOD $$$
(📞 508-778-6500; www.nakedoyster.com; 410 Main St; lunch $11-20, dinner mains $22-38; ⏰ noon-10pm Mon-Sat) 🌱 Limited ingredient travel times are preferred at this upmarket joint, where the eponymous bivalves come from the restaurant's oyster farm in Barnstable Harbor. They keep fine company in the raw bar: shrimp, littlenecks, lobster. The menu borrows global flavors to dress up fresh seafood – Thai shrimp, *moules frites*, fish tacos, curried scallops – with fine results.

🍷 Drinking & Entertainment

⭐ **Cape Cod Beer** BREWERY
(📞 508-790-4200; www.capecodbeer.com; 1336 Phinneys Lane; ⏰ 10am-6pm Mon-Fri, 11am-4pm Sat) Not just a place for beer connoisseurs (although they'll be pretty happy), this brewery is a fun spot to while away some time. Free

brewery tours happen daily (except Sunday) at 11am, but you can stop in for tastings ($6) any time. Check the website for events, from bring-your-pet 'yappy hour' to painting classes, live music and comedy nights.

Embargo COCKTAIL BAR
(📞 508-771-9700; www.embargorestaurant.com; 453 Main St; ⏰ 4:30pm-1am) Live jazz accompanies creative tapas dishes during dining hours, then DJs hit the decks from 10pm. Signature martinis and a long cocktail list keep the crowds happy.

Cape Cod Melody Tent LIVE MUSIC
(📞 508-775-5630; www.melodytent.org; 21 W Main St; ⏰ late May-early Sep) The Melody Tent is just that – a giant tent, seating 2300 people – with nobody sitting more than 50ft from the revolving stage. From Memorial Day to Labor Day it headlines acts such as Vince Gill and ZZ Top.

ℹ Information

Visitor Center (📞 508-775-7778; www.hyannis.com; 367 Main St; ⏰ 10am-4pm daily late May–mid-Oct) The Hyannis Chamber of Commerce runs a tourist visitor center on Main St.

ℹ Getting There & Away

Hyannis is the Cape's transportation hub.

AIR

Also known as Hyannis airport, the **Barnstable Municipal Airport** (📞 508-775-2020; www.townofbarnstable.us/airport; 480 Barnstable Rd) sits only a mile or so north of Hyannis Main St. **Cape Air** (📞 800-227-3247; www.capeair.com) flies several times a day year-round between Hyannis and Boston and Nantucket, plus Martha's Vineyard from May to October. In summer, JetBlue (www.jetblue.com) has flights that connect Hyannis with New York's JFK Airport.

BOAT

Hyannis is the jumping-off point for ferries to Nantucket (p161), operated by **Hy-Line Cruises** (📞 508-778-2600; www.hylinecruises.com) and **Steamship Authority** (📞 508-548-5011; www.steamshipauthority.com) from **South St Dock** (69 South St). Parking lots near the docks cater to those traveling to the island (in peak season, there are large parking lots in town that are connected to the docks by shuttle). Parking costs $5 to $20 per day, depending on the season.

BUS

Hyannis Transportation Center (HTC; 📞 800-352-7155; www.capecodrta.org; 215 Iyannough Rd/MA 28) is Cape Cod's bus transportation hub. Frequent buses connect Hyannis with Boston (including Logan airport), or run further out to Provincetown (calling at Cape towns en route). Heading west, there are connections from Boston to Providence and New York City.

Sample one-way fares from Hyannis:

Boston ($21, 1¾ hours)
Logan airport ($27, two hours)
Provincetown ($12, 80 minutes)

Find schedules and fares at Plymouth & Brockton (p160) and Peter Pan (www.peterpanbus.com).

TRAIN
The **Cape Flyer** (☑ 508-775-8504; www.capeflyer.com; one-way tickets $5-22; ☺ late May-Aug) is a weekend train service operating from Memorial Day to Labor Day (late May to mid-October), connecting Boston's South Station with Hyannis. It operates on Friday evenings, Saturday and Sunday. From Boston to Hyannis takes about 2½ hours (one way/round trip $22/40).

ℹ Getting Around

At summer's peak, the Hyannis Trolley (www.capecodrta.org/hyannis-trolley.htm) provides shuttle service from the Hyannis Transportation Center to Main St, the **Ocean St docks** (220 Ocean St) and the Steamship Authority ferry docks. It can be flagged down on its route (wherever it's safe to do so).

Yarmouth

☑ 508, 774 / POP 23,300

There are two Yarmouths, and the experience you have depends on what part of town you find yourself in. The north side of town, along MA 6A, called Yarmouth Port, is green and genteel, with shady trees, antique shops and gracious old homes. The second Yarmouth, to the south, where MA 28 crosses the villages of West Yarmouth and South Yarmouth, is a flat world of mini-golf, strip malls and endless motels. Both have their charms, depending on what kind of vacation you're looking for.

◉ Sights

★ **Captains' Mile**   HISTORIC BUILDING
(http://www.hsoy.org/thecaptainsmile-1-1-1; along MA 6A, Yarmouth Port) Nearly 50 historic sea captains' homes are lined up along MA 6A (the Old King's Hwy) in Yarmouth Port, on a 1.5-mile stretch known as the Captains' Mile. Most of them are family homes these days (or genteel B&Bs), so you'll be doing much

of your viewing from the sidewalk. You can download a walking tour brochure from the website of the Historical Society of Old Yarmouth (HSOY), which admirably outlines the history of many of the houses.

Whydah
Pirate Museum   MUSEUM
(☑ 508-534-9571; www.discoverpirates.com; 674 MA 28, West Yarmouth; adult/youth 5-17yr/child 4yr & under $18.95/14.95/free; ☺ 10am-5pm Apr-Nov, only Wed-Sun Dec, only Sat & Sun Mar; 👪) Of the more than 3000 shipwrecks off the Cape's coast, the *Whydah* is one of the best documented and is the subject of this family-friendly museum. Captained by 'Black Sam' Bellamy, the *Whydah* sank in 1717 and to this day remains the only authenticated pirate ship ever salvaged. A local expedition recovered more than 100,000 items of booty – coins, jewelry, weapons – and some of these are on display here. There's other general pirate info as well.

Gray's Beach   BEACH
(Center St, Yarmouth Port) Gray's Beach, also known as Bass Hole, is no prize for swimming, but a terrific 0.25-mile-long boardwalk extends over a tidal marsh and creek, offering a unique vantage for viewing all sorts of sea life. It's also a fine spot for picnics and sunsets, and the parking is free. To get there, take Center St off MA 6A, just west of the playground in the center of the village.

Seagull Beach   BEACH
(Seagull Rd, West Yarmouth) Long and wide Seagull Beach, off South Sea Ave from MA 28, is the town's best south-side beach. The scenic approach to the beach runs alongside a tidal river that provides a habitat for osprey and shorebirds; bring your binoculars. Facilities include a bathhouse and a snack bar. Parking costs $15 in summer.

Edward Gorey House   MUSEUM
(☑ 508-362-3909; www.edwardgoreyhouse.org; 8 Strawberry Lane, Yarmouth Port; adult/child $8/2; ☺ 11am-4pm Thu-Sat, noon-4pm Sun mid-Apr–Jun, 11am-4pm Wed-Sat, noon-4pm Sun Jul-early Oct, 11am-4pm Fri & Sat, noon-4pm Sun mid-Oct–Dec) Near the post office on MA 6A sits the former home of the brilliant and somewhat twisted author and graphic artist Edward Gorey. He illustrated the books of Lewis Carroll, HG Wells and John Updike but is most widely recognized for his offbeat pen-and-ink

animations used in the opening of the PBS *Mystery!* series. The museum honors Gorey, the artist and the person, with exhibits of fabulous works from his archives, plus details of his devotion to animal welfare.

🛏 Sleeping & Eating

Village Inn   B&B $$
(☑508-362-3182; www.thevillageinncapecod.com; 92 MA 6A, Yarmouth Port; r $195-345; ❄☎) Antique charm and modern comforts pair well at this relaxed B&B occupying a 200-year-old house that's on the National Register of Historic Places. Set on a 1-acre lot, the inn provides lots of common space and eight guest rooms of varying sizes (including configurations for families). There's a two- or three-night minimum stay during summer's peak.

Jack's Outback   DINER $
(☑508-362-6690; 161 Main St, Yarmouth Port; mains $10-13; ⊙6:30am-2pm Mon-Sat, to 1pm Sun) People rave about the breakfast at this unpretentious restaurant and bakery off Main St in Yarmouth Port. Even Rachael Ray called it out as one of her favorite budget spots on the Cape. Cash only.

Inaho   JAPANESE $$$
(☑508-362-5522; 157 MA 6A, Yarmouth Port; mains $16-35; ⊙5-10pm Tue-Sat) Beloved of locals, this serene year-round restaurant has an impeccable pedigree for putting seafood to great use. Sushi and sashimi are fresh and delicate, but teriyaki and tempura are also first-class. Reservations recommended.

ℹ Information

Yarmouth Chamber of Commerce (☑508-778-1008; www.yarmouthcapecod.com; 424 MA 28, West Yarmouth; ⊙9am-5pm Mon-Fri, plus 10am-3pm Sat & Sun May-Oct) You can find plenty of information at this large office right on MA 28.

ℹ Getting There & Away

Yarmouth town sprawls across three villages: Yarmouth Port on Cape Cod Bay (accessed via MA 6A) and West Yarmouth and South Yarmouth on the Cape's south side (accessed by MA 28). The most direct link between north and south is via Station Ave/Union St.

Dennis
☑508 / POP 14,000

Like neighboring Yarmouth, Dennis has a distinctly different character from north to south. Heavily trafficked MA 28, which cuts through the villages of West Dennis and Dennisport on the south side of town, is lined with motels, casual eateries and mini-golf. There are some scenic river-outlet areas for water sports like kayaking, too. The classier north side, the village of Dennis, runs along MA 6A, with handsome old sea captains' homes living second lives as inns, galleries and antique shops.

⊙ Sights & Activities

Chapin Memorial Beach   BEACH
(Chapin Beach Rd; 🅿) Families will love the gently sloping waters at this dune-backed beach. Not only is it ideal for wading, but all sorts of tiny sea creatures can be explored

---

CAPE COD RAIL TRAIL

The mother of all Cape bicycle trails, the **Cape Cod Rail Trail** (CCRT; www.mass.gov/locations/cape-cod-rail-trail) runs 22 glorious paved miles through forest, past cranberry bogs and along sandy ponds ideal for a dip. This rural route, formerly used as a railroad line, is one of the finest bike trails in all of New England.

The path begins in Dennis on MA 134 and continues through Nickerson State Park (p144) in Brewster, into Orleans and across the Cape Cod National Seashore (p150), all the way to South Wellfleet.

There's a hefty dose of Ye Olde Cape Cod scenery en route and you'll have opportunities to detour into villages for lunch or sightseeing. If you have only enough time to do part of the trail, begin at Nickerson State Park and head for the National Seashore – the landscape is unbeatable.

Bicycle rentals are available at the trailheads in Dennis and Wellfleet and opposite the National Seashore's visitor center in Eastham. There's car parking at all four sites (free except for a $10 charge at Nickerson).

in the tide pools. At low tide, you can walk way out onto the sandy tidal flats – it takes a hike just to reach water up to your knees. This mile-long beach is also perfect for sunsets and walks under the light of the moon.

West Dennis Beach BEACH
(Lighthouse Rd, off MA 28, West Dennis) Extending one gorgeous mile along Nantucket Sound, this is the south side's mecca for swimmers, windsurfers and kiteboarders. It's a good bet for finding a parking space on even the sunniest of days, as the parking lot ($20 to $25) extends the full length of the beach, with room for 1000 cars.

Scargo Tower TOWER
(Scargo Hill Rd; ◷6am-10pm) FREE Built in 1902 on the highest spot in the area – 120ft above sea level – this 38-step, stone tower rising above Scargo Lake gives you grand views of Cape Cod Bay. On clear days you can see all the way to Sandwich and across to Provincetown. To get here, take MA 6A to Scargo Hill Rd.

Cape Cod Waterways KAYAKING
(☑508-398-0080; www.capecodwaterways.org; 16 Main St/MA 28, Dennisport; kayak rental per 90min/1 day $20/59; ◷May–mid-Oct; ▦) Right on the scenic Swan Pond River (close to MA 134), this outfitter can set you up for a paddle: kayaks, canoes, stand up paddle surfboards and electric-powered paddleboats (perfect for families with small kids) are available for hire. Rates are based on 90 minutes, the general amount of time it takes for a leisurely round-trip paddle from the boathouse.

🛏 Sleeping & Eating

★**Isaiah Hall Inn** B&B $$
(☑508-385-9928; www.isaiahhallinn.com; 152 Whig St; r $165-300; ▦▦) Occupying an 1857 farmhouse, this year-round country-style inn offers homey comforts in a quiet yet central neighborhood. The house has sloping wood floors, canopied beds and a 12ft-long breakfast table ideal for convivial chatter with fellow guests. Prices reflect the season, room size and whether you opt for extras, like balconies or fireplaces. It's just behind the Cape Playhouse area.

Scargo Manor B&B $$
(☑508-385-5534; www.scargomanor.com; 909 Main St/MA 6A; r $195-310; ▦▦) The sea captain who built this grand house in 1895 scored a prime locale on Scargo Lake, and

you're free to paddle off in the owner's canoe or kayaks whenever the mood strikes. For places you can't paddle to, you can pedal to, using the inn's loaner bikes. The antiques-laden house has seven rooms, each with its own character.

Captain Frosty's Fish & Chips SEAFOOD $
(☑508-385-8548; www.captainfrosty.com; 219 MA 6A; mains $9-21; ◷11am-8pm mid-Apr–May & Sep–mid-Oct, to 9pm Jun-Aug) Don't be misled by the 1950s ice-cream shack appearance: this simple seafood takeout joint does it right. Forget frozen food – there's none in this kitchen. Order fish and chips and you'll be munching on cod caught in nearby Chatham. And yes, there's still a dairy bar (soft-serve ice cream a specialty).

★**Sesuit Harbor Cafe** SEAFOOD $$
(☑508-385-6134; www.sesuit-harbor-cafe.com; 357 Sesuit Neck Rd; mains $13-31; ◷7am-2:30pm mid-Apr–mid-Oct, to 8:30pm mid-May–mid-Sep) This is the Cape Cod you won't find on the highway: an idyllic shack tucked into Sesuit Harbor serving freshly caught seafood at picnic tables smack on the water. The scrumptious lobster rolls, like everything else, taste like they just crawled onto your plate. BYOB; cash only. Take Bridge St north off MA 6A.

🍷 Drinking & Entertainment

Harvest Gallery Wine Bar WINE BAR
(☑508-385-2444; www.harvestgallerywinebar.com; 776 Main St/MA 6A; ◷4pm-midnight Thu-Sun) Tip your glass with class at this combo wine bar and art gallery behind the Dennis village post office. There's live music several nights weekly (jazz, blues, folk etc), and a tempting grazing menu of tapas plates, oysters and pizza.

★**Cape Cinema** CINEMA
(☑508-385-2503; www.capecinema.com; 35 Hope Lane, off MA 6A; tickets adult/child $9.50/6) On the grounds of the Cape Playhouse, this vintage movie theater shows foreign and independent films. It's a true art house: the entire ceiling is covered in an art-deco mural of the heavens painted by American realist painter Rockwell Kent.

Cape Playhouse THEATER
(☑box office 508-385-3911; www.capeplayhouse.com; 820 Main St/MA 6A; tickets $19-79; ◷early Jun-early Sep; ▦) The Cape Playhouse is the oldest operating professional summer theater (since 1927) in the US. Bette Davis

once worked here as an usher, and some of the biggest names in showbiz have appeared on its stage. It hosts a different production every two weeks – everything from *Hairspray* to Hitchcock – and also has a children's theater, with classics, puppetry and more.

ⓘ Information

Dennis Chamber of Commerce (☑ 508-398-3568; www.dennischamber.com; 242 Swan River Rd, West Dennis; ⊙ 10am-4pm Mon-Fri, to 2pm Sat late May–mid-Oct, 10am-4pm Mon-Fri late Oct–mid-May) A helpful office with plenty of brochures and recommendations for local businesses.

ⓘ Getting There & Away

Dennis town sprawls across five villages: the main Dennis village is on Cape Cod Bay (accessed via MA 6A), bordered by East Dennis and South Dennis. On the Cape's south side (accessed by MA 28) are West Dennis and Dennisport. The most direct link between north and south is via MA 134.

Brewster
☑ 508 / POP 9900

Woodsy Brewster, on the Cape's bay side, makes a good base for outdoorsy types. The Cape Cod Rail Trail cuts clear across town, and there's first-rate camping and water activities. Brewster also has fine restaurants, out of proportion to the town's small size, as well as a bevy of antique stores and galleries. Everything of interest is on or just off MA 6A (also called Main St), which runs the length of the town.

◉ Sights

Nickerson State Park STATE PARK
(☑ 508-896-3491; www.mass.gov/dcr; 3488 MA 6A; parking $15; ⊙ dawn-dusk; 🐾) This 2000-acre oasis has eight freshwater ponds with sandy beaches ideal for swimming and boating, as well as miles of cycling and walking trails. Bring along a fishing pole to catch your own trout dinner or just pack a lunch and enjoy the picnic facilities; book ahead to camp.

Cape Cod Museum of Natural History MUSEUM
(☑ 508-896-3867; www.ccmnh.org; 869 MA 6A; adult/child $15/6; ⊙ 9:30am-4pm Jun-Aug, 11am-3pm Sep, shorter hours Oct-May; 🐾) This family-friendly museum offers exhibits on the Cape's flora and fauna, including an aquarium and a butterfly house. It has a fine **boardwalk trail** across a salt marsh to a remote beach with tide pools. The museum has a calendar rich with naturalist-led walks, talks and kids' programs.

Brewster Store HISTORIC BUILDING
(☑ 508-896-3744; www.brewsterstore.com; 1935 Main St/MA 6A; ⊙ 6am-10pm Jun-Sep, 7am-5pm Mon-Fri, 6am-4pm Sat, to 2pm Sun Oct-May) The Brewster Store, in the heart of town, is a sight in itself. The old-fashioned country store opened in 1866, and it's barely changed since: penny candy is still sold alongside the local newspaper. Don't miss the half-hidden stairs that lead to the 2nd floor, where you'll discover a stash of museum-quality memorabilia as old as the building.

Brewster Historical Society Museum MUSEUM
(☑ 508-896-9521; www.brewsterhistoricalsociety. org; 739 Lower Rd; $5; ⊙ 1-4pm Sat late May–mid-Oct, also 1-4pm Thu & Fri & 4-7pm Wed late Jun-Aug) FREE Brewster's active historical society has moved its impressive collection of local artifacts to the restored 1799 Captain Elijah Cobb House. Visit to see a treasure trove of trinkets brought back by sea captains, colonial tools and other bits of Brewster's centuries-old history.

🛏 Sleeping

★ Nickerson State Park Campground CAMPGROUND $
(☑ info 508 896-3491, reservations 877-422-6762; www.reserveamerica.com; 3488 MA 6A; tent & RV sites $35, yurts $60-70; ⊙ May–mid-Oct; 🐾) Head here for Cape Cod's best camping, with more than 400 wooded campsites and a handful of yurts set in pond- and trail-filled grounds. It often fills up, so reserve your spot early. You can make reservations up to six months in advance.

★ Old Sea Pines Inn B&B $$
(☑ 508-896-6114; www.oldseapinesinn.com; 2553 Main St/MA 6A; r $130-170, ste $210-425; @ 🖳) Staying here is a bit like staying at Grandma's house: antique fittings, sleigh beds and sepia photographs on the bureau. This former girls' boarding school dating from 1840 has 24 rooms: some small; others commodious, with fireplace; some suited to families. Mosey out to the rocking chairs on the porch and soak up the yesteryear atmosphere.

ANTIQUES & AMERICANA ON HWY 6A

Nearly anything you can imagine – from nautical antiques to art-deco kitsch – can be found on the tightly packed shelves of Cape Cod's 100-plus antique shops. The key to antiquing on the Cape is to follow MA 6A, also known as the **Old King's Highway**. The oldest continuous stretch of historic district in the USA, the road is lined with old sea-captains' homes, many of which have been converted to quality antique shops. You'll find the best hunting on the section between Barnstable and Brewster.

Then there are the auctions. The high roller on the scene, **Eldred's** (☑ 508-385-3116; www.eldreds.com; 1483 MA 6A, East Dennis; ⊗ 8:30am-5pm Mon-Fri Apr-Oct, to 4:30pm Nov-Mar), specializes in fine arts and appraised antiques; five-figure bids here barely raise an eyebrow. More homespun is the **Sandwich Auction House** (☑ 508-888-1926; www.sandwichauction.com; 15 Tupper Rd), which handles estate sales where you might find anything from antique Sandwich glass to old Elvis albums.

Of course, if you just want to spend an afternoon picking through piles of treasure, head to **Antiques by the Bay** (☑ 774-323-3962; 1424 Main St/MA 6; ⊗ 11am-5pm daily May-Oct, Sat & Sun only rest of year) in Brewster, a perfectly cluttered shop spread out over a charming old house.

🍴 Eating & Drinking

Cobie's　　　　　　　　SEAFOOD $$
(☑ 508-896-7021; www.cobies.com; 3260 Main St/MA 6A; mains $7-24; ⊗ 11:30am-7:30pm May–mid-Oct, to 9pm Jun-Aug; 🖑) Just off the Cape Cod Rail Trail, this bustling roadside clam shack dishes out fried seafood that you can crunch and munch at outdoor picnic tables, as well as non-fishy fare like burgers and hot panini sandwiches. Great ice cream.

★ Brewster Fish House　　　SEAFOOD $$$
(☑ 508-896-7867; www.brewsterfishhouse.com; 2208 Main St/MA 6A; mains $28-38; ⊗ 11:30am-3pm & 5-9:30pm) It's not an eye-catcher from the outside, but it's heaven inside for seafood lovers. Start with the chunky lobster bisque. From there it's safe to cast your net in any direction; dishes are fresh and creative. Just a dozen tables, and no reservations, so try lunch (mains $17 to $19) or an early dinner to avoid long waits.

Snowy Owl　　　　　　　　COFFEE
(☑ 774-323-0605; www.socoffee.co; 483 Main St/MA 6A; ⊗ 6:30am-5pm Mon-Fri, from 7:30am Sat & Sun) Things are extra cozy at the Snowy Owl, just off of Main St in Brewster proper. The interior of this coffee shop with an on-site roaster is all warm woods and pleasant vibes. Head to the back, where you'll find a herbalist shop.

ℹ️ Information

Brewster Chamber of Commerce (☑ 508-896-3500; www.brewster-capecod.org; 2198 Main St/MA 6A; ⊗ 9am-3pm Jun-early Sep, to 1pm Tue-Fri mid-Sep–May) This office inside Brewster Town Hall has tourist information and sells beach parking permits in summer.

ℹ️ Getting There & Away

Brewster stretches along Cape Cod Bay between Dennis and Orleans. Access is best via MA 6A. From the Cape's south, take MA 124 or MA 137 from Harwich.

Harwich

☑ 508, 774 / POP 12,200

Harwich occasionally feels overshadowed by Chatham, its more well-known neighbor to the east, but this quiet hamlet is well worth visiting in its own right. It has good beaches, a few killer restaurants and one of the Cape's most photographed spots – yacht-packed Wychmere Harbor.

Most of what you'll need is along MA 28, which runs through the south side of town.

Harwich has fine beaches, although many of them restrict parking to residents. But fret not: to get to one of the prettiest, park your car for free at the municipal lot behind the information center and then walk five minutes to the end of Sea St, which terminates at glistening Sea St Beach.

🛏️ Sleeping & Eating

★ Wequassett Resort　　　RESORT $$$
(☑ 508-432-5400; www.wequassett.com; 2173 MA 28, East Harwich; r with/without breakfast for 2 from $545/495; ❄️ @ 🛜 🏊) The Cape's priciest, most prestigious lodging offers pretty much anything you could ask of a full-service, five-star resort: flower-filled gardens, a private

golf course, fine dining and a full menu of watery activities. On the grounds you'll be soothed with gorgeous views of Pleasant Bay, north of Chatham. The in-room Jacuzzis and fireplaces spell romance; families also welcome (kids' club on-site).

Brax Landing   SEAFOOD $$
(☑508-432-5515; www.braxrestaurant.com; 705 MA 28, Harwich Port; mains $10-23; ⊙11:30am-10pm Mon-Sat, from 10am Sun) Head to this casual harborside gem for water-view dining and fresh seafood at honest prices. The menu's broad, but stick with the local catch, like the Chatham scrod or the hefty lobster rolls. Grab yourself a seat on the outdoor deck overlooking Saquatucket Harbor for the best drink-with-a-view in town.

★Buca's Tuscan Roadhouse   TUSCAN $$$
(☑508-432-6900; www.bucasroadhouse.com; 4 Depot Rd; mains $24-36; ⊙5-10pm Mon-Sat, to 9pm Sun) You'll need a reservation (or to be pals with Martin at the front) most nights of the week at this beloved Italian restaurant. The basic central Italian dishes on the menu are prepared with modern flair, but don't worry: they still have hearty flavors and generous portions.

ⓘ Information

Harwich Information Center (☑508-432-1600; www.harwichcc.com; cnr 1 Schoolhouse Rd & MA 28, Harwich Port; ⊙9am-5pm Mon-Fri, 10am-4pm Sat, 10am-2pm Sun Jun-early Sep, shorter hours rest of year)

ⓘ Getting There & Away

Freedom Cruise Line (☑508-432-8999; www.nantucketislandferry.com; 702 MA 28 at Saquatucket Harbor, Harwich Port; round trip adult/child $76/51; ⊙late May-late Sep) Operates a summer passenger ferry to Nantucket from Saquatucket Harbor in Harwich Port. It's conveniently scheduled for day-tripping, and offers free parking (for day-trippers only). Services operate one to three times daily in each direction (80 minutes), from late May to late September. Bookings advised.

Chatham

☑508 / POP 6170

The patriarch of Cape Cod towns, Chatham has a genteel reserve that is evident along its shady Main St: the shops are upscale and the lodgings tastefully swank. That said, there's something for everyone here – families flock

to town for seal-watching and birders migrate to the wildlife refuge. And then there are all those beaches. Sitting at the 'elbow' of the Cape, Chatham has an amazing 60 miles of shoreline along the ocean, the sound and countless coves and inlets.

MA 28 leads right to Main St, where the lion's share of shops and restaurants are lined up. Chatham is a town made for strolling. You'll find free parking along Main St and in the parking lot behind the Chatham Squire restaurant (but you'll have to fight for a space in summer).

⊙ Sights

Chatham Shark Center   MUSEUM
(☑508-348-5901; www.atlanticwhiteshark.org; 235 Orleans Rd, North Chatham; $5; ⊙10am-4pm Fri, Sat & Mon, from 11am Sun Jun, 10am-4pm Mon-Sat, from 11am Sun Jul & Aug, 10am-4pm Sat, from 11am Sun Sep-early Oct) Stop here for the lowdown on one of the Cape's most intriguing summer residents: the great white shark. Interactive exhibits and videos aimed at kids and adults attempt to demystify the animal given a good deal of bad PR in the Cape Cod–set movie, *Jaws*. It's under the auspices of the Atlantic White Shark Conservancy (motto: 'Awareness inspires conservation').

Lighthouse Beach   BEACH
(Main St) Directly below Chatham Light is Lighthouse Beach, an endless expanse of sea and sandbars that offers some of the finest beach strolling on Cape Cod. Swimming isn't recommended – there are strong currents and no lifeguards. Plus, as signs warn, great white sharks live in these waters.

Monomoy National
Wildlife Refuge   WILDLIFE RESERVE
(☑508-945-0594; www.fws.gov/refuge/monomoy; 30 Wikis Way; ⊙sunrise-sunset) Take Morris Island Rd beyond the Chatham lighthouse to reach this 7600-acre wildlife refuge, spreading from Morris Island to encompass the shifting sands of the uninhabited North Monomoy and South Monomoy barrier islands. The refuge is a haven for shorebirds and seabirds (nearly 300 species nest here; 10 times that number pass through on migrations). It's one of the most important ornithological stops on the Atlantic seaboard. There's a visitor center, a nature trail and access to the Morris Island shore.

North and South Monomoy Islands are accessible only by boat. **Monomoy Island Ferry** (☑508-237-0420; www.monomoyisland

ferry.com; 80 Bridge St, Stage Harbor Marine; seal-watching tour adult/child $35/30; ⊙May-Oct) offers a wildlife boat tour.

Chatham Marconi Maritime Center   MUSEUM

(☑508-945-8889; www.chathammarconi.org; 847 Orleans Rd/MA 28, North Chatham; adult/child $10/free; ⊙10:30am-4:30pm Tue-Sat, 1-4pm Sun Jun-Aug, also 10:30am-4:30pm Mon late Jul-early Aug) Communication in all its guises is the focus at this museum dedicated to the history of WCC, a short-wave radio station that operated for many years in Chatham. WCC was the busiest coast station in the public ship-to-shore radio service for most of the 20th century; during WWII it had the vital role of intercepting coded signals from German U-boats. An Enigma machine is part of a cool exhibit on coding and encryption.

Chatham Light   LIGHTHOUSE

(37 Main St/Shore Rd; ⊙1-3:30pm Wed May-Oct) FREE For dramatic vistas of sand and sea, head to the lighthouse viewing area on Shore Rd. The landmark lighthouse dates to 1878; its light is visible 15 miles out to sea. No reservations are taken for the tours, so just show up. Note that in May, June, September and October, the tours take place on the first and third Wednesdays of the month, while in July and August they happen every Wednesday.

Chatham Railroad Museum   MUSEUM

(☑508-945-5100; www.chathamrailroadmuseum. com; 153 Depot Rd; by donation; ⊙10am-4pm Tue-Sat mid-Jun–mid-Sep; 🚻) Train buffs won't want to miss the 1910 caboose and assorted memorabilia at Chatham's original 1887 railroad depot. The Victorian building is an architectural treasure worth a visit in itself.

🛏 Sleeping

Chatham Guest Rooms   APARTMENT $$

(☑508-945-1660; www.chathamguestrooms.com; 1409 Main St/MA 28; ste $125-175; ❄🖥) 🐾 A top-shelf budget option in pricey Chatham. Here, above the Maps of Antiquity store, three suites are available at a bargain price. The Garden Suite and Main Suite can each sleep four: the Main Suite has a full kitchen and laundry facilities; the Garden Suite, a private porch. The owners are fonts of information, with commendable environmental policies.

CHATHAM FISH PIER

In the mid- to late afternoon, head to **Chatham Fish Pier** (cnr Shore Rd & Barcliff Ave), 1 mile north of Chatham Light, to watch the fishing fleet unload its daily catch. This is a prime time to see seals, which swim around the boats as the haul is brought in. The pier is well worth a visit any day, but if you're lucky enough to be there on a summer weekend, you'll likely find seasoned fishers hanging around to regale visitors and locals alike with real-deal fish stories.

Bow Roof House   B&B $$

(☑508-945-1346; www.facebook.com/TheBow RoofHouse; 59 Queen Anne Rd; r $161; 🖥) It's hard to find places like this anymore. This homey, six-room, c 1780 house is delightfully old-fashioned in price and offerings, and within easy walking distance of the town center and Oyster Pond Beach. Except for a few modern-day conveniences, like the added private bathrooms, the house looks nearly the same as it did in colonial times.

Chatham Bars Inn   RESORT $$$

(☑508-945-0096; www.chathambarsinn.com; 297 Shore Rd; r from $530; 🅿❄🖥🐾🏊) The grand dame of Cape lodging, century-old Chatham Bars sprawls over 25 seaside acres. A campus of cottages and buildings houses 217 sophisticated rooms and suites and loads of high-end trimmings: spa, restaurants, fitness center, children's programs, a boat to shuttle guests to the National Seashore, and a pool area directly on the private beach. Minimum stays in peak summer.

🍴 Eating

Marion's Pie Shop   BAKERY $

(☑508-432-9439; www.marionspieshopof chatham.com; 2022 Main St/MA 28; small/large pies from $9/15; ⊙8am-6pm late May-Aug, to 5pm rest of year, closed late Dec–mid-Feb) It's all about pie here, both sweet (wild blueberry, lemon meringue, strawberry peach, all made with fresh fruit) and savory (chicken, beef steak, clam). They're available in 6in and 9in sizes. Breakfast muffins and cinnamon nut rolls are huge and delicious as well.

Red Nun Bar & Grill
BURGERS $

(☑508-348-0469; www.rednun.com; 746 Main St; sandwiches & burgers $10-14; ☺11:30am-1am May-Sep, from 4:30pm Mon-Thu, from 11:30am Fri & Sat, from noon Sun Oct-Apr) If burgers are your thing, step into this unassuming joint and order the Nun Burger. It starts with a half-pound of Angus beef placed in an oversize English muffin, which is then piled with cheddar, bacon, sauteed onions and mushrooms. Burgers are the headline act, but beer-friendly dishes like nachos and wings play a fine supporting role.

★Chatham Pier Fish Market
SEAFOOD $$

(☑508-945-3474; www.chathampierfishmarket. com; 45 Barcliff Ave; mains $12-24; ☺10am-7pm mid-May–mid-Nov) If you like it fresh and local, this salt-sprayed fish shack with its own sushi chef and day-boats is for you. The chowder's incredible, the fish so fresh it was swimming earlier in the day. It's all takeout, but there are shady picnic tables where you can watch fishers unloading their catch and seals frolicking as you savor dinner.

Bluefins
SUSHI $$

(☑508-348-1573; www.bluefinschatham.com; 513 Main St; mains $13-31; ☺5-10pm Mon-Thu, from 11:30am Fri-Sun) You won't find a basic California roll on the menu at Bluefins. This ultra-chic spot on Chatham's Main St specializes in unique rolls such as Surf & Turf, which has both shrimp tempura and grilled Kobe beef smothered in a trio of spicy sauces. It also has a menu of pan-Asian dishes and a great cocktail list.

Del Mar
AMERICAN $$

(☑508-945-9988; www.delmarbistro.com; 907 Main St; mains $24-32; ☺5-9:30pm Jun-Sep, to 9pm Tue-Sat Oct-May) The creative menu at this stylish bistro swings from thin-crust fig-and-prosciutto pizza to maple-glazed duck and beyond. Global influences enhance fine local produce: Portuguese steamed littlenecks, seafood gumbo, wood-fired Wellfleet Bay scallops. The bar's a good place for solo diners, or simply for a cocktail.

🍷 Drinking & Entertainment

Chatham Bars Inn
COCKTAIL BAR

(☑508-945-0096; www.chathambarsinn.com; 297 Shore Rd; ☺11am-9pm mid-Jun–Aug) Drink in the seaside views from the veranda of this refined resort (built in 1914), or join the fun at the Beach House, where cocktails, clambakes and cookouts rock summer evenings.

Chatham Orpheum
CINEMA

(☑508-945-4900; www.chathamorpheum.org; 637 Main St; tickets adult/child $11/8) A beautifully restored, two-screen movie house dating from 1916. There's a cool cafe inside.

❶ Information

Bassett House Visitor Center (☑508-945-5199; www.chathaminfo.com; 2377 Main St/ MA 28; ☺10am-2pm Wed-Sat Apr-Jun, to 5pm Mon-Sat Jul-Aug, to 2pm Mon-Sat Sep-Oct) For local info, stop at the chamber of commerce's Bassett House Visitor Center as you drive into town.

❶ Getting There & Away

Chatham sits at the 'elbow' of the Cape. MA 28 is the main route through it; it becomes Main St in the downtown area. MA 137 connects Chatham with US 6.

Orleans

☑508 / POP 5820

Those in the know will tell you that Orleans is more than the place where MA 6A and MA 28 converge and US 6 continues onward as the sole road to Provincetown. A few popular beaches are accessed from the otherwise sleepy town, including the exhilarating surfer's paradise of Nauset Beach. There's also the untouched Nauset Marsh, offering a unique kayaking experience through one of the Cape's richest ecosystems. Meanwhile, the small downtown contains some choice restaurants and cute shops.

◉ Sights

Skaket Beach
BEACH

(Skaket Beach Rd; 🅿) On the bay side of town, calm Skaket Beach is a magnet for families – kids love wading in the shallow waters to dig for hermit crabs. Its generous sands triple in size when the tide goes out – at low tide you can walk the flats all the way to Brewster and back. Sunsets are often photo-worthy.

Nauset Beach
BEACH

(Beach Rd, East Orleans) Dune-backed and gloriously wide and sandy, this wild barrier beach extends for miles along the open Atlantic. Nauset is one of the Cape's best beaches for surfing, bodysurfing, long walks, ace sunrises and just plain partying. You'll find a good clam shack and full facilities. Swing by on a Monday night in July and August for a rocking sunset concert.

Daily parking costs $20 in summer (late May to mid-September); tickets can be purchased at the parking lot gate.

Rock Harbor
WATERFRONT

(Rock Harbor Rd) A favorite spot for sunset-watchers, this scenic inlet on the bay has docks and a small fishing fleet, plus a few summertime charter boats offering excursions. There's a small sandy beach, and free parking that can fill fast on a sunny day. There are some highly regarded lobster shacks in the immediate neighborhood.

French Cable Station Museum
MUSEUM

(📞 508-240-1735; www.frenchcablestationmuseum.org; 41 S Orleans Rd/MA 28; ⏰ 1-4pm Fri-Sun Jun-Sep) FREE The first cable connection between Europe and the US was established in 1879 by the French Telegraph Company on a windswept bluff in Eastham. When conditions there proved inhospitable, the station was moved to Orleans in 1891, and until the mid-20th century the French Cable Station transmitted communications via a 3000-mile-long cable between Orleans and Brest, France. Charles Lindbergh's arrival in Paris was among the messages relayed. This museum contains all the original equipment; staff help explain everything.

🛏 Sleeping & Eating

Cove Motel
MOTEL $$

(📞 508-255-1203; www.thecoveorleans.com; 13 S Orleans Rd/MA 28; r $174-244; 🐾❄️) A good choice for those who want to be on the water but within strolling distance of the town center. Rooms are well equipped, but many are built motel-style around a parking lot. Others have a more Cape Cod-cottage look, set back overlooking a cove. For the best water views, request rooms 20 to 25.

Ship's Knees Inn
B&B $$

(📞 508-255-1312; www.shipskneesinn.com; 186 Beach Rd, East Orleans; r $225-350; ⏰ Apr-Dec; 🐾❄️🐾) This place packs in excellent amenities and appealing period decor. Best of all, it's just a quarter-mile walk to Nauset Beach. The 17 rooms in this old sea captain's home have nautical themes. Sea captains were accustomed to close quarters: some of the rooms are tight on elbow room, others are generous suites.

Lobster Claw
SEAFOOD $$

(📞 508-255-1800; www.lobsterclaw.com; 42 MA 6A/Cranberry Hwy; mains $12-30; ⏰ 11:30am-9pm Apr-mid-Oct; 🍴) Super family-friendly and decidedly retro, the Lobster Claw has a cute nautical interior and a menu of steamed clams, mussels and littlenecks, plus lobster every which way. One warning: kids may just want to take home a plush lobster toy from the gift shop.

ℹ Information

Orleans Chamber of Commerce (📞 508-255-7203; https://orleanscapecod.org; 44 Main St; ⏰ 9am-4pm Mon-Fri) Dispenses information from its downtown location.

ℹ Getting There & Away

Orleans is where MA 6A and MA 28 converge; US 6 continues as the only road to Provincetown.

Eastham

📞 508, 774 / POP 4900

Eastham is not only the southern entrance to the Cape Cod National Seashore (p150), but it's also home to a handful of historic sites and some great hiking and viewpoints. Don't be fooled by the bland commercial development along US 6 – slip off the highway and you'll find an unspoiled world of beaches, marshes and trails.

👁 Sights

★ Salt Pond Visitor Center
MUSEUM

(📞 508-255-3421; www.nps.gov/caco; 50 Nauset Rd, cnr US 6; ⏰ 9am-4:30pm year-round) FREE The Salt Pond Visitor Center is the place to start exploring the National Seashore – and it has a great view to boot. Here you'll find exhibits and short films on the Cape's ecology, history and ever-changing landscape. Helpful staff can provide maps to the park's trails, both **hiking** and **cycling**, some of which begin right at the center. Ask about the daily schedule of ranger-guided walks, talks, open houses at historic buildings, canoe trips and more (reservations often required).

Coast Guard Beach
BEACH

(Ocean View Dr) All roads lead to the National Seashore's Coast Guard Beach. The main road from the Salt Pond Visitor Center deposits you here, as do cycling and hiking

CAPE COD NATIONAL SEASHORE

Extending some 40 miles around the curve of the Outer Cape, **Cape Cod National Seashore** (☑ 508-255-3421; www.nps.gov/caco; pedestrian/cyclist/motorcycle/car per day $3/3/10/20) encompasses the Atlantic shoreline from Orleans all the way to Provincetown. Under the auspices of the National Park Service, it's a treasure trove of unspoiled beaches, dunes, salt marshes, nature trails and forests. Thanks to the backing of President John F Kennedy, this vast area was set aside for preservation in the 1960s, just before a building boom hit the rest of his native Cape Cod.

Access to the park sights is easy: everything of interest is on or just off MA 6. The year-round Salt Pond Visitor Center (p149) in Eastham is the place to start. The Province Lands Visitor Center (p155) in Provincetown is smaller and open seasonally, but it has similar services to the Eastham center plus a fabulous ocean view.

Beach parking permits cost $20 per day or $60 per season and are valid at all National Seashore beaches, so you can use the same permit to spend the morning at one beach and the afternoon at another; pedestrians and cyclists pay $3, motorcyclists $10. The fees are collected only in summer – from late June through early September, when lifeguards are on duty – and on weekends and holidays from Memorial Day (late May) to the end of September. Outside these times, beach parking is free.

trails. And it's for good reason: this grand beach, backed by a classic coast guard station, is a stunner that attracts everyone from beachcombers to hard-core surfers. Bird-watchers also flock to Coast Guard Beach for the eagle-eye view of **Nauset Marsh**.

Nauset Light LIGHTHOUSE
(☑ 508-240-2612; www.nausetlight.org; Ocean View Dr; ⊙ tours 1-4pm Sun May-Oct, plus 4:30-7pm Tue & Wed Jun-Aug) FREE Nauset Light is a picturesque red-and-white lighthouse guarding the shoreline at the Nauset Light Beach. Look familiar? You may have seen it on all the Cape Cod potato-chip packets!

It's open to the public for free tours Sundays from May to October and on Tuesdays and Wednesdays in June through August.

Fort Hill VIEWPOINT
(Fort Hill Rd) Don't miss the commanding view of expansive Nauset Marsh from Fort Hill. It's a favorite place to be at dawn, but the view is memorable any time of the day. And bring your walking shoes for the 2-mile **Fort Hill Trail**. It leads down scenic Fort Hill toward the coast and then skirts inland to meander along raised boardwalks over a unique red-maple swamp. It's one of the nicest walks in the National Seashore, especially in fall.

First Encounter Beach BEACH
(Samoset Rd; 🚻) First Encounter Beach, where Samoset Rd meets Cape Cod Bay, is a fine place to watch the sunset. With its vast

tidal flats and kid-friendly, calm, shallow waters, it offers a night-and-day contrast to the National Seashore beaches on Eastham's wild Atlantic side. Parking costs $18 to $20 in summer.

And the name of the beach? It's the site of the first encounter between the Pilgrims and the local Native Americans, in 1620, prior to the Pilgrims settling in Plymouth.

Eastham Windmill LANDMARK
(☑ 508-255-1798; www.eastham-ma.gov/eastham-windmill; 2515 US 6; ⊙ 10am-5pm Mon-Sat, from 1pm Sun Jul & Aug) FREE Eastham's landmark windmill is the oldest structure in town, although it was actually built in Plymouth (MA) in 1680. It sits in a pretty park by the side of US 6. Parking on-site is very limited.

🛏 Sleeping

⭐ **Inn at the Oaks** B&B $$
(☑ 508-255-1886; www.innattheoaks.com; 3085 US 6; r $195-325; 🅿🐾📶❄) This inn has 13 antique-filled guest rooms, set in a converted sea captain's house from 1870. There's a room for every taste; the roomy suites in the carriage house are the pick. Expect a lot of stylishly relaxed charm: rockers on the wraparound porch, sprawling grounds and lots of common areas. It's not far from Salt Pond Visitor Center.

Eagle Wing Inn MOTEL $$
(☑ 508-240-5656; www.eaglewingmotel.com; 960 US 6; r $225-282; 🅿🐾📶❄) Spacious squeaky-clean rooms, comfy beds and quiet grounds

are the draw at this boutique motel geared for adults. Opt for one of the rooms with a rear deck and watch the rabbits raid the backyard flowers. There's even a free laundry and complimentary bikes for guests – handy for covering the 2 miles to the National Seashore.

✗ Eating

Arnold's Lobster & Clam Bar
SEAFOOD $$

(☑508-255-2575; www.arnoldsrestaurant.com; 3580 US 6; meals $5-25; ☺11:30am-8pm mid-May–mid-Oct; ⊕) Fried seafood is the staple (plus renowned onion rings); there's also salads, baked cod and steamed lobster on the menu. Everything is fresh, and at night this place adds on a raw bar, separating it from other counter-service seafood shacks along the highway. It's super family-oriented, with kids' dishes served on Frisbees. Also has a mini-golf course and an ice-cream stand.

Friendly Fisherman
SEAFOOD $$

(☑508-255-6770; www.friendlyfishermaneastham.com; 4580 MA 6; meals $10-21; ☺restaurant 11:30am-3pm mid-May–mid-Sep, to 9pm Sun-Thu, to 9:30pm Fri & Sat Jul & Aug, market 10am-6pm Mon-Sat, from noon Sun mid-May–mid-Sep; ⊕) This simple seafood spot, attached to a fish market, has outdoor picnic tables and serves the perfect lobster roll: huge, overflowing with sweet chunks of claw and tail meat, and with just enough mayo to hold it all together. The fried clams here are impressive, too. BYOB. Kids playground on-site.

ℹ Information

Eastham Visitor Information Booth (☑508-255-3444; www.easthamchamber.com; 1700 MA 6, cnr Governor Prence Rd; ☺9am-5pm late May–mid-Oct) This summertime information booth is on MA 6, just north of the Fort Hill turnoff. When it's closed, there are maps and guides available.

ℹ Getting There & Away

US 6 is the arterial through Eastham for cars; the Cape Cod Rail Trail (p142) is perfect for two-wheeled travel. A shuttle runs from Salt Pond Visitor Center to Coast Guard Beach in summer (it's free, but note that you must pay to access the National Seashore).

Wellfleet
☑508, 774 / POP 2740

Art galleries, primo surfing beaches and those famous Wellfleet oysters lure visitors to this seaside village. Actually, there's not much Wellfleet doesn't have, other than crowds. It's a delightful throwback to an earlier era, from its drive-in movie theater to its unspoiled town center, which has barely changed in appearance since the 1950s.

Most of Wellfleet east of US 6 is part of the Cape Cod National Seashore. To get to the town center, turn west off US 6 at either Main or School Sts.

☉ Sights & Activities

Marconi Beach
BEACH

(off US 6) Part of the Cape Cod National Seashore, Marconi is a narrow Atlantic beach backed by sea cliffs and undulating dunes. Facilities include changing rooms, restrooms and showers. It's named for famous Italian inventor Guglielmo Marconi, who sent the first transatlantic wireless message from a station nearby in 1903. Parking costs $20 in summer (the permit fee to access the National Seashore). The **Atlantic White Cedar Swamp Trail** is a 1.5-mile nature trail that's worth exploring.

Wellfleet Bay Wildlife Sanctuary
NATURE RESERVE

(☑508-349-2615; www.massaudubon.org; 291 US 6, South Wellfleet; adult/child $5/3; ☺trails 8am-dusk, nature center 8:30am-4:30pm late May-early Oct; ⊕) Birders flock to Mass Audubon's 940-acre sanctuary, where 5 miles of trails cross tidal creeks, salt marshes and beaches. The most popular is the **Goose Pond Trail** (1.5-mile round trip), which leads out to a salt marsh and offers abundant opportunities for spotting marine and birdlife. The sanctuary also offers guided walks and kayaking tours, seal cruises and summer kids' programs.

Little Capistrano Bike Shop
CYCLING

(☑508-349-2363; www.littlecapistranobikeshop. com; 1446 US 6, South Wellfleet; 24hr rental $30; ☺9am-4pm Jun-early Sep) The northern end of the Cape Cod Rail Trail is at Lecount Hollow Rd near its intersection with US 6. You can rent bikes in summer here, right near the trailhead, and pedal south (grab some goodies from nearby PB Boulangerie & Bistro for the journey). Kids' bikes and trailers available.

✷ Festivals & Events

Wellfleet OysterFest　　　FOOD & DRINK
(www.wellfleetoysterfest.org; ⊘mid-Oct) During the Wellfleet OysterFest, held on a weekend in mid-October, the entire town center becomes a food fair, with a beer garden, an oyster-shucking contest and, of course, belly-busters of the blessed bivalves. It's a wildly popular event and a great time to see Wellfleet at its most spirited.

🛏 Sleeping

Surfside Cottages　　　COTTAGE $$
(☑508-349-3959; www.surfsidecottages.com; Ocean View Dr) This agency oversees the rental of a community of cottages just back from Lecount Hollow Beach (and full marks to the website, which specifies how many *steps* each place is to the beach!). Cottages vary in capacity and aesthetic, from simple old-school beach shack to a more modern fit-out and furnishings. Prices reflect this; rentals are generally by the week.

Even'Tide Motel　　　MOTEL $$
(☑508-349-3410; www.eventidemotel.com; 650 US 6, South Wellfleet; r $149-280, cottages per week $1500-2900; ⊘May–mid-Oct; ✳ 🛜 🛋) This highly regarded motel, set back from the highway in a grove of pine trees, has an assortment of options: regular motel rooms, plus 10 diverse cottages that can each accommodate two to 10 people (week-long minimum in the summer). Pluses include a large, indoor heated pool and 5 acres of wooded grounds that harbor sports and picnic facilities.

★Wagner at Duck Creek　　　INN $$$
(☑508-942-8185; www.thewagneratduckcreek.com; 70 Main St; r $217-373; ✳ 🛜) Energetic owners have breathed new life into this iconic inn – no small undertaking, given it encompasses 27 rooms housed in three antique timber buildings spread over lovely grounds. The result is a boutique feel, with pretty, well-equipped rooms plus an on-site tavern, open year-round. Future plans think big: bike rental, kayaks for guest use, a pool and a spa.

🍴 Eating

★PB Boulangerie & Bistro　　　BAKERY $
(☑508-349-1600; www.pbboulangeriebistro.com; 15 Lecount Hollow Rd, South Wellfleet; pastries $3-5; ⊘bakery 7am-6pm Wed-Sun, bistro 5-9:30pm Wed-Sat, 10:30am-2pm Sun) A Michelin-starred French baker setting up shop in tiny Wellfleet? You might think he'd gone crazy, if not for the line out the door. You can't miss PB: it's painted pink and set back from US 6. Scan the cabinets full of fruit tarts, chocolate-almond croissants and filled baguettes and you'll think you've died and gone to Paris.

Mac's on the Pier　　　SEAFOOD $$
(☑508-349-9611; www.macsseafood.com; 265 Commercial St, Wellfleet Town Pier; mains $8-33; ⊘11am-8:30pm late May-early Oct; ☑ 🛋) Head here for fish-market-fresh seafood at bargain prices. Fried-fish standards join the likes of oyster po'boys, sushi rolls and grilled striped-bass dinners. You order at a window and chow down at picnic tables overlooking Wellfleet Harbor.

Wicked Oyster　　　AMERICAN $$
(☑508-349-3455; www.thewickedo.com; 50 Main St; dinner mains $15-28; ⊘7:30am-2pm & 5-10pm) Hang out here for the likes of filet mignon with a bourbon caramel sauce, buttermilk-fried calamari and, of course, several incarnations of Wellfleet oysters. Although the chef works his magic at dinner, you can also start your day here with a wicked omelet or a smoked-salmon bagel (breakfast mains $6 to $14).

🍷 Drinking & Entertainment

★Beachcomber　　　BAR
(☑508-349-6055; www.thebeachcomber.com; 1120 Cahoon Hollow Rd; ⊘11:30am-1am late May-early Sep) If you're ready for some serious partying, 'Da Coma' is *the* place to rock the night away. It's a bar. It's a restaurant. It's a dance club. It's the coolest summertime hangout on the entire Cape. It's set in a former lifeguard station right on Cahoon Hollow Beach, and you can watch the surf action till the sun goes down.

Wellfleet Drive-In　　　CINEMA
(☑508-349-7176; www.wellfleetcinemas.com; 51 US 6, South Wellfleet; tickets adult/child $12/9; ⊘late May–mid-Sep; 🛋) By night, park your car at the 1950s-era Wellfleet Drive-In, where everything except the feature flick is true to the era. Grab a bite to eat at the old-fashioned snack bar, hook the mono speaker over the car window (or tune your car's stereo to the dedicated frequency) and settle in for a double feature. Cash only.

Wellfleet Harbor Actors Theater
THEATER

(WHAT; ☑508-349-9428; www.what.org; 2357 US 6) WHAT's happening! The Cape's most celebrated theater always has something going on in its state-of-the-art Julie Harris Stage. The contemporary, experimental plays staged here are always lively, occasionally bawdy and often the subject of animated conversation.

🛈 Information

Wellfleet Chamber of Commerce (☑508-349-2510; www.wellfleetchamber.com; 1410 US 6, South Wellfleet; ⊙9am-5pm mid-May–mid-Oct) Has an information booth by the South Wellfleet post office at Lecount Hollow Rd.

🛈 Getting There & Away

Most of Wellfleet east of US 6 is part of the Cape Cod National Seashore. To get to the town center, turn west off US 6 at either Main or School Sts.

Truro

☑508, 774 / POP 2000

Squeezed between Cape Cod Bay on the west and the open Atlantic on the east, narrow Truro abounds with views of the water. An odd collection of elements coexist here peacefully: strip motels along the highway, trophy homes in the hills and dales west of US 6, and pine forests and beaches to the east.

To reach Truro's historic sites, which are on the ocean side, take Highland or South Highland Rds off US 6. Or, for fun, just take any winding road off the highway and let yourself get a little lost, soaking in the distinctive scenery.

◉ Sights & Activities

Truro Vineyards
WINERY, DISTILLERY

(☑508-487-6200; www.trurovineyardsofcapecod.com; 11 Shore Rd/MA 6A, North Truro; tastings $10; ⊙11am-5pm Mon-Sat, from noon Sun May-Oct, Fri-Mon Apr, Nov & Dec) This boutique vineyard, the first on the Outer Cape, is worth a stop. In recent times it has added a boutique distillery, South Hollow Spirits, producing amber rum and gin. From May to October, tastings take place every half-hour (a pricey $10 for five tastes); free **tours** are held at 1pm and 3pm. The grounds are a pretty spot for a lazy afternoon, especially if the food truck operated by BlackFish sets up (mains $14 to $30).

Head of the Meadow Beach
BEACH

(Head of the Meadow Rd) Part of the Cape Cod National Seashore (p150), this wide, dune-backed beach has limited facilities, but there are lifeguards in summer. If you happen to be there at low tide, you might catch a glimpse of old shipwrecks that met their fate on the shoals. There are two entrances: the National Seashore beach (parking $20) is to the left and open to the public. The other entrance is for local residents only.

Cape Cod Highland Light
LIGHTHOUSE

(☑508-487-1121; www.capecodlight.org; Highland Light Rd; lighthouse tour $6; ⊙10am-5:30pm mid-May–mid-Oct) Sitting on the Cape's highest elevation (a mere 120ft!), Cape Cod Highland Light dates to 1797 and casts the brightest beam on the New England coast. Admission includes a 10-minute video, an exhibit in the keeper's house and a climb up the lighthouse's 69 steps to a sweeping vista. Children must be at least 48in tall to make the climb.

Pilgrim Heights
WALKING

(US 6, North Truro) You'll find two short trails with broad views at this historic site within the Cape Cod National Seashore (p150). Both trails start at the same parking lot, and each takes about 20 minutes to walk. The signposted turnoff into Pilgrim Heights is along the northeast side of US 6. Poison oak has been reported along the trails so pants are recommended.

🛏 Sleeping & Eating

★ North of Highland Camping Area
CAMPGROUND $

(☑508-487-1191; www.capecodcamping.com; 52 Head of the Meadow Rd, North Truro; tent sites $44; ⊙late May–mid-Sep) Little Truro harbors one of the most secluded campgrounds on all of Cape Cod, with 237 sites spread over 60 pine-fresh acres a short walk from the beach. You don't have to worry about setting up your tent next to an RV – it's tents only. Amenities include metered hot showers, a camp store, a laundry, a rec hall and a kids' playground.

HI Truro
HOSTEL $

(☑508-349-3889; www.hiusa.org; 111 N Pamet Rd; dm/tr $45/149; ⊙late Jun–early Sep; [P]🕸) Budget digs don't get more atmospheric than this former coast-guard station perched amid undulating dunes within the Cape Cod National Seashore (p150). It's so remote that wild turkeys are the only traffic along the road – and it's but a stroll to a quiet beach. There are just 42 beds, so book early to avoid disappointment.

Days' Cottages
COTTAGE $$

(☎508-487-1062; www.dayscottages.com; 271 Shore Rd/MA 6A, North Truro; per week $1700-1950; ☺May–mid-Oct) The 23 identical cottages, lined up like ducks in a row, are an architectural landmark dating to 1931. You can't get closer to the water – each cottage is just inches from the shoreline. In recent years many have been sold off privately (to become condominiums); some new owners have renovated, and many of the cottages are still for rent, at varying prices.

Box Lunch
SANDWICHES $

(☎508-487-4545; http://boxlunchcapecod.com; 300 US 6; sandwiches $8-12; ☺7am-6pm daily late May-Sep, to 4pm rest of year, closed Sun Dec-Mar) Light on the wallet and handy for a quick lunch, this simple roadside operation attached to a farm stand offers an array of roll-up sandwiches, the best of which is the Californian: a turkey, avocado and tomato combo that hits the mark. Box Lunch is a Cape chain: there are a few other stores around, with the same budget-friendly menu.

★ BlackFish
MODERN AMERICAN $$

(☎508-349-3399; 17 Truro Center Rd; mains $26-39; ☺5-10pm Fri-Wed, to midnight Thu mid-May–early Nov; ☑) Local ingredients meet urban sophistication at Truro's top dinner restaurant. From the nautical decor to the out-of-the-ordinary menu choices, everything clicks. Perhaps you'll want to start with the crispy skin haddock and finish with the blackberry bread pudding and brandy ice cream. Try the house specialty, tuna Bolognese. There are always some creative vegetarian options as well. Bookings advised.

☆ Entertainment

Payomet Performing Arts Center
LIVE MUSIC, THEATER

(☎508-487-5400; www.payomet.org; 29 Old Dewline Rd, North Truro; ☑) The center's theme – 'national talent on a local stage' – rings true, with performances by everyone from folk icons Arlo Guthrie and Ani DiFranco to African music legends Ladysmith Black Mambazo. The setting, inside a large tent surrounded by woods, is as cool as the performers. Theater productions, circus classes and children's workshops also take place here in the summer.

❶ Information

Truro Chamber of Commerce (☎508-487-1288; www.trurochamberofcommerce.com; 2 Head of the Meadow Rd, cnr MA 6, North Truro; ☺9am-6pm Jun-Oct) Has a visitor information booth on MA 6, at the turning to Head of the Meadow Beach.

❶ Getting There & Away

From Truro, US 6 presses on to Provincetown and the tip of the Cape. A more scenic drive is via MA 6A, which follows the bay shore.

Provincetown

☑508, 774 / POP 3000

This is it: Provincetown is as far as you can go on the Cape, and more than just geographically. The draw is irresistible. Fringe writers and artists began making a summer haven in Provincetown a century ago. Today this sandy outpost has morphed into the hottest LGBTIQ+ destination in the Northeast. Flamboyant street scenes, brilliant art galleries and unbridled nightlife paint the town center. But that's only half the show. Provincetown's untamed coastline and vast beaches also beg to be explored. Sail off on a whale-watch, cruise the night away, get lost in the dunes – it's all easy to do in Provincetown.

Summers, specifically between June and August, are when the town shines brightest, but you'll still find plenty of nature adventure opportunities and cute guys in the spring and fall. Whenever you decide to come, make sure you don't miss this unique, welcoming corner of New England.

◉ Sights & Activities

★ Provincetown Art Association & Museum
MUSEUM

(PAAM; ☎508-487-1750; www.paam.org; 460 Commercial St; adult/child $10/free; ☺11am-5pm Sat-Thu, to 10pm Fri Jun & Sep, to 8pm Mon-Thu, to 10pm Fri, to 5pm Sat & Sun Jul & Aug, noon-5pm Thu-Sun Oct-May) Founded in 1914 to celebrate the town's thriving art community, this vibrant museum showcases the works of hundreds of artists who have found their inspiration on the Lower Cape. Chief among them are Charles Hawthorne, who led the early Provincetown art movement, and Edward Hopper, who had a home and gallery in the Truro dunes.

★Pilgrim Monument & Provincetown Museum   MUSEUM
(📞508-487-1310; www.pilgrim-monument.org; 1 High Pole Hill Rd; adult/child $12/4; ⊗9am-5pm Apr, May & Sep-Jan, to 7pm Jun-Aug) Climb to the top of the country's tallest all-granite structure (253ft) for a sweeping view of town, the beaches and the spine of the Lower Cape. The climb is 116 steps plus 60 ramps and takes about 10 minutes at a leisurely pace. At the base of the c 1910 tower is an evocative, but quite Eurocentric, museum depicting the landing of the *Mayflower* Pilgrims and other Provincetown history.

MacMillan Pier   PIER
The central town wharf is the hub of water-going traffic, like passenger ferries to and from Boston, whale-watching cruises, fishing charters and schooners taking passengers on a sunset sail.

Provincetown Public Library   LIBRARY
(📞508-487-7094; www.provincetownlibrary.org; 356 Commercial St; ⊗10am-5pm Mon & Fri, to 8pm Tue-Thu, 1-5pm Sat & Sun; 🖥) Erected in 1860 as a church, this building was turned into a museum a century later, complete with a half-size replica of Provincetown's famed race-winning schooner *Rose Dorothea*. When the museum went bust, the town converted the building to a library. One catch: the boat, which occupies the building's upper deck, was too big to remove – so it's still there, with bookshelves built around it. Pop upstairs and take a look.

Province Lands Visitor Center   MUSEUM
(📞508-487-1256; www.nps.gov/caco; 171 Race Point Rd, off US 6; ⊗9am-5pm mid-Apr–mid-Oct) Overlooking Race Point Beach, this Cape Cod National Seashore visitor center has displays on dune ecology and a rooftop observation deck with an eye-popping 360-degree view of the outermost reaches of Cape Cod. The park stays open to midnight, so even after the visitor center closes you can still climb to the deck for sunset views and unobstructed stargazing.

Race Point Beach   BEACH
(Race Point Rd) On the wild tip of the Cape, this Cape Cod National Seashore (p150) beach is a breathtaking stretch of sand, crashing surf and undulating dunes as far as the eye can see. Kick off your sandals, kids – the soft, grainy sand makes for a fun run. This is the kind of beach where you could walk for miles and see no one but the occasional angler casting for bluefish.

Parking costs $20 in summer (the National Seashore fee).

Herring Cove Beach   BEACH
(Province Lands Rd) Swimmers favor the relatively calm (though certainly brisk) waters of Herring Cove Beach, part of the Cape Cod National Seashore (p150). The long, sandy beach is popular with everyone. Though technically illegal, nude sunbathers head left to the south section of the beach; families usually break out the picnic baskets closer to the parking lot. The entire beach faces west, making it a spectacular place to be at sunset. Parking costs $20 in summer (the National Seashore fee).

Long Point Beach   BEACH
Home to the Cape's most remote grains of sand, Long Point Beach is reached by a two-hour walk (each way) along the stone dike at the western end of Commercial St. There are no facilities, so bring water. Be sure to time your walk carefully, as the dike is submerged at extreme high tide. Or do it the easy way and hop on the Long Point Shuttle (www.flyersboats.com), which ferries sunbathers across the bay from June to September ($10).

Stellwagen Bank National Marine Sanctuary   WILDLIFE RESERVE
(www.stellwagen.noaa.gov) Provincetown is the perfect launch point for whale-watching, since it's the closest port to Stellwagen Bank National Marine Sanctuary, the summer feeding ground for humpback whales. Some 17 species have been seen at one time or another; many of the estimated 350 remaining North Atlantic right whales, one of the world's most endangered whale species, frequent these waters. Take a whale-watching boat tour (p156) to scour the sanctuary waters for life.

Dune Shacks Trail   HIKING
(crn MA 6 & Snail Rd; ⊗dawn to dusk) FREE Pull off MA 6 and after a short walk you'll find yourself surrounded by dunes as far as you can see. There's no one trail (keep walking relatively straight and you'll get to a lovely beach) so you can wander the sand hills as you wish. Make sure to bring lots of sunscreen and note the location where you began your walk.

👉 Tours

★Art's Dune Tours   TOURS
(📞508-487-1950; www.artsdunetours.com; 4 Standish St; day tours adult/child $32/20, sunset

Provincetown

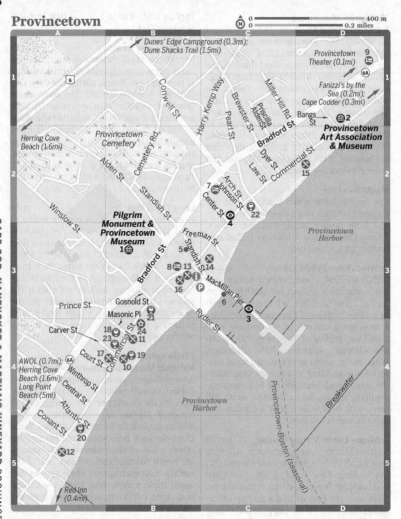

tours adult/child $49/27) Art's offers 4WD tours that are surprisingly informative and scenic. And talk about local – the same family has been running these tours since 1946. The basic hour-long daytime tour takes you along a remote stretch of beach before heading off to explore the dunes. For more drama, take the two-hour sunset tour (add a clambake option for extra local flavor).

★ **Dolphin Fleet Whale Watch**　WILDLIFE
(☎ 800-826-9300, 508-240-3636; www.whale watch.com; 307 Commercial St; adult/child $52/31; ☺ mid-Apr–Oct; ⊕) ♂ Dolphin Fleet offers as many as 10 whale-watch tours daily in peak

season, each lasting three to four hours. You can expect a lot of splashy fun. Humpback whales have a flair for acrobatic breaching and come surprisingly close to the boats. The naturalists on board are both informative and play a vital role in monitoring whale populations.

🎊 Festivals & Events

Provincetown International Film Festival　FILM
(www.ptownfilmfest.org; ☺ mid-Jun) A fine excuse for Hollywood to come to Province-

Provincetown

◎ Top Sights
1 Pilgrim Monument & Provincetown Museum B3
2 Provincetown Art Association & Museum D1

◎ Sights
3 MacMillan Pier C3
4 Provincetown Public Library C2

◆ Activities, Courses & Tours
5 Art's Dune Tours B3
6 Dolphin Fleet Whale Watch C3

⊟ Sleeping
7 Carpe Diem C2
8 Moffett House B3
9 Roux D1

✕ Eating
10 Aquarium Marketplace B4
11 Canteen B4

12 Joon A5
13 Kung Fu Dumplings B3
14 Lobster Pot C3
15 Mews Restaurant & Cafe D2
16 Portuguese Bakery B3
17 Spiritus Pizza B4

◎ Drinking & Nightlife
18 A-House B4
19 Aqua Bar B4
20 Boatslip Beach Club A5
21 Crown & Anchor B3
22 Harbor Lounge C2
23 Nor'East Beer Garden B4

✪ Entertainment
Provincetown Art House .... (see 23)
24 Waters Edge Cinema B4

CAPE COD, NANTUCKET & MARTHA'S VINEYARD PROVINCETOWN

town. You can usually count on director John Waters to show.

Provincetown Carnival
LGBTIQ+

(www.ptown.org/provincetown-carnival; ☉ Aug) Mardi Gras, drag queens, flowery floats: this is the ultimate LGBTIQ+ party event in this LGBTIQ+ party town, attracting some 90,000 revelers over the entire third week of August.

Women's Week
LGBTIQ+

(www.womensweekprovincetown.com; ☉ Oct) A weeklong celebration of women, sponsored by the Women Innkeepers of Provincetown (www.womeninnkeepers.com), with events and entertainment from big-name performers and comics in LGBTIQ+ culture.

⊟ Sleeping

Dunes' Edge Campground
CAMPGROUND $

(☎508-487-9815; www.thetrustees.org; 386 US 6; tent/RV sites with hookups from $49/61; ☉mid-May–Sep; P🐾) Camp amid the dunes and shady pines at this family-friendly campground on the north side of US 6, between the National Seashore and town. With just 100 sites, it gets booked solid in midsummer, so reserve well in advance (book online). There's a seven-night minimum in the high season. Facilities are decent: coin showers, a coin laundry, a camp store.

Cape Codder
GUESTHOUSE $

(☎508-487-0131; www.capecodderguests.com; 570 Commercial St; r without bath $85-119; ☉May-Oct; P🐾🛜♨🐾) Definitely think budget – this is a very simple place that makes no pretense to be anything more. The 14 rooms share four bathrooms, there are no TVs or phones, and there's the occasional wall crack and threadbare bedspread. But heck, for these prices in this town it's a steal. You can't beat the private beach and sundeck.

Race Point Lighthouse
INN $$

(☎855-722-3959; www.mybnbwebsite.com/racepointlighthouse; Race Point; d without bath $175-205; ☉May-Nov) 🏆 Want to *really* get away? If unspoiled sand dunes and a 19th-century lighthouse sound like good company, book one of the three upstairs bedrooms in the old lighthouse-keeper's house. It's a cool place: totally off the grid, powered by solar panels and a wind turbine, and literally on the outer tip of the Cape, miles from the nearest neighbor.

Moffett House
GUESTHOUSE $$

(☎508-487-6615; www.moffetthouse.com; 296a Commercial St; d $115-159, without bath $75-114; P❄@🛜) Set back on an alleyway, this guesthouse is not only quiet but also has another bonus: every room comes with two bicycles for your stay. Rooms are basic – it's more like crashing with a friend than a hotel – but you get kitchen privileges, bagels and

PT IS TO MA WHAT SF IS TO CA

While other cities have their LGBTIQ+ districts, in Provincetown the entire town is the LGBTIQ+ district. You will see plenty of theme parties or even entire themed weeks, but overall there is a sense of camaraderie among the LGBTIQ+ community here, regardless of age, body type, or gender expression. Following are some of the highlights of the scene:

A-House (Atlantic House; ☎508-487-3169; www.ahouse.com; 4 Masonic Pl; ⊙Little Bar noon-1am, Macho Bar & club 10pm-1am) This landmark club offers many nightlife experiences: there's a casual bar to have a drink and chat, as well as several larger dance venues that host regular parties.

Boatslip Beach Club (☎508-487-1669; www.boatslipresort.com; 161 Commercial St; ⊙tea dances daily from 4pm Jun-early Sep, Fri-Sun mid-Sep–May) Provincetown's famous tea dances are held at this harborside club. It's the perfect place to mingle.

Crown & Anchor (☎508-487-1430; www.onlyatthecrown.com; 247 Commercial St; ⊙hours vary) Everything from a piano bar to a leather bar can be found at this complex.

coffee in the morning (in summer), and lots of opportunities to meet fellow travelers.

★AWOL
BOUTIQUE HOTEL $$$

(☎508-413-9820; www.awolhotel.com; 59 Province Lands Rd; r $399-639; ⊙May-Oct; P❄🖐🛜🏊) Overlooking the salt marsh and away from the bustle of Provincetown's main drag is AWOL, a new boutique hotel with a tropical 1960s vibe. Wood and wicker furniture is featured both in the rooms and on the large front lawn, which is set up with lounge chairs and fire pits, perfect for sipping a tiki cocktail under the moonlight.

★Roux
B&B $$$

(☎508-487-1717; www.rouxprovincetown.com; 210 Bradford St; r $277-459; P❄🛜) A fabulously warm welcome combines with a riot of color and animal print at this still relatively new (by Provincetown standards) hotel in the local scene. Owners Ali and Ilene oversee six character-filled rooms decked out with artistic flair, and their creativity extends to the excellent breakfast dishes. For unwinding, there are art-filled common areas, a garden and happy hour.

Carpe Diem
BOUTIQUE HOTEL $$$

(☎508-487-4242; www.carpediemguesthouse.com; 12-14 Johnson St; r $349-599; P❄🛜) Sophisticated yet relaxed, this boutique inn blends a soothing mix of smiling Buddhas, orchid sprays and artistic decor. Each guest room is inspired by a different LGBTIQ+ literary genius; the room themed on poet Raj Rao, for example, has sumptuous embroidered fabrics draped over the modern

furniture. The on-site spa includes a Finnish sauna, a hot tub and massage therapy.

🍴 Eating

★Canteen
MODERN AMERICAN $

(☎508-487-3800; www.thecanteenptown.com; 225 Commercial St; mains $10-16; ⊙11am-9pm Sun-Thu, to 10pm Fri & Sat; 🖐🪑) Cool and casual, but unmistakably gourmet – this is your optimal P-town lunch stop. Choose from classics like lobster rolls and barbecued pulled-pork sandwiches, or innovations like cod *bahn mi* and shrimp sliders. We strongly recommend you add crispy Brussels sprouts and a cold beer to your order and then take a seat at the communal picnic table on the sand.

Aquarium Marketplace
FOOD HALL $

(205 Commercial St; ⊙11am-10pm) This 1920s building was originally a garage, then an aquarium, and is now a food court, with a variety of vendors serving crowd-pleasing dishes, including Connie's Bakery, Big Daddy's Burritos, I Dream of Gelato and Two Southern Sissies BBQ. Pop in for a browse and a bite, then settle in for a front-seat waterfront cocktail at the Aqua Bar.

Kung Fu Dumplings
ASIAN $

(☎774-538-7106; www.kfdumplings.com; 293 Commercial St; dishes $7-12; ⊙11am-10pm Sun & Tue-Thu, to 11pm Fri & Sat) Scoring low for aesthetics but high for flavor and value, this central place has a selection of dumplings (choose steamed or pan-fried) plus a short menu of Asia-roaming dishes like chicken teriyaki, lo mein and kimchi. It offers delivery, too ($5).

Spiritus Pizza
PIZZA **$**

(📞 508-487-2808; www.spirituspizza.com; 190 Commercial St; slices/pizzas $3/20; ⊘ 11:30am-2am) This is the place to pick up a late-night slice, or a late-night date if you haven't been lucky at one of the clubs. While the cruising is top rate, the pizza's just middling. Best bet is to see what's fresh out of the oven and order by the slice. Regardless, it remains the only late-night restaurant in P-town.

Portuguese Bakery
BAKERY **$**

(📞 508-487-1803; 299 Commercial St; snacks $3-6; ⊘ 7am-11pm) This old-school bakery has been serving *malassada* (sweet fried dough), spicy linguica (sausage) sandwiches and Portuguese soups for more than a century. True local flavor.

Fanizzi's by the Sea
SEAFOOD **$$**

(📞 508-487-1964; www.fanizzisrestaurant.com; 539 Commercial St; mains $11-29; ⊘ 11:30am-9:30pm Mon-Sat, from 10am Sun; 🐾) Consistent food, an amazing water view and reasonable prices make this restaurant a local favorite. The extensive menu has something for everyone, from fresh seafood and salads to comfort food; there's even a kids' menu. So why is it cheaper than the rest of the pack? It's less central – about a 15-minute walk northeast of the town center.

★ Joon
AMERICAN **$$$**

(📞 508-413-9336; https://joonbar.com; 133 Commercial St; mains $26-40; ⊘ 5:30-10:30pm Tue-Sun late May-Aug, reduced hours rest of year) It's worth squeezing yourself into Joon's petite and stylish dining room: the food here is wonderful. There are exciting small plates and classic American mains, like halibut with whipped potatoes and broccoli, all seasoned and cooked to perfection. Wine and cocktail buffs will have lots to choose from on the drinks menu.

★ Mews
Restaurant & Cafe
MODERN AMERICAN **$$$**

(📞 508-487-1500; www.mews.com; 429 Commercial St; mains $19-44; ⊘ 5-10pm, also 10am-2pm Sun mid-May–Sep) A fantastic water view, the hottest martini bar in town and scrumptious food add up to Provincetown's finest dining scene. There are two sections: opt to dine gourmet on lobster risotto and filet mignon downstairs, where you're right on the sand, or go casual with a juicy Angus burger from the bistro menu upstairs. Reservations recommended.

Lobster Pot
SEAFOOD **$$$**

(📞 508-487-0842; www.ptownlobsterpot.com; 321 Commercial St; sandwiches $13-21, mains $25-35; ⊘ 11:30am-9pm Apr-Nov) True to its name, this busy fish house overlooking the harbor is *the* place for lobster, and many have been lured by its retro neon sign. Start with the lobster bisque, then put on a bib and crack open the perfect boiled lobster (there's a full gluten-free menu, too). The best way to beat the crowd is to come mid-afternoon.

🍷 Drinking & Nightlife

Red Inn
BAR

(📞 508-487-7334; http://theredinn.com; 15 Commercial St; ⊘ hours vary, closed Jan-Apr) The happy hour at this harbor-front hotel bar is a must. There is a large patio, but even inside the bar you'll have a great view of the waning summer sun over the water while you sip a craft cocktail and nibble on something from the great happy-hour small plates menu.

Nor'East Beer Garden
PUB

(📞 508-487-2337; www.thenoreastbeergarden.com; 206 Commercial St; ⊘ 11:30am-11:30pm Mon-Fri, from 10am Sat & Sun mid-May–Oct) The cocktails always flow in P-town, but it's not immune from the craft-brew explosion. This delightful main-street oasis features 16 draft beers from all over the US, and adds extra appeal with garden-inspired cocktails (eg tequila with housemade rhubarb syrup and lime juice), plus some impressive kitchen output.

Aqua Bar
BAR

(📞 774-593-5106; www.facebook.com/aquabar ptown; 207 Commercial St; ⊘ 10:30am-10pm Sun-Thu, to midnight Fri & Sat May-Oct) Imagine a food court where the options include a raw bar, sushi, gelato and other international delights. Add a fully stocked bar with generous bartenders pouring the drinks. Now put the whole place in a gorgeous seaside setting, overlooking a little beach and a beautiful harbor. Now imagine this whole scene at sunset. That's Aqua Bar.

Harbor Lounge
COCKTAIL BAR

(📞 508-413-9527; www.theharborlounge.com; 359 Commercial St; ⊘ noon-11pm Apr-Dec) The Harbor Lounge takes full advantage of its seaside setting, with floor-to-ceiling windows and a boardwalk stretching out into the bay. Candlelit tables and black leather sofas constitute the decor – nothing else is needed. The cocktails are surprisingly affordable, with many martini concoctions to sample.

☆ Entertainment

Waters Edge Cinema CINEMA
(☑ 508-413-9369; www.watersedgecinema.org; 237 Commercial St; tickets adult/child $12/10) Upstairs at the Whaler's Wharf complex, this cinema shows mainstream and art-house films – a good option on a rainy day.

Provincetown Theater THEATER
(☑ 508-487-7487; www.provincetowntheater.org; 238 Bradford St) This stellar performing arts center, 1 mile northeast of the town center, always has something of interest happening – sometimes Broadway musicals, sometimes offbeat local shows.

Provincetown Art House THEATER
(☑ 508-487-9222; www.ptownarthouse.com; 214 Commercial St) The Art House has two state-of-the-art stages featuring a variety of edgy theater performances, drag shows and cabarets.

ℹ Information

Provincetown Chamber of Commerce
(☑ 508-487-3424; www.ptownchamber.com; 307 Commercial St; ◷ 9am-5pm) The town's helpful tourist office is right at MacMillan Pier.

ℹ Getting There & Away

AIR
Provincetown Municipal Airport (☑ 508-487-0241; www.provincetown-ma.gov; 176 Race Point Rd) The closest airport is northwest of town and connected year-round to Boston via frequent flights with Cape Air (www.capeair.com).

BOAT
From around May to October, boats connect Provincetown's MacMillan Pier (p155) with Boston and Plymouth. Schedules are geared to day-trippers, with morning arrivals into Provincetown and late-afternoon departures. No ferries carry cars, but bikes can be transported for a fee (around $16 round trip in addition to your regular ticket). Advance reservations are recommended, especially on weekends and in peak summer.

Bay State Cruise Co (☑ 617-748-1428; www.boston-ptown.com; round trip adult/child $95/72) Fast ferry (1½ hours) operates three times daily from Boston's World Trade Center Pier.

Boston Harbor Cruises (☑ 617-227-4321; www.bostonharborcruises.com; round trip adult/child $93/65) Fast-ferry service (1½

hours) from Long Wharf in Boston up to three times daily.

Plymouth-to-Provincetown Express Ferry (☑ 508-927-5587; www.captjohn.com; round trip adult/child $53/32) Ferry from Plymouth (1½ hours, once daily) to Provincetown's MacMillan Pier.

BUS
Plymouth & Brockton (☑ 508-746-0378; www.p-b.com) Bus service from Boston that runs several times daily (one way $38, three to 3½ hours) and services other Cape towns. To get all the way to Provincetown you must switch buses in Hyannis.

CAR
From the Cape Cod Canal via US 6, it takes about 1½ hours to reach Provincetown (65 miles), depending on traffic.

ℹ Getting Around
In P-town everything is within walking distance. The town is heaving in summer and on-street parking is next to impossible, but you may be able to find space in the main public parking lot at MacMillan Pier ($3.50 per hour, $35 for a 24-hour period). Town parking is free from November through March. Commercial St is narrow and crowded with pedestrians, so you'll want to do most of your driving along the more car-friendly Bradford St. It's a good idea to leave your car at your accommodation and walk or cycle – or ask advice from your accommodation on parking lots. There are a number of central bike-hire places.

From late May to late September, the **Provincetown Shuttle** (☑ 800-352-7155; www.capecodtransit.org/ptown-route.htm; single ticket/day pass $2/6) travels up and down Bradford St, and to MacMillan Pier, Herring Cove Beach, Province Lands Visitor Center and Race Point Beach, and North Truro. Bike racks are available.

Taxi fares are fairly standard at about $7 per person anywhere within town and $9 between the airport and town. Cape Cab (508-487-2222; www.capecabtaxi.com) is a reliable company.

NANTUCKET & AROUND

One need not be a millionaire to visit Nantucket, but it couldn't hurt. This compact island, 30 miles south of Cape Cod, grew rich from whaling in the 19th century. In recent decades it's seen a rebirth as a summer getaway for CEOs, society types and other well-heeled visitors from Boston and New York.

It's easy to see why. Nantucket is New England at its most rose-covered, cobblestoned, picture-postcard perfect. Nantucket town has the biggest draw for its fine dining, lively bars and one-of-a-kind history you can experience on just about every street. Elsewhere on the island outdoor activities abound. Even in summer you'll be able to find uncrowded stretches of sandy beach. All on an island that is close enough to reach without much hassle, but still feels deliciously remote.

ⓘ Getting There & Away

The most common way to reach Nantucket is by the Steamship Authority (p140) and Hy-Line Cruises (p140) ferries from Hyannis.

The Steamship Authority runs frequent, year-round ferries between Hyannis and Nantucket from Steamboat Wharf (p167). There are two options:

➡ The traditional ferry takes 2¼ hours and operates three to six times daily in each direction (round trip adult/child/bike $37/19/14). It carries cars (round trip $288 to $400 depending on size and season), but the high fares aim to discourage visitors from adding to traffic congestion on Nantucket's narrow streets. If you are bringing a car, book *well* in advance.

➡ The high-speed ferry carries passengers only, not vehicles, and operates four to five times daily from mid-April to early January (round trip adult/child/bike $69/35/14). Journey time is one hour. If you take the high-speed ferry as a same-day trip on Monday to Thursday, the return fare drops to $50/25 for adults/children.

Hy-Line Cruises operates a fast passenger ferry from Hyannis to Nantucket from Straight Wharf year-round. The journey time is one hour; there are five to nine sailings daily (round trip adult/child/bike $77/51/14).

Hy-Line also operates a daily summer ferry between Nantucket and Oak Bluffs on Martha's Vineyard (round trip adult/child/bicycle $65/45/14); travel time is 70 minutes. Unfortunately, the times don't allow an easy day trip to the Vineyard from Nantucket.

Seastreak (📞 800-262-8743; www.seastreak. com) operates high-speed passenger ferries in summer (mid-May to early September) to Nantucket daily from New Bedford, MA (round trip adult/child/bike $90/50/20, two hours), and weekend services from New Jersey and New York City (round trip adult/child/bike $260/155/30, 6¼ to 7¾ hours).

ⓘ Getting Around

No destination on the island is more than 8 miles from town; thanks to Nantucket's relatively flat terrain and dedicated bike trails, cycling is an unbeatable way to explore. Bike paths connect the town with the main beaches and the villages of Madaket and 'Sconset (Siasconset) – no place is more than an hour's pedal away.

Rentals are available at **Young's Bicycle Shop** (📞 508-228-1151; www.youngsbicycleshop. com; 6 Broad St; bike rental per 24hr/week $35/100; ⊗ 8:30am-6pm daily Jun-Aug, 9am-5pm May & Sep-Oct, closed Wed Mar-Apr & Oct-Dec).

Nantucket Regional Transit Authority (📞 508-228-7025; www.nrtawave.com; single fare $2-3) runs handy shuttle buses (known as 'the Wave') all over the island, connecting Nantucket Town with 'Sconset in the east, Madaket in the west and beach destinations in between. Most routes operate every 20 to 60 minutes throughout the day, from Memorial Day to Columbus Day. Fares depend on the destination and are paid via electronic fare boxes; exact fare is advised. Buses have racks for two bikes.

Nantucket Town

📋 508.774 / POP 11.300

The town of Nantucket (called 'Town' by locals) is the island's only real population center. Once home port to the world's largest whaling fleet, the town's storied past is reflected in the gracious period buildings lining its leafy streets. It has the nation's largest concentration of houses built prior to 1850 and is the only place in the US where the entire town is a National Historic Landmark. It's a thoroughly enjoyable place to amble about the cobblestone streets and soak up the atmosphere.

There are two ferry terminals: Straight Wharf and Steamboat Wharf. Walk off Straight Wharf and you're on Main St; Steamboat Wharf is just a few blocks north. The majority of restaurants, inns and other visitor facilities are within a 10-minute walk of the wharves.

◉ Sights & Activities

★**Nantucket Whaling Museum** MUSEUM
(📞 508-228-1894; www.nha.org; 13 Broad St; museum & sites/all access $20/25; ⊗ 9am-5pm late May–mid-Oct, 10am-4pm mid-Oct–Dec & Apr–mid-May, 10am-4pm Thu-Sun early Feb-Mar, closed Jan) One of the island's highlights, this evocative museum occupies an 1847 spermaceti (whale oil) candle factory and the excellent exhibits relive Nantucket's 19th-century heyday as the whaling center of the world. There's a worthwhile, albeit long

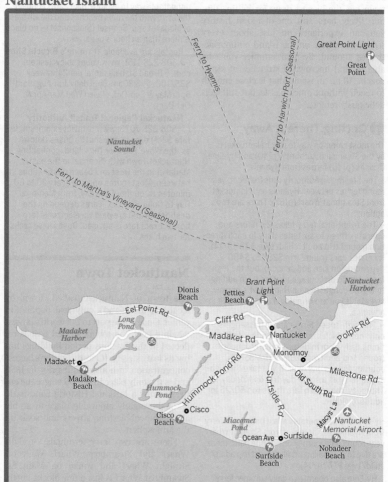

Nantucket Sound

Ferry to Hyannis

Ferry to Harwich Port (Seasonal)

Great Point Light

Great Point

Ferry to Martha's Vineyard (Seasonal)

Dionis Beach

Jetties Beach

Brant Point Light

Nantucket Harbor

Eel Point Rd

Cliff Rd

Long Pond

Madaket Harbor

Madaket Rd

Nantucket

Polpis Rd

Madaket

Monomoy

Milestone Rd

Madaket Beach

Hummock Pond Rd

Hummock Pond

Old South Rd

Macy's La

Surfside Rd

Cisco Beach

Cisco

Miacomet Pond

Nantucket Memorial Airport

Ocean Ave

Surfside

Nobadeer Beach

Surfside Beach

(54 minutes), documentary on the island, incredible scrimshaw exhibits (engravings and carvings done by sailors on ivory, whalebone or baleen), and a 46ft sperm whale skeleton rising above it all. Be sure to head to the rooftop deck for lovely views.

★ **Brant Point Light** LIGHTHOUSE
(Easton St) Welcoming ferries into Nantucket Harbor, this lighthouse was established in 1746 and is still in operation. It's quite tiny (only 26ft), but impossibly photogenic – you may see many wedding parties using it as a backdrop. It's well worth the walk or cycle.

★ **Nantucket Atheneum** HISTORIC SITE
(☑ 508-228-1110; www.nantucketatheneum.org; 1 India St; ☺ 9:30am-1pm Mon, to 5pm Tue, Wed & Fri, to 7:30pm Thu, to 4pm Sat) FREE More than just the public library, this stately Greek Revival edifice is a sight in itself. The 2nd-floor **Great Hall** has hosted such notables as Ralph Waldo Emerson and abolitionist Frederick Douglass. Nationally known opinion makers still speak here today; ask about the summer **lecture series**, and look out for classes and concerts (there's a useful calendar online).

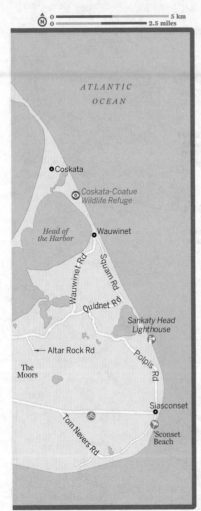

is the town's oldest building still on its original foundation. It's in a traditional 'salt box' style, with south-facing windows to catch the winter sun and a long, sloping roof to protect the home from harsh north winds. It's a half-mile northwest of the town center via W Chester St.

Hadwen House   HISTORIC BUILDING

(www.nha.org; 96 Main St; houses & sites/Whaling Museum $15/20; ⊙9am-5pm daily late May–early Oct, 10am-4pm mid-Oct–Dec) A walk through the Nantucket Historical Association's Hadwen House, a Greek Revival home built in 1845 by a whaling merchant, provides testimony to just how lucrative the whaling industry was in its heyday. The house also hosts rotating exhibits on various topics relating to Nantucket's history.

Museum of African American History   MUSEUM

(☑508-228-9833; www.afroammuseum.org; 29 York St; adult/teen/child $10/8/free; ⊙10am-4pm Tue-Fri, to 2pm Sat, noon-4pm Sun Jun-Sep, 11am-4pm Thu-Sun Oct-Dec, only Fri-Sun Jan-May) The Nantucket campus of this museum stands as testimony to the influential African American community that thrived on the island in the 19th century. It includes the **African Meeting House**, built in 1820, which is the second-oldest African American meeting house in the nation. At the time of writing there were plans to expand the museum to other buildings on the campus for exhibits.

Nantucket Lightship Basket Museum   MUSEUM

(☑508-228-1177; www.nantucketlightshipbasket museum.org; 49 Union St; adult/child $7/3; ⊙10am-4:30pm Tue-Sat late May-late Oct) What the lighthouse is to the New England coast, the lightship was to the sea – essentially a floating lighthouse to warn of dangerous shoals or sandbars below. Sailors would stay aboard the lightships for weeks on end, and to combat boredom they created beautiful, intricate baskets that have become emblems of Nantucket. This small museum highlights these craftspeople and their products.

🏃 Tours

Nantucket Historical Association Walking Tours   WALKING

(☑508-228-1894; www.nha.org; 13 Broad St; adult/child $10/4; ⊙11:30am & 1:30pm mid-May–Oct) Guides from the Nantucket Historical Association lead 90-minute

⭐**First Congregational Church**   CHURCH

(☑508-228-0950; www.nantucketfcc.org; 62 Centre St; suggested donation adult/child $5/1; ⊙10am-2pm Tue-Fri May–mid-Oct) Everyone comes to this church, which traces its roots to the early 1700s, for the eagle-eye view from the top of the steeple. It's well worth the 94-step climb! You can also attend services at 10am on Sundays.

Jethro Coffin House   HISTORIC BUILDING

(☑508-228-1894; www.nha.org; 16 Sunset Hill; houses & sites/Whaling Museum $15/20; ⊙9am-5pm daily late May–early Oct, 10am-4pm mid-Oct–Dec) Built in 1686, the Jethro Coffin House

Nantucket Town

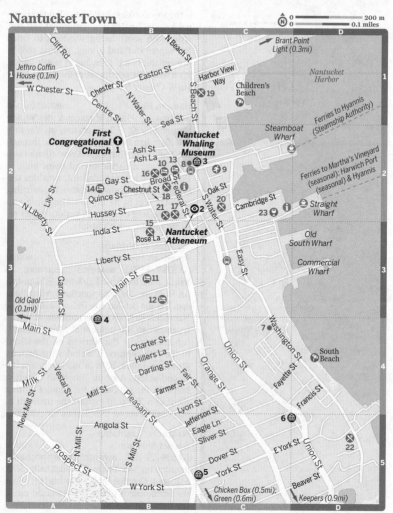

history-themed walking tours of the town twice daily. Confirm schedules and purchase tickets at the Nantucket Whaling Museum (p161), which is the departure point for walks (no reservations taken; walks offered rain or shine).

Nantucket Bike Tours

CYCLING

(📞508-784-6690; www.nantucketbybike.com; 31 Washington St; tour incl bike $65-85) Garnering glowing reviews, this company helps you explore the bike paths and hidden gems of Nantucket, with a little history thrown in. Tours are generally 2½ to three hours; classic tours include a spin around Nan-

tucket town or out to 'Sconset, a sunset tour (order a wine and cheese basket) or a pedal to Cisco Brewers (p168). Customized tours arranged.

Raven's Walk

WALKING

(📞508-257-4586; www.ravens-walk.com; most tours adult/child $20/10; 🚶) History-filled walking tours with a twist are offered by storytelling Robin and her raven. Choose from a variety of tours: a nighttime ghost walk, a children's pirate-themed tour, or perhaps a walk that explores the lives of women in Nantucket while their husbands were out whaling. Departure times and locations vary.

Nantucket Town

⊙ Top Sights
1 First Congregational Church.................. B2
2 Nantucket Atheneum............................. B2
3 Nantucket Whaling Museum................. B2

⊙ Sights
4 Hadwen House.. A4
5 Museum of African American
    History.. C5
6 Nantucket Lightship Basket
    Museum... D5

⊙ Activities, Courses & Tours
7 Nantucket Bike Tours............................ C4
8 Nantucket Historical Association
    Walking Tours..................................... B2
9 Young's Bicycle Shop............................ C2

⊜ Sleeping
10 21 Broad... B2
11 76 Main... B3
12 Barnacle Inn... B3
13 Greydon House..................................... B2
14 Sherburne Inn....................................... A2

⊗ Eating
15 Black-Eyed Susan's............................. B3
16 Brotherhood of Thieves....................... B2
17 Company of the Cauldron..................... B2
18 Corner Table... B2
19 Lola 41°.. C1
20 Nautilus.. C2
21 Proprietors... B2
22 Sayle's Seafood.................................... D5

⊜ Drinking & Nightlife
23 Gazebo.. C2

🎊 Festivals & Events

Daffodil Festival CULTURAL
(www.daffodilfestival.com; ⊙late Apr) The island goes yellow in the last weekend of April with three million blooms, plus art shows, tours and exhibitions. A highlight is the antique car parade that makes its way to 'Sconset for a tailgate picnic.

Nantucket Film Festival FILM
(www.nantucketfilmfestival.org; ⊙ Jun) Celebrities flood the island each June for the Nantucket Film Festival, which focuses on the art of screenwriting.

🛏 Sleeping

⭐**Greydon House** BOUTIQUE HOTEL $$$
(☎508-228-2468; http://greydonhouse.com; 17 Broad St; r $449-819; ❄🐾🏱) Everything about Greydon House, a relative newcomer to Nantucket's hotel scene, is top rate. The interiors are a warm mix of dark wood and white linens and packed with luxury amenities – noise machines, Bluetooth speakers, plush robes – that make it well worth the splurge for one of its rooms or luxury suites (per night $1249).

⭐**76 Main** BOUTIQUE HOTEL $$$
(☎508-228-2533; www.76main.com; 76 Main St; r $463-753; ⊙late Apr-Dec; ❄🏱) In the ultra-refined neighborhood at the top of Main St, 76 Main shines with great design detail and nautical accents: elegant wallpapers, fabrics and bed headboards are a feature, and the courtyard with a fire pit is a coveted retreat.

Facilities are first-rate and fun (including a cocktail mixer bar). The suites off the courtyard are especially nice.

Barnacle Inn B&B $$$
(☎508-228-0332; www.thebarnacleinn.com; 11 Fair St; r $450, without bath $330; ⊙late Apr-early Nov; ❄🏱) This is what old Nantucket is all about: folksy owners and quaint accommodations that hearken back to earlier times. Rooms in this turn-of-the-19th-century inn don't have phones or TVs, but they do have good rates for Nantucket Town, particularly if you opt for a shared bathroom.

21 Broad BOUTIQUE HOTEL $$$
(☎508-228-4749; www.21broadhotel.com; 21 Broad St; r $503-693; ⊙late Apr-Dec; ❄🏱) A summery, light-filled design is the result of this inn's extreme makeover. Fun splashes of seaside colors (blues and yellows) and glitzy common areas (including an alfresco deck with a fire pit, and a lounge with a turntable) combine with well-equipped rooms featuring soft linens, guest iPads and fridges.

Sherburne Inn B&B $$$
(☎508-228-4425; www.sherburneinn.com; 10 Gay St; r $419-533; ❄🏱) Sit in the parlor by the Victorian fireplace and share travel tips with fellow guests at this gracious inn. Built in 1838, the inn flawlessly fuses period appeal with modern amenities. Rooms are comfy, with four-poster beds. The street is quiet, yet the inn is just a two-minute stroll from the town center.

✕ Eating

★ Corner Table
CAFE $

(☑508-228-2665; www.nantucketculinary.com; 22 Federal St; mains $11-19; ☸7am-9pm) 🍴 A real local gathering place, this sweet cafe has great coffee, a cabinet full of high-quality eats to have here or take away (black bean and sweet potato salad, Bolognese, mascarpone raspberry cheesecake), daily soups and sandwiches, a sofa or two, and a sustainable, community-minded ethos.

Green
CAFE $

(☑508-228-1100; www.thegreennantucket.com; 5 W Creek Rd; mains $9-13; ☸6:30am-3pm Mon-Fri, from 7:30am Sat, 8:30am-2pm Sun; 🖋) Gluten-free baked goods, organic smoothies, veggie wraps and damn good coffee can all be found at this cute cafe in the center of the island. It is most popular for its breakfast burritos and sandwiches, which can be made anywhere on the spectrum of vegan to carnivore.

★ Proprietors
MODERN AMERICAN $$

(☑508-228-7747; www.proprietorsnantucket.com; 9 India St; plates $17-35; ☸5:30pm-late Mon-Sat, 10:30am-2pm Sun Apr-Oct) 🍴 Creative, globally inspired cooking and fine cocktails go down a treat at this bar-restaurant that proudly flaunts local farm-to-table fare. Your eyes may be bigger than your belly when reading the small-plates-focused menu: the house-made charcuterie is a worthy choice, as are kimchi pancakes, roasted bone marrow and tuna crudo. Return on Sundays for the lauded brunch.

Keepers
AMERICAN $$

(☑508-228-0009; www.keepersnantucket.com; 5 Amelia Dr; mains $16-22; ☸5-9pm Thu-Mon) Fun updates to American classics (think bacon-wrapped meatloaf) are served in a warm dining room at Keepers, one of the island's best bets for food outside of Nantucket Town.

Lola 41°
INTERNATIONAL $$

(☑508-325-4001; www.lola41.com; 15 S Beach St; mains $17-30; ☸11:30am-2pm & 5pm-1am) We tip our hat to anywhere beloved by locals for both burgers *and* high-grade sushi. Lola 41° is named after Nantucket's latitude, and the menu borrows from others along that parallel, including Spain, Italy and, especially, Japan. The bistro menu has plates large and small (shrimp tempura, gnocchi Bolognese, kung pao chicken), and the sushi menu is creative and delicious.

Brotherhood of Thieves
PUB FOOD $$

(☑508-228-2551; www.brotherhoodofthieves.com; 23 Broad St; mains $16-32; ☸11:30am-10pm) A longtime favorite of locals, who come for the friendly tavern atmosphere (set off with brick and dark woods) and some of the island's best burgers. Not in a burger mood? How about a fish burrito made with local cod, or some broiled Nantucket scallops? The craft beers on tap, some island-brewed, go down easy.

Sayle's Seafood
SEAFOOD $$

(☑508-228-4599; www.saylesseafood.com; 99 Washington St Extension; mains $12-25; ☸10am-9pm) For the island's best fried clams, cheapest lobster dinners and other seafood treats, head to this combo fish market-clam shack on the south side of town. It's all takeout, but there's outdoor seating where you can enjoy your feast.

★ Company of the Cauldron
MODERN AMERICAN $$$

(☑508-228-4016; www.companyofthecauldron. com; 5 India St; 4-course dinners $60-89; ☸6:30-10pm Mon-Sat mid-May–Jan) A splendid choice for a romantic dinner, this intimate restaurant has attentive service and top-rated food. It offers only reserved seating times and four-course prix-fixe dinners, with the likes of rosemary-skewered shrimp followed by beef tournedos. As the chef concentrates his magic on just one menu each evening, it's done to perfection. Book early for Lobster Monday.

Nautilus
ASIAN $$$

(☑508-228-0301; https://nautilusnantucket.com; 12 Cambridge St; small plates $12-19, mains $27-33; ☸5:30pm-1am Jun-Sep, 5:30pm-1am Wed-Sat, also 11:30am-2:30pm Fri & Sat, 11:30am-2:30pm Sun Nov-late Feb, Apr & May) In a sea of, well, seafood restaurants, Nautilus offers a tantalizing alternative with its menu of global-minded (but decidedly Asian focused) dishes. It offers hearty mains, such as thick and satisfying *dandan* noodles, as well as a bevy of fun small plates like scallion pancakes and harissa-spiced lamb chops. Killer cocktails, too.

Black-Eyed Susan's
MODERN AMERICAN $$$

(☑508-325-0308; www.black-eyedsusans.com; 10 India St; mains breakfast $10-14, dinner $26-29; ☸7am-1pm daily & 6-10pm Mon-Sat Apr-Oct; 🖋) It's hard to find anyone who doesn't adore this petite, long-running, quietly gourmet place. At breakfast, try the sourdough

French toast topped with cinnamon pecans and orange butter; at dinner, sit at the bar to watch chefs perform magic in a *tiny* space. The fish of the day often takes top honors (with strong competition). BYOB and cash only.

Drinking & Entertainment

Gazebo
BAR

(☑ 508-228-1266; www.nantuckettavern.com/gazebo; 4 Harbor Sq, Straight Wharf; ⊙ 11:30am-9:30pm mid-May–mid-Oct) Great stargazing (both kinds) at this bustling open-air bar right on the wharf. You can keep one eye on who's getting off the ferry and the other on your cocktail.

Chicken Box
LIVE MUSIC

(☑ 508-228-5625; www.thechickenbox.com; 16 Dave St; ⊙ noon-1am) This former fried-chicken shack has evolved into a roadhouse for live jazz and blues. Actually, depending on who's on the island, these days it can cover the full spectrum, especially rock and reggae. The college crowd meets here, too. It's located 1 mile south of town via Pleasant St. See the website for events.

ℹ Information

Visitor Services & Information Bureau
(☑ 508-228-0925; www.nantucket-ma.gov; 25 Federal St; ⊙ 9am-5pm daily mid-Apr–mid-Oct, Mon-Sat rest of year) has everything you'll need, including public restrooms and a list of available accommodations. The folks here also maintain a summertime **kiosk** (⊙ 9am-5pm late May-early Sep) on Straight Wharf.

ℹ Getting There & Away

Flights arrive at the island's airport 3 miles southwest of town. Ferries (p161) dock at either Steamboat Wharf or Straight Wharf.

ℹ Getting Around

Cycling is the best way to explore the town and the island. Buses (p161) are also excellent, and operate from Memorial Day to Columbus Day. Nantucket Island Rent A Car (www.nantucketislandrentacar.com) operates from the airport, and Affordable Rentals (☑ 508-228-3501; www.affrentals.com) offers cars, jeeps and mopeds from a location near **Steamboat Wharf**.

Note that there are separate bus stops for NRTA Wave buses bound for eastern destinations like **'Sconset** and western destinations such as **Madaket**.

Siasconset
☑ 508, 774 / POP 205

Although this village is barely 7 miles from town, it thinks of itself as worlds apart. Nantucket Town may seem uncrowded and un-hurried compared with the rest of the US, but Siasconset (aka 'Sconset) takes it to another level.

The petite village centers on a cozy dinner restaurant, a tiny general store and a stamp-size post office. It's a wonderful place for lunch and a walk – but the secret's out, so get there early. The old cottages in this seaside village are a watercolor artist's dream, with white-picket fences and climbing pink roses on gray cedar shingles. You'll find some of the loveliest cottages on Broadway, near the village center. Many of them, including the Lucretia M Folger House, at the corner of Main St and Broadway, date to the 18th century. All are private homes now, so do your peeking from a respectful distance.

⊙ Sights & Activities

Sankaty Head Light
LIGHTHOUSE

(www.sconsettrust.org; Baxter Rd) About 1.5 miles north of the village, the 1850 Sankaty Head Light stands photogenically in its new position since 2007, having been relocated due to erosion. It is still operating. A couple of times a year, the lighthouse is open for visitors and offers free tours to the top; see the 'Sconset Trust's website for dates.

'Sconset Beach
BEACH

(🚶) Take a short walk from 'downtown' Siasconset to this pleasant beach with a popular nearby playground. Parking is free, but very limited.

'Sconset Bluff Walk
WALKING

(27 Bank St) This easy-to-walk trail, starting by the beach on Bank St, runs through the backyard of many of 'Sconset's nicest homes along a bluff overlooking the sea and will be a thrill for ocean-view lovers and architecture fanatics (obviously respect for the privacy of the owners of the homes is expected).

🛏 Sleeping & Eating

Summer House Cottages
COTTAGE $$$

(☑ 508-257-4577; www.summerhousecottages.com; 17 Ocean Ave; r & ste $275-695, cottages $450-2000; ☎ ❄) A refined getaway of low-key elegance. Stay in one of 'Sconset's signature rose-covered cottages (sizes vary, and

ISLAND BREW

Enjoy a hoppy pint of Whale's Tale pale ale at the friendliest brewery you'll likely ever see. **Cisco Brewers** (☑508-325-5929; www.ciscobrewers.com; 5 Bartlett Farm Rd; tours $20; ☺noon-7pm Mon-Thu, from 11am Fri & Sat, noon-6pm Sun year-round) is the 'other' Nantucket, a laid-back place where fun banter loosens those stiff upper lips found in primmer quarters. In addition to the brewery, there's a small distillery, casual indoor and outdoor bars, regular food trucks and live music.

The brewery tours and entertainment typically happen around 4pm, so let your hair down and plan accordingly (tours include free samples). There's a free shuttle bus running from town in season. Tour times change throughout the year; see the website for details and daily events.

include in-demand three-bedroom options) and relax by the pool or just drink in the ocean view. Some rooms have fireplace and Jacuzzi. Breakfast is included in the rates. A piano bar, a bistro and a fine-dining restaurant round out the high-class facilities.

★**Chanticleer**
Restaurant & Gardens AMERICAN $$$
(☑508-257-4499; http://chanticleernantucket.com; 9 New St; mains $38-50; ☺11:30am-2pm & 6-9:30pm daily late May-Aug, closed Wed Sep–mid-Oct) Eating here is a fully realized dining experience. The restaurant is set in a whimsical garden setting and the menu of New England–inspired seasonal cuisine is superb, featuring everything from roasted Vermont chicken to an upscale take on an old-school patty melt. Reservations are highly recommended.

ⓘ Getting There & Away

The nicest way to reach 'Sconset is by bike, but there's a summertime bus (p161), too.

South Shore

Outside of Nantucket Town, communities like Surfside and Cisco consist almost entirely of private homes, but visitors head here for the long, broad beaches, which are among the island's best. Some excellent restaurants have also been popping up in the areas near the airport, making it worth the trip away from town.

ⓞ Sights & Activities

Madaket Beach BEACH
There's not a lot to see at Nantucket's western outpost, but this beach, at the end of its namesake bike path, is the island's ace place to watch sunsets. The strong currents and heavy surf make it less than ideal for swimming, but there's some attractive beach walking to be done.

Surfside Beach BEACH
Surfside Beach, 3 miles from Nantucket Town at the end of Surfside Rd, is a top draw with the college and 20-something set. It has full facilities, including a snack shack, and a moderate-to-heavy surf that can make for good bodysurfing.

Nantucket Island
Surf School SURFING
(☑508-560-1020; www.nantucketsurfing.com; Cisco Beach; 1hr lesson $60-80, half-day rental surfboard/SUP $35/70; ☺8am-8pm mid-Jun–mid-Sep) At Cisco Beach, at the end of Hummock Pond Rd, this outfitter handles everything you'll need for hitting the waves: rental of surfboards and stand up paddle surfboards, as well as bodyboards and wetsuits. Surfing lessons are offered, too – private or group, for all ages and skill levels. Advance reservations are required for lessons and rentals.

🛏 Sleeping & Eating

★**Bartlett's Farm** MARKET $
(☑508-228-4403; www.bartlettsfarm.com; 33 Bartlett Farm Rd; sandwiches $8-12; ☺8am-6pm; ☑) 🍴 From a humble farm stand this family operation has grown into a huge gourmet market, with salads, tempting desserts and sandwiches (including a great lobster roll). It's the perfect place to grab everything you'll need for a lunch or sunset picnic on the beach. Events are held here, too – like regular farm-to-table dinners and free farm tours.

ⓘ Getting There & Away

Those who can shouldn't pass up the opportunity to visit the south shore beaches by bike. For everyone else there are summertime bus (p161) connections, too.

MARTHA'S VINEYARD

Bathed in unique beauty, Martha's Vineyard attracts wide-eyed day-trippers, celebrity second-home owners, and urbanites seeking a restful getaway; its 15,000 year-round residents include many artists, musicians and back-to-nature types. The Vineyard remains untouched by the kind of rampant commercialism found on the mainland – there's not a single chain restaurant or cookie-cutter motel in sight. Instead you'll find cozy inns, chef-driven restaurants and a bounty of green farms and grand beaches. And there's something for every mood here – fine dining in gentrified Edgartown one day and hitting the cotton candy and carousel scene in Oak Bluffs the next.

Martha's Vineyard is the largest island in New England, extending some 23 miles at its widest. Although it sits just 7 miles off the coast of Cape Cod, Vineyarders feel themselves such a world apart that they often refer to the mainland as 'America.'

🛈 Getting There & Away

AIR
Martha's Vineyard Airport (MVY; ☑ 508-693-7022; www.mvyairport.com; 71 Airport Rd, Vineyard Haven) is in the center of the island, about 6 miles south of Vineyard Haven, and is served by buses. It has year-round service to Boston and Nantucket and seasonal services to Hyannis, New Bedford, MA and New York. Check Cape Air (www.capeair.com) for schedules. Delta and JetBlue also offer seasonal services from New York's JFK Airport.

BOAT
Steamship Authority (www.steamshipauthority.com) operates a frequent, year-round ferry service to Martha's Vineyard. It connects Vineyard Haven with Woods Hole, south of Falmouth on the Cape (a 45-minute voyage). This is the only ferry that carries vehicles – if you're bringing a car, book well in advance (round-trip car passage is $87 to $162, depending on size and season). There are up to 14 services daily in each direction.

The are also summer connections to the Vineyard. Reservations are recommended:

Woods Hole to Oak Bluffs From mid-May to mid-October, Steamship Authority also has ferries from Woods Hole to Oak Bluffs (four or five daily, 45 minutes). The fares are the same as to Vineyard Haven.

Falmouth to Oak Bluffs From late May to mid-October, the passenger-only ferry **Island Queen** (☑ 508-548-4800; https://islandqueen.com; round trip adult/child/ bike $22/12/8; ⊙ late May–mid-Oct) sails up to seven times daily between Oak Bluffs and Falmouth Harbor (35 minutes).

Falmouth to Edgartown From late May to early September, the **Falmouth-Edgartown Ferry** (www.falmouthedgartownferry.com; one-way adult/child/bike $30/20/5; ⊙ mid-Jun–early Sep) operates from Falmouth Harbor to Edgartown. There are up to five services daily from mid-June to early September, and also weekend services from late May to mid-June.

Hyannis to Oak Bluffs From May through October, **Hy-Line Cruises** (www.hylinecruises.com; round-trip adult/child/bike $59/39/14; ⊙ May-Oct) operates a high-speed ferry from Hyannis to Oak Bluffs (one hour) two to six times daily.

New Bedford to Oak Bluffs From mid-May to mid-October, **Seastreak** (www.seastreak.com) runs a handful of times daily from New Bedford, MA (one hour), to Oak Bluffs. Tickets are cheaper for travel on a weekday.

Oak Bluffs to Nantucket From late May to early October, Hy-Line Cruises also operates an interisland ferry up to three times daily in each direction (70 minutes), making a day trip possible in July and August (round trip adult/ child/bike $65/45/14).

GETTING AROUND
Year-round, the **Martha's Vineyard Regional Transit Authority** (☑ 508-693-9440; www.vineyardtransit.com; fare 1 town/2 towns/ day pass 1.50/2.50/8) operates a network of buses from the Vineyard Haven ferry terminal to villages throughout the island. It's a practical way to get around and even serves out-of-the-way destinations such as the Aquinnah Cliffs.

Bus 13 travels frequently between the three main towns: Vineyard Haven (aka Tisbury), Oak Bluffs and Edgartown.

Fares are $1.50 per town, each way, including town of origin (so Vineyard Haven to Oak Bluffs is $2.50, to Edgartown is $3.75).

Vineyard Haven

☑ 508, 774 / POP 2120

Although it's the island's commercial center, Vineyard Haven is a town of considerable charm. Its harbor has more traditional wooden schooners and sloops than any harbor of its size in New England.

Central Vineyard Haven (aka Tisbury) is just four or five blocks wide and about a half-mile long. Main St, dotted with galleries and boutiques, is the place to meander while looking for souvenirs or a place to pop in for a bite. Steamship Authority ferries dock at the end of Union St, a block from Main St.

Martha's Vineyard

5 km
2.5 miles

Nantucket Sound

Cape Poge Lighthouse

Cape Poge Wildlife Refuge

Cape Poge Bay

Wasque Reservation

Katama Bay

Chappaquiddick Island

Chappaquiddick Rd

Ferry to Nantucket (Seasonal)

Ferry to Falmouth (Seasonal)

Edgartown Harbor

Edgartown Lighthouse

Edgartown

Katama Rd

Katama Beach (South Beach)

Herring Creek Rd

Ferry to Falmouth (Seasonal)

Ferry to Hyannis (Seasonal)

Joseph Sylvia State Beach

Felix Neck Wildlife Sanctuary

Oak Bluffs

County Rd

Meetinghouse Way

Edgartown–West Tisbury Rd

Ferry to Woods Hole

East Chop Lighthouse

Beach Rd

Edgartown–Vineyard Haven Rd

Edgartown Great Pond

Sengekontacket Pond

Lagoon Pond

West Chop Lighthouse

Main St

Vineyard Haven (Tisbury)

Lake Tashmoo Owen Park

Airport Rd

Airport

Martha's Vineyard Airport

Long Point Wildlife Refuge

ATLANTIC OCEAN

Ferry to New Bedford (Seasonal)

Lamberts Cove Rd

State Rd

Manuel F Correllus State Forest

Edgartown–West Tisbury Rd

Lambert's Cove

Old County Rd

Tisbury Great Pond

Indian Hill Rd

Cedar Tree Neck Sanctuary

State Rd

West Tisbury

South Rd

Naushon Island

Vineyard Sound

Polly Hill Arboretum

Middle Rd

South Rd

North Rd

Tabor House Rd

Menemsha Cross Rd

Lucy Vincent Beach

ELIZABETH ISLANDS

Buzzards Bay

Westend Pond

Menemsha Beach

Menemsha

Menemsha Harbor

Chilmark

Menemsha Pond

Pasque Island

Lobsterville Beach

Lobsterville Rd

Lighthouse Rd

South Rd

Aquinnah

Squibnocket Pond

Nashawena Island

Aquinnah Cliffs

Gay Head Lighthouse

Aquinnah Public Beach

Moshup Trail

Rhode Island Sound

From the terminal, Water St leads to the infamous 'Five Corners' intersection: five roads come together and no one really has the right of way. Good luck.

◉ Sights & Activities

Martha's Vineyard Museum   MUSEUM
(☑508-627-4441; www.marthasvineyardhistory.org; 151 Lagoon Pond Rd, Vineyard Haven; adult/child $10/5; ⊙10am-5pm Mon-Sat, from noon Sun late May–mid-Oct, 10am-4pm Mon-Sat rest of year) This well-done museum has a fascinating collection of whaling paraphernalia and scrimshaw, and puts the history of Martha's Vineyard into context. Don't miss the lighthouse display, which includes the huge, 1000-prism Fresnel lens that sat in the Gay Head Lighthouse for a century until electrical power arrived in 1951.

Wind's Up   WATER SPORTS
(☑508-693-4252; www.windsupmv.com; 199 Beach Rd; 1hr kayak/canoe/sailboat rental $20/35/55; ⊙10am-5:30pm Jun, 9am-6pm Jul-Aug, 10am-5pm Wed-Sat, noon-4pm Sun Sep) Vineyard Haven has windsurfing action for all levels. Lagoon Pond, south of the drawbridge between Vineyard Haven and Oak Bluffs, has good wind and enclosed waters suitable for beginners and intermediates. Vineyard Harbor, on the ocean side, is good for advanced windsurfers. Wind's Up, at the drawbridge, rents windsurfing gear, stand up paddle surfboards and kayaks. Lessons also arranged.

🛏 Sleeping

Martha's Vineyard
Family Campground   CAMPGROUND $
(☑508-693-3772; www.campmv.com; 569 Edgartown Rd; tent/RV sites $62/68, 4-/6-person cabins $155/175; ⊙mid-May–mid-Oct) This woodsy place offers the island's only camping and has basic cabins. Book early, especially for weekends. It's 2 miles south of the ferry terminal.

★ Nobnocket
Boutique Inn   BOUTIQUE HOTEL $$$
(☑508-696-0859; www.nobnocket.com; 60 Mt Aldworth Rd; r $350-495; P✲🛜) At Nobnocket there's an emphasis on the meeting place between classic and contemporary. The building is an antique, but the interior design is full of clean, white surfaces with pops of color and pattern carefully selected for each space. It's a dream for lovers of interior design; guests also rave about the

outstanding service and amenities (bikes, snacks, robes etc).

Clark House   B&B $$$
(☑800-696-8633; www.clarkhouseinn.com; 20 Edgartown Rd; r $260-290; ⊙May-Oct; ✲🛜) This homey colonial inn close to town has helpful innkeepers and a nice variety of rooms, from small to commodious. A couple of rooms can accommodate up to five people.

🍴 Eating

★ ArtCliff Diner   CAFE $
(☑508-693-1224; 39 Beach Rd, Vineyard Haven; mains $9-14; ⊙7am-2pm Thu-Tue) 🖉 Hands down the best place in town for breakfast and lunch. Chef-owner Gina Stanley, a grad of the prestigious Culinary Institute of America, adds flair to everything she touches, from the almond-encrusted French toast to the fresh fish tacos. The eclectic menu utilizes farm-fresh island ingredients. Expect a line, but it's worth the wait.

Waterside Market   CAFE $
(☑508-693-8899; www.watersidemarket.com; 82 Main St; mains $10-16; ⊙7:30am-4pm Sat-Thu, to 8:30am Fri, to 9pm daily late May-Aug) Quality sandwiches and salads are made to order at this popular lunch spot located in a beautiful old house on Main St. The inside seating can be a bit hectic, so try to grab a spot on the large wraparound porch outside. Check online to see if it's currently doing two-for-one burger nights, which are typically on Friday from 5pm to 8:30pm.

Scottish Bakehouse   BAKERY $
(☑508-693-6633; http://scottishbakehousemv.com; 977 State Rd; pastries $2-4, mains $5-15; ⊙6am-7:30pm Jun-Sep, to 6:30pm Oct-May) While the name may conjure up images of shortbread and tea cakes, the Scottish Bakehouse serves a wonderful variety of baked goodies in its cozy digs on State Rd. It also has a well-rounded menu of breakfast sandwiches and burritos and hearty lunch options. Make sure to try the Brazilian favorite *pão de queijo* (cheese bread).

La Choza Burritos   FAST FOOD $
(☑508-693-9050; www.lachozaburritos.com; 4 Main St; burritos $7-11; ⊙11am-9pm Mon-Sat; 🖉) Bumper bespoke burritos are the order of the day at this corner spot on Main St, not far from the ferry terminal. The signs step you through the process, and the results are delicious. Veggie and gluten-free options, too. Cash only.

WORTH A TRIP

CHILMARK & MENEMSHA

Occupying most of the western side of the island between Vineyard Sound and the Atlantic, Chilmark is a place of pastoral landscapes and easygoing people. Its chief destination is the picture-perfect fishing village of **Menemsha**, with its harbor lined with shanty shacks selling seafood straight from the boat. Across the way, undulating dunes meander down to the delightful public beach which remains virtually unchanged since its flirtation with global stardom in the cult classic film, *Jaws*. But don't let that dissuade you: the shark was fake, sunsets here are spectacular and the **fish market** (☑508-645-2282; www.menemshafishmarket.net; 54 Basin Rd, Menemsha; lobster meals $14-35; ⊘11am-5:30pm) will feed you a lunch of kick-ass chowder and lobster fresh from the pot.

Should you decide to linger a little longer, **Menemsha Inn** (☑508-645-2521; 12 Menemsha Inn Rd; r $425-465, cottage per week $2600-5190; ⊘May–mid-Nov; P❈🔊) has oodles of country island charm, from the original 1923 inn-buildings to the clutch of cosy cottages dotted carefully about on its sprawling hilltop perch, overlooking the wild Atlantic.

The other reason to make the trip across the island is to dine at the celebrated **Chilmark Tavern** (☑508-645-9400; www.chilmarktavern.com; 9 State Rd; mains $30-52; ⊘5:30-10pm Thu-Mon mid-May–mid-Jun & Sep–mid-Oct, 5:30-10pm Thu-Tue late Jun-Aug) – for those who fancy foodie food, but don't like silly menus and overzealous sommeliers.

Bus 4 from West Tisbury will get you here, if you don't have wheels.

❶ Information

Martha's Vineyard Chamber of Commerce (☑508-693-0085; www.mvy.com; 24 Beach Rd; ⊘9am-5pm Mon-Fri) The island's year-round visitor center. Pick up a free island-wide guide here, and additional info. If you haven't booked your accommodation, the chamber keeps an up-to-date list of lodging vacancies for the week (available online).

❶ Getting There & Around

Although Oak Bluffs is a popular ferry destination, Vineyard Haven is the main port for the island; the year-round vehicle ferry (p169) from Woods Hole docks here.

The bus stop is beside the ferry terminal. This is a major arrival and departure point for buses (p169) all over the island.

Oak Bluffs

☑508, 774 / POP 4680

Odds are, this ferry-port town – where the lion's share of summer day-tripping boats arrive – will be your introduction to the island. Welcome to the Vineyard's summer-fun mecca: a place to wander with an ice-cream cone in hand, poke around honky-tonk sights and go clubbing at night.

All ferries dock in the center of town; the Steamship Authority boats along Seaview Ave and the other ferries along Circuit Ave Extension. The two roads connect together

as a single loop. The area between the two docks is filled with trinket shops, eateries and bike-rental outlets.

◉ Sights & Activities

★**Campgrounds & Tabernacle**　　　　　　HISTORIC SITE
(☑508-693-0525; www.mvcma.org) Oak Bluffs started out in the mid-19th century as a summer retreat by a revivalist church, whose members enjoyed a day at the beach as much as a gospel service. They first camped out in tents, then built some 300 wooden cottages, each adorned with whimsical filigree trim.

Cottage Museum　　　　　　　　　　MUSEUM
(☑508-693-5042; www.mvcma.org; 1 Trinity Park; adult/child $3/50¢; ⊘10am-4pm Mon-Sat, from 1pm Sun Jun–mid-Oct) You can visit a typical Campground cottage, complete with period furnishings, thanks to the Cottage Museum. It's filled with Camp Meeting Association history and artifacts.

Joseph Sylvia State Beach　　　　　　　　　BEACH
(Bend-in-the-Road Beach; Beach Rd; 🏖) A mile south of the Oak Bluffs Town Beach is this popular spot, which has calm waters suitable for kids. The Edgarton-side portion of the beach is also referred to as Bend-in-the-Road Beach.

Flying Horses Carousel
HISTORIC SITE

(☑508-693-9481; www.mvpreservation.org; Oak Bluffs Ave; per ride/10 rides $3/25; ⏰11am-4:30pm Sat & Sun May–mid-Jun, 10am-10pm daily mid-Jun–Aug, 11am-4:30pm Sep-early Oct; ⌨) Take a nostalgic ride on this National Historic Landmark, which has been captivating kids of all ages since 1876. It's the USA's oldest continuously operating merry-go-round, and these antique horses have manes of real horse hair.

✦ Festivals & Events

Grand Illumination Night
CULTURAL

(www.mvcma.org; ⏰mid-Aug) It's all about lights. If you're lucky enough to be in Oak Bluffs on the third Wednesday in August, you'll see the Campground cottages adorned with colorful Chinese and Japanese lanterns; a sing-along and a concert is held in the Tabernacle. The lanterns are lit at dusk – it's quite magical.

🛏 Sleeping

★ Summercamp
HOTEL $$$

(☑508-693-6611; www.summercamphotel.com; 70 Lake Ave; r $389-579; ⏰May-Oct; ✿🐾) We dare you not to smile in response to the detail of this fun place, the incarnation of an iconic 1879 hotel that borders the Tabernacle area. The nostalgic summer-camp theme extends from the Astroturfed games room to the canteen selling retro snacks. And there's even a twin room with bunks. Decor is fresh and inspired, location is ace.

✕ Eating & Drinking

Biscuits
BREAKFAST $

(☑508-693-2033; 26 Lake Ave; mains $5-11; ⏰7am-2:30pm Mon-Fri, to 3pm Sat & Sun May-early Oct) If you're wondering what Biscuits specializes in, you needn't look further than its name. This Southern-inspired breakfast and lunch spot is a favorite for its namesake baked good, which are big and fluffy and can be turned into a variety of sandwiches or enjoyed on their own.

Linda Jean's
DINER $

(☑508-693-4093; www.lindajeansrestaurantmv. com; 25 Circuit Ave; mains $9-17; ⏰6am-8pm; 🖋⌨) The town's best all-around inexpensive eatery rakes in the locals with unbeatable blueberry pancakes, juicy burgers and simple but filling dinners. Kids' menu available.

Martha's Vineyard Chowder Company
SEAFOOD $$$

(☑508-696-3000; www.mvchowder.com; 9 Oak Bluffs Ave; mains lunch $13-18, dinner $27-29; ⏰11am-10pm Sun-Thu, to 11pm Fri & Sat) The namesake clam chowder is pretty impressive – rich, creamy and a frequent award-winner. But the rest of the large menu is also impressive, from the raw bar offerings to the lobster roll. It's fish-focused, but not to the exclusion of meaty mains (eg baby back ribs, NY strip steak).

VINEYARD ROOTS

African Americans have deep, proud roots on the Vineyard. Arriving as slaves in the late 1600s, they integrated themselves into the community here long before slavery ended on the mainland. In 1779 a freed slave named Rebecca Amos became a landowner when she inherited a farm from her Wampanoag husband. Her influence on the island was widespread – Martha's Vineyard's only Black whaling captain, William Martin, was one of her descendants.

During the Harlem Renaissance, African American tourism to the Vineyard took off. Writer Dorothy West, author of *The Wedding,* was an early convert to the island's charms. Oak Bluffs soon became a prime vacation destination for East Coast African American movers and shakers.

The cadre of African Americans gathered on the Vineyard during the 1960s was so influential that political activist Joe Overton's Oak Bluffs home became known as the 'Summer White House' of the Civil Rights movement. His guest list ranged from Malcolm X to Jackie Robinson and Harry Belafonte. It was at Overton's home that Martin Luther King Jr worked on his famous 'I Have a Dream' speech. The term 'Summer White House' took on new meaning in 2009 when America's first Black president, Barack Obama, took his summer vacation on the Vineyard.

Learn more about the Vineyard's Black heritage at www.mvheritagetrail.org.

★ **Offshore Ale Co** MICROBREWERY
(📞 508-693-2626; www.offshoreale.com; 30 Kennebec Ave; ⏰ 11:30am-8:30pm Sun-Thu, to 9:30pm Fri & Sat) Join the throngs of locals and visitors at this popular microbrewery – enjoy a pint of Hop Goddess ale, some superior pub grub (including a knockout lobster roll) and the kind of laid-back atmosphere where boats are suspended from the ceiling and peanut shells are thrown on the floor.

ℹ️ Information

Visitor Information Booth (📞 508-693-4266; cnr Circuit & Lake Aves; ⏰ 9am-5pm late May–mid-Oct) The town hall staffs this convenient summertime info booth near the carousel.

ℹ️ Getting There & Around

Oak Bluffs is a busy summertime port from mid-May to mid-October, when ferries (p169) from Hyannis, Falmouth, Woods Hole and New Bedford bring day-trippers across.

Pick up public island buses (p169) in front of Ocean Park, 200yd south of the Oak Bluffs ferry terminal.

Edgartown

📞 508, 774 / POP 4320

Perched on a fine natural harbor, Edgartown has a rich maritime history and a patrician air. At the height of the whaling era it was home to more than 100 sea captains, whose fortunes built the grand old homes that still line the streets today. Unlike Oak Bluffs and Vineyard Haven, which have substantial ferries carting folks in and out, Edgartown only has a small ferry to the mainland. Of the three north-shore towns it's the one most geared to upmarket travelers.

All roads into Edgartown lead to Main St, which extends down to the harbor. Water St runs parallel to the harbor. Most restaurants and inns are on or near these two streets.

🔵 Sights

Cape Poge Wildlife Refuge WILDLIFE RESERVE
(📞 508-627-7689; Dike Bridge Rd, Chappaquiddick; adult/child Jun-early Oct $5/free; ⏰ daily year-round) On the eastern edge of Chappaquiddick sits this idyllic reserve that contains coastal forests, estuaries, rolling dunes and miles of pristine coastline. Many visitors come for the Cape Poge Lighthouse, which is about a 2-mile walk (or ride if you have an over-sand vehicle) from the park's gate.

The better way to go is by tour to the lighthouse (adult/child $35/18) organized by local conservation group the Trustees (www.thetrustees.org).

Chappaquiddick ISLAND
Accessed by frequent ferry (the 'Chappy Ferry') from Edgartown harbor, Chappaquiddick is a small island with a big history, thanks to a fatal accident in 1969 that involved Senator Ted Kennedy. The island's population is around 180; it's a popular spot with visitors for its beaches, cycling, hiking, fishing and birding. Bring a bike and a picnic over on the ferry and go exploring (there is one shop and no restaurants). Mytoi, a beautiful Japanese-style garden, is free and worth a visit if you're in the area.

Felix Neck
Wildlife Sanctuary NATURE RESERVE
(📞 508-627-4850; www.massaudubon.org; 100 Felix Neck Dr; adult/child $4/3; ⏰ trails dawn-dusk, visitor center 9am-4pm Mon-Fri mid-Sep–Mar, also 10am-2pm Sat Apr-May & 10am-3pm Sat & Sun Jun–mid-Sep; 🚸) Mass Audubon's Felix Neck Wildlife Sanctuary, 3 miles northwest of Edgartown center, is a birder's paradise, with miles of trails skirting fields, marshes and ponds. Because of the varied habitat, this 194-acre sanctuary harbors an amazing variety of winged creatures, including ducks, oystercatchers, wild turkeys, ospreys and red-tailed hawks. Bring your binoculars.

The sanctuary also offers nature tours, from family kayak trips to marine discovery outings – especially in July and August. See the website for details.

Katama Beach BEACH
(Katama Rd) Although they're convenient, Edgartown's in-town beaches are just kids' stuff. For the real deal head to Katama Beach, aka South Beach, about 3 miles south of Edgartown center. Kept in a natural state, this barrier beach stretches for three magnificent miles. Rugged surf will please surfers on the ocean side; many swimmers prefer the protected salt ponds on the inland side.

There's a bike path connecting Edgartown with Katama Beach – excellent for avoiding parking hassles.

Edgartown Lighthouse LIGHTHOUSE
(www.mvmuseum.org/edgartown.php; 121 N Water St; adult/child $5/free; ⏰ 10am-4pm Sat & Sun late May–mid-Jun & Sep-early Oct, daily late Jun-Aug) It's not a long climb to the top, but the Ed-

gartown Lighthouse does have a pretty spectacular panoramic view of the town harbor and Chappaquiddick.

🛏 Sleeping & Eating

⭐ The Christopher   BOUTIQUE HOTEL $$$
(📱508-627-4784; www.thechristophermv.com; 24 S Water St; r/ste from $493/653; ⊙May-early Dec; P❋🛜) The central Victorian Inn has been reborn as the Christopher, and the makeover has been quite something: bright, bold and boutique in the best possible way. Edgartown is just outside your doorstep, but inside it's about high-tech gadgets, stylish nooks and a cool outdoor courtyard with a fire pit. Fifteen rooms are spread over three floors (note: no elevator).

Edgartown Inn   B&B $$$
(📱508-627-4794; www.edgartowninn.com; 56 N Water St; r $250-375; ⊙mid-Apr-Oct; P❋🛜) The best bargain in town, with 14 straightforward rooms spread across the main inn and garden house. The inn dates to 1798 and claims Nathaniel Hawthorne and Daniel Webster among its earliest guests. Rooms have changed only a bit since then, but most have private bathrooms. Ask about last-minute specials; you might score a discount if things are slow.

Back Yard Taco   TACOS $
(📱774-549-6944; www.facebook.com/backyard tacomv; 33 Winter St; tacos $4.50-5.50; ⊙noon-12:30am Apr-Oct; 🍴) Back Yard Taco is a favorite of Martha's Vineyard's cooler set and considering it serves some of the island's best tacos, it's not hard to see why. Seating inside is limited, but as the name suggests, there's a nice backyard space to chow down in. Lots of veggie and vegan options as well.

Among the Flowers Café   CAFE $$
(📱508-627-3233; 17 Mayhew Lane; lunch $10-21, dinner mains $24-35; ⊙8am-4pm mid-Apr-Oct, to 10pm Jun-Aug; 🍴) Join the in-the-know crowd on the garden patio (under cute striped awnings and – yes – among the flowering plants) for homemade soups, waffles, sandwiches, crepes and even lobster rolls. Although everything's served on paper or plastic, it's still kinda chichi. In summer, it serves dinner as well, and the kitchen kicks it up a notch.

Port Hunter   GASTROPUB $$$
(📱508-627-7747; www.theporthunter.com; 55 Main St; mains $16-32; ⊙5:30pm-12:30am Jun-Sep, closed Mon May & Oct) Set in a high-ceiling building with an industrial vibe that harkens back to Edgartown's past as a busy harbor, Port Hunter has a diverse menu of high-end pub food and a killer cocktail list. Expect a wait even on weeknights.

ℹ Information

Edgartown Visitors Center (29 Church St; ⊙8:30am-6pm Jun-Sep) This operation at the bus terminal has restrooms and a post office.

ℹ Getting There & Around

Summertime ferries (p169) connect Edgartown with Falmouth on the Cape. The **Chappy Ferry** (www.chappyferry.com; 53 Dock St; round trip per person/bike/car $4/6/12; ⊙6:45am-midnight late May–mid-Oct, to 11:15pm rest of year) links Edgartown with Chappaquiddick (a distance of only 527ft). It runs more-or-less continuously year-round from 6:45am to 11pm (later in summer). Cars and bikes can travel on it (round trip car/bike and driver $12/6); bikes are a better option.

In Edgartown, the public bus terminal is in the town center on Church St, near Main St. Some key buses (p169):

Bus 8 Katama (South) Beach (half-hourly)

Bus 13 Oak Bluffs and Vineyard Haven (half-hourly)

West Tisbury
📱508, 774 / POP 2900

The island's agricultural heart has a white church, calm ponds and a vintage general store, all evoking an old-time sensibility. West Tisbury also has some worthwhile artists' studios and galleries sprinkled throughout, the most well known being the beloved Martha's Vineyard Glassworks.

⊙ Sights

Grange Hall   HISTORIC BUILDING
(1067 State Rd) The 1859 Grange Hall is a historic meetinghouse, most visited these days for markets and events. This post-and-beam structure is also a venue for concerts, lectures and other events.

There's usually something interesting going on here in summer. Stop by for an excellent farmers market, and also for regular artisan fairs (more info at www.vineyard artisans.com).

Polly Hill Arboretum   NATURE RESERVE
(📱508-693-9426; www.pollyhillarboretum.org; 809 State Rd; adult/child $5/free; ⊙grounds sunrise-sunset) This 60-acre refuge celebrates

woodlands and wildflower meadows, and is particularly pretty in the fall. The visitor center is open from 9:30am to 4pm from Memorial Day to Columbus Day. You can explore on your own or join an hourlong guided tour (daily at 10am in July and August).

Alley's General Store   HISTORIC BUILDING
(☑508-693-0088; 1041 State Rd; ⊙7am-7pm Mon-Sat, to 6pm Sun late May-Aug, to 6pm Mon-Sat, to 5pm Sun rest of year) Part food shop ('dealers in almost everything'), part historic landmark, Alley's General Store is a favorite local gathering place and has been since 1858. Lots of souvenirs and gifts available.

Long Point Wildlife Refuge   NATURE RESERVE
(☑508-693-7392; www.thetrustees.org; off Edgartown–West Tisbury Rd; adult/child $5/free; ⊙9am-5:30pm mid-Jun–mid-Sep, sunrise-sunset rest of year) Pond, cove and ocean views all open up on a mile-long trail that leads to a remote beach. Along the way birders can expect to spot nesting osprey and other raptors, from northern harriers to the more common red-tailed hawks. Kayaks and stand up paddle surfboards can be hired to explore Long Cove Pond. From mid-June to mid-September, there's a $10 fee to park at the refuge. It pays to check the website for directions.

Cedar Tree
Neck Sanctuary   NATURE RESERVE
(☑508-693-5207; www.sheriffsmeadow.org; Obed Daggett Rd; ⊙8:30am-5:30pm) FREE Cedar Tree Neck's inviting 2.5-mile hike crosses native bogs and forest to a coastal bluff with views of Cape Cod and the Elizabeth Islands. Be sure to take the short detour to Ames Pond to enjoy a meditative moment with painted turtles and peeping tree frogs (but note that swimming is forbidden).

Martha's Vineyard Glassworks   GALLERY
(☑508-693-6026; www.mvglassworks.com; 683 State Rd; ⊙10am-5pm May-Oct, 11am-4pm Oct-May) Master glassblowers turn sand into colorful creations at the Martha's Vineyard Glassworks. If you can stand the heat, you can watch them work their magic. Call ahead before visiting in the off-season.

🛏 Sleeping & Eating

HI Martha's Vineyard   HOSTEL $
(☑508-693-2665; www.hiusa.org; 525 Edgartown–West Tisbury Rd; dm/d/tr $41/119/159; ⊙mid-May–early Oct; P@🛜) Reserve early for a bed at this popular, purpose-built hostel in the center of the island. It has everything you'd expect: a solid kitchen, a games room, bike delivery, no curfew and friendly staff. The public bus stops out front and it's right on the bike path. Dorms and private rooms are available.

Lambert's Cove Inn   INN $$$
(☑800-535-0272; https://lambertscoveinn.com; 90 Manaquayak Rd; r $399-599; ⊙Apr-early Dec) It's a long drive through the woods to reach Lambert's Cove Inn: but for anyone looking to really get away it's worth it. The inn and its grounds have the air of an English country manor. The rooms are luxurious, but tasteful, and there's a slew of amenities (pool, access to a nearby private beach) to cap everything off.

West Tisbury Farmers Market   MARKET $
(www.wtfmarket.org; 1067 State Rd; ⊙9am-noon Sat Jun–mid-Oct, plus Wed Jul & Aug, 10am-1pm Sat late Oct–mid-Dec) Be sure to head to the Grange Hall in the center of West Tisbury on market days for fresh-from-the-farm produce. The best time to go is Saturday, when it's a full-on community event, with live fiddle music and alpacas for the kids to pet. There's a winter market on Saturdays at the New Agricultural Hall, also in West Tisbury.

ⓘ Getting There & Around

It's 7 miles from Vineyard Haven to West Tisbury, and 8.5 miles from Edgartown. Roads, bike paths and buses (routes 2 and 3 from Vineyard Haven, route 6 from Edgartown) lead here.

Aquinnah

☑508, 774 / POP 327

Aquinnah is about as far south as you can go on Martha's Vineyard without ending up in the ocean. Apart from its isolation, Aquinnah's chief attraction is the windswept cliffs that form a jagged face down to the Atlantic – astonishing in the colorful variety of sand, gravel, fossils and clay that reveal aeons of geological history.

Aquinnah also has a rich Native American history, and it's here more than anywhere else on the island that you'll notice the influence of the island's Wampanoag people.

⦿ Sights

Aquinnah Cliffs   LANDMARK
(Aquinnah Circle) Also known as the Gay Head Cliffs, these clay cliffs, overlooking a

5-mile-long beach, were formed by glaciers 100 million years ago. Rising 150ft from the ocean, they're dramatic any time of day but are at their very best in the late afternoon, when they glow in the most amazing array of colors. The beach area directly below the cliffs is off-limits.

Gay Head Lighthouse   LIGHTHOUSE
(📞508-645-2300; www.gayheadlight.org; adult/child $6/free; ⊙10am-4pm mid-Jun–mid-Oct, Sat & Sun only May–mid-Jun) Built in 1844 with a state-of-the-art Fresnel lens, this red-brick structure on the Gay Head Cliffs is arguably the most scenic lighthouse on the Vineyard. In 2015 it was carefully moved 134ft back from its eroding cliff edge, buying at least 150 years before erosion may require another move inland. Islanders raised $3 million for the relocation.

Aquinnah Cultural Center   MUSEUM
(📞508-645-7900; www.wampanoagtribe.net; 35 Aquinnah Circle; adult/child $5/3; ⊙11am-4pm mid-Jun–early Oct) A short walk from the Gay Head Cliffs is a lovingly preserved historic house that contains a museum dedicated to the culture and history of the Wampanoag Tribe of Gay Head. It's just a few rooms of artifacts and information, but it's well worth a visit to gain some first-hand knowledge about some of Martha's Vineyard's original inhabitants.

🛏 Sleeping & Eating

⭐**Outermost Inn**   INN $$$
(📞508-645-3511; www.outermostinn.com; 81 Lighthouse Rd; r $360-430; ⊙mid-May–mid-Oct; ❇🐾) Be a guest of Hugh Taylor (musician James Taylor's younger brother) at this attractive seven-room inn near Gay Head Lighthouse. The hilltop setting and ocean views are grand, and the Taylors make you feel at home. Dinner at the inn's restaurant, prepared by an accomplished chef, is open to the public and in hot demand, so phone reservations are essential.

Aquinnah Shop   AMERICAN $$
(📞508-645-3867; www.theaquinnahshop.com; 27 Aquinnah Circle; mains $14-36; ⊙8:30am-3pm daily, also 5:30-8:30pm Wed-Mon late May-Sep) Although this restaurant caters to tourists who come to the southern tip of Martha's Vineyard to take in the majestic Gay Head Cliffs, the food is surprisingly good. Tables on the patio overlooking the cliffs are obviously in high demand, so be prepared to wait if you want to dine alfresco.

❶ Getting There & Around

Bus 5 runs here from West Tisbury.

Central Massachusetts & the Berkshires

📍 508, 413

Includes ➡

Worcester	180
Sturbridge	181
Springfield	183
Northampton	187
Amherst	190
Great Barrington & Around	194
Lenox	199
Pittsfield	202
Williamstown	203

Best Places to Eat

➡ Nudel (p201)

➡ Gypsy Apple Bistro (p192)

➡ Armsby Abbey (p181)

➡ Chef Wayne's Big Mamou (p185)

➡ Gould's Sugar House (p192)

Best Places to Stay

➡ Stonover Farm B&B (p200)

➡ Guest House at Field Farm (p204)

➡ Starlight Llama B&B (p188)

➡ Hotel on North (p203)

➡ Porches Inn (p206)

Why Go?

Artfully blending the cultural and cosmopolitan with the rural and rustic, the Pioneer Valley and the Berkshires offer a tantalizing mix of artistic offerings, verdant hills and sweet farmland.

Stretch your quads on hiking trails up Massachusetts' highest mountain and through nature preserves that blanket the surrounding hills. Or, ramble through estate homes of the once famous, listen to world-class musicians from a picnic blanket on a well-manicured lawn, and feast on farm-to-table cuisine at chef-driven restaurants. You could easily spend an entire summer hopscotching the patchwork of wilderness areas, while taking in a dance festival here, an illustrious music series there and summer theater all over the place.

At every turn, you'll come across college towns with shady campuses, bohemian cafes and exceptional art museums. And those lucky enough to be here in autumn will find apples ripe for the picking and hillsides ablaze in brilliant foliage.

When to Go
Worcester

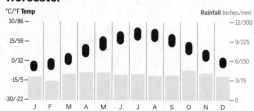

May Prices are lower and college towns are still lively during these quieter months.

Jun–Aug Cultural attractions, summer theater, dance and concert festivals.

Sep–Oct Gorgeous colors, but traffic jams up on weekends.

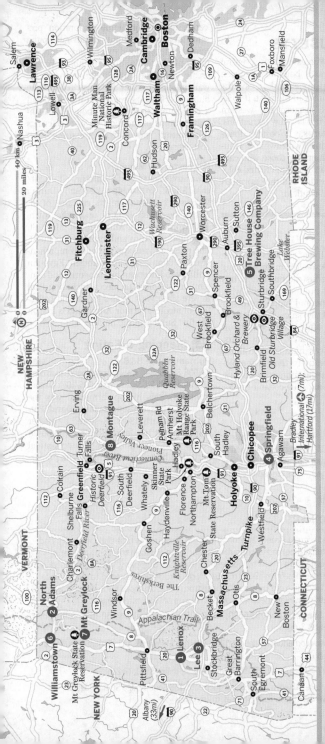

Central Massachusetts & the Berkshires Highlights

1 Tanglewood (p201) Listening to the Boston Symphony as you picnic on the lawn at Lenox's legendary music festival.

2 MASS MoCA (p205) Rambling about the USA's largest contemporary art museum.

3 Jacob's Pillow (p198) Watching an outdoor performance at one of the top summer dance festivals.

4 Springfield Museums (p184) Exploring a heady mix of fine arts, history, motorcycles and the world of Dr Seuss.

5 Tree House Brewing Company (p183) Waiting in line to sample the ales at this craft beer hot spot.

6 Williamstown (p203) Relishing stellar art museums and summer theater.

7 Mt Greylock (p207) Ascending to the summit for a wild vista of five states.

8 Montague Bookmill (p191) Whiling away an afternoon contemplating fine books and river views.

CENTRAL MASSACHUSETTS

Also referred to as Worcester County, central Massachusetts marks a boundary between Boston's suburbs to the east and vast swaths of farm and hill country to the west. It lacks the visual charm of eastern and western Massachusetts, but it has a few attractions. The city of Worcester (say 'Wooster') dominates the area, offering a worthwhile art museum and classic diners for those who care to stop. A bigger draw is the re-created colonial village of Sturbridge and the enormous antiques market at Brimfield.

Worcester

⚐ 508 / POP 185,700

Welcome to 'Worm Town,' as locals affectionately call their city. A wealthy manufacturing center during the industrial revolution, this place invented and produced barbed wire, the modern envelope and more. Worcester has struggled mightily since factories began shutting down after WWII, with scant urban renewal victories in recent years. Nonetheless, the city's nine small colleges inject youth and creativity, though the biggest draw might be the numerous historic diners that have slung blue-collar eggs for generations.

◉ Sights

EcoTarium   MUSEUM
(www.ecotarium.org; 222 Harrington Way; adult/child $18/14, planetarium $5; ◷10am-5pm Tue-Sat, noon-5pm Sun; 🖪) This museum and 'center for environmental exploration' presents an array of exhibits to intrigue young minds. The outdoor exhibit area features many places to dig, build, climb, move and create – and that's in addition to the scenic walking trails. Other kid favorites include bubbles, dinosaurs, rocks and minerals, and a cool interactive exhibit about Mt Washington. Some of the most exciting offerings (planetarium shows, explorer express train) cost extra.

Worcester Art Museum   MUSEUM
(www.worcesterart.org; 55 Salisbury St; adult/child $16/6; ◷10am-4pm Wed-Sun) During Worcester's golden age, its captains of industry bestowed largess upon the town. The Worcester Art Museum, off Main St, remains a generous and impressive bequest. The museum's unexpected and comprehensive collection ranges from ancient Egyptian artifacts to European masterworks and contemporary American pieces, including Paul Revere silverwork. It also has a wild collection of medieval armor. Admission is free on the first Sunday of the month.

🛏 Sleeping & Eating

Putnam House B&B   B&B $
(⚐508-865-9094; www.putnamhousebandb.com; 211 Putnam Hill Rd, Sutton; r/ste $95/105) Dating from 1737, this hilltop farmstead was the home of Massachusetts senator David Putnam in the early 1800s. Restored by master carpenters, it has large fireplaces, exposed beams and an enormous red centennial barn. The hosts exemplify the term, preparing generous breakfasts.

DON'T MISS

WORCESTER DINERS

Worcester nurtured a great American icon: the diner. Here, in this rust-belt city, you'll find a dozen old relics tucked behind warehouses, underneath old train trestles, and steps from dicey bars. Some were made by Worcester Lunch Car Company, which produced 650 prefabricated beauties from 1906 to 1961. Models from the '30s tend to incorporate rich wood trim and look like old train cars. Those from the '50s shoot for a sleek 'streamlined' aesthetic, with gleaming metal exteriors. Visit one of Worcester's finest:

Miss Worcester Diner (⚐508-753-5600; 300 Southbridge St; mains $8.50-16; ◷5am-2pm Mon-Fri, 6am-2pm Sat & Sun)

Corner Lunch (www.cornerlunchdiner.net; 133 Lamartine St; mains $4-11; ◷6am-1pm Mon & Wed-Sat, 7am-1pm Sun)

Boulevard Diner (⚐508-791-4535; 155 Shrewsbury St; mains $5-11; ◷24hr)

George's Coney Island (www.coneyislandlunch.com; 158 Southbridge St; hot dogs $2; ◷10am-8pm Mon, Wed & Thu, to 9pm Fri & Sat, to 7pm Sun)

Beechwood Hotel
HOTEL **$$**

(☑508-754-5789; www.beechwoodhotel.com; 363 Plantation St; r $200-245, ste $265-285; 🕸🛜🐾) This hotel is well known to business travelers and wedding guests for its attentive service. With 52 rooms, the place is small enough to retain a personal atmosphere, while still offering all the services and amenities you would expect. It's a cylinder-shaped building east of the city center along MA 9 near the Massachusetts Biotechnology Park.

Belmont Vegetarian
VEGAN **$**

(www.belmontvegetarian.com; 157 Belmont St; mains $13-15; ⏱11am-8pm Tue-Sat; ☑) Proof positive that beautiful flowers can bloom in the most unassuming of places, Belmont offers huge portions of Jamaican-inspired vegan fare with enough soulful flavor to convert the most hardened carnivore. You can't go wrong with soy pepper steak.

★Armsby Abbey
AMERICAN **$$**

(☑508-795-1012; www.armsbyabbey.com; 144 Main St; sandwiches $14-18, cheese plates $10-23; ⏱kitchen 11:30am-10pm Mon-Thu, 11:30am-11pm Fri, 10am-11pm Sat, 10am-10pm Sun; 🛜) The Abbey rakes in all sorts of awards for its locally sourced, slow-food menu and stellar selection of craft beers on tap. Think comfort food with a gourmet twist. They are very big on farmstead cheeses here; choose from more than a dozen cheesy wedges, served with fresh-baked bread from the next-door bakery. The setting is hip, urban and welcoming.

🍸 Drinking & Nightlife

Ralph's Chadwick Square Diner
CLUB

(www.ralphsrockdiner.com; 148 Grove St; ⏱4pm-2am) Hands down the most interesting night spot in Worcester, this old diner attached to a rock club serves chili dogs, great burgers and cheap booze. But above all, it hosts some sweet gigs, mostly local and often talented. The place attracts college kids, bikers, rockers, goths and yuppies – and everyone gets into the vibe.

MB Lounge
GAY

(www.mblounge.com; 40 Grafton St; ⏱5pm-2am; 🛜) Depending on the night, this gay lounge runs the gamut from casual neighborhood karaoke bar to bass-thumping dance club.

ℹ Information

Blackstone Heritage Corridor Visitor's Center (☑508-341-0741; 3 Paul Clancy Way; ⏱9am-5pm Mon-Sat, noon-5pm Sun)

LIKE BEER?

So do the locals. So much so, they've dedicated the **Western Mass Beer Week** (www.westernmassbeerweek.org; ⏱Jun) to celebrating the local craft beer scene and all things ale. Stop by for a week of fun and informative (well...about beer...) events held at breweries and other venues in Western Mass. Expect live music, social functions, brewery tours and plenty of tastings. Hurrah!

ℹ Getting There & Away

Peter Pan Bus Lines (www.peterpanbus.com) operates buses from **Union Station** (2 Washington Sq) to destinations throughout New England.

Amtrak trains (www.amtrak.com) stop in Worcester en route between Boston and Chicago. MBTA (www.mbta.com) runs frequent commuter trains to/from Boston ($12.50, 90 minutes). Trains for both rails leave from Union Station.

Massport operates **Worcester Regional Airport** (ORH; www.massport.com; 375 Airport Dr), 5 miles west of the city center (a taxi costs about $20). JetBlue (www.jetblue.com) has daily flights to Fort Lauderdale, Orlando and New York's JFK airport; American Airlines (www.aa.com) has flights to its hub in Philadelphia; and Delta (www.delta.com) operates a service to Detroit.

Sturbridge
☑508 / POP 9850

Sturbridge's main attraction – the living museum at Old Sturbridge Village – has preserved an example of a traditional Yankee community; at the same time, the town itself is lined with motor inns, fast-food chains, gas stations and roadside shops, which sprouted up to meet the needs of museum visitors. So while the town may not have the same historic atmosphere or rural charm as some of its westerly neighbors, at least we all can appreciate the irony here.

In any case, families and history buffs will enjoy the excellent museum. In town, there is no shortage of amenities for visitors, though traffic on Main St is often a nightmare. Welcome to the 21st century.

👁 Sights

Old Sturbridge Village
MUSEUM

(www.osv.org; 1 Old Sturbridge Village Rd; adult/child $28/14; ⏱9:30am-5pm daily May-Aug, to 4pm Wed-Sun Mar-Apr & Sep-Nov, 9:30am-4pm

Sat & Sun Jan & Feb, hours vary Dec; ⊛) Historic buildings from throughout the region have been moved to this site to re-create a New England town from the 1830s, with 40 restored structures filled with antiques. Rather than labeling the exhibits, this museum has 'interpreters' – people who dress in costume, ply the trades of their ancestors and explain to visitors what they are doing.

Hyland Orchard   FARM
(www.hylandorchard.com; 195 Arnold Rd; ⊙noon-6pm Sat & Sun mid-Sep–late Oct; ⊛) **FREE** Come fall, when the apples are ripe, Hyland Orchard opens its doors for pick-your-own and a host of other activities. The kids will be flat our with the petting farm, wagon rides and craft activities such as pumpkin painting, while the bucolic setting, live music and craft brews from on-site Rapscallion Brewery will appeal to older members of the family.

Brimfield Antique Show   ANTIQUES
(www.brimfieldshow.com; US 20, Brimfield; ⊙6am-dusk Tue-Sun) Six miles west of Sturbridge is the Brimfield Antique Show, the largest outdoor antiques fair in North America. How big is it? The fair takes place on 23 farmers' fields, where 6000 sellers and 130,000 buyers gather to do business. The town has shops open year-round, but the major antiques shows are held in mid-May, early July

FARM-TO-TABLE FINE DINING
Located in a homestead built in around 1740, **Salem Cross Inn** (www.salemcrossinn.com; 260 W Main St/MA 9, West Brookfield; mains lunch $12-19, dinner $16-29; ⊙11:30am-9pm Tue-Fri, 5-9pm Sat, noon-8pm Sun Apr-Dec, Thu & Fri only Feb & Mar, Fri only Jan) is set on 600 acres of lush countryside. Feast on specialties such as calf's liver with bacon and onions or lavender duck. In addition to the main dining room there's also the Hexmark Tavern, which cooks up comfort food like chicken pot pie.

Besides offering traditional New England meals, the inn hosts special events ranging from a colonial-style fireplace feast cooked on an open hearth to a theatrical murder-mystery dinner. To get here follow US 20 to MA 148 north; 7 miles along, turn left onto MA 9 and go 5 miles.

and early September, usually from Tuesday through Sunday. Most of the fields are free to enter, but the 'premium' fields may charge an admission fee, especially early in the day.

Russian Icon Exhibit   MUSEUM
(St Anne Shrine; www.stannestpatrickparish.com; 16 Church St; ⊙10am-5pm) **FREE** The collection of 60 rare works preserved at St Anne Shrine's Russian icon exhibit is an unusual treasure. Monsignor Pie Neveu, a Roman Catholic Assumptionist bishop, collected valuable Russian icons when he ministered to a diocese in Russia from 1906 to 1936. The collection was augmented by acquisitions brought to the USA by the Assumptionist fathers who served as chaplains at the US embassy in Moscow between 1934 and 1999.

🛏 Sleeping

Wells State Park   CAMPGROUND $
(📷877-422-6762; www.mass.gov/dcr; MA 49; tent sites $27, yurts $60-70; ⊙May-Oct) This campground offers 60 wooded sites – some on the shores of Walker Pond – on its 1470 acres. It's north of I-90, 5 miles from Old Sturbridge Village.

Nathan Goodale House   B&B $
(📷413-245-9228; www.brimfield.org; 11 Warren Rd/MA 19N, Brimfield; r $100-150; 🛜) In a large and simple Victorian Italianate house, this B&B has tasteful rooms that are decked out with antiques, likely procured at the nearby Brimfield Antique Show. It's nicely situated in a residential area, just a few blocks from the show – an ideal base for your antiquing outing. Rates rise during antique shows.

Publick House Historic Inn   INN $$
(📷508-347-3313; www.publickhouse.com; 140 Main St/MA 131; motel r from $69, inn r/ste from $109/139; ❄🛜🐾) Here is Sturbridge's most famous historic inn, the 1771 Publick House, near the village common. Three separate buildings make up the property: your best bet is the Publick Inn itself, with its canopy beds and 18th-century decor. For budget travelers, the on-site Country Motor Lodge looks like it sounds – generic but affordable.

🍴 Eating & Drinking

Annie's Country Kitchen   BREAKFAST $
(www.anniescountrykitchen.com; 140 Main St/MA 131; mains $4-10; ⊙6am-2pm Mon-Fri, to noon Sat & Sun; ⊛) If you're big on breakfast and nuts about home fries, this local shack is the place to jump-start your day. The omelets

are huge, but it's the pancakes – filled with everything from wild blueberries to chocolate chips – that will bust your gut. You might not get hungry until dinner.

Publick House
Historic Tap Room AMERICAN **$$**
(www.publickhouse.com; 277 Main St/MA 131; mains $17-32; ⊙11:30am-8:30pm Sun-Thu, to 9pm Fri & Sat) The historic inn's original dining room features a rustic atmosphere, enhanced by the enormous wide-hearth fireplace. Here you can order a traditional Thanksgiving turkey dinner any day of the year, or turn it up a notch with classic pot roast or lobster pie. While the food is fine, it isn't quite as good as the history.

Rapscallion Brewery MICROBREWERY
(www.drinkrapscallion.com; 195 Arnold Rd; ⊙5-9pm Mon, 3-10pm Tue-Fri, noon-10pm Sat, noon-8pm Sun) In a picture-perfect red farm barn, this craft brewery produces a dozen different beers, including a tempting honey and a seasonal ale made with locally foraged birch twigs and sap. There's often live music, and on weekends a food truck serves flatbreads, hot dogs and other bites ($5 to $10).

ℹ Information

Sturbridge Area Tourist Association (☑508-347-2761; www.sturbridgetownships.com; 46 Hall Rd; ⊙9am-5pm Mon-Fri)

ℹ Getting There & Away

Most travelers arrive in Sturbridge by car via the Mass Pike, I-90. Take exit 9 onto I-84, and it will deposit you onto Main St (US 20), not far from the gate of Old Sturbridge Village.

PIONEER VALLEY

With the exception of gritty Springfield, the Pioneer Valley offers a gentle landscape of college towns, picturesque farms and old mills that have been charmingly converted into modern use. The uber-cool burg of Northampton provides the region's top dining, nightlife and street scenes, while the other destinations offer unique museums, geological marvels and a few unexpected roadside gems.

ℹ Getting There & Around

Most travelers are likely to reach this region by driving from Boston, Hartford or New York. The Pioneer Valley Transit Authority (www.pvta.com) provides bus services to the Five Colleges

WORTH A TRIP

TREE HOUSE BREWING COMPANY

Beer enthusiasts consider **Tree House Brewing Company** (www.treehouse brew.com; 129 Sturbridge Rd/US 20, Charlton; ⊙2-8pm Tue, noon-8pm Wed-Fri, 11am-7pm Sat, noon-5pm Sun) to be among the top breweries in the country, and since its beers are not sold elsewhere, expect to wait in line behind other thirsty hopheads. It's a sleek operation, located in sharply designed premises with views of the brew kettles from the shop and bar, and outdoor seating in landscaped wooded grounds. It's 4.5 miles northeast of Sturbridge, off US 20.

area (the central part of the Pioneer Valley) and to Springfield. The Northampton–Amherst route has the most frequent service. But you'll want your own vehicle if you intend to explore the more rural areas.

Springfield

🗺 413 / POP 153,700

Springfield is a city on the rise. A $960 million MGM casino complex is at the heart of a major regeneration of the formerly rundown city center, and at weekends the city swells with visitors who come to try their luck at the slot machines and gaming tables.

Downtown, you'll find some striking reminders of the city's 19th-century wealth, including some excellent museums, a grand symphony hall and stately Romanesque Revival buildings at Court Sq. The Amazing World of Dr Seuss museum and sculpture garden will delight visitors young and old, and up the hill there's an intriguing armory dating back to the American Revolution. And, as all local grade-schoolers know, basketball originated in Springfield, which explains the presence of the Hall of Fame.

What's more, Springfield also supports a lively night scene, not to mention one of the best Cajun eateries this side of New Orleans.

◉ Sights

★**Naismith Memorial Basketball Hall of Fame** MUSEUM
(☑877-446-6752; www.hoophall.com; 1000 Hall of Fame Ave; adult/child $24/16; ⊙10am-5pm daily Jul & Aug, reduced hours rest of year; 🅿🚼) It

DON'T MISS

SPRINGFIELD MUSEUMS

The **Springfield Museums** (www.springfieldmuseums.org; 21 Edwards St; adult/child $25/13; ◷10am-5pm Tue-Sat, 11am-5pm Sun; P ♿) surround Museum Quadrangle, two blocks northeast of Court Sq. Out front, look for the Augustus Saint-Gaudens statue The Puritan. One ticket (adult/child $25/13) grants entrance to all five museums, giving a good dose of art, fine arts, history and science. Access to the grounds (and the Dr Seuss National Memorial Sculpture Garden) is free.

Amazing World of Dr Seuss (☑413-263-6800; www.seussinspringfield.org; ◷10am-5pm Mon-Sat, from 11am Sun) This innovative museum is dedicated to the life and work of Springfield native Theodore Geisel, aka Dr Seuss. On the 1st floor, interactive exhibits use the stories of Dr Seuss to engage children with rhyming games and storytelling. Upstairs, galleries display original artwork, a moving collection of letters from the author to his great nephew, and a reproduction of Geisel's studio.

Smith Art Museum This museum has exterior windows designed by Tiffany Studios and a fine collection of 19th-century American and European paintings, textiles, ceramics and more. The samurai armor collection is among the finest outside of Japan. In the Hasbro Discovery Center, kids can explore the art in a hands-on way (drawing and tracing, trying on costumes and armor, playing games).

Museum of Springfield History Showcasing the city's distant heyday, this museum is home to the Esta Mantos Indian Motocycle collection (the world's largest). There's also a huge assortment of firearms, including more Smith & Wesson guns than you'll see anywhere else. And there's a fabulous automobile collection that includes a couple of early Rolls-Royce roadsters that were built right here in Springfield.

Museum of Fine Arts The 20 galleries of this art deco–style building are filled with lesser paintings of the great European masters and better works of lesser masters. The impressionist collection includes works by Pissarro and Renoir, while the contemporary gallery includes pieces by Georgia O'Keeffe and Picasso. One of the best-known pieces is The Historical Monument of the American Republic, a grand work by Erastus Salisbury Field that depicts US history using architectural towers.

Springfield Science Museum This museum possesses a respectable, if slightly outdated, range of natural history and science exhibits. The Dinosaur Hall has a full-size replica of a Tyrannosaurus rex, the African Hall covers evolution and ecology, and the Seymour Planetarium has shows daily.

was Springfield where, in 1891, a young Canadian physical education instructor called James Naismith first invented basketball. The game is celebrated at this state-of-the art museum. Though the emphasis at the basketball hall of fame seems to be more hoopla than hoops – there's an abundance of multiscreened TVs and disembodied cheering – devotees of the game will be thrilled to shoot baskets, feel the center-court excitement and learn about the sport's history and great players.

Springfield Armory
National Historic Site   HISTORIC SITE
(☑413-734-8551; www.nps.gov/spar; cnr State & Federal Sts; ◷9am-5pm daily May-Oct, 9am-5pm Wed-Sun Nov-Mar; P) FREE This National Historic Site preserves what remains of the USA's greatest federal armory, built under the command of General George Washington during the American Revolution. Nowadays, it holds one of the world's largest collections of firearms, including Remingtons, Colts, Lugers and even weapons from as early as the 1400s. In other words, guns galore. For the weirdest sculpture you might ever see, don't miss the Organ of Muskets, composed of 645 rifles.

✦ Festivals & Events

Springfield Jazz & Roots Festival   MUSIC
(www.springfieldjazzfest.org; ◷Aug) FREE This free outdoor festival celebrates the diverse cultural heritage of Springfield's population, with a day of performances by mostly local and regional performers. The music runs the gamut, from Dixieland jazz to R & B and Latin rhythms. It all goes down on Court Sq on the first or second Saturday in August.

Big E

FAIR

(www.thebige.com; 1305 Memorial Ave/MA 147, West Springfield; adult/child day pass $15/10, unlimited entry $40/20; ☺mid-Sep) In mid-September, sleepy West Springfield explodes into activity with the annual Eastern States Exposition, better known as the Big E. It's 17 days of farm exhibits and horse shows, carnival rides and parades, concerts and circus performances, mass consumption of food on sticks, and one giant dairy-themed sculpture out of butter. It's the largest event of its kind in New England. Discounts available for advance purchase; carnival rides cost extra.

🛏 Sleeping & Eating

La Quinta Inn & Suites

HOTEL $

(☎413-781-0900; www.lq.com; 100 Congress St; r from $110; P❄☎🐾) Plain but practical, the spacious rooms at this hotel won't win any design awards but offer good value in a central location. Rates include a hot breakfast.

Naomi's Inn

B&B $$

(☎413-433-6019; www.naomisinn.net; 20 Springfield St; r $120-200; P❄☎🐾) With a broad porch and shady trees, this large home overlooks a hospital compound 1.5 miles northwest of the city center. The seven rooms are ample and comfortable, each with a different decorating scheme (some veer toward the gaudy). To get there, follow signs to Bay State Medical Center; the inn is opposite the hospital. Prices include a hot breakfast.

★ Chef Wayne's Big Mamou

CAJUN $$

(☎413-732-1011; www.chefwaynes-bigmamou. com; 63 Liberty St; mains $10-26; ☺11am-8:30pm Mon-Thu, to 9:30pm Fri, noon-4pm & 5-9:30pm Sat) Don't be fooled by its meager appearance – this hole in the wall serves up fabulous home-style Cajun fare. Highlights include the barbecued pulled pork, crayfish quesadillas and blackened catfish. One caveat: you'll want to get here early at dinner, especially on weekends, when lines form outside the door. Reservations are not taken. You can BYO alcohol.

Nadim's Mediterranean Grill

MIDDLE EASTERN $$

(☎413-737-7373; www.nadims.com; 1390 Main St; mains $16-26; ☺11am-10pm Mon-Fri, 3-11pm Sat, 2-8pm Sun; 🐾) The upscale setting and Mediterranean menu attract a business crowd at this downtown restaurant. Lebanese standards are done well, including *fattoush*, *kafta* and kebabs. Fan favorites include hummachos (hummus dip with meat, feta and veggies), fried wings (drizzled with cilantro, garlic and lemon) and the 'famous' lentil soup. Service is friendly and efficient.

Student Prince Cafe & Fort Restaurant

GERMAN $$

(www.studentprince.com; 8 Fort St; mains $17-29; ☺11am-9pm Mon-Wed, to 11pm Thu-Sat, to 8pm Sun) The Student Prince has been scratching those schnitzel and sauerkraut itches since 1935 and shows no signs of slowing down. Even if you're not in the mood for heavy starches, come by anyway to admire the impressive beer steins lining the walls (one was owned by a Russian czar). You'll also find some satisfying brews on tap.

☆ Entertainment

★ Theodore's

BLUES

(www.theobbq.com; 201 Worthington St; ☺11am-2am Mon-Fri, 5pm-2am Sat & Sun) Offering 'booze, blues and BBQ,' this joint is a gem. Truly great blues and jazz acts get booked

DR SEUSS & FRIENDS

The writer and illustrator responsible for such nonsensically sensible classics as *The Cat in the Hat* was born Theodor Seuss Geisel in 1904 in Springfield, Massachusetts. Geisel credits his mother for inspiring his signature rhyming style; she would lull him and his sister to sleep by chanting pie lists she remembered from her bakery days back in Germany.

After graduating from Dartmouth College, Geisel made his living primarily as a political cartoonist and ad man. His first children's book, *And to Think That I Saw It on Mulberry Street*, was rejected by dozens of publishers before one bit. Geisel's first major success came with the publication of *The Cat in the Hat*, which he wrote after reading Rudolf Flesch's 'Why Johnny Can't Read', an article that asserted children's books of the day were boring and 'antiseptic,' and called upon people like Geisel (and, er, Walt Disney) to raise the standard of primers for young children. By the time he died in 1991, Geisel had published 44 books and his work had been translated into more than 20 languages. His classic *Green Eggs and Ham* is still ranked as one of the top-selling English-language books.

Springfield

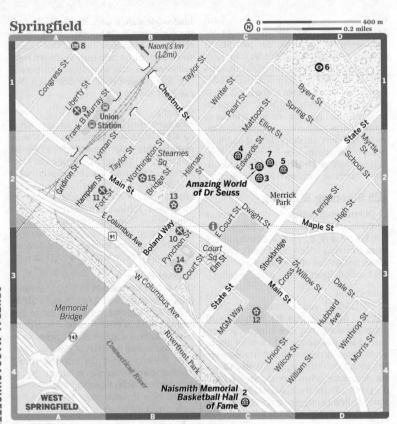

in the bar, and the barbecue is finger-lickin' good. There's usually music from Tuesday to Saturday. Wednesday is open-mike night but the others are guaranteed winners. A jazzy mural captures its illustrious history (the Blues Foundation once named Theodore's the best blues club in the country).

MGM Springfield　　　　　　　　CASINO
(www.mgmspringfield.com; 1 MGM Way) The MGM casino complex features an outdoor plaza and events space centered on the re-furbished state armory, a building dating from 1895 that hosts live comedy nights. As well as a gaming floor with slot machines, gaming tables and a poker room, the casino complex houses a cinema and bowling alley.

**Springfield
Symphony Orchestra**　　　CLASSICAL MUSIC
(www.springfieldsymphony.org; 1441 Main St; tick-ets $30-75; ⊙box office 9:30am-4:30pm Mon-Fri) This respected symphony orchestra – New

England's largest outside of Boston – does monthly performances at **Symphony Hall** (☑413-788-7033; www.symphonyhall.com; 34 Court St). The repertoire is diverse, includ-ing holiday extravaganzas, internationally themed concerts and special guests.

ⓘ Information

Springfield Regional Visitor Center (☑413-787-1548; www.explorewesternmass.com; 1319 Main St; ⊙10am-6pm Tue-Sat)

ⓘ Getting There & Away

Peter Pan Bus Lines (www.peterpanbus.com) connects Springfield with cities throughout New England. The **bus station** (www.spring fieldunionstation.com; 55 Frank B Murray St) is a 10-minute walk northwest of Court Sq. In the same terminal, the Pioneer Valley Transit Authority (www.pvta.com) runs routes to 23 communities in the region, including all of the five colleges.

Springfield

⊙ **Top Sights**
1 Amazing World of Dr Seuss..................C2
2 Naismith Memorial Basketball
   Hall of Fame.......................................C4

⊙ **Sights**
3 Museum of Fine Arts...........................C2
4 Museum of Springfield History...........C2
5 Smith Art Museum...............................C2
6 Springfield Armory National
   Historic Site.......................................D1
7 Springfield Museums...........................C2
   Springfield Science
   Museum......................................(see 7)

🛏 **Sleeping**
8 La Quinta Inn & Suites........................A1

🍴 **Eating**
9 Chef Wayne's Big Mamou....................A1
10 Nadim's Mediterranean Grill...............B3
11 Student Prince Cafe & Fort
   Restaurant...A2

🎭 **Entertainment**
12 MGM Springfield...................................C3
13 Springfield Symphony
   Orchestra...B2
14 Symphony Hall......................................B3
15 Theodore's..B2

Amtrak (www.amtrak.com) operates between Boston and Springfield **Union Station** (www. springfieldunionstation.com; 66 Lyman St), which is a 10-minute walk northwest of Court Sq. The *Lake Shore Limited,* the daily train running between Boston and Chicago, stops in Springfield, as does the daily *Vermonter,* which runs between St Albans, VT, and Washington, DC. The Hartford Line (www.hartfordline.com) has five trains daily connecting Springfield and New Haven Union Station in Connecticut.

ℹ Getting Around

From Wednesday through Sunday the Pioneer Valley Transit Authority (www.pvta.com) runs a free electric bus service called the Loop, with buses every hour from 10am to 10pm, connecting Union Station, Springfield Museums, MGM Springfield and the Basketball Hall of Fame. **Valley Bike share** (📞1-833-825-2453; www. valleybike.org; single trip/day pass $2/6) has 14 stations in and around the city center.

Northampton

📞413 / POP 28,600

In a region famous for its charming college towns, you'd be hard-pressed to find anything more appealing than the crooked streets of downtown Northampton. Old redbrick buildings and lots of pedestrian traffic provide a lively backdrop for your wanderings, which will likely include cafes, rock clubs and bookstores (which explains why locals call their town 'NoHo'). Move a few steps outside of the picturesque commercial center and you'll stumble onto the bucolic grounds of Smith College. Northampton is a well-known liberal enclave in these parts. The lesbian community is famously outspoken, and rainbow flags wave wildly all over town.

⊙ Sights

Smith College Museum of Art   MUSEUM
(📞413-585-2760; www.smith.edu/artmuseum; 20 Elm St; adult/child $5/free; ⊙10am-4pm Tue, Wed, Fri & Sat, to 8pm Thu, noon-4pm Sun) This impressive campus museum boasts a 25,000-piece collection. The collection is particularly strong in 19th- and 20th-century European and North American paintings, including works by Degas, Winslow Homer, Picasso and James Abbott McNeill Whistler. Another highlight is the so-called 'functional art': the remarkable restrooms and the eclectic collection of benches (that you can actually sit on) – all designed and created by contemporary American artists.

Smith College   COLLEGE
(📞413-584-2700; www.smith.edu; Elm St) Founded 'for the education of the intelligent gentlewoman' in 1875, Smith College is one of the largest women's colleges in the country, with 2600 students. The verdant 125-acre campus holds an eclectic architectural mix of nearly 100 buildings, set on a pretty pond. Notable alums of the college include Sylvia Plath, Julia Child and Gloria Steinem. After exploring the campus, take a stroll around Paradise Pond and snap a photo at the Japanese tea hut.

Lyman Conservatory   GARDENS
(www.smith.edu/garden; 15 College Lane; ⊙8:30am-4pm) FREE Visitors are welcome to explore Smith College's collection of Victorian greenhouses, set opposite Paradise Pond, which are packed to the brim with odd things in bloom. There's a popular 'bulb show' in spring and a 'mum show' in the fall. A handy campus map also shows the way to the campus arboretum and half a dozen other more formal gardens.

🏃 Activities

Manhan Rail Trail   CYCLING
(www.manhanrailtrail.org) The Manhan section of the Mass Central Rail Trail connects

CENTRAL MASSACHUSETTS & THE BERKSHIRES NORTHAMPTON

HOLYOKE & HADLEY

There's not much to do in the towns of Hadley and South Hadley, in the shadow of modest Mt Holyoke, but if you find yourself nearby, it's worth a visit, if only to enjoy a slower pace and to admire the pretty landscape and architecture.

In South Hadley, **Mount Holyoke College** (www.mtholyoke.edu; 50 College St) is the nation's oldest women's college, founded in 1837. The great American landscape architect Frederick Law Olmsted laid out the center of the park-like, 800-acre campus, regarded as one of the most beautiful college campuses in the country. Bucolic and small, the college has an enrollment of just 2200 students.

Once you've had a look around, why not ascend the equally bucolic and relatively small Mount Holyoke, part of **Skinner State Park** (☑413-586-0350; www.mass.gov/locations/skinner-state-park; 10 Skinner State Park Rd, Hadley; summit parking $10; ◷9am-8pm May-Aug, to 6pm Sep, to 4pm Oct-Nov) **FREE**. It's high enough to earn the visitor panoramic views of the Connecticut River (and Valley) and the distant smudge of Mt Greylock to the west. At its peak you'll find **Summit House** (Skinner State Park Rd; ◷10am-4:30pm Sat & Sun late May-late Sep) **FREE**, a former hotel dating from 1861, now a museum and visitor center.

A 1.5-mile road to the top is open to hikers year-round and to vehicles from May to October. The park is north of South Hadley off MA 47 in Hadley.

Northampton with Easthampton, 5 miles south. From Northampton, the paved walking and cycling trail runs alongside the forest and meadows of the Arcadia Wildlife Sanctuary before crossing the Manhan river and passing Lower Mill Pond.

Beerology　　　　　　　　　　　BEER
(☑413-829-2337; www.beerology.beer; 342 Pleasant St; class/guided tasting $35/40; ◷11am-6pm Tue-Fri, to 5pm Sat & Sun) If tasting New England's craft beers has inspired you to brew your own, head to Beerology to take a homebrewing class and pick up supplies (fermentation vessels and kegs, as well as 40 malts and grains, 40 hop varieties and 50 yeast strains). Check the website for a list of upcoming classes, which include homebrewing, cidermaking and guided beer tastings.

🛏 Sleeping

★ Starlight Llama B&B　　　　　B&B $$
(☑413-584-1703; www.starlightllama.com; 940 Chesterfield Rd, Florence; r $115; ☎) ✈ Five miles outside Northampton, near the town of Florence, Starlight offers the ultimate back-to-nature sleep. This off-the-grid, solar-powered farm sits amid 65 acres of llama pastures, hiking trails and friendly barnyard creatures. Owner John Clapp built the house and much of the Shaker-style furniture found in the three guest rooms. Breakfast

features the farm's own free-range eggs and organic produce.

Hotel Northampton　　　　　　HOTEL $$
(☑413-584-3100; www.hotelnorthampton.com; 36 King St; r $185-286; P☎) This old-timer is perfectly situated smack in the center of Northampton and has been the town's best bet since 1927. The 106 rooms are airy and well fitted, with traditional furnishings and floral quilts and curtains. There's a quiet grandeur to the place. And mailing a postcard via an antiquated letterbox system always feels good.

🍴 Eating

Woodstar Cafe　　　　　　　　　CAFE $
(www.woodstarcafe.com; 60 Masonic St; mains $5.50-9.30; ◷7am-6pm Mon, to 7pm Tue-Fri, 8am-7pm Sat, 8am-6pm Sun; ☎🖉) Students flock to this family-run bakery-cafe, just a stone's throw from campus, for tasty sandwiches made on the freshest of bread and named after local towns and landmarks. Save room for dessert, as the pastries – made on-site – are divine.

Herrell's Ice Cream　　　　　ICE CREAM $
(Old South St, Thornes Marketplace; cones $2-5; ◷noon-11pm Sun & Thu, to 10:30pm Mon-Wed, to 11:30pm Fri & Sat) Steve Herrell began scooping out gourmet ice cream in this place in 1980. Even before that, he had invented 'Smoosh-ins,' which is when a topping (any

topping) is manually smushed into the ice cream (any flavor) using a scoop and spade and special board. Highly recommended.

Bela
VEGETARIAN $

(☑413-586-8011; www.belaveg.com; 68 Masonic St; mains lunch/dinner $10/15; ⊘noon-8:30pm Tue-Sat; 🖋🚼) 🍴 This cozy vegetarian restaurant puts such an emphasis on fresh ingredients that the chalkboard menu changes daily depending on what local farmers are harvesting. Think home-cooked comfort food and a setting that welcomes families – there's even a collection of toys for the kids! Cash only.

🍷 Drinking

Northampton Brewery
MICROBREWERY

(☑413-584-9903; www.facebook.com/northamp tonbrewery; 11 Brewster Ct; ⊘11:30am-1am Mon-Sat, from noon Sun; 🐾) This brewpub claims to be the oldest operating in New England. At any given time, there are about a dozen fresh and tasty beers on offer, along with a solid menu of pub grub and pizzas. The interior is warm and welcoming, but it's the generously sized rooftop deck that draws the crowds.

Dirty Truth
BAR

(www.facebook.com/dirtytruthbeerhall; 29 Main St; ⊘4pm-midnight Mon-Wed, to 1am Thu & Fri, 11am-1am Sat, to midnight Sun) Slide into a high-top under some decent contemporary art to choose from the impressive list of available draft beers scrawled on the chalkboard menu. When the weather is fine, the front windows open up for fresh air and people-watching.

☆ Entertainment

Academy of Music Theatre
THEATER, CINEMA

(☑413-584-9032; www.academyofmusictheatre. com; 274 Main St; tickets $7-50; ⊘box office 3-6pm Tue-Fri) This balconied theater is one of the oldest movie houses in the USA (1890), and one of the most beautiful. It shows first-run independent films, plus books all sorts of music concerts from folk to cabaret as well as theatrical troupes.

Iron Horse Music Hall
CONCERT VENUE

(☑413-586-8686; www.iheg.com; 20 Center St; tickets $12-40; ⊘box office 10am-6pm Mon-Sat, noon-5pm Sun) The town's top venue for folk, rock and jazz with performers from Judy Collins to Dar Williams. Table seating means the atmosphere is pretty relaxed, though the food and drinks are overpriced and underwhelming.

ℹ Information

Greater Northampton Chamber of Commerce (☑413-584-1900; www.explorenorth ampton.com; 99 Pleasant St; ⊘9am-5pm Mon-Fri, plus 10am-2pm Sat & Sun May-Oct) Get all your questions answered at the local chamber.

ℹ Getting There & Away

Northampton is 18 miles north of Springfield on I-91. If you don't score a parking spot on Main St, you'll find public parking at **Thornes Marketplace** (www.thornesmarketplace.com; 150 Main St; ⊘10am-6pm Mon-Wed, to 8pm Thu-Sat, noon-5pm Sun) in the town center.

Pioneer Valley Transit Authority (www.pvta. com) provides bus services (with bike racks) throughout the Five College area, with the

---

BREWERIES OF EASTHAMPTON

Massachusetts loves the microbrew, and nowhere quite as much as the Pioneer Valley, and in particular the town of Easthampton – which likely won't be on your radar unless you're also a brew-fan and have a hankering to check out the town's three breweries:

Abandoned Building Brewery (www.abandonedbuildingbrewery.com; 142 Pleasant St; ⊘5-10pm Thu & Fri, noon-10pm Sat, 1-6pm Sun; 🐾) An atmospheric craft microbrewery in an industrial space, furnished with rustic, recycled furniture. Try the Hoppy Valley IPA.

New City Brewery (www.newcitybrewery.com; 180 Pleasant St; ⊘4-10pm Mon-Thu, 4-11pm Fri, 1-11pm Sat, 1-8pm Sun; 🚼) Housed in a renovated mill building with outdoor seating, it's a family-friendly space with outdoor seating. Sample a variety of tasting flights or take a tour.

Fort Hill Brewery (www.forthillbrewery.com; 30 Fort Hill Rd; ⊘4-7pm Thu & Fri, 2-8pm Sat, 2-6pm Sun) A brew-house in a big red barn with live bands Thursday to Sunday. German brewing techniques are the secret here.

LOCAL KNOWLEDGE

ICE-CREAM BREAK?

A popular stop for homemade ice cream in Easthampton is **Mt Tom's** (www.mttoms.com; 34 Cottage St, Easthampton; cone $4-5; ⊙11:30am-9pm Sun-Thu, to 9:30pm Fri & Sat), near Nashawannuck Pond. The more than 50 available flavors include black cherry, coconut almond fudge and maple walnut, as well as various flavors of vegan gelato.

Northampton–Amherst route having the most frequent service.

Amherst

⌲ 413 / POP 40,500

This quintessential college town is home to the prestigious Amherst College, a pretty 'junior ivy' that borders the town green, as well as the hulking University of Massachusetts and the cozy liberal-arts Hampshire College. Start your explorations at the town green, at the intersection of MA 116 and MA 9. In the surrounding streets, you'll find a few small galleries, a bookstore or two, countless coffeehouses and a few small but worthwhile museums (several of which are associated with the colleges).

◉ Sights

**Leverett
Peace Pagoda**   PAGODA

(www.newenglandpeacepagoda.org; 100 Cave Hill Rd, Leverett; ⊙dawn-dusk) FREE The world can always do with a little more peace. A group of monks, nuns and volunteers are doing their part in an unexpected spot in the woods near the pea-sized town of Leverett. Run by the non-proselytizing Nipponzan Myohoji sect of Buddhism, the Leverett Peace Pagoda was the first in the Western Hemisphere. The centerpiece is a stupa, a 100ft-tall white bell-shaped monument to Buddha – meant to be circumambulated, not entered. Nearby, prayer flags wave above a frog-filled pond.

Emily Dickinson Museum   MUSEUM

(⌲413-542-8161; www.emilydickinsonmuseum. org; 280 Main St; guided tour adult/child $15/free; ⊙10am-5pm Wed-Mon Jun-Aug, 11am-4pm Wed-Sun Mar-May & Sep-Dec) During her lifetime, Emily Dickinson (1830–86) published only seven poems, but more than 1000 were discovered and published posthumously, and her verses on love, nature and immortality have made her one of the USA's most important poets. Dickinson spent most of her life in near seclusion in this stately home near the center of Amherst. Worthwhile guided tours (one hour) focus on the poet and her works, visiting both the Dickinson Homestead and the adjacent Evergreens.

**Eric Carle Museum
of Picture Book Art**   MUSEUM

(⌲413-559-6300; www.carlemuseum.org; 125 W Bay Rd; adult/child $9/6; ⊙10am-4pm Tue-Fri, to 5pm Sat, noon-5pm Sun; ⍟) Co-founded by the author and illustrator of *The Very Hungry Caterpillar,* this superb museum celebrates book illustrations from around the world with rotating exhibits in three galleries, as well as a permanent collection. All visitors (grown-ups included) are encouraged to express their own artistic sentiments in the hands-on art studio.

West Cemetery   CEMETERY

(Triangle St; ⊙dawn-dusk) FREE For a peek at Amherst's colorful past, make your way to the West Cemetery, between Triangle St and N Pleasant St. Here you'll find the graves of Amherst's notables, including Emily Dickinson. To spot her stone, follow the main paved path to the southern end of the cemetery; the Dickinson family plot borders the left side of the path.

Amherst College   COLLEGE

(www.amherst.edu; 220 South Pleasant St) Founded in 1821, Amherst College has retained its character and quality partly by maintaining its small size (1850 students). The scenic campus lies just south of the town common. Get information on guided campus tours or pick up a self-guided walking tour brochure at the admissions office. There are also a few museums on campus, including the small but fantastic **Mead Art Museum** (⌲413-542-2335; www.amherst.edu/ museums/mead; 41 Quadrangle, Amherst College; ⊙9am-5pm Tue-Sun, to 8pm Fri) FREE and the equally fascinating **Beneski Museum of Natural History** (⌲413-542-2165; www.amherst.edu/museums/naturalhistory; 11 Barrett Hill Dr; ⊙11am-4pm Tue-Fri, 10am-5pm Sat & Sun; ⍟) FREE.

🛏 Sleeping & Eating

★ Inn on Boltwood   INN $$
(☑ 413-256-8200; www.lordjefferyinn.com; 30 Boltwood Ave; r $180-320; ❄ 🐾) 🐾 The finest place to lay your head in Amherst is this boutique operation, in a classic setting overlooking Amherst Green. The Colonial-era inn masterfully fuses traditional fittings with mod conveniences, with additional welcome perks such as organic toiletries. The library, with its open fire and comfy nooks, must be the coziest spot in town.

Amherst Inn   B&B $$
(☑ 413-253-5000; www.allenhouse.com; 257 Main St; r $105-195; ❄🐾) A stately, three-story Victorian with handsome Tudor detailing, this classic B&B also offers plenty of appeal in price and comfort. It books heavily with return guests but a nearby sister operation, the Allen House, adds another half-dozen rooms to the mix. The rate includes a sumptuous breakfast, served in the elegant dining room.

Antonio's Pizza by the Slice   PIZZA $
(☑ 413-253-0808; www.antoniospizza.com; 31 N Pleasant St; slices $2.65-4.15; ⊙10am-2am) Amherst's most popular pizza place features excellent slices made with a truly vast variety of toppings. Bizarre as some offerings are (black bean avocado), the place comes across as authentic, set in an old brick building graced with a white-and-red awning.

🍷 Drinking & Entertainment

Moan & Dove   BAR
(www.moananddovebar.com; 460 West St; ⊙3pm-1am Mon-Fri, 1pm-1am Sat & Sun) The folks at this small, dark saloon near Hampshire College know their beer. Choose from 150 bottles and 20 draft beers. No food is served, unless you count free peanuts, but you can bring your own grub. The place attracts a crowd, and sometimes the barkeepers have trouble keeping up, but if you order right, it's worth the wait.

Amherst Cinema   CINEMA
(www.amherstcinema.org; 28 Amity St; tickets $10-11; ♿) 🐾 Here's an independent, non-profit theater that uses solar panels to help power the films. That's all good, but the real reason to come here is for the cutting-edge programming – classic films, foreign flicks, art-house hits, documentaries and shorts, not to mention retrospectives and talks by contemporary filmmakers.

UMass Fine Arts Center   PERFORMING ARTS
(http://fac.umass.edu; 151 Presidents Dr, UMass campus) This striking concert hall is the region's largest venue, located on the University of Massachusetts campus. It offers a full program of classical and world music concerts, theater and dance.

ℹ Information

Amherst Area Chamber of Commerce
(☑ 413-253-0700; www.amherstarea.com; 35 S Pleasant St; ⊙8:30am-4:30pm Mon-Fri) In the heart of town, opposite the common.

ℹ Getting There & Away

Peter Pan (www.peterpanbus.com) runs long-distance buses to Springfield, Boston and New York. The Pioneer Valley Transit Authority (www.pvta.com) provides bus service around Amherst and to Northampton and other nearby towns.

MONTAGUE BOOKMILL

Montague Bookmill (www.montaguebookmill.com; 440 Greenfield Rd, Montague; ⊙10am-6pm Sun-Wed, to 8pm Thu-Sat) promises 'books you don't need in a place you can't find.' Luckily, both claims are slightly exaggerated. Housed in a converted cedar gristmill from 1842, the Bookmill's maze of rooms are packed with used books and comfy couches. Westward-facing walls are punctuated by large windows that overlook the roiling Sawmill River and its waterfall.

An art gallery and casual cafe share the same awesome river view, making it a fun place to join locals whiling away a lazy afternoon. From Amherst, take MA 63 to the Montague Center exit. Take a left off the exit and turn right onto Main St. Continue through the town center, bearing left after the village green onto Greenfield Rd; the mill is on the left.

Shelburne Falls

📍 413 / POP 1700

Pretty Shelburne Falls is home to a small but vibrant community of artists and musicians. The village's main drag – Bridge St – is tiny and charming, only three blocks long but with a passel of interesting galleries and craft shops. Forming the background are Massaemett Mountain, the Deerfield River and a pair of picturesque bridges that cross it – one made of iron, the other covered in flowers.

◉ Sights

Glacial Potholes   WATERFALL
(Deerfield Ave) FREE Stones trapped swirling in the roiling Deerfield River have been grinding into the rock bed at this location ever since the ice age. The result: 50 near-perfect circles in the riverbed, including the largest known glacial pothole (39ft diameter) in the world.

Bridge of Flowers   BRIDGE
(www.bridgeofflowersmass.org; ⊙ Apr-Oct) FREE Since 1929, volunteers have maintained this bridge of blooms over the Deerfield River. It's one photogenic civic centerpiece. More

ZIP LINING & RAFTING WITH ZOAR OUTDOOR

Heading west from Shelburne Falls along MA 2 for about 9 miles, you'll come to to this fun, family-friendly operator, **Zoar Outdoor** (📞800-532-7483; www.zoaroutdoor.com; 7 Main St/MA 2, Charlemont; kayak $45-50, rafting $71-122, zip lining $79-94; ⊙9am-5pm daily Apr–mid-Oct, 10am-4pm Mon-Sat mid-Oct–Mar; ▣), which offers zip lining and all sorts of splashy fun from Class II and III white-water rafting to canoeing and kayaking the Deerfield River. No experience? No problem. Zoar's enthusiastic guides adeptly provide newbies with all the ABCs. Three-hour zip-lining outings take you through the treetops above the Deerfield River Valley, including rappels and a series of zips.

To do zip lining, children must be at least 10 years old and weigh a minimum of 70 pounds, but there are rafting activities suitable for children as young as five.

than 500 varieties of flowers, shrubs and vines flaunt their colors on the 400ft-long span from early spring through late fall. Access to the bridge is from Water St.

🛏 Sleeping

Dancing Bear Guest House   GUESTHOUSE $$
(📞413-625-9281; www.dancingbearguesthouse.com; 22 Mechanic St; r $129-149; ▣ 🗗) Everything the town has to offer is within easy walking distance of this c 1850 guesthouse. The owners are welcoming, the breakfast home-cooked and the rooms squeaky clean. It's like staying with old friends – a perfect choice for travelers who truly want a local experience.

🍴 Eating & Drinking

Foxtown Diner   DINER $
(www.facebook.com/foxtowndiner; 25 Bridge St; mains $5-8; ⊙5am-7pm Mon-Fri, to 5pm Sat & Sun) Here is your classic small-town diner, where staff are on a first-name basis with most of the customers and know their order before they place it. Pancakes and omelets for breakfast, and soup and sandwiches for lunch. There are usually a half-a-dozen homemade pies on offer for dessert – definitely a highlight.

★**Gould's Sugar House**   BREAKFAST $$
(www.facebook.com/GouldsSugarHouse; 570 Mohawk Trail; mains $8-12; ⊙8:30am-2pm Mar-Apr & Sep-Nov) The standard order at this family-run farm is fluffy pancake perfection, drizzled with maple heaven. Other highlights include the sugar pickles (yes, you read that right), maple ice cream and corn fritters. While you wait, you can watch the syrup being made. Located right on the Mohawk Hwy, east of the Shelburne Falls turnoff.

★**Gypsy Apple Bistro**   FUSION $$
(📞413-625-6345; www.gypsyapplebistro.com; 65 Bridge St; mains $22-30; ⊙5-9pm Thu-Sun) This is an unexpected dining delight in Shelburne Falls. The tiny place artfully blends New England ingredients, French flavors, impeccable service and an inviting atmosphere. The menu is short and sweet – featuring classic dishes like rack of lamb and roasted chicken – but it's all perfectly prepared. The place is small: be sure to reserve.

HISTORIC DEERFIELD VILLAGE

The main street of **Historic Deerfield Village** (www.historic-deerfield.org; 84 Old Main St; adult/child $18/5; ⊙9:30am-4:30pm Apr-Dec), 6 miles north of the modern-day township of South Deerfield (pop 5100), escaped the ravages of time and now presents a noble prospect: a dozen houses dating from the 1700s and 1800s, well preserved and filled with period furnishings that reflect their original occupants. There's also a museum stuffed with artifacts and several active workshops. In various buildings you might see (and try) old-fashioned cooking, woodworking or farming techniques.

It's worth taking a look at the **Memorial Hall Museum** (www.americancenturies.mass. edu; 8 Memorial St; adult/child $6/3; ⊙11am-4:30pm Sat & Sun May, Tue-Sun Jun-Oct), the original building of the Deerfield Academy (1798), now a local history museum. Puritan and Native American artifacts include carved and painted chests, embroidery, musical instruments and glass-plate photographs. Most dramatically, this is where you can see the so-called Indian House Door, a relic from the famous 1704 Deerfield Raid, when some 50 villagers were killed by French and Native American attackers.

If you feel like spending the night, the **Deerfield Inn** (☑413-774-5587; www. deerfieldinn.com; 81 Old Main St; r $200-315; ❈ ❀ ❀) has 11 rooms with various floral decoration schemes and furnished with antiques, in a grand Greek Revival farmhouse, and a further 13 rooms in outbuildings. Rates include a hot, hearty breakfast and after-noon tea and cookies. It's restaurant, **Champney's** (☑413-772-3087; www.champneys restaurant.com; mains $12-25; ⊙noon-9pm Sun-Thu, to 10pm Fri & Sat) sources locally.

Grab local info and maps from the **Hall Tavern Visitor Center** (www.historic-deer field.org; 84 Old Main St; ⊙9:30am-4:30pm) when you arrive.

Mocha Maya's CAFE
(☑413-625-6292; www.mochamayas.com; 47 Bridge St; ⊙7am-5pm; ☎) No matter what your thirst, Mocha Maya's is the place, pouring everything from organic fair-trade coffee to locally crafted beer. Live music and poetry readings take place on Friday and Saturday evenings after hours.

ⓘ Information

Shelburne Falls Visitor Center (☑413-625-2526; www.shelburnefalls.com; 75 Bridge St; ⊙10am-4pm Mon-Sat, noon-3pm Sun May-Oct) Helps with accommodations in the area.

ⓘ Getting There & Away

Shelburne Falls is on the south side of MA 2, about 27 miles east of North Adams. Heading south, MA 112 turns into Main St, which runs into Bridge St.

THE BERKSHIRES

Few places in America combine culture and country living as deftly as the Berkshire hills, home to world-class music, dance and theater festivals – the likes of Tanglewood and Jacob's Pillow – as well as miles of hiking trails and acres of farmland.

Extending from the highest point in the state – Mt Greylock – southward to the Connecticut state line, the Berkshires have been a summer refuge for more than a century, when the rich and famous arrived to build summer 'cottages' of grand proportions. Many of these mansions survive as inns or performance venues. And still today, on summer weekends when the sidewalks are scorching in Boston and New York, crowds of city dwellers jump in their cars and head for the Berkshire breezes.

ⓘ Getting There & Away

Most travelers are likely to reach this region by driving from Boston, Hartford or New York. It is possible to arrive by bus or train, but you'll want your own vehicle if you intend to visit the more rural areas. If not, the Berkshire Regional Transit Authority (www.berkshirerta.com) runs buses between major Berkshire towns. A ride costs $1.75 for short trips and $4 for longer journeys.

Great Barrington & Around

📍 413 / POP 2300

Great Barrington's Main St used to consist of Woolworth's, hardware stores, thrift shops and a run-down diner. These have given way to artsy boutiques, antique shops, coffeehouses and restaurants. Nowadays, the town boasts the best dining scene in the region, with easy access to hiking trails and magnificent scenery in the surrounding hills.

The Housatonic River flows through the center of town just east of Main St/US 7, the central thoroughfare.

◉ Sights

Most of your time in town will be spent strolling along Main St, with its mild bustle, handful of stores and dozen or so restaurants. After an hour or two's rest in small-town America, you might consider a hike in the hills.

Windy Hill Farm FARM
(www.windyhillfarminc.com; 686 Stockbridge Rd/US 7; ⊙9am-5pm Apr-Dec) If you hop in the car and drive, you're bound to find several farms where you can pick seasonal produce at harvest times. The setting can be overwhelmingly beautiful in the fall. A favorite is Windy Hill Farm, about 5 miles north of Great Barrington, where more than a score of apple varieties, from pucker-sour to candy-sweet, are yours for the autumn picking. Summer is blueberry picking season.

Beartown State Forest FOREST
(☑413-528-0904; www.mass.gov/dcr; 69 Blue Hill Rd, Monterey; parking $15) This lovely state park is centered on Benedict Pond, a perfect spot for swimming, fishing, canoeing and kayaking. There are miles of hiking trails, including a piece of the Appalachian Trail. The furthest reaches of this forest are home to deer, bears, bobcats and fishers. Less ambitious hikers can stroll the 1.5-mile **Benedict Pond Loop**.

🏃 Activities

★ Monument Mountain HIKING
(www.thetrustees.org; US 7; parking $5; ⊙sunrise-sunset) Less than 5 miles north of Great Barrington center on US 7 is Monument Mountain, which has hiking trails to the 1642ft summit of Squaw Peak. Turning right from the parking lot, the 3-mile circular route ascends steeply via the **Hickey trail** and runs along the cliff edge to Squaw Peak and the Devil's Pulpit lookout. From the top you'll get fabulous views all the way to Mt Greylock to the northwest and to the Catskills in New York.

Bartholomew's Cobble HIKING
(www.thetrustees.org; US 7, Sheffield; adult/child $5/1; ⊙sunrise-sunset) South of Great Barrington, it's easy to kill a few hours at the 329-acre Bartholomew's Cobble, a 'cobble' being a high, rocky knoll of limestone, marble or quartzite. Five miles of hiking trails provide routes for enjoying the cobble and the woods, including the strenuous route to the top of **Hurlburt's Hill**, and the **Ledges Trail**, which weaves along the Housatonic River.

Keep your eyes peeled for some of the 200 species of birds who fly around here. Bartholomew's Cobble is 10 miles south of Great Barrington along US 7 and MA 7A toward Ashley Falls.

Housatonic River Walk WALKING
(www.gbriverwalk.org; ⊙sunrise-sunset Apr-Nov) FREE The picturesque Housatonic River flows through the center of Great Barrington, with the half-mile River Walk offering a perfect perch from which to admire it. Access the walking path from Main St (behind Rite-Aid) or from Bridge St.

✯ Festivals & Events

Aston Magna MUSIC
(www.astonmagna.org; tickets $30-50; ⊙Jun-Jul) Listen to Bach, Brahms, Buxtehude and other early classical music at a number of venues in Great Barrington, including Mahaiwe Performing Arts Center (p196). Now in its fifth decade!

🛏 Sleeping

Beartown State Forest Campground CAMPGROUND $
(☑413-528-0904; www.mass.gov/dcr; 69 Blue Hill Rd, Monterey; tent sites $20) It's mostly backpackers who stay at this quiet campground on the Appalachian Trail, 8 miles east of Great Barrington via MA 23. It has 12 basic sites that overlook 35-acre Benedict Pond.

Lantern House Motel MOTEL $$
(☑413-528-2350; www.thelanternhousemotel.com; 256 Stockbridge Rd/US 7; r $65-200; ❈ 🛜 ☲) The decor's a bit dated, for sure, but the cheerful operators of this independent family-run motel keep everything spotlessly clean and

the place is darn comfortable. Most of the rooms are spacious, too, so if you've got kids, you won't be tripping over them here.

Wainwright Inn
B&B $$

(☎ 413-528-2062; www.wainwrightinn.com; 518 S Main St; r $140-230; ▣ ☎) Great Barrington's finest place to lay your head, this inn (c 1766) exudes historical appeal from its wraparound porches and spacious parlors to the period room decor in the nine guest rooms. Breakfast is a decadent experience. The inn is a short walk from the center of town on a busy road.

Old Inn on the Green
INN $$$

(☎ 413-229-7924; www.oldinn.com; 134 Hartsville-New Marlborough Rd/MA 57, New Marlborough; Old Inn r $285, Thayer House r $385; ⊙ restaurant 5:30-9:30pm Wed-Mon Jul-Oct, Wed-Sun Nov-Jun; ▣ ☎ ▤) Once a relay stop on a post road, the Old Inn (c 1760) is exactly what most people picture when they think New England country inn. The dining rooms are lit entirely by candlelight (mains $29 to $46), and guest rooms have wide-plank floors, four-poster beds and fireplaces. Breakfast features treats such as homemade granola, fresh fruit and warm pastries.

✗ Eating

Berkshire Co-op Market Cafe
CAFE $

(www.berkshire.coop; 42 Bridge St; sandwiches $5.50-8; ⊙ 8am-8pm; ▯) ✔ You don't need to spend a bundle to eat green, wholesome and local. This cafe inside the Berkshire Co-op Market, just off Main St, has a crunchy farm-fresh salad bar, generous made-to-order sandwiches (both meat and veggie), fresh juices and fair-trade coffees.

Baba Louie's
PIZZA $

(☎ 413-528-8100; www.babalouiespizza.com; 286 Main St; small pizzas $10-14; ⊙ 11:30am-3pm & 5-9:30pm; ☎) Baba's is known for its organic sourdough crust. There's a pizza for every taste, running the gamut from the fan-favorite Dolce Vita with figs, gorgonzola and prosciutto to the dairy-free Vegetazione with artichoke hearts, broccoli, tofu and soy mozzarella.

Prairie Whale
MODERN AMERICAN $$

(www.facebook.com/PrairieWhale; 178 Main St; mains $18-30; ⊙ 5-10pm Mon, Thu & Fri, 11am-3pm & 5-10pm Sat & Sun) Dimly lit and atmospheric, this bar and restaurant occupies a former family home, with outdoor seating on the porch and an inventive menu. The owners are committed to using local

The Berkshires

BISH BASH FALLS

In the very southwest corner of the state, near the New York state line, is **Bash Bish Falls** (www.mass.gov/locations/bash-bish-falls-state-park; Falls Rd, Mt Washington; ☉ sunrise-sunset), the largest waterfall in Massachusetts. The water feeding the falls runs down a series of gorges before the torrent is sliced in two by a massive boulder perched directly above a pool. There it drops as a picture-perfect double waterfall. These 60ft-high falls are a popular spot for landscape painters to set up their easels.

A short, steep trail leads directly to the falls from the Massachusetts parking lot. For a gentler walk, continue driving 1 mile west across the state border to the New York parking lot, from where a more level path takes you to the water's edge. Hikes from both starting points take about 20 minutes each way.

To get there from Great Barrington, take MA 23 west to South Egremont. Turn onto MA 41 south and then take the immediate right onto Mt Washington Rd (which becomes East St) and continue for 7.5 miles. Turn right onto Cross Rd, then right onto West St and continue 1 mile. Turn left onto Falls Rd and follow that for 1.5 miles. The parking lot and trailhead will be on your left.

suppliers, including sheep and laying hens from their own farm. Hand-reared farm animals and organic produce don't come cheap, however; prices are on the high side.

With a mean cocktail menu (served with locally grown garnishes, of course) and an excellent wine and beer list, the Prairie Whale is also one of the best places in town for a drink.

John Andrews Restaurant　　　　MODERN AMERICAN **$$$**
(☏ 413-528-3469; www.jarestaurant.com; 224 Hillsdale Rd, Egremont; mains $24-36; ☉ 5-9pm Sun-Tue & Thu, to 10pm Fri & Sat, closed Wed May-Nov, closed Tue & Wed Dec-Apr; 🖉) 🍴 Raised in an Iowa farm family, chef Dan Smith was a pioneer of the farm-to-table movement in the Berkshires. His restaurant turns out a fine Italian–New American menu featuring delicious lamb and other items from nearby farms. The setting, a rustic 19th-century farmhouse overlooking a garden, makes a perfect match for the menu.

🍸 Drinking & Entertainment

Barrington Brewery　　　　MICROBREWERY
(☏ 413-528-8282; www.barringtonbrewery.net; 420 Stockbridge Rd/US 7; mains $10-22; ☉ 11:30am-9:30pm Mon-Thu, to 10pm Fri & Sat, to 9pm Sun; 🛜) 🍴 You can rest easy, knowing your beer was brewed with solar power. The frothy, hoppy brews are the star of the show here, but the grass-fed beef burgers make a decent complement and the outdoor seating takes it up a notch on a balmy summer night.

★**Guthrie Center**　　　　LIVE MUSIC
(☏ 413-528-1955; www.guthriecenter.org; 4 Van Deusenville Rd; concert tickets $25-60; ☉ Troubadour concerts Fri-Sun Jun-Oct) The old church made famous in Arlo Guthrie's *Alice's Restaurant* hosts a beloved Troubadour series, featuring folk concerts by the likes of Tom Chapin, Tracy Grammer, Tom Rush and, occasionally, local boy Arlo himself. It's a cozy setting with just 100 seats, so book in advance.

Mahaiwe Performing Arts Center　　　　PERFORMING ARTS
(www.mahaiwe.org; 14 Castle St) Culture vultures will find an eclectic menu of events at this classic theater, from jazz vocals to classic movies and modern dance.

ℹ️ Information

Southern Berkshire Chamber of Commerce
(☏ 413-528-1510; www.southernberkshire chamber.com; 362 Main St; ☉ 10am-6pm Thu-Mon) Maintains a kiosk on Main St (at the corner of St James Pl) that's well stocked with maps, restaurant menus and accommodations lists.

ℹ️ Getting There & Away

Most travelers arrive by car on US 7, which runs through the center of town. Otherwise, **Peter Pan** (www.peterpanbus.com; 362 Main St) buses run to/from Pittsfield and Greenfield, MA, as well as Canaan, CT. The bus stop is outside CVS Pharmacy (near the Chamber of Commerce information booth). Bus route 21, operated by the Berkshire Regional Transit Authority (www.berkshirerta.com), connects Great Barrington with Stockbridge and Lee.

Stockbridge

📍 413 / POP 1870

Take a good look down Stockbridge's wide Main St. Notice anything? More specifically, notice anything missing? Not one stoplight interrupts the view; not one telephone pole blights the picture-perfect scene – it looks very much the way Norman Rockwell might have seen it.

In fact, Rockwell did see it – he lived and worked in Stockbridge during the last 25 years of his life. Nowadays, Stockbridge attracts summer and fall visitors en masse, who come to stroll the streets, inspect the shops and sit in the rockers on the porch of the historic Red Lion Inn. And they come by the busload to visit the Norman Rockwell Museum on the town's outskirts.

All that fossilized picturesqueness comes at a price. Noticeably absent from the village center is the kind of vitality that you find in the neighboring towns.

◉ Sights

★ Norman Rockwell Museum   MUSEUM

(📞 413-298-4100; www.nrm.org; 9 Glendale Rd/MA 183; adult/child $20/free; ⊙ 10am-5pm May-Oct, to 4pm Nov-Apr) Born in New York City, Norman Rockwell (1894–1978) sold his first magazine cover illustration to the *Saturday Evening Post* in 1916. In the following half-century he did another 321 covers for the *Post,* as well as illustrations for books, posters and many other magazines on his way to becoming the most popular illustrator in US history. This excellent museum has the largest collection of Rockwell's original art, as well as Rockwell's studio.

Chesterwood   MUSEUM

(www.chesterwood.org; 4 Williamsville Rd; adult/child under 13yr $20/free; ⊙ 10am-5pm late May–mid-Oct) This pastoral 122-acre plot was 'heaven' to its owner Daniel Chester French (1850–1931), the sculptor best known for his great seated statue of Abraham Lincoln in the Lincoln Memorial in Washington, DC. French's public works, mostly monumental, made him a wealthy man. His house and studio are substantially as they were when he lived and worked here, with nearly 500 pieces of sculpture, finished and unfinished, in the barnlike studio. Guided tours run at 11am, noon, 1pm and 2pm.

Naumkeag   HOUSE

(www.thetrustees.org; 5 Prospect St; house or garden tour adult/child $20/5, house & garden tour adult/child $25/10; ⊙ 10am-5pm daily mid-May–late Oct, 10am-5pm Sat & Sun mid-Apr–mid-May) Designed by the renowned architect Stanford White in 1885, this 44-room Gilded Age 'cottage' was the summer retreat of Joseph Hodges Choate, a former US ambassador to England. The estate retains so much of its original character that you might expect Choate to be sitting at the breakfast table. The influence of his travels abroad are visible not only in the home's rich and eclectic interior but also in the acres of surrounding formal gardens with their fountains, sculpture and themed plantings.

Mission House   HISTORIC BUILDING

(www.thetrustees.org; 19 Main St; adult/child $5/free; ⊙ 11am-2pm Sat & Sun Jul & Aug) Swing by this classic 1739 Colonial home, a National Historic Landmark, if just to view it from the outside. It was home to John Sergeant, the first missionary to the region's native Mohicans. The interior contains a collection of 18th-century American furniture and decorative arts. The house is on the corner of Main and Sergeant Sts, just west of the Red Lion Inn.

✦✦ Festivals & Events

Berkshire Theatre Festival   THEATER

(📞 413-997-9444; www.berkshiretheatre.org; 83 E Main St; ⊙ Jun-Oct) Experimental theater is held at venues in Stockbridge and Pittsfield.

Stockbridge Main Street at Christmas   CHRISTMAS

(www.stockbridgechamber.org; Main St; adult/child $5/free; ⊙ Dec) On the first Sunday in December, Stockbridge's Main St is closed to traffic and vintage cars are parked in their place as Norman Rockwell's iconic Christmas scene is recreated. Weekend activities include horse-drawn carriage rides, carol concerts and house tours of historic properties in the village.

🛏 Sleeping & Eating

Red Lion Inn   HISTORIC HOTEL $$

(📞 413-298-5545; www.redlioninn.com; 30 Main St; r with/without bath from $180/120; ✴ @ 🛜 🛝 🐾) This aging white-frame hotel is at the very heart of Stockbridge village, marking the intersection of Main St and MA 7. It's been the town's focal point since 1773, though it was completely rebuilt after a fire in 1897.

Rooms in the main building have old print wallpaper, classic moldings and white linens; some also feature fireplaces.

Stockbridge Country Inn INN $$$
(413-298-4015; www.stockbridgecountryinn.com; 26 Glendale Rd/MA 183; r $300-450; ☎ ✉) Occupying a 19th-century estate house, this is the closest inn to the Norman Rockwell Museum. Antique fittings, four-poster beds and 4 acres of pretty grounds set the tone. But it's the full country breakfast served on a sunny porch overlooking flowery gardens that sets it apart.

★**Once Upon a Table** AMERICAN $$
(413-298-3870; www.onceuponatablebistro.com; 36 Main St; mains lunch $10-12, dinner $15-28; ⊙11:30am-3pm & 5-8:30pm Sun-Thu, to 9pm Fri & Sat) This bright spot in the Mews shopping arcade serves upscale fare in a sunny dining room. It's the best place in town for lunch, with choices like daily-changing omelets and sophisticated sandwiches. The dinner menu features reliably delicious treats such as pecan-crusted rainbow trout and fine dessert pastries.

Red Lion Inn AMERICAN $$$
(413-298-5545; www.redlioninn.com; 30 Main St; tavern mains $18-24, dining room mains $26-39; ⊙8-10am, noon-4:30pm & 5:30-9pm Mon-Thu, to 9:30pm Fri-Sun) The Red Lion is the main eating venue in Stockbridge. On the stodgy side is the formal dining room, where you can indulge in a roasted native turkey while sitting under a crystal chandelier. More relaxed is the Widow Bingham Tavern, a rustic pub that serves gourmet sandwiches and many variations on cow.

🍷 Drinking & Nightlife

Stockbridge Coffee & Tea COFFEE
(www.stockbridgecoffeeandtea.com; 6 Elm St; ⊙7am-5pm) Call in to this cozy cafe for quality, single origin coffee, specialty tea and freshly baked pastries; then browse the shelves of the adjoining used bookstore. Look out for monthly poetry and literary reading events.

Lion's Den PUB
(www.redlioninn.com; 30 Main St; mains $12-18; ⊙4-10pm Mon-Thu, to 11pm Fri, noon-11pm Sat, noon-10pm Sun) Downstairs at the Red Lion Inn, this dark, cozy bar has a friendly crowd and live music most nights. It serves daily pub specials like chicken pot pie, Hungarian goulash and turkey dinner. In fair weather you can dine in the courtyard out back.

ℹ Information

Stockbridge Chamber of Commerce (413-298-5200; www.stockbridgechamber.org; Main St; ⊙9am-5pm Mon, Wed & Fri) You can also pick up brochures at the small kiosk opposite the library on Main St in the town center. It's often unstaffed, but the door's always open.

ℹ Getting There & Away

The center of Stockbridge is at the intersection of MA 102 and MA 7. In town, MA 102 becomes Main St.

Operated by the Berkshire Regional Transit Authority (www.berkshirerta.com), buses connect Stockbridge to the other towns in the region. Peter Pan buses (www.peterpanbus.com) go to Great Barrington, Lenox and Sturbridge, as well as New York City.

Lee
413 / POP 2040

Welcome to the towniest town in the Berkshires. A main street, both cute and gritty, runs through the center, curving to cross some railroad tracks. On it you'll find a hardware store, a bar and a few places to eat including a proper diner favored by politicians desiring photo ops with working-class folks. Most travelers pass through Lee simply because it's near a convenient exit off the Mass Pike. The main draw is the prestigious Jacob's Pillow dance festival on the outskirts of town.

◎ Sights & Events

October Mountain State Forest FOREST
(413-243-1778; www.mass.gov/dcr; 317 Woodland Rd; ⊙sunrise-sunset) FREE Most out-of-towners head to Mt Greylock, and leave October Mountain State Forest to the locals. This 16,500-acre state park is the largest tract of open space in Massachusetts, and it's rife with opportunities for outdoor adventure. Hidden amid the hardwoods, **Buckley Dunton Reservoir** – a small body of water stocked with bass – is a great spot for canoeing. For hikers, a 9-mile stretch of the Appalachian Trail pierces the heart of the forest through copses of hemlocks, spruces, birches and oaks.

Jacob's Pillow DANCE
(413-243-9919; www.jacobspillow.org; 358 George Carter Rd, Becket; tickets $25-78; ⊙mid-Jun–late Aug) Founded by Ted Shawn in an old barn in 1932, Jacob's Pillow is one of the premier summer dance festivals in the USA. Through

the years, Alvin Ailey, Merce Cunningham, the Martha Graham Dance Company and other leading interpreters of dance have taken part. A number of free shows, classes and talks allows even those on tight budgets to join in the fun. Look especially for free performances on the Inside/Out stage. The festival theaters are in the village of Becket, 8 miles east of Lee along US 20 and MA 8.

🛏 Sleeping & Eating

October Mountain
State Forest Campground　　CAMPGROUND $
(📋 413-243-1778; www.mass.gov/dcr; Center St; tent sites $17, yurts $60-70; 🕙 late May-early Oct) This state forest campground, near the shores of the Housatonic River, has 47 sites with hot showers as well as four- and six-bed yurts (reserve well ahead). To find the campground, turn east off US 20 onto Center St and follow the signs.

Chambery Inn　　　　　　　　　INN $$
(📋 413-243-2221; www.chamberyinn.com; 199 Main St; ste $150-450) Formerly a school house run by French nuns, this 1885 building retains many original features, such as the tin ceilings and the separate staircases for girls and boys. There is no shortage of modern comfort in the nine suites, which have four poster beds and period furnishings. Breakfast is a basket of freshly baked muffins and scones, delivered to your door.

🍴 Eating & Drinking

Joe's Diner　　　　　　　　　　DINER $
(📋 413-243-9756; 85 Center St; mains $3.50-15; 🕙 6am-4pm Mon, to 8pm Tue-Fri, to 3:30pm Sat, to 1pm Sun) There's no better slice of blue-collar Americana in the Berkshires than Joe's Diner, at the north end of Main St. Norman Rockwell's famous painting of a policeman sitting at a counter talking to a young boy, *The Runaway* (1958), was inspired by this diner. Joe's has barely changed a wink – not the bar stools and not the old-fashioned diner fare.

Locker Room Sports Pub　　　　　PUB
(www.lockerroomsportsbar.com; 232 Main St; mains $8-18; 🕙 kitchen 11am-9pm Sun-Thu, to 10pm Fri & Sat, bar 11am-midnight; 🛜🍴) For a drink with the locals, head to this friendly pub on the main drag. Tables in cute wooden booths have views of the sports screens and there's a good selection of bottled, canned and draft beer, including local craft beers on tap. Rea-

sonable pub food – sandwiches, burgers and snacks – is served; there's also a kids menu.

ℹ Information

Lee Chamber of Commerce (📋 413-243-1705; www.leechamber.org; 3 Park Pl; 🕙10am-4pm Mon-Sat Jun-Oct)

ℹ Getting There & Away

Just off I-90 at exit 2, Lee is the gateway to Lenox, Stockbridge and Great Barrington. US 20 is Lee's main street, and leads right into Lenox, about a 15-minute drive away.

Operated by the Berkshire Regional Transit Authority (www.berkshirerta.com), bus route 21 connects Lee with Stockbridge and Great Barrington to the south; route 2 serves Lenox and Pittsfield to the north.

Lenox
📋 413 / POP 1700

This appealing, wealthy town is a historical anomaly: firstly, its charm was not destroyed by the industrial revolution; and then, prized for its bucolic peace, the town became a summer retreat for wealthy families with surnames like Carnegie, Vanderbilt and Westinghouse, who had made their fortunes by building factories in other towns.

As the cultural heart of the Berkshires, Lenox's illustrious past remains tangibly present today. The superstar among its attractions is the Tanglewood Music Festival, an incredibly popular summer event drawing scores of visitors from New York City, Boston and beyond.

⊙ Sights & Activities

Mount　　　　　　　　　　　HISTORIC SITE
(www.edithwharton.org; 2 Plunkett St; adult/child $20/free; 🕙10am-5pm Mar-Oct, 11am-4pm Sat & Sun Nov-Feb) Almost 50 years after Nathaniel Hawthorne left his home in Lenox, another writer found inspiration in the Berkshires. Edith Wharton (1862–1937) came to Lenox in 1899 and proceeded to build her palatial estate, the Mount. When not writing, she would entertain literary friends here, including Henry James. Wharton was also a keen horticulturist; many visitors come here just to wander the magnificent formal gardens, which, thanks to a $3 million restoration effort, have regained much of their original grandeur.

Pleasant Valley Wilderness Sanctuary
NATURE RESERVE

(☑ 413-637-0320; www.massaudubon.org; 472 W Mountain Rd; adult/child $5/3; ☺ 10am-4pm Tue-Sun Nov-Apr, daily May-Oct, trails dawn-dusk year-round) This 1300-acre wildlife sanctuary has 7 miles of pleasant walking trails through forests and meadows, as well as a challenging hike to the summit of Lenox Mountain. It's not uncommon to see beavers on the viewing platform near Pike's Pond. A nature center is open daily.

Berkshire Scenic Railway Museum
MUSEUM

(www.berkshirescenicrailroad.org; 10 Willow Creek Rd; ☺ 10am-2pm Sat late May-early Sep; 🚗) FREE This museum of railroad lore is set up in Lenox's 1903 vintage railroad station. Its model-railroad display is a favorite with kids, as is the chance to ride a train across the museum yard. The museum is 2 miles east of Lenox center, via Housatonic St.

Kripalu Center
YOGA

(☑ 413-448-3400; www.kripalu.org; West St/MA 183; day pass $105-135) ⚑ The premier yoga institute in the northeast, Kripalu breathes tranquility. Set on a lush estate overlooking a calm cerulean lake, the center is in a wonderful setting for those wanting to take some time off to pursue inner peace.

Although serious students spend weeks here at a time, the center also offers day passes, which allow guests to join the yoga classes, meditation sessions and other holistic offerings and include three healthy delicious meals at the Kripalu Kitchen. You don't need to be buy a pass to eat at the restaurant or have a massage at the healing arts center (50-minute treatment from $90; reserve ahead).

Arcadian Shop
OUTDOORS

(☑ 413-637-3010; www.arcadian.com; 91 Pittsfield Rd/US 7; per day bike/kayak/skis $50/35/30; ☺ 9:30am-6pm Mon-Wed, Fri & Sat, to 7pm Thu, 11am-5pm Sun) The Arcadian Shop rents out high-end mountain and road bikes, kayaks, paddleboards, cross-country skis and snowshoes. Kennedy Park, just north of downtown Lenox on US 7, is popular with mountain bikers in summer and cross-country skiers in winter. You might also explore the Berkshires' many miles of stunning back roads or paddle down the Housatonic River.

🛌 Sleeping

Cornell Inn
B&B $$

(☑ 413-637-4800; www.cornellbb.com; 203 Main St; d $130-315; @ 🖥) Spread across three historic houses, this B&B offers good value in a pricey town. When it's not full, the manager might even bargain a little – so ask about specials. It's no gilded mansion, but the rooms are cozy with the expected amenities, staff is friendly and hot breakfast is served on the porch overlooking the picturesque pond.

Hampton Inn & Suites Berkshires-Lenox
MOTEL $$

(☑ 413-499-1111; www.hamptoninn3.hilton.com; 445 Pittsfield Rd/US 7; r from $155; @ 🖥 ❄) Top choice among the area's motels, the Hampton Inn sits in a quiet location 3 miles north of town. The tasteful but traditional rooms are comfortable but not luxurious.

⭐ Stonover Farm B&B
B&B $$$

(☑ 413-637-9100; www.stonoverfarm.com; 169 Under Mountain Rd; ste $385-585; ❄ @ 🖥) If you're looking for a break from musty Victorians with floral wallpaper, you'll love this contemporary inn wrapped in a century-old farmhouse. The three suites in the main house groan with casual luxury. Oversized hot tubs, marble bathrooms, wine and cheese in the evening – this is pampering befitting its Tanglewood neighborhood setting. There are also two private stand-alone cottages.

Birchwood Inn
INN $$$

(☑ 413-637-2600; www.birchwood-inn.com; 7 Hubbard St; r $208-399; ❄ 🖥 ❄) A pretty hilltop inn a couple of blocks from the town center, Birchwood occupies the oldest (1767) home in Lenox. The 11 spacious rooms vary in decor: some swing with a vintage floral design, others are more country classic, but all are romantic and luxurious. Deluxe rooms feature king-size beds and wood-burning fireplaces.

An afternoon tea of homemade cookies, cakes and hot cider or iced tea is served in a fireside drawing room or on the sunny porch. Breakfast is another highlight, with several courses of delicious treats like baked pear with mascarpone and pumpkin seed crunch, and avocado, bacon and brie rolled omelet.

Canyon Ranch
SPA HOTEL $$$

(☑ 413-637-4100; www.canyonranchlenox.com; 165 Kemble St; r per person from $865; ❄ 🖥 ❄) The well-heeled come from around the world to unwind and soak up the spa facilities at

UNTANGLE YOURSELF

Dating from 1934, the **Tanglewood Music Festival** (☑888-266-1200; www.tanglewood.org; 297 West St/MA 183, Lenox; lawn tickets from $21; ⊙late Jun-early Sep) is among the most esteemed summertime music events in the world. Symphony, pops, chamber music, jazz and blues are performed from late June through early September. You can count on renowned cellist Yo-Yo Ma, violinist Joshua Bell and singer James Taylor to perform each summer, along with a run of world-class guest artists and famed conductors.

Performance spaces include the 'Shed,' which is anything but – a 6000-seat concert shelter with several sides open to the surrounding lawns. The weekend Boston Symphony Orchestra concerts pack the largest crowds. Most casual attendees – up to 8000 of them – arrive three or four hours before concert time, staking out good listening spots on the lawn outside the Shed, then break out picnics until the music starts. Pack a picnic from a local store like **Nejaime's Wine Cellar** (☑413-637-2221; www.nejaimeswine.com; 60 Main St; ⊙9am-9pm Mon-Sat, 11am-6pm Sun) or order in advance from Tanglewood Cafe.

Families should check out Kids Corner, offered on weekends, where children can participate in musical, arts and crafts projects.

Tanglewood is easy to find – just follow the car in front of you! From Lenox center, head west on West St/MA 183 for about 1.5 miles. Ample free concert parking is available, but remember that parking – and, more importantly, unparking – 6000 cars can take time. If your lodging is close, consider walking.

this famed resort. The all-inclusive rates include healthy gourmet meals (including vegetarian options), luxury spa treatments, fitness classes, outdoor activities, cooking demonstrations, creativity workshops and oodles of saunas, pools and quiet paths.

✗ Eating

★ **Haven Cafe & Bakery**   CAFE $
(☑413-637-8948; www.havencafebakery.com; 8 Franklin St; mains $7.50-15.50; ⊙7:30am-3pm Mon-Fri, 8am-3pm Sat & Sun; 🛜✎) It looks like a casual cafe, but the sophisticated food evokes a more upscale experience. For breakfast, try croissant French toast or inventive egg dishes like salmon scramble; for lunch there are fancy salads and sandwiches – all highlighting local organic ingredients. Definitely save room for something sweet from the bakery counter.

Bagel & Brew   BAGELS $
(www.facebook.com/BagelandBrew; 18 Franklin St; bagels $5-9; ⊙bagels 7am-1pm, bar 5-11pm Sat & Sun) Bagels by day, brews by night. Tasty bagel sandwiches are served for breakfast and lunch; then there's a dozen different beers on tap – most of them regional – served in the beer garden, starting around the dinner hour. The food that accompanies the brew is not bagels, but truly delicious pub grub. This place has a great vibe.

★ **Nudel**   AMERICAN $$
(☑413-551-7183; www.nudelrestaurant.com; 37 Church St; mains $18-26; ⊙5-9:15pm) Nudel is a driving force in the area's sustainable food movement, with just about everything on the menu seasonally inspired and locally sourced. The back-to-basics approach rings through in inventive dishes, which change daily but never disappoint. Incredible flavors. Nudel has a loyal following, so reservations are recommended. The last seating is at 9:15pm.

Kripalu Kitchen   HEALTH FOOD $$
(www.kripalu.org; 57 Interlaken Rd; breakfast/lunch/dinner $13/16/19; ⊙7-8:30am, 11:30am-1:30pm & 5:30-7pm) The restaurant at the Kripalu Center is open to everyone. Buffet meals are prepared with organic, seasonal, locally sourced ingredients. Whole grains, fresh vegetables and pulses form the basis of the dishes, with optional fish, dairy and poultry available, too. Menus are influenced by Ayurvedic principles. Breads are freshly baked on-site.

Tanglewood Cafe   CAFETERIA $$
(☑advance orders 413-637-5152; Lion's Gate Entrance, Hawthorne Rd, Tanglewood campus; mains from $22; ✎🛜) On the Tanglewood campus, the eponymous cafe (open when performances are on) has a menu of locally sourced light fare. Alternatively, order online 48 hours in advance (google 'Tanglewood Meals to Go' for daily menus and

prices); options range from internationally themed sandwiches and salads to more elaborate feasts of local meat, fish and produce.

Bistro Zinc
FRENCH $$$

(☑ 413-637-8800; www.bistrozinc.com; 56 Church St; mains lunch $9-18, dinner $18-34; ☺ 11:30am-3pm & 5:30-10pm) The postmodern decor here is all metal surfaces and light woods, with tin ceilings, black-and-white tile floors and wine-crate doors. Tempting French offerings include steak *frites,* beef bourguignon and trout meunière, all with a nouveau twist. Tasty cocktails, too.

☷ Drinking & Entertainment

Brava
WINE BAR

(www.facebook.com/BravaBarLenox; 27 Housatonic St; tapas $7-17, pizzas $15-17; ☺ 5pm-1am) This cozy little place calls itself a wine and beer bar, and backs it up with a bulging wine cellar, a good choice of *vino* by the glass, and more than 80 craft beers from around the world. Spanish and Italian-style tapas and pizza are served until midnight but the bar stays open until 1am (late for these parts).

Bookstore
WINE BAR

(Get Lit Wine Bar; www.bookstoreinlenox.com; 11 Housatonic St; ☺ 10am-6pm Mon-Sat, to 4pm Sun, longer hours Jul & Aug) We've all been to bookstores that serve coffee, but this one serves wine. Good wine. Which is a perfect complement to the good books that are also on sale here. The proprietor, Matt, is a charming host who loves to talk about books and other important things.

Olde Heritage Tavern
PUB

(www.facebook.com/OldeHeritageTavern; 12 Housatonic St; mains $7-15; ☺ 11:30am-12:30am Mon-Fri, 8am-12:30am Sat & Sun; ☷) Come to this upbeat tavern for local microbrews on tap, a friendly atmosphere and decent pub fare. Shady outdoor seating is a welcome option.

Shakespeare & Company
THEATER

(☑ box office 413-637-3353; www.shakespeare.org; 70 Kemble St) This renowned company often updates the Bard's plays to a contemporary setting, which is a fun twist. The company stages plays in its three on-site theaters: the Tina Packer Playhouse, the Elayne P Bernstein Theatre, and the tented outdoor Rose Footprint, a replica of Shakespeare's first London playhouse.

❶ Information

Visit Lenox (☑ 413-637-3646; www.lenox. org; 4 Housatonic St; ☺ 10am-4pm Wed-Sat Sep-Jun, to 6pm daily Jul-Aug) This office is a clearinghouse of information on everything from inns to what's going on.

❶ Getting There & Away

Lenox is on MA 7A, just off US 7. The nearest airports are Bradley International in Connecticut and Albany International in New York. **Peter Pan Bus Lines** (www.peterpanbus.com; 5 Walker St) operates between Lenox and Boston. Amtrak trains stop in nearby Pittsfield.

Berkshire Regional Transit Authority (www. berkshirerta.com) operates bus route 2, connecting Lenox with Lee and Pittsfield.

Pittsfield

☑ 413 / POP 44,700

Welcome to the service city of the Berkshires, where the trains stop and the people shop (for things like vacuum cleaners, not art). Jokes about the name of this town are easy to make, and not without a modicum of accuracy. Still, travelers who pause here are often delighted by the interesting museums, and they wil eat well while they are here, too.

◉ Sights & Activities

Hancock Shaker Village
MUSEUM

(☑ 413-443-0188; www.hancockshakervillage.org; 1843 W Housatonic St; adult/teen/child $20/8/free; ☺ 10am-5pm Jul-Oct, to 4pm Apr-Jun & Nov-Dec; ☷) This evocative museum illustrates the lives of the religious sect that founded the village in 1783. The Shakers believed in communal ownership, the sanctity of work and celibacy, the latter of which proved to be their demise. Known as the City of Peace, the village was occupied by Shakers until 1960. At its peak in 1830, the community numbered some 300 members.

Berkshire Museum
MUSEUM

(www.berkshiremuseum.org; 39 South St; adult/child $13/6; ☺ 10am-5pm Mon-Sat, noon-5pm Sun; ☷) This museum hosts some worthwhile temporary exhibitions and also displays a rotating permanent collection of international artworks and artifacts, many of them brought back to the Berkshires over the years by traveling locals. It also has a solid collection of Hudson River School artwork, as well as kid-friendly attractions like an aquarium and a hands-on science center.

Jiminy Peak Mountain Resort SKIING
(☑413-738-5500; www.jiminypeak.com; 37 Corey Rd, Hancock; day pass adult/child $61/41, lift tickets from $81/61; ⊙9am-10pm) 🏂 In keeping with the Berkshires' ecofriendly green vibe, Jiminy Peak proudly claims the title of being the first wind-power-operated ski resort in the country. Its 253ft wind turbine generates up to half the resort's electrical usage. And with 45 trails, and a Left Bank run of 2 miles, Jiminy offers the area's finest skiing.

It's an activity center in summer as well, when lift-served mountain biking and a ropes course take over the slopes. Jiminy Peak is 12 miles north of Pittsfield via US 7.

🛏️ Sleeping & Eating

⭐**Hotel on North** BOUTIQUE HOTEL $$
(☑413-358-4741; www.hotelonnorth.com; 297 North St; r from $170; 🅿️❄️🛜) Hints of Pittsfield's 19th-century heyday can be seen in this listed former department store turned boutique hotel. Exposed brick walls, tin ceilings and original columns have been combined with contemporary furnishings to create stylish spaces. Rooms are huge, modern and feature large bathrooms. Common areas include a double-height atrium with books and board games.

Marketplace Cafe SANDWICHES $
(www.ourmarketplacecafe.com; 53 North St; sandwiches $8-10; ⊙8am-8pm Mon-Sat, 9am-5pm Sun; 🍴) If you like sandwiches, you'll love this downtown lunch spot. There's something about a funny local name that makes a sandwich taste better. Case in point: Bartholomew's Gobble is not a turkey sandwich but a turkey dinner, complete with stuffing and cranberry, which happens to come between bread.

District Kitchen & Bar GASTROPUB $$
(www.district.kitchen; 40 West St; mains $13-30; ⊙4pm-midnight) Industrial-style decor, moody lighting and striking local artwork make this an atmospheric place. Come for dinner (tasty gastropub fare such as grilled Moroccan chicken, risotto and mac 'n' cheese), or a stop by for a cocktail and snacks (cheese boards and small plates $6 to $17).

Elizabeth's ITALIAN $$
(☑413-448-8244; 1264 East St; mains $22.50; ⊙5-9pm Wed-Sun) Don't be put off by the out-of-town location, nor by the deceptively casual interior. Folks travel from New York and Boston to sample Tom and Elizabeth Ellis' innovative Italian fare. Super-fresh ingredients and lots of love go into these dishes, most of which are vegetarian friendly.

🍷 Drinking & Nightlife

Methuselah BAR
(www.methbar.com; 391 North St; ⊙5pm-1am Mon-Sat) The name might be a little pretentious (Methuselah was a biblical figure who lived to the age of 969), but thankfully the bar itself is relaxed and welcoming, with a Scandi-style wooden interior and candles. Bar staff will guide you through the long list of organic and biodynamic wines, 16 craft beers on tap and responsibly sourced cocktails.

The menu runs from cheese boards and olives to sandwiches and tacos (mains $9 to $12).

ℹ️ Information

1 Berkshire (☑413-499-1600; www.1berkshire.com; 66 Allen St; ⊙9am-5pm Mon-Fri) Has information on Pittsfield and the rest of the Berkshires.

ℹ️ Getting There & Away

Pittsfield is 7 miles north of Lenox on US 7, at the intersection with MA 9. Peter Pan buses (www.peterpanbus.com) operate out of the **Pittsfield Bus Terminal** (1 Columbus Ave), traveling south to Lenox or north to Williamstown and North Adams. Longer-distance buses go to Boston and New York.

Berkshire Regional Transit Authority (www.berkshirerta.com) operates buses to Lenox, Lee, Great Barrington and North Adams.

Amtrak (www.amtrak.com) trains also stop here on their way to Boston or Albany, NY.

Williamstown

☑413 / POP 4300

Small but pretty Williamstown is nestled within the heart of the Purple Valley, so named because the surrounding mountains often seem shrouded in a lavender veil at dusk. Folks congregate in the friendly town center, which is only two blocks long, while dogs and kids frolic in the ample green spaces.

Williamstown is a quintessential New England college town, its charming streets and greens dotted with the stately brick and marble buildings of Williams College. Cultural life is rich, with a pair of exceptional art museums and one of the region's most respected summer theater festivals.

◉ Sights

★ Clark Art Institute — MUSEUM

(📱413-458-2303; www.clarkart.edu; 225 South St; adult/child $20/free; ⊙10am-5pm Tue-Sun Sep-Jun, daily Jul & Aug) Even if you're not an avid art lover, don't miss this gem, set on 140 gorgeous acres of expansive lawns, flower-filled meadows and rolling hills. The building – with its triple-tiered reflecting pool – is a stunner. The collections are particularly strong in the impressionists, with significant works by Monet, Pissarro and Renoir. Mary Cassatt, Winslow Homer and John Singer Sargent represent contemporaneous American painting.

Robert Sterling Clark (1877–1956), a Yale engineer whose family made a fortune in the sewing-machine industry, began collecting art in Paris in 1912. He and his wife eventually housed their impressive collection in Williamstown in a white marble temple built expressly for the purpose. 'The Clark,' as everyone in town calls it, is less than 1 mile south of the intersection of US 7 and MA 2.

Williams College Museum of Art — MUSEUM

(📱413-597-2429; https://wcma.williams.edu; 15 Lawrence Hall Dr; ⊙10am-5pm, to 8pm Thu, closed Wed Sep-May) FREE In the center of town is this worthwhile – and free! – art museum. It has a collection of some 15,000 pieces, with substantial works by notables such as Edward Hopper (*Morning in a City*), Winslow Homer and Grant Wood, to name only a few. The photography collection is also noteworthy. Temporary exhibitions are accompanied by academic talks. To find the museum, look for the huge bronze eyes by Louise Bourgeois, embedded in the front lawn on Main St.

Williams College — UNIVERSITY

(📱413-597-3131; www.williams.edu; 880 Main St) Here is the Berkshires' quintessential college campus, with wide green lawns and graceful academic architecture, surrounded by a sleepy town and the rolling hills beyond. Williams is one of the 'Little Ivies' – a highly rated, super-selective and beautifully located liberal arts college.

★☆ Festivals & Events

Williamstown Theatre Festival — THEATER

(📱box office 413-458-3200; www.wtfestival.org; 1000 Main St; ⊙Jun-Aug) Stars of the theater world descend upon Williamstown every year from the third week in June to the third week in August. Widely considered the best summer theater in the area, the Williamstown Theatre Festival was the first to win the Regional Theatre Tony Award.

The festival mounts the region's major theatrical offerings with a mix of classics and contemporary works by up-and-coming playwrights. Kevin Kline, Richard Dreyfuss and Gwyneth Paltrow are but a few of the well-known thespians who have performed here. Besides the offerings on the Main Stage and Nikos Stage, there are cabaret performances in area restaurants and family nights when kids can attend performances for free.

⨋ Sleeping

River Bend Farm B&B — B&B $$

(📱413-458-3121; www.riverbendfarmbb.com; 643 Simonds Rd/US 7; r $120; ⊙Apr-Oct; 🅿🛜) Step back in time to 1770, when this Georgian Colonial was a local tavern owned by Benjamin Simonds. The house owes its painstaking restoration to hosts Judy and Dave Loomis. Four simple, comfortable doubles share two bathrooms with claw-foot tubs. Breakfast is served in the wood-paneled taproom, next to the wide stone fireplace. A truly atmospheric place to stay.

Maple Terrace Motel — MOTEL $$

(📱413-458-9677; www.mapleterrace.com; 555 Main St; d $120-200, ste $150-230; 🛜🏊) The Maple Terrace is a simple yet cozy place on the eastern edge of town, with family-friendly suites equipped with kitchenettes, and spacious gardens that make you want to linger. There's nothing fancy going on here, but the place is comfortable and service is warmly attentive. A simple breakfast is included. Discounts offered in winter and spring.

★ Guest House at Field Farm — INN $$$

(📱413-458-3135; www.thetrustees.org/field-farm; 554 Sloan Rd; r $250-350; @🛜🏊) About 6 miles south of Williamstown, this one-of-a-kind inn offers an artful blend of mid-20th century modernity and timeless mountain scenery. The six rooms are spacious and fitted with handcrafted furnishings that reflect the modernist style of the house. The sculpture-laden grounds feature miles of lightly trodden walking trails and a pair of Adirondack chairs set perfectly for unobstructed stargazing.

The house was built in 1948 in spare, clean-lined Bauhaus style on 300 acres of woods and farmland facing Mt Greylock. The original owners, art collectors Lawrence and Eleanor Bloedel, bequeathed the estate to the Trustees of Reservations, which now operates it.

✗ Eating & Drinking

Pappa Charlie's Deli DELI $
(✐413-458-5969; 28 Spring St; sandwiches $5-7; ⊘8am-8pm Mon-Sat, to 7pm Sun) Here's a welcoming breakfast spot where locals really do ask for 'the usual.' The stars themselves created the lunch sandwiches that bear their names. The Mary Tyler Moore is a favorite (bacon, lettuce, tomato and avocado); the actress later went vegetarian, so you can also get a version with soy bacon. Order a Politician and get anything you want.

Moonlight Diner & Grille DINER $
(✐413-458-3305; www.facebook.com/Moonlight Diner; 408 Main St; mains $6-15; ⊘7am-3pm Sun-Tue, to 8pm Wed & Thu, to 9pm Fri & Sat) This old-school diner on the east side of town dishes up all the classics at honest prices. The retro 1950s decor is fun and though the food is nothing extraordinary, sometimes you just need a huge juicy burger or a cheesy omelet with no fancy business.

★ Mezze Bistro & Bar FUSION $$
(✐413-458-0123; www.mezzerestaurant.com; 777 Cold Spring Rd/US 7; mains $16-28; ⊘5-9pm Sun-Thu, to 9:30pm Fri & Sat) You don't know exactly what you're going to get at this contemporary restaurant – the menu changes frequently – but you know it's going to be good. Situated on 3 spectacular acres, Mezze's farm-to-table approach begins with an edible garden right on-site. Much of the rest of the seasonal menu, from small-batch microbrews to organic meats, is locally sourced as well.

Tunnel City Coffee CAFE
(www.tunnelcitycoffee.com; 100 Spring St; ⊘6am-6pm; 🛜) A bustling den of cramming students and mentoring professors. Besides liquid caffeine, some seriously delicious desserts like triple-layer chocolate mousse cake will get you buzzing.

ℹ Information

Williamstown Chamber of Commerce
(✐413-458-9077; www.williamstownchamber. com; 100 Spring St; ⊘11am-6pm Mon-Sat Jun-Aug) Operates a seasonal information booth.

ℹ Getting There & Away

The bus station is in the lobby of the Williams Inn, at the intersection of US7 and MA 2. Peter Pan Bus Lines (www.peterpanbus.com) runs buses to Albany, NY, and Pittsfield, Lenox, Lee and Springfield. Berkshire Regional Transit Authority (www.berkshirerta.com) operates hourly buses to North Adams (25 minutes).

North Adams
☑ 413 / POP 13,500

At first glance, North Adams' beautiful and bleak 19th-century downtown seems out of sync with the rest of the Berkshires. It's not so lively and the amenities are limited. But it doesn't take long to discover the appeal – mainly, Mass MoCA, an exemplary contemporary art museum of staggering proportions. Indeed, the place is big enough to be its own village, and its grounds do in fact contain some of the city's best dining, drinking and shopping options.

◉ Sights & Activities

★ MASS MoCA MUSEUM
(Massachusetts Museum of Contemporary Art; ✐413-662-2111; www.massmoca.org; 1040 Mass MoCA Way; adult/child $20/8; ⊘10am-6pm Sun-Wed, to 7pm Thu-Sat Jul & Aug, 11am-5pm Wed-Mon Sep-Jun) MASS MoCA sprawls over 13 acres of downtown North Adams – one-third of the entire business district. After the Sprague Electric Company closed in 1985, some $31 million was spent to modernize the property into 'the largest gallery in the United States.' The museum encompasses 222,000 sq ft in 25 buildings, including art construction areas, performance centers and 19 galleries. Long-term exhibitions include a gallery of wall paintings by Sol LeWitt. Thought-provoking guided tours run daily at 1pm and 3pm.

In addition to carrying description-defying installation pieces and cutting-edge temporary exhibitions, the museum has evolved into one of the region's key venues for theater, documentary films and avant-garde dance performances. Families with budding artists should check out the museum's Kidspace, where children can create their own masterpiece.

North Adams Art Walk
PUBLIC ART

(www.downstreetart.org) **FREE** When you're done exploring the art spaces at Mass MoCA, don't miss the arresting murals in the streets nearby. Highlights include *Justice* by Alaa Awad, with ancient Egyptian motifs, and *Imaginarium,* a colorful work by Yu-Baba. Take them in on a self-guided art walk; pick up a free map from the booth near the main entrance to Mass MoCA.

Hoosac Range Trail
HIKING

(Mohawk Trail /MA 2) **FREE** Near North Adams, there is an easy 1.6-mile trail to Sunset Rock, where you can pick blueberries in season. If you have more time, take the moderate 6.2-mile trail to Spruce Hill, where you'll be rewarded with open ledges and long views. The trail is known for rocky glacial cliffs and creepy tree formations, caused by wind and ice. The trailhead is at the Western Summit of the Mohawk Trail, located on MA 2 about 4 miles east of North Adams.

✦✦ Festivals & Events

Northern Berkshire Fall Foliage Parade
PARADE

(www.1berkshire.com; ☉Oct) Usually held on the first Sunday in October, this annual event showcases local marching bands, dance schools, emergency services and sports teams, and – if you're lucky – features an appearance by the prince and princess of the Adams Aggie Fair. If that doesn't get you excited, there's also a dog parade. All surrounded by brilliantly colored trees.

🛏 Sleeping

Clarksburg State Park
CAMPGROUND $

(☑413-664-8345; www.mass.gov/dcr; 1199 Middle Rd, Clarksburg; tent sites $27) With views of the Berkshire hills and the Green Mountains, this is a scenic spot to pitch your tent. The 45 campsites in wooded grounds have access to bathrooms with hot showers, as well as about 10 miles of walking trails and opportunities for kayaking, canoeing and swimming in Mauserts Pond. The park is 3 miles north of North Adams.

Savoy Mountain State Forest
CAMPGROUND $

(☑413-663-8469; www.mass.gov/dcr; 260 Central Shaft Rd, Florida; tent sites/cabins $27/65; ⊛) This wooded campground has 45 sites and four very rustic log cabins in one of the best state parks for mountain biking. The campground is 9 miles southeast of North Adams.

★ Porches Inn
BOUTIQUE HOTEL $$$

(☑413-664-0400; www.porches.com; 231 River St; d $220-300, ste $310-420; ⊛⊕⊛) Across the street from MASS MoCA, the artsy rooms here combine well-considered color palettes, ample lighting and retro styling. The accommodations are inside a row of 19th-century houses with traditional front porches complete with rocking chairs, perfect for post-museum contemplation. A highlight is the heated swimming pool and hot tub open year-round. Rates include a cooked breakfast.

✗ Eating & Drinking

Lickety Split
CAFE $

(www.licketysplitatmassmoca.com; 1040 Mass MoCA Way; mains $9-11.50; ☉9am-5pm Mon & Wed-Sat, 10am-6pm Sun) A convenient place for museum-goers to eat is at this pretty cafe inside MASS MoCA, offering satisfyingly good homemade soups and sandwiches, as well as breakfast fare and free-trade coffee. Alert: premium ice cream made in-house is served on-site. Opens for dinner when there are evening performances at Mass MoCA.

★ Public Eat & Drink
PUB FOOD $$

(☑413-664-4444; www.publiceatanddrink.com; 34 Holden St; mains $12-27; ☉11:30am-10pm) With exposed-brick walls and big windows overlooking the street, this airy pub is the most popular dinner spot in North Adams. Come for an excellent selection of craft beers and gourmet pub fare, like brie burgers, flatbread pizzas and bistro steak. Some decent vegetarian options as well.

Bright Ideas Brewing
BREWERY

(www.brightideasbrewing.com; 111 Mass MoCA Way; ☉noon-8pm Sun-Wed, to 10pm Thu, to 11pm Fri & Sat) Beer and art go together perfectly it turns out. They'll prove it to you at this brewery in the Mass MoCA compound. Exposed-brick walls, concrete floors and radical artwork constitute the decor in the former industrial space. There are a few tasty sandwiches and snacks for noshing, and the beer is delicious. What a bright idea!

❶ Getting There & Away

North Adams sits along MA 2, about 6 miles east of Williamstown. Berkshire Regional Transit Authority buses (www.berkshirerta.com) stop here along their loop around the Berkshire towns.

Mt Greylock State Reservation

At a modest 3491ft, the state's highest peak can't hold a candle altitude-wise to its western counterparts, but a climb up the 92ft-high **War Veterans Memorial Tower** at its summit rewards you with a panorama stretching up to 80 verdant miles, across the Taconic, Housatonic and Catskill ranges, and over five states. Even if the weather seems drab from the foot, a trip to the summit may well lift you above the gray blanket, and the view with a layer of cloud floating between tree line and sky is simply magical.

The reservation has some 45 miles of hiking trails. Frequent trail pull-overs on the road up – including some that lead to waterfalls – make it easy to get at least a little hike in before reaching the top of Mt Greylock. The road to the top is closed from November to late May, but the trails are open year-round.

⊙ Sights

Mt Greylock State Reservation Visitor Center   VISITOR CENTER
(☑ 413-499-4262; www.mass.gov/locations/mount-greylock-state-reservation; 30 Rockwell Rd, Lanesborough; ⊙ 9am-4:30pm Jun-early Oct, shorter hours rest of year) FREE Stop in at the visitor center for trail maps, bird lists and answers to any of your other questions. There is also an introductory film and exhibits on the park's topography, flora, fauna and history (the mountain road and lodge were constructed by the Civilian Conservation Corps in the 1930s as part of President Roosevelt's New Deal).

🍴 Sleeping & Eating

Bascom Lodge   LODGE $
(☑ 413-743-1591; www.bascomlodge.net; 1 Summit Rd; dm/d/tr/q without bath $40/125/170/190; ⊙ Sat & Sun May–mid-Jun, daily mid-Jun–Oct; 🅿) High atop Mt Greylock, this lodge was built as a federal work project in the 1930s. In the lobby, inviting leather sofas are arranged

---

HIKING MT GREYLOCK

Mt Greylock has hikers of all levels covered. Take your pick from 45 miles of hiking trails, along 13 marked routes, including a portion of the Appalachian Trail.

A stretch of wildflower-strewn meadow, named after a man called Seth Jones who farmed here in the 1800s, is the starting point for this fairly strenuous, 8.5-mile day hike. From the trailhead on Rockwell Rd, the **Jones Nose Trail** begins in open meadow; look out for butterflies. Ledges along this section of the trail offer views to the south and west of the Berkshire hills, Taconic Range and Catskills.

Follow the blue markers uphill for 1.2 miles to join the **Appalachian Trail**, heading north. From here, you'll hike 2.9 miles along the legendary trail to the Mt Greylock summit.

By the time you join the Appalachian Trail, the path has entered the trees as it climbs up toward the summit of **Saddle Ball Mountain** (3247ft). The trail continues through boreal forest; red spruce and balsam fir are dominant.

At the summit, views extend for some 80 miles in clear weather. Climb the 92ft **Veterans War Memorial Tower** for a 360-degree outlook. Nearby, **Adams Overlook** offers a bird's-eye view of the town of Adams, the Hoosic River and the surrounding farmland. You can get lunch at Bascom Lodge.

For the route back down, follow the Appalachian Trail 0.7 miles south to the **Hopper Trail**, to the west of Rockwell Rd, and follow it to Sperry Rd (1.2 miles).

From here there is the option of a 2-mile round-trip detour along Sperry Rd to **Stony Ledge**. Follow signs past the campsite to reach the ledge with views of the Hopper, a steep valley that was largely inaccessible to loggers and contains old-growth forest.

At the junction of Sperry Rd and Rockwell Rd, cross over to the **CCC Dynamite Trail** and follow the trail south for 1.6 miles, past ferns and wildflowers, to rejoin the Jones Nose Trail. Continue downhill for half a mile to return to the trailhead.

The Jones Nose trailhead is off the Rockwell Rd, on the southern side of the mountain, 3.7 miles from the Rockwell Rd entrance and the visitor center. There is a small parking lot at the trailhead.

around a stone fireplace – a sociable place for a drink come nightfall. Rooms have shared bathrooms, comfortable beds and wonderful views.

The meals – fresh, hot and individually prepared – are excellent and filling, providing perfect sustenance for hikers. Reserve ahead for dinner.

Mt Greylock State
Reservation Campsite CAMPGROUND $

(☑ 413-499-4262; www.reserveamerica.com; Sperry Rd; tent sites $10) It's a 1.3-mile hike from the parking lot to the primitive, wooded sites on Mt Greylock. There are composting toilets and pumped-in water but no showers. The sites are about halfway up the mountain, and are accessed via Rockwell Rd.

Bascom Lodge Restaurant AMERICAN $$$

(www.bascomlodge.net; mains lunch $7-9, dinner $36-39; ⊙ 11am-4:30pm, dinner 7pm) Drop in for a tasty and filling lunch made with locally sourced ingredients at this welcoming mountain-top lodge with predictably stunning views. Book ahead for dinner, served at 7pm; guests are usually seated at communal tables making it a sociable experience, though prices are on the high side. Wine and local craft beers are served, too.

❶ Getting There & Away

There are two entrances to Mt Greylock State Reservation: Rockwell Rd Gate near Lanesborough (follow the signs 2 miles north of town; the visitor center is located at this entrance), and Notch Rd Gate, near North Adams (from North Adams take the MA2 west, and follow signs). From both entrances, a paved road winds up to the summit (watch out for frequent trail crossings). Parking at the top costs $10.

Rhode Island

♪ 401 / POP 1.06 MILLION

Includes ➡

Providence 212
Blackstone
River Valley 219
Bristol 221
Tiverton 222
Newport 223
Narragansett
& Point Judith 233
Westerly
& Watch Hill 234
Block Island 235

Best Places to Eat

➡ birch (p217)

➡ Boat House (p222)

➡ Matunuck Oyster Bar (p234)

➡ Anthony's Seafood (p230)

➡ Simpatico Jamestown (p232)

Best Places to Stay

➡ The Chanler at Cliff Walk (p230)

➡ Weekapaug Inn (p235)

➡ Ocean House (p235)

➡ Dean Hotel (p215)

➡ Graduate Providence (p216)

Why Go?

Rhode Island, the smallest of the US states, isn't actually an island. Although it only takes about an hour to traverse, this little wonder packs in over 400 miles of coastline with white-sand swimming beaches and some of the country's finest historic architecture, galleries and museums. What's more, Rhode Islanders are about as friendly as folks come.

Hugging the rugged shoreline before heading inland, sea-side resorts, quaint Colonial villages and extravagant country homes give way to lush fields of berry farms, vineyards and horse studs. Rhode Island's main cities – Providence, with working-class roots, and Newport, born of old money the likes of which most cannot conceive – are each among New England's finest.

With year-round cultural attractions, festivals, events, top-notch restaurants and seriously cool bars, it's no wonder the nouveau riche continue to flock here for summer shenanigans. While visiting Rhode Island ain't cheap, it's worth every penny.

When to Go
Providence

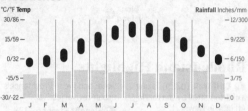

Jun This is the Ocean State: join the crowds who flock to the state's many gorgeous beaches.

Jul & Aug Newport's festival season is in full swing with classical, jazz and folk music.

Dec Providence's Federal Hill comes alive for the Christmas holiday.

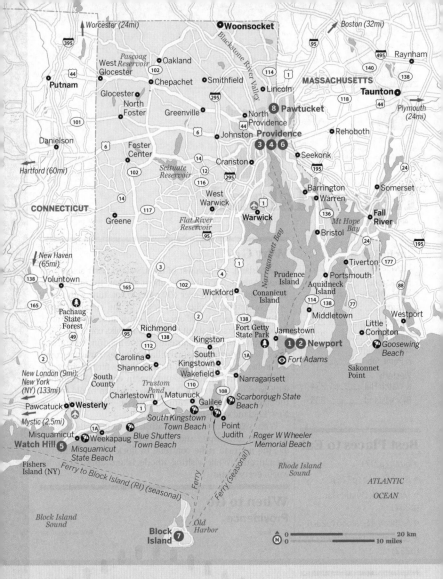

Rhode Island Highlights

1 Cliff Walk (p229) Taking a cliff-top stroll by the roaring Atlantic in Newport.

2 Preservation Society of Newport County (p227) Touring the palatial manors collectively known as the Newport Mansions.

3 WaterFire (p216) Celebrating the elements of water and fire in Providence's urban-revival festival.

4 Benefit Street (p212) Uncovering Providence's rich architectural heritage.

5 Watch Hill (p234) Dreaming about having your own country estate.

6 John Brown House Museum (p213) Wandering through the wonderfully furnished rooms of Brown's historic Providence mansion.

7 Glass Float Project (p238) Searching for treasure amid the dunes.

8 Slater Mill (p220) Recounting a nation's history where the American industrial revolution began.

History

Ever since it was founded in 1636 by Roger Williams, a religious outcast from Boston, Providence has enjoyed an independent frame of mind. Williams' guiding principle, the one that got him ostracized from Massachusetts, was that all people should have freedom of conscience. He put his liberal beliefs into practice when settling Providence, remaining on friendly terms with the local Narragansett Native Americans after purchasing from them the land for a bold experiment in tolerance and peaceful coexistence.

Williams' principles would not last long. As Providence and Newport grew and merged into a single colony, competition and conflict with area tribes sparked several wars, leading to the decimation of the Wampanoag, Pequot, Narragansett and Nipmuck peoples. Rhode Island was also a prolific slave trader and its merchants would control much of that industry in the years after the Revolutionary War.

The city of Pawtucket birthed the American industrial revolution, with the establishment of the water-powered Slater Mill in 1790. Industrialism impacted the character of Providence and surrounds, particularly along the Blackstone River, creating urban density. As with many small East Coast cities, these urban areas went into a precipitous decline in the 1940s and '50s as manufacturing industries (textiles and costume jewelry) faltered. In the 1960s, preservation efforts salvaged the historic architectural framework of Providence and Newport. Today, Newport has flourished into one of the nation's most attractive historical centers.

Providence also rerouted its destiny to emerge as a lively and stylish city with a dynamic economy and vibrant downtown core, largely due to the work of Buddy Cianci, twice-convicted felon and twice-elected mayor (1975–84, 1991–2002). Cianci is credited with saving the city from industrial and urban decline with a large-scale revitalization project that uncovered and rerouted previously subterranean river tributaries into a central artificial pond. The spectacle of today's wildly popular WaterFire festival (p216) is a powerful symbol of the city's phoenix-like rebirth along the confluence of the three rivers that gave it life. Cianci died in 2016, aged 74.

ⓘ Getting There & Around

Providence has excellent transportation options. But elsewhere in the state, public transport can be slow and infrequent. Rhode Island's twisty-turvy shape alone, with so much meandering shoreline, means that by far the best way to explore the state is with the freedom of having your own wheels.

AIR

TF Green Airport (p219) Twenty minutes' drive south of downtown Providence, this airport is served by major US airlines and car-rental companies. The airport is connected to road and rail arteries via the Interlink transportation hub.

Westerly State Airport (☑ 401-596-2357; www.pvdairport.com; 56 Airport Rd) Managed by the Green Airport Authority, this small airport operates flights to and from Block Island.

BOAT

Block Island Ferry (p239) Runs a high-speed ferry from Point Judith in Narragansett (adult/child $38/22, 30 minutes) and a traditional ferry ($26/13, one hour). The latter is the only car ferry: vehicle reservations are essential and additional fees apply. There are also high-speed ferries from Newport ($51/26, one hour) and Fall River, MA ($60/30, two hours). Rates listed are for round-trip dates on different dates. Same-day round-trip fares are marginally cheaper.

Block Island Express (p239) Operates services from New London, CT, to Old Harbor, Block Island (round-trip adult/child $47.50/23.75, 75 minutes) between May and September.

BUS

Providence and Newport are well serviced, and some buses depart direct from Green Airport.

Peter Pan Bus Lines (www.peterpanbus.com) Operates routes that connect Providence with New York City (from $32, 3¾ hours) and Boston (from $16, one hour), as well as Newport to Boston (from $26, 1½ hours).

Greyhound (www.greyhound.com) Connects to Greyhounds extensive national network, serving similar routes at similar rates.

Rhode Island Public Transit Authority (RIPTA; www.ripta.com) Rhode Island's regional transportation network links Providence's Kennedy Plaza with most towns and cities around the state.

CAR & MOTORCYCLE

I-95 cuts diagonally across the state, providing easy access from coastal Connecticut to the south and Boston to the north. From Worcester take Rte 146 to Providence. There's no shortage of car-rental companies operating out of Providence and Newport.

TRAIN

Amtrak (www.amtrak.com) trains operate between New York's Penn Station and Boston Back Bay Station, stopping in Westerly (five daily), Kingston (eight daily) and Providence (eight daily). The additional high-speed *Acela Express* train stops only in Providence.

Massachusetts Bay Transportation Authority (www.mbta.com) operates a commuter train between Providence and Boston ($11, one hour), and Providence and Green Airport ($11, 1½ hours).

PROVIDENCE

📋 401 / POP 180,393

Atop the confluence of the Providence, Moshassuck and Woonasquatucket Rivers, Rhode Island's capital city offers some of the finest urban strolling in New England: around Brown University's historic campus on 18th-century College Hill, along the landscaped Riverwalk trail, and through downtown's handsome streets and lanes with their hip cafes, art-house theaters, fusion restaurants and trendsetting bars.

Once destined to become an industrial relic, Providence's fate was spared when Buddy Cianci, its then controversial two-time mayor, rolled out a plan to revitalize the downtown core by rerouting subterranean rivers, reclaiming land and restoring historic facades. It created a city where history's treasures are not simply memorialized but rather integrated into a creative present; three centuries of architectural styles are unified in colorful urban streetscapes that are at once bold, beautiful and cooler than cool.

Providence's large student population helps keep the city's social and arts scenes cutting edge. Play it cool.

⊙ Sights

★ RISD Museum of Art   MUSEUM

(📋 401-454-6500; www.risdmuseum.org; 20 N Main St; adult/under 18yr $15/free; ⊙ 10am-5pm Tue-Sun, to 9pm 3rd Thu of month; P ♿) Wonderfully eclectic, the Rhode Island School of Design's art museum showcases 19th-century French paintings; classical Greek, Roman and Etruscan art; medieval and Renaissance works; and examples of 19th- and 20th-century American painting, furniture and decorative arts. It also has visiting exhibitions and events. Pop in before 1pm on a Sunday and admission is free. Check out the excellent website before you go.

★ Rhode Island State House   NOTABLE BUILDING

(📋 401-222-3983; www.sos.ri.gov; 82 Smith St; ⊙ self-guided tours 8:30am-4:30pm Mon-Fri, guided tours 9am, 10am, 11am, 1pm & 2pm Mon-Fri; P) FREE Designed by McKim, Mead and White in 1904, the Rhode Island State House rises above the Providence skyline, easily visible from miles around. Modeled in part on St Peter's Basilica in Vatican City, it has the world's fourth-largest self-supporting marble dome and houses one of Gilbert Stuart's portraits of George Washington, which you might want to compare to a dollar bill from your wallet.

★ Benefit Street   STREET

(Benefit St) Immediately east of Providence's downtown, you'll find College Hill, where you can see the city's Colonial history reflected in the 18th-century houses that line Benefit St on the East Side. These are mostly private homes, but many are open for tours one weekend in June during the annual Festival of Historic Houses (p215). Benefit St is a fitting symbol of the Providence renaissance, rescued by local preservationists in the 1960s from misguided urban-renewal efforts that would have destroyed it.

★ Providence Athenaeum   LIBRARY

(📋 401-421-6970; www.providenceathenaeum.org; 251 Benefit St; ⊙ 10am-7pm Mon-Thu, to 6pm Fri-Sat, 1-5pm Sun) FREE One of the most prominent buildings on Benefit St, the Greek Revival Providence Athenaeum was designed by William Strickland and completed in 1838. This is a library of the old school with plaster busts and oil paintings filling in spaces not occupied by books. Edgar Allen Poe used to court ladies here. Pick up a brochure for a self-guided Raven Tour of the building's artwork and architecture.

Prospect Terrace Park   PARK

(184 Pratt St) A great spot from which to get an overview of Providence is this elevated, compact green space known as Prospect Terrace Park. In warm weather, you'll find students throwing Frisbees, office workers picnicking and, if you arrive at the transitional point between day and the arrival

PROVIDENCE ARCHITECTURE

Come to Providence and you'll find an urban assemblage of unsurpassable architectural merit – at least in the USA. It's the only American city to have its *entire* downtown listed on the National Registry of Historic Places. The beaux-arts City Hall makes an imposing centerpiece to Kennedy Plaza, and the stately white dome of the Rhode Island State House remains visible from many corners of the city – its arcade is modeled after Parisian antecedents. These impressive structures, along with the grand art-deco **Industrial National Bank Building** (111 Westminster St) skyscraper, now empty and shockingly earmarked for demolition, are only a few of the city's many showcase buildings. The more ordinary 19th-century brick structures that fill in the spaces between their famously designed neighbors work together to create a landscape of harmonious scale, beauty and craftsmanship.

Other treasures include the 1708 **Stephen Hopkins House** (☑ 401-421-0694; www.stephenhopkins.org; 15 Hopkins St; donations accepted; ⊙ 11am-2pm Wed year-round & 10am-4pm Sat Apr-Nov), named for the 10-time governor and Declaration of Independence signer, and the clean Greek Revival lines of William Strickland's 1838 Providence Athenaeum.

Also on College Hill, the brick John Brown House Museum, described as the 'most magnificent and elegant mansion that I have ever seen on this continent' by president John Quincy Adams, was built in 1786.

of night, a sunset view. The monumental statue facing the city is that of Providence founder Roger Williams, whose remains were moved to this site in 1939.

Rhode Island School of Design
UNIVERSITY

(RISD; ☑ 401-454-6300; www.risd.edu; 20 N Main St; P) FREE Perhaps the top art school in the USA, RISD's imprint on Providence is easily felt, with students' creativity extending across the cityscape. Open to the public are the extraordinary collections of the school's Museum of Art.

Brown University
UNIVERSITY

(☑ 401-863-1000; www.brown.edu; 1 Prospect St) FREE Dominating the crest of the College Hill neighborhood on the East Side, Brown University's campus exudes Ivy League charm. **University Hall**, a 1770 brick edifice used as a barracks during the Revolutionary War, sits at its center. To explore the campus, start at the wrought-iron gates at the intersection of College St and Prospect St and make your way across the green toward Thayer St.

Waterplace Park
PARK

(1 Financial Way) The landscaped cobblestone paths of the Providence Riverwalk (p214) lead along the Woonasquatucket River to Waterplace Park's central pool and fountain, overlooked by a stepped amphitheater where outdoor artists perform in warm weather. Take a look at the historical maps and photos mounted on the walls of the

walkway beneath Memorial Blvd. Waterplace Park also serves as a nucleus for the unmissable WaterFire (p216) festival.

John Brown House Museum
MUSEUM

(☑ 401-331-8575, ext 362; www.rihs.org/museums/john-brown-house/; 52 Power St; adult/child $10/6; ⊙ tours 1:30pm & 3pm Tue-Fri, 10:30am, noon, 1:30pm & 3pm Sat Apr-Nov; P) The ruddy-brick John Brown House, built in 1786 atop College Hill, now houses yet another impressive Rhode Island local history museum. This one is lovingly curated by the Rhode Island Historical Society. Both docent-led and audio-guide tours (around an hour) are available as you walk your way through beautiful, authentically furnished period rooms of the mansion.

Providence Children's Museum
MUSEUM

(☑ 401-273-5437; www.childrenmuseum.org; 100 South St; $12; ⊙ 9am-6pm Tue-Sun, daily Apr-Labor Day; P) This well-designed, hands-on museum genuinely delights its intended guests, who can enter a giant kaleidoscope, do experiments with water fountains, pretend to be a veterinarian or play with marionettes made by some renowned puppeteers. It's aimed at pre-schoolers to pre-teens.

Providence City Hall
NOTABLE BUILDING

(☑ 401-680-5000; 25 Dorrance St) Visitors are free to enter the working City Hall and wander its hallways, although there's not much to see on the inside except city offices.

Providence

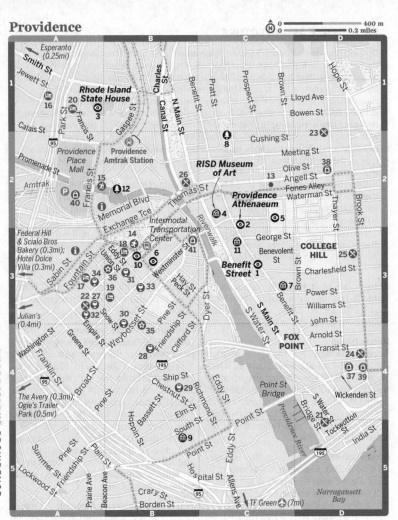

🏃 Activities

Providence Riverwalk
WALKING

Radiating out from Waterplace Park (p213), Providence Riverwalk consists of three quarters of a mile of paved pedestrian walkways and Venetian-styled bridges that hug the river. There are usually street artists and food vendors along the way and the place is packed for front-row seats when WaterFire (p216) takes place.

Providence Rink
ICE SKATING

(☎ 401-331-5544; https://theprovidencerink.com/; 2 Kennedy Plaza, Bank of America City Center; adult/ child $6/3, skate rental $4; ⊙ 10am-10pm Mon-Fri, from 11am Sat & Sun mid-Nov–mid-Mar; 🚶) This outdoor rink at the Bank of America City Center occupies prime downtown real estate in the shadow of the Graduate (p216) hotel and the Fleet Building. Be prepared to skate to some seriously loud pop songs. College students skate for $3 on Wednesday night.

👉 Tours

⭐ Rhode Island Historical Society
WALKING

(RIHS; ☎ 401-273-7507; www.rihs.org/walking -tours/; 52 Power St; adult/child $15/10; ⊙ Apr-Nov)

Providence

⊙ Top Sights
1 Benefit Street C3
2 Providence Athenaeum C2
3 Rhode Island State House A1
4 RISD Museum of Art C2

⊙ Sights
5 Brown University C2
6 Industrial National Bank Building B3
7 John Brown House Museum C3
8 Prospect Terrace Park C2
9 Providence Children's Museum B5
10 Providence City Hall B3
Rhode Island School of Design ...... (see 4)
11 Stephen Hopkins House C3
12 Waterplace Park B2

❸ Activities, Courses & Tours
13 Brown University Admissions Office C2
14 Providence Rink B3
15 Providence Riverwalk A2
Rhode Island Historical Society ..... (see 7)

🛏 Sleeping
16 Christopher Dodge House A1
17 Dean Hotel A3
18 Graduate Providence B3
19 Hotel Providence B3
20 Renaissance Providence Hotel A1

⊗ Eating
21 Al Forno D5
22 birch A3
23 East Side Pockets D2
24 Friends Market D4
Haven Brothers Diner .... (see 10)
25 Louis Family Restaurant D3
26 New Rivers B2

❷ Drinking & Nightlife
27 Dark Lady & Alley Cat A3
28 Ego B4
29 Mirabar B4
30 Providence Eagle B3
31 Salon B3
32 The Bar at AS220 .... A3
33 The Eddy B3
34 The Stable A3

❷ Entertainment
35 Providence Performing Arts Center B4
36 The Strand Ballroom & Theatre B3

⬡ Shopping
37 Blick Art Materials D4
38 Brown University Bookstore D2
39 Nostalgia Antiques and Collectibles D4
40 Providence Place A2
41 risd|works B3

The historical society runs guided tours of College Hill's premier historic home, the John Brown House Museum (p213), and a range of other tours including Benefit St's 'Mile of History,' an informed amble on Riverwalk, and summer walks along S Main St. Departure points vary for each tour, but all can be booked online.

Brown University Admissions Office TOURS
(☑ 401-863-2378; www.brown.edu/about/visit; 45 Prospect St) Free tours of the Brown University (p213) campus depart from the Corliss Brackett House building five times daily on weekdays, and on Saturday mornings from mid-September to mid-November. Just show up, or contact the admissions office in advance to confirm a place on the tour.

✹ Festivals & Events

★ **Gallery Night Providence** ART
(www.gallerynight.org) Held every third Thursday of the month from March to November from 5pm to 9pm. Twenty-three galleries and museums around the city open their doors for free viewings. Check out the website before you go and find out where to hop on the shuttle, hook up with a guide or sign up for a free celebrity-guided tour.

Festival of Historic Houses CULTURAL
(www.ppsri.org/programs-events/signature-events/festival-of-houses/; ⊗ Jun) FREE Each year, the general public has the opportunity to tour some of Providence's fabulous 18th-century homes during this 'doors-open' festival.

Rhode Island International Film Festival FILM
(www.film-festival.org; ⊗ Aug) For five days every August, cool kids from Rhode Island School of Design and beyond screen hundreds of original independent shorts and feature-length films in venues around town.

🛏 Sleeping

★ **Dean Hotel** BOUTIQUE HOTEL $
(☑ 401-455-3326; http://thedeanhotel.com; 122 Fountain St; d from $109) The Dean epitomizes all that is design in Providence. It features a beer hall, a karaoke bar, a cocktail den and a beer hall downstairs; upstairs has eight quirky, design-themed rooms that provide a stylish urban oasis from the fun and frivolity downstairs. If you're a cool kid and you know it, you belong here.

Hotel Dolce Villa
HOTEL **$**

(☎ 401-383-7031; www.dolcevillari.com; 63 DePasquale Sq; d/ste from $99/139; P❂) Three of this hotel's 14 suites have balconies perched directly over Federal Hill's DePasquale Sq, a lively plaza covered with terrace seating for nearby restaurants: perhaps too noisy for some. Rooms range from standard hotel-style options to one- and two-bedroom suites with full kitchens. Aside from a feature wall offering a splash of color, everything is white!

Christopher Dodge House
B&B **$**

(☎ 401-351-6111; www.providence-hotel.com; 11 W Park St; d from $139; P) Though its exterior is somewhat austere, the interior of this charming 1858 Federal-style house is cozy and inviting, furnished with early American reproduction furniture and marble fireplaces. Rooms are elegantly proportioned with large, shuttered windows, hardwood floors and private bathrooms.

Esperanto
HOSTEL **$**

(Providence Hostel & Guesthouse; ☎ 401-216-8807; www.providencehostel.com; 62 Nolan St; dm/d from $36/79) Providence's only hostel has clean five-bed dorms and private rooms with shared facilities. Staff are friendly and helpful. The hostel is about 1 mile west of Rhode Island State House (p212), off Smith St.

Graduate Providence
HISTORIC HOTEL **$$**

(☎ 401-421-0700; www.graduatehotels.com/providence; 11 Dorrance St; d from $189; P❂) The granddaddy of Providence's hotels, the property dates from the 1920s, although its 294 oversized guestrooms and suites have been thoroughly refurbished to a high standard, stretching many stories above the old city: ask for a room on a high floor. The lobby, both intimate and regal, nicely combines dark wood, twisting staircases and chandeliers, harking back to a lost age.

Renaissance Providence Hotel
HISTORIC HOTEL **$$**

(☎ 401-276-0010; www.renaissance-hotels.marriott.com/renaissance-providence-downtown-hotel; 5 Ave of the Arts; d from $237; P❂❂) Built as a Masonic temple in 1929, this monster stood empty for 77 years before it opened as a hotel in 2007. Some rooms overlook the Rhode Island State House (p212) and are decorated in forceful colors that attempt, with limited success, to evoke Masonic traditions.

Hotel Providence
BOUTIQUE HOTEL **$$**

(☎ 401-861-8000; www.hotelprovidence.com; 139 Mathewson St; d/ste from $179/259; P❂❂) This boutique hotel with 80 guestrooms and 16 suites is perfectly located in the heart of the city. It's just large enough for privacy but small enough for the excellent staff to make you feel special. Guestrooms are comfortable and stylish with crisp white linens and red velvet accents. If you can book in advance they offer excellent value.

✖ Eating

Louis Family Restaurant
DINER **$**

(☎ 401-861-5225; www.louisrestaurant.org; 286 Brook St; mains $5-12; ⊙5am-3pm; ❂) Wake up early to watch bleary-eyed students and carpenters eat strawberry-banana pancakes and drink drip coffee at their favorite greasy spoon long before the rest of College Hill shows signs of life.

East Side Pockets
MEDITERRANEAN **$**

(☎ 401-453-1100; www.eastsidepocket.com; 278 Thayer St; mains $5-9; ⊙10am-1am Mon-Thu, to 2am Fri & Sat, to 10pm Sun; ❂) Fabulous falafels and baklava at student-friendly prices.

Friends Market
DELI **$**

(☎ 401-861-0345; 126 Brook St; sandwiches $4-8; ⊙9am-6pm Tue-Sun; ❂) This old-world-style grocery is tucked in among the trendy coffeehouses, salons and galleries of the Fox Point neighborhood and is a great place to

WATERFIRE

During summer and on a handful of dates in the cooler months, much of downtown Providence transforms into a carnivalesque festival during the popular **WaterFire** (☎ 401-273-1155; www.waterfire.org; ⊙dates vary) art installation created by Barnaby Evans in 1994. Marking the convergence of the Providence, Moshassuck and Woonasquatucket rivers, 100 flaming braziers illuminate the water, overlooked by crowds strolling over the bridges and along the riverside.

WaterFire occurs about 15 times a year from April to November and begins at sunset. A schedule is posted on the website. Occasionally there's a lighting around the New Year.

pick up provisions for picnicking in a Providence park.

Haven Brothers Diner
DINER $

(☑401-603-8124; www.havenbrothersmobile.com; cnr Dorrance & Fulton Sts; meals $5-12; ⊗5pm-3am) Parked next to City Hall, this Providence institution is basically a diner on the back of a truck that has rolled into the same spot every evening for decades. Climb up a rickety ladder to get basic diner fare alongside everyone from drunks to prominent politicians and college kids pulling an all-nighter. The murder burger comes recommended.

Scialo Bros Bakery
ITALIAN $

(☑401-421-0986; www.scialobakery.com; 257 Atwells Ave; sweets $2-5; ⊗8am-7pm Mon-Thu & Sat, to 8pm Fri, to 5pm Sun; ☑) Since 1916, the brick ovens at this Federal Hill relic have turned out top-notch butterballs, *torrone* (a nougat and almond combo), amaretti, and dozens of other kinds of Italian cookies and pastries.

Julian's
MODERN AMERICAN $$

(☑401-861-1770; www.juliansprovidence.com; 318 Broadway; brunch $6-14, mains $18-25; ⊗9am-1am; ☜☑🍴) A messy combination of neon, exposed brick and ductwork in Federal Hill; come here for tattooed cooks preparing a stellar brunch (served until 5pm) with changing blackboard specials (goat's cheese, caper, tomato and mushroom hash), along with a variety of poached eggs and plenty of vegetarian- and vegan-friendly options.

★birch
MODERN AMERICAN $$$

(☑401-272-3105; www.birchrestaurant.com; 200 Washington St; 4-course dinner $60, beverage pairings $40; ⊗5-10pm Thu-Mon) With a background at Noma in Copenhagen and the Dorrance at the Biltmore, chef Benjamin Sukle and his wife, Heidi, now have their own place: the understated but fabulously good birch. Its intimate size and style (seating surrounds a U-shaped bar) means attention to detail is exacting in both the decor and the food, which focuses on under-utilized, hyper-seasonal produce.

Al Forno
ITALIAN $$$

(☑401-273-9760; www.alforno.com; 577 S Main St; mains $18-40; ⊗5-10pm Tue-Sat; ℙ) Our most recent visit featured scallops with blackened bacon so perfect that they were celestial. Also enjoy wood-grilled leg of lamb, handmade *cavatelli* with butternut squash and prosciutto, and incredible desserts (such as limoncello cake with candied citrus peel).

PAWTUCKET ARTS FESTIVAL

Held over the month of September each year, the **Pawtucket Arts Festival** (www.pawtucketartsfestival.org; Slater Park, Pawtucket) FREE hosts a slew of family-friendly dance, music, theater, film, visual and folk-traditional arts events in Slater Park and at venues around town. Check the website for current programming.

Pawtucket, gateway to the Blackstone River Valley (p219), is a zippy 5 miles north of Providence on the I-95.

Budget-minded folks can order wood-fired pizzas ($20) big enough for two to split. Make a reservation.

New Rivers
MODERN AMERICAN $$$

(☑401-751-0350; www.newriversrestaurant.com; 7 Steeple St; mains $18-38; ⊗5:30-10pm Mon-Sat) Every bit as good as they say, this New American bistro has a seasonal menu featuring dishes like rabbit loin with sweet-pea sauce, roasted sole, and beef tenderloin with mushrooms and pearl onions. With soft lighting, walls painted in rich hues of green, red and yellow, and a well-conceived wine list, it's worth a splurge.

🍷 Drinking & Nightlife

★The Eddy
COCKTAIL BAR

(☑401-831-3339; www.eddybar.com; 95 Eddy St; ⊗4pm-1am) Providence's classiest cocktail concoctions are served at the Eddy alongside a healthy selection of on-tap and bottled beers and an impressive wine list. Dress to impress.

★Ogie's Trailer Park
BAR

(☑401-383-8200; www.ogiestrailerpark.com; 1155 Westminster St; ⊗4pm-1am Mon-Thu, 3pm-2am Fri & Sat, noon-1am Sun) This place is just so awesome and unexpected that we almost want to keep it to ourselves. Let's just say that in terms of thematics and design, if you crossed the *Brady Bunch* with *Mad Men* with *Breaking Bad,* you'd be somewhere in the vicinity. Eat, drink and love.

★The Avery
BAR

(☑401-751-5920; www.averyprovidence.com; 18 Luongo Sq; ⊗4pm-midnight Mon-Fri, from 5pm Sat & Sun) Tucked into a quiet residential neighborhood in West Providence, the Avery is easy to miss. But inside there's a jaw-droppingly

LGBTIQ+ PROVIDENCE

Providence has a lively LGBTIQ+ scene for a city of its size and you should have no problems with discrimination here.

There's a number of gay venues on Snow St between Washington and Weybosset streets, including one of North America's few remaining leather bars, the **Providence Eagle** (☑401-421-1447; www.providenceeagle.com; 124 Snow St; ☉5pm-late). If it's your cup of tea, Providence also has two men-only gay saunas: ask around and someone might even show you the way.

Popular bars include **Dark Lady & Alley Cat** (☑401-272-6369; 19 Snow St; ☉9pm-3am), which caters to a mixed crowd, the **Stable** (☑401-272-6950; 125 Washington St; ☉2pm-1am), for an older, classier vibe, and for those who just wanna dance like everyone is watching there's **Ego** (☑401-383-1208; www.egopvd.com; 73 Richmond St; ☉10pm-3am Thu-Sun): say no more. There are no women-only bars here, but women will probably feel most at home at **Mirabar** (☑401-331-6761; www.mirabar.com; 15 Elbow St; ☉3pm-1am Mon-Thu, to 2am Fri & Sat, 1pm-1am Sun).

And if you're not so much of a scene queen, you can't beat Ogie's Trailer Park – a cool place for cool people to hang out and meet each other.

gorgeous varnished-wood interior, with backlit art-nouveau wood cuttings and an elegant, curved bar that's lit from beneath and lined with black-vinyl stools.

Salon
CLUB
(☑401-865-6330; www.thesalonpvd.com; 57 Eddy St; ☉7pm-1am Tue-Thu, to 2am Fri & Sat) The Salon mixes ping-pong tables and pinball machines with 1980s pop and pickleback shots (whiskey with a pickle juice chaser) upstairs, with live shows, open mikes, DJs and dance parties downstairs. If you get hungry, there are PB&J sandwiches.

The Bar at AS220
BAR
(☑401-831-9327; www.as220.org; 115 Empire St; ☉5pm-1am Tue-Fri, 4pm-2am Sat) A long-standing outlet for all forms of Rhode Island art, AS220 (say 'A-S-two-twenty') books experimental bands, hosts readings and provides gallery space for a very active community. If you need a cup of coffee, a vegan cookie or a slice of spinach pie, it also operates a cafe.

☆ Entertainment

★ Providence
Performing Arts Center
PERFORMING ARTS
(☑401-421-2787; www.ppacri.org; 220 Weybosset St; ticket prices vary) This popular venue for touring Broadway musicals and other big-name performances is in a former Loew's Theater dating from 1928. It has a lavish art-deco interior. Rush tickets, with discounts of up to 50%, are typically available to students and seniors two hours before shows upon presentation of a valid ID.

The Strand Ballroom & Theatre
LIVE MUSIC
(☑401-331-5876; http://thestrandri.com/; 79 Washington St) Providence's legendary music venue (formerly known as Lupo's) was expanded and rebranded as the Strand. Over $1 million worth of refurbishments to the historic theater mean better sound and bigger acts; past performers include Bloc Party, Ani DiFranco, Marilyn Manson and Rihanna.

🛍 Shopping

Nostalgia Antiques and Collectibles
VINTAGE
(☑401-400-5810; www.nostalgiaprovidence.com; 236 Wickenden St; ☉11am-7pm) Three floors of cheap vintage and retro gear, on consignment to a bunch of sellers, under one roof. It's hectic, hotch-potch and lots of fun.

Blick Art Materials
ARTS & CRAFTS
(☑401-331-3780; www.dickblick.com; 200 Wickenden St; ☉9am-8pm Mon-Fri, to 6pm Sat) One of the best art-supply stores in the Northeast.

Providence Place
MALL
(☑401-270-1000; www.providenceplace.com; 1 Providence Pl; ☉10am-9pm Mon-Sat, 11am-6pm Sun) This shopping mall is in the heart of downtown.

risd|works
DESIGN
(☑401-277-4949; www.risdworks.com; 10 Westminster St; ☉10am-5pm Tue-Sun; ♿) RISD maintains several fine galleries. A design showcase is risd|works, a shop displaying an assortment of goods (jewelry, photographic prints, flatware, coffee tables, children's books) made by faculty members and alumni.

RHODE ISLAND PROVIDENCE

Brown University Bookstore BOOKS
(☑ 401-863-3168; www.brown.edu/campus-life/
support/bookstore/; 244 Thayer St; ⊘9am-6pm
Mon-Fri, 10am-6pm Sat, 11am-5pm Sun) Providence's most comprehensive bookstore.

❶ Information

Providence Visitor Information Center
(☑ 401-751-1177; www.goprovidence.com; 1
Sabin St, Rhode Island Convention Center;
⊘9am-5pm Mon-Sat) Stop by for maps and
glossy print travel info. There's also a Satellite
Visitor Information Center (☑ 401-456-0200;
10 Memorial Blvd, IGT Center; ⊘9am-5pm).

❶ Getting There & Away

With hills, two interstates and two rivers defining
its downtown topography, Providence can be a
confusing city to find your way around. Parking
can be difficult downtown and near the train
station. For a central lot, try the huge garage at
Providence Place and get a merchant to validate
your ticket. On the East Side, you can usually
find metered street parking quite easily.

Major car-rental companies have both airport
and downtown locations.

AIR
➤ **TF Green Airport** (☑ 888-268-7222; www.
pvdairport.com; 2000 Post Rd) is in Warwick,
about 20 minutes south of Providence. Green is
served by most major airlines.

➤ Taxi services include Airport Taxi (https://
www.airporttaxiri.com/).

➤ RIPTA buses 1, 14 and 20 ($2, 20 to 30 min-
utes) run to downtown Providence. The service
is frequent on weekdays until 11pm. On Saturday and Sunday it is significantly reduced.

BUS
➤ All long-distance buses and most local routes
stop at the central **Intermodal Transportation Center** (Kennedy Plaza; ⊘6am-7pm).
Greyhound and Peter Pan Bus Lines have ticket
counters inside and there are maps outlining
local services.

➤ Peter Pan connects Providence and Green
Airport with Boston's South Station (from $9,
one hour, 12 daily) and Boston's Logan International Airport (from $18, 70 minutes, 10 daily).

➤ Greyhound buses depart for Boston (from
$9, 65 minutes), New York City (from $15, 5½
to six hours) and elsewhere.

TRAIN
➤ Amtrak trains, including high-speed Acela
trains, connect Providence with Boston (from
$12, 50 minutes) and New York (from $54,
three to 3½ hours).

➤ MBTA commuter rail has regular scheduled
services to Boston ($12, 60 to 75 minutes).

❶ Getting Around

Providence is small, pretty and walkable, so
once you arrive it makes sense to get around
on foot.

RIPTA operates two 'trolley' routes. The Green
Line runs from the East Side through downtown
to Federal Hill. The Gold Line runs from the
Providence Marriott Downtown hotel south to
the hospital via Kennedy Plaza, and stops at the
Point St Ferry Dock. Fares are $2 per ride.

BLACKSTONE RIVER VALLEY

This attractive river valley in the northeast
corner of the state is named for its first
European settler, the Reverend William
Blackstone, who arrived here in 1635. But
it wasn't until the invention of the water-
powered spinning jenny, which was brought
to the area in the 1790s, that the region really began to boom. Fueled by the Blackstone
River, small wool and cotton textile mills
proliferated, becoming the valley's dominant industry. Be sure to check out Slater
Mill, credited with beginning the industrial
age in America.

After the decline of the Rhode Island textile plants, the area fell on hard economic
times, but recently, after communities band-
ed together to repair the natural beauty of
the region, Blackstone has become an in-
creasingly popular destination for outdoor
enthusiasts. For the lowdown on this hard-
to-pin-down area just outside Providence,
focused around Pawtucket, and sections of
which are in Massachusetts, visit www.tour
blackstone.com.

❶ Getting There & Away

Pawtucket is the gateway town and the largest
community in the area known as the Blackstone
River Valley, although Pawtucket proper feels
much like a suburb of Providence, only 5 miles
to the south. From Newport (38 miles) or Providence, take the I-95 north to exit 28.

Other key communities within the region include Smithfield and Woonsocket.

Woonsocket

☑ 401 / POP 41,759

It's thought that Woonsocket Falls was settled as early as 1660, though its heyday came
in the 1830s when the American industrial
revolution took hold.

WORTH A TRIP

SLATER MILL

On the banks of the lower Blackstone River, **Slater Mill** (☑401-725-8638; www.facebook.com/slater.mill; 67 Roosevelt Ave, Pawtucket; adult/child $12/6.50; ☉10am-4pm Wed-Sun May-Jul & Sep-Nov, 10am-4pm Wed-Mon Jul-Sep, 11am-3pm Sat & Sun Mar, Apr & Nov; P) has been dubbed the 'Birthplace of the American Industrial Revolution' – with good cause. It was here that, in 1793, Samuel Slater built the first successful water-powered cotton-spinning mill in North America, which effectively shaped the world we live in today. The site comprises the lovingly restored 1793 Old Slater Mill, the 1810 Wilkinson Mill and Sylvanus Brown's 1758 early Pawtucket cottage, housing exhibits on cotton-spinning and local history.

Today, the town is known as Woonsocket and remains centered on its eponymous though not-so-scenic waterfalls. It's the second largest of the Blackstone River Valley communities and one of Rhode Island's northernmost settlements, lying just across the border with Massachusetts.

Woonsocket features some gently fading historic buildings and an interesting museum or two. It makes a great spot to stop for lunch if you're exploring the valley by car, either for diner-style old-school Americana or farm-fresh produce. One gets the feeling that the town is on the verge of a renaissance of sorts, with young folks snapping up and renovating cheap historic real estate.

⊙ Sights & Activities

★St. Ann Arts
& Cultural Center   CULTURAL CENTER
(☑401-356-0713; www.stannartsandcultural center.org; 84 Cumberland St; tours adult/child $10/8; ☉1-4pm Sun) It's a real surprise to find something of this rarity and beauty in sleepy Woonsocket. Now home to a busy arts and cultural center, the former Church of St. Ann features walls and ceilings decorated with North America's largest collection of fresco paintings: imagine the Blackstone River Valley's version of the Sistine Chapel and you'll be in the ballpark. Tours, held every Sunday, are worth every

penny. Check the website for details of coming events.

Museum of Work and Culture   MUSEUM
(☑401-769-9675; 42 S Main St; adult/child $10/ free; ☉10am-4pm Tue-Sat, from noon Sun; P) This large museum tells the stories of the settlers, mostly French Canadians, who came to Rhode Island's mill towns in the 19th and 20th centuries in search of a better life.

Blackstone River Bikeway   CYCLING
(www.dot.ri.gov/community/bikeri/blackstone. php) FREE This largely riverside bike path is Rhode Island's second longest, featuring 11.6 miles of continuous path from Cumberland to Woonsocket and a section of 4.7 miles of shared-use path between Woonsocket and Providence. Download a PDF map of the path from the website, or check in with the folks at the Blackstone Valley Visitor Center in Pawtucket for hard copies.

🛏 Sleeping & Eating

**Holiday Inn
Express Woonsocket**   HOTEL $
(☑401-769-5000; www.holidayinn.com; 194 Fortin Dr; d from $149; P❄🛜🏊) Guest rooms in this new-build Holiday Inn on the outskirts of town are light and bright. Although they're fairly generic, they represent some of Woonsocket's best-value accommodations. There's even an indoor pool.

★**Beef Barn**   AMERICAN $
(☑401-762-9880; www.thebeefbarn.com; 1 Greenville Rd, North Smithfield; sandwiches $2-4.50; ☉11am-9pm Mon-Sat, from noon Sun; P) Folks flock from far and wide to get gristly at the iconic Beef Barn on the outskirts of Woonsocket, where slow-cooked roast-beef sandwiches go out the door as quickly as happy travelers can get in. It's kitsch, family-run fun unless you abstain from carnivorous dining, in which case, it won't be your idea of a good time.

★**Wright's Dairy
Farm & Bakery**   BAKERY $
(☑401-767-3014; www.wrightsdairyfarm.com; 200 Woonsocket Hill Rd, North Smithfield; baked goods $2-14; ☉8am-5pm Fri-Wed; P) If you can stand the smell of cow manure, make a beeline to this working dairy farm in a pretty location in the hills just outside Woonsocket. Why? For freshly baked pastries, cakes and cookies, plus farm-fresh dairy products, including some pretty dreamy and creamy ice-cream flavors.

Ye Olde English Fish & Chips   SEAFOOD $$
(☑401-762-3637; www.yeoldeenglishfishandchips.
com; 25 S Main St; mains $6-20; ⊙11am-6pm
Tue-Sat; [P]) What's not to love about an old-
school wood-panelled diner that's been fry-
ing fish and chips in a British batter made
to a family recipe since 1922? Calorie count,
OK, check, but otherwise? Did we mention
they also serve fried chicken, clam strips
and lobster rolls? You know you gotta...

ℹ️ Information

Pawtucket's **Blackstone Valley Visitor Center**
(☑401-724-2200; www.tourblackstone.com;
175 Main St; ⊙10am-5pm Mon-Fri, to 4pm Sat &
Sun) is your nearest port of call for advice, maps
and pamphlets.

Online, try www.woonsocketri.org/visitors for
a general overview of the city and links to official
government portals.

ℹ️ Getting There & Away

Woonsocket is 7 miles northeast of Smithfield
and 17 miles northwest of Pawtucket.

EAST BAY

Rhode Island's jagged East Bay captures the
early American story in microcosm, from the
graves of early settlers in Little Compton to
the farmsteads and merchant homes of whal-
ers and farmers in Warren and Barrington,
and the mansions of slave traders in Bristol.

Aside from Barrington's historic and
picturesque **Tyler Point Cemetery**, set be-
tween the Warren and Barrington Rivers,
and Warren's clutch of early stone and clap-
board churches (built in the 18th and 19th
centuries), the most interesting of the three
communities is Bristol. Further south is
Sakonnet, the Wampanoag's 'Place of Black
Geese,' a rural landscape of pastures and
woods centered on the two tiny communi-
ties of Tiverton and Little Compton.

The East Bay is proudly protected by its
residents and represents a fascinating, large-
ly unpromoted region for the discerning in-
dependent traveler interested in American
history and New England's natural delights.

Bristol

☑401 / POP 22,290

One fifth of all slaves transported to the USA
were brought in Bristol ships and by the 18th
century the town was one of the country's

major commercial and shipbuilding ports.
For most visitors today, Bristol is somewhere
you simply drive past on the main road be-
tween Providence and Newport.

The history of slavery and elusive access
aside, it's worth making the detour, as Bris-
tol has some excellent museums, a pretty
downtown and the fabulous Colt State Park,
which is widely regarded as Rhode Island's
most scenic park. It's also the stepping-off
point for adventures to the delightfully
non-touristy Prudence Island (p222).

⊙ Sights

★**Colt State Park**   STATE PARK
(☑401-253-7482;   www.riparks.com/Locations/
LocationColt.html;   Rte 114;   ⊙dawn-dusk;   [P])
FREE Bristol's Colt State Park is Rhode Is-
land's most scenic park, with its entire west-
ern border fronting Narragansett Bay. The
parks is fringed by 4 miles of cycling trails
and has over 400 shaded picnic tables (you
read that correctly!) set among 464 acres
of groomed fruit trees, flowerbeds and lush
greenery.

Blithewold Mansion   HISTORIC BUILDING
(☑401-253-2707;   www.blithewold.org;   101 Ferry
Rd; adult/child $15/6; ⊙mansion 10am-4pm Tue-
Sat, to 3pm Sun Apr–mid-Oct; gardens 10am-5pm
year-round; [P]) Local resident Augustus Van
Wickle bought a 72ft Herreshoff yacht for
his wife Bessie in 1895, but having nowhere
suitable to moor it, he then had to build
Blithewold Mansion. The arts-and-crafts
mansion sits in a peerless position on Nar-
ragansett Bay and is particularly lovely in
spring, when daffodils line the shore.

MOUNT HOPE FARMERS MARKET

Held every Saturday year-round,
the wonderful **Mount Hope Farm-
ers Market** (☑401-254-1745; www.
mounthopefarm.org; 250 Metacom Ave;
⊙9am-1pm Sat) takes place amid
200 acres of pristine farmland on the
Mount Hope Farm in Bristol. Off-season
markets have a smaller selection on
offer, but stalls at the summer markets
sell everything from freshly squeezed
lemonade to bean salads, fruit pre-
serves, honey and farm-fresh organic
produce.

PRUDENCE ISLAND

Idyllic **Prudence Island** (☑401-683-0430; www.prudencebayislandstransport.com; ☻ferries 5:45am-6pm Mon-Fri, 7:30am-6pm Sat & Sun) sits in the middle of Narragansett Bay, an easy 25-minute ferry ride (adult/child $5.40/1.90) from Bristol. Originally used for farming and later as a summer vacation spot for families from Providence and New York, who traveled here on the Fall River Line Steamer, the island now has only 88 inhabitants. There are some fine Victorian and beaux-arts houses near Stone Wharf, plus a lighthouse and a store, but otherwise it's wild and unspoiled.

It's perfect for mountain biking, barbecues, fishing and paddling.

Herreshoff Marine Museum   MUSEUM
(☑401-253-5000; www.herreshoff.org; 1 Burnside St; adult/child $15/10; ☻10am-5pm May-Oct; P) The world-class Herreshoff Marine Museum showcases some of the country's finest yachts, including eight built for the America's Cup. Featuring the **America's Cup Hall of Fame** and a fascinating display of boatbuilding techniques, there's likely to be something of interest here, even if you aren't much of a mariner.

🛏 Sleeping & Eating

Governor Bradford House   INN $$
(☑401-254-1745; www.mounthopefarm.org/stay/governor-bradford-house; 250 Metacom Ave; r from $169; P❀❈) Administered by the Mount Hope Trust, the Governor Bradford offers four individually styled rooms and one suite in a 300-year-old Georgian farmhouse. Once owned by the Haffenreffer family, of beer-brewing fortune, the house is located in the Mount Hope Farm complex.

Beehive   CAFE $
(☑401-396-9994; www.thebeehivecafe.com; 10 Franklin St; mains $7-14; ☻7am-4pm Sun-Wed, to 9pm Thu-Sat) There's a real buzz in Bristol about this beehive whose busy bees buy local wherever possible, bake their own breads and make everything (but the ketchup) from scratch. Best for breakfast and light lunches, this crafty kitchen serves a limited dinner menu from Thursday to Sunday and brews organic coffee round the clock. Sensible pricing adds to its appeal.

The Lobster Pot   SEAFOOD $$$
(☑401-253-9100; www.lobsterpotri.com; 119 Hope St; mains $15-40; ☻noon-9pm Mon-Thu & Sun, to 10pm Fri-Sat) Since 1929 the Lobster Pot has been serving fresh seafood from its prime location on the Bristol waterfront, with fine alfresco dining in the warmer months and a busy, upscale dining room year-round.

🛈 Getting There & Away

RI 114 links Providence and Newport. Bristol is smack bang in the middle.

Tiverton
☑401 / POP 15,874

The sprawling community of Tiverton stretches out lazily alongside the Sakonnet River, with views of distant sailing vessels and Aquidneck Island. The further south you explore on RI 77, the prettier the landscape becomes with ramshackle farm stands selling fresh produce, rolling fields extending in all directions and tantalizing flashes of the ocean in the distance.

A rare-for-the-area traffic light marks Tiverton's historic Four Corners (www.tivertonfourcorners.com). This crossroads represents the hub of the community where shops, restaurants and provision stores cluster.

There are no accommodations in Tiverton itself, but the ubiquitous chain motels of Middletown and the fine selection of Newport lodgings are just over the bridge.

🍴 Eating

Evelyn's Nanaquaket Drive-In   DINER $$
(☑401-624-3100; www.evelynsdrivein.com; 2335 Main Rd; mains $8-24; ☻11:30am-8pm; P🐾🍽) On the north stretch of Rte 77, you'll find this gray-shingled drive-in, a traditional roadside eatery from another era, perched alongside marshy Nanaquaket Pond. Park on the crushed-shell driveway to devour lobster rolls (cool, mildly spiced claw and tail meat on a hot dog bun) and more traditional diner favorites.

★Boat House   SEAFOOD $$$
(☑401-624-6300; www.boathousetiverton.com; 227 Schooner Dr; mains $18-44; ☻11:30am-9pm; P) If you're looking for a good all-rounder, it's hard to fault the Boat House for its fresh, locally sourced and inventively prepared seafood and produce, reasonable prices, and a magnificent setting on the banks of the Sakonnet River. Indoor and

alfresco diners all enjoy the fantastic views and killer sunsets. A classic New England experience.

ⓘ Getting There & Away

To reach Tiverton from Providence (26 miles) take I-95 south and connect with RI 24. For Newport (15 miles), take RI 24 over the Sakonnet Bridge, then follow RI 114 south.

Little Compton

📞 401 / POP 3518

Fiercely protected by its close-knit community, and often overlooked for its lack of 'attractions,' Little Compton is one of the oldest and loveliest villages in New England.

As you drive south from Tiverton, the large wood-framed homes become older, grayer and statelier, just as an increasing number of stone walls crisscross the green landscape with its hand-hewn clapboard houses and the white-steepled United Congregational Church overlooking the Old Commons Burial Ground. Here, Elizabeth Padobie, daughter of *Mayflower* pilgrims Priscilla and John Alden, and the first settler born in New England, is buried.

Though many visitors are content just driving or biking around town, a pair of beaches also competes for your attention. To find them, turn right after arriving at the United Congregational Church, continue to Swamp Rd, make a left and head for the water.

◎ Sights

Wilbor House Museum HISTORIC SITE
(📞 401-635-4035; www.littlecompton.org; 548 W Main Rd; adult/child $6/3; ⊙1-5pm Thu-Sun Apr-Oct, 9am-3pm Tue-Fri Nov-Mar) Seventeenth-century Wilbor House belonged to early settler Samuel Wilbor, who crossed the Sakonnet River from Portsmouth in 1690 and built this big square home, which served his family for eight generations. The home and its outbuildings have been meticulously and lovingly preserved and now house this unique local history museum. Serious history buffs should inquire about a docent-led private tour.

Carolyn's Sakonnet Vineyard VINEYARD
(📞 401-635-8486; www.sakonnetwine.com; 162 West Main Rd; ⊙11am-6pm Sun-Thu, to 8pm Fri & Sat late May–mid-Oct, 11am-5pm daily rest of year; 🅿) This popular vineyard has free guided tours, a seasonal cafe and daily tastings for $14: great value for sampling seven local wines.

🛏 Sleeping & Eating

Stone House Inn HISTORIC HOTEL $$$
(📞 401-635-2222; www.newportexperience.com/stonehouse; 122 Sakonnet Point Rd; d from $279; 🅿➔❄🕾) When this unashamedly upscale inn opened its doors in 2016, Little Compton's notoriously private elite feared it meant the out-of-towners were coming. With only 13 rooms (lavish as they may be), it's hardly cause for an invasion. If you have cash and the inclination, this is your chance to take a peek at how the other half live.

★**Commons Lunch** DINER $$
(📞 401-635-4388; 48 Commons; mains $8-21; ⊙6am-7pm) Serving local old-world classics such as New England corned beef and cabbage alongside quahog stuffies (stuffed clams), New Englanders come from far and wide for the Johnny cakes (a kind of flat cornmeal pancake), which have been a Little Compton breakfast staple for centuries.

ⓘ Getting There & Away

Little Compton is at the end of the road. Take RI 77 south from Tiverton (10 miles).

NEWPORT

📞 401 / POP 24,942

Established by religious moderates, 'new port' flourished in the independent colony of Rhode Island, which declared itself a state here in 1776. Downtown, shutterbugs snap excitedly at immaculately preserved Colonial-era architecture and landmarks at seemingly every turn.

Fascinating as Newport's early history is, the real intrigue began in the late 1850s, when wealthy industrialists began building opulent summer residences along cliff-top Bellevue Ave. Impeccably styled on Italianate palazzi, French châteaux and Elizabethan manor houses, these gloriously restored mansions filled with priceless antiques and their breathtaking location must be seen to be believed. The curiosity, variety and extravagance of this spectacle is unrivaled.

Honoring its maritime roots, Newport remains a global center for yachting. Put simply, summers here sparkle: locals have excellent taste and know how to throw a shindig. There's always something going on, including a series of cross-genre festivals that are among the best in the USA.

◉ Sights

★ The Breakers   HISTORIC BUILDING

(Map p225; ☑401-847-1000; www.newportman
sions.org; 44 Ochre Point Ave; adult/child
$24/8; ⊙9am-5pm Apr–mid-Oct, hours vary
mid-Oct–Mar; ℗) A 70-room Italian Renaissance megapalace inspired by 16th-century
Genoese palazzi, the Breakers is the most
magnificent of Newport's grandiose mansions. At the behest of Cornelius Vanderbilt
II, Richard Morris Hunt did most of the design (though craftspeople from around the
world perfected the decorative program).
The building was completed in 1895 and
sits at Ochre Point, on a grand oceanside
site. The furnishings, most made expressly
for the Breakers, are all original.

★ Rough Point   HISTORIC BUILDING

(Map p225; ☑401-849-7300; www.newportrestor
ation.org/roughpoint/; 680 Bellevue Ave; adult/
child $25/free; ⊙9:30am-2pm Thu-Sun Apr-early
May, 9:30am-3:30pm Tue-Sun early May-early Nov;
℗) While the peerless position and splendor
of the grounds alone are worth the price of
admission, this faux-English manor house
also contains heiress and philanthropist
Doris Duke's impressive art holdings, including medieval tapestries, furniture owned by
French emperors, Ming dynasty ceramics,
and paintings by Renoir and Van Dyck.

★ The Elms   HISTORIC BUILDING

(Map p226; ☑401-847-1000; www.newportman
sions.org/explore/the-elms; 367 Bellevue Ave;
adult/child $17.50/8, servant life tours adult/child

$18/7.50; ⊙10am-5pm Apr–mid-Oct, hours vary
mid-Oct–Mar; ℗🚻) Designed by Horace
Trumbauer in 1901, the Elms is a replica of
Château d'Asnières, built near Paris in 1750.
Here you can take a 'behind-the-scenes'
tour that will have you snaking through
the servants' quarters and up onto the
roof. Along the way you'll learn about the
activities of the army of servants and the
architectural devices that kept them hidden
from the view of those drinking port in the
formal rooms.

★ Redwood Athenaeum   LIBRARY

(Map p226; ☑401-847-0292; www.redwoodlibrary.
org; 50 Bellevue Ave; ⊙9:30am-5:30pm Mon-
Wed, Fri & Sat, to 8pm Thu, 1-5pm Sun; ℗) FREE
Founded by Abraham Redwood in 1747 as
an important archive of American history
and architecture, this beautiful neoclassical
library was designed and built by architect
Peter Harrison – honored within by a room
devoted to significant American portraiture.
There's also a gallery with revolving exhibits and a quiet reading room. In the warmer
months, genteel concerts and garden parties
are frequently held here: check the home-
page for what's on.

★ Newport Car Museum   MUSEUM

(☑401-848-2277; www.newportcarmuseum.org;
1847 W Main Rd, Portsmouth; adult/child $18/8;
⊙10am-4pm; ℗) Located in Portsmouth,
6 miles north of Newport, on the site of a
former missile manufacturing plant, this
fantastic museum showcases more than
60 vintage, classic, hot-rod and muscle

NEWPORT'S BEST BEACHES

Newport's public beaches are on the eastern side of the peninsula along Memorial Blvd.
All are open 9am to 6pm in summer.

Easton Beach (First Beach; www.cityofnewport.com/departments/beach-parking; Memorial
Blvd; beach parking Mon-Fri/Sat & Sun $10/20; ℗) This is the largest beach with a pseudo-
Victorian pavilion containing bathhouses and showers, a snack bar and a large carousel.
You can rent umbrellas, chairs and surfboards at the pavilion.

Second (Sachuest) Beach (☑401-846-6273; http://parks.middletownri.com/sachuest-
aka-second-beach-and-third-beach/; Sachuest Point Rd, Middletown; beach parking Mon-Fri/Sat
& Sun $15/25) The most beautiful beach on Aquidneck Island curves around Sachuest
Bay and is backed by the 450-acre Norman Bird Sanctuary.

Third Beach (☑401-846-6273; http://parks.middletownri.com/sachuest-aka-second-beach
-and-third-beach/; beach parking Mon-Fri/Sat & Sun $15/25) Popular with families because it
is protected from the open ocean, Third Beach also appeals to windsurfers because the
water is calm and the winds are steady.

Gooseberry Beach (130 Ocean Ave; parking $20) A quiet white-sand beach in a little cove
with calm waters. It has a restaurant too.

Newport Area

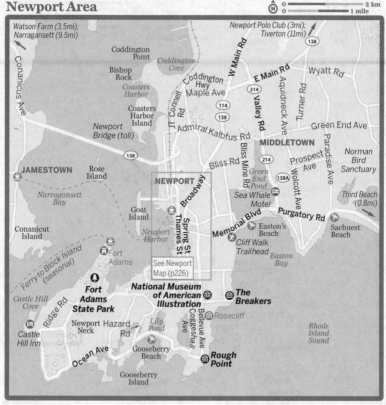

cars that will elicit sighs of envy from any self-respecting rev-head. The state-of-the-art 50,000-sq-ft exhibition space features meticulously preserved European and American cars dramatically lit in the style of a contemporary art gallery. Accompanying displays show tech specs and tell the stories behind the cars.

★ **Fort Adams State Park**   STATE PARK
(Map p225; ☑ 401-847-2400; www.riparks.com/Locations/LocationFortAdams.html; Harrison Ave; overnight parking $6; ⊘ dawn-dusk) **Fort Adams** (Map p225; ☑ 401-841-0707; www.fortadams.org; 90 Fort Adams Dr; tours adult/child $12/6; ⊘ 10am-4pm late May–Oct, reduced hours Nov & Dec) is America's largest coastal fortification and the centerpiece of this gorgeous state park, which juts out into Narragansett Bay. It's the venue for the Newport jazz (p228) and folk festivals (p228) and numerous special events. A beach, picnic and fishing areas, and a boat ramp are open daily.

★ **National Museum of American Illustration**   MUSEUM
(Map p225; ☑ 401-851-8949; www.americanillustration.org; 492 Bellevue Ave; adult/child $20/10; ⊘ 11am-5pm Thu-Sun Jun-Aug, 11am-5pm Fri Sep-May; ℗) This acclaimed museum features an impressive collection of 'the most American of American Art' including Maxfield Parrish's impossibly luminous works in color, NC Wyeth prints, Norman Rockwell's nostalgia and the illustrations of other American graphic heavyweights. If you can, take the free guided tour on Friday (3pm; available year-round), which sheds light on the stories behind the images and how they molded American culture through the decades.

Rosecliff   HISTORIC BUILDING
(Map p225; ☑ 401-847-1000; www.newportmansions.org; 548 Bellevue Ave; adult/child $17.50/8; ⊘ 9am-4pm Apr–mid-Oct, hours vary mid-Oct–Mar; ℗) Built for Mrs Hermann Oelrichs, an heiress of the Comstock Lode silver

Newport

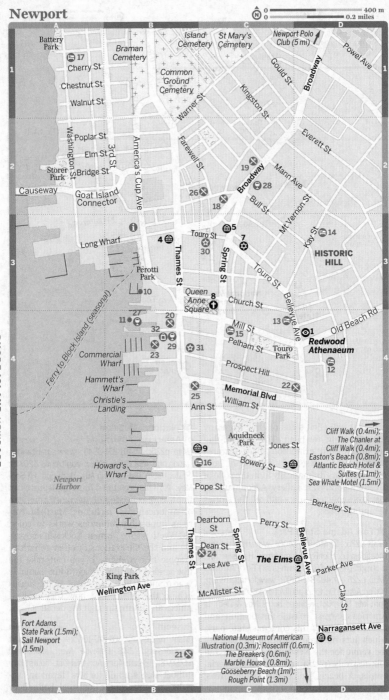

Battery Park

Island Cemetery

St Mary's Cemetery

Newport Polo Club (5 mi)

Powel Ave

17 Cherry St

Braman Cemetery

Common Ground Cemetery

Broadway

Chestnut St

Warner St

Kingston St

Gould St

Everett St

Walnut St

Washington St

Poplar St

America's Cup Ave

Farewell St

Elm St

3rd St

Bridge St

Storer Park

Goat Island Connector

Causeway

Broadway 19

28 Bull St

Mann Ave

Mt Vernon St

Kay St 14

Long Wharf

26 18

Touro St 30

5 7

HISTORIC HILL

4

Thames St

Spring St

Touro St

Bellevue Ave

Perotti Park

10

Queen Anne Square

8 Church St

13

1

Redwood Athenaeum

Old Beach Rd

11 27 20 32 29 23

Mill St 15

31

Pelham St

Touro Park

12

Commercial Wharf

Hammett's Wharf

Christie's Landing

Prospect Hill

22

Memorial Blvd

25

William St

Ann St

Aquidneck Park

Jones St

Cliff Walk (0.4mi);
The Chanler at
Cliff Walk (0.4mi);
Easton's Beach (0.8mi);
Atlantic Beach Hotel &
Suites (1.1mi);
Sea Whale Motel (1.5mi)

Ferry to Block Island (seasonal)

Howard's Wharf

Newport Harbor

9

16

Bowery St

3

Pope St

Berkeley St

Dearborn St

Perry St

Thames St

Dean St

24

Spring St

The Elms 2

Bellevue Ave

Parker Ave

Lee Ave

King Park

McAlister St

Clay St

Wellington Ave

Fort Adams
State Park (1.5mi);
Sail Newport
(1.5mi)

21

National Museum of American
Illustration (0.3mi); Rosecliff (0.6mi);
The Breakers (0.6mi);
Marble House (0.8mi);
Gooseberry Beach (1mi);
Rough Point (1.3mi)

Narragansett Ave

6

Newport

◎ **Top Sights**
1 Redwood Athenaeum............................D4
2 The Elms...D6

◎ **Sights**
3 Kingscote C5
4 Museum of Newport History
at Brick Market...............................B3
5 Newport Museum of Art.....................C3
6 Preservation Society of
Newport County.............................D7
7 Touro Synagogue National
Historic Site...................................C3
8 Trinity Church......................................C3
9 Whitehorne House Museum................B5

⊕ **Activities, Courses & Tours**
10 America's Cup Charters.......................B3
11 Classic Cruises of Newport.................B4
Newport Historical
Society Walking Tours................(see 4)

⊜ **Sleeping**
12 Attwater...D4
13 Hotel Viking...C4
14 Marshall Slocum Inn...........................D3
15 Mill Street Inn.....................................C4

16 Newport International
Hostel.. B5
17 Stella Maris Inn A1

◎ **Eating**
18 Boru...C2
19 Corner Cafe...C2
20 Fluke Newport.....................................B4
21 Mamma Luisa.......................................B7
22 Meg's Aussie Milk Bar........................D4
23 Mooring...B4
24 Scales & Shells....................................C6
25 The Red Parrot.....................................B4
26 White Horse Tavern.............................C2

⊜ **Drinking & Nightlife**
27 Black Pearl...B4
28 Pour Judgement C2
29 The Wharf B4

⊕ **Entertainment**
30 Jane Pickens Theater...........................C3
31 Newport Blues Café B4

⊜ **Shopping**
32 Bannister's Wharf................................B4

treasure, Rosecliff was designed by Stanford White to look like the Grand Trianon at Versailles, and its palatial ballroom (Newport's largest) and landscaped grounds quickly became the setting for some truly enormous parties. Houdini entertained at one. Today it's managed by the **Preservation Society of Newport County** (Newport Mansions; Map p226; 5-site tickets adult/child $35/12), which offers discounted tickets for visits to other mansions in its custodianship.

Kingscote HISTORIC BUILDING
(Map p226; ☑ 401-847-1000; www.newportman sions.org/explore/kingscote; 253 Bellevue Ave; adult/child $17.50/8; ⊙10am-5pm Jul–mid-Oct; ℗) An Elizabethan fantasy complete with Tiffany glass, Kingscote was Newport's first 'cottage' strictly for summer use, designed by Richard Upjohn in 1841 for George Noble Jones of Savannah, GA. It was later bought by China-trade merchant William H King, who gave the house its name.

Newport Museum of Art GALLERY
(Map p226; ☑ 401-848-8200; www.newportart museum.org; 76 Bellevue Ave; adult/child $15/ free; ⊙10am-5pm Tue-Sat, from noon Sun) This vibrant city art museum has a permanent collection of around 2600 artworks focusing on American and contemporary art

from the 18th century to the present day, but it's better known for its calendar of regularly changing visiting exhibitions and workshops. See the website for current programming.

**Museum of Newport
History at Brick Market** MUSEUM
(Map p226; ☑ 401-841-8770; www.newporthistory. org; 127 Thames St; suggested donation adult/child $4/2; ⊙10am-5pm) Newport's excellent local history museum, housed in the 1762 Brick Market building, brings the city's fascinating past to life with an award-winning collection of displays and memorabilia. Contact the museum to inquire about the scheduling of its local walking tours and to make bookings.

**Touro Synagogue
National Historic Site** SYNAGOGUE
(Map p226; ☑ 401-847-4794; www.tourosyna gogue.org; 85 Touro St; adult/student/child $12/8/ free; ⊙10:30am-2:30pm Sun-Fri May & Jun, 9:30am-4:30pm Sun-Fri Jul & Aug, 9:30am-2:30pm Sun-Fri Sep & Oct, 11:30am-2:30pm Sun Nov-Apr) Designed by Peter Harrison (architect of the Athenaeum and King's Chapel, Boston), this synagogue is the finest example of 18th-century Georgian architecture in Newport. Its large glass windows illuminate an interior that treads the line between austere and

lavish. Built by the nascent Sephardic Orthodox Congregation Yeshuat Israel in 1763, it has the distinction of being North America's oldest synagogue.

Whitehorne House Museum MUSEUM

(Map p226; 401-847-2448; www.newportrestoration.org/whitehornehouse/; 416 Thames St; by appointment) A few decades ago, Colonial Newport was decaying and undervalued. Enter Doris Duke, who used her fortune to preserve many of the buildings that now attract people to the city. One of them is Whitehorne, a Federal period estate. Rooms contain a collection of extraordinary furniture crafted by Newport's famed cabinetmakers, including pieces by Goddard and Townsend. At the time of writing, the museum was closed for general admission. Private group tours are available and occasional open-house events are held.

Trinity Church CHURCH

(Map p226; 401-846-0660; www.trinitynewport. org; 1 Queen Anne Sq; suggested donation $5; 10am-4pm Mon-Fri, to 3pm Sat mid-Jun–mid-Oct, 11am-2pm May–mid-Jun) On Queen Anne Sq, Trinity follows the design canon of Sir Christopher Wren's Palladian churches in London. Built between 1725 and 1726, it has a fine wineglass-shaped pulpit, Tiffany stained glass, traditional box pews (warmed by the bottoms of many celebrity guests including George Washington, Queen Elizabeth II and Archbishop Desmond Tutu) and an organ once played by Handel.

Tours

Newport Historical Society Walking Tours WALKING

(Map p226; 401-841-8770; www.newporthistorytours.org; 127 Thames St; tours adult/child from $15/5; departures vary;) Newport Historical Society will guide you on a walking tour of Historic Hill. Periodically, the society offers themed heritage tours, where you'll learn about 'Rogues & Scoundrels,' or Jewish or African American history. Tours begin at the Museum of Newport History at Brick Market; see the website for departure times.

America's Cup Charters BOATING

(Map p226; 401-846-9886; www.americascup charters.com; 49 America's Cup Ave, Newport Harbor Hotel & Marina; 2-hour sail adult/child $75/40; May–mid-Oct;) Take the ultimate waterborne tour aboard a 12m America's Cup racing yacht. Ticketed, two-hour sunset sails and private charters are available daily in season and offer an unforgettably thrilling experience.

Classic Cruises of Newport BOATING

(Map p226; 401-847-0298; www.cruisenew port.com; 24 Bannister's Wharf; adult/child from $25/20; May-Oct) This popular operater runs good-value excursions on the *Rum Runner II,* a Prohibition-era bootlegging vessel, and *Madeleine,* a 72ft schooner. The narrated tour will take you past mansions and former speakeasies.

Festivals & Events

★ Newport Music Festival MUSIC

(401-849-0700; www.newportmusic.org; tickets $25-50; mid-Jul) This internationally regarded festival offers a wide program of classical music concerts performed in the spectacular settings of some of the Newport Mansions, as well as other visually delicious and acoustically satisfying venues around town.

Newport Folk Festival MUSIC

(www.newportfolk.org; late Jul) Big-name stars and up-and-coming groups perform at Fort Adams State Park (p225) and other venues around town during one of the top folk festivals in the USA. Not just limited to music, this popular festival has a family-friendly, carnival-like atmosphere and features workshops, exhibitions and pop-up shops. Check the website for current pricing.

Newport Jazz Festival MUSIC

(www.newportjazz.org; tickets adult/child from $65/15; Aug) This classic festival usually takes place on an August weekend, with concerts at Fort Adams State Park (p225) and smaller gigs in venues around town. Popular shows can sell out a year in advance.

Newport Flower Show FAIR

(401-847-1000; www.newportmansions.org/ events/newport-flower-show; 548 Bellevue Ave; Jun) Held in the grounds of the stunning Rosecliff (p225) mansion, this annual three-day flower festival and competition features exhibits, special events and vendors celebrating all things floral and botanical.

Newport International Boat Show SAILING

(www.newportboatshow.com; Newport Yachting Center, 4 Commercial Wharf; adult/child from $20/free, parking $20; Sep) Held over three days in mid-September, this is one of the largest in-water boat shows in the country,

BELLEVUE AVENUE & CLIFF WALK

During the 19th century, the wealthiest New York bankers and business families chose Newport as their summer playground, building their fabulous mansions along Bellevue Ave. Ten of the mansions (not including Rough Point or Ochre Court) are under the management of the Preservation Society of Newport County (p227), and are open seasonally between June and November. Some are open year-round. Combination tickets are better value if you intend visiting several of the properties, and some tours require advance booking, which is advisable during high season. Tickets can be purchased online or onsite. The society also offers a range of food- and wine-themed events.

Alternatively, hire a bike and cruise along Bellevue Ave enjoying the view of the mansions or saunter along the famed **Cliff Walk** (www.cliffwalk.com; Memorial Blvd), a pedestrian path that runs along the headland between the mansions and their sea views.

featuring 850 exhibitors. If you're not in the market to buy a boat, you can always get inspiration for what your life might look like if you won the lottery.

🛏 Sleeping

Atlantic Beach Hotel & Suites   HOTEL **$**
(📞401-847-5330; www.atlanticbeachhotelri.com; 34 Wave Ave, Middletown; d from $99; 🅿✳@🛜) There's nothing flashy or particularly luxurious about the guestrooms and apartment-style suites of this creaky, rust-shingled beachfront hotel, but it's hard to beat for it's *el-primo* location on Easton's Beach, great-value rates and friendly, helpful service, which it doles out in spades.

Mill Street Inn   HOTEL **$**
(Map p226; 📞401-849-9500; www.millstreetinn. com; 75 Mill St; studio/ste from $134/154) Located in the heart of downtown Newport, studio and one-bedroom suites in this former mill with exposed brickwork, high ceilings and neutral color palettes, offer excellent value.

Marshall Slocum Inn   B&B **$**
(Map p226; 📞401-841-5120; www.marshall slocuminn.com; 29 Kay St; d/apt from $110/135; 🛜) This clapboard Colonial house, a former parsonage, is situated in a quiet residential street between Historic Hill and downtown Newport. The period feel is wonderfully preserved in gorgeous rooms featuring canopy beds, linen bed sheets, wide wooden floorboards and shuttered windows. There's also a quaint apartment adjacent to the main house. Excellent value means you're well advised to book ahead.

Newport International Hostel   HOSTEL **$**
(William Gyles Guesthouse; Map p226; 📞401-369-0243; www.newporthostel.com; 16 Howard St; dm/d from $29/79; ⊗May-Nov; 🛜) Book as early as you can to get into Rhode Island's only hostel, run by an informal and knowledgeable host. The tiny guesthouse contains the fixings for a simple breakfast, plus a laundry machine and clean digs in a dormitory room.

Stella Maris Inn   INN **$**
(Map p226; 📞401-849-2862; www.stellamarisinn. com; 91 Washington St; d from $125; 🅿) This quiet stone-and-frame inn has numerous fireplaces, lashings of black-walnut furnishings, Victorian bric-a-brac and no shortage of floral upholstery. Rooms with garden views rent for less than those overlooking the water. Check the website for what's available.

Hotel Viking   HISTORIC HOTEL **$$**
(Map p226; 📞401-847-3300; www.hotelviking. com; 1 Bellevue Ave; d/ste from $169/270; 🅿⊖✳@🛜) This iconic hotel, Newport's largest, stands at the start of Bellevue Ave and has survived the test of time. Guestrooms have benefitted from a thorough refurbishment, shedding a period feel in favor of a more neutral, contemporary seaside look in line with the chic, modern styling of the lobby, bar-restaurant and common areas. Great rates can be found off-season.

Sea Whale Motel   MOTEL **$$**
(Map p225; 📞888-257-4096; www.seawhale. com; 150 Aquidneck Ave, Middletown; d midweek/weekend from $149/209; 🅿🛜) This owner-occupied motel is a lovely place to stay with rooms facing Easton's Pond and flowers everywhere. Rooms are neat and comfortable with simple furnishings, fridges, microwaves, and tea and coffee provided. Everything is within easy walking distance and the owner is a fount of information and recommendations.

RHODE ISLAND NEWPORT

★ **Castle Hill Inn**   INN $$$

(Map p225; ☎888-466-1355; www.castlehill
inn.com; 590 Ocean Ave; d/cottage/suite from
$399/655/795; P❋☎) Occupying a land-
mark Victorian mansion with 40 acres of
waterfront land overlooking the mouth of
Narragansett Bay, a short drive from New-
port, this celebrated upscale inn has a vari-
ety of luxurious rooms and suites individu-
ally furnished in New England country-chic
style. Lovelier still are the handful of se-
cluded, semi-private beach cottages on the
water's edge, great for romancin'.

★ **The Chanler**
at Cliff Walk   BOUTIQUE HOTEL $$$

(☎401-847-1300; www.thechanler.com; 117 Memorial Blvd; d/ste from $325/525; P❋❋☎) Don't
pull up in less than a BMW at this beautiful boutique hotel, worthy of its place on
any 'Best Hotels' list. Affording a remarkable cliff-top position near the beginning of
Newport's legendary Cliff Walk (p229), the
Chanler is a gorgeous 19th-century mansion
boasting sumptuous rooms. Several luxury
villa suites are hidden in its immaculate gardens. Service is appropriately first-class.

★ **Attwater**   BOUTIQUE HOTEL $$$

(Map p226; ☎401-846-7444; www.theattwater.
com; 22 Liberty St; r $139-659; P❋☎) New-
port's newest hotel has the bold attire of a
midsummer beach party with turquoise,
lime green and coral prints, ikat headboards
and snazzily patterned geometric rugs. Pic-
ture windows and porches capture the sum-
mer light and rooms come furnished with
thoughtful luxuries such as iPads, Apple TVs
and beach bags.

✘ **Eating**

Corner Cafe   CAFE $

(Map p226; ☎401-846-0606; www.cornercafenew
port.com; 110 Broadway; mains $9-18; ⊙7am-
2:30pm Mon-Thu, to 10pm Fri & Sat, to 8pm Sun; ▢)
This cheery cafe has good coffee and some
of the best-value breakfasts in Newport,
including a memorable eggs Benedict and
some good vegetarian options.

Meg's Aussie Milk Bar   AUSTRALIAN $

(Map p226; ☎401-619-4811; www.megsmilkbar.
com; 111 Bellevue Ave; breakfast $6-12, shakes
from $4.20; ⊙8am-3pm Mon-Sat, to 2pm Sun)
American Meg and her Aussie hubby have
created this Australiana-themed cafe where
you can sample Vegemite on toast, tuck into
a freshly baked meat pie, or choose from a

wide selection of fresh sandwiches, burgers,
soups and salads. Oh, and milkshakes – the
Aussie way: with lots of ice cream and tons
of syrup. Delish!

★ **Scales & Shells**   SEAFOOD $$

(Map p226; ☎401-846-3474; www.scalesandshells.
com; 527 Thames St; mains $14-34; ⊙5-9pm) Only
opening for dinner and exclusively serving
seafood has allowed this casual, often packed
eatery to hone its skills. This is one of the best
places in town to have your seafood almost
any way you like it. It's been so successful that
the restaurant has expanded to include a bar
and oyster room next door.

★ **Anthony's Seafood**   SEAFOOD $$

(☎401-846-9620; www.anthonysseafood.net; 963
Aquidneck Ave; mains $12-32; ⊙11am-8pm Mon-
Sat, from noon Sun) Lauded by locals and fea-
tured on TV's *Diners, Drive-ins and Dives*,
this wholesale, takeout and dine-in seafood
joint tucked away from the main drag in
Middletown is always hopping, testament to
the quality and freshness of the seafood. It's
a great place to try a quahog (also known as
'stuffies' or stuffed clams).

Boru   NOODLES $$

(Map p226; ☎401-846-4200; www.borunoodle
bar.com; 36 Broadway; noodles $12-16; ⊙noon-
10pm Tue-Sun) Queue at this newcomer on
the Newport restaurant scene for Japanese
ramen noodles with a twist, such as Thai
seafood ramen with sweet potato in a green
curry broth. Ramen purists might prefer the
spicy miso ramen.

The Red Parrot   SEAFOOD $$

(Map p226; ☎401-847-3800; www.redparrot
restaurant.com; 348 Thames St; mains $14-34;
⊙11:30am-10pm) One of Newport's most
popular pub-restaurants, the Red Parrot has
three levels of dining and a huge menu with
a focus on seafood (particularly lobster) but
all the other good stuff as well: pizza, pasta,
surf 'n' turf, chicken, cocktails and dreamy
desserts.

Mamma Luisa   ITALIAN $$

(Map p226; ☎401-848-5257; www.mammaluisa.
com; 673 Thames St; mains $20-34; ⊙5-10pm
Thu-Tue; ▢) This low-key, loved-by-locals
pasta house is as cozy and romantic as it is
authentic, and it's also a great place to escape the Newport crowds. There are classic
pasta dishes (cheese ravioli with fava beans,
spaghetti *alle vongole*), as well as a range of
hearty meat and fish dishes.

★ **Fluke Newport** SEAFOOD $$$
(Map p226; ☑401-849-7778; www.flukenewport.
com; 41 Bowens Wharf; mains $24-36; ⊙5-11pm
May-Oct, 5pm-10pm Wed-Sat Nov-Apr) Fluke's
Scandinavian-inspired dining room, with
blond wood and picture windows, offers
an accomplished seafood menu featuring
roasted monkfish, seasonal striped sea bass
and plump scallops. Upstairs, the Harbor
View Bar overlooking the docks and the
bay, serves rock-and-roll cocktails, beer and
pours from an extensive wine list. Reserva-
tions are recommended.

★ **Mooring** SEAFOOD $$$
(Map p226; ☑401-846-2260; www.mooringres
taurant.com; 1 Sayer's Wharf; sandwiches $12-26,
mains $25-45; ⊙11:30am-10pm Sun-Thu, to 11pm
Fri & Sat) A harborfront setting and a menu
brimming with fresh seafood make Mooring unbeatable for dining by the water in
true Newport style. If it's packed, and you've
not done the sensible thing and reserved a
table, squeeze up to the bar, grab a stool and
order the meaty clam chowder and a 'bag of
doughnuts' (tangy lobster fritters).

White Horse Tavern AMERICAN $$$
(Map p226; ☑401-849-3600; www.whitehorsenew
port.com; 26 Marlborough St; mains lunch $12-29,
dinner $24-42; ⊙11am-9pm Sun-Thu, to 10pm Fri &
Sat) If you'd like to eat at a 17th-century tav-
ern that once served as an annual meeting
place for the Colonial Rhode Island General
Assembly, try this historic, gambrel-roofed
beauty. Dinner menus might include baked
escargot, truffle-crusted Atlantic halibut or
beef Wellington. Service can be hit or miss de-
spite the dress code: business-casual for din-
ner; no sportswear or swimwear for lunch.

🍷 Drinking & Nightlife

Black Pearl TAVERNA
(Map p226; ☑401-846-5264; www.blackpearl
newport.com; 1 Bannister's Wharf; ⊙11am-1am)
Tucked away among the docks of **Bannis-
ter's Wharf** (☑401-846-4500; www.bannisters
newport.com) you'll find this uber-popular
bar. Its sprawling outdoor patio is perfect
for watching all the action on the harbor or
soaking up the sun with a beer in hand. If
you get peckish, there are casual and more
upscale dining options to boot.

Pour Judgement BAR
(Map p226; ☑401-619-2115; www.pourjudge
mentnewport.com; 32 Broadway; ⊙noon-1am)
This little bar serves homebrews and tasty

pub-style fare in a rather more authentic at-
mosphere than is usually found in the many
nautical- or heritage-themed watering holes
geared toward the tourist market.

The Wharf PUB
(Map p226; ☑401-619-5672; www.thewharfpub
newport.com; 37 Bowen's Wharf; ⊙noon-midnight)
This rustic waterfront tavern frequently fea-
tures live music and serves seafood (includ-
ing a raw bar) and comfort food.

☆ Entertainment

Newport Blues Café LIVE MUSIC
(Map p226; ☑401-841-5510; www.newportblues.
com; 286 Thames St; ⊙7pm-1am Wed-Sun) This
popular rhythm and blues bar and restau-
rant draws top acts to an old brownstone
that was once a bank. It's an intimate space
where you can dine on quahogs (stuffed
clams), house-smoked ribs or pork loins at
tables adjoining the small stage. Dinner is
offered from 7pm to 10pm; the music starts
at 9:30pm.

Jane Pickens Theater CINEMA
(Map p226; ☑401-846-5252; www.janepickens.
com; 49 Touro St; ticket prices vary) This beauti-
fully restored one-screen cinema used to be
an Episcopalian church, built around 1834.
Simple, pretty and old, the theater contains
an organ and a balcony. It screens both pop-
ular and art-house films.

ℹ Information

Newport Visitor's Center (Map p226; ☑401-
845-9131; www.discovernewport.org; 23
America's Cup Ave; ⊙9am-5pm) Offers maps,
brochures, local bus information, tickets to
major attractions, public restrooms and an
ATM. There's free parking for 30 minutes
adjacent to the center.

ℹ Getting There & Away

Parking can be tough in Newport. Free street
parking spaces do pop up, but check to make
sure any non-metered spots aren't reserved for
Newport residents.

An excellent parking resource is www.discover
newport.org/blog/post/the-ultimate-guide-to
-parking-in-newport-ri/.

BOAT

Block Island Ferry (p239) Between June and
September high-speed ferries depart three
times daily from a dock near Fort Adams to
Block Island.

BUS

Peter Pan Bus Lines operates buses to Boston (from $22, 1¾ to two hours, four to five daily) from the Newport Visitor Center.

RIPTA bus 60 serves Providence ($2, one hour) almost every hour. For the West Kingston Amtrak station, take bus 64 ($2, one hour, five buses Monday to Friday, three on Saturday). Bus 14 serves TF Green airport ($2, one hour) in Warwick. Most RIPTA buses arrive and depart from the Newport Visitor Center.

ⓘ Getting Around

Most people get around Newport by car, but if you prefer two wheels to four:

Scooter World (☑ 401-619-1349; www.scooterworldri.com; 12 Christie's Landing; scooter hire from $50 for first hour, $35 each additional hour; ☺ 9am-7pm)

Newport Bicycle (☑ 401-846-0773; www.newportbicycleri.com; 130 Broadway; rentals per hour/day from $7/35)

JAMESTOWN & CONANICUT ISLAND

Linked to the mainland by the Jamestown Verrazzano Bridge to the west and the Claiborne Pell Newport Bridge to the east, rural Conanicut Island feels worlds apart.

Its first inhabitants were Quaker farmers, shepherds and pirates – Captain Kidd spent considerable time here and is said to have buried his treasure on the island, but it's never been found. The real treasure lies in Conanicut's rustic, laid-back settlement, Jamestown, whose waterfront seems to draw you to its edge for a stroll, or to admire the sweeping views across the bay to Newport, Fort Adams and the awesome sight of the Claiborne Pell Bridge itself.

Aside from its natural and scenic bounty, there are no blockbuster attractions on the island to speak of, but most visitors find coming over for a day trip a worthwhile experience.

◎ Sights

Beavertail Lighthouse Museum LIGHTHOUSE
(☑ 401-423-3270; www.beavertaillight.org; Beavertail Rd, Jamestown; donations welcome; ☺ 10am-4:30pm Jun-Sep; ℗) Located in **Beavertail State Park** (☑ 401-423-9941; www.riparks.com/Locations/LocationBeavertail.html; ☺ dawn-dusk; ℗) **FREE** and built in 1749, Jamestown's Beavertail Lighthouse is one of the oldest

along the Atlantic coast, and still signals ships into Narragansett Bay. Inside there's a small maritime museum and visitors can climb to the top for a small donation. The lighthouse is generally open to the public from June to September, but dates and times are subject to change: check the website.

Watson Farm FARM
(☑ 401-423-0005; www.historicnewengland.org/property/watson-farm/; 455 North Rd, Jamestown; adult/child $6/3; ☺ 1-5pm Tue, Thu & Sun Jun–mid-Oct; ✐) It's a delight to wander around the 265-acre Watson Farm, which has been tended by five generations of the descendants of Job Watson since 1796. The farm welcomes visitors and continues to practice traditional farming methods, grazing Red Devon cattle across its seaside pastures. A self-guided walking map is provided. Note that the farmhouse is private property and not open to visitors.

🛏 Sleeping & Eating

Fort Getty Campground CAMPGROUND $
(☑ 401-423-7211; www.jamestownri.gov/town-departments/parks-rec/fort-getty; Fort Getty Rd, Jamestown; tent/RV sites $27/40; ℗) This pleasant 41-acre predominantly RV park occupies a pretty pocket of land on the west coast of Conanicut Island. There are 83 RV sites, 24 tent sites on a grassy field, a dock for fishing and a view of the squat Dutch Lighthouse. Follow RI 138 over the Newport Bridge and take the Jamestown exit, making your way to Fort Getty Rd.

Wyndham Bay Voyage Inn HOTEL $$
(☑ 401-423-2100; www.wyndhambayvoyageinn.com; 150 Conanicus Ave, Jamestown; studios from $149; ℗✳❄☂) On the waterfront overlooking Narragansett Bay toward Newport, this former 19th-century inn turned hotel and timeshare resort has a variety of self-contained studios and suites, plus an excellent seasonal outdoor pool (June to September). The location is perfect if you're looking for tranquility: it's just 10 minutes' drive from downtown Newport.

★ Simpatico Jamestown AMERICAN $$
(☑ 401-423-2000; www.simpaticojamestown.com; 13 Narragansett Ave, Jamestown; mains $18-24; ☺ 5-9pm Tue-Sat) Sample the likes of shrimp paella, comfort chicken and citrus-barbecued pork tenderloin from a menu that includes seafood, but is refreshingly not limited to it. Apart from the quality and

presentation of its cooking, the best thing about Simpatico is its wonderfully romantic yet casual ambience, especially when dining alfresco under the fairy lights on the split-level patio.

Chopmist Charlies
DINER $$

(☑ 401-423-1020; www.chopmistcharlie.com; 40 Narragansett Ave, Jamestown; mains $17-25; ⊙ noon-9pm) Chopmist Charlies is a refreshing alternative to dining in Newport, where restaurants of its ilk can feel too pricey, too crowded or too stuffy. Charlies is patronized by locals and accessible to everyone. Expect fresh seafood and diner-style favorites, plus a warm, convivial atmosphere.

ⓘ Getting There & Away

Jamestown and Conanicut Island are connected to Newport (6 miles) via the Claiborne Pell Newport Bridge. There's a $4 toll each way to cross the bridge. Heading west over the Verrazzano Bridge, also an impressive feat of engineering but for which there is no toll, you can pick up RI 1A and drop south to reach Narragansett (12 miles).

The **Jamestown Newport Ferry** (☑ 401-423-9900; www.jamestownnewportferry.com; 1 E Ferry Wharf, Jamestown; return adult/child $26/10; ⊙ May-Oct) sails between Jamestown and Newport with stops at Fort Adams and Rose Island. It's the best deal going for a harbor tour.

SOUTHERN RHODE ISLAND

South of Matunuck the tribal lands of the Narragansett Nation spread south across 1800 acres of woods and fields encompassing Charlestown on the coast and, to the north, Richmond with its white-clapboard mill villages of Carolina and Shannock.

In the westernmost corner of the state, Westerly sits on the Pawcatuck River, which marks the boundary between Rhode Island and Connecticut. Once a wealthy 19th-century town, it's now a quiet commuter community, upstaged by its own affluent Watch Hill enclave.

Narragansett & Point Judith

Named after one of the most powerful Native American tribes in New England, Narragansett, meaning literally 'People of the Small Point,' is the essence of Rhode Island.

Surrounded by miles of sandy beaches and punctuated by salt ponds and mudflats, it became a popular beach resort at the end of the 19th century. At that time, large oceanfront hotels were constructed alongside a holiday pier (which was rebuilt in the 1970s) along with the Stanford White–designed Towers Casino, of which only the twin towers remain standing. But you're not here for the architecture.

After you've plunged your person in the chilly Atlantic and baked yourself bronze, head on down Ocean Rd to the pretty village of Point Judith, where there's not much to do other than gorge yourself on the freshly caught bounty of the deep. Sound like a tough day?

◉ Sights

Narragansett Town Beach
BEACH

(☑ 401-783-6430; 39 Boston Neck Rd, Narragansett; entry/season pass $6/25; parking Mon-Fri/Sat & Sun $12/14; ⊙ admission office 8:30am-5:30pm; ℗) This mile-long stretch of beach tends to be crowded because it's an easy walk from Narragansett Pier. It's popular with surfers thanks to its soft curling waves, and is serviced by two pavilions, changing rooms and restrooms. It's the only beach in Rhode Island that charges a per-person admission fee on top of parking.

Scarborough State Beach
BEACH

(☑ 401-789-2324; www.riparks.com/Locations/LocationScarborough.html; 970 Ocean Rd, Narragansett; parking Mon-Fri/Sat & Sun $12/14; ⊙ dawn-dusk May-Oct; ℗) Scarborough (sometimes written as 'Scarboro') is considered by many to be the best beach in the state. A massive, castle-like pavilion, generous boardwalks, a wide and long beachfront, on-duty lifeguards and great, predictable surf make Scarborough special. On a hot summer day, expect hordes of beachgoers.

🛏 Sleeping & Eating

★ Fishermen's Memorial State Park
CAMPGROUND $

(☑ 401-789-8374; www.riparks.com/Locations/LocationFishermens.html; 1011 Point Judith Rd, Narragansett; tent sites RI residents/nonresidents $14/20; ⊙ May-Oct; ℗) Fishermen's Memorial State Park in Galilee is so popular that many families return year after year to the same site. There are only 180 tent sites at Fishermen's, so it's wise to reserve early by requesting the necessary form from the park management or the Division of Parks & Recreation.

★Matunuck Oyster Bar   SEAFOOD $$
(☎401-783-4202; www.rhodyoysters.com; 629
Succotash Rd, South Kingstown; mains $18-28, oys-
ters from $2 each; ☺11:30am-9pm) This small,
indoor-outdoor seafood-centric restaurant
sits on a spit of land opposite Galilee on
Point Judith Pond. Considering that the
parking lot is carpeted in shells, it's no sur-
prise that this oyster bar specializes in local
bivalves – all ultra-fresh and some raised in
the restaurant's own farm at Potter Pond Es-
tuary out back. The oyster sampler ($20) lets
you try 12 varieties, all from Rhode Island
and its immediate environs.

★Champlin's Seafood   SEAFOOD $$
(☎401-783-3152; 256 Great Rd, Point Judith;
mains $10-26; ☺11am-9pm summer, shorter hours
off-season) At Champlin's Seafood, order a
lobster roll, stuffed clams, scallops or one
of many sea critters breaded and fried, and
hang out on its 2nd-floor deck, which sits
inches from the harbor's channel. The sway-
ing masts of rusty fishing vessels give you
the feeling that this a real working fishing
port, which somehow makes the fresh catch
taste even better.

❶ Information

Narragansett Chamber of Commerce (☎401-
783-7121; www.narragansettcoc.com; 36
Ocean Rd, Narragansett; ☺9am-5pm Mon-Fri)
For information on the town of Narragansett
and its vicinity. It also operates a very useful
free shuttle from an out-of-town parking lot to
the downtown and pier areas during summer
weekends.

❶ Getting There & Away

Narragansett is 25 miles east of Westerly on US
1 and 15 miles from Newport (via Jamestown) on
the other side of Narragansett Bay.

Rhode Island's port for car ferries to Block
Island is at Galilee State Pier, at the southern
end of RI 108 in the village of Galilee, near Point
Judith.

Westerly & Watch Hill

☎401 / POP 22,567

Westerly sits on Rhode Island's western
border, sharing the banks of the Pawcatuck
River with Connecticut. In the 19th century it was a town of some wealth thanks to
its high-grade granite quarries and textile
mills. That heyday is long gone, although
the area's beaches still attract huge weekend
crowds in season. The town's main draw is

the wealthy enclave of Watch Hill, featuring
some of the country's most lavish and beautiful private homes...owned by weekenders,
can you believe!

◉ Sights

★Watch Hill   AREA
A 5-mile drive southwest of Westerly town
center, you'll come to the cloistered community known as Watch Hill, where New
York's rich and/or famous have lavish and
beautiful cliff-top mansions overlooking the
wild Atlantic Ocean. Parking here is tricky,
but the best thing to do is find a spot for
your chariot, then stroll the hilly streets
and lanes, respectfully taking a peek at how
the other half live: a good place to start is
around the Ocean House hotel.

★Misquamicut State Beach   BEACH
(☎401-322-8910; www.riparks.com/Locations/
LocationMisquamicut.html; 257 Atlantic Ave; parking Mon-Fri/Sat & Sun $12/14; ☺dawn-dusk May-
late Oct) With good surf and close proximity
to the Connecticut state line, Misquamicut
draws huge crowds. It offers families low
prices and convenient facilities for changing, showering and eating.

Napatree Point
Conservation Area   NATURE RESERVE
(☎401-315-5399; www.thewatchhillconservancy.
org/napatree.html; Fort Road) For a leisurely beach walk, the half-mile stroll to the
westernmost tip of Watch Hill is unbeatable. With the Atlantic on one side and the
yacht-studded Little Narragansett Bay on
the other, Napatree is a protected conservation area, so walkers are asked to stay on the
trails and off the dunes.

Flying Horses Carousel   RIDE
(151 Bay St; rides $1; ☺11am-9pm Mon-Fri, from
10am Sat & Sun May-Oct; ♿) This antique
merry-go-round has been in this location
since 1883. It boasts a unique design: its
horses are suspended on chains so that
they really do 'fly' outward as the carousel spins around. The flying horses have a
mane of real horsehair and leather saddles.
Sorry adults: no riders over 12 years old.

⨁ Sleeping

Margin St Inn   B&B $$
(☎401-348-8710; www.marginstreetinn.com; 4
Margin St; d from $225; ⓟ☻☎) This hand-
some historic home (well, two homes ac-
tually) has been converted into a classy

B&B with 10 fresh, beautifully furnished rooms spread across the two houses and their pretty gardens. There's not an air of stuffiness or floral chintz about the place. It's the closest accommodations to downtown Westerly.

★ **Weekapaug Inn** BOUTIQUE HOTEL $$$
(☑ 401-637-7600; www.weekapauginn.com; 25 Spray Rock Rd; d/ste from $325/655; P❄ ✱ 🐾 ✈) A member of the luxury Relais & Châteaux group of boutique hotels, this gorgeous, intimate country inn leaves nothing to be spared. Modern, casual comfort complements luxe furnishings, so you can truly relax and enjoy being pampered without the airs, graces and stuffiness of some high-end hotels in this moneyed cloister of New England.

★ **Ocean House** HOTEL $$$
(☑ 401-584-7000; www.oceanhouseri.com; 1 Bluff Ave; d/ste from $415/755; P✱❄🐾✈) This visually striking hotel sits like a frosted yellow wedding cake, dominating the bluffs above East Beach. Though designed to emulate the grandeur of a previous era, the Ocean House is a recent construction with ultra-luxe modern amenities, including fireplaces, private terraces, Italian-woven linens and so on. All rooms include complimentary 'resort activities' from yoga to cooking classes.

Watch Hill Inn INN $$$
(☑ 401-348-6300; www.watchhillinn.com; 38-44 Bay St; d/ste from $290/485; ⊘ May-late Oct; P✱❄) Rooms in this central, thoroughly renovated and well-equipped inn overlook the bobbing boats floating in the harbor across the street. The property's three fully equipped suites are excellent for families or small groups traveling together. As you'd expect in this neck of the woods, these are luxe accommodations and, despite higher-than-elsewhere prices, they sell out fast.

✕ Eating

The Cooked Goose CAFE $
(☑ 401-348-9888; www.thecookedgoose.com; 92 Watch Hill Rd; lunches $8-14; ⊘ 7am-7pm May-Sep, to 3pm Oct-Apr) With its appealing selection of Benedicts, omelets, baked goods (*pain au chocolat*, house-made doughnuts) and exotic sandwiches (consider the Nirvana, with baked tofu, honey-ginger dressing, cheddar cheese and sprouts on wholewheat bread), this is a favorite of the Watch Hill

elite. Prices are reasonable and its location across from the harbor makes it good for boat-watching.

St Clair's Annex ICE CREAM $
(☑ 401-348-8407; www.stclairannexrestaurant.com; 141 Bay St; cones from $3; ⊘ 8am-9pm May-Oct; ✈) This ice-cream shop has been run by the same family since 1887, and features several dozen flavors of homemade ice cream. On top of traditional light breakfast fare (omelets and the like), it serves seaside specialties such as lobster rolls, hot dogs and lemonade.

Olympia Tea Room BISTRO $$$
(☑ 401-348-8211; www.olympiatearoom.com; 74 Bay St; mains $14-38; ⊘ 11:30am-9pm May–mid-Oct) The most atmospheric restaurant in Watch Hill, the Olympia is an authentic 1916 soda-fountain-turned-bistro with wooden booths, pink walls and black-and-white checkered floor tiles. Its antique marble-topped soda fountain still remains. Dine on calf livers, broiled flounder or sausages.

❶ Getting There & Away

Westerly is 8 miles east of Mystic, CT, on US 1, and 5 miles north of the mansions of Watch Hill. Charlestown is 13 miles east along the coast.
New England Airlines (☑ 401-596-2460; www.blockislandairline.com; 56 Airport Rd) flies from Westerly airport to Block Island, with one-way/return flights from $59/109.

BLOCK ISLAND

POP 1051

From the deck of the ferry, a cluster of mansard roofs and gingerbread houses rises picturesquely from the commercial village of Old Harbor, where little has changed since 1895, short of adding electricity and flushing toilets! If you remain after the departure of the masses on the last ferry, the scale and pace of the island will delight or derange you: some find it blissfully quiet, but others get island fever fast.

Block Island's simple pleasures center upon strolling the beach, which stretches for miles to the north of Old Harbor, biking around the island's rolling farmland and getting to know the calls of the many bird species that make the island home. During off-season, when the population dwindles to a few hundred, the landscape has the spare, haunted feeling of an Andrew Wyeth

Block Island

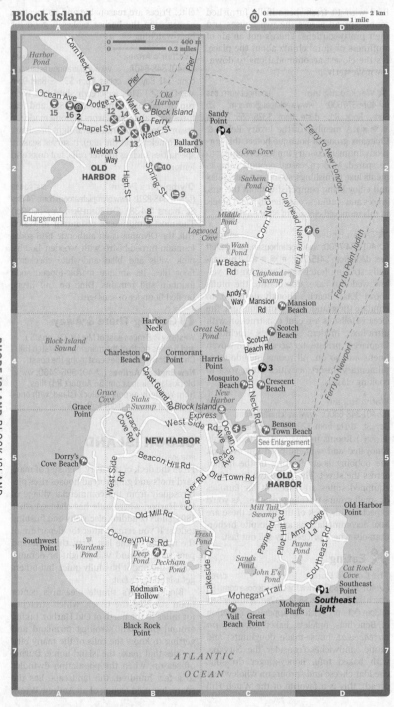

Enlargement

Harbor Pond

Corn Neck Rd

Pier

Pier

Ocean Ave

Dodge St

Water St

Old Harbor

15 16 2 12 14

Chapel St

Block Island Ferry

Water St

Weldon's Way

11 13

Ballard's Beach

OLD HARBOR

High St

Spring St

10

9

8

Sandy Point

4

Cow Cove

Sachem Pond

Middle Pond

Logwood Cove

Wash Pond

W Beach Rd

Clayhead Swamp

Clayhead Nature Trail

Corn Neck Rd

6

Ferry to New London

Ferry to Point Judith

Andy's Way

Mansion Rd

Mansion Beach

Harbor Neck

Great Salt Pond

Scotch Beach

Block Island Sound

Charleston Beach

Cormorant Point

Harris Point

Scotch Beach Rd

3

Ferry to Newport

Mosquito Beach

Crescent Beach

Grace Cove

Coast Guard Rd

Siahs Swamp

New Harbor

Corn Neck Rd

Grace Point

Grace's Cove Rd

Block Island Express

West Side Rd

Ocean Ave

5

Benson Town Beach

NEW HARBOR

Beacon Hill Rd

Center Rd

Beach Ave

Old Town Rd

OLD HARBOR

See Enlargement

Dorry's Cove Beach

West Side Rd

Old Harbor Point

Southwest Point

Old Mill Rd

Fresh Pond

Mill Tail Swamp

Payne Rd

Pilot Hill Rd

Amy Dodge La

Southeast Rd

Cooneymus Rd

Deep Pond

7

Peckham Pond

Lakeside Dr

Sands Pond

John E's Pond

Payne Pond

Cat Rock Cove

Southeast Point

Rodman's Hollow

Mohegan Trail

Mohegan Bluffs

1

Southeast Light

Black Rock Point

Vail Beach

Great Point

ATLANTIC

OCEAN

Block Island

⊙ Top Sights
1 Southeast Light D6

⊙ Sights
2 Block Island Historical Society A1
3 Block Island State Beach C4
4 North Lighthouse C2

⊕ Activities, Courses & Tours
5 Block Island Fishworks C5
6 Clayhead Nature Trail D3
7 Rodman's Hollow B6

⊜ Sleeping
8 Atlantic Inn B3

9 Sea Breeze Inn B2
10 The 1661 Inn B2

⊗ Eating
11 Aldo's Bakery & Homemade Ice
    Cream B2
12 Eli's B1
13 Finn's Seafood B2
14 Rebecca's B1

⊙ Drinking & Nightlife
15 Captain Nick's A1
16 Poor People's Pub A1
17 Yellow Kittens A1

painting, with stone walls demarcating centuries-old property lines and few trees interrupting the spectacular ocean vistas.

⊙ Sights

★**Southeast Light**   LIGHTHOUSE
(☑401-466-5009; 122 Mohegan Trail, New Shoreham; ⊙10am-4pm Jun-Jan; Ⓟ) FREE You'll likely recognize the red-brick lighthouse known as the Southeast Light from postcards of the island. Set dramatically atop 200ft-high red-clay cliffs called Mohegan Bluffs south of Old Harbor, the lighthouse was moved back from the eroding cliff edge in 1993. With waves crashing below and sails drifting across the Atlantic offshore, it's probably the best place on the island to watch the sunset. Just south of it a steep stairway descends to a narrow beach backed by the bluffs.

Block Island Historical Society   MUSEUM
(☑401-466-2481; www.blockislandhistorical.org; 18 Old Town Rd, Old Harbor; adult/child $6/free; ⊙11am-4pm Tue-Sun) This excellent local history society runs a compact but top-notch museum covering all things Block Island. If you're around on a Tuesday, don't miss one of their walking tours (adult/child $15/5), which depart at 10am from in front of the Chamber of Commerce, rain or shine, and conclude at the museum.

North Lighthouse   LIGHTHOUSE
(Corn Neck Rd, New Shoreham; ⊙museum 10am-4pm Tue-Mon Jun-Sep; Ⓟ) FREE At Sandy Point, the northernmost tip of the island, this pretty little beacon stands at the end of a long sandy path lined with beach roses. At the trailhead, you'll find Settler's Rock, a

small monument that lists the names of the island's original English settlers at the spot where they landed in 1661. The 1867 lighthouse contains a small maritime museum and interpretive center with information about famous island wrecks, but there is no access to the modest tower.

Block Island State Beach   BEACH
(www.blockislandinfo.com/maps/beaches-parks -map; Old Harbor; Ⓟ) The island's east coast, north of Old Harbor, is lined with this glorious 3-mile stretch of beach. The southern part, Fred Benson Town Beach, sits closest to Old Harbor, and is supplied with changing and showering stalls, a snack stand, and umbrella and boogie-board rentals. Heading north, you'll next hit Crescent Beach, then Scotch Beach and finally the grand curve of Mansion Beach.

🏃 Activities

★**Greenway Walking Trails**   HIKING
Explore Block Island's unique ecosystems (dune fields, morainal grasslands, salt ponds and kettle-hole ponds) along 28 miles of public-access greenway walking trails. The trails meander over the southern half of the island through Nathan Mott Park, the Enchanted Forest and Rodman's Hollow.

The numerous trailheads can be hard to find at first – get trail maps and guides from the Block Island Hospitality Center (p239) or talk to the friendly folks at the Block Island Conservancy (p239).

Clayhead Nature Trail   HIKING
(off Corn Neck Rd, New Shoreham) About 3 miles north of Old Harbor, this scenic trail follows a maze-like series of paths cut into low

GLASS FLOAT PROJECT

This wonderful interactive Glass Float Project (www.glassfloatproject.com), akin to a grown-up version of hide-and-seek, was started by Rhode Island artist and glassblower, Eben Horton, to promote the natural beauty of Block Island. Initially, 550 numbered, hand-blown glass orbs have been hidden along Greenway Walking Trails across the island. The rules are simple: if you find an orb, keep it and register your find with the Block Island Hospitality Center; if you find another, leave it for the next sleuth. Donations welcome.

vegetation that attracts many bird species then veers through high clay bluffs to the beachfront. To reach the trailhead, turn east off Corn Neck Rd and look for the big yellow farmhouse: a marker opposite indicates the start of the trail.

Rodman's Hollow   HIKING
(Cooneymus Rd, New Shoreham) In the south of the island, this 230-acre glacial outwash plain is dotted with walking trails offering panoramic vistas over the Atlantic, with direct access to Black Rock Beach. We're told it's a hot spot for orb-seekers joining in the fun of the Glass Float Project.

Block Island Fishworks   FISHING
(☑401-466-5392; www.sandypointco.com; 40 Ocean Ave, New Harbor; half-/full-day charters from $375/750) Fishing charters on a small boat with a Coast Guard–licensed captain. Possible catches include striped bass, bluefish, bonito, false albacore, tuna, shark, scup, sea bass and fluke.

🛏 Sleeping

★Sea Breeze Inn   INN $$
(☑401-466-2275; www.seabreezeblockisland.com; 71 Spring St, New Shoreham; d with/without bath from $230/95; P🐕) Some rooms in these charming hillside cottages have uninterrupted views over a tidal pond and the ocean beyond. Others face inward toward a country garden. Inside, airy rooms have eccentric, rustic furnishings, cathedral ceilings, and no electronic distractions such as TVs and clocks. Breakfast comes served in a basket, which can be enjoyed on the porch. Open April to September.

The 1661 Inn   INN $$$
(☑401-466-2063; www.blockislandresorts.com; 5 Spring St, New Shoreham; d low season $125-399, high season $250-875; P😊🐕) Set on a sunset-facing hill overlooking the sea, The 1661 Inn has one of the best locations on the island and is open year-round. Its nine rooms are decorated in antique style with charming floral wallpaper, brass and four-poster beds, and some stunning private decks. You can just walk across the road for one of the island's finest dinners.

Room rates vary dramatically by season: check the website for pricing.

Atlantic Inn   INN $$$
(☑401-466-5883; www.atlanticinn.com; 359 High St, New Shoreham; d low season $180-240, high season $225-335; P🐕) This 1879 establishment commands a gentle perch on a grassy hilltop, with ocean and town vistas. The gracefully appointed Victorian inn features a wide porch, a fine-dining restaurant and Adirondack chairs strewn across a spacious lawn. The 21 rooms vary in size, with some on the small side, but all are quaintly decorated with quilts and lace curtains.

🍴 Eating

Rebecca's   SEAFOOD $
(☑401-466-5411; www.rebeccasseafood.com; 435 Water St, Old Harbor; sandwiches & burgers $3-8, seafood dinners $12-16; ⊙7am-2am Thu-Mon, to 8pm Tue & Wed) This snack stand serves burgers, chowder, grilled-cheese sandwiches, deep-fried clams, fish, scallops and more to hungry tourists seated at picnic tables under umbrellas. It's one of the reliable, open-when-you-need-it, island eateries that won't break your budget.

Aldo's Bakery &
Homemade Ice Cream   ICE CREAM $
(☑401-466-2198; www.aldosbakery.com; 130 Weldon's Way, Old Harbor; ice cream and pastries $2.50-6; ⊙6am-11pm May–mid-Oct) Family-friendly Aldo's has been serving homemade ice cream and pastries, including delicious Portuguese sweetbread, to Block Island tourists for over 40 years. It even operates a 'pastry boat' so you can have freshly baked muffins delivered right to your deck.

Finn's Seafood   SEAFOOD $$
(☑401-466-2473; www.finnsseafood.com; 212 Water St, Old Harbor; mains $12-26; ⊙11:30am-

10pm) Finn's is an island institution, its bunting-draped deck the first cheerful sight that greets arrivals at the ferry dock. Come here for New England–style chowder, clams, lobster rolls, steamers and broiled fish that still taste of the ocean. There's a takeout window, too.

★ **Eli's**   MODERN AMERICAN $$$
(☑ 401-466-5230; www.elisblockisland.com; 456 Chapel St, Old Harbor; mains $19-32; ☺ 6-10pm Fri-Sun; ☑) The locally caught sea-bass special (tender fillets over scallions, grapes and beans) tastes so fresh and mildly salty and sweet that its memory will haunt you for weeks. For real. The room is cramped, crowded and casual with lots of pine wood and some well-conceived art.

🍸 Drinking & Nightlife

Poor People's Pub   PUB
(☑ 401-466-8533; www.pppbi.com; 33 Ocean Ave, Old Harbor; ☺ noon-11pm) Poor People's Pub with its barbecue, beer and bands is a hit with everyone, not just the handful of visitors who actually have a budget!

Captain Nick's   BAR
(☑ 401-466-5670; www.captainnicksbi.com; 34 Ocean Ave, Old Harbor; ☺ 4pm-1am) Built of reclaimed wood, this is the island's most raucous bar. It has live music six days a week in season – sometimes acoustic, often rock (there's even a weekly disco night). There's sushi Thursday through Sunday.

Yellow Kittens   BAR
(☑ 401-466-5855; www.yellowkittens.com; Corn Neck Rd; ☺ 11am-11pm) Just north of Old Harbor, Yellow Kittens attracts bands from around New England and keeps rowdy patrons happy with pool, table tennis and darts. It's been called Yellow Kittens since 1876!

🛈 Information

Block Island Conservancy Education Center
(☑ 401-466-3111; www.biconservancy.org; 235 Weldon's Way, Old Harbor) This excellent little education center teaches kids about conservancy in general and particularly focuses on the island's unique ecosystems and natural resources. Drop in for information on the island's extensive Greenway Walking Trails (p237) network.

Block Island Hospitality Center (☑ 401-466-2982; www.blockislandchamber.com; 1 Water St, Old Harbor Ferry Landing; ☺ 9am-5pm late May-early Sep, 10am-4pm rest of year) The Block Island Chamber of Commerce operates this visitor center next to the ferry dock, where you'll also find public restrooms.

🛈 Getting There & Away

You don't need a car to get around Block Island and, aside from hotel parking lots, there aren't many places to put one. You'll save a ton of money by leaving it behind in the well-organized parking lots at Point Judith ($10 per day). Besides, why mess with the island's pristine ecology and laid-back, bike-riding vibe? **Island Moped and Bike Rentals** (☑ 401-466-2700; www.bimopeds.com; 41 Water St, Old Harbor; per day bikes/mopeds from $20/45; ☺ 9am-8pm May-Oct) offers everything from mountain bikes to mopeds.

If you simply can't live without your car, the one-way surcharge to bring your vehicle on the ferry is $39.60, excluding the driver. Bikes are $3.50. Reservations for vehicle crossings are essential.

AIR

New England Airlines (p235) flies between Westerly State Airport, on Airport Rd off RI 78, and Block Island State Airport (12 minutes; one way/return $59/109).

BOAT

Block Island Ferry (☑ 401-783-7996; www.blockislandferry.com) runs a high-speed ferry from Point Judith in Narragansett (round-trip adult/child $38/22, 30 minutes) from Memorial Day (May 25) to mid-October, and a year-round traditional ferry (adult/child $26/13, one hour). The latter is the only car ferry (additional fares apply). Reservations for vehicle crossings are essential.

There are additional high-speed ferries from Newport (adult/child $51/26, one hour) and Fall River, MA ($60/30, two hours).

Block Island Express (☑ 860-444-4624; www.goblockisland.com) operates services from New London, CT, to Old Harbor, Block Island (round-trip adult/child $47.50/23.75, 75 minutes) between May and September.

🛈 Getting Around

Up until recently, Block Island didn't use normal US street addresses: each house was assigned a fire number instead. Useful if you're delivering mail or tracking down a blaze, but not much help to travelers. Nowadays, you'll find standard street names and numbers in the Old and New Harbor areas. Either way, be sure to grab an island map from the ferry!

Connecticut

☏ 860, 959 / 860, 959 / POP 3.6 MILLION

Includes ➡

Hartford	241
East Haddam	249
Chester	251
Essex	251
New London	253
Mystic	255
Stonington	259
New Haven	261
Westport	268
Litchfield Hills	271

Best Places to Eat

➡ Mockingbird Kitchen & Cafe (p272)

➡ Captain Daniel Packer Inne (p258)

➡ Trumbull Kitchen (p247)

➡ Whelk (p268)

➡ ZINC (p265)

Best Places to Stay

➡ Inn at Stonington (p259)

➡ White Hart Inn (p269)

➡ Boardman House Inn (p250)

➡ Silas W. Robbins House (p246)

➡ Study at Yale (p264)

Why Go?

Known for its commuter cities, New York's neighbor is synonymous with the affluent lanes and mansions of *The Stepford Wives* and TV's *Gilmore Girls*. In old-moneyed Greenwich, the Litchfield Hills and the Quiet Corner, these representations ring true.

Many regard the state as a mere stepping stone to the 'real' New England, from whose tourist boom Connecticut has been spared. The upside is that the state retains a more 'authentic' feel. The downside is a slow decaying of former heavyweights like Hartford and New London, where visitors can ponder the price of progress and learn about urban renewal. New Haven is one such place rewiring itself as a vibrant cultural hub.

Rich in maritime, literary and national history, as well as the farm-to-table food movement, celebrity chefs and enough waterfalls and state parks for the most avid outdoors folk, the Nutmeg State unfolds in incredible layers the longer you stick around.

When to Go
Hartford

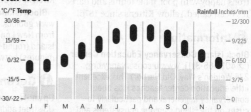

Jun Enjoy New Haven's International Festival of Arts and Ideas and coastal beach-going.

Jul The Litchfield Jazz Festival briefly interrupts the peace and quiet of the Litchfield Hills.

Sep–Oct Norwalk's much-loved Oyster Festival and brilliant fall foliage across the state.

History

A number of Native American tribes (notably the Pequot and the Mohegan, whose name for the river became the name of the state) were here when the first European explorers, primarily Dutch, appeared in the early 17th century. The first English settlement was at Old Saybrook in 1635, followed a year later by the Connecticut Colony, built by Massachusetts Puritans under Thomas Hooker. A third colony was founded in 1638 in New Haven. After the Pequot War (1637), the Native Americans were no longer able to check Colonial expansion in New England, and Connecticut's English population grew. In 1686 Connecticut was brought into the Dominion of New England.

The American Revolution swept through Connecticut, leaving scars with major battles at Stonington (1775), Danbury (1777), New Haven (1779) and Groton (1781). Connecticut became the fifth state in 1788. It embarked on a period of prosperity, propelled by its whaling, shipbuilding, farming and manufacturing (firearms to bicycles to household tools) industries, which lasted well into the 19th century.

The 20th century brought world wars and the Depression but, thanks in no small part to Connecticut's munitions industries, the state was able to fight back. Everything from planes to submarines were made in the state, and when the defense industry began to decline in the 1990s, the growth of other businesses (such as insurance) helped pick up the slack. Today, two booming casinos are a key source of income for the state – $7 billion since 1997 – so much so that a third casino has been approved by legislators.

ⓘ Getting There & Away

AIR

Bradley International Airport (BDL; ☑ 860-292-2000; www.bradleyairport.com; Schoephoester Rd), 12 miles north of Hartford in Windsor Locks (I-91 exit 40), is served by American Airlines, Delta, JetBlue, Southwest Airlines and United Airlines.

Connecticut Transit buses (www.cttransit. com) connect the airport with Windsor Locks and Windsor train stations, both of which are served by Amtrak. Route 30, the Bradley Flyer, provides an express service to downtown Hartford ($1.50, 30 minutes, hourly).

BOAT

Ferries from New London are an easy way to get your car, or yourself, to Block Island (RI), Fisher's Island and Long Island, avoiding the long drive around.

TRAIN

➤ Metro-North trains (www.new.mta.info/mnr) make the run between New York City's Grand Central Terminal and New Haven (peak/off-peak $22/16.50, from one hour 50 minutes), with services to Greenwich ($13/9.75, 45 minutes) and South Norwalk ($15.50/11.75, one hour). There is a connecting line north to Danbury, but its infrequency makes it difficult to rely on.

➤ Peak fares apply to weekday trains arriving in Grand Central Terminal between 5am and 10am and departing Grand Central Terminal between 4pm and 8pm.

➤ Shore Line East (www.shorelineeast.com), Connecticut's commuter rail service, travels along the shore of Long Island Sound, connecting with Metro-North and Amtrak lines at New Haven.

➤ Amtrak (www.amtrak.com) trains depart New York City's Penn Station for Connecticut on three lines.

HARTFORD

☑ 860 / POP 125,020

Connecticut's capital, one of America's oldest cities, is famed for the 1794 birth of the lucrative insurance industry, conceived when a local landowner sought fire insurance. Policy documents necessitated printing presses, which spurred a boom in publishing that lured the likes of Mark Twain, Harriet Beecher Stowe and Wallace Stevens. In 1855 Samuel Colt made the mass production of the revolver commercially viable. Big business boomed in Hartford.

It's ironic that the industries responsible for the city's wealth (insurance and guns) have contributed to its slow decline: Hartford has a gritty track record for crime. Although things are improving, keep this in mind. Old money has left a truly impressive legacy of fine historic attractions worthy of any New England itinerary. Visit during spring when the darling buds burst to life or in summer when trees are green and skies are blue, and you're likely to be pleasantly surprised.

⊙ Sights

★ **Wadsworth Atheneum**   MUSEUM

(☑ 860-278-2670; https://thewadsworth.org; 600 Main St; adult/child $15/free; ⊙ 11am-5pm Wed-Fri, 10am-5pm Sat & Sun) In 2015 the nation's oldest public art museum completed a five-year, $33-million renovation, renewing 32 galleries and 15 public spaces. The Wadsworth

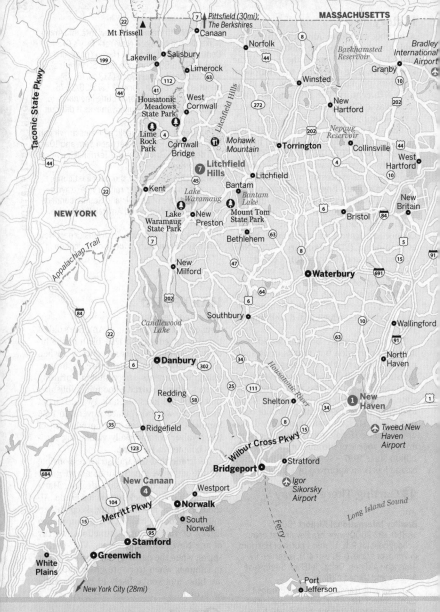

Connecticut Highlights

1 Yale University (p261)
Exploring world-class
museums and the hopping
student scene in New Haven.

**2 Mystic Seaport
Museum** (p255) Delighting

budding mariners at Mystic's
marvelous maritime world.

3 Wadsworth Atheneum
(p241) Gawking at this
magnificent historic collection
of art and artifacts in Hartford.

**4 Philip Johnson Glass
House** (p269) Peering
through walls at this iconic
architectural treasure.

5 New London (p253)
Marveling at faded

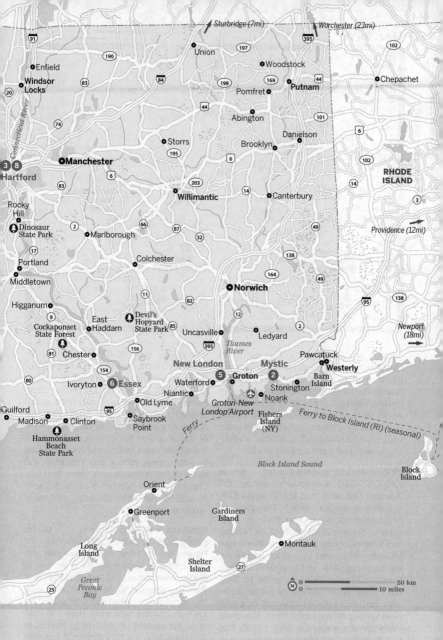

architectural gems and pondering progress before dining by the waterfront.

6 **Essex Steam Train & Riverboat Ride** (p252) Jumping on board for the romance of steam along the Connecticut River.

7 **Litchfield Hills** (p271) Cozying up in country inns, hiking forested hills and fishing the Housatonic.

8 **Mark Twain House & Museum** (p244) Walking through the corridors of the former home of a literary legend.

Hartford

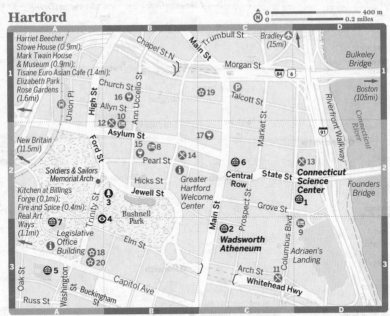

houses nearly 50,000 pieces of art in a castle-like Gothic Revival building. On display are paintings by members of the Hudson River School, including some by Hartford native Frederic Church; 19th-century impressionist works; 18th-century New England furniture; sculptures by Connecticut artist Alexander Calder; and an outstanding array of surrealist, postwar and contemporary works.

⭐ **Connecticut Science Center**   MUSEUM
(☑ 860-520-2160; www.ctsciencecenter.org; 250 Columbus Blvd; adult/child $24/17, movies $7/6; ⊙10am-5pm Tue-Sun; Ⓟ🚼) Designed by Argentinian architect Cesar Pelli, the Connecticut Science Center is both an exciting architectural space and an absorbing museum for adults and kids alike. Innovative, interactive exhibits and programs abound; there's a dedicated KidsZone on the 1st floor; films, stage shows and special events are on offer; and there's always a fascinating world-class visiting themed exhibition. You could easily spend a whole day here, but it's best to arrive after 2pm when the school groups clear out. Check the website for what's on.

⭐ **Mark Twain House & Museum**   MUSEUM
(☑ 860-247-0998; www.marktwainhouse.org; 351 Farmington Ave, parking at 385 Farmington Ave; guided house tours adult/child $20/11, Living History/Ghost tours $25/12, museum only $6; ⊙9:30am-5:30pm, closed Tue Jan & Feb; Ⓟ) For 17 years, encompassing the most productive period of his life, Samuel Langhorne Clemens (1835–1910) and his family lived in this striking orange-and-black brick Victorian house, which then stood in the pastoral area of the city called Nook Farm. Architect Edward Tuckerman Potter lavishly embellished it with turrets, gables and verandas, and some of the interiors were done by Louis Comfort Tiffany. Admission to the house is by guided tour only; advance purchase is recommended.

Elizabeth Park Rose Gardens   GARDENS
(☑ 860-231-9443; www.elizabethparkct.org; cnr Prospect & Asylum Aves; ⊙dawn-dusk daily, concert times vary) Known for its collection of 15,000 rose bushes, the 102-acre Elizabeth Park was donated to the city by a wealthy industrialist, who asked that it be named for his wife. Planted with more than 900 varieties, the gardens are covered in blooms in June and July, but they flower, if less profusely, well into fall. During the summer months, concerts are held at the park.

Museum of Connecticut History   MUSEUM
(☑ 860-757-6535; www.museumofcthistory.org; 231 Capitol Ave; ⊙9am-4pm Mon-Fri, to 2pm Sat)

Hartford

◎ Top Sights
1 Connecticut Science Center D2
2 Wadsworth Atheneum C3

◎ Sights
3 Bushnell Park B2
4 Bushnell Park Carousel A3
5 Museum of Connecticut History........A3
6 Old State House C2
7 State Capitol A3

🛏 Sleeping
8 Goodwin B2
9 Hartford Marriott Downtown D3
10 Homewood Suites by Hilton
Downtown...B2

✕ Eating
11 Bear's Smokehouse C3
12 Black-Eyed Sally's BBQ & Blues........B2
13 ON20 ....D2
14 Trumbull Kitchen B2

🍷 Drinking & Nightlife
15 Bin 228 ....B2
16 Russian Lady B1
17 Vaughan's Public House C2

🎭 Entertainment
Aetna Theater ....(see 2)
18 Bushnell A3
19 Hartford Stage C1
20 Hartford Symphony............................A3

FREE This museum, housed in the Connecticut State Library on Capitol Hill and renowned for its impressive genealogy library, packs a punch for US history buffs. It also holds Connecticut's original royal charter of 1662, a prime collection of Colt firearms (which were manufactured in Hartford), coins, and the table at which Abraham Lincoln signed the Emancipation Proclamation.

Children's Museum   MUSEUM

(☑ 860-231-2824; www.thechildrensmuseumct. org; 950 Trout Brook Dr, West Hartford; adult/child $14.75/13.75; ⊙ 10am-4pm Tue-Sat, 11am-4pm Sun; P♿) Founded in 1927 and relocated here in 1958, this not-for-profit museum aims to educate kids about science and nature in a fun, hands-on way. It features the museum itself, a planetarium, a wildlife sanctuary and Conny the Sperm Whale, a life-size replica of Connecticut's state animal. Behind-the-scenes tours for future veterinarians aged 10-plus are available with advance planning.

Wethersfield Museum at the
Keeney Memorial Cultural Center   MUSEUM

(☑ 860-529-7656; www.wethersfieldhistory.org; 200 Main St, Wethersfield; ⊙ 10am-4pm Tue-Sat, 1-4pm Sun) FREE This local history museum brings together a wide range of pieces from the Wethersfield Historical Society's impressive collection of photographs, documents and artifacts.

Bushnell Park Carousel   RIDE

(1 Jewell St; rides $1; ⊙ May–mid-Oct; ♿) This vintage 1914 merry-go-round designed by Stein and Goldstein, in Bushnell Park, continues to delight young and old.

Old State House   HISTORIC BUILDING

(☑ 860-522-6766; www.ctoldstatehouse.org; 800 Main St; adult/child $6/3; ⊙ 10am-5pm Tue-Sat Jul-Sep, Mon-Fri Oct-Jun; ♿) Connecticut's original capitol building (from 1797 to 1873) was designed by Charles Bulfinch, who also designed the Massachusetts State House in Boston, and was the site of the trial of the *Amistad* prisoners. Gilbert Stuart's famous 1801 portrait of George Washington hangs in the senate chamber. The space houses interactive exhibits aimed at kids, as well as a **Museum of Curiosities** that features a two-headed calf, Mark Twain's bicycle, a narwhal's horn and a variety of mechanical devices.

Bushnell Park   PARK

(☑ tours 860-232-6710; www.bushnellpark.org; monthly tours by donation; ⊙ dawn-dusk) The Capitol overlooks the 37-acre Bushnell Park, the first public park in the USA built with taxpayers' money. It was designed by Jacob Weidenmann and opened in 1861. Weidenmann's unique vision – an informal, natural style – broke from the traditional New England central green, and included 157 varieties of trees and shrubs from around North America, Europe and East Asia. In July, the park hosts the nation's longest-running free jazz concert series (http://hartfordjazzsocie ty.com) and the annual jazz festival (p246).

Over time, additions were made to the park, including the Gothic Soldiers & Sailors Memorial Arch, which frames the Trinity St entrance and is accessible only by tour (noon Thursdays, May to October). The Bushnell Park Carousel delights children.

Harriet Beecher-Stowe Center   MUSEUM

(☑ 860-522-9258; www.harrietbeecherstowe.org; 77 Forest St; adult/child $16/10; ⊙ 9:30am-5pm Mon-Sat, noon-5pm Sun; P) Hartford was home to Harriet Beecher Stowe, author of the antislavery book *Uncle Tom's Cabin.* Upon meeting Stowe, Abraham Lincoln reputedly said, 'So this is the little lady who made this big war.' The facility centers on Stowe House, built in 1871, which reflects the author's strong ideas about decorating and domestic efficiency, as expressed in her bestseller *American Woman's Home* (nearly as popular as her famous novel).

Combination tickets with Mark Twain House (p244) next door can save you a few dollars if you wish to tour both.

State Capitol   HISTORIC BUILDING
(☑860-240-0222; www.cga.ct.gov; cnr Capitol Ave & Trinity St; ◷hourly tours 9:15am-1:15pm Mon-Fri Sep-Jun, plus 2:15pm Jul-Aug) FREE Built of New England granite and white marble and topped by an ostentatious gold-leaf dome, the Gothic palace that is Connecticut's State Capitol (1879) was designed by Richard Upjohn and took over a decade to complete. Because of the variety of architectural styles it reflects, it's been called 'the most beautiful ugly building in the world.' Frank Lloyd Wright dismissed it as 'ridiculous.' You be the judge. Guided tours depart from the southwest entrance of the Legislative Office Building (☑860-240-1000; 300 Capitol Ave).

🎭 Festivals & Events

Greater Hartford Festival of Jazz   MUSIC
(www.hartfordjazz.org; Bushnell Park; ◷Jul) The largest free jazz event in New England is held at Bushnell Park over a weekend in July.

Taste of Hartford   FOOD & DRINK
(www.ctnow.com; ◷dates vary) Usually held once in winter and once in summer. Reservations are recommended during this week-long extravaganza of prix-fixe meals dished up across the city at a multitude of restaurants.

🛏 Sleeping

**Homewood Suites
by Hilton Downtown**   HOTEL $$
(☑860-524-0223; www.hilton.com; 338 Asylum St; d from $169; P✦❀❀) Occupying a 1913 heritage building, this tasteful, modern hotel offers studio and one- and two-bedroom suites, all with full kitchens. The one- and two- bedroom suites feature separate living areas. Daily breakfast is included and there's

a 24-hour convenience store on-site. Polite and helpful staff. Conveniently located next to Black-Eyed Sally's (☑860-278-7427; www.blackeyedsallys.com; 350 Asylum St; mains $10-20; ◷11:30am-10pm Mon-Sat, noon-8pm Sun), a Southern restaurant and bar.

Hartford Marriott Downtown   HOTEL $$
(☑860-249-8000; www.marriott.com; 200 Columbus Blvd; d/ste from $159/279; P◉@❀❀) This colossal Marriott hotel is in the Adriaen's Landing district overlooking the Connecticut River and linked to the convention center. There are 401 stylish rooms spread over 22 stories alongside an indoor rooftop pool and fitness center. There's also an affiliated spa, an upscale restaurant and a slick bar on the ground floor.

⭐**Goodwin**   BOUTIQUE HOTEL $$$
(☑860-246-1881; www.goodwinhartford.com; 1 Haynes St; r from $359) This historic building has been redone in modern New York chic by the same folks who run Norwalk's Hotel Zero Degrees. The Queen Anne terra-cotta facade exudes the building's 19th-century origins while the inside oozes 21st-century cool. Convenient to the downtown scene, the Goodwin gives you no reason to leave the premises with its own charming bar-restaurant Porrón and Piña, managed by chef Tyler Anderson.

⭐**Silas W. Robbins House**   B&B $$$
(☑860-571-8733; www.silaswrobbins.com; 185 Broad St, Wethersfield; d $195-325; P❀❀) About 6 miles south of downtown Hartford in the charming historic village of Wethersfield, you'll find this beautiful and opulent 1873 French Second Empire home. Its common areas and five plush rooms, with their soaring ceilings and light-filled windows overlooking the manicured grounds, have been refurbished in the style of the period.

🍴 Eating

Kitchen at Billings Forge   CAFE $
(☑860-727-8066; www.billingsforgeworks.org; 559 Broad St; items $6-10; ◷8am-4pm Mon-Fri) 🍃 Providing training and employment opportunities for the Billings Forge/Hartford community, this bright, forward-thinking cafe works with local farmers to source fresh seasonal produce (in addition to what is available from the community garden and farmers market) to create a truly sustainable dining experience. Menu items, including salads,

ART IN NEW BRITAIN

Not technically a part of the Connecticut River Valley, and not really a suburb of Hartford either, New Britain is hard to situate and easy to miss. Indeed, this small formerly industrial city has seen better days. Even so, the city's truly wonderful art museum, **New Britain Museum of American Art** (☑ 860-229-0257; www.nbmaa.org; 56 Lexington St; adult/child/student $15/free/10; ☺ 11am-5pm Sun-Wed & Fri, to 8pm Thu, 10am-5pm Sat), is reason enough to visit. Its collection features some outstanding pieces, including Thomas Benton's stunning *Arts of Life* murals, painted at the height of the Great Depression. Works are presented according to 'schools', giving a fantastic overview of the development of modern American art.

Follow it up with an all-American soda pop at **Avery's Beverages** (☑ 860-224-0830; www.averysoda.com; 520 Corbin Ave; ☺ 8:30am-5:30pm Tue-Wed & Fri, to 7pm Thu, to 3pm Sat, hours vary Mon). Its 30-plus flavors of sodas and seltzers (including the hysterical 'Totally Gross' soda range) are still made with 1950s technology in the original red barn where it all started back in 1904. The water is pure well and the sugar is pure cane – no high-fructose corn syrup here. If your group is at least five strong, be sure to call ahead to arrange a make-your-own-soda tour (price varies). You'll go upstairs to the Mixing Room and create three bottles of soda to your exact flavor specifications and then watch the conveyor-belt machine downstairs add the water and CO_2 and affix the cap. Sodas are sold by the case (within which you can mix and match flavors), and there are also six-packs and single bottles available.

From Hartford, New Britain is an 18-mile drive via I-84 and CT 9 S, or a 30-minute trip on bus 101, 102 or 928.

soups, sandwiches and fresh baked goods, are usually under $10.

Quaker Diner
DINER $

(☑ 860-232-5523; 319 Park Rd, West Hartford; meals $5-16; ☺ 6am-2:30pm Mon-Fri, 7am-1:30pm Sat & Sun) Get in early and squeeze into a slightly uncomfortable cyan-colored booth for a taste of real old-school Americana at this ancient cafe that has hardly changed since opening in 1931, including the Formica counter splashed with coffee. Undoubtedly Hartford's most authentic and good-value breakfast experience. Make sure you take home some meatloaf for dinner.

Fire and Spice
VEGAN $

(☑ 888-367-7970; www.firenspiceveganrestaurant. com; 491 Capitol Ave; meals $9-14; ☺ 8am-9pm Mon-Sat, 10am-2pm Sun) Just outside of the downtown core, Hartford has one notable restaurant catering to nonmeat eaters, lovers of vegetables and those with food intolerances. Raw foods and salads complement a variety of spicy and not-so-spicy options, sandwiches on freshly baked bread, and smoothies. Healthy and cheap.

★ Trumbull Kitchen
MODERN AMERICAN $$

(www.maxrestaurantgroup.com/trumbull; 150 Trumbull St; mains $13-30; ☺ noon-11pm Mon-Sat, 4-10pm Sun) TK's smart-yet-casual fine-dining

atmosphere awaits, with excellent service and a wonderfully executed, diverse menu, making it a great alternative to some of Hartford's upscale joints. Drop in for a cocktail and some fabulous appetizers, or save that appetite for fish, chicken, burgers and steak, freshly prepared and presented like works of art: dressed-up comfort food. The interior is flash, too.

Bear's Smokehouse
BARBECUE $$

(☑ 860-724-3100; www.bearsbbq.com; 89 Arch St; mains $10-20; ☺ 11am-9pm) Locals love this wood-smoked Kansas-style barbecue famed for brisket, baby back ribs and pulled pork. Vegetarians might want to head elsewhere, although there are some kick-ass sides: collard greens, broccoli salad and mac 'n' cheese. Carnivores will dig the Moink balls (a little bit of 'moo' crossed with a little bit of 'oink'): bacon-wrapped meatballs with your choice of sauce.

Tisane Euro Asian Cafe
CAFE $$

(☑ 860-523-5417; www.mytisane.com; 537 Farmington Ave; mains $10-20; ☺ 11:30am-1am Mon-Thu, to 2am Fri & Sat, 10am-midnight Sun) This odd – and locally loved – coffeehouse-cum-restaurant-cum-bar somehow manages to morph from one beast to another throughout its long business day. For lunch and dinner there are Asian noodle dishes alongside Italian-style flatbreads and American-style hamburgers. Later still, Tisane becomes a full-service bar, serving cocktails until last call, with DJs and karaoke.

★ON20 FUSION $$$

(📞860-722-5161; www.ontwenty.com; 400 Columbus Blvd; mains $30-45, chef tasting menu $95; ⊙11:30am-1:30pm Mon-Fri, 5:30-9:30pm Thu-Sat) On the 20th floor of the Hartford Steam Boiler Inspection and Insurance Co, contemporary ON20 serves an elegant fusion menu with peerless views of the city. An ever-evolving menu with dishes like Rohan duck and poached halibut are executed with precision and immaculately presented with bright drizzles, microgreens and flowers.

Reservations are recommended and a 20% service charge is added to all checks. Dress to impress.

🍸 Drinking & Nightlife

Russian Lady BAR

(📞860-247-5239; www.therussianladyhartford. com; 191 Ann Uccello St; ⊙4pm-1am Tue-Thu, to 2am Fri & Sat) Nobody actually knows who the Russian Lady, is but the youngsters who like to drink, dance and party the night away all swear she's their new best friend. She looks like a pub, but as the night wears on becomes more like a club with each passing drink. Or perhaps its just that all four floors merge into one after a while...

Bin 228 WINE BAR

(📞860-244-9463; www.bin228winebar.com; 228 Pearl St; ⊙11:30am-10pm Mon-Thu, to midnight Fri, 4pm-midnight Sat, 4-10pm Sun) It's a wine bar that serves real-deal Italian fare – toasted freshly baked panini with tomato and buffalo mozzarella, cheese platters and small plates – alongside its expansive all-Italian wine list. After a few killer reds, you'll appreciate the food even more: on weekends, the kitchen stays open until midnight.

Vaughan's Public House PUB

(📞860-882-1560; www.irishpublichouse.com; 59 Pratt St; ⊙11:30am-1am) This popular Irish pub serves a full pub menu – including beer-battered cod and chips, Guinness lamb stew and farmhouse pie – at a long wooden bar. There are also two taps of Guinness, an excellent happy hour (3pm to 6pm Monday to Friday) and an amusing mural celebrating famous Irish men and women, including James Joyce and Sinéad O'Connor.

☆ Entertainment

Real Art Ways CINEMA

(RAW; 📞860-232-1006; www.realartways.org; 56 Arbor St; adult/student $11/8; ⊙gallery 12:30-9pm) FREE Contemporary-media works find an outlet at this consistently offbeat and adventurous gallery/cinema/performance space/lounge. Sip wine or beer as you watch a hot documentary, listen to an all-female chamber-rock quintet or contemplate performance art. Networkers will love talking the talk with Hartford's art community at the Creative Cocktail Hour, held on the third Thursday of every month ($10, 6pm to 10pm).

Hartford Symphony CLASSICAL MUSIC

(📞860-244-2999; www.hartfordsymphony.org; 166 Capitol Ave, the Bushnell; ticket prices vary) The well-respected Hartford Symphony stages performances in the Bushnell all year-round.

Aetna Theater CINEMA

(📞860-278-2670; www.thewadsworth.org; 600 Main St; films adult/senior & student $10/9) Within the Wadsworth Atheneum (p241), this handsome art-deco theater shows independent and art films, as well as hosting music, dance, and drama performances, throughout the year.

Hartford Stage THEATER

(📞860-527-5151; www.hartfordstage.org; 50 Church St; ticket prices vary; ⊙box office noon-5pm Mon-Fri) Staging around six major productions and one or two summer productions each season, this respected theater attracts recognized actors to Hartford. Plays include classic dramas and provocative new works. Venturi & Rauch designed the striking theater building of red brick with darker red zigzag details.

Bushnell CONCERT VENUE

(📞860-987-5900; www.bushnell.org; 166 Capitol Ave; ⊙box office 10am-5pm Mon-Fri, to 2pm Sat) Hosting more than 500 events a year, Bushnell plays a major role in the state's cultural life. This landmark historic building is the go-to for most ballet, symphony, opera and chamber-music performances.

ℹ Information

Greater Hartford Welcome Center (Greater Hartford Arts Council; 📞860-244-0253; www.letsgoarts.org; 100 Pearl St; ⊙9am-5pm Mon-Fri) The bulk of tourist services can be found at this centrally located office.

ℹ️ Getting There & Around

Central **Union Station** (www.amtrak.com; 1 Union Pl) is the city's transportation hub. Catch trains, airport shuttles, intercity buses and taxis from here.

Bradley International Airport (p241) is in Windsor Locks. The Bradley Flyer connects the airport with downtown Hartford (Convention Center, Union Station, $1.75, 30 minutes, hourly).

Amtrak (www.amtrak.com) trains connect Hartford to Boston (from $62, four hours via New Haven) and New York's Penn Station (from $39, 2¾ hours).

Connecticut Transit (www.cttransit.com) operates citywide bus services. A general all-day bus pass costs $3.50.

CONNECTICUT RIVER VALLEY

The Connecticut River, New England's longest, flows southwards for 410 miles from its humble source at Fourth Connecticut Lake, just 300 yards from the Canadian border in New Hampshire. It forms the state boundary between Vermont and New Hampshire, before snaking its way through Massachusetts and Connecticut until it meets the Atlantic at Long Island Sound. Mercifully, it escaped the bustle of industry and commerce that marred many of the northeast's rivers.

The river is anchored by Hartford in the north, and well-preserved historic towns grace the river's banks to the south, notably Old Lyme, Essex, Ivoryton, Chester and East Haddam. Together, they enchant visitors with gracious country inns, fine dining, train rides and river excursions that allow authentic glimpses into provincial life on the Connecticut.

East Haddam

📞 860 / POP 9150

Surrounded by the Seven Sisters hills, East Haddam is a quiet, pretty town on the banks of the Connecticut River. You'll find a handful of worthwhile attractions in town and some great spots to picnic in the surrounding countryside.

The town came into the spotlight at the turn of the 20th century on account of two of its more flamboyant residents, actor William Hooker Gillette (of *Sherlock Holmes* fame) and wealthy local banker and merchant William Goodspeed. Goodspeed's philanthropy

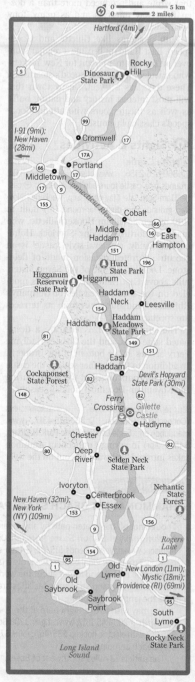

Connecticut River Valley

indirectly led to the formation of a company that wrote and produced more than a dozen Broadway musicals and as many Tony Award–winning shows.

With residents like Gillette and Goodspeed, East Haddam became a regular stopover on the summer circuit for New Yorkers, who traveled up on Goodspeed's steamship. These days, it's a sweet, sleepy town that will most interest history and nature buffs, as well as theatergoers who attend Goodspeed's classic playhouse.

◎ Sights & Activities

Gillette Castle CASTLE
(☑ 860-526-2336; www.ct.gov; 67 River Rd; grounds free, castle tours adult/child $6/2; ⊙ castle 11am-5pm late May-early Sep, weekends Nov-Dec, grounds 8am-dusk year-round; P) Built in 1919 by actor William Hooker Gillette, who made his fortune playing Sherlock Holmes, this gaudy, medieval-style 'castle' is an eccentric turreted mansion made of fieldstone. Looming on one of the Seven Sisters hills above East Haddam, the folly is modeled on the medieval castles of Germany's Rhineland and the views from its terraces are spectacular.

The surrounding 125 acres are a designated state park, and the Chester-Hadlyme Ferry arrives at the bottom of the property. In addition to the summer season, the castle is open for tours on select weekends during the November–December holiday season.

Eagle & Osprey Cruise BIRDWATCHING
(Connecticut Audubon; ☑ 860-575-4317; www.ctaudubon.org; Eagle Landing State Park, Haddam; $45; ⊙ Apr) In spring Connecticut Audubon takes intrepid bird-watchers out on the river for close-ups of the national bird, the majestic bald eagle, as well as ospreys and other waterbirds. Three decks allow for good viewing, a naturalist is aboard to explain things and there's a heated cabin if your buns need warming. Its just across the water from the opera house.

🛌 Sleeping & Entertainment

★ **Boardman House Inn** B&B $$
(☑ 860-873-9233; www.boardmanhouse.com; 8 Norwich Rd; r from $199-269; P❋🐾) If you're in town for the opera, make a weekend of it and stay at the elegant, hard-to-fault Boardman House Inn in East Haddam. Book the light-filled garden suite if you can. The house is a spectacular 1860 Second Empire mansion with a deep porch, tall French windows and a rose-laden garden.

☆ Entertainment

Goodspeed Opera House THEATER
(☑ 860-873-8668; www.goodspeed.org; 6 Main St; tickets $29-85, tours adult/child $5/1; ⊙ performances Wed-Sun Apr-Dec) This 1876 Victorian music hall is known as 'the birthplace of the American musical,' and it still produces a full schedule of shows: *Man of La Mancha* and *Annie* premiered here before going on to national fame. The fascinating riverfront building is worth a look even if you aren't able to catch a performance; on summer Saturdays one-hour tours are available.

❶ Getting There & Away

East Haddam is almost midway between Hartford (28 miles) and Old Lyme (21 miles) by car, including an optional ride on the vehicle-friendly Chester–Hadlyme Ferry, when it's running.

WORTH A TRIP

HAMMONASSET BEACH STATE PARK

Though not off the beaten path by any means, the two full miles of flat, sandy beach at **Hammonasset Beach State Park** (☑ 203-245-2785; www.ct.gov; 1288 Boston Post Rd, Madison; weekdays/weekends $15/22; ⊙ 8am-sunset; P) handily accommodate summer crowds. This is the ideal beach (the state's largest) at which to set up an umbrella chair, crack open a book and forget about the world. The surf is tame, making swimming superb. Restrooms and showering facilities are clean and ample, and a wooden boardwalk runs the length of the park.

You may wish to overnight here at the **Hammonasset Beach State Park Campground** (☑ 203-245-1817; www.ct.gov; 1288 Boston Post Rd; campsites residents/nonresidents $20/30, with electric hookup $35/45, cabins $70/80; P❋), as the park offers Connecticut's only beach camping.

The park is 13 miles southwest of Essex.

Chester

📞 860 / POP 3840

Cupped in the valley of Pattaconk Brook, Chester is a placid riverside village with a general store, a post office, a library and a few shops accounting for most of the action.

🍴 Eating & Drinking

Simon's Marketplace   CAFE $
(📞 860-526-8984; www.simonsmarketplaceches ter.com; 17 Main St; items from $4; ⊗ 8am-6pm; 🖉 🐾) For casual eats, Simon's is part cafe, part eatery, part ice-cream parlor, part candy shop and part general store. It's a great spot to grab a quick meal or supplies for a sunny picnic, or to load up the kids on sugary treats for a fun-filled day on the road. Try the fresh loaves of salt bread and the mac 'n' cheese.

Otto   PIZZA $$
(📞 860-526-9445; www.ottochester.com; 69 Main St; large pizzas $19-25; ⊗ 5-9pm Mon-Thu, to 10pm Fri, 11:30am-9pm Sat & Sun) A new, more reasonably priced and homey offer on Main St: wood-oven-fired pizzas in a variety of red and white sauces and toppings. Will you have room for the homemade tiramisu, though?

⭐ River Tavern   BISTRO $$$
(📞 860-526-9417; www.rivertavernrestaurant. com; 23 Main St; lunches $12-22, meals $20-34; ⊗ 11:30am-2:30pm & 5-9pm Sun-Thu, to 10pm Fri & Sat) This popular wood-accented bistro with a bar and dining-room menu dishes up impeccable food with a variety of inflections. The menu changes, but if it's in season you should definitely order shad, caught from the Connecticut River. Save room for Toshi's made-to-order date pudding with dark rum caramel sauce – order ahead.

Little House Brewing Co   BREWERY
(www.littlehousebrewing.com; 16 Main St; ⊗ 3-8pm Wed & Thu, 2-9pm Fri, noon-9pm Sat, noon-6pm Sun) Vassar college pals Sam and Carlisle have already created a buzz in their first year crafting 10 different beers, mostly from Connecticut cash crops. Try the brown ale. Carlisle learned the trade at Cottrell Brewing Company up the road in Pawcatuck.

🛍 Shopping

Chester Farmers Market   MARKET
(https://chestersundaymarket.jimdo.com; Main St; ⊗ 10am-1pm Sun mid-Jun–mid-Oct & mid-Nov–early Dec) Main St closes down in summer for

---

CHESTER-HADLYME FERRY

In summer, you can cross the Connecticut River on the historic **Chester–Hadlyme Ferry** (www.ctvisit.com/listings/chesterhadlyme-ferry; car/pedestrian $6/2; ⊗ 7am-6:45pm Mon-Fri, 10:30am-5pm Sat & Sun Apr-Nov). A service has been operating here (seasonally) since 1769, making it one of the oldest continuously operating ferry services in the USA. The five-minute river crossing on the *Selden III* affords great views of Gillette Castle and deposits passengers at the foot of the castle in East Haddam. In the opposite direction it's a fun way to link up with the Essex Steam Train (p252), which runs between Chester and Essex.

---

the Chester Sunday Market, a weekly townwide farmers market hawking produce, meats, cheeses and breads from small-scale farmers and local businesses. A more seasonal holiday market runs from November to December in the same spot.

❶ Getting There & Away

By car, Chester is a short diversion off I-95 between New Haven (35 miles) and New London (26 miles). From Hartford (30 miles), take I-91 south and pick up scenic CT 9, which runs right through town.

In summer, you can cross the Connecticut River on the car and pedestrian Chester–Hadlyme Ferry.

Essex

📞 860 / POP 6700

Tree-lined Essex, established in 1635, stands as the chief town of the Connecticut River Valley region. It's worth a visit if only to gawk at the beautiful, well-preserved Federal-period houses, legacies of rum and tobacco fortunes made in the 19th century. The town has a strong following with steam train and riverboat enthusiasts, and also has lovely St John's church, a picturesque riverside park, and a handful of galleries and antique dealers.

◎ Sights

Essex Park   PARK
(Main St) This beautiful shoreline park is centered on a gazebo and features an illustration explaining the 25 tree species lining the

perimeter. You can launch kayaks from here, too. It's a peaceful respite in any weather, and as an added bonus, it has a public bathroom!

Connecticut River Museum MUSEUM

(☑ 860-767-8269; www.ctrivermuseum.org; 67 Main St; adult/child $10/6; ⊙ 10am-5pm, closed Mon Oct-May; P 🐾) Adjacent to Essex's Steamboat Dock, this museum's meticulously presented exhibits recount regional history and include a reproduction of the world's first submarine, the *American Turtle*: a hand-propelled, barrel-like vessel built by Yale student David Bushnell in 1776 and launched at nearby Old Saybrook. The museum also hosts visiting exhibitions, runs summer workshops and organizes river paddles – dates and prices vary.

🖝 Tours

★ Essex Steam
Train & Riverboat Ride TOURS

(☑ 860-767-0103; www.essexsteamtrain.com; 1 Railroad Ave; adult/child $20/10, incl cruise $30/20; ⊙ daily May-Oct, seasonal events year-round; 🐾) This wildly popular attraction features a steam locomotive and antique carriages. The journey travels 6 scenic miles to Deep River, where you can cruise to the Goodspeed Opera House (p250) in East Haddam, before returning to Essex via train. The round-trip train ride takes about an hour; with the riverboat ride it's 2½ hours. This train also connects with Connecticut Audubon for special bird-watching trips in the fall.

A variety of themed excursions are available – consult the website for fares, times and details. If you're staying in Essex, where nightly dining options are limited, you might elect to take the **Essex Clipper Dinner Train**. The $80 (tax included) round-trip fare includes a 2½-hour train ride and four-course meal with a cash bar.

🛏 Sleeping & Eating

Griswold Inn INN $$

(☑ 860-767-1776; www.griswoldinn.com; 36 Main St; d/ste from $195/240; P 🛜) The 'Gris' is one of the country's oldest continually operating inns, Essex' physical and social centerpiece since 1776. The buffet-style Hunt Breakfast (11am to 1pm Sunday) is a tradition dating from the War of 1812, when British soldiers occupying Essex demanded to be fed. Two main buildings were refurbished and are connected, eliminating walks between in inclement weather.

Essex Coffee and Tea Company CAFE $

(www.essexcoffee.com; 51 Main St; pastries $3-5; ⊙ 7am-5pm Mon-Sat, 8am-5pm Sun) A pleasant, jazz-filled cafe with a range of coffee drinks, loose-leaf tea and killer macaroons – they've won some awards and it's clear why. Local art adorns the walls and local intellectuals while the hours away.

ⓘ Getting There & Away

By road, from scenic CT 9 you'll come into the town center and eventually find yourself deposited onto Main St. The ferry (p251) at Chester will take you across the river to Hadlyme.

Old Lyme

POP 7600

Near the mouth of the Connecticut River and perched on the smaller Lieutenant River, Old Lyme was home to some 60 sea captains in the 19th century. Since the early 20th century, however, Old Lyme has been known as the center of the Lyme Art Colony, which cultivated the nascent American impressionist movement. Numerous artists, including William Chadwick, Childe Hassam, Willard Metcalfe and Henry Ward Ranger, came here to paint, staying in the mansion of local art patron Florence Griswold.

Worth a look-in if you're nearby, Old Lyme is a pleasant town with some pretty historic buildings, which will appeal most to folks with a particular interest in American art. Famed nature writer Roger Tory Peterson made his home here for four decades and the nearby Estuary Center managed by Connecticut Audubon bears his name.

◉ Sights & Tours

Florence Griswold Museum MUSEUM

(☑ 860-434-5542; www.florencegriswoldmuseum. org; 96 Lyme St; adult/student/child $10/8/free; ⊙ 10am-5pm Tue-Sat, 1-5pm Sun; P) Florence Griswold's house, which her artist friends decorated with murals (often in lieu of paying rent), is now the Florence Griswold Museum. The 'home of American impressionism' exhibits 6000 works, with solid collections of American impressionist and Barbizon paintings, as well as sculpture and decorative arts. The estate consists of Griswold's Georgian-style house, the Krieble Gallery, the Chadwick studio and Griswold's beloved gardens.

Roger Tory Peterson Estuary Center BIRDWATCHING
(☎860-598-4218; www.ctaudubon.org; 90 Halls Rd/US 1, Big Y Shopping Center) This branch of the Connecticut Audubon focuses on education and public programs such as hiking and boat tours of the estuary and its bountiful wildlife. Its location in a shopping center is a bit weird.

🛏 Sleeping & Entertainment

⭐ **Bee & Thistle Inn** INN $$
(☎860-434-1667; www.beeandthistleinn.com; 100 Lyme St; r $150-289; P🐾) Occupying a handsome, Dutch Colonial farmhouse dating from 1756, this classy establishment has beautiful, well-tended gardens that stretch down to the Lieutenant River. Most of its 11 plush, well-appointed rooms feature abundant antiques and a canopy or four-poster bed.

Sidedoor JAZZ
(☎860-434-2600; http://thesidedoorjazz.com; 85 Lyme St, Old Lyme Inn; from $35) Top-notch jazzers have been taking the stage at Ken Kitching's 75-seat venue since its 2011 inception in the renovated Old Lyme Inn. Kitchings, the spirit behind the revival of New London's Garde Arts Center (p255), has created a much more intimate venue here, where microphones are hardly needed to capture the interplay of the onstage combos.

❶ Getting There & Away

Accessible by road, Old Lyme is just off I-95, between New Haven (34 miles) and New London (16 miles).

SOUTHEASTERN CONNECTICUT

The southeastern corner of Connecticut is home to the state's number-one tourist attraction and the country's largest maritime museum, Mystic Seaport. Built on the site of a former shipbuilding yard in 1929, the museum celebrates the area's seafaring heritage, when fisherers, whalers and clipper-ship engineers broke world speed records and manufactured gunboats and warships for the Civil War.

To the west of Mystic, you'll find the submarine capital of the USA, Groton, where General Dynamics built WWII subs, and, across the Thames River, New London. To the east is the historic fishing village of Stonington, extending along a narrow mile-long peninsula into the sea. It's one of the most charming seaside villages in New England, where Connecticut's only remaining commercial fleet operates and yachties come ashore in summer to enjoy the restaurants on Water St.

New London
☎860 / POP 27,620

During its golden age in the mid-19th century, New London, then home to some 200 whaling vessels, was one of the largest whaling centers in the USA and one of the wealthiest port cities. In 1858 the discovery of crude oil in Pennsylvania sent the value of whale oil plummeting and began a long period of decline for the city, from which it has never fully recovered. Even so, New London retains strong links with its seafaring past (the US Coast Guard Academy and US Naval Submarine Base are here) and its downtown is listed on the National Register of Historic Places.

Despite lacking the sanitized tourism push of nearby Mystic and Stonington, remnants of New London's glorious and opulent times are still evident throughout the city, making it one of Connecticut's most surprising destinations for those interested in history, architecture and urban sociology. Hip Bank St is a hopeful sign of rejuvenation.

◉ Sights & Activities

Hygienic Art GALLERY
(☎860-443-8001; www.hygienic.org; 79 Bank St; ◷2-7pm Tue-Fri, noon-7pm Sat, noon-4pm Sun) FREE Done up in a Greek Revival style replete with a sculpture garden, a mural plaza, fountains and a large performance area, this not-for-profit art space hosts poetry readings, film screenings, a summer concert series and an annual art show attracting nearly 500 artists. The gardens and amphitheater are open during daylight hours.

Connecticut College Arboretum GARDENS
(☎860-439-5020; 270 Mohegan Ave; ◷dawn-dusk) FREE More than 750 acres of native plants, ornamentals and trees from around the world are spread over this college campus. Free guided tours happen at 10am on the first and third Sunday of the month, April to November, at Olin Science Center,

and there are also self-guided tours via an app. Two hundred acres have been left completely undisturbed as hemlock/oak forest and tidal marsh.

Custom House Maritime Museum MUSEUM
(☑ 860-447-2501; www.nlmaritimesociety.org; 150 Bank St; suggested donation adult/child $7/5, tours $5; ☺ 1-5pm Wed-Sun Apr-Dec, 1-5pm Thu-Sun Jan-Mar) Near the ferry terminal, this 1833 building is the oldest operating customhouse in the country, in addition to functioning as a museum. Its front door is made from the wood of the USS *Constitution*. Tours must be reserved in advance. Lighthouse excursions can be organized from here, as well.

Ocean Beach Park BEACH
(☑ 860-447-3031; www.ocean-beach-park.com; 98 Neptune Ave; pedestrian walk-in price $7) At the southern end of Ocean Ave, this popular beach and amusement area has waterslides, a picnic area, miniature golf, an arcade, a swimming pool and an old-fashioned boardwalk. The parking fee ($17/23 weekdays/weekends) includes admission for up to five people. The pool and attractions all cost extra, but the kids will be begging not to leave. For a breather from the madness, a nice nature trail winds through the tall grasses to an observation deck.

**US Coast Guard
Academy & Museum** MUSEUM
(☑ 860-444-8511; www.uscg.mil/Resources/Library; 15 Mohegan Ave; ☺ 9am-4pm Mon-Fri) FREE Located in Waesche Hall on the grounds of the US Coast Guard Academy is this small, unattended museum. Plans are afoot for the first National Coast Guard Museum to open in a separate location (see www.coastguardmuseum.org), though construction had not commenced at the time of writing. Visitors are free to stroll the grounds of one of the five military academies in the country. Pick up a self-guided walking tour booklet at the museum.

Little Pink House HOUSE
(Kelo House; 36 Franklin St) Susette Kelo took on pharmaceutical giant Pfizer in 2000 when they tried to exercise eminent domain and tear down her little pink house. The case went all the way to the US Supreme Court, where Kelo finally lost, but she succeeded in forcing local governments to enact more stringent eminent domain laws around the country, and her story became a movie in 2017, starring Catherine Keener as Kelo.

🛏 Sleeping & Eating

Holiday Inn New London HOTEL $
(☑ 860-443-7000; www.holidayinn.com/newlondonct; 35 Governor Winthrop Blvd; ☺ d from $90; 🅿 ❄ 🤖 ♨) New London's only downtown hotel received a complete renovation in 2013 and is still in pretty good shape. Beds and showers do what they're supposed to do well, and a range of room types, including four suites, is available. Convenient to the ferry and the train.

Muddy Waters Cafe CAFE $
(☑ 860-444-2232; 42 Bank St; sandwiches $5-12; ☺ 7am-3pm Mon-Fri, 9am-3pm Sat & Sun; 🐾) This coffee bar is the heart of the downtown lunchtime scene, serving a full coffee menu alongside generous sandwiches and pastries. The outdoor deck overlooks the river and there are stacks of board games, magazines and books scattered around the couches. One drawback is that you have to ask for a real coffee cup; otherwise it's a tacky paper cup.

★ On the Waterfront SEAFOOD $$
(☑ 860-444-2800; www.onthewaterfrontnl.com; 250 Pequot Ave; mains $15-28; ☺ noon-9pm Tue-Thu & Sun, to 10pm Fri & Sat; 🐾) A spectacular lobster bisque and other delights from the deep, like pistachio-crusted salmon and Montauk-jumbo-stuffed shrimp, are served up with water views from a multitude of windows. The bar is a popular spot with locals who don't like it rowdy. A diverse menu and friendly staff help to accommodate die-hard landlubbers and those with food intolerances.

**★ Captain Scott's
Lobster Dock** SEAFOOD $$
(☑ 860-439-1741; www.captscotts.com; 80 Hamilton St; mains $7-21; ☺ 11am-9pm May-Oct; 🐾) The Coast Guard knows a bit about the sea, and you'd be remiss if you didn't follow its cadets to *the* place for summer seafood. The setting's just picnic tables by the water (BYOB), but you can feast on succulent (hot or cold) lobster rolls, followed by steamers, fried whole-belly clams, scallops or lobsters, and two kinds of chowdah.

🍷 Drinking & Entertainment

Social New London CRAFT BEER
(☑ 860-442-6900; www.socialnewlondon.com; 208 Bank St; ☺ 4-10pm Mon-Wed, 3pm-midnight Thu & Fri, 11am-midnight Sat) In the heart of the hopeful Bank St scene, Social popped

up in 2016, with 50 microbrews (yup!), live rock, jazz, acoustic open mike and stand-up comedy, as well as a menu that leans toward healthy local and even veggie options. Hand-crafted burgers and cocktails in New London, you say? Yes, it's so.

Garde Arts Center   THEATER
(☎ 860-444-7373; www.gardearts.org; 325 State St; ☺ box office 10am-5pm Mon-Fri) The centerpiece of this arts complex is the one-of-a-kind 1472-seat Garde Theater, a former vaudeville house, built in 1926, with a restored Moroccan interior. Today, the theater presents everything from Broadway plays and operas to national music acts and film screenings.

ⓘ Information

New London Mainstreet (☎ 860-444-2489; www.newlondonmainstreet.org; 147 State St; ☺ 9am-5pm Mon-Fri) This downtown revitalization organization maintains a useful up-to-date website and produces a downloadable downtown map and brochure.

ⓘ Getting There & Away

New London's transport hub is **Union Station** (www.amtrak.com; 47 Water St), which is served by Amtrak. Conveniently, the bus station is in the same building and the ferry terminal (for boats to Long Island, Block Island and Fishers Island) is next door.

I-95 runs right through the center of town. New London's commercial district is just southwest of Union Station along Bank St. Follow Ocean Ave to reach Ocean Beach Park.

BOAT

Cross Sound Ferry (☎ 860-443-5281; www.longislandferry.com; 2 Ferry St) operates car ferries (passenger only, one way adult/child $16.25/6, 1½ hours) and high-speed passenger ferries (one way adult/child $21.50/9, 40 minutes) year-round between Orient Point, Long Island, NY, and New London. From late June through Labor Day, ferries depart each port every hour on the hour from 7am to 9pm (last boats at 9:45pm).The 'auto and driver' fare is $55; for bicycles it's $5.

Fishers Island Ferry (☎ 860-442-0165; www.fiferry.com; 5 Waterfront Park; adult/senior & child/car mid-May–mid-Sep $25/18/58, mid-Sep–mid-May $19/14/40) runs cars and passengers from New London to Fishers Island, NY, several times a day year-round.

Block Island Express (☎ 860-444-4624; www.goblockisland.com; 2 Ferry St; adult/child/bike $26/13/10; ☺ May-Sep) operates summer-only services between New London and Block Island, RI.

TRAIN

Amtrak (www.amtrak.com) trains between New York City (from $39, 2½ hours) and Boston (from $29, 1½ hours) stop at New London.

Mystic

☎ 860 / POP 4200

A skyline of masts greets you as you arrive in town on US 1. They belong to the vessels bobbing ever so slightly in the postcard-perfect harbor. There's a sense of self-satisfied calm and composure in the air – until suddenly a heart-stopping steamer whistle blows, followed by the cheerful cling of a drawbridge bell. You know you've arrived in Mystic.

From simple beginnings in the 17th century, the village of Mystic grew to become a prosperous whaling center and one of the great shipbuilding ports of the East Coast. In the mid-19th century, Mystic's shipyards launched clipper ships, gunboats and naval transport vessels, many from the George Greenman & Co Shipyard, now the site of Mystic Seaport Museum, Connecticut's largest tourist attraction. Some great food and drink spots have grown up around the tourism, including the state's hottest bakery (p257) and a quaint Irish pub (www.harpandhound.com; 4 Pearl St; ☺ 11:30am-1am Mon-Thu, to 2am Fri, 10am-2am Sat & Sun).

⊙ Sights

★ **Mystic Seaport Museum**   MUSEUM
(☎ 860-572-0711; www.mysticseaport.org; 75 Greenmanville Ave; adult/child $29/19; ☺ 9am-5pm Apr-Oct, 10am-4pm Thu-Sun Nov-Mar; P ⓟ) More than a museum, Mystic Seaport is a re-creation of an entire New England whaling village spread over 17 acres of the former George Greenman & Co Shipyard. To re-create the past, 60 historic buildings, four tall ships and almost 500 smaller vessels are gathered along the Mystic River. Interpreters staff the site and are glad to discuss traditional crafts and trades. Most illuminating are the demonstrations on such topics as ship rescue, oystering and whaleboat launching.

Coogan Farm   FARM
(☎ 860-536-1216; www.dpnc.org; 162 Greenmanville Ave; ☺ 9am-8pm; P ⓟ) Ⓕ FREE Opened in September 2014, this public-access, 45-acre historic farm and nature center affords sweeping views of the Mystic River. Maintained by volunteers, the property features

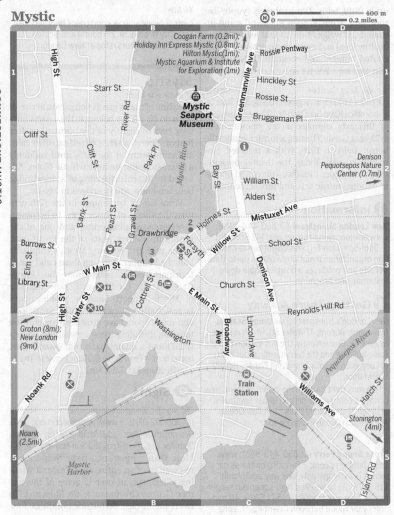

Coogan Farm (0.2mi);
Holiday Inn Express Mystic (0.8mi);
Hilton Mystic(1mi);
Mystic Aquarium & Institute
for Exploration (1mi)

miles of walking tracks and protects two Stonington watersheds (wildlife habitats containing 10 species listed with a high conservation property) and historic farm buildings that have been restored for educational use. A mile-long walking trail connects the farm with the Denison Pequotsepos Nature Center.

Denison Pequotsepos
Nature Center NATURE RESERVE
(☑ 860-536-1216; www.dpnc.org; 109 Pequotsepos Rd; ☺ 9am-5pm; P ♠) **FREE** Linked by walking trails to Coogan Farm, this nature center and natural history museum has more than

10 miles of walking trails and an animal rehabilitation facility. It runs an array of educational programs for adults and kids alike. The center was inaugurated in 1946 and is staffed mainly by volunteers.

Mystic Aquarium
& Institute for Exploration AQUARIUM
(☑ 860-572-5955; www.mysticaquarium.org; 55 Coogan Blvd; adult/child/teen $37/27/31; ☺ 9am-5:50pm Apr-Aug, to 4:50pm Mar & Sep-Nov, 10am-4:50pm Dec-Feb; ♠) This state-of-the-art aquarium boasts more than 6000 species of sea creatures, as well as an outdoor viewing area for watching seals and sea lions below

Mystic

◎ **Top Sights**
1 Mystic Seaport Museum......................B1

➕ **Activities, Courses & Tours**
2 Argia Mystic Cruises B3
3 Historic Harbor Tours of Mystic B3

🛏 **Sleeping**
4 Steamboat Inn.....................................B3
5 Taber Inn & Suites D5
6 Whaler's Inn..B3

✖ **Eating**
7 Captain Daniel Packer Inne.................A4
8 Engine Room B3
9 Harbour House Restaurant.................D4
10 Oyster Club..A3
11 Sift Bake Shop.....................................A3

🍷 **Drinking & Nightlife**
12 Harp and Hound.................................B3

the waterline, and a penguin pavilion. The aquarium's most famous (and controversial) residents are the three beluga whales, who reside in the Arctic Coast exhibit. Animal-welfare groups claim it is debilitating to keep whales in enclosed containers.

👉 Tours

Argia Mystic Cruises　　　　　　CRUISE
(📞 860-536-0416;　www.argiamystic.com;　12 Steamboat Wharf; adult/child $52/42; ☺ May-Oct) This outfit offers two- to three-hour daytime or sunset cruises down the Mystic River to Fishers Island Sound on the 19th-century replica schooner *Argia*.

Historic Harbor Tours of Mystic　　CRUISE
(The Mystic Express; 📞 860-222-5037; www.mystic harbortours.com; 1 Holmes St; adult/child/teen $25/10/15; ☺ May–early Oct) Pay on board for a 40-minute narrated scenic tour of the Mystic River on the *Mystic Express*. Departs from the dock of the S&P Oyster Co, near the drawbridge.

🛏 Sleeping

Taber Inn & Suites　　　　　　INN $$
(📞 866-822-3746;　www.taberinne.com;　66 Williams Ave;　d/ste $165/255, townhouses $365; P ❄ 🤖 🏊) This property has downtown Mystic prices, family charm and a range of accommodations. It's somewhat aging in places, and bathrooms are on the smallish side in the standard rooms, but you can choose a suite or two-bedroom town house

for more comfort. As a bonus, it has one of the few heated pools in town.

Hilton Mystic　　　　　　　HOTEL $$
(📞 860-572-0731; www.hiltonmystic.com; 20 Coogan Blvd, Olde Mistick Village; d from $184; P ➔ ❄ 🤖 🏊) Updated in 2015, Mystic's only true full-service hotel has 183 fresh, understated guest rooms and suites in an enviable location near a bunch of family-friendly shops and restaurants. There's an indoor pool and a bar with a killer happy hour (4pm to 6pm Monday to Friday).

Holiday Inn Express Mystic　　HOTEL $$
(📞 860-536-4493; www.ihg.com; 6 Coogan Blvd, Olde Mistick Village; d from $189; P ➔ ❄ @ 🤖 🏊) Featuring oversized guest rooms (some with jetted tubs), complimentary parking, breakfast and wi-fi, this well-located chain hotel offers excellent value. Kids love the indoor heated pool.

Whaler's Inn　　　　　　　INN $$
(📞 860-536-1506; www.whalersinnmystic.com; 20 E Main St; d $159-299; P 🤖 @ 🤖) Beside Mystic's historic drawbridge, this hotel combines an 1865 Victorian with a reconstructed adults-only luxury hotel from the same era (the landmark 'Hoxie House' burned down in the 1970s) and a modern motel known as Stonington House. Seasonal packages available including dinners and area attractions. Rates include continental breakfast at respected Bravo Bravo next door, a small gym and complimentary bicycles.

⭐ Steamboat Inn　　　　　　INN $$$
(📞 860-536-8300;　www.steamboatinnmystic. com; 73 Steamboat Wharf; d $220-350; P ❄ 🤖) Located in the heart of downtown Mystic, the 11 rooms and suites of this historic inn have wraparound water views and luxurious amenities, (some) hot tubs, cable TV and fireplaces. Some have stunning floor-to-ceiling windows overlooking the river. Antiques lend the interior a romantic, period feel, and service is top-notch with baked goods for breakfast, complimentary bikes and boat docks.

🍴 Eating

Sift Bake Shop　　　　　　　BAKERY $
(📞 860-245-0541; www.siftbakeshopmystic.com; 5 Water St; desserts $4-7, sandwiches $8-10; ☺ 7am-7pm) When pastry chef Adam Young won the Food Network's Best Baker award in 2018, things blew up at this Water St location.

WHERE THE LOCALS EAT LOBSTER

Locals know that the best place to head for fresh seafood is the tiny fishing village of **Noank**, situated on Morgan Point between Mystic and Groton. Almost the entire village is listed on the National Register of Historic Places thanks to its 18th- and 19th-century houses and shipyards, but the real treat in Noank is its seafood shacks. In fact, the quaint marine-side lobster shack covered in rainbow-colored buoys, featured in the film *Mystic Pizza*, is Noank's **Ford's Lobster** (☑ 860-536-2842; 15 Riverview Ave; mains $25-40; ⊘ 11.30am-9pm). Here you can sit at an outdoor bar framing the dock and devour delicious buttered lobster rolls, clam chowder and mussels in white wine. Further down the road are the classic shacks, **Abbott's** (☑ 860-536-7719; www.abbottslobster.com; 117 Pearl St; mains $11-25; ⊘ 11:30am-7pm daily Jun-Sep, 11:30-7pm Fri-Sun May & Oct) and (you guessed it) **Costello's** (☑ 860-572-2779; www.costellosclamshack.com; 145 Pearl St; dishes $10-30; ⊘ 11:30am-8:30pm daily Jun-Aug, 11:30am-8:30pm Fri-Sun May & Sep), only open seasonally. If you can't get a seat or for something even more casual, head to Captain Scott's Lobster Dock (p254) in nearby New London.

Baguettes, ciabattas, chocolate croissants, brioche and specialties like pumpkin cheesecake are all so good, it may be worth the (long) line. *So* good.

Engine Room   BURGERS $$
(☑ 860-415-8117; www.engineroomct.com; 14 Holmes St; mains $12-25; ⊘ 11am-10pm Mon-Thu, to 11pm Fri & Sat; 🖉 🖶) Promising beer, bourbon and burgers, this place delivers. Evocatively set in the old Lathrup Marine Engine building, it's an excellent place to eat and drink, even for vegetarians. The chicken and waffles are much beloved.

★**Oyster Club**   SEAFOOD $$$
(☑ 860-415-9266; www.oysterclubct.com; 13 Water St; oysters $2-2.50, lunch mains $13-20, dinner mains $18-40; ⊘ noon-3pm & 5-10pm Fri & Sat, 10am-3pm & 5-9pm Sun, 5-9pm Mon-Thu; 🅿 🕸) Offering casual fine dining at its best, this is the place locals come to knock down oysters on the deck out back. Grilled lobster and pan-roasted monkfish or flounder feature alongside veal, steak and a drool-worthy burger. If oysters are an aphrodisiac, anything could happen at the bar after the daily happy hour (4pm to 6pm), when shucked oysters are a buck each.

★**Captain Daniel
Packer Inne**   AMERICAN $$$
(☑ 860-536-3555; www.danielpacker.com; 32 Water St; mains $19-34; ⊘ 11am-4pm & 5-10pm) This 1754 historic house has a low-beam ceiling and creaky floorboards. On the lower pub level, you'll find bar denizens, live music, a good selection of tap beer and excellent pub grub: try the fish and chips. Upstairs, the dining room has river views and an imaginative American menu, including petite filet

mignon with Gorgonzola sauce and walnut demi-glace. Reservations recommended.

Harbour House Restaurant   AMERICAN $$$
(☑ 860-536-8140; www.innatmystic.com/harbour-house; 3 Williams Ave; mains $25-40; ⊘ 11:30am-9pm Mon-Thu, to 10pm Fri, 8am-9pm Sat & Sun) Reserve a window table with a view overlooking the grounds of the Inn at Mystic or grab a seat by the wood-fired oven for upscale yet informally presented fare. The seafood crepes are exquisite, the pasta fresh and steaks attentively prepared. Wednesday is build-your-own mac 'n' cheese night.

❶ Information

Stop in at the **Greater Mystic Chamber of Commerce** (☑ 860-572-9578; www.mysticchamber.org; 62 Greenmanville Ave; ⊘ 9am-6pm Jun-Sep, reduced hours Oct-May) or its kiosk in the train depot, or head to the **Mystic & Shoreline Tourist Information Center** (☑ 860-536-1641; www.mysticinfocenter.com; 27 Coogan Blvd; ⊘ 10am-5pm Mon-Sat, 11am-4pm Sun) in Olde Mistick Village.

❶ Getting There & Away

Mystic's **train station** (2 Roosevelt Ave) is served by Amtrak trains (www.amtrak.com) to New York (from $41, 2½ hours) and Boston (from $49, one to 1½ hours). It's less than a mile south of Mystic Seaport Museum. Nearby New London (about 15 minutes by taxi) has more frequent services.

The Groton-New London airport is 8 miles from Mystic and has flights from Philadelphia; the Providence, RI, airport, about 45 minutes by car, has more frequent and varied flights.

Mystic is just south of I-95 between New London and the Rhode Island border.

Stonington

☑ 860 / POP 930

Five miles east of Mystic on US 1, Stonington is Connecticut's oldest 'borough' and one of the most appealing towns on the coast. Laid out on a peninsula that juts into Long Island Sound, the town's compact footprint is scattered with photogenic 18th- and 19th-century houses, many of which were once sea captains' homes. It's a somewhat quieter alternative to Mystic during the summer madness.

◉ Sights

★Velvet Mill   ARTS CENTER

(☑ 917-915-6340; www.americanvelvetmill.com; 22 Bayview Ave; ⊗ 9am-5pm; P) This community arts center hosts a weekend farmers market (10am to 1pm Saturday, October to May) and an artisan/vendor market (10am to 4pm Saturday and Sunday, year-round), and is a hub for local artists, small businesses (including some locavore food vendors), and practitioners of yoga and other healing arts. Delicious discoveries include a brewer (p260), a baker (p260) and wood-fired pizza maker.

★Saltwater Farm Vineyard   WINERY

(☑ 860-415-9072; www.saltwaterfarmvineyard. com; 349 Elm St; tastings $10; ⊗ 11am-5pm Wed & Thu, to 3pm Fri-Sun) Housed in a striking 1930s aluminum airport hangar, Saltwater Farm is one of the newest vineyards in Connecticut. Surrounded by tidal marshes and cooled by salty coastal breezes, the cabernet franc, merlot, chardonnay and sauvignon blanc vintages benefit from a unique microclimate and are only sold locally. The real joy is sampling wines on terraces overlooking lush green vines and Wequetequock Cove.

Barn Island Wildlife Management Area   PARK

(Palmer Neck Rd, Pawcatuck; P) FREE Canoeists, kayakers, hikers and birders enjoy over 300 acres of salt- and freshwater marshes at Barn Island. Inhabited by hundreds of species of bird (it's designated an Important Bird Area by the Audubon Society), 4 miles of hiking trails snake between placid pools and reed beds and offer beautiful views over Little Narragansett Bay and Wequetequock Cove. A dog-lover's delight.

Old Lighthouse Museum   MUSEUM

(☑ 860-535-1440; www.stoningtonhistory.org; 7 Water St; adult/child $10/6; ⊗ 10am-5pm Thu-Tue May-Oct) Climb the winding iron staircase of this squat, granite lighthouse for 360-degree views from the lantern room. Afterward browse the small museum, which recounts unsuccessful British assaults on the harbor during the American Revolution and the War of 1812, as well as hosting exhibits on whaling, Native American artifacts and curios from the China trade.

Captain Nathaniel Palmer House   HISTORIC SITE

(☑ 860-535-8445; www.stoningtonhistory.org; 40 Palmer St; adult/child $10/6; ⊗ 1-5pm Mon, Tue & Thu-Sat May-Oct) The 16-room Captain Nathaniel Palmer House is one of the finest houses in town and the former home of the first American to see the continent of Antarctica (at the tender age of 21, no less). Guided tours operate on the hour. Admission includes entry to the Old Lighthouse Museum.

Portuguese Holy Ghost Society Building   HISTORIC BUILDING

(☑ 860-535-3855; www.holyghostclub.com; 26 Main St; ⊗ by appointment) Built in 1836, the club building of the Portuguese Holy Ghost Society is a reminder of the contributions Portuguese whalers have made to Stonington since they settled in the village in the 19th century. Although the club is not open to the public, the society continues its century-long, open-house tradition of spring and autumn Friday fish fries (11:30am to 7:30pm, until mid-November). In August, the Holy Ghost Festival offers an opportunity for a weekend-long feast of traditional food and music.

🛏 Sleeping

Stonington Motel   MOTEL $

(☑ 860-599-2330; www.stoningtonmotel.com; 901 Stonington Rd/US 1; d $55-70; P ✳ 🛜 🐾) This owner-run, old-school motel is Stonington's most affordable accommodations, and is simple, convenient and quaint. The 13 no-frills rooms have satellite TV, microwave and fridge. It's an easy and pleasant bike ride into town and is well located for Saltwater Farm and Barn Island.

★Inn at Stonington   INN $$$

(☑ 860-535-2000; www.innatstonington.com; 60 Water St; d $290-490; P ✳ @ 🛜) Offering an easy sophistication, this romantic inn, long lauded by those in the know, continues to stay at the top of its game. From windows overlooking Stonington Harbor you can watch the sunrise or yachties tying up at the hotel dock of an evening. Elegant, country-style rooms feature plump sofas, four-poster beds, soaking tubs and fireplaces. Bikes, kayaks, free beach access and massages are available.

Orchard Street Inn
B&B $$$

(☑ 860-535-2681; www.orchardstreetinn.com; 41 Orchard St; d $250-295; P ❄ 🤍) This unpretentious five-room inn is quiet and elegant, within easy walking distance of the town center. Free use of bicycles is provided for jaunts around town. Although fitting the local look, these buildings were constructed from the ground-up in 2008, so have all the most modern conveniences. Fresh Portuguese muffins comprise part of the ample breakfasts. Check out the widow's walk 360-degree view!

✖ Eating & Drinking

Zest! Fresh Pastry
BAKERY $

(☑ 860-381-0771; www.zestfreshpastry.com; 22 Bayview Ave; pastries $3-5; ☺ 9am-4pm Wed-Sun) Gabriella's been whipping up the good stuff here for more than five years. There are dozens of palate-pleasers on offer, such as orange-almond macarons, some of the gluten-free and vegan variety. They also have a cafe in neighboring Ledyard. Another nice option inside the ever-surprising Velvet Mill (p259).

Noah's
CAFE $$

(☑ 860-535-3925; www.noahsfinefood.com; 113 Water St; mains $12-27; ☺ 7:45am-9pm Tue-Sun; 🍽) Noah's is a popular, informal place, with two small rooms topped with original stamped-tin ceilings. It's famous for its seafood (especially chowder and scallops) and pastries, like the mouthwatering apple-spice and sour-cream coffee cakes. Lunchtime is a family-friendly affair, while dinner is more formal. Book ahead at weekends.

Water St Cafe
AMERICAN $$$

(☑ 860-535-2122; www.waterstcafe.com; 143 Water St; mains $18-30; ☺ 5:30-9:30pm Mon-Thu, to 10:30pm Fri & Sat, 10am-9pm Sun) North of Grand St, this crimson-walled cafe set in a post-and-beam house offers a creative, modern menu. The restaurant's seafood dishes, often with Asian-influenced preparations (think black-bean roast salmon and miso-glazed halibut), are the big draw, but basics – like the shoestring fries – also stand

out. Chef Walter is a graduate of the CIA (Culinary Institute of America, that is).

Beer'd Brewing Co
CRAFT BEER

(22 Bayview Ave; ☺ 3-8pm Thu, 3-9pm Fri, 11am-7pm Sat, 11am-5pm Sun) This cozy microbrewery, inside the Velvet Mill (p259), offers three free sips to determine your brew of choice. Reasonable and tasty beers, a mellow vibe, and you can order pizza from Woodfellas down the hall, who make their crust with Beer'd's beer! The 9.2% Hobbit Juice will put a glide in your stride, and you can take cans and growlers to go.

ⓘ Getting There & Away

The only way to reach Stonington is by road (off I-95). It's possible to take an Amtrak (www.amtrak.com) train to Mystic, then catch a local SEAT bus (www.seatbus.com), but services are somewhat infrequent and may not connect well (route 10 connects the two towns). You can also get off Amtrak in Westerly, RI (5 miles away).

THE QUIET CORNER

Wedged between the Quinebaug and Shetucket Rivers Valley, Connecticut's Quiet Corner is known locally as 'the last green valley' between Boston and Washington. The 12 miles of CT 169 between Brooklyn and Woodstock induce sighs of contentment and frequent pullovers.

Incorporated in 1713, Pomfret is at the heart of the Quiet Corner. It's one of the oldest towns in the state and today includes the villages of Abington, Elliotts, Pomfret Center and Pomfret Landing. There is no formal town center, but a scattering of interesting things to do and see can be found here.

⊙ Sights & Activities

★ Roseland Cottage
MUSEUM

(Bowen House; ☑ 860-928-4074; www.historicnewengland.org; 556 CT 169, Woodstock; adult/student $10/5; ☺ 11am-4pm Wed-Sun Jun 1-Oct 15) This colorful museum was once the summer home of Henry Bowen and his family. Meticulously maintained by the fabulous people at Historic New England, the 1846 Gothic Revival–style mansion featuring pointed arches, crockets and stained-glass windows is complemented by a delightful garden. It's a pleasure to frolic through the bountiful flower beds bordered by formal boxwood parterres laid out according to the

1850 plan. Other follies include an aviary, a summerhouse, an icehouse and a vintage bowling alley.

Sharpe Hill
WINERY

(☑ 860-974-3549; http://sharpehill.com; 108 Wade Rd, Pomfret; tastings $10-15; ☺ 11am-5pm Fri-Sun) Arguably Connecticut's finest vineyard: Sharpe Hill's wines have been awarded over 250 international medals. Take a walk through the vines before sitting down to a gourmet farm-to-table meal ($40 to $55) at the vineyard's Fireside Tavern. That is, if you phoned ahead well in advance – lunch and dinner hours vary and reservations are essential.

Woodstock Orchards
FARM

(☑ 860-928-2225; 494 CT 169, Woodstock; ☺ 9am-6pm) Stop at the old-fashioned Woodstock Orchards to pick your own blueberries (late summer) and apples (fall), and to stock up on jams, fresh cider and honey at the farm stand. The stand closes when apples run out, usually about April. The orchards are next to the Inn at Woodstock Hill.

Grassland Bird Conservation Center
BIRDWATCHING

(Connecticut Audubon Center at Pomfret; www.ctaudubon.org; 218 Day Rd, Pomfret Center) Connecticut Audubon manages this small grassland property as well as the adjacent 700-acre Bafflin Sanctuary. The 2.5-mile loop trail around Bafflin is a moderate trek over rolling, easy terrain, but the trail itself isn't terribly well marked, so be forewarned. Views of hemlock groves, cornfields and marshes make it well worthwhile.

🛏 Sleeping & Eating

Inn at Woodstock Hill
INN $$$

(☑ 860-928-0528; www.woodstockhill.com; CT 169 & Plaine Hill Rd; r from $190; P ❄ 🛜) The Bowen family has owned this property, now a 21-room inn with its own vegetable garden and a beautiful sitting room/library, since 1816. Some rooms have fireplaces and four-poster beds, and you'll be spoiled by the dining room, which serves up fresh American-European fare like heritage pork chops.

Vanilla Bean Cafe
MODERN AMERICAN $

(www.thevanillabeancafe.com; 450 Deerfield Rd, Pomfret; mains $6.50-16; ☺ 7am-3pm Mon-Thu, to 8pm Fri & Sat, 8am-4pm Sun; 🖉) Families, cyclists and Sunday drivers regularly make the pilgrimage to 'The Bean' for creative casual dining, live music (including open

mikes and well-known folkies) and artful surroundings. The acoustic balance of the room and local artwork can't help but get your head right.

❶ Getting There & Around

Mostly, you have to drive a car to make any significant headway in the Quiet Corner. Pomfret, one of the spokes in the QC wheel, is a pleasant drive north of Norwich (29 miles) on CT 169. From Hartford (43 miles) take the I-84 to exit 79, past Tolland, then follow signs to Willington, Ashford and Pomfret.

Peter Pan Bus Lines (www.peterpanbus.com) operates routes across New England with services connecting to Storrs, the location of University of Connecticut. Greyhound (www.greyhound.com) also stops in Storrs.

To get between local towns, Northeast Connecticut Transit District has a few different bus lines (www.nectd.org).

NEW HAVEN

☑ 203 / POP 130,660

Connecticut's second-largest city radiates out from pretty New Haven Green, laid by Puritan settlers in the 1600s. Around it, Yale University's over-300-year-old accessible campus offers visitors a wealth of world-class attractions, from museums and galleries to a lively concert program and walking-tour tales of secret societies.

As you admire Yale's gorgeous faux-Gothic and Victorian architecture, it's hard to fathom New Haven's struggle to shake its reputation as a dangerous, decaying seaport – but the city is successfully repositioning itself as a thriving home for the arts, architecture and the human mind.

While Yale may have put New Haven on the map, there's much to savor beyond campus. Well-aged dive bars, ethnic restaurants, barbecue shacks and cocktail lounges make the area almost as lively as Cambridge's Harvard Sq, but with better pizza and less ego.

◉ Sights

★ Yale University
UNIVERSITY

(☑ 203-432-2300; www.yale.edu/visitor; 149 Elm St) FREE Each year, thousands of high-school students make pilgrimages to Yale, nursing dreams of attending the country's third-oldest university, which boasts such notable alums as Noah Webster, Eli Whitney and Samuel Morse, and presidents William

H Taft, George HW Bush, Bill Clinton and George W Bush. You don't need to share the students' ambitions in order to take a stroll around the campus – just pick up a map at the visitor center or join a free, one-hour guided tour (p267).

★ **Yale Center for British Art** MUSEUM
(☑203-432-2800; www.ycba.yale.edu; 1080 Chapel St; ⊙10am-5pm Tue-Sat, noon-5pm Sun) FREE
Reopened in 2016 after extensive restoration, this fabulous gallery was architect Louis Kahn's last commission and is the setting for the largest collection of British art outside the UK. Spanning three centuries from the Elizabethan era to the 19th century, and arranged thematically as well as chronologically, the collection gives an unparalleled insight into British art, life and culture. A visit is an absolute must for anyone interested in beautiful things. And yes, it's free.

★ **Yale University Art Gallery** MUSEUM
(☑203-432-0600; http://artgallery.yale.edu; 1111 Chapel St; ⊙10am-5pm Tue-Fri, to 8pm Thu, 11am-5pm Sat & Sun) FREE This outstanding museum was architect Louis Kahn's first commission and houses the oldest university art collection in the country; it includes Vincent van Gogh's *The Night Café* and European masterpieces by Frans Hals, Peter Paul Rubens, Manet and Picasso. In addition there are displays of American masterworks by Winslow Homer, Edward Hopper and Jackson Pollock, silver from the 18th century, and art from Africa, Asia, and the pre- and post-Columbian Americas. Best of all, it won't cost you a penny to take a peek.

★ **Shore Line Trolley Museum** MUSEUM
(☑203-467-6927; www.shorelinetrolley.org; 17 River St, East Haven; adult/child $10/7; ⊙10:30am-4:30pm daily Jul & Aug, Sat & Sun May, Jun, Sep & Oct; ⊕) For a unique take on East Haven's shoreline, take a ride on this open-sided antique trolley – the oldest continuously running suburban trolley line in the country – along 3 miles of track that takes you from River St in East Haven to Short Beach in Branford. Enjoy the museum and its beautifully maintained carriages when you're done. Bring a picnic lunch.

Beinecke Rare Book & Manuscript Library LIBRARY
(☑203-432-2977; www.library.yale.edu; 121 Wall St; ⊙10am-7pm Mon, 9am-7pm Tue-Thu, 9am-5pm Fri) FREE Built in 1963, this extraordinary piece of architecture is the largest building in the world designed for the preservation of rare manuscripts. The windowless cube has walls of Danby marble that subdue the effects of light, while inside the glass stack tower displays sculptural shelves of books, including one of only 48 surviving Gutenberg Bibles (1455) and original manuscripts by Charles Dickens, Benjamin Franklin and Goethe. Open weekends when there is an exhibition.

PEZ Visitor Center & Museum LANDMARK
(https://us.pez.com; 35 Prindle Hill Rd, Orange; $5; ⊙10am-5pm Mon-Sat, noon-5pm Sun) PEZ dispensers are iconic American kitsch, but their origins are in Austria. You'll glean this and a few other factoids here, but the real gems are the hundreds of dispensers on view in this 'museum,' ranging from all the US presidents to various cartoon and cultural legends. Some days, you can see the candy-making process through the thick glass windows. Worth the short wander off the freeway.

Lighthouse Point Park PARK
(www.cityofnewhaven.com/parks; 2 Lighthouse Rd; ⊙7am-sunset) This pretty seaside park a few minutes' drive from Tweed New Haven Airport features the handsome 1840s Five Mile Point Lighthouse, listed on the National Register of Historic Places, and a beautiful 1916 carousel (rides 50¢) and pavilion. Parking fees apply in season (April to October).

Grove Street Cemetery CEMETERY
(www.grovestreetcemetery.org; 227 Grove St; ⊙9am-4pm) Three blocks north of the green, this cemetery holds the graves of several famous New Havenites behind its grand Egyptian Revival gate, including rubber magnate Charles Goodyear, telegraph inventor Samuel Morse, lexicographer Noah Webster and cotton-gin inventor Eli Whitney. Machu Picchu 'discoverer' Hiram Bingham lurks below, too. Around the turn of the 19th century Yale medical students would sneak in at night to dig up bodies for dissection, but you can simply join the free **walking tour** (⊙10am Sat Apr-Oct).

Peabody Museum of Natural History MUSEUM
(☑203-432-5050; www.peabody.yale.edu; 170 Whitney Ave; adult/child $13/6; ⊙10am-5pm Tue-Sat, noon-5pm Sun; ℗⊕) It's hard not to be fascinated by this vast collection of animal, vegetable and mineral specimens, including wildlife dioramas, meteorites and minerals.

New Haven

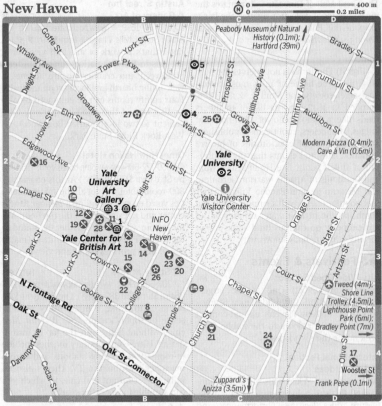

New Haven

◎ Top Sights
1 Yale Center for British Art	B3
2 Yale University	C2
3 Yale University Art Gallery	B2

◎ Sights
4 Beinecke Rare Book & Manuscript Library	B2
5 Grove Street Cemetery	C1
6 Tomb	B2

✦ Activities, Courses & Tours
7 Grove Street Cemetery Tour	C1

🛌 Sleeping
8 New Haven Hotel	B4
9 Omni New Haven Hotel	C3
10 Study at Yale	A2

✕ Eating
11 Atticus Bookstore Café	B3
12 Booktrader Cafe	A3

13 Cheese Truck	C2
14 Claire's Corner Copia	B3
15 Louis' Lunch	B3
16 Mamoun's Falafel Restaurant	A2
17 Sally's Apizza	D4
18 Union League Café	B3
19 York St Noodle House	A3
20 ZINC	B3

🍷 Drinking & Nightlife
21 116 Crown	C4
22 BAR	B3
23 Ordinary	B3

✪ Entertainment
24 Café Nine	C4
25 New Haven Symphony Orchestra	C2
26 Shubert Theater	B3
27 Toad's Place	B2
28 Yale Repertory Theatre	B3

The Great Hall of Dinosaurs illuminates the museum's fossil collection against the backdrop of the Pulitzer Prize–winning mural *The Age of Reptiles*.

Tomb
HISTORIC BUILDING

(64 High St) The Tomb is not open to the public. This is the home of Yale's most notorious secret society, the Skull & Bones Club, founded in 1832, and its list of members reads like a 'who's who' of high-powered judges, financiers, politicians, publishers and intelligence officers. Stories of bizarre initiation rites and claims that the Tomb is full of stolen booty, like Hitler's silverware and the skulls of Apache warrior Geronimo and Mexican general Pancho Villa, further fuel popular curiosity. It's rumored that the Tomb has the highest water utilities bill of any property on campus (and some say in the city)...and nobody knows why.

🎭 Festivals & Events

City-Wide Open Studios
ART

(www.cwos.org; ☉Oct) One of the largest events of its kind, City-Wide Open Studios sees some of New Haven's up-and-coming talent open their doors to the public for a peek inside their workspaces.

International Festival of Arts & Ideas
ART

(www.artidea.org; ☉Jun) This engaging, jam-packed festival, held in mid- to late June, feature tours, lectures, performances and master classes by artists and thinkers from around the world.

Music on the Green
MUSIC

(www.infonewhaven.com; ☉Jul) This free outdoor concert series (mid- to late July) has presented the likes of Soul Asylum, Regina Belle, Debbie Gibson and En Vogue.

🛏 Sleeping

★ New Haven Hotel
BOUTIQUE HOTEL $$

(☎800-644-6835; www.newhavenhotel.com; 229 George St; d from $169) This robust downtown hotel is both simply stylish and affordable. It's nice to see a private operator raising the bar. The hotel occupies a handsome mid-last-century brick building with bright, modern common areas, while guest rooms are airy with large windows, clean lines, dark woods and sink-into-me bedding. Reasonable rates mean it's understandably popular. Book in advance.

Austin Street Inn & Gallery of Art
BOUTIQUE HOTEL $$

(☎203-387-1699; www.austinstreetinn.net; 9 Austin St, Westville Village; r from $179; P �s) A hotel that's a work of art, and vice versa, the Austin features parlors done in tasteful blue/green and cranberry/ochre accents, a welcoming hearth and local art on the walls. Four comfy rooms can be enhanced by also renting one of the adjoining parlors. Convenient to two lovely parks: Edgewood and West Rock Ridge State Park.

Omni New Haven Hotel
BUSINESS HOTEL $$

(☎860-772-6664; www.omnihotels.com; 155 Temple St; d from $179; P ❄ s) At this enormous, 309-room hotel you get all the smart amenities you'd expect, including a 24-hour fitness center and a restaurant on the top floor. Ask for a room with a view of either the sound or the green. The 19th-floor restaurant (mains $16 to $28) provides booze and views.

★ Study at Yale
HOTEL $$$

(☎203-503-3900; www.thestudyatyale.com; 1157 Chapel St; r $250-389; P s) The Study at Yale manages to evoke a mid-century modern sense of sophistication (call it '*Mad Men* chic') without being over the top or intimidating. Ultra-contemporary touches include in-room iPod docking stations and cardio machines with built-in TV. There's also an in-house restaurant and cafe, to which you can stumble for morning snacks.

🍴 Eating

★ Pantry
AMERICAN $

(☎203-787-0392; 2 Mechanic St; breakfast $11-24; ☉7am-2pm Mon-Sat, 8am-3pm Sun) The secret is already out about New Haven's ah-mazing little breakfast-lunch joint. You'll most likely have to line up then rub shoulders with a bunch of hungry students (who'd probably rather we kept this one to ourselves), but persevere if you can: you won't find a better-value, more drool-worthy breakfast for miles. Take your pick: it's *all* good.

Cheese Truck
FOOD TRUCK $

(Caseus; ☎203-850-3504; www.thecheesetruck.com; Grove St & Hillhouse Ave; sandwiches $3-5; ☉11:30am-2pm Tue-Fri; ☍) While the flagship Caseus bistro has shuttered its doors (its former staff have opened Olmo in its place, at 95 Whitney St), its cheese truck rolls on, delivering jaw-dropping grilled cheese sandwiches and tomato soup to the masses.

Mamoun's
Falafel Restaurant MIDDLE EASTERN $
(📞201-656-0310; www.mamouns.com; 85 Howe St; dishes $6-18; ⏰11am-3am) This hole-in-the-wall Middle Eastern joint serves fresh, cheap, delicious food in a simple restaurant with loads of character (and characters). It must be good brain food: locations near NYU and Princeton are off-the-charts popular, too.

Atticus Bookstore Café CAFE $
(📞203-776-4040; www.atticusbookstorecafe.com; 1082 Chapel St; salads & sandwiches $6-12; ⏰7am-9pm Tue-Sat, 8am-8pm Sun-Mon) On the fringe of the Yale campus, come here to get your bearings and mingle with the alumni over great coffee, artisanal sandwiches, stellar breads, soup and salad, surrounded by an immaculately presented, eclectic selection of books.

Chip's BREAKFAST $
(📞203-795-5065; www.chipsrestaurants.com; 321 Boston Post Rd/US 1, Orange; pancakes $8-12; ⏰6am-9:30pm) A Connecticut staple since 1966, these buttermilk pancakes are somehow light as a feather, and topped with a choice of boysenberries, pecans or maple syrup – hard to resist. Sure, there's other stuff on the menu, but why bother?

Louis' Lunch BURGERS $
(📞203-562-5507; www.louislunch.com; 261-263 Crown St; burgers $6; ⏰11am-3:45pm Tue-Wed, noon-2am Thu-Sat) A New Haven institution since 1895, it's all about the atmosphere and reputation of being the 'birthplace of the hamburger sandwich.'

Booktrader Cafe CAFE $
(📞203-787-6147; www.booktradercafe.net; 1140 Chapel St; sandwiches $8-10; ⏰7:30am-9pm Mon-Fri, 9am-9pm Sat, to 7pm Sun; 🛜📶) This light-filled, new-and-used book-filled atrium (you won't believe how many books there are) is a delightful place to devour scrumptious sandwiches and spellbinding literature. In nice weather, there's a shady patio.

Claire's Corner Copia VEGETARIAN $
(📞204-562-3888; www.clairescornercopia.com; 1000 Chapel St; mains $9-12; ⏰8am-9pm Mon-Fri, 9am-9pm Sat & Sun; 🛜📶) Bright, airy and always packed, this has been the best vegetarian restaurant in town since 1975. The soups, salads and quiches are excellent, though the sandwiches can be a bit bland. Try something off the Mexican section of the menu or just come for a sweet treat, like the Lithuanian coffee cake ($3.60).

York St Noodle House ASIAN $
(📞203-776-9675; 166 York St; dishes $6-7; ⏰11:30am-10pm) If you're looking for a quick meal that's both filling and inexpensive, look no more. This small eatery is usually filled with chatty students slurping huge bowls of soupy and stir-fried noodles. There are also delicious dumplings, rice dishes and lots of veggies. Sullen staff get no points, however.

★ZINC AMERICAN $$$
(📞203-624-0507; www.zincfood.com; 964 Chapel St; mains $12-28; ⏰noon-2:30pm & 5-9pm Tue-Fri, 5-10pm Sat & Mon) Whenever possible, this trendy bistro's ingredients hail from local organic sources, but the chef draws inspiration from all over, notably Asia and the Southwest. There's a constantly changing

---

LOCAL KNOWLEDGE

NEW HAVEN PIZZA

Frank Pepe (📞203-865-5762; www.pepespizzeria.com; 157 Wooster St; pizzas $8-29; ⏰11am-10pm; 📶👶) The granddaddy of the New Haven pizza scene since 1925.

Sally's Apizza (📞203-624-5271; www.sallysapizza.com; 237 Wooster St; pizzas from $7.50; ⏰5-10pm Tue-Fri, to 11pm Sat & Sun) Some say Sal's spicier sauce puts his pies ahead of the competition.

Modern Apizza (📞203-776-5306; www.modernapizza.com; 874 State St; pizzas $10-20; ⏰11am-11pm Tue-Sat, 3-10pm Sun) Hardly new, Modern has been slinging its Italian Bomb since 1934. If gluten is not your friend, don't fret! There's no surcharge for a gluten-free pie base at Modern Apizza.

Zuppardi's Apizza (📞203-934-1949; www.zuppardisapizza.com; 179 Union Ave, West Haven; pizzas from $7.50; ⏰11am-9pm Mon-Thu, to 10pm Fri & Sat, noon-8:30pm Sun) Octogenarian Zuppardi's is in the quieter neighborhood of West Haven.

'market menu,' but for the most rewarding experience, share several small plates, like smoked duck nachos or *prosciutto Americano crostini*. Reservations are advised.

Union League Café
FRENCH $$$

(☑203-562-4299; www.unionleaguecafe.com; 1032 Chapel St; mains $23-38; ⊙11:30am-9:30pm Mon-Fri, 5-10pm Sat) An upscale French bistro in the historic Union League building. Expect a menu featuring continental classics like *cocotte de joues de veau* (organic veal cheeks with sautéed wild mushrooms; $25) along with those of nouvelle cuisine. If your budget is tight, try a sinful dessert like *crêpe soufflé au citron* (lemon crepes) washed down with a glass from the exquisite wine list.

🍸 Drinking & Nightlife

★ Ordinary
COCKTAIL BAR

(☑203-907-0238; www.ordinarynewhaven.com; 990 Chapel St; ⊙4pm-midnight Mon-Thu, to 1am Fri & Sat) Ordinary is anything but. It's tall, dark and handsome, ineffably stylish and a treat for the senses. Its patrons often also fall into at least one of these categories. They come for cheese boards, charcuterie and cocktails. Put on your fancy pants and join them.

116 Crown
BAR

(☑203-777-3116; www.116crown.com; 116 Crown St; ⊙5pm-1am Tue-Sun) Upscale contemporary design, DJ sets, expertly mixed cocktails and an international wine list draw the style crowd to this Ninth Sq bar. Small plates and a raw bar keep you from toppling off your stool, but style this chic doesn't come cheap.

Cave à Vin
WINE BAR

(☑203-777-6206; www.caveavinwinebar.com; 975 State St; ⊙4-11:30pm) This jovial little wine bar is a top spot for a tipple, with an extensive wine list and expert sommelier to take the pressure off (or put it on) you (or whoever is footing the bill). Naturally, appropriately paired small plates are also served. Weekends feature live music.

BAR
CLUB

(☑203-495-1111; www.barnightclub.com; 254 Crown St; ⊙11:30-1am Wed-Sun, 5pm-1am Mon-Tue) This restaurant-club-pub encompasses the Bru Room (New Haven's first brewpub), the Front Room, the video-oriented BARtropolis Room and other enclaves. Taken

in toto, you're set for artisanal beer and brick-oven pizza, a free pool table, and either live music or DJs spinning almost every night of the week.

☆ Entertainment

Café Nine
LIVE MUSIC

(☑203-789-8281; www.cafenine.com; 250 State St; free-$20) An old-school beatnik dive with a roadhouse feel, this is the heart of New Haven's local music scene (it dubs itself the 'musician's living room'). It's an offbeat place where banjo-playing hippies rub shoulders with jazzers, all in the name of good music.

New Haven Symphony Orchestra
CLASSICAL MUSIC

(☑203-776-1444; www.newhavensymphony.org; cnr College & Grove Sts; ticket prices vary) Yale's Woolsey Hall is home to most performances by this orchestra, whose season runs from October through April. Outside of season, crowds flock to the New Haven Green for the special outdoor summer concert series (featuring Beethoven, Tchaikovsky and Mendelssohn). The box office is now combined with the **Long Wharf Theatre** (☑203-787-4282; www.longwharf.org; 222 Sargent Dr).

Shubert Theater
THEATER

(☑203-562-5666; www.shubert.com; 247 College St) Dubbed 'Birthplace of the Nation's Greatest Hits,' the Shubert has, since 1914, been hosting ballet and Broadway musicals on their trial runs before heading off to New York City. In recent years it has expanded its repertoire to include a broader range of events, including a series of interviews, films and musical performances.

Yale Repertory Theatre
THEATER

(☑203-432-1234; www.yalerep.org; 1120 Chapel St) Performing classics and new works in a converted church, this Tony-winning repertory company has mounted more than 90 world premieres. Its varied program is presented by graduate student actors from the Yale School of Drama (Meryl Streep and Sigourney Weaver are alums) as well as professionals.

Toad's Place
LIVE MUSIC

(☑203-624-8623; www.toadsplace.com; 300 York St) Toad's is arguably New England's premier music hall, having earned its rep hosting the likes of the Rolling Stones, U2 and Bob Dylan. These days, an eclectic range of performers work the intimate stage, including They Might Be Giants and Martin & Wood.

ⓘ Information

INFO New Haven (☎203-773-9494; www.infonewhaven.com; 1000 Chapel St; ⏱10am-9pm Mon-Sat, noon-5pm Sun) This downtown bureau offers maps and helpful advice.

Yale University Visitor Center (☎203-432-2300; http://visitorcenter.yale.edu; 149 Elm St; ⏱9am-4:30pm Mon-Fri, 11am-4pm Sat & Sun) Offers free one-hour tours at 10:30am and 2pm weekdays, and at 1:30pm on weekends.

ⓘ Getting There & Away

➡ New Haven is 141 miles southwest of Boston, 36 miles south of Hartford, 75 miles from New York and 101 miles from Providence, via interstate highways.

➡ Avis, Budget and Hertz rent out cars at Tweed New Haven Airport.

AIR

Tweed New Haven Airport (☎203-466-8833; www.flytweed.com; 155 Burr St, East Haven) services a global network of more than 330 cities. However, flights out of airports in New York City and Hartford are significantly cheaper, and ground transportation to both cities is easy and inexpensive. Connecticut Transit (www.cttransit.com) bus G gets you to the airport ($3.25, 15 minutes). A taxi costs around $20.

BOAT

Bridgeport & Port Jefferson Steamboat Company (☎Connecticut 888-443-3779, Long Island 631-473-0286; www.88844ferry.com; 1 Ferry Access Rd, Bridgeport) operates daily car ferries year-round between Bridgeport, 10 miles southwest of New Haven, and Port Jefferson on Long Island, about every 1½ hours. The one-way 1½-hour voyage costs $19 for adults, $16 for seniors, and is free for children aged 12 and under. The fee for a car is $58, including the driver but not including passengers.

BUS

Peter Pan Bus Lines (www.peterpanbus.com) connects New Haven with New York City (from $12, two hours, eight daily), Hartford (from $12, one hour, six daily) and Boston (from $11, four to five hours, seven daily), as does Greyhound (www.greyhound.com). Buses depart from inside New Haven's Union Station.

Connecticut Limousine (www.ctlimo.com) is an airport shuttle servicing Hartford's Bradley airport, New York's JFK and LaGuardia airports, and New Jersey's Newark airport. Pick-up and drop-off is at Union Station and select downtown New Haven hotels. Services to Newark attract a higher rate.

TRAIN

Metro-North (www.mta.info/mnr) trains make the run between **Union Station** (50 Union Ave) and New York City's Grand Central Terminal (peak/off-peak $23.25/17.50, two hours) almost every hour from 7am to midnight.

Shore Line East (www.shorelineeast.com) runs regional trains up the shore of Long Island Sound to Old Saybrook (45 minutes) and New London (70 minutes), as well as Commuter Connection buses that shuttle passengers from Union Station (in the evenings) and from State St Station (in the mornings) to New Haven Green.

Amtrak (www.amtrak.com) trains run express from New York City's Penn Station to New Haven (from $32, 1¾ hours).

ⓘ Getting Around

Go New Haven Go (www.gonhgo.org) is a good resource for car-free travel.

GOLD COAST

This southwestern corner of Connecticut was home to potato farmers and fishers until 19th-century railroads and lower taxes brought New Yorkers north. With their blue-chip companies they transformed Fairfield County into one of the wealthiest regions in the USA, with affluent Greenwich at its heart. Now financial firms, yacht clubs and gated communities line the shore.

It's been the setting for suburban ennui in novels such as *The Swimmer* and *The Ice Storm*, among others. Darien (if you don't know how to say it, you'll be scorned) was ranked the state's 'snobbiest' town by local press.

You must ply further north to New Canaan, Ridgefield and Redding for the original Colonial flavor of the area, although the perfectly clipped lawns and spotless clapboards are telltale signs that many New Yorkers also have second homes here.

Further north along the coast, Stamford, once a stagecoach stop on the New York-to-Boston post road, is the area's commercial and industrial hub, while Norwalk and Westport have quietly thriving cultural communities with radically different characters.

NORWALK

Straddling the Norwalk River and encrusted with the salt spray of Long Island Sound, Norwalk is fiercely proud of its maritime tradition. The area supported a robust oystering industry in the 18th and 19th centuries, and is still the state's top oyster producer.

The past decade saw the redevelopment of the crumbling waterfront in South Norwalk (SoNo), where a clutch of galleries, boutiques and restaurants opened around Washington, Main and Water Sts, but overall the town appears a little crumbly again. Norwalk, although pleasant enough, isn't likely to excite and delight, unless you're an inquisitive youngster: the **Stepping Stones Museum for Children** (☑203-899-0606; www.steppingstonesmuseum.org; 303 West Ave, Mathews Park; $15; ☉10am-5pm, closed Mon Sep-May; 🅿) and the Custom House Maritime Museum (p254) are great for those young minds who aren't glued to digital devices.

Otherwise, you could time your visit with the **Oyster Festival** (www.seaport.org; Veterans Memorial Park; ☉Sep) or enjoy a round-trip cruise to Sheffield Island on the **Sheffield Island Ferry** (☑203-838-9444; www.seaport.org; 4 North Water St; adult/child under 5yr/child over 5 $26.50/5/16.50; ☉May-Sep, sailings vary), including a tour of the island's historic 1868 lighthouse, beach walks and nature trails. Acoustic music cruises, sunset cruises and clambakes happen on select summer nights, and family discounts are available. Ferries depart just down the dock from the aquarium.

Norwalk is about 32 miles southwest of New Haven on I-95. Metered parking around town is about $2 per hour.

Westport

☑203 / POP 26,600

Affluent Westport has been dubbed 'Beverly Hills East' for its popularity as a retreat for artists, writers and film stars. Despite its links to the rich and famous, the town otherwise bears no resemblance to Beverly Hills whatsoever.

Joanne Woodward, with her late husband Paul Newman, established the well-respected Westport Country Playhouse; Martha Stewart built her media empire from her Westport drawing room. There's a Tiffany's here for a reason.

Although there aren't any conventional tourist sights, Westport has a lovely location on the Saugatuck River (perfect for kayaking) and a drool-worthy main street of high-end boutiques with a small-town country flavor.

⊙ Sights & Activities

★ **Westport Arts Center**   ARTS CENTER
(☑203-222-7070; www.westportartscenter.org; 51 Riverside Ave; exhibits free; ☉10am-5pm Mon-Sat; 📶) The Westport Arts Center is right on the river and has a busy schedule of changing exhibits, kids' classes and performances.

Westport Historical Society   MUSEUM
(☑203-222-1424; https://westporthistory.org; 25 Avery Pl; ☉10am-4pm Mon-Fri, noon-4pm Sat; 🅿) **FREE** The Westport Historical Society organizes local walks and guided tours based on a historical theme. The once-a-year Hidden Garden tour is a green-thumber's dream. Its headquarters, situated in the 1795 Bradley-Wheeler House, has four period rooms on permanent display and hosts various small exhibitions.

✗ Eating

★ **Whelk**   SEAFOOD $$
(☑203-557-0902; www.thewhelkwestport.com; 575 Riverside Ave; mains $14-28; ☉4:30-9:30pm Tue-Thu, noon-10:30pm Fri & Sat) The flagship seafood restaurant from talented chef Bill Taibe continues to turn heads with its fresh presentation of oceanic delights. There's a raw bar (oysters!), a real bar (martinis!) and a fun crew of on-the-ball chefs and servers. If you're a lover of aquatic delicacies, and like fine food without the pretense, this one is a must.

Boathouse   MODERN AMERICAN $$$
(☑203-221-7475; www.saugatuckrowing.com; 521 Riverside Ave; mains $22-29; ☉11:30am-3pm & 5-9pm Tue-Fri, 5-9pm Sat) Don your chinos and boaters and pop in to this waterfront favorite at the Saugatuck Rowing Club. Sip on wine, dine in the sunshine on a selection of small farmers plates and a medley of tasty starters, or go for a romantic dinner with a small menu of beautifully presented chicken, fish, steak and veal, with definite Italian influences.

☆ Entertainment

★ Westport Country Playhouse   THEATER

(☎203-227-4177;   www.westportplayhouse.org;
25 Powers Ct; ⊙box office performance weeks
noon-7pm Tue, to 8pm Wed-Fri, 11am-8pm Sat &
Sun) Since its founding in 1931 this well-
respected playhouse has staged hundreds
of productions attracting big-name Broadway talent. It's hardly surprising when the
converted former barn was given a state-of-
the-art overhaul by Joanne Woodward and
her late husband Paul Newman, and a few
other deep-pocketed donors, in 2005.

❶ Getting There & Away

➤ To access Westport by road, take US 1 east
from Norwalk (4 miles).

➤ It's just over one hour from Grand Central
Terminal by Metro-North train (off-peak/peak
$13.50/18).

Ridgefield

☑203 / POP 24,700

Ridgefield serves as the poster child for
a Norman Rockwell painting with its old
Yankee charm and cultural sophistication.
Tree-lined Main St is fronted by stately 18th-
and 19th-century mansions and quaint
local shops. Aldrich museum is well worth
a morning or afternoon visit, and nearby
Weir Farm (☎203-834-1896; www.nps.gov/
wefa; 735 Nod Hill Rd; ⊙grounds sunrise-sunset,
visitor center 10am-4pm Wed-Sun May-Oct) FREE
in Wilton is also worth a trip.

◉ Sights

Aldrich Contemporary
Art Museum   MUSEUM

(☎203-438-4519; www.aldrichart.org; 258 Main
St; adult/child $10/free; ⊙noon-5pm Wed-Mon,
10am-5pm Sat; ℗) Swing into the parking lot
of this spotless white clapboard mansion,
which was once the town store and is now
a brilliant contemporary gallery. Photography, sculpture, painting and mixed-media
installations are displayed in cutting-edge
temporary exhibitions, which have previously featured notable names such as Cy Twom-
bly, Robert Rauschenberg, Anslem Kiefer
and Tom Sachs. Workshops for children are
held downstairs in light-filled rooms and the
museum also runs summer camps.

🛏 Sleeping & Eating

West Lane Inn   B&B $$

(☎203-438-7323; www.westlaneinn.com; 22 West
Lane/CT 35; d $215-255; ℗❄🛜) Quaintness
mixes with modernity in a town where two
well-known lodgings have closed in recent
years: the West Lane is an 1849-built home

CONNECTICUT RIDGEFIELD

WORTH A TRIP

NEW CANAAN

Smack-dab on the New York border, New Canaan has two attractions well worth heading out here for: the mid-century-modern architectural icon of Philip Johnson's **Glass
House** (☎866-811-4111; www.theglasshouse.org; 199 Elm St; tours from $25; ⊙9:30am-
5:30pm Thu-Mon May 1-Nov 30, last tour 2pm), with its accompanying artwork and grounds,
and the blissful sanctuary of **Grace Farms** (☎203-920-1702; www.gracefarms.org; 365
Lukes Wood Rd) FREE, created by New Canaanites themselves to put the brakes on a
McMansion-style development project.

Daily tours allow you to explore sections of the Glass House, along with its stunning
gardens; reservations are highly recommended. The visitor center is conveniently located
across the street from the New Canaan train station, making it an easy day trip from NYC's
Grand Central Terminal. During off-peak hours you may need to change trains at Stamford.

Grace Farms is dedicated to education, justice, community and nature. Included are an
extensive library, walking trails, a cafe and permanent art that blends seamlessly into the
lay of the land. The spectacular **River Building**, designed by Pritzker Prize–winning Japanese architectural firm SANAA, winds downhill, comprising several sub-buildings en route.

You might also want to spend the night nearby: the **White Hart Inn** (☎860-435-
0030; www.whitehartinn.com; 15 Undermountain Rd, Salisbury; d/ste from $250/365; ℗❄🛜)
is worth a look-see. Renovated completely in 2014, WHI radiates country luxury (marble
bathrooms, flat-screen tellies etc) and its dining room, managed by renowned British chef Annie Wayte, gets high marks – Wayte has been called a 'soup genius' in the
popular press.

just blocks from the Aldrich museum (p269) and a sedate stroll from the center. Bathrooms on the 1st floor are a bit tight, so if you want a postshower stretch, opt for the 2nd or 3rd floors.

★ **Hoodoo Brown BBQ**   BARBECUE $$
(https://hoodoobrownbbq.com; 967 Ethan Allen Hwy/CT 7; mains $11-15; ☺ 4-10pm Tue-Thu, 11:30am-10pm Fri-Sun) A Texas road trip inspired this unlikely Connecticut cult classic, where brisket falls off your fork and leaves you speechless (because maybe your mouth is crammed full of it). Gunslinger photos and steer horns linger above the picnic-style tables, but the real star is the smoked meat, with sandwiches like Battle of Ridgefield (brisket, crispy pork, coleslaw) winning the day.

Located where Route 7 meets Route 35.

❶ Getting There & Away

You can take the Danbury Metro-North train from nearby Branchville and switch in South Norwalk for a two-hour trip to Manhattan. Some prefer to drive to neighboring Katonah, NY, and take a one-hour direct trip from there. Route 35 is the main way into town from New York.

HOUSATONIC VALLEY

North of the Gold Coast, the Housatonic River Valley unfurls languidly between forested mountain peaks, picturesque ponds and rural Colonial villages. The area is anchored by industrial Danbury in the south; beyond its sprawling suburbs, Connecticut's prettiest rural landscapes line the valley's main north–south byway, scenic US 7. The centerpiece of the region is the Litchfield Hills with its centuries-old farms, winding country roads, abundant autumn fairs and hospitable country inns.

Candlewood Lake

With a surface area of 8.4 sq miles, Candlewood Lake is the largest lake in Connecticut. Created in the 1920s with water from the Housatonic River, its shoreline is shared by the four towns of Brookfield, New Milford, Sherman and New Fairfield, and is dotted with private cottages and a smattering of country inns. It's prettiest in the spring or fall.

Visitors head to lakefront **Squantz Pond State Park** (☑ 203-312-5023; www.ct.gov; 178 Shortwoods Rd, New Fairfield; weekdays/weekends May-Sep $15/22; ☺ 8am-sunset; ℗ ⊛) for picnicking, while in Brookfield and Sherman you'll find quiet vineyards with acres of gnarled grapevines lining the hillsides.

Just south of Candlewood Lake, Danbury is the closest large town to the Housatonic Valley and a good base for midrange mainstream accommodations and dining options.

◉ Sights & Activities

White Silo Farm   WINERY
(☑ 860-355-0271; www.whitesilowinery.com; 32 CT 37, Sherman; tastings $8; ☺ 11am-6pm Fri-Sun Jun-Dec; ℗ ⊛) Stop in at White Silo Farm winery for a tasting of specialty wines made from farm-grown fruit. Lisa and Eric also host local art showings and quarterly farm-to-table dinners, and produce an eclectic mix of *vino* from nontraditional sources like blackberry, quince and even rhubarb.

Lover's Leap State Park   HIKING
(☑ 860-424-3200; Still River Dr, New Milford; ☺ 8am-sunset) FREE A surprising little gem just south of New Milford town, Lover's Leap is home to Falls Bridge, one of the state's five remaining iron lenticular truss bridges (it's a vision in rusty red). The bridge leads to a three-quarter-mile moderately easy walk past the lookout and down to the Housatonic River (aka Lake Lillinonah).

◴ Sleeping & Eating

Crowne Plaza Danbury   HOTEL $$
(☑ 203-794-0600; www.cpdanbury.com; 18 Old Ridgebury Rd, Danbury; r from $99) This hulking chain hotel doesn't look much from the outside (in fact, it's quite ugly), but the good thing about old hotels is their oversize rooms. Inside, it has been fully refurbished to brand standards with plush bedding and amenities. Great rates make it a sensible base for exploring the Housatonic Valley, if you must stay in Danbury, or need a convenient stop just off I-84.

❶ Getting There & Away

North of Danbury, CT 39 mostly hugs the lake's western shore. From New Milford, you can drop down on US 7 and then Candlewood Lake Rd to get back to Danbury by the eastern shore.

Litchfield Hills

The rolling hills in the northwestern corner of Connecticut are sprinkled with lakes and dotted with forests and state parks. Historic Litchfield is the hub of the region, but lesser-known Bethlehem, Kent and Norfolk boast similarly illustrious lineages and are just as photogenic.

An intentional curb on development continues to preserve the area's rural character. Accommodations are limited. Volunteers staff a useful information booth on Litchfield's town green from June to November.

If you have your own car, there's no shortage of postcard-perfect country roads to explore in the Litchfield Hills. One particularly delightful stretch is from Cornwall Bridge taking CT 4 west and then CT 41 north to Salisbury. Gourmands will also find this area surprisingly rich in good food.

Lake Waramaug

Among the plentiful lakes and ponds in the Litchfield Hills, Lake Waramaug, north of New Preston, stands out. Gracious inns dot its shoreline, parts of which are a state park.

◉ Sights

Hopkins Vineyard WINERY
(☑ 860-868-7954; www.hopkinsvineyard.com; 25 Hopkins Rd, New Preston; tastings $12; ◷ 10am-5pm Mon-Fri, to 7pm Sat, 11am-6pm Sun May-Dec, 10am-5pm Fri-Sun Jan-Feb, 10am-5pm Wed-Sun Mar & Apr) On the northern shore of Lake Waramaug, Hopkins Vineyard produces eminently drinkable wines from predominant-ly French American hybrid grapes. Come for wine tastings with views of the lake from its bar. There's a nice cheese bar upstairs, too, to pair with your bottle. Call ahead during the low season, a good time to taste the ice wine, made from frozen grapes.

🛏 Sleeping

Lake Waramaug State Park CAMPGROUND $
(☑ 860-868-0220; www.ct.gov; 30 Lake Waramaug Rd; campsites $17-27) Lake Waramaug State Park has 77 campsites, both wooded and open, many of them lakeside. There's a snack bar in the park and a small beach for swimming. Book well in advance.

★**Hopkins Inn** INN $$
(☑ 860-868-7295; www.thehopkinsinn.com; 22 Hopkins Rd, Warren; r $140-150, without bath $130, apt $160-250; 🅿 ❄ 🐾) The 19th-century Hopkins Inn boasts a well-regarded restaurant with Austrian-influenced country fare (the second-generation chef whips up a mean schnitzel and mouthwatering pastries) and a variety of lodging options, from simple rooms with shared bathrooms to lake-view apartments. Whatever the season, there's something magical about sitting on the porch gazing upon Lake Waramaug and the hills beyond.

🍴 Eating & Drinking

★**Community Table** MODERN AMERICAN $$$
(Ct; ☑ 860-868-9354; http://communitytablect.com; 223 Litchfield Turnpike/US 202, Washington; brunch $22-28, mains $26-42; ◷ 5-9:30pm Sat, 10am-2pm & 3:30-9pm Sun; 🅿) The name of this Scandinavian-inspired restaurant

---

CONNECTICUT'S WINE & BEER TRAILS

Connecticut's agricultural reputation paved an easy path to it becoming a heady beer and wine region. The Connecticut Beer Trail (www.connecticut.beer) hops around the state from Litchfield to Stonington and points between: highlights include drinking in an **old post office** (☑ 860-423-6777; www.willibrew.com; 967 Main St, Norwich; ◷ 11:30am-1am Tue-Thu & Sun, to 2am Fri & Sat, 4pm-1am Mon) and a converted factory space (p260).

The Connecticut Wine Trail (www.ctwine.com) will give you all the info you need on the state's 40+-plus vintners, from scenic Litchfield lake overlooks to salt-sprayed coastal varietals (p259). Like its parallel neighbor, Long Island, Connecticut turned other farmland over to wine production in the 1970s with a range of grapes from cabernet franc and chardonnay to pinot gris and riesling. A 'passport book' is a fun way to track your groggy progress.

If you're continuing your vintage education up into Rhode Island and Massachusetts, the Coastal Wine Trail (www.coastalwinetrial.com) will guide you to 14 different vineyards, terminating at the end of Cape Cod.

DINNER & A MOVIE?

If you're looking for a fun night out in the Hills, head to the village of Bantam, 3 miles southwest of Litchfield, where you'll find the **Mockingbird Kitchen & Cafe** (☑ 860-361-6730; www.mockingbirdkitchenandbar.com; 810 Bantam Rd; mains $18-30). Produce can hardly get any fresher: it comes from the gardens out back and seven local farms. Chef Sam dishes out pan-Asian delights, like Laotian khao soi noodles, covered in a magical blend of red curry, peanuts, turmeric, onion and coconut milk. But this is New England, so you'll find a zesty rendition of seafood chowder too. If the kitchen is closed, there are other options nearby.

Time your visit with a screening at **Bantam Cinema** (☑ showtimes 860-567-0006, box office 860-567-1916; www.bantamcinema.com; 115 Bantam Lake Rd/CT 209). Housed in a converted red barn on the shores of Lake Bantam, the oldest continuously operating movie theater in Connecticut is a real Litchfield experience. The well-curated screenings focus on independent and foreign films, and the 'Meet the Filmmaker' series features guest directors, actors and producers, many of whom live nearby.

comes from the 300-year-old black-walnut table, where you can sit down to Sunday brunch. The modern American menu is locally sourced.

Kent Falls Brewing Co. BREWERY
(☑ 860-398-9645; https://kentfallsbrewing.com; 33 Camps Rd, Kent; ⊘ 2-7pm Wed & Fri, noon-5pm Sat) This converted barn-brewery has a down-home vibe, and the Coffee Milk Stout tastes damn fine, too. They fill growlers and sell cans and bottles of about a dozen different brews. Family-friendly atmosphere, and you can bring your own food (or buy some of their farm-raised pork and poultry, right in a cooler out front).

🛈 Getting There & Away

Lake Waramaug is a winding 10-mile drive east from Kent. It's about 14 miles from Litchfield, to the northeast, via US 202.

Litchfield

☑ 860 / POP 8460

Litchfield is Connecticut's best-preserved late-18th-century town and the site of the nation's first law school. The town itself converges on a long oval green, and is surrounded by lush swaths of protected land just asking to be hiked through and picnicked on.

Founded in 1719, Litchfield prospered from 1780 to 1840 on the commerce brought by stagecoaches en route between Hartford and Albany, NY. In the mid-19th century, railroads did away with the coach routes, and industrial water-powered machinery drove Litchfield's artisans out of the mar-

kets, leaving the town to languish in faded gentility. Today, farming and tourism rule the roost.

👁 Sights & Activities

Litchfield History Museum MUSEUM
(☑ 860-567-4501; www.litchfieldhistoricalsociety. org; 7 South St; ⊘ 11am-5pm Tue-Sat, 1-5pm Sun mid-Apr–Nov) FREE This museum features a small permanent collection, including a modest photographic chronicle of the town and a dress-up box with Colonial clothes for children to try on, plus some local-interest rotating exhibits.

Lourdes of Litchfield SHRINE
(☑ 860-567-1041; 50 Monfort Rd; ⊘ dawn-dusk) FREE Whether you're seeking enlightenment or just a peaceful stroll on wooded paths, this beautiful fieldstone replica of the Grotto Lourdes in France, constructed by Litchfield's Monfort Brothers seminarians in the 1950s, provides a bit of solace. Open-air masses are held May to October but the grounds are open year-round.

Litchfield Distillery Batchers DISTILLERY
(☑ 860-361-6503; www.litchfielddistillery.com; 569 Bantam Rd; ⊘ 11am-6pm, last tour 5pm) FREE In just a few years David and Jack have produced some prime hooch: award-winning bourbons, gins and vodkas (100% Connecticut corn!) made in small batches here in the Litchfield Hills. Some (but not all) secrets of the distiller's trade are revealed in a short but interesting tasting tour. Reservations advised.

Lee's Riding Stable · HORSEBACK RIDING

(☑ 860-567-0785; www.windfieldmorganfarm.com/lees.html; 57 E Litchfield Rd, off CT 118; trail rides $50; ⊙ 9am-5pm) What better way to see the rolling hills around Litchfield than on a trail ride from local riding stable Lee's? Sweet-natured ponies and horses make for gentle rides with experienced guide Heather. The stable caters to children seven years and up and also offers lessons in its indoor and outdoor schools ($50 for 30 minutes).

White Memorial
Conservation Center · WALKING

(☑ 860-567-0857; www.whitememorialcc.org; 80 Whitehall Rd, off US 202; park free, museum adult/child $6/3; ⊙ park dawn-dusk, museum 9am-5pm Mon-Sat, noon-5pm Sun) **FREE** Made up of 4000 supremely serene acres, this park has two dozen trails (0.2 miles to 6 miles long) that crisscross the center, including swamp paths on a raised boardwalk. The center also manages three campgrounds and there's a small nature museum. It's 2 miles west on US 202 from Litchfield.

🛏 Sleeping & Eating

Litchfield Inn · INN $$

(☑ 860-567-4503; www.litchfieldinnct.com; 432 Bantam Rd; d from $169; P ⊛ ❄ 🖤) Litchfield's largest lodgings feature 32 well-appointed hotel-style rooms and a range of fantastic themed suites that are so varied you'll need to check out the website to see what tickles your fancy (two have hot tubs). Rates vary dramatically between the off and peak season. There's also an elegant library and excellent on-site bar-restaurant, and breakfast (omelets! waffles!) is included.

Tollgate Hill Inn · INN $$

(☑ 866-567-1233; www.tollgatehill.com; 571 Torrington Rd/US 202; d/ste from $120/225; @ 🖤) About 2 miles east of town, this 1745 property used to be the main way station for travelers between Albany and Hartford. Divided between three buildings, including one of the oldest schoolhouses in Connecticut (which was relocated to here in 1920), rooms have a private deck and pull-out couch (great for families), while the suites afford a wood-burning fireplace, canopy bed, fridge and bar.

★ Peaches 'N Cream · ICE CREAM $

(☑ 860-496-7536; www.peachesncreamicecream.com; 632 Torrington Rd; scoops $3; ⊙ noon-9pm) This old-fashioned ice-cream parlor with peppermint trim on the road to Torrington has been serving up homemade ice cream for decades. Seasonal flavors include the eponymous peaches 'n' cream, cashew cream, maple walnut and Kahlúa chocolate. It also makes a neat ice-cream sandwich.

Village · PUB FOOD $$$

(☑ 860-567-8307; www.village-litchfield.com; 25 West St; dinner mains $18-36; ⊙ 11:30am-9:30pm Wed-Sun; 🍴) This restaurant-cum-taproom on Litchfield's town green is both a casual, welcoming hometown pub and – if eating in the dining room – a place to go for a special-occasion meal. The menu has something for everyone, from well-composed salads, to burgers and sandwiches, to pan-seared sea scallops. There's a children's menu and an excellent sangria for the liquid-lunch crowd.

West Street Grill · AMERICAN $$$

(☑ 860-567-3885; www.weststreetgrill.com; 43 West St; mains $25-40; ⊙ 11:30am-9pm Wed-Sun) A Parisian-style bistro on Litchfield's historic green, this is one of the state's top restaurants. Over the years its inventive modern American cooking has earned it nods from *Gourmet* magazine and the *New York Times*. The Asian chicken salad with cabbage and mango is a crunchy delight.

❶ Getting There & Away

Litchfield lies 34 miles west of Hartford and 36 miles south of Great Barrington, MA, in the Berkshires. The town green is at the intersection of US 202 and CT 63.

No buses stop in Litchfield proper, but Peter Pan Bus Lines (www.peterpanbus.com) will get you from New York City to Torrington ($34, 2½ hours), the closest major town, from where you'll need your own wheels.

Kent

☑ 860 / POP 3000

Lazing by the banks of the Housatonic River, Kent is arguably the loveliest town in the Hills, although Litchfielders would disagree. It's a popular stop for hikers on the Appalachian Trail (www.appalachiantrail.org), which intersects CT 341 about 2 miles northwest of town. Unlike much of the trail, the Kent section offers a mostly flat 5-mile river walk alongside the Housatonic, the longest riverside ramble of the whole trail.

During summer and fall, city folk flock to Kent's small but respected clutch of art galleries, its shops and its scenic countryside.

Especially popular is Kent Falls State Park, about 5 miles north of town, where the water drops 250ft over a quarter-mile before joining up with the Housatonic River. Hike the easy trail to the top of the cascade, or just settle into a sunny picnic spot at the bottom, near the red covered bridge.

● Sights

Sculpturedale   SCULPTURE

(☑860-927-3429;   www.deniscurtisssculptor. com; 3 Carter Rd, cnr Kent Cornwall Rd/US 7; ☺7am-dusk) Denis Curtiss has turned his yard into a veritable menagerie of cast-iron giraffes, hippos, turtles, elephants, herons and even a few people. They're crafted in Denis' on-site workshop, and many are for sale. If you think you recognize the work, you probably do – he's sold pieces around the world. A worthwhile stop before or after Kent Falls.

Kent Falls State Park   WATERFALL

(462 Kent Cornwall Rd/CT 7; Mon-Fri free, Sat & Sun $15; ☺8am-sunset) A rather amazing and popular site, you can walk a quarter-mile to the top – where there's a gushing 70ft waterfall – stopping at various platforms along the way to view the series of different minifalls. There are more easily graded switchback trails through the pine forest if you want to descend a bit more gently, and at the bottom, you can dip your feet in the cool mountain water. Nice picnic spot, too.

Connecticut
Industrial Museum   MUSEUM

(☑860-927-0050;   www.ctamachinery.com;   31 Kent Cornwall Rd; suggested donation adult/child $3/1.50; ☺10am-4pm Wed-Sun May-Oct; 🖈) Kids love this hands-on outdoor free-for-all cared for by the Connecticut Antique Machinery Association, with all manner of steam-powered locomotives, machines and demonstrations.

Sloane-Stanley Museum   MUSEUM

(☑860-927-3849;   www.ericsloane.com/museum.htm; 31 Kent Cornwall Rd; adult/child $8/5; ☺10am-4pm Wed-Sun May-Oct) Traditional, though quirky, Sloane-Stanley Museum is a barn full of early American tools and implements – some dating from the 17th century – lovingly collected and arranged by artist and author Eric Sloane. The museum is about 2 miles north of Kent on the left.

🍽 Sleeping & Eating

Starbuck Inn   INN $$$

(☑860-927-1788; www.starbuckinn.com; 88 N Main St, Kent; d $220-250) A B&B with a modern twist, including central air-conditioning and cable TV. Peter Starbuck, your host, makes sure you get a freshly prepared breakfast every day, sometimes featuring the house's famed blueberry pancakes. A lovingly prepared high tea is served at 4pm, and you're walking distance from all of Kent's shops and attractions.

J.P. Gifford Market   MODERN AMERICAN $

(☑860-592-0200;   www.jpgifford.com/kent;   12 N Main St; mains $10-12; ☺7am-6pm Mon-Sat, to 3pm Sun) Gifford has expanded to two Litchfield locations, and the Kent market is a handy spot to get all-day breakfast burritos and intriguing sandwiches like the Chicken Cutlet Apple Melt. They also offer a few variations on the traditional burger and noodle bowls, all for a pretty decent price.

Fife 'n' Drum   DINER $$

(☑860-927-3509;   www.fifendrum.com;   53 Main St; mains $8-24; ☺11:30am-10pm Mon-Sat, to 3pm Sun; 🅿) If you're a fan of 1950s Americana, you'll love this dark woodsy restaurant-cum-diner-cum-bar attached to an inn of the same name. It's delightfully olde worlde, serving hearty comfort food to get you through a day's driving around the Litchfield Hills, or to put you to sleep (if you're the lucky one in the passenger seat) for said day's driving.

● Getting There & Away

Kent is 29 miles north of Danbury on US 7 and about 3 miles from the New York state line on scenic Route 341.

Cornwall

Home to a picturesque covered bridge, Cornwall (which includes Cornwall Bridge, West Cornwall and Cornwall Village) attracts nature-lovers, birders, skiers and hikers thanks to the lazy Housatonic River and nearby Mohawk Mountain.

● Sights & Activities

West Cornwall
Covered Bridge   BRIDGE

(Covered Bridge; West Cornwall) You'll want to venture down to the river's edge to photograph this quaint covered bridge, built in

1864 and famed for allowing the passengers of horse-drawn carriages to have a moment of sheltered canoodling, which earned it the nickname 'Kissing Bridge.' This is one of two covered bridges in the state you can drive across; the other, Bull's Bridge, is just 17 miles south, in Kent.

Housatonic River Outfitters FISHING

(☎860-672-1010; www.dryflies.com; 24 Kent Rd South/CT 7, Cornwall Bridge; ⊗8am-5pm Sun-Thu, to 6pm Fri & Sat) Runs guided fishing trips with gourmet picnics, and sells the gear to match.

Mohawk Mountain Ski Area SKIING

(☎860-672-6100; www.mohawkmtn.com; 46 Great Hollow Rd, West Cornwall) In winter the Mohawk Mountain Ski Area is the largest ski resort in the state, with 24 slopes and trails.

Sleeping

Cornwall Inn INN $$

(☎860-672-6884; www.cornwallinn.com; 270 Kent Rd/US 7, Cornwall Bridge; d/ste from $159/259; P🅿🛜🏊) The tranquil, 14-room historic property at Cornwall Inn consists of a six-room inn and the more rustic-flavored eight-room lodge. Evenings feature wine and cocoa, and madness around the 1950s foosball table and the Pacman machines in the games room. There is also a pool and hot tub.

❶ Getting There & Away

Heading south, US 7 links Cornwall with Kent (13 miles).

Vermont

📞 802 / POP 623,650

Includes ➡

Brattleboro	278
Bennington	282
Manchester	285
Woodstock & Quechee Village	289
Killington Mountain	293
Middlebury	295
Burlington	301
Stowe & Smugglers Notch	310
Montpelier	316

Best Places to Eat

➡ Hen of the Wood (p315)

➡ Von Trapp Bierhall (p314)

➡ American Flatbread (p298)

➡ Revolution Kitchen (p307)

➡ TJ Buckley's (p281)

Best Places to Stay

➡ Inn at Shelburne Farms (p305)

➡ Grafton Inn (p286)

➡ Inn at Round Barn Farm (p300)

➡ Old Schoolhouse of Isle La Motte (p304)

➡ On the Creek B&B (p296)

Why Go?

Whether seen under blankets of snow, patchworks of blazing fall leaves or the exuberant greens of spring and summer, Vermont's blend of bucolic farmland, mountains and picturesque small villages make it one of America's most appealing states. Hikers, bikers, skiers and kayakers will find four-season bliss, on the expansive waters of Lake Champlain, the award-winning Kingdom Trails Network, the 300-mile Long and Catamount Trails, and the fabled slopes of Killington, Stowe and Mad River Glen.

Foodies will love it: small farmers have made Vermont a locavore paradise, complemented by America's densest collection of craft brewers. But most of all, what sets Vermont apart is its independent spirit: the only state with a socialist senator and the only one without a McDonald's in its capital city, Vermont remains a haven for quirky creativity, a champion of grassroots government and a bastion of 'small is beautiful' thinking, unlike anyplace else in America.

When to Go
Burlington

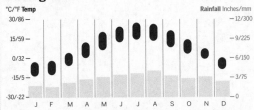

Dec–Mar Play with 'Powder Hounds' at New England's paramount ski resorts.

Jun–Aug Climb a mountain, paddle on a lake and frolic with fireflies in a Vermont State Park.

Sep & Oct Marvel at the colors and savor the flavors of fall, during leaf season.

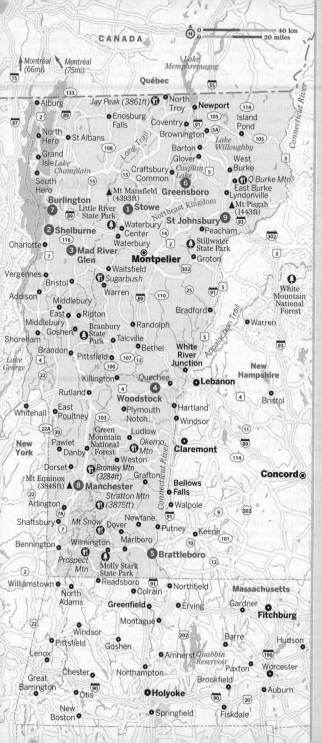

Vermont Highlights

1 Stowe Recreation Path (p314) Sauntering along Stowe's spectacular riverside ramble.

2 Shelburne Museum (p301) Exploring a 19th-century lighthouse, schoolhouse and steamship and then some.

3 Mad River Glen (p298) Gawking at the fall foliage from America's sole surviving single chairlift.

4 Billings Farm & Museum (p290) Celebrating the harvest, befriending brown cows or taking a sleigh ride.

5 Brattleboro Farmers Market (p279) Catching a taste of Vermont's thriving locavore food culture.

6 Hill Farmstead Brewery (p318) Making the dirt-road pilgrimage to this world-class remote brewery in Greensboro.

7 Church Street Marketplace (p301) Shopping and bar-hopping through downtown Burlington.

8 Hildene (p286) Exploring the Lincoln family mansion and its magnificent grounds.

9 Dog Mountain (p319) Cavorting with canines outside Stephen Huneck's whimsical hilltop Dog Chapel.

History

Frenchman Samuel de Champlain explored Vermont in 1609, becoming the first European to visit these lands long inhabited by the native Abenaki.

Vermont played a key role in the American Revolution in 1775 when Ethan Allen led a local militia, the Green Mountain Boys, to Fort Ticonderoga, capturing it from the British. In 1777 Vermont declared independence as the Vermont Republic, adopting the first New World constitution to abolish slavery and establish a public school system. In 1791 Vermont was admitted to the USA as the 14th state.

The state's independent streak is as long and deep as a vein of Vermont marble. Long a land of dairy farmers, Vermont is still largely agricultural and has the lowest population of any New England state.

❶ Getting There & Away

Vermont is not particularly large, but it is mountainous. Although I-89 and I-91 provide speedy access to certain areas, the rest of the time you must plan to take it slow and enjoy the winding roads and mountain scenery.

AIR

Vermont's only major airport is in Burlington (p310), served by Delta, JetBlue, United and American Airlines. Cape Air also flies from Boston to the smaller commercial airports in **Rutland** (RUT; ☑ 802-786-8881; www.flyrutlandvt. com) and Lebanon, NH (the latter just across the Vermont/New Hampshire state line).

BOAT

Lake Champlain Ferries (p310) runs ferries between Plattsburgh, NY, and Grand Isle; between Port Kent, NY, and Burlington; and between Essex, NY, and Charlotte. The teeny-tiny Fort Ti Ferry (www.forttiferry.com) runs from Larrabees Point in Shoreham, VT, to Ticonderoga Landing, NY, from early May to October.

BUS

Greyhound (www.greyhound.com), Megabus (www.megabus.com) and Vermont Translines (www.vttranslines.com) provide limited long-distance bus service to and from Vermont. The most convenient schedules serve Brattleboro (from New York City and points in between), Burlington (from Boston, Montreal and New York) and Bennington (from Albany, NY).

TRAIN

Amtrak operates two trains in Vermont. The *Ethan Allen Express* (www.amtrak.com/ethan-allen-express-train) departs New York City and stops in Fair Haven and Rutland. The more scenic *Vermonter* (www.amtrak.com/vermonter-train) heads from Washington, DC, and New York City to Brattleboro, Bellows Falls, Windsor, White River Junction, Randolph, Montpelier, Waterbury, Burlington–Essex Junction and St Albans. If you're a cyclist, you can buy one ticket on the *Vermonter* and get on and off as many times as you like, as long as you reserve a space for yourself and your bicycle ahead of time.

SOUTHERN VERMONT

White churches and inns surround village greens throughout historic southern Vermont, a region that's home to several towns that predate the American Revolution. In summer the roads between the three 'cities' of Brattleboro, Bennington and Manchester roll over green hills; in winter, they wind their way toward the ski slopes of Mt Snow, southern Vermont's cold-weather playground. For hikers, the Appalachian and Long Trails pass through the Green Mountain National Forest here, offering a colorful hiking experience during the fall foliage season.

Brattleboro

☑ 802 / POP 11,500

Perched at the confluence of the Connecticut and West Rivers, Brattleboro is a little gem that reveals its facets to those who stroll the streets and prowl its dozens of independent shops and eateries. An energetic mix of aging hippies and the latest crop of pierced and tattooed hipsters fuels the town's sophisticated eclecticism, keeping the downtown scene percolating and skewing its politics decidedly leftward.

Whetstone Brook runs through the south end of town, where a wooden stockade dubbed Fort Dummer was built in 1724, becoming the first European settlement in Vermont (theretofore largely a wilderness populated exclusively by the native Abenaki people).

At Brattleboro's old Town Hall, celebrated thinkers and entertainers, including Oliver Wendell Holmes, Horace Greeley and Mark Twain, held forth on civic and political matters. Rudyard Kipling married a Brattleboro woman in 1892, and while living here he wrote *The Jungle Book*.

⦿ Sights & Activities

★ Brattleboro Farmers Market
MARKET

(www.brattleborofarmersmarket.com; 570 Western Ave; ⊙9am-2pm Sat May-Oct) ⚑ Offering a crash course in Vermont food, the market has more than 50 local vendors selling cheese, free-range beef and lamb, honey, pastries, maple syrup, fruit, veggies and healthy snacks to nibble on as you wander. Live music and an active crafts scene round out the experience. From downtown, head west on VT 9 and continue 1.5 miles to the Creamery Bridge.

Retreat Farm
FARM

(☑802-490-2270; www.retreatfarm.org; 45 Farmhouse Sq; adult/child $8/6, recreational trails free; ⊙10am-4pm Wed-Sat, from noon Sun late May–Aug, 10am-4pm Fri & Sat, from noon Sun Sep & Oct; ⊕) Pet, groom and say hello to over four dozen barnyard animals at this farm 1 mile north of town on VT 30. Look for the large cluster of red barns (or listen for the goats!). Out back, you can also walk, run, bike, ski or snowshoe on the farm's network of recreational trails. Summer food trucks and a year-round calendar of special events add to the appeal.

Robb Family Farm
FARM

(☑farm 802-257-0163, sugar house 802-258-9087; www.robbfamilyfarm.com; 822 Ames Hill Rd; ⊙10am-5pm Mon-Fri, to 4pm Sat, 11am-3pm Sun; ⊕) Run by the same family for more than a century, this 400-acre farm hosts maple-sugaring demonstrations in early spring; it also offers free sugar-house tours and sells maple products and organic beef in its gift shop year-round. From Brattleboro, follow VT 9 west to Greenleaf St, then continue 3 miles up Ames Hill Rd and look to the right.

West River Trail
OUTDOORS

(www.westrivertrail.org; Spring Tree Rd) This lovely multipurpose trail, still partially under construction, follows 36 miles of a former railway bed along the West River between Brattleboro and South Londonderry. The 3.5-mile lower section, easily accessible from the Marina Trailhead just north of Brattleboro's marina, is open to walkers, cyclists, skiers and snowshoers. Check the website for maps and progress reports on the trail's completion.

Gallery Walk
WALKING

(☑802-257-2616; www.gallerywalk.org; ⊙5:30-8:30pm 1st Fri of month) Join like-minded folk each month on the immensely popular Gal-

Brattleboro

Brattleboro

⊕ Activities, Courses & Tours
1 Gallery Walk B3

⊜ Sleeping
2 Latchis Hotel B2

⊗ Eating
3 Amy's Bakery Arts Cafe B2
4 Brattleboro Food Co-op B3
5 TJ Buckley's A3
6 Whetstone Station B2

⊖ Drinking & Nightlife
7 McNeill's Brewery A2

⊕ Entertainment
Latchis Theatre .... (see 2)

lery Walk. Since the mid-1990s, galleries and businesses have opened their spaces to artists from an ever-increasing geographic reach and renown.

A free monthly publication, available throughout town and on the website, maps the locations for this self-guided tour. Many venues keep their Gallery Walk exhibits on display all month.

WORTH A TRIP

NEWFANE

Vermont is rife with pretty villages, but Newfane, 12 miles north of Brattleboro on VT 30, is near the top of everyone's list. All the postcard-perfect sights you'd expect in a Vermont town are here: tall old trees, white high-steepled churches, gracious old houses and an adorable inn. In spring Newfane is busy making maple sugar; in summer, the town buzzes around its flea market; fall lures leaf peepers; and winter brings couples seeking cozy rooms in warm hideaways.

A short stroll exposes Newfane's core: you'll see the stately **Congregational Church** (1839), the **Windham County Courthouse** (1825), built in Greek Revival style, and a few antique shops. If your budget permits, you might even consider staying in the **Four Columns Inn** (www.fourcolumnsvt.com), a multicolumned 19th-century beauty on the village green, **Newfane Common**.

To loop back to Brattleboro via a more scenic route, head southwest from Newfane to Williamsville, passing the village's old general store and crossing through a historic covered bridge dating to 1870. At South Newfane, branch south onto Augur Hole Rd and follow its hard-packed dirt surface 8 miles along the river, pausing at beautiful Olallie Daylily Farm before continuing toward Marlboro. Turn left on VT 9 and make your way back downhill into Brattleboro.

✯ Festivals & Events

Strolling of the Heifers   PARADE
(www.strollingoftheheifers.com; ☺ early Jun; 👪) Brattleboro's fun-spirited June celebration of community agriculture begins with flower-garlanded heifers mooing their way down Main St. Then come the bagpipes, 4H'-ers, Vermont politicians, bad cow jokes from the parade's commentators, excrement-scooping superheroes (complete with capes!), antique tractors and synchronized shopping-cart performances by the local food co-op. Don't miss the crowning of Miss Ver-mooont, prettiest heifer of them all!

🛏 Sleeping

Kampfires
Campground & Inn   CAMPGROUND, INN $
(📞 802-254-2098; www.kampfires.com; 792 US 5, Dummerston; tent sites $39, RV sites $39-60, inn r $129-159; 🅿 ❄ 🛜) If you like the campground vibe but you're not big on tents, then unpack your bags inside one of the four modern rooms at pleasantly hip Kampfires. Each room is assigned its own outdoor picnic area. Amenities include mini-golf, a playground and an ice-cream stand. On weekends, burgers, poutine and craft beer are served from the **Whetstone Station** (📞 802-490-2354; www.whetstonestation.com; 36 Bridge St; beer garden mains $4-13, restaurant mains $12-22; ☺ 11:30am-10pm Sun-Wed, to 11pm Thu-Sat) food truck.

Close to Brattleboro, Kampfires is an easy 20 miles west of downtown Keene.

Latchis Hotel   HOTEL $$
(📞 802-254-6300; www.latchishotel.com; 50 Main St; r $100-210, ste $190-240; 🛜) You can't beat the location of these 30 reasonably priced rooms and suites, in the center of downtown and adjacent to the historic theater of the same name. The hotel's art-deco overtones are refreshing, and wonderfully surprising for New England.

★ Inn on Putney Road   B&B $$$
(📞 802-536-4780; www.vermontbandbinn.com; 192 Putney Rd; r $169-309; @ 🛜) Designed to resemble a miniature chateau, this sweet 1930s-vintage B&B north of town has a glorious landscaped yard, five cozy, beautifully appointed rooms and one luxurious suite with fireplace. Overlooking the West River estuary, it offers opportunities for walking, biking and boating right on its doorstep, and plenty of rainy-day activities, including billiards, board games, DVDs and a guest library.

🍴 Eating

Amy's Bakery Arts Cafe   BAKERY, CAFE $
(📞 802-251-1071; 113 Main St; sandwiches, soups & salads $6-12; ☺ 8am-6pm Mon-Sat, 9am-5pm Sun; 🍴) Brattleboro's favorite bakery inspires poetic accolades for its breakfast breads, cakes, pastries and coffee with views of the Connecticut River. At lunchtime, the focus shifts to salads, soups and sandwiches, including many vegetarian options. Rotating exhibitions of art (all for sale) by local artists cover the walls.

Marina

AMERICAN $$

(☎ 802-257-7563; www.marina.restaurant; 28 Spring Tree Rd; mains $11-25; ⊙ 11:30am-9pm Mon-Wed, to 10pm Thu-Sat, 10am-9pm Sun) The sublime location on the banks of the West River makes this one of Brattleboro's most pleasant places to grab a bite. The varied menu features burgers, seafood, salads, pasta and sandwiches. The outdoor deck is a perennial favorite for summer sundowners and Sunday brunch. It's 1 mile north of downtown, on the west side of US 5.

★ TJ Buckley's

AMERICAN $$$

(☎ 802-257-4922; www.tjbuckleysuptowndining. com; 132 Elliot St; mains incl salad $45; ⊙ 5:30-9pm Thu-Sun year-round, plus Wed mid-Jun–early Oct) ⌀ Chef-owner Michael Fuller founded this exceptional, upscale little eatery in an authentic 1925 Worcester dining car over 30 years ago. Ever since, he's been offering a verbal menu of four seasonally changing items, sourced largely from local farms. Locals rave that the food here is Brattleboro's best. The diner seats just 18 souls, so reserve ahead. No credit cards.

🍷 Drinking & Entertainment

McNeill's Brewery

PUB

(☎ 802-254-2553; www.facebook.com/mcneills brewery; 90 Elliot St; ⊙ 4pm-2am Mon-Thu, from 3pm Fri, from 1pm Sat & Sun) This classic pub is inhabited by a lively, friendly local crowd. With 10 varieties, plus a few seasonal options, there's a beer for every taste. Offerings include its namesake microbrew, McNeill's, its flagship Firehouse Amber and award-winning Pullman Porter. There's also frequent live music.

Latchis Theatre

CINEMA

(☎ 802-246-2020; http://theater.latchis.com; 50 Main St) The nicely restored, art-deco Latchis Building houses this theater, where you can see mainstream and indie films on four screens nightly, listen to live music (such as a string quartet) or catch Metropolitan Opera performances broadcast live from New York City.

ℹ Information

Brattleboro Chamber of Commerce (☎ 802-254-4565; www.brattleborochamber.org; 180 Main St; ⊙ 9am-5pm Mon-Fri) Dependable year-round source of tourist info.

ℹ Getting There & Away

By car, the scenic 40-mile drive across VT 9 from Brattleboro to Bennington takes about an hour.

From Brattleboro to Northampton, MA, it's a 45-minute, 40-mile cruise down I-91.

Greyhound (www.greyhound.com) runs one bus daily to New York City (from $32, 5¾ hours) via Northampton, MA ($12, one hour) and Hartford, CT ($21, three hours). For the best fares, buy tickets in advance on Greyhound's website.

Amtrak's scenic daily *Vermonter* train (www.amtrak.com/vermonter-train) connects Brattleboro with points north and south, including Montpelier ($30, 2¾ hours), Burlington/Essex Junction ($34, 3½ hours), New York City ($67, 5½ hours) and Washington, DC ($99, nine hours). See Amtrak's website for details.

Wilmington

📞 802 / POP 1800

Nestled in the upper Deerfield Valley at the foot of the Green Mountains, Wilmington was one of Vermont's earliest settlements, chartered by New Hampshire governor Benning Wentworth in 1751 and named for England's Earl of Wilmington. Picturesquely sited at the confluence of two branches of the Deerfield River, the town built its economy around agriculture, lumber milling and its strategic position on the old stage road between Brattleboro and Bennington.

These days, Wilmington is best known as the access point for **Mt Snow** (☎ 800-245-7669; www.mountsnow.com; 39 Mt Snow Rd, West Dover; lift tickets adult/child $110/88; ⊙ 9am-4pm Mon-Fri, from 8am Sat & Sun), one of New England's best ski resorts and an excellent summertime mountain-biking and golfing spot. Many restaurants and stores cater to families, who are the resort's main clientele. Aside from its ski-town allure, Wilmington's main claim to fame is as the southern gateway to scenic VT 100, Vermont's favorite road-trip destination.

🛏 Sleeping & Eating

Nutmeg

B&B $$

(☎ 802-380-6101; www.thenutmegvermont.com; 153 W Main St/VT 9; r $130-190, ste $190-255; ☎) Located just west of Wilmington, this 18th-century farmhouse has 10 rooms and four suites with antiques and reproduction pieces. Most luxurious is the Grand Deluxe King Suite, with skylights and a marble bath.

CHEESEMAKING

Local cheesemakers have been around since Colonial times in Vermont, but it's only in the last few decades that artisanal cheese has come into vogue and become more widely available. Sheep's and goat's milk are now used in addition to cow's milk, adding variety to the traditional staples of cheddar and Colby. Vermont Cheese Council (www.vtcheese.com) lists nearly four dozen cheese producers on its online Cheese Trail map; two of the best and easiest to visit are Shelburne Farms (p301) and the **Grafton Village Cheese Company** (☑802-246-2221; www.graftonvillagecheese.com; 400 Linden St/ VT 30; ⊙10am-6pm).

Serious cheese connoisseurs can learn more about the state's smaller producers in Ellen Ecker Ogden's *The Vermont Cheese Book*. You'll also find a huge selection of local cheeses at places like the **Brattleboro Food Co-op** (☑802-257-0236; www.brattleboro foodcoop.coop; 2 Main St; deli items $5-9; ⊙7am-9pm Mon-Sat, from 9am Sun), Montpelier's Hunger Mountain Co-op (p317) and City Market (p305) in Burlington.

Dot's
DINER $

(☑802-464-7284; www.dotsofvermont.com; 3 E Main St; breakfast $4-9, lunch $4-11, dinner $13-19; ⊙5:30am-8pm Sun-Thu, to 9pm Fri & Sat) This venerable down-home diner has been a beloved Wilmington fixture since 1930. Recently rebuilt from scratch after a devastating flood, it's famous for its early-bird breakfasts and specialties like Vermont maple-berry chicken, homemade meatloaf and award-winning chili. There's a second location near the Mt Snow ski slopes in **West Dover** (☑802-464-6476; www.betseysdots ofdover.com; 2 Mountain Park Plaza/VT 100; mains $5-15; ⊙6am-3pm).

★ Folly
BISTRO $$$

(☑802-464-1333; www.vtfolly.com; 33 W Main St; mains $25-35; ⊙5:30-9pm Fri-Sun) Book ahead for this fabulous little bistro, which only opens three nights a week. The inspired menu changes weekly, drawing on a diversity of ingredients and international influences – from quail to octopus to wild mushrooms, and from Alpine to Italian to South American – but delivering consistently interesting, delicious and beautifully presented results.

ℹ Information

Southern Vermont Deerfield Valley Chamber of Commerce (☑802-464-8092; www. visitvermont.com; 21 W Main St; ⊙9am-4pm Mon-Fri, from 10am Sat & Sun) Has information on accommodations and activities.

ℹ Getting There & Away

Wilmington sits halfway between Brattleboro and Bennington on VT 9, southern Vermont's main east–west highway; it's a winding 20-mile

(half-hour) drive across the mountains to either town. Wilmington also sits astride scenic VT 100, which runs north past Haystack and Mt Snow to Killington (75 miles, 1¾ hours) and Stowe (146 miles, 3½ hours).

Bennington

☑ 802 / POP 15,000

Bennington is a mix of historic Vermont village (Old Bennington), workaday town (Bennington proper) and college town (North Bennington). It is also home to the Bennington Battle Monument, which commemorates the crucial Battle of Bennington during the American Revolution.

The charming hilltop site of Colonial Old Bennington is studded with 80 Georgian and Federal houses (dating from 1761 – the year Bennington was founded – to 1830). The poet Robert Frost is buried here and a museum in his old homestead pays eloquent tribute.

As Bennington is within the bounds of the Green Mountain National Forest, there are many hiking trails nearby, including the grandparents of them all: the Appalachian and Long Trails.

◉ Sights & Activities

Bennington Museum
MUSEUM

(☑802-447-1571; www.benningtonmuseum.org; 75 Main St; adult/child $10/free; ⊙10am-5pm daily Jun-Oct, Thu-Tue Nov-May) Bennington's standout attraction, this museum features the world's largest public collections of Grandma Moses paintings and Bennington pottery, along with a rich array of Vermont paintings, decorative arts and folk art from the 18th century to the present, encompassing everything from Vermont's Gilded Age to Bennington modernism to outsider art. The Works on Paper Gallery displays prints, lithographs, photography and more by nationally recognized regional artists. Don't miss the vintage Martin Wasp, a 1925 luxury car manufactured here in Bennington.

Bennington Battlefield Historic Site
HISTORIC SITE

(☑518-860-9094; www.nysparks.com/historic-sites/12/details.aspx; NY 67, Walloomsac, NY; ☺8am-sunset May–mid-Nov) FREE Just west of the Vermont/New York border, this was the site of a crucial American Revolutionary War battle in 1777. Had Colonel Seth Warner and Vermont's 'Green Mountain Boys' not helped weaken British defenses here, the American colonies might well have been split. To reach the battlefield, head 8 miles northwest from Old Bennington, following the 'Bennington Battlefield' signs through a historic covered bridge to North Bennington, then continuing west on VT 67. Picnic tables are provided.

Park-McCullough House Museum
MUSEUM

(☑802-442-5441; www.parkmccullough.org; 1 Park St, North Bennington; guided tour adult/child/teen $15/8/12, grounds free; ☺hourly tours 10am-2pm Fri, to 4pm Sat, from noon Sun May-Oct, other times by appointment, grounds dawn-dusk year-round) Just off VT 67A in North Bennington, this magnificent 35-room mansion, built in 1865, is filled with period furnishings and a fine collection of antique dolls, toys and carriages. Stroll the grounds during daylight any time of year, or visit the house on a guided tour (regularly scheduled on Fridays and Saturdays in warm weather, by appointment at other times).

Old First Church
HISTORIC SITE

(☑802-447-1223; www.oldfirstchurchbenn.org; cnr Monument Ave & VT 9; ☺10am-4pm Mon-Sat, from 1pm Sun Jul–mid-Oct, weekends only late May–Jun) FREE Gracing the center of Old Bennington, this historic church was built in 1805 in Palladian style. Its churchyard holds the remains of five Vermont governors, numerous American Revolution soldiers and poet Robert Frost (1874–1963) – the best-known, and perhaps best-loved, American poet of the 20th century – buried beneath the inscription 'I Had a Lover's Quarrel with the World.'

Bennington Battle Monument
HISTORIC SITE

(☑802-447-0550; www.benningtonbattlemonument.com; 15 Monument Circle, Old Bennington; adult/child $5/1; ☺9am-5pm late Apr–Oct) Commemorating the Battle of Bennington, a crucial American Revolutionary War battle fought near here in 1777, Vermont's loftiest structure offers an unbeatable 360-degree view of the countryside with peeks at covered bridges and across to New York. And you won't have to strain hamstrings climbing this 306ft-tall obelisk: an elevator whisks you painlessly to the top.

Robert Frost Stone House Museum
MUSEUM

(☑802-447-6200; www.frostfriends.org; 121 VT 7A, Shaftsbury; adult/child $10/5; ☺11am-5pm Wed-Sun May-Oct) When he moved his family to Shaftsbury (4 miles north of Bennington), poet Robert Frost was 46 years old and at the height of his career. This modest museum opens a window into the poet's life, with one entire room dedicated to his most famous work, 'Stopping by Woods on a Snowy Evening,' which he penned here in the 1920s.

Sugar Shack & Norman Rockwell Exhibition
MUSEUM

(☑802-375-6747; www.sugarshackvt.com/norman-rockwell-exhibit; Sugar Shack Lane, Arlington; ☺10am-4:30pm Mon-Fri, 9am-4pm Sat & Sun Mar–late Dec) FREE In Arlington, a 10-mile drive north of Bennington, this tiny maple-syrup shop houses an exhibition of *Saturday Evening Post* covers from Norman Rockwell's years in Arlington (1939–53), along with photos and written remembrances from former Arlington residents who posed for Rockwell. You can also see a short film about the artist.

Prospect Mountain Cross-Country Ski Touring Center
SKIING

(☑802-442-2575; www.prospectmountain.net; VT 9, Woodford; trail pass adult/child $22/17; ☺9am-5pm) About 7 miles east of Bennington, Prospect Mountain has more than 18 miles of groomed trails. It offers ski rentals and lessons as well as snowshoe rentals.

🛏 Sleeping

Camping on the Battenkill
CAMPGROUND $

(☑802-375-6663; www.campingonthebattenkillvt.com; VT 7A, Arlington; tent site/lean-to/cabin $33/42/46, RV site $39-43; ☺late Apr–mid-Oct)

LUDLOW, WESTON & THE OKEMO VALLEY

On the Green Mountains' eastern slopes, the Okemo Valley is one of Vermont's most attractive year-round vacation destinations.

At the heart of it all is the low-key ski village of **Ludlow**, home to the family-friendly **Okemo Mountain Resort** (📞 802-228-5222; www.okemo.com; 77 Okemo Ridge Rd, Ludlow). With 121 trails, the East's longest superpipe, excellent snowmaking facilities and high-speed lifts (including the heated six-seater Sunburst Six), Okemo appeals to skiers and snowboarders of all levels.

Downtown Ludlow is home to a variety of restaurants and accommodations, including the wonderful **Homestyle Hostel** (📞 802-975-0030; www.homestylehostel.com; 119 Main St, Ludlow; d $125, dm/tw/d/q with shared bath $40/75/89/115). Inviting and warm, the hostel has a variety of accommodation levels, from dorms to family rooms, and serves up a delicious locally sourced breakfast.

Eleven miles south of Ludlow, the picturesque village of **Weston** – built along the banks of the West River and anchored by a grassy common graced with towering maples and a bandstand – is most famous for its beloved **Vermont Country Store** (📞 802-824-3184; www.vermontcountrystore.com; 657 Main St/VT 100; ⏰ 8:30am-7pm Jul–mid-Oct, 9am-6pm rest of year). Founded in 1946 and still owned by the original Orton family, this creaky-floored Main St enterprise has morphed from a traditional country store into a vast all-purpose emporium selling everything from flannel nighties, lilac lotion and vintage games to penny candies, cookies and cheeses (there are seemingly endless free samples – don't be shy!). In summer, Weston is equally popular for its **Weston Playhouse** (📞 802-824-5288; www.westonplayhouse.org; 703 Main St; ⏰ performances late Jun–early Sep), Vermont's oldest professional theater.

Weston has a couple of historic inns and a family-friendly B&B-motel, all spread out along a two-mile stretch of VT 30. You can browse Weston's limited dining options in a five-minute walk from the playhouse south along Main St.

Stop by the **Okemo Valley Chamber of Commerce** (📞 802-228-5830; www.yourplaceinvermont.com; 57 Pond St, Ludlow; ⏰ 8:30am-4:30pm Mon-Sat) for more information about Weston, Ludlow, Grafton and eight surrounding communities, including the historic stone village of Chester.

Fishing is the forte at this campground just north of Arlington, which has 100 sites split between forest, meadow and open areas. Call early to reserve the popular riverside sites. Multiday stays are required during peak periods.

Greenwood
Lodge & Campsites   HOSTEL, CAMPGROUND $
(📞 802-442-2547; www.campvermont.com/greenwood; 311 Greenwood Dr, Woodford; 2-person tent/RV sites $30/39, dm $35-38, r $79; ⏰ mid-May–late Oct; 🛜) Nestled in the Green Mountains in Woodford, this 120-acre space with three ponds is home to one of Vermont's best-sited hostels. Accommodations include 17 budget beds and 40 campsites. You'll find it 8 miles east of Bennington, just off VT 9 near the Prospect Mountain ski area. Facilities include hot showers and a games room.

South Shire Inn   INN $$
(📞 802-447-3839; www.southshire.com; 124 Elm St; r $135-255; 🛜) This centrally located, antique-filled Victorian inn has nine plush, spacious and high-ceilinged rooms, including some with fireplace, scattered across a main house and carriage house. Complimentary afternoon tea held in the grand mahogany library enhances the refined atmosphere.

Four Chimneys Inn   B&B $$$
(📞 802-447-3500; www.fourchimneys.com; 21 West Rd/VT 9; r $199-429; 🛜) Old Bennington's only B&B, this grand white 1910 mansion surrounded by 11 acres of manicured lawns has a variety of spacious rooms, many with fireplace and porch. The best suite is a two-story revamped former icehouse with a spiral staircase. The attached restaurant, open August to October, has seated such guests as Walt Disney, Richard Burton and Elizabeth Taylor.

✖ Eating & Drinking

Blue Benn Diner
DINER $

(☑ 802-442-5140; 314 North St; mains breakfast $4-10, lunch & dinner $6-11; ⊙ 6am-5pm Mon & Tue, to 8pm Wed-Fri, to 4pm Sat, from 7am Sun; ☑) This classic 1950s-era diner serves breakfast all day and a healthy mix of American, Asian and Mexican fare, including vegetarian options. Enhancing the retro experience are little tabletop jukeboxes where you can play Willie Nelson's 'Moonlight in Vermont' or José Feliciano's 'Feliz Navidad' till your neighbors scream for mercy.

★ Pangaea
INTERNATIONAL $$

(☑ 802-442-7171; www.vermontfinedining.com; 1 Prospect St, North Bennington; mains $9-31; ⊙ lounge 5-10pm daily, restaurant to 9pm Tue-Sat) Whether you opt for the casual lounge, the riverside terrace or the more upscale dining room, you can expect exceptional food at this cozy North Bennington favorite. The varied menu ranges from burgers, salads, crab cakes, eggplant parmigiana and Thai stir-fries on the lounge side to herb-crusted halibut, roast duck and rack of lamb in the tastefully decorated restaurant.

Marigold Kitchen
PIZZA $$

(☑ 802-445-4545; www.marigoldkitchen.info; 25 Main St, North Bennington; pizzas $10-22; ⊙ 4-10pm; 🖲) This homegrown neighborhood pizzeria in North Bennington makes the best pizzas in town, with your choice of stone-ground wheat-flour or gluten-free crusts and organic toppings sourced from a dozen local farms.

Madison Brewing Co Pub & Restaurant
PUB FOOD $$

(☑ 802-442-7397; www.madisonbrewingco.com; 428 Main St; mains $11-20; ⊙ 11:30am-9pm Sun-Thu, to 10pm Fri & Sat) With 14 of its own brews on tap, this bustling two-level pub features fare ranging from sandwiches and burgers to steak, meatloaf, salads and pasta. The small upstairs deck is a popular summer hangout.

South Street Café
CAFE

(☑ 802-447-2433; www.southstreetcafe.com; 105 South St; ⊙ 7am-7pm Mon-Sat, 8am-6pm Sun; 🖲) Sink into a velvet sofa and sip a cup of locally roasted joe in this inviting, high-ceilinged cafe with boldly colored walls and vintage patterned tinwork. Located smack in Bennington's center at the corner of VT 9 and US 7, it's an oasis for soups, sandwiches, quiche, bakery treats and warm mugs of deliciousness.

ℹ Information

Bennington Welcome Center (☑ 802-447-2456; www.informationcenter.vermont.gov; 100 VT 279; ⊙ 7am-9pm) Bennington's spiffy tourist office has loads of information, long hours, and free coffee and tea for motorists; it's at the highway interchange where VT 279 and US 7 meet.

ℹ Getting There & Away

Bennington is 40 miles west of Brattleboro via VT 9, or 25 miles south of Manchester via US 7. Vermont Translines (www.vttranslines.com) offers once-daily bus service north to Manchester ($6, 35 minutes), Middlebury ($22.50, 2½ hours) and Burlington ($32, four hours), and west to Albany, NY ($10, one hour).

Manchester

☑ 802 / POP 4250

Manchester has been a fashionable resort town for almost two centuries. These days, the draw is mostly winter skiing and upscale outlet shopping (there are dozens of shops, from J Crew to Marimekko to Armani).

Two families put Manchester on the map. The first was native son Franklin Orvis (1824–1900), who became a New York businessman but returned to Manchester to establish the Equinox House Hotel (1849).

MAPLE SUGARING

Ranking first among states in maple-syrup production, Vermont regularly produces between one and two million gallons of the sweet stuff per year – nearly half the entire output of the US. This is particularly impressive considering Vermont's diminutive size and the fact that almost 40 gallons of sap must be tapped from maple trees for a mere quart of syrup. Demonstrations can be seen and samples tasted at the Robb Family Farm (p279), Shelburne Farms (p301), Merck Forest (p287) and dozens of other farms around Vermont during **Maple Open House Weekend** (www.vermontmaple.org/maple-open-house-weekend), held in late March or early April, when the sap is flowing.

Franklin's brother, Charles, founded the Orvis Company, makers of fly-fishing equipment, in 1856. The Manchester-based company now has a worldwide following.

The second family was that of Abraham Lincoln (1809–65). His wife, Mary Todd Lincoln (1818–82), and their son Robert Todd Lincoln (1843–1926), came here during the Civil War, and Robert returned to build a mansion – Hildene – a number of years later.

◉ Sights

★ Hildene HISTORIC SITE

(☑ general info 800-578-1788, tour reservations 802-367-7968; www.hildene.org; 1005 Hildene Rd/VT 7A; adult/child $23/6, guided tour $7.50 extra; ◎ 9:30am-4:30pm) Outside Manchester, the 24-room Georgian Revival mansion of Robert Todd Lincoln, son of Abraham and Mary Lincoln, is a national treasure. Lincoln family members lived here until 1975, when it was converted into a museum and filled with the family's personal effects and furnishings.

These include a vintage 1908 Aeolian pipe organ (still functioning), one of Abraham Lincoln's famous top hats, and remarkable brass casts of his hands, the right one swollen from greeting well-wishers while campaigning for the presidency.

Southern Vermont Arts Center MUSEUM

(☑ 802-362-1405; www.svac.org; 930 SVAC Dr; ◎ 10am-5pm Tue-Sat, from noon Sun) FREE In addition to excellent outdoor sculptures, this center's 10 galleries of classic and contemporary art feature touring shows of sculpture, paintings, prints and photography. Other attractions include walking trails, the on-site Garden Cafe, lectures and numerous musical events, including jazz concerts and the Manchester Music Festiva, where classical music is the focus.

American Museum of Fly Fishing MUSEUM

(☑ 802-362-3300; www.amff.org; 4070 Main St/ VT 7A; adult/child $5/3; ◎ 10am-4pm Tue-Sun Jun-Oct, Tue-Sat Nov-May) This museum has perhaps the world's best display of fly-fishing equipment, including fly collections and rods used by Ernest Hemingway, Babe Ruth, Bing Crosby and several US presidents, including Herbert Hoover. If you can believe it, the latter penned the tome *Fishing for Fun & To Wash Your Soul.*

Activities

Equinox Preserve HIKING

(☑ 802-366-1400; www.equinoxpreservationtrust. org; W Union St) FREE The Equinox Preservation Trust maintains this 914-acre woodland preserve on the eastern slopes of 3848ft Mt

---

WORTH A TRIP

GRAFTON

The bucolic village of Grafton owes its graceful beauty in part to the private Windham Foundation, which established a restoration and preservation program for the entire village in the 1960s. The foundation's initiatives included burying all electrical and telephone lines, which helps account for Grafton's lost-in-time appearance.

Today visitors come not only for Grafton's picture-postcard New England charm but also to ski and bike at the **Grafton Trails & Outdoor Center** (☑ 802-843-2350; www.graftoninnvermont.com/grafton-trails; 783 Townshend Rd) and to taste one of Vermont's best cheddar cheeses, produced by the **Grafton Village Cheese Company** (☑ 800-472-3866; www.graftonvillagecheese.com; 533 Townshend Rd; ◎ hours vary) FREE.

When you're here, why not overnight at the village's loveliest landmark, the **Grafton Inn** (☑ 802-843-2248; www.graftoninnvermont.com; 92 Main St; r $159-279; ☎), to join the ranks of such notable guests as Rudyard Kipling, Theodore Roosevelt and Ralph Waldo Emerson? While the original brick inn is quite formal, many of the 45 guest rooms and suites – scattered around houses within the village – are less so. As is the **Phelps Barn** (☑ 802-234-8718; www.graftoninnvermont.com/dining/phelps-barn; mains $13-28; ◎ 4-8:30pm Sun-Thu, to 9:30pm Fri & Sat), the inn's historic tavern.

Grafton lies at the junction of VT 121 and VT 35, about 27 miles north of Brattleboro and 45 miles southeast of Manchester.

MERCK FOREST & FARMLAND CENTER

Encompassing 3200 acres of high-country meadow and forest, the sprawling **Merck Forest & Farmland Center** (☑ 802-394-7836; www.merckforest.org; 3270 VT 315, Rupert; ⊙ visitor center 9am-4pm; ⛺) offers a blissful vision of Vermont's natural beauty and agricultural heritage. The park's centerpiece is a working organic farm with animals, vegetable gardens, renewable-energy installations and a sugar house where you can watch maple syrup being produced during sugaring season. It's hidden away on a gorgeous hilltop, only 25 minutes from busy VT 7 but a world apart from Manchester's designer outlet hustle and bustle.

Equinox. Hikers will appreciate the well-signposted network of trails, the most dramatic of which is the 3.1-mile, 2840ft climb to the top of Mt Equinox via the Blue Summit Trail. Park at the W Union St trailhead, or in the lot behind Equinox resort (p288).

Get trail maps at the self-serve kiosk adjacent to the Equinox parking lot.

Bromley Mountain
SKIING

(☑ 802-824-5522, snow conditions 866-856-2201; www.bromley.com; 3984 VT 11, Peru; lift ticket adult/teen/child $87/58/44; ⛺) Approximately 5 miles east of Manchester, 3284ft Bromley Mountain is a family-oriented resort featuring 46 downhill ski runs and nine lifts. Summer attractions include the Alpine Slide (one of the world's longest), Sun Mountain Flyer (New England's longest zipline), an aerial adventure park, a climbing wall, trampolines, Vermont's longest waterslide, a children's adventure park and access to the Long/Appalachian Trail.

Stratton Mountain
SKIING

(☑ 802-297-4000; www.stratton.com; 5 Village Lodge Rd, Stratton; lift ticket adult $129, child $50-80; ⊙ 9am-4pm Mon-Fri, from 8:30am Sat & Sun) This all-season recreational playground, 16 miles southeast of Manchester, has 97 trails, 11 lifts (including a summit gondola), 670 acres of skiable terrain and a vertical drop of 2003ft on a 3875ft mountain. There are also over 7 miles of groomed cross-country trails. Summer activities include golf, tennis, kayaking, swimming, stand-up paddleboarding, hiking, biking and scenic gondola rides.

Mt Equinox Skyline Drive
SCENIC DRIVE

(☑ 802-362-1114; www.equinoxmountain.com; VT 7A, btwn Manchester & Arlington; car/motorcycle & driver $20/12, each additional passenger $5, under 10yr free; ⊙ 9am-4pm late May–Oct) For exceptional views, climb the insanely steep 5-mile Skyline Dr, a private toll road that leads to

the summit of 3848ft Mt Equinox, the highest mountain in the Taconic Range; it's just off VT 7A, south of Manchester.

Battenkill Bicycles
CYCLING

(☑ 802-362-2734; www.battenkillbicycles.com; 99 Bonnet St; bike rental per day $40; ⊙ 9:30am-5:30pm Apr-Oct, 10am-5pm Wed-Sun Nov-Mar) Just north of Manchester Center, this bike shop rents road, mountain, hybrid and fat-tire demo bikes.

★☆ Festivals & Events

Manchester Music Festival
MUSIC

(☑ 802-362-1956; www.mmfvt.org; ⊙ mid-Jul–mid-Aug) Presents a month-long summer series of classical concerts by renowned international musicians at the Southern Vermont Arts Center.

🛏 Sleeping

Inn at Manchester
INN $$

(☑ 802-362-1793; www.innatmanchester.com; 3967 Main St/VT 7A; r $155-245, ste $235-315; ❋@🛜🏊) This restored inn and its two carriage barns offer 21 rooms and suites with quilted comforters and country furnishings, each named after a herb or flower. There's a big front porch, an expansive backyard and comfortable common rooms, one with a wee pub. Full country breakfasts feature the inn's fluffy 'cottage cakes,' sinfully delicious pancakes made with cottage cheese.

Aspen at Manchester
MOTEL $$

(☑ 802-362-2450; www.aspenvt.com; 5669 Main St/VT 7A; r $89-199, 6-person cottage $289-369; ❋🛜🏊) An affordable standout, this family-run motel set back serenely from the road has 27 comfortable rooms, a swimming pool and a convenient location within walking distance of Manchester Center. Two adjacent cottages sleeping up to six make an attractive option for families.

BEST BOOKS

Forming both the geographic and the intellectual center of the Manchester community, the thriving **Northshire Bookstore** (☑802-362-2200; www.northshire.com; 4869 Main St; ⊙10am-7pm Sun-Thu, to 9pm Fri & Sat) is the best in Vermont, with a sprawling collection of titles on every subject imaginable (including an entire section on Vermont and New England) and an impressive array of readings and author events.

Barnstead Inn
INN $$

(☑802-362-1619; www.barnsteadinn.com; 349 Bonnet St; r $109-199, ste $275-310; 🖨🕸) Barely a half-mile from Manchester Center, this converted 1830s hay barn exudes charm and is in a good location. Rooms have refrigerators and homey braided rugs, while the porch has wicker rockers for watching the world pass by.

Casablanca Motel
MOTEL, CABINS $$

(☑802-362-2145; www.casablancamotel.com; 5927 Main St/VT 7A; cabins 1 room $75-169, 2 rooms $150-250; 🕸@🕸) This tidy collection of cabins on the northern fringes of town has units with microwave, fridge and coffeemaker, each decorated in a different country theme.

Inn at Ormsby Hill
INN $$$

(☑802-362-1163; www.ormsbyhill.com; 1842 Main St/VT 7A; r $215-545; 🕸) Just southwest of Manchester, adjacent to the Hildene estate, this sprawling place built around an 18th-century home is arguably one of the most welcoming inns in all of New England. Fireplaces, two-person Jacuzzis, flat-screen TVs, antiques, gracious innkeepers and 2.5 acres of lawn are among the features that draw repeat guests.

Equinox
RESORT $$$

(☑802-362-4700; www.equinoxresort.com; 3567 Main St/VT 7A; r $240-716; 🕸@🕸) Manchester's most famous resort encompasses many worlds: cottages with woodburning fireplace, luxury town houses with full kitchen, the main house's elegant suites, and the Federal-style 1811 House's antique-filled rooms, canopied beds and oriental rugs. High-end extras abound: an 18-hole golf course, two tennis courts, a state-of-the-art fitness center, a full-service spa and endless activities, including falconry, archery and snowmobiling.

Eating

⭐ Moonwink
BURMESE $

(☑802-768-8671; www.facebook.com/moonwinkvt; 4479 Main St; mains $12-13; ⊙11:30am-7pm Tue-Sat) Nothing fancy here, but Moonwink – owned by Burmese-born chef May Stannard and her Vermonter husband Wes – makes some of the best authentic Asian food you'll find in rural New England. Order a Burma bowl (rice and sprouted peas with curry), a delicious vegetarian or vegan salad, or daily specials such as fish stew or coconut chicken noodle soup.

Little Rooster Cafe
CAFE $

(☑802-362-3496; 4645 Main St/VT 7A; dishes $6-12; ⊙7am-2:30pm Thu-Tue) This colorful spot serves an eclectic mix of dishes, including pan-seared salmon, roast leg of lamb, spinach salad, and focaccia sandwiches with tasty ingredients like roasted portobello mushrooms and grilled eggplant. It's also popular for its delicious breakfast entrees, such as the trademark Cock-A-Doodle-Doo (poached eggs with smoked salmon and dill-mustard-caper sauce on sourdough toast).

Ye Olde Tavern
AMERICAN $$$

(☑802-362-0611; www.yeoldetavern.net; 5183 Main St; mains $19-34; ⊙5-9pm) Hearthside dining at candlelit tables enhances the experience at this gracious roadside 1790s inn. The menu is wide-ranging: 'Yankee favorites' like traditional pot roast cooked in the tavern's own ale; New England scrod baked with Vermont cheddar, bread crumbs, sherry and lemon; and local venison (a regular Friday special) seal the deal.

ℹ Information

Green Mountain National Forest Ranger Station (☑802-362-2307; www.fs.usda.gov/gmfl; 2538 Depot St, Manchester Center; ⊙8am-4:30pm Mon-Fri) Stop by for info about the Appalachian and Long Trails, trail maps and details about shorter day hikes.

Manchester Visitors Center (www.manchestervermont.com; 18 Depot St; ⊙1-4pm Mon-Thu, from 10am Fri-Sun)

ℹ Getting There & Away

Manchester sits 25 miles (30 minutes) north of Bennington and 65 miles (1½ hours) south of Middlebury on US 7. For a more scenic (and not much slower) drive, take VT 7A to Bennington or VT 30 to Middlebury. Brattleboro is 48 miles (1¼ hours) southeast across the Green Mountains via VT 30.

Vermont Translines (www.vttranslines. com) offers once-daily bus service north to Middlebury ($16.50, two hours) and Burlington ($25.50, 3¼ hours), and south to Bennington ($6, 35 minutes) and Albany, NY ($16, 1½ hours).

Dorset

📞 802 / POP 1950

Six miles northwest of Manchester along VT 30, Dorset is a pristinely beautiful Vermont village, originally settled in 1768, with a stately inn (the oldest in Vermont), a lofty church and a village green. The sidewalks and many other buildings are made of creamy marble from the nearby quarry, about a mile south of the village center on VT 30. Dorset supplied much of the marble for the grand New York Public Library building and numerous other public edifices. These days the quarry is filled with water and makes a lovely place to picnic.

Dorset is best known as a summer playground for well-to-do city folks (a role it has played for over a century) and the home of a renowned theater, the **Dorset Playhouse** (📞 802-867-5570; www.dorsetplayers.org; 104 Cheney Rd), which draws a sophisticated audience for the **Dorset Theatre Festival** (www.dorsettheatrefestival.org; ⊙ mid-Jun–Aug).

🛏 Sleeping & Eating

Dorset Inn   INN $$$

(📞 802-867-5500; www.dorsetinn.com; 8 Church St; r $165-355, ste $235-485; 🅟🛜❄) In business since 1796, Vermont's oldest continuously operating lodging is still going strong. Facing the village green, this traditional but updated inn has 31 renovated guest rooms. The front-porch rockers provide a nice setting for watching the comings and goings of this sleepy but upscale Vermont town. Opt for rates that include dinner, as the chef-owned restaurant is highly regarded.

Dorset Rising   SANDWICHES $

(📞 802-867-7021; www.dorsetrising.com; 3239 VT 30; sandwiches $7-15; ⊙ 8am-4pm) Stenciled tables, woven cushions and ceramic platters hung on the mustard-yellow walls create a folksy backdrop at this popular breakfast and lunch hangout. Scrumptious apple-cider doughnuts and blueberry scones share the menu with a variety of sandwiches, from avocado toast to Vietnamese banh mi to classic bacon, egg and cheese.

ⓘ Getting There & Away

Dorset is on VT 30, 7 miles (15 minutes) north of Manchester and 58 miles (1¼ hours) south of Middlebury.

CENTRAL VERMONT

Vermont's heart features some of New England's most bucolic countryside. Cows begin to outnumber people just north of Rutland (Vermont's second-largest city, with a whopping 15,500 residents). Lovers of the outdoors make frequent pilgrimages to central Vermont, especially to the resort areas of Killington, Sugarbush and Mad River Glen, which attract countless skiers and summer hikers. For those interested in indoor pleasures, antique shops and art galleries dot the back roads.

Woodstock & Quechee Village

POP 2930

Chartered in 1761, Woodstock has been the highly dignified seat of scenic Windsor County since 1766. Many grand houses surround the oval village green, and four of Woodstock's churches can claim bells cast by Paul Revere. Senator Jacob Collamer, a friend of Abraham Lincoln's, once observed, 'The good people of Woodstock have less incentive than others to yearn for heaven.'

Today Woodstock is still very beautiful and very wealthy. Spend some time walking around the green, surrounded by Federal and Greek Revival homes and public buildings, or along the Ottauquechee River, spanned by three covered bridges. The Rockefellers and the Rothschilds own estates in the surrounding countryside, and the well-to-do come to stay at the grand Woodstock Inn & Resort.

About a five-minute drive east of Woodstock, small, twee Quechee Village is home to Quechee Gorge – Vermont's diminutive answer to the Grand Canyon – as well as some outstanding restaurants.

⊙ Sights

★**Quechee Gorge**   CANYON

(US 4, Quechee) FREE Lurking beneath US 4, less than a mile east of Quechee Village, the gorge is a 163ft-deep scar that cuts about 3000ft along a stream that you can view from a bridge or easily access by footpaths from the road. A series of well-marked, undemanding trails, none of which should take more than an hour to cover, lead down into the gorge.

Just upstream from the gorge, the tranquil waters of Dewey's Mill Pond are another lovely spot, bordered by a pretty expanse of reeds and grasses. The pond is named for AG Dewey, who set up a prosperous woolen mill here in 1869.

Marsh-Billings-Rockefeller National Historical Park
PARK

(☑ 802-457-3368; www.nps.gov/mabi; 54 Elm St, Woodstock; mansion tours adult/child $8/free, trails & carriage roads free; ☺ visitor center & tours 10am-5pm late May–Oct, trails & carriage roads year-round) Built around the historic home of early American conservationist George Perkins Marsh, Vermont's only national park examines the relationship between land stewardship and environmental conservation. The estate's 20 miles of trails and carriage roads are free for exploring on foot, horseback, cross-country skis or snowshoes. There's an admission fee to the mansion itself, where tours are offered every 30 minutes.

Billings Farm & Museum
FARM

(☑ 802-457-2355; www.billingsfarm.org; 69 Old River Rd, Woodstock; adult/child $16/8; ☺ 10am-5pm daily Apr-Oct, to 4pm Sat, Sun & holidays Nov-Feb; ☕) A mile north of Woodstock's village green, this historic farm founded by 19th-century railroad-magnate Frederick Billings delights children with hands-on activities related to old-fashioned farm life. Farm animals, including pretty cows descended from Britain's island of Jersey, are abundant. Family-friendly seasonal events include wagon & sleigh rides, pumpkin and apple festivals, and old-fashioned Halloween, Thanksgiving and Christmas celebrations.

VINS Nature Center
WILDLIFE RESERVE

(Vermont Institute of Natural Science; ☑ 802-359-5000; www.vinsweb.org; 149 Natures Way, Quechee; adult/child $15.50/13.50; ☺ 10am-5pm mid-Apr–Oct, to 4pm Nov–mid-Apr; ☕) This science center near Quechee houses two dozen species of raptors, ranging from the tiny, 3oz saw-whet owl to the mighty bald eagle. The birds that end up here have sustained permanent injuries that prevent them from returning to the wild. On offer are regular educational presentations and three self-guided nature trails, delightful for summer hiking and winter snowshoeing.

Sugarbush Farm
FARM

(☑ 802-457-1757; www.sugarbushfarm.com; 591 Sugarbush Farm Rd, Woodstock; ☺ 9am-5pm; ☕) **FREE** At the end of a bucolic mountain road, this working 550-acre farm – complete with animals for kids to pet – processes sap from its 9000 maple trees, and ships up to 100 tons of cheese annually. Watch a video of the maple-sugaring process and sample four grades of syrup along with 14 varieties of cheddar – from mild sage or spicy jalapeño-cayenne to the prize-winning hickory and smoked varieties. The adjacent shop sells wax-coated bars of cheese designed for easy transport.

🏃 Activities & Tours

Suicide Six
SKIING

(☑ 802-457-6661; www.woodstockinn.com/mountain; 247 Stage Rd, South Pomfret; lift ticket adult/child weekend $72/55, midweek $35/30; ☺ 9am-4pm mid-Dec–Mar) In 1934 Woodstockers installed the first mechanical ski tow in the USA, and skiing is still important here. Three miles north of Woodstock, this resort is known for challenging downhill runs, although the lower slopes are fine for beginners. Midweek lift tickets are among the cheapest you'll find anywhere in New England. In summer, mountain bikers enjoy these same trails.

There are 24 trails (30% beginner, 40% intermediate, 30% expert) served by two chairlifts and a J-bar.

Woodstock Inn & Resort Nordic Center
SNOW SPORTS

(☑ 802-457-6674; www.woodstockinn.com/do/things-to-do/woodstock-nordic-center; VT 106, Woodstock; trail pass adult/child $25/18; ☺ 9am-4pm mid-Dec–mid-Mar) Just south of town, this outfit at the Woodstock Country Club rents Nordic skis, snowshoes and fat bikes and has over 40km of groomed touring trails spread out between 1080ft Mt Peg and 1250ft Mt Tom.

Discovery Bicycle Tours
CYCLING

(☑ 802-457-3553; www.discoverybicycletours.com; 2174 Maxham Meadow Way, Woodstock) Formerly known as Bike Vermont, this family-run, Woodstock-based company operates two- to five-night bike tours in the area, including inn-to-inn tours.

🛏 Sleeping

Silver Lake State Park
CAMPGROUND $

(☑ 802-234-9451; www.vtstateparks.com/htm/silver.htm; 20 State Park Beach Rd, Barnard; camp-

VERMONT'S STATE PARKS

With more than 150,000 acres of protected land set aside in more than 50 state parks, Vermont isn't called the Green Mountain State for nothing! Finding an exceptional and often underutilized state park in Vermont is about as easy as breathing. Whether you're interested in swimming, hiking, snowshoeing, cross-country skiing, camping or fishing, you'll find plenty of places that fit the bill. For complete details on all state parks, contact Vermont State Parks (www.vtstateparks.com).

Here are some of our favorite off-the-beaten-track state-park campgrounds in Vermont.

Burton Island State Park (☑ 802-524-6353; www.vtstateparks.com/burton.html; 2714 Hathaway Point Rd, St Albans; day use adult/child $4/2, campsite/lean-to $20/39; ☉ late May–late Sep; ☝) Only accessible by ferry, this island state park in the middle of Lake Champlain (35 miles north of Burlington) has lakeside campsites and lean-tos, walking trails, boat rentals, a cafe and a nature center.

Seyon Lodge State Park (☑ 802-584-3829; www.vtstateparks.com/seyon.html; 2967 Seyon Pond Rd, Groton; day use adult/child $4/2, d $85-95; ☉ closed mid-Mar–mid-Apr & mid-Nov–late Dec) The only park of its kind in Vermont, Seyon Lodge (30 miles east of Montpelier) offers private rooms in its rustic lodge on the shores of Noyes Pond and also serves meals, including three-course dinners made with locally sourced produce. There's great fly-fishing in the pond and hiking or skiing on the network of trails just outside the front door.

Jamaica State Park (☑ 802-874-4600; www.vtstateparks.com/jamaica.html; 48 Salmon Hole Lane, Jamaica; day use adult/child $4/2, campsites $20-22, lean-tos $27-29; ☉ early May–mid-Oct) With campsites directly adjacent to the rushing West River, this is one of only two riverside state parks in Vermont. It's especially popular with kayakers and rafters for its annual white-water weekends. It's 27 miles north of Brattleboro via VT 30.

Underhill State Park (☑ 802-899-3022; www.vtstateparks.com/underhill.html; 352 Mountain Rd, Underhill; day use adult/child $4/2, campsite $20-22, lean-to $27-29; ☉ late May–mid-Oct) This teeny park on the western slopes of Mt Mansfield (25 miles northeast of Burlington) is the perfect jumping-off point for the classic climb to Vermont's highest summit via the Sunset Ridge Trail.

sites $20-22, lean-tos $27-29; ☉ late May–early Sep) This 34-acre park, 10 miles north of Woodstock off VT 12, has 39 tent/trailer sites, seven lean-tos, a beach, boat and canoe rentals, and fishing.

Shire HOTEL $$
(☑ 802-457-2211; www.shirewoodstock.com; 46 Pleasant St/US 4, Woodstock; r $119-259; ❀ ☎ ☒) Within walking distance of Woodstock's town center on US 4, this recently expanded hotel has 50 comfortable rooms, the best of which come with fireplaces, Jacuzzis and/or decks with rockers looking out over the Ottauquechee River. New beds and linens offer a comfy night's sleep, and most units have river views (the ones from room 405 are especially dreamy).

Sleep Woodstock Motel MOTEL $$
(☑ 802-332-6336; www.sleepwoodstock.com; 4324 W Woodstock Rd/US 4, Woodstock; r $88-178, 6-person ste $250-450) Prices are generally high in the Woodstock area, so this remodeled motel 5 miles west of town comes as a welcome surprise. The clean, comfy rooms have big-screen TV, coffeemaker, minifridge and microwave, service is attentive, and – outside foliage season and busy holiday weekends – the nightly rate rarely exceeds $145.

★ **Blue Horse Inn** INN $$$
(☑ 802-457-9999; www.thebluehorseinn.com; 3 Church St, Woodstock; d $179-359, ste $299-389; ☎ ☒) Jill and Tony Amato completely renovated and reopened this grand Federal Greek Revival inn in the heart of Woodstock. Set on 2 acres of grassy lawns sloping down to riverside Adirondack chairs, the red-brick and white-clapboard 19th-century home conceals a sprawling collection of fireplace-equipped common areas and carpeted guest rooms gazing out over the yard or downtown Woodstock.

Woodstock Inn & Resort

RESORT $$$

(☑ 802-332-6853; www.woodstockinn.com; 14 The Green, Woodstock; r $369-539; ✻ 🛜 🏊) Woodstock's grande dame and one of Vermont's most luxurious hotels, this resort has extensive grounds, a formal dining room, an 18-hole golf course, tennis courts, cross-country skiing, a spa and an indoor sports center. A fire blazes in the huge stone fireplace during chilly periods, enhancing the welcoming ambience. Rooms are decorated in soft, muted colors and Vermont-crafted wood furnishings.

🍴 Eating & Drinking

Mon Vert Cafe

CAFE $

(☑ 802-457-7143; www.monvertcafe.com; 28 Central St, Woodstock; breakfast $7-13, lunch $9-11; ⊙ 7:30am-5:30pm Mon-Thu, to 6:30pm Fri & Sat, 8am-5:30pm Sun) Pop into this cheerful two-level cafe for croissants, scones, egg sandwiches and maple lattes in the morning, or settle in on the front patio for salads and panini at lunchtime. A large map of Vermont and New Hampshire highlights the multitude of farms and food purveyors that provide the restaurant's locally sourced ingredients.

★ Skunk Hollow Tavern

AMERICAN $$

(☑ 802-436-2139; www.skunkhollowtavernvt.com; 12 Brownsville Rd, Hartland Four Corners; mains $13-32; ⊙ 5-10pm Wed & Fri, to 9pm Thu, Sat & Sun) Few Vermont eateries are as atmospheric as this tiny 200-year-old crossroads tavern 8 miles south of Woodstock, with worn wooden floors that ooze history. Enjoy burgers, fish and chips or shepherd's pie downstairs at the bar or in the more intimate space upstairs. Friday evenings, when there's live music and the band takes up half the room, are a special treat.

Worthy Kitchen

PUB FOOD $$

(☑ 802-457-7281; www.worthyvermont.com/kitchen; 442 Woodstock Rd/US 4, Woodstock; mains $13-32; ⊙ 4-9pm Mon-Thu, to 10pm Fri, from 11:30am Sat, to 9pm Sun) A couple of miles east of town, this laid-back brewpub draws crowds with its tasty burgers, organic salads and farm-to-table comfort food. Daily specials – from buttermilk-fried chicken to mac-and-cheese with local Plymouth cheddar – are scrawled on giant blackboards, along with a frequently rotating lineup of 18 microbrews (mostly from Vermont or elsewhere in New England).

White Cottage Snack Bar

AMERICAN $$

(☑ 802-457-3455; www.whitecottagesnackbar.com; 863 W Woodstock Rd, Woodstock; fast food $3-9, seafood $6-27; ⊙ 11am-10pm early May–mid-Oct) A Woodstock institution, this glorified snack shack has been serving loyal locals fried clams, burgers and ice cream by the riverside since 1957.

★ Mangalitsa

BISTRO $$$

(☑ 802-457-7467; www.mangalitsavt.com; 61 Central St; mains $26-32; ⊙ 5-9pm) Launched to universal acclaim, this sweet, chef-owned bistro is a welcome addition to Woodstock's dining scene. The ever-changing menu of small and large plates draws on seasonal ingredients like fiddlehead ferns, house-butchered meats, whole fish and produce from local purveyors such as Fat Sheep Farm. With only 22 seats it fills up fast; book ahead.

★ Simon Pearce Restaurant

MODERN AMERICAN $$$

(☑ 802-295-1470; www.simonpearce.com; 1760 Quechee Main St, Quechee; mains lunch $14-19, dinner $23-33; ⊙ 11:30am-2:45pm & 5:30-9pm) Few views in Vermont compare with those from the window tables overlooking spectacular Ottauquechee Falls in Simon Pearce's dining room, suspended over the river in a converted brick mill. Local ingredients are used to fine effect in salads, cheese plates and dishes such as braised lamb shoulder or cider-brined chicken. The restaurant's stemware is hand-blown in the adjacent **glass workshop** (☑ 802-295-2711; www.simonpearce.com; 1760 Quechee Main St, Quechee; ⊙ 10am-9pm).

Long Trail Brewing Company

BREWERY

(☑ 802-672-5011; www.longtrail.com; 5520 US 4 at VT 100A, Bridgewater Corners; ⊙ 10am-7pm) Halfway between Killington and Woodstock, the brewer of 'Vermont's No 1 Selling Amber' draws crowds for self-guided brewery tours and a sunny riverside deck where you can enjoy sandwiches, burgers, salads (mains $12 to $17) and, of course, beer. Order a four-beer sampler ($7 or $8) to taste a mix of classic and seasonal brews.

ℹ Information

Quechee Gorge Visitors Center (☑ 802-295-7900; www.hartfordvtchamber.com; 5966 Woodstock Rd, Quechee; ⊙ 9am-5pm Jun-Oct, 10am-4pm Nov-May) Well-stocked tourist office just east of the Quechee Gorge bridge, dispensing information about Quechee and the gorge.

Woodstock Welcome Center (☎802-457-3555; www.woodstockvt.com; 3 Mechanic St, Woodstock; ◉9am-5pm) Woodstock's welcome center is housed in a lovely red building on a riverside backstreet, two blocks from the village green. There's also a small information booth on the village green itself. Both places can help with accommodations.

ℹ Getting There & Away

For drivers, it's a straight shot from Woodstock to Burlington (1¾ hours, 95 miles) via US 4 east and I-89 north. For Killington (20 miles, 30 minutes), take US 4 west.

Greyhound buses (www.greyhound.com) from Boston and Amtrak trains (www.amtrak.com/vermonter-train) from New York and Washington, DC, stop at nearby White River Junction. From either station, it's a 15-mile trip to Woodstock. Vermont Translines (www.vttranslines.com) runs once-daily buses from Woodstock to Quechee ($1.50, 15 minutes), White River Junction ($3.50, 30 minutes) and Killington ($5, 40 minutes).

Killington Mountain

POP 770

The largest ski resort in the East – with a season that typically runs from October to May – Killington spans seven mountains, dominated by Vermont's second highest summit, 4241ft Killington Peak. Killington boasts the largest snowmaking system in North America, with numerous outdoor activities centrally located on the mountain, a host of services concentrated along Killington Rd just below and lodging for more than 20,000 people within a 20-mile radius. The surrounding community lacks the historic charm and village atmosphere of places like Stowe and the Mad River Valley – but if skiing is your primary focus, Killington may be exactly what you're looking for.

🏃 Activities

★ Killington Resort   SKIING

(☎info 800-734-9435, reservations 800-621-6867; www.killington.com; 4763 Killington Rd; lift tickets adult/child/senior $124/95/105) Known as the 'Beast of the East,' Vermont's prime ski resort is enormous, yet runs efficiently enough to avoid overcrowding. It has five separate lodges, each with a different emphasis, as well as 29 lifts and 92 miles of trails. The ski season runs from November through early May, enhanced by America's largest snowmaking system.

More than 200 runs snake down Killington's seven mountains (4241ft Killington Peak, 3967ft Pico Mountain, 3800ft Skye Peak, 3610ft Ramshead Peak, 3592ft Snowdon Peak, 3295ft Bear Mountain and 2456ft Sunrise Mountain), covering 1977 acres of slopes. A quarter are considered easy, a third moderate and the rest difficult. Snowboarders will find six challenging terrain parks, including superpipes with 18ft walls.

K-1 Lodge has the K-1 Express Gondola, which transports up to 3000 skiers per hour in heated cars along a 2.5-mile cable and is the highest lift in Vermont. **Snowshed Lodge** is an ideal base for adults looking for lessons or refresher courses. Free-ride enthusiasts should check out **Bear Mountain Lodge** for pipe action, tree skiing or rail jibbing, not to mention the double-black-diamond Outer Limits, the longest, steepest mogul run in the east. **Ramshead Lodge** caters to children and families, as well as those looking for easier terrain, while **Skyeship Lodge** is the home of the Skyeship Gondola, a two-stage gondola with quick and direct access to Skye Peak. Each lodge has food courts, restaurants, bars and ski shops.

In summer, there's mountain biking and golfing, and in fall, leaf-peepers can ride the resort's famous K-1 Express Gondola to Killington Peak for spectacular views.

Killington Mountain
Bike Park   MOUNTAIN BIKING

(☎802-422-6232; 4763 Killington Rd; full-day lift ticket & trail pass adult/child $60/45, incl bike rental $165/125; ◉late Jun–mid-Oct) Bikers can take the Snowshed Express Quad to access Killington Resort's newest trails for beginning and intermediate riders, or the classic 1.25-mile K-1 gondola ride to the summit of Killington Peak where 45 miles of trails await, including plenty of challenging free-ride terrain. The Killington Bike Shop at Snowshed Lodge rents out top-quality mountain bikes.

🛏 Sleeping

Gifford Woods
State Park   CAMPGROUND $

(☎802-775-5354; www.vtstateparks.com/gifford.html; 34 Gifford Woods Rd; campsites $20-22, lean-tos $27-29, cabins $50; ◉mid-May–mid-Oct) A half mile north of US 4 and VT 100, this park has four cabins, 19 lean-tos and 21 tent/trailer sites set on 114 acres. Added bonuses

DON'T MISS

VERMONT LEAF PEEPS

Here are a few spots to see Vermont's famous fall foliage at its best.

Mt Mansfield Vermont's highest peak is gorgeous when draped in fall colors, especially when an early snowfall dusts the summit white. The best panoramic perspectives are from Stowe, Jeffersonville, Cambridge and Underhill. Hikers can also experience the full sweep of color from the mountaintop; one of the prettiest routes is the Sunset Ridge Trail in Underhill State Park.

Grafton Villages don't get any cuter than Grafton, which looks like it was airlifted in from an earlier century. The white clapboard buildings are even more photogenic when contrasted against fiery leaves and a brilliant blue sky.

Lake Willoughby (p318) The technicolor majesty of changing maples looks especially dramatic on the steep slopes surrounding this fjord-like lake in Vermont's Northeast Kingdom.

Mad River Glen (p298) Ride the nation's last commercially operating single chairlift – the same one that whisks skiers to the mountaintop in winter – to admire spectacular panoramic views of the Mad River Valley's fall foliage.

Vermont Rte 100 A road-tripper's dream, this classic driving route through the heart of the Green Mountains shows off Vermont's farm country in its full autumnal splendor.

Merck Forest (p287) Climb to the barn meadow at this environmental education center in southwestern Vermont for breathtaking vistas of the Taconic Mountains in bright rainbow colors.

---

are the playground, fishing in Kent Pond and hiking trails, including easy access to the Appalachian Trail.

★**Killington Motel** MOTEL $$
(☑802-773-9535; www.killingtonmotel.com; 1946 US 4; r May-Oct $72-124, Nov-Apr $78-178; ✯ ☎) Way more welcoming than your typical motel thanks to the personal attention of longtime owners Stephen and Robin, this clean, well-maintained place just west of the VT 100/US 4 junction offers some of Killington's best rates. Breakfast features home-baked breads and muffins, and coffee roasted on-site in small batches by Stephen himself.

Vermont Inn INN $$
(☑802-775-0708; www.vermontinn.com; 78 Cream Hill Rd, Mendon; d $110-275; @ ☎ ✹) This 19th-century red clapboard inn straddles a 5-acre parcel in the Green Mountains 10 minutes west of Killington. It's popular with skiers not only for its proximity to the slopes, but also for its sauna, hot tub, full country breakfast, afternoon tea and fireplaces in many guest rooms. Summertime draws include a swimming pool and outdoor children's play area.

Killington Mountain Lodge HOTEL $$
(☑802-422-4302; www.killingtonmountainlodge.com; 2617 Killington Rd; r $139-289; @ ☎) Well situated a third of the way up the mountain, this hotel has all the modern conveniences, in addition to a Jacuzzi, exercise rooms, tennis courts and a spa.

✖ Eating

Sunup Bakery BAKERY $
(☑802-422-3865; www.sunupbakery.com; 2250 Killington Rd; sandwiches $5-9; ⊗7am-5pm Nov-Apr, reduced hours May-Oct) Skiers flock here at the crack of dawn for freshly baked muffins, sticky buns and bagels, breakfast sandwiches, New England–roasted coffees, soy lattes, smoothies and juices. The bakery also makes sandwiches and box lunches to go.

Liquid Art Coffeehouse INTERNATIONAL $$
(☑802-422-2787; www.liquidartvt.com; 37 Miller Brook Rd; mains breakfast & lunch $5-11, dinner $11-25; ⊗8am-9pm Mon & Tue, to 10pm Wed-Fri, from 7am Sat & Sun) Much more than a coffeehouse, Liquid Art serves everything from delicious breakfast and lunch sandwiches to dinners of mussels, lasagna, roasted garlic tofu or filet mignon with Gorgonzola. Good coffee drinks and 'warm-me-up' cocktails

such as Bacardi-infused spiced cider round out the experience, all served in a bright, high-ceilinged barnlike space with classic post-and-beam architecture.

Sushi Yoshi JAPANESE, CHINESE $$
(☎802-422-4241; www.vermontsushi.com; 1807 Killington Rd; mains $14-25; ⊗11:30am-10pm Sun-Thu, to 11pm Fri & Sat) A gourmet Chinese restaurant that has successfully added Japanese hibachi fare to its repertoire, Sushi Yoshi is a perennial favorite along Killington's main drag.

🍸 Drinking & Entertainment

Jax Food & Games Bar BAR
(☎802-422-5334; www.jaxfoodandgames.com; 1667 Killington Rd; ⊗3pm-2am) Combines an indoor game-room-bar with live music, burgers, a good beer selection and an outdoor deck.

McGrath's Irish Pub LIVE MUSIC
(☎802-775-7181; www.innatlongtrail.com/mcgraths-irish-pub.html; 709 US 4; ⊗3-11pm Mon-Thu, to midnight Fri, from 11:30am Sat, to 11pm Sun) Guinness on tap, Vermont's largest selection of Irish whiskies, and live Irish music on Friday and Saturday evenings.

Pickle Barrel LIVE MUSIC
(☎802-422-3035; www.picklebarrelnightclub.com; 1741 Killington Rd; ⊗8pm-2am Oct–mid-Apr, Fri & Sat only rest of year) With four bars, three stages and two dance floors, this popular three-story club showcases great rock-and-roll bands and other national-caliber acts. Best of all, there's a free shuttle bus to get you home in one piece.

❶ Information

Killington Central Reservations (☎800-621-6867; www.killington.com; 4763 Killington Rd; ⊗8am-5pm Mon-Fri, to 4pm Sat & Sun) Advice on accommodations, including package deals.
Killington Welcome Center (☎802-773-4181; www.killingtonpico.org; 2319 US 4; ⊗9am-5pm Mon-Fri, 10am-2pm Sat & Sun) General tourist information, conveniently located on US 4.

❶ Getting There & Away

To reach Killington from Burlington (1¾ hours, 95 miles) take US 7 south to VT 4 east. From Manchester, VT (70 minutes, 45 miles), take US 7 north and VT 4 east.

Vermont Translines (www.vttranslines.com) offers once-daily bus service from Killington to Woodstock and other points east and west along US 4.

Middlebury
📍802 / POP 8600

Built astride the falls of Otter Creek in the late 18th century, Middlebury is surrounded by the rolling farmland of Vermont's Champlain Valley. In 1800 Middlebury College was founded here, and it has been synonymous with the town ever since. Poet Robert Frost (1874–1963) owned a farm in nearby Ripton and cofounded the college's renowned Bread Loaf School of English in the hills above town. The college is also famous for its summer foreign language programs, which have been drawing linguists here for over a century. Middlebury's history of marble quarrying is evident in the college's architecture: many buildings are made with white marble and gray limestone.

Modern-day Middlebury is the seat of Addison County, whose role as Vermont's leading agricultural producer is reflected in the wealth of fresh produce at the local food co-op and the profusion of orchards and farms in the surrounding countryside.

⊙ Sights

★**Otter Creek Falls** WATERFALL
The village of Middlebury grew up around the broad falls of Otter Creek, whose roaring waters provided power for a number of 19th-century mills. For gorgeous views, head down to the pedestrian bridge at the foot of the falls, accessed via Mill St or the pedestrian path off Printer's Alley (opposite Middlebury's town green).

Henry Sheldon Museum MUSEUM
(☎802-388-2117; www.henrysheldonmuseum.org; 1 Park St; adult/child $5/3; ⊗10am-5pm Tue-Sat year-round, from 1pm Sun late May–mid-Oct) This 1829 Federal-style brick mansion-turned-museum owes its existence to Henry Sheldon, a town clerk, church organist, storekeeper and avid collector of 19th-century Vermontiana. His collection runs the gamut from folk art and furniture to paintings and bric-a-brac, but is highlighted by an upstairs room devoted to such curios as a cigar holder made of chicken claws and Sheldon's own teeth.

Middlebury College Museum of Art MUSEUM
(☎802-443-5007; http://museum.middlebury.edu; 72 Porter Field Rd; ⊗10am-5pm Tue-Fri, from noon Sat & Sun) FREE This small but diverse

museum presents rotating exhibitions alongside a fine permanent collection that includes an Egyptian sarcophagus, Cypriot pottery, 19th-century European and American sculpture, and works by such luminaries as Pablo Picasso, Salvador Dalí, Alice Neel and Andy Warhol.

University of Vermont Morgan Horse Farm
FARM
(☏802-388-2011; www.uvm.edu/morgan; 74 Battell Dr, Weybridge; adult/teen/child $5/4/2; ⊙9am-4pm May-Oct; ᵢ) See registered Morgan horses and tour their stables at this farm 3 miles north of Middlebury. Known for their strength, agility, endurance and longevity, and named after Justin Morgan, who brought his thoroughbred Arabian colt to Vermont in 1789, these little horses became America's first native breed, useful for heavy work, carriage draft, riding and even war service.

Champlain Orchards
FARM
(☏802-897-2777; www.champlainorchards.com; 3597 VT 74 W, Shoreham; ⊙9am-5pm; ᵢ) 🍎 This century-old orchard 16 miles southwest of Middlebury sells sweet and hard cider year-round, with pick-your-own cherries, peaches, plums and berries starting in June. Its busiest season is fall, when more than 100 varieties of apples are ripe for the picking and the annual Harvest Festival fills the air with fiddle tunes and family fun.

🏃 Activities

Middlebury College Snow Bowl
SKIING
(☏802-443-7669; www.middleburysnowbowl. com; VT 125; lift ticket Mon-Fri $35, Sat & Sun $55; ⊙9am-4pm Mon-Fri, 8:30am-4:30pm Sat & Sun Dec-Mar; ᵢ) One of Vermont's most affordable, least crowded ski areas, this college-owned facility has only three lifts, but with trails for all levels, nonexistent lift lines and prices half of what you'd pay elsewhere, who's complaining? Middlebury's 'graduation on skis' takes place here each February: graduates slalom down the slopes in full valedictory regalia, their dark robes fluttering amid the snowflakes.

Rikert Nordic Center
SKIING
(☏802-443-2744; www.rikertnordic.com; 106 College Cross Rd, Ripton; trail pass $25; ⊙8:30am-4:30pm Nov-Mar; ᵢ) Middlebury College's cross-country ski center offers over 30 miles of trails in Green Mountain National Forest, in a gorgeous mountain setting along VT 125, an easy 12-mile drive from Middlebury.

🛏 Sleeping

★On the Creek B&B
B&B $
(☏802-388-6517; www.onthecreekbedandbreakfast.com; 284 Pulp Mill Bridge Rd, Weybridge; d $125, cottage for 2/4 people $175/275) At this lovely 19th-century brick home overlooking Otter Creek, two upstairs rooms blend character and comfort, with polished plank

---

HIKING VERMONT'S LONG LONG TRAIL

Built between 1912 and 1930 as America's first long-distance hiking trail, the Long Trail of Vermont follows the south–north ridge of the Green Mountains for 264 miles, from Massachusetts to Canada. A little less than half of the trail is located inside the **Green Mountain National Forest** (☏802-747-6700; www.fs.usda.gov/gmfl).

Often only 3ft wide, the trail traverses streams and forests, skirts ponds and weaves up and down mountains to bare summits like Mt Abraham, Mt Mansfield and Camel's Hump. From up top, hikers enjoy exceptional vistas, with wave after wave of hillside gently rolling back to a sea of green dotted with the occasional pasture or meadow.

Three excellent guides to the trail – *Long Trail Guide*, the *Day Hiker's Guide to Vermont* and *The Long Trail End-to-Ender's Guide* – are published by the venerable Green Mountain Club (GMC), which originally constructed the trail and still maintains it. All three guides are packed with nitty-gritty details on equipment sales and repairs, mail drops and B&Bs that provide trailhead shuttle services.

The GMC maintains more than 60 rustic lodges and lean-tos along the trail, all spaced at 5- to 7-mile intervals. Hikers can easily walk from one shelter to the next in a day, but it's imperative to bring a tent as shelters often fill up.

While the trail is wonderful for multiday excursions, it's also popular for day hikes. Call or drop by the Green Mountain Club Visitors Center (p316), or visit its website for information and itinerary planning advice.

floors, down comforters and bedside lamps. Friendly hosts Zelia and Gary serve full breakfasts featuring fresh-squeezed OJ and home-baked scones, and offer free use of bikes and a canoe for the half-hour paddle into town. The adjacent self-catering cottage sleeps four.

Inn on the Green
INN **$$**

(☑ 802-388-7512; www.innonthegreen.com; 71 S Pleasant St; r $149-259; ⊛ @ 🛜) Lovingly restored to its original stateliness, this 1803 Federal-style home has spacious rooms and suites in the main house and in an adjoining carriage house (the latter's rooms are more modern). One of its signature treats is a continental breakfast delivered to your room each morning.

Swift House Inn
INN **$$**

(☑ 802-388-9925; www.swifthouseinn.com; 25 Stewart Lane; r $165-299; 🛜) Two blocks north of the town green, this grand white Federal mansion (1814) is surrounded by formal lawns and gardens. Luxurious standard rooms in the main house and adjacent carriage house are supplemented by suites with fireplaces, sitting areas and Jacuzzis. Other welcome luxuries include a steam room and sauna, a cozy pub, a library and a sun porch.

Middlebury Inn
INN **$$**

(☑ 802-388-4961; www.middleburyinn.com; 14 Court Sq/VT 7; r $175-241; 🛜) Directly opposite the town green, this inn's fine old main building (1827) has beautifully restored formal public rooms and charming guest rooms with all the modern conveniences. The adjacent Porter Mansion, with Victorian-style rooms, is also full of attractive architectural details. Lower-priced units in the motel-like modern annex out back are considerably less appealing.

✖ Eating

Middlebury Bagel & Deli
BAKERY **$**

(☑ 802-388-0859; www.facebook.com/middleburybagel; 11 Washington St; breakfasts $4-10; ⊙6am-2pm Mon-Fri, to 1pm Sat & Sun) Since 1979, the Rubright family has been showing up at 4am daily to bake some of New England's finest doughnuts and bagels. Skiers on their way to the slopes, workers en route to the job site and professors headed for class all converge here for warm-from-the-oven apple fritters, doughnuts and bagel sandwiches, along with omelets and other breakfast treats.

BLUEBERRIES WITH A VIEW

About 15 miles southeast of Middlebury, an unpaved forest service road leads to the **Green Mountain National Forest Blueberry Management Area**, one of central Vermont's best-kept secrets. This vast hillside patch of wild blueberries is ripe for the picking between late July and early August, and the view over the surrounding mountains is fantastic.

Otter Creek Bakery
BAKERY **$**

(☑ 802-388-3371; www.ottercreekbakery.com; 14 College St; sandwiches & salads $6.50-9.50; ⊙7am-5:30pm Mon-Sat, to 3pm Sun) This bakery with outdoor seating is popular for takeout pastries, strong coffee and creative sandwiches. Traveling with a pooch? It'll lick your face if you buy it a Twisted Puppy Biscuit.

A&W Drive-in
BURGERS **$**

(☑ 802-388-2876; www.awrestaurants.com; 1557 US 7; mains $3-10; ⊙11:30am-8pm late May–Sep) For a slice of retro Americana, stop at Middlebury's A&W Drive-In. Among the few remaining New England branches of this century-old national chain, it's the only one where carhops on roller skates still deliver root-beer floats, cheeseburgers, onion rings and other artery-clogging goodness directly to your car window.

🍷 Drinking & Nightlife

Stonecutter Spirits
COCKTAIL BAR

(☑ 802-388-3000; www.stonecutterspirits.com; ⊙noon-8pm Thu-Sat, to 4pm Sun) Free samples of Stonecutters' heritage cask whiskey and single barrel gin are the top draw at this Middlebury-based distillery, but it's worth sticking around for the creative cocktails ($11) and a game or two of shuffleboard. The award-winning gin, flavored with cardamom, orange peel, juniper, green tea and rose, is the real standout.

Woodchuck Cider House
BREWERY

(☑ 802-385-3656; www.woodchuck.com/ciderhouse; 1321 Exchange St; ⊙11am-6pm Wed-Fri, to 5pm Sat & Sun) North America's largest cidery (producer of hard cider) offers pints, cider cocktails, bar snacks and tastes (four for $3) at its state-of-the-art production facility 2 miles north of Middlebury. The rotating lineup of 20 ciders on tap ranges from classics

DON'T MISS

ECO PIZZA & GOURMET BEER

In this neck of the woods, uttering the name 'American Flatbread' to a local will always elicit an 'ooh' or a 'yum,' followed usually by some proud rhetoric and possibly a little drool. And deservedly so. The home grown concept is simple: a menu revolving around farm-fresh salads and custom-made flatbreads (don't call it pizza or they'll come after you with the paddle) topped with locally sourced organic cheeses, meat and veggies, accompanied by Vermont microbrews and set in inspiring surroundings that make you just want to tuck in deeper, especially in winter.

The original location (there are now three others) on pretty **Lareau Farm** (☑802-496-8856; www.americanflatbread.com/restaurants/waitsfield-vt; 46 Lareau Rd, Waitsfield; flatbread $14-22; ⊙5-9:30pm Thu-Sun; 🏠) in the Mad River Valley has been firing the oven against its gorgeous Green Mountain backdrop for over twenty years.

The **Middlebury** (☑802-388-3300; www.americanflatbread.com/restaurants/middle bury-vt; 137 Maple St; flatbreads $9-25; ⊙5-9pm Tue-Sat) location occupies a cavernous marble-block building with a bustling bar and blazing fire that keeps things cozy. There's a 'hearth' (branch) in **Burlington** (☑802-861-2999; www.americanflatbread.com; 115 St Paul St; flatbreads $14-23; ⊙11:30am-3pm & 5-11:30pm Mon-Fri, 11:30am-11:30pm Sat & Sun) as well.

like pear, raspberry and amber (Wood-chuck's flagship apple cider) to experimental and seasonal flavors like pumpkin, ginger and smoked apple.

Otter Creek Brewing BREWERY
(☑802-388-0727; www.ottercreekbrewing.com; 793 Exchange St; ⊙11am-6pm Sat-Thu, to 7pm Fri) One of New England's best breweries, Otter Creek makes fine craft beers, from year-round favorites like Berner IPA to seasonal brews like Oktoberfest and Drip Drop Coffee Stout. At the company's brewpub, OCB Pub Space, sip a flight of four 5oz pours ($8) and watch the brewers through viewing windows. There's free live music Fridays from 5pm to 7pm.

ℹ Information

Addison County Chamber of Commerce
(☑802-388-7951; www.addisoncounty.com; 93 Court St; ⊙9am-5pm Mon-Fri) About half a mile south of the town green, this place dispenses information about Middlebury and the rest of Addison County.

ℹ Getting There & Away

Middlebury is right on US 7. To drive here from Burlington (50 minutes, 35 miles), take US 7 south; from Manchester (1½ hours, 65 miles), take US 7 or VT 30 north.

ACTR (www.actr-vt.org) runs early-morning and evening buses north to Burlington ($4, 1½ hours), while Vermont Translines (www.vttrans lines.com) has once-daily service south to Manchester ($16.50, two hours) and Bennington ($22.50, 2½ hours).

Mad River Valley

POP 1680 (WARREN); 1700 (WAITSFIELD)

North of Killington, VT 100 is one of the finest stretches of road in the country: a bucolic mix of rolling hills, covered bridges, white steeples and fertile farmland. Here you'll find the Mad River Valley, where the pretty villages of Waitsfield and Warren nestle in the shadow of two major ski areas, Sugarbush and Mad River Glen.

For tantalizing valley perspectives, explore the glorious back roads on either side of VT 100. Leave the pavement behind and meander up the valley's eastern side, following Brook, E Warren, Common, North and Pony Farm Rds from Warren north to Moretown; or head west from Warren over Lincoln Gap Rd, the highest, steepest and perhaps prettiest of all the 'gap roads' that run east to west over the Green Mountains. Stop at Lincoln Gap (2424ft) for the scenic 3-mile hike up the **Long Trail** to Mt Abraham (4017ft), Vermont's fifth-highest peak.

🏃 Activities

★**Mad River Glen** SKIING
(☑802-496-3551; www.madriverglen.com; VT 17, Waitsfield; lift tickets adult/child $89/72) The most rugged lift-served ski area in the East, Mad River is also one of the quirkiest. Managed by an owner cooperative, not a major ski corporation, it largely eschews artificial snowmaking, prohibits snowboarding and proudly continues to use America's last

operating single chairlift, a vintage 1948 model. It's 6 miles west of Waitsfield.

Sugarbush
SKIING

(☑802-583-6300; www.sugarbush.com; 102 Forrest Dr, Warren; adult/child lift tickets $97/77) Lincoln Peak (3975ft) and Mt Ellen (4083ft) are the main features of this large resort 6 miles southwest of Waitsfield. In all, 16 lifts afford skiers and snowboarders access to three terrain parks, 97 acres of woods and 111 trails, including backcountry runs like Paradise and Castlerock, which hurtle through a tapestry of maple, oak, birch, spruce, pine and balsam.

Clearwater Sports
BICYCLE RENTAL, WATER SPORTS

(☑802-496-2708; www.clearwatersports.com; 4147 Main St/VT 100, Waitsfield; ⊘10am-6pm Mon-Fri, from 9am Sat, 10am-5pm Sun) This friendly shop rents river-floating tubes, canoes, kayaks, stand-up paddleboards, hybrid bikes, snowshoes, rocket sleds, telemark demo gear and many other types of sports equipment. It also organizes guided kayak trips on the Winooski and Mad Rivers, along with custom tours and even yoga classes on stand-up paddleboards in a mountain lake!

Sugarbush Soaring
GLIDING

(☑802-496-2290; www.sugarbushsoaring.com; 2355 Airport Rd, Warren; 15/20/30/45min rides $109/134/175/209; ⊘mid-May–Oct) This outfit can take you soaring quietly through the skies, far above the mountains and river valleys, in a glider, which is kept aloft by updrafts of warm air. It's especially beautiful in early October, when central Vermont's trees are fully ablaze.

Vermont Icelandic Horse Farm
HORSEBACK RIDING

(☑802-496-7141; www.icelandichorses.com; 3061 N Fayston Rd, Waitsfield; 1-3hr rides $60-120, full day incl lunch $220, multiday treks $675-1695; ⊘by appointment; ⊕) Explore the scenic hills above Waitsfield on beautiful, gentle and easy-to-ride Icelandic horses. Rides range from hour-long jaunts to multiday inn-to-inn treks.

Ole's Cross Country Ski Center
SKIING

(☑802-496-3430; www.olesxc.com; 2355 Airport Rd, Warren; adult/child ski pass $18/15, snowshoe pass $12/10; ⊘9am-5pm) This friendly local Nordic ski center up near Warren's airport has 20 miles of groomed cross-country ski trails.

🛏 Sleeping

★ Tevere Hostel
HOSTEL $

(☑802-496-9222; www.hosteltevere.com; 203 Powderhound Rd, Warren; dm $35-40; ☜) One of New England's coolest hostels, Tevere spreads across two floors of an artfully renovated old farmhouse in Warren, just downhill from Sugarbush resort. Four-to seven-bed dorms with comfy mattresses and colorful walls are complemented by a lounge with a blazing woodstove and an animated bar-restaurant that hosts live music on Saturdays throughout the ski season.

Mad River Barn
INN $$

(☑802-496-3310; www.madriverbarn.com; 2849 Mill Brook Rd/VT 17, Waitsfield; r $140-220; ☜⊕) Owners Heather and Andrew (assisted by their Welsh corgi, Gizmo) have thoroughly revamped this family-friendly, 1940s-era lodge between Sugarbush and Mad River Glen ski areas, using recycled materials to rustic-chic effect while amping up comfort and amenities. The refurbished central barn houses a spacious, welcoming pub with Vermont microbrews on tap, warm wood paneling and a massive stone fireplace.

Waitsfield Inn
INN $$

(☑802-496-3979; www.waitsfieldinn.com; 5267 Main St/VT 100, Waitsfield; d $125-170; ☜) In the heart of Waitsfield village, this converted parsonage has 12 tastefully decorated rooms as well as various nooks and dining areas to unwind in. All rooms have private bathrooms and some even have four-poster beds.

DON'T MISS

BARTLETT FALLS

Where do locals head when the mercury starts hitting devilish highs? One popular spot is **Bartlett Falls**, a heavenly swimming hole hidden just off the main road near Bristol, halfway between Warren and Middlebury. This gorgeous natural pool sits at the foot of a pretty waterfall, flanked by cliffs that make a popular jumping-off point for local youths. With shallow and deep sections and plenty of forested shade, it's perfect for all ages.

Look for the parked cars along Lincoln Gap Rd, a half-mile east of VT 116.

Mad River Inn
INN $$

(☑ 802-496-7900; www.madriverinn.com; 243 Tremblay Rd, Waitsfield; r $115-150; ❄ 🛜) This 19th-century Victorian farmhouse overlooking pretty gardens and cornfields has seven simple, old-fashioned rooms and a two-room suite, complemented by a Queen Anne dining room where guests enjoy the included three-course breakfasts and afternoon tea by the fireside.

Sugarbush Village
ACCOMMODATION SERVICES $$

(☑ 802-583-3000; www.sugarbushvillage.com; 145 Mountainside Dr, Warren; 1-bedroom condo per night from $150) A large selection of slope-side condos is rented out by Sugarbush Village, right at the ski area. Rental prices depend on condo size and location, and your date of arrival and length of stay.

★ Inn at Round Barn Farm
INN $$$

(☑ 802-496-2276; www.theroundbarn.com; 1661 E Warren Rd, Waitsfield; r $179-359; 🛜 ❄) This place gets its name from the adjacent 1910 round barn – among the few authentic examples remaining in Vermont. The decidedly upscale inn has antique-furnished rooms with mountain views, gas fireplaces and canopy beds. All overlook the meadows and mountains. In winter guests leave their shoes at the door to preserve the hardwood floors. The country-style breakfast is huge.

✗ Eating

★ Warren Store
SANDWICHES $

(☑ 802-496-3864; www.warrenstore.com; 284 Main St, Warren; sandwiches & light meals $5-9; ☺ 7:45am-7pm) This atmospheric country store serves the area's best sandwiches along with delicious pastries and breakfasts. In summer, linger over coffee and the *New York Times* on the front porch, or eat on the deck overlooking the waterfall, then descend for a cool dip among river-sculpted rocks. Browsers will love the store's eclectic upstairs collection of clothing, toys and jewelry.

Peasant
MODERN AMERICAN $$

(☑ 802-496-6856; www.peasantvt.com; 40 Bridge St, Waitsfield; mains $25-28; ☺ 5:30-9pm Thu-Mon) Living up to its tagline 'a simple feast,' Peasant delivers seasonal farm-to-table treats that can vary from hearty cassoulet in the dead of winter to maple-glazed salmon with locally grown veggies in summer, all complemented by an ample choice of beer, wine and cocktails. Look for it in a cozy slate-blue house in the village center.

🍷 Drinking & Entertainment

★ Lawson's Finest Liquids
MICROBREWERY

(☑ 802-496-4677; www.lawsonsfinest.com; 155 Carroll Rd, Waitsfield; ☺ noon-7pm) For years, Mad River locals would line up for special releases of Sean and Karen Lawson's homebrew, dispensed from a converted maple-sugar shack at their home in Warren. Then the Lawsons opened this cavernous timber-framed brewery, taproom and store in Waitsfield, with 16 beers on tap, a convivial bar and fireside seating indoors and out. Beer-lovers, rejoice!

Big Picture Café-Theater
CINEMA

(☑ 802-496-8994; www.bigpicturetheater.info; 48 Carroll Rd) This popular community hangout screens movies five nights a week – doubling as a cafe where skiers warm up with coffee, breakfast and delicious homemade maple doughnuts each morning, and return for burgers and beer after a day on the slopes.

❶ Information

Mad River Valley Visitor Information (☑ 802-496-3409; www.madrivervalley.com; cnr Main & Bridge Sts, Waitsfield; ☺ 10am-5pm Wed-Sat, to 3pm Sun) The valley's new info center in downtown Waitsfield can assist with lodging and the latest skiing info.

❶ Getting There & Away

From Waitsfield, take VT 100 to Stowe (40 minutes, 24 miles); for Montpelier (30 minutes, 19 miles), take VT 100B north and US 2 east.

NORTHERN VERMONT

Northern Vermont is home to the state's largest city, Burlington, and the state capital, Montpelier. Even so, this area still has all the rural charms found elsewhere in the Green Mountain State. Even within Burlington, cafe-lined streets coexist with scenic paths along Lake Champlain and the Winooski River. Further north, the pastoral Northeast Kingdom offers a full range of outdoor activities, from skiing to biking, in the heart of the mountains.

Burlington

📞 802 / POP 42,250

Perched on the shores of Lake Champlain, Vermont's largest city would be considered tiny in most other states, but its relatively diminutive size is one of Burlington's charms. With the University of Vermont (UVM) swelling the city by 13,000 students and contributing to its vibrant cultural and social life, Burlington has a spirited, youthful vibe and more ethnic diversity than anywhere else in Vermont.

Burlington's walkable downtown, bike paths, farmers market, fabulous food co-op, and proximity to nature earn it accolades as one of America's greenest and most livable cities. The city's ongoing Great Streets Initiative (www.greatstreetsbtv.com) aims to sustain that momentum, with wider sidewalks, enhanced green spaces and reduced pollution.

Burlington makes an attractive base for exploring the rest of northwestern Vermont. Two of Vermont's crown jewels, Shelburne Farms and the Shelburne Museum, lie just 15 minutes south, while Stowe and the Green Mountains are within an hour's drive.

◎ Sights

★ Intervale Center   FARM

(📞 802-660-0440; www.intervale.org; 180 Intervale Rd) FREE You'd never guess it standing on a busy Burlington street corner, but one of Vermont's most idyllic green spaces is less than 2 miles from downtown. Tucked among the lazy curves of the Winooski River, Burlington's Intervale encompasses half a dozen organic farms and a delightful trail network, open 365 days a year for hiking, biking, skiing, bird-watching, paddling and more.

★ Shelburne Farms   FARM

(📞 802-985-8686; www.shelburnefarms.org; 1611 Harbor Rd, Shelburne; adult/child $8/5 mid-May–mid-Oct, free rest of year; ⊙ 9am-5:30pm mid-May–mid-Oct, 10am-5pm rest of year; 🚼) 🌿 In 1886 William Seward Webb and Lila Vanderbilt Webb built themselves a magnificent country estate on the shores of Lake Champlain. The 1400-acre farm, designed by landscape architect Frederick Law Olmsted (who also designed New York's Central Park and Boston's Emerald Necklace), was both a country house for the Webbs and a working farm, with stunning lakefront perspectives.

The 24-bedroom English-style country manor (completed in 1899), now an inn (p305), is surrounded by working farm buildings inspired by European romanticism.

★ Shelburne Museum   MUSEUM

(📞 802-985-3346; www.shelburnemuseum.org; 6000 Shelburne Rd/US 7, Shelburne; adult/child $25/14 May-Oct, $10/5 Nov-Apr; ⊙ 10am-5pm daily May-Dec, Wed-Sun Jan-Apr; 🚼) This extraordinary 45-acre museum, 9 miles south of Burlington, showcases the priceless Americana collections of Electra Havemeyer Webb (1888–1960) and her parents – 150,000 objects in all. The mix of folk art, decorative arts and more is housed in 39 historic buildings, most of them moved here from other parts of New England to ensure their preservation.

★ Church Street Marketplace   MARKET

(www.churchstmarketplace.com; 🚼) Burlington's pulse can often be taken along this four-block pedestrian zone running from Pearl to Main Sts. When the weather's good, buskers (licensed by the town), food and craft vendors, soapbox demagogues, restless students, curious tourists and kids climbing on rocks mingle in a vibrant human parade.

Waterfront   WATERFRONT

A five-minute walk from downtown, Burlington's delightfully uncommercialized waterfront features a scenic, low-key promenade, a 7.5-mile bike path, a pier for Lake Champlain boat trips and the family-friendly Echo aquarium.

Shelburne Vineyard   WINERY

(📞 802-985-8222; www.shelburnevineyard.com; 6308 Shelburne Rd/US 7, Shelburne; guided tour free, tasting $8; ⊙ 11am-6pm May-Oct, to 5pm Nov-Apr, tours daily May-Oct, Sat only Nov-Apr) One of Vermont's best tasting rooms, this converted barn offers samples of Shelburne's award-winning whites and reds. Afternoon tours of the vineyard and the energy-efficient winery building are available year-round.

Magic Hat Brewery   BREWERY

(📞 802-658-2739; www.magichat.net; 5 Bartlett Bay Rd, South Burlington; ⊙ 11am-7pm Mon-Sat, noon-5pm Sun) Drink in the history of one of Vermont's most dynamic microbreweries on the fun, free, self-guided 'Artifactory' Tour (once you see the whimsical labels, this name makes perfect sense) and learn all the nuances of the beer-making process. Afterward, sample a few experimental brews

Burlington

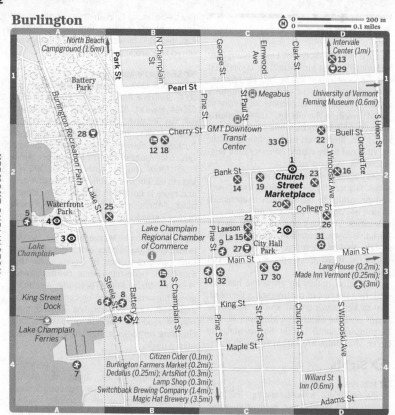

from the four dozen taps in the on-site Growler Bar, or grab a six-pack to go. The brewery is 3.5 miles south of downtown Burlington, on the west side of US 7.

Echo Leahy Center
for Lake Champlain
AQUARIUM

(✆802-864-1848; www.echovermont.org; 1 College St; adult/child $14.50/11.50; ⊙10am-5pm; ▯) This kid-friendly lakeside museum examines the colorful past, present and future of Lake Champlain. A multitude of aquariums wriggle with life, and nature-oriented displays invite inquisitive minds and hands to splash, poke, listen and crawl. Regular rotating exhibits focus on scientific themes – from wind power to giant insects, and dinosaurs to cadavers – with plenty of hands-on activities.

Ethan Allen Homestead
HISTORIC SITE

(✆802-865-4556; www.ethanallenhomestead. org; 1 Ethan Allen Homestead; adult/child $10/6; ⊙10am-4pm May-Oct) American Revolution hero Ethan Allen lived in this 18th-century colonial homestead, 1 mile north of Burlington on VT 127. Be sure to take the guided tour (included in the entrance fee; tour times vary) of the historic house. The center features multimedia exhibits documenting the exploits of Allen's Green Mountain Boys and also has walking trails behind the house.

Burlington City Arts Center
ARTS CENTER

(BCA Center; ✆802-865-7166; www.burlingtoncityarts.org/bca-center; 135 Church St; ⊙noon-5pm Tue-Thu & Sun, to 8pm Fri & Sat, closed Sun Nov-Apr) FREE Under the auspices of Burlington City Arts, the BCA Center is an exciting locus for art exhibits, classes and discussions. Ongoing open studios involve the community with an artist in residence. A community darkroom has open-studio hours, classes and discussions.

Burlington

◉ Top Sights
1 Church Street Marketplace C2

◉ Sights
2 Burlington City Arts Center C3
3 Echo Leahy Center for Lake
    Champlain..A3
4 Waterfront..A3

◉ Activities, Courses & Tours
5 Burlington Community
    Boathouse A3
6 Burlington Greenway..............................B3
7 Lake Champlain Paddlers Trail A4
8 Local Motion B3
9 North Star Sports.....................................C3
10 Ski Rack...C3
   Spirit of Ethan Allen II.....................(see 5)
   Whistling Man Schooner
       Company...(see 5)

◉ Sleeping
11 Burlington Hostel B3
12 Hotel Vermont B2

◉ Eating
13 iDuino! (Duende).....................................D1
14 A Single Pebble.......................................C2

15 American Flatbread................................C3
16 City Market D2
17 Gryphon...C3
18 Hen of the Wood B2
19 Henry's Diner..C2
20 Leunig's Bistro C2
21 Monarch & the Milkweed C3
22 Penny Cluse Cafe....................................D2
23 Revolution Kitchen D2
24 Shanty on the Shore...............................B4
25 Skinny Pancake B2
26 Stone Soup D2

◉ Drinking & Nightlife
27 Drink C3
28 Foam Brewers A2
29 Radio Bean..D1

◉ Entertainment
30 Flynn Center for the Performing
    Arts C3
   Light Club Lamp Shop....................(see 29)
31 Nectar's...D3
32 Vermont Comedy Club C3

◉ Shopping
33 Outdoor Gear Exchange C2

VERMONT BURLINGTON

University of Vermont Fleming Museum MUSEUM

(☏802-656-2090; www.flemingmuseum.org; 61 Colchester Ave; adult/student & senior $5/3; ☉10am-4pm Tue, Thu & Fri, to 7pm Wed, noon-4pm Sat & Sun, closed university holidays) A mile east of City Hall Park, on the verdant campus of UVM (New England's fifth-oldest university, chartered in 1791), this museum has an international collection of over 20,000 objects, from African masks to samurai armor. The American collection includes works by Alfred Stieglitz, Winslow Homer and Andy Warhol.

Vermont Teddy Bear Factory FACTORY

(☏802-985-3001; www.vermontteddybear.com; 6655 Shelburne Rd, Shelburne; adult/under 13yr $4/free; ☉9am-6pm mid-Jun–Aug, to 5pm Sep–mid-Oct, 10am-4pm rest of year; 🎫) Tours of this thriving, touristy factory demonstrate the entire teddy-bear life cycle, from designers' sketches, to stuffing and stitching, to the bear 'hospital,' which patches up tattered beasts for their devoted owners.

🏃 Activities

Burlington Greenway OUTDOORS

(www.enjoyburlington.com/place/burlington-green way) The Burlington Greenway, a popular 7.5-mile recreation path for walking, biking, in-line skating and general perambulating, runs along the waterfront, through the Waterfront Park and promenade.

Whistling Man Schooner Company BOATING

(☏802-825-7245; www.whistlingman.com; 1 College St; cruises day adult/child $50/35, sunset/moonlight adults only $55/35; ☉late May–early Oct) Sail around Lake Champlain with the breeze in your hair and a Vermont microbrew in your hand on the *Friend Ship*, a classic 43ft New England beauty that can hold 17 passengers. Captains are knowledgeable about the area, and encourage passengers to bring food and drink on board. Private charters are also available (from $500 for two hours). Reserve ahead.

Lake Champlain Paddlers Trail BOATING

(☏802-658-1414; www.lakechamplaincommittee. org) ✎ There's no finer way to enjoy Lake Champlain than on a multiday paddling trip, overnighting at one or more of the 600-plus camping spots around the lake. Paddlers are encouraged to join the ecofriendly Lake Champlain Committee ($45 per year), for which they receive an essential, annually

BIKING AROUND BURLINGTON

Burlington's core is pedestrian central. You could also spend your entire Burlington vacation on a bike – if you're staying for a number of days during the nonsnowy months, consider renting a bike for your entire stay (you'll fit in well with the ever-so-green locals, who passionately use bikes as a primary mode of transport). Bike paths cover the entire city and most suburbs, and vehicles generally give cyclists plenty of breathing space.

Local Motion (☑ 802-861-2700; www.localmotion.org; 1 Steele St; adult/tandem/child bike per 4hr $25/42/16, per 24hr $38/62/24; ☺ 10am-6pm Mon-Fri, from 9am Sat & Sun Jun, from 9am daily Jul-Sep; ⊞), a nonprofit group with its own trailside center downtown, spearheads ongoing efforts to expand bike trails and sustain existing ones. It also offers encyclopedic advice on where to cycle in the local area, along with bike rentals, maps, tours and refreshments. Highly recommended is the 12-mile **Island Line Trail**. It combines with the waterfront Burlington Recreation Path, beginning just south of the boathouse and extending onto the narrow Colchester causeway that juts 5 miles out into the lake.

You can even extend your adventure at trail's end by catching Local Motion's **Island Line bike ferry** (one-way/round trip $5/8) north to the Champlain Islands; it runs from late May through early October (daily mid-June to early September, weekends rest of the season).

You can also rent bikes (or in-line skates or roller-skis for that matter!) at **Ski Rack** (☑ 802-658-3313; www.skirack.com; 85 Main St; ☺ 10am-7pm Mon-Sat, 11am-5pm Sun) and **North Star Sports** (☑ 802-863-3832; www.northstarsportsvt.com; 100 Main St; ☺ 10am-6pm Mon-Sat, noon-5pm Sun).

updated guidebook detailing the trails, campsites and rules of the nautical road.

Burlington Community Boathouse
BOATING

(☑ 802-865-3377; www.enjoyburlington.com/place/community-boathouse-marina; 1 College St; ☺ mid-May–mid-Oct) The departure point for boat cruises and rentals is Burlington Community Boathouse, a popular hangout fashioned after Burlington's original 1900s yacht club – easy to spot from Burlington's waterfront recreational path.

Spirit of Ethan Allen II
CRUISE

(☑ 802-862-8300; www.soea.com; 1 College St; cruises day adult/child $23/9, sunset adult/child $24/16; ☺ mid-May–mid-Oct) This ship plies the lake with scenic 1½-hour day cruises (three to four times daily), lunch and dinner excursions, and 2½-hour sunset cruises.

🎎 Festivals & Events

First Friday Art Walk
ART

(www.artmapburlington.com; ☺ 5-8pm 1st Fri of month) Dozens of Burlington artists and arts venues open their doors to the public on the first Friday of each month.

Discover Jazz Festival
MUSIC

(☑ 802-863-7992; www.discoverjazz.com; ☺ early Jun) Burlington plays host to jazz for 10 days in early June at the waterfront and various venues around town.

★ Vermont Brewers Festival
BEER

(www.vtbrewfest.com; $45; ☺ mid-Jul) Meet Vermont's artisan craft brewers and sample their wares during this mid-July weekend event on Burlington's waterfront. Tickets go on sale three months in advance and sell out quickly.

🛏 Sleeping

★ Old Schoolhouse of Isle La Motte
B&B, HOSTEL $

(☑ 802-928-3053; www.theoldschoolhouseofilm.com; 172 School St, Isle La Motte; dm/d $40/125; ☺ Jun-Oct; ⊞ 🐾) For cyclists or fans of historic schoolhouses, this hybrid hostel-B&B on Isle La Motte (around 40 miles north of Burlington) is a dream come true. Dating to the 1930s, the white clapboard building has two private rooms and one four-bed dorm – all with original blackboards – plus a DVD library and musical instruments for entertainment. It's the perfect halfway stop for cyclists traveling from Burlington to Montréal.

Burlington Hostel
HOSTEL $

(☑ 802-540-3043; www.theburlingtonhostel.com; 53 Main St, 2nd fl; dm midweek/weekend $39/49; ☺ mid-Feb–Nov; ⊞ @ 🐾) Hidden behind an unassuming facade just minutes from the action centers of Church St and Lake Champlain, Burlington's hostel accommodates up to 48 guests in four- to eight-bed mixed and women-only dorms. There's an invitingly open kitchen and lounge area where breakfast (coffee and waffles) is served each morning.

North Beach Campground CAMPGROUND $

(☎802-862-0942; www.enjoyburlington.com/type/campground; 60 Institute Rd; tent & RV sites $37-45; ☺May–mid-Oct; ☎) Nature lovers should make a beeline for this wonderful campground, with 137 sites on 45 wooded acres bordering Lake Champlain. From Burlington's downtown waterfront, follow Battery St and North Ave (VT 127) 2km north to Institute Rd. All sites have picnic tables and fire rings, with access to hot showers, a playground, a bike path and a natural sand beach.

★Willard Street Inn INN $$

(☎802-651-8710; www.willardstreetinn.com; 349 S Willard St; r $155-305; ☎) Perched on a hill within easy walking distance of UVM and the Church Street Marketplace (p301), this mansion, fusing Queen Anne and Georgian Revival styles, was built in the late 1880s. It has a fine-wood and cut-glass elegance, yet radiates a welcoming warmth. Many of the guest rooms overlook Lake Champlain.

Lang House B&B $$

(☎802-652-2500; www.langhouse.com; 360 Main St; r $189-299; ❀@☎) This elegant B&B occupies a centrally located, tastefully restored 19th-century Victorian home and carriage house with 11 spacious rooms, some with fireplace. Pampering touches include robes in each room, and sumptuous breakfasts served in an alcove-laden room decorated with old photographs of the city. Reserve ahead for one of the 3rd-floor rooms with lake views.

Hotel Vermont HOTEL $$$

(☎802-651-0080; www.hotelvt.com; 41 Cherry St; r/ste from $259/439) Burlington's newest downtown hotel, in a LEED-certified energy-efficient building halfway between Church St and Lake Champlain, pampers guests with 125 bright modern rooms filled with high-end amenities. There's a pair of excellent on-site restaurants and regular live jazz in the lobby.

Made Inn Vermont B&B $$$

(☎802-399-2788; www.madeinnvermont.com; 204 S Willard St; r $234-369) This 19th-century hillside mansion with gorgeous period features is way trendier than your typical New England B&B, thanks to the creative flair of owner Linda Wolf (a former home-stager in Santa Fe, NM). Jazzy touches include a backyard hot tub, vintage record players with a vast collection of vinyl, loaner Fender guitars and chalkboard walls where guests can express themselves.

✗ Eating

★City Market MARKET $

(☎802-861-9700; www.citymarket.coop; 82 S Winooski Ave; cold & hot buffet per lb $7.99; ☺7am-11pm; ☒) ✔ If there's a food co-op heaven, it must look something like this. Burlington's gourmet natural-foods grocery (recently expanded to a second location in the city's South End) is chock-full of local produce and products, with hundreds of Vermont-based producers represented. Especially noteworthy are the huge takeout deli and hot bar, and the massive microbrew-focused beer section.

DON'T MISS

THE INN AT SHELBURNE FARMS

One of New England's top 10 places to stay, the **Inn at Shelburne Farms** (☎802-985-8498; www.shelburnefarms.org/staydine; 1611 Harbor Rd, Shelburne; r $270-530, without bath $160-230, cottages & houses $270-850; ☺early May–late Oct; ☎), 7 miles south of Burlington off US 7, was once the summer mansion of the wealthy Webb family. It now welcomes guests, with rooms in the gracious, welcoming country manor house by the lakefront, as well as four independent, kitchen-equipped cottages and guesthouses scattered across the property (p301).

Relive the Webbs' opulent lifestyle by taking tea (served every afternoon) or eating in the inn's fabulous restaurant (dinner mains range from $28 to $36; most of the menu is built around produce from the surrounding 1400-acre farm). Or chill out playing billiards or relaxing in one of the common areas, complete with elegant, original furnishings. If you're feeling more energetic, the hiking trails, architect-designed barns and vast grounds are also worthy of several hours' exploration.

VILLAGES FROZEN IN TIME

Many Vermont villages have a lost-in-time quality, thanks to their architectural integrity and the state's general aversion to urban sprawl. Some, like Grafton, Newfane, Woodstock and Dorset, are well-known to outsiders. Others are further off the beaten track.

Brownington (Northeast Kingdom) This sleeping beauty 40 miles north of St Johnsbury is full of 19th-century buildings reposing under the shade of equally ancient maple trees. The Old Stone House Museum (p318) here pays tribute to educational trailblazer Alexander Twilight. The first African American college graduate in the US, he built Brownington's boarding school and ran it for decades.

Peacham (Northeast Kingdom) This idyllically sited village 15 miles southwest of St Johnsbury was originally a stop on the historic Bayley–Hazen Military Rd – intended to help Americans launch a sneak attack on the British during the Revolutionary War. These days it's just a pretty spot to admire pastoral views over the surrounding countryside.

Plymouth Notch (Central Vermont) President Calvin Coolidge's boyhood home, preserved as the **President Calvin Coolidge State Historic Site** (☎802-672-3773; www.historicsites.vermont.gov; 3780 Rte 100A, Plymouth Notch; adult/child $10/2; ☺10am-5pm late May–mid-Oct), looks much as it did a century ago, with a church, one-room schoolhouse, cheese factory and general store gracefully arrayed among old maples on a bucolic hillside. It's 15 miles southwest of Woodstock.

★**Penny Cluse Cafe**   CAFE $
(☎802-651-8834; www.pennycluse.com; 169 Cherry St; mains $6-14; ☺6:45am-3pm Mon-Fri, from 8am Sat & Sun) This ever-popular downtown eatery serves pancakes, biscuits and gravy, omelets and tofu scrambles, along with sandwiches, tacos, salads and delightful drinks ranging from smoothies to Bloody Marys. Don't miss its decadent Bucket-o-Spuds (home-fried potatoes with cheddar, salsa, sour cream and scallions) and *chiles rellenos* – among the best you'll find anywhere east of the Mississippi. Expect an hour's wait on weekends.

ArtsRiot Food Trucks   FOOD TRUCK $
(400 Pine St; snacks from $5; ☺5-8pm Fri late May–early Oct) Burlingtonians kick off their summer weekends with snacks and drinks at this stellar Friday-evening gathering of food trucks, held in the parking lot behind the ArtsRiot (p309) bar-restaurant-performance space.

Skinny Pancake   CREPES $
(☎802-540-0188; www.skinnypancake.com; cnr Lake & College Sts; crepes $6-13; ☺8am-8pm Sun-Thu, to 10pm Fri & Sat) What started as a humble Church St food cart is now a Burlington institution, serving its delicious crepes at multiple locations, including this main lakeshore branch. Regionally sourced savory crepes like the Lumberjack (Vermont apples, ham and Cabot cheddar) share the menu with dessert classics like the Lovemaker (Nutella and strawberries). There's live entertainment nightly, plus a Sunday jazz brunch.

Rustic Roots   AMERICAN $
(☎802-985-9511; www.rusticrootsvt.com; 195 Falls Rd, Shelburne; mains $10-15; ☺9am-3pm Wed-Sun, 6-7:30pm Fri & Sat) Rustic wood decor, cheery burgundy walls and warm service make this Shelburne's favorite brunch spot, perfect for a break between stints at nearby Shelburne Museum (p301). Farm-to-table freshness is the constant in a wide-ranging menu whose highlights include house-cured salmon and burlap bacon, breakfast sandwiches, butternut-squash soup, poached-pear salad, maple-bourbon turkey and pastrami on rye.

Stone Soup   VEGETARIAN $
(☎802-862-7616; www.stonesoupvt.com; 211 College St; buffet per lb $11.75, sandwiches from $10; ☺7am-9pm Mon-Fri, from 9am Sat; ☎✐) Going strong for over two decades, this enduring local favorite is best known for its excellent vegetarian- and vegan-friendly buffet, but also serves homemade soups, salads, sandwiches on home-baked bread, pastries and locally raised meats.

Shanty on the Shore   SEAFOOD $
(☎802-864-0238; www.shantyontheshore.com; 181 Battery St; mains $13-29; ☺11am-9pm) With its fine lake views, this combo seafood market and eatery serves fresh lobster, fish and

shellfish. The outdoor deck is wonderful in summer, and the array of potent drinks enhances the sunset.

Henry's Diner
DINER $

(☎802-862-9010; www.henrysdinervt.com; 155 Bank St; mains $6-14; ☺6am-4pm) A Burlington fixture since 1925, this old-school diner has breakfast all day and a variety of weekend specials.

★ Revolution Kitchen
VEGAN, VEGETARIAN $$

(☎802-448-3657; www.revolutionkitchen.com; 9 Center St; mains $14-18; ☺5-9pm Tue-Thu, to 10pm Fri & Sat; ☑) Vegetarian fine dining? And romantic atmosphere to boot? Yep, they all come together at this cozy brick-walled restaurant that makes creative use of Vermont's abundant organic produce. Asian, Mediterranean and Latin American influences abound in house favorites like Revolution tacos, crispy seitan piccata and the laksa noodle pot. Most items are (or can be adapted to be) vegan.

Gryphon
BISTRO $$

(☎802-489-5699; www.gryphonvt.com; 131 Main St; mains $9-26; ☺11:45am-11pm Mon-Thu, to midnight Fri, from 11am Sat, 10am-10pm Sun) Housed in a beautifully refurbished former hotel with high coffered ceilings, leather couches and antique lighting running the length of the bar, this unpretentious family-run spot serves killer seafood chowder and a multitude of other American classics – NY strip steaks, burgers, green-tomato BLTs, shrimp and grits – with a few wild cards thrown in, such as homemade pierogi and Cuban sandwiches.

Monarch & the Milkweed
BAKERY $$

(☎802-310-7828; www.monarchandthemilkweed.com; 111 St Paul St; mains $8-16; ☺8am-11pm Mon-Thu, to 1am Fri & Sat, to 5pm Sun) Part bakery and part cocktail bar, this cute little spot gazing across at Burlington's City Hall Park serves an all-day brunch menu featuring scrumptious pastries (don't miss the banana cream tarts) alongside breakfast sandwiches featuring homemade bagels, eggs and artisanal Vermont meats and cheeses. Come evening, attention shifts to colorful cocktails and CBD-laced chocolate truffles.

¡Duino! (Duende)
INTERNATIONAL $$

(☎802-660-9346; www.radiobean.com/duino-info; 10 N Winooski Ave; mains $12-18; ☺4-10:30pm Sun-Thu, to midnight Fri, from 10am Sat, to 10:30pm

Sun; ☑) This funky round-the-world street-food-inspired spot has everything from Salvadoran *pupusas* (corn tortillas filled with cheese, beans, meat or vegetables) to Korean bulgogi to Cuban sandwiches, falafel, tacos and gyros. Burlington's finest veggie burger wins rave reviews, as do the stellar Belgian-style *frites* (fries) with garlic aioli. It's all served in a chill space with dark tables and crimson walls.

Leunig's Bistro
FRENCH $$

(☎802-863-3759; www.leunigsbistro.com; 115 Church St; mains lunch $15-27, dinner $18-31; ☺11am-10pm Mon-Thu, to 11pm Fri & Sat, 10am-10pm Sun) 'Live well, laugh often and love much' advises the sign over the bar at this stylish and convivial Parisian-style brasserie with an elegant, tin-ceilinged dining room and sidewalk seating on busy Church St. A long-standing Burlington staple, it's as much fun for the people-watching and occasional live jazz as for its excellent wine list and food.

A Single Pebble
CHINESE $$

(☎802-865-5200; www.asinglepebble.com; 133 Bank St; mains lunch $9-14, dinner $11-25; ☺11:30am-1:45pm Thu-Sun, 5-11pm daily; ☑) Run by Taiwanese photojournalist-turned-chef Chiuho Duval, A Single Pebble sprawls over two adjoining clapboard houses and offers up sumptuous MSG-free fare to the strains of traditional Chinese music. The dim sum is particularly satisfying. Be sure to try the mock eel (made with shiitake mushrooms), and look for its food truck around town throughout summer and fall.

Hen of the Wood
GASTRONOMY $$$

(☎802-540-0534; www.henofthewood.com; 55 Cherry St; mains $22-35; ☺restaurant 5-10pm, bar 4-11pm) An offshoot of Waterbury's legendary Hen of the Wood (p315) restaurant, this high-end dining mecca and its acclaimed chef Jordan Ware have repeatedly won 'Best in Burlington' awards since their debut in 2013. For a taste of the restaurant's classy ambience on a smaller budget, drop by the bar for $1 oysters daily between 4pm and 5pm or 10pm and 11pm.

🍷 Drinking & Nightlife

★ Foam Brewers
MICROBREWERY

(☎802-399-2511; www.foambrewers.com; 112 Lake St; ☺noon-9pm Mon-Thu, 11am-11pm Fri & Sat, to 7pm Sun) Housed in an attractive brick building with exposed post-and-beam

WORTH A TRIP

LAKE CHAMPLAIN ISLANDS

Unfolding like a ribbon just north of Burlington lie the Champlain Islands, a 27-mile-long stretch of three largely undeveloped isles – South Hero (also known as Grand Isle), North Hero and Isle La Motte – all connected by US 2 and a series of bridges and causeways. It's an easy day trip from Burlington, perfect for aimless meandering. Here are a few highlights.

Snow Farm Winery (☑️802-372-9463; www.snowfarm.com; 190 W Shore Rd, South Hero; ⊙11am-5pm daily May-Oct, to 4pm daily Nov & Dec, to 4pm Sat & Sun Jan-Apr) Vermont's first vineyard has a sweet tasting room and a free summer concert series on the lawn beside the vines.

Allenholm Orchards (☑️802-372-5566; www.allenholm.com; 111 South St, South Hero; ⊙9am-5pm late May–Christmas Eve; 🍴) Pick-your-own apples, plus a petting zoo and playground for kids.

Grand Isle State Park (☑️802-372-4300; www.vtstateparks.com/grandisle.html; 36 E Shore South, Grand Isle; tent & RV sites $20-22, lean-tos $27-29, cabins $50; ⊙mid-May–mid-Oct) Waterfront living in four cabins, 36 lean-tos and 117 tent/trailer sites.

Hyde Log Cabin (☑️802-372-4024; 228 US 2, Grand Isle; adult/child $3/free; ⊙11am-4pm Fri-Sun late May–mid-Oct; 🍴) One of the oldest (1783) log cabins in the US.

Hero's Welcome (☑️802-372-4161; www.heroswelcome.com; 3537 US 2, North Hero; ⊙6:30am-7pm Mon-Fri, from 7am Sat & Sun mid-Jun–early Sep, shorter hours rest of year) A quirky, jam-packed general store with a good deli and dockside seating out front.

North Hero House (☑️888-525-3644; www.northherohouse.com; 3643 US 2, North Hero; r $125-250, ste $295-350; 🐾) A country inn with incomparable, front-row lake views of the water and a fantastic restaurant. **Steamship Pier Bar & Grill** (☑️802-372-4732; www. northherohouse.com/dining-wine; 3643 US 2, North Hero; mains $11-22; ⊙Jun–early Oct), serving burgers, fish tacos, lobster rolls and cocktails on the pier.

Old Schoolhouse of Isle La Motte (p304) A perfect halfway stop for cyclists traveling from Burlington to Montréal, this former schoolhouse has been converted to a delightful hostel and B&B.

woodwork and a dreamy terrace looking out toward Lake Champlain, Foam was founded by a group of local beer aficionados looking to unleash their improvisational spirit. The result: one of Burlington's liveliest new brewpubs, with a rotating selection of inventive craft beers and live music six nights a week.

★**Citizen Cider**　　MICROBREWERY
(☑️802-497-1987; www.citizencider.com; 316 Pine St; ⊙11am-10pm Mon-Sat, to 7pm Sun) Tucked into an industrial-chic building with painted concrete floors and long wooden tables, this homegrown success story uses tankfuls of apples trucked in from Vermont orchards to make its ever-growing line of hard ciders. Taste test a flight of five for $7, including perennial favorites such as the ginger-and-lemon-peel-infused Dirty Mayor, or go for one of the inventive cider-based cocktails.

★**Radio Bean**　　BAR
(☑️802-660-9346; www.facebook.com/radiobean; 8 N Winooski Ave; ⊙8am-2am Mon-Fri, from 10am Sat & Sun; 🐾) This is Burlington's social hub for arts and music. Espressos, beer and wine keep things jumping at the all-day cafe, while nightly live performances (jazz, acoustic, Afro-Cuban and more) animate two stages, here and at the semi-attached Light Club Lamp Shop. Radio Bean is also noteworthy for having cofounded the Radiator, Burlington's fabled low-power indie radio station (105.9 FM, www.bigheavy world.com/live-stream-intro).

When hunger strikes, segue into international snacks at Radio Bean's in-house sister eatery ¡Duino! (Duende) (p307).

**Switchback Brewing
Co Tap Room**　　MICROBREWERY
(☑️802-651-4114; www.switchbackvt.com; 160 Flynn Ave; ⊙tours 1pm & 2pm Sat, taproom 11am-8pm Sun-Thu, to 9pm Fri & Sat) One of Vermont's

finest microbreweries, Switchback is best known for its trademark reddish-amber ale and the lighter-bodied Connector IPA. You'll see both on bar menus statewide, but there's nothing like getting them here at the source, in Switchback's Burlington taproom, where you can also enjoy live music on Friday nights and free brewery tours on Saturday afternoons.

Dedalus WINE BAR
(✔802-865-2368; www.dedaluswine.com; 388 Pine St; ☺wine bar 4-10pm daily, shop from 10am Mon-Sat, from 11am Sun) After a decade in business, this purveyor of fine wines (mostly Italian and French, many organic) has recently expanded into seductively spacious new digs in Burlington's South End. Gourmet deli items are sold alongside wines by the bottle in the classy wine shop next door.

Drink WINE BAR
(✔802-860-9463; www.vtdrink.com; 135 St Paul St; ☺4:30pm-2am Mon-Fri, from 3pm Sat & Sun) A lengthy wine list dominates, complemented by an armada of nightly special cocktails (mojitos, cosmopolitans and more) for those in search of stiffer treatment. Small plates of New England delicacies (scallops wrapped in bacon, mini crab cakes) complement the drinks admirably.

☆ Entertainment

★ Flynn Center
for the Performing Arts PERFORMING ARTS
(✔802-863-5966; www.flynncenter.org; 153 Main St) Broadway hits, international acts, music, dance and theater grace the stage at this art-deco masterpiece. Expect anything from King Lear to Ladysmith Black Mambazo.

ArtsRiot LIVE MUSIC
(✔802-540-0406; www.artsriot.com; 400 Pine St; ☺4:30pm-late Tue-Sat) This brick-walled, exuberantly frescoed former timber warehouse in Burlington's South End is the venue for myriad events, from live music to storytelling. In the late afternoons it's a convivial bar-restaurant with early-bird specials till 5:30pm; come nightfall the door opens onto the performance space and dance floor. On Fridays in summer a host of food trucks (p306) parks out back.

Light Club Lamp Shop LIVE MUSIC
(✔802-660-9346; www.radiobean.com/light-club -info; 12 N Winooski Ave; ☺7pm-late Sun-Thu, 6pm-2am Fri & Sat) This cool and quirky place

doubles – well, OK, *triples* – as a lamp shop (witness the amazing, densely packed lighting collection suspended from the walls and ceiling), a bar and a performance space. Shows run the gamut from indie singer-songwriter to jazz to poetry. It's attached to sister nightspot Radio Bean; a single cover charge grants admission to both venues.

Vermont Comedy Club COMEDY
(✔802-859-0100; www.vermontcomedyclub.com; 101 Main St; ☺5-11pm Wed, Thu & Sun, to midnight Fri & Sat) Burlington's headquarters for stand-up and improv comedy, with shows five nights per week.

Nectar's LIVE MUSIC
(✔802-658-4771; www.liveatnectars.com; 188 Main St; ☺7pm-2am Sun-Tue, from 5pm Wed-Sat) Indie darlings Phish got their start here and the joint still rocks out with the help of aspiring acts. Grab a vinyl booth, chill at the bar or dance upstairs at Club Metronome (www.clubmetronome.com), which hosts a slew of theme nights along with larger live acts.

🛍 Shopping

Burlington Farmers Market MARKET
(www.burlingtonfarmersmarket.org; 345 Pine St; ☺8:30am-2pm Sat May-Oct, from 10am Sat Nov-Apr) Every Saturday from May through October, downtown Burlington bursts into life with this enormously popular farmers market. All vendors must grow or make precisely what they sell: expect fresh produce, prepared food, cheeses, breads, baked goods and crafts. During the rest of the year, the market moves indoors to the Davis Center at the University of Vermont (590 Main St).

Lamp Shop VINTAGE
(✔802-864-6782; www.shopthelamp.com; 424 Pine St; ☺10:30am-5:30pm Tue-Fri, to 4pm Sat) In the heart of Burlington's artsy South End, the Lamp Shop sells an inspirational array of lamps and light fixtures, from the vintage to the cutting-edge.

Outdoor Gear
Exchange SPORTS & OUTDOORS
(✔802-860-0190, 888-547-4327; www.gearx.com; 37 Church St; ☺10am-7pm Mon-Thu, to 8pm Fri & Sat, to 6pm Sun) This place rivals major outdoor-gear chains for breadth of selection, and trumps them on price for a vast array of used, closeout and even new gear and

clothing. Name the outdoor pursuit and staff can probably outfit you.

ⓘ Information

Lake Champlain Regional Chamber of Commerce (☑877-686-5253, 802-863-3489; www.vermont.org; 60 Main St; ☺8:30am-4:30pm Mon-Thu, to 3pm Fri) Staffed tourist office in the heart of downtown.

ⓘ Getting There & Away

To get here from Boston (3½ hours, 216 miles), take I-93 to I-89. It's another 1¾ hours (95 miles) north from Burlington to Montréal.

All Burlington's car-rental companies (Hertz, Avis, Enterprise, National, Thrifty, Budget and Alamo) are located at Burlington International Airport. The best option for Amtrak passengers arriving in Essex Junction is to take a taxi 5 miles to the airport and rent a car there. **Green Cab VT** (☑802-864-2424; www.green cabvt.com; 10 Gregory Dr), recommended for its fuel-efficient fleet, can shuttle people from Essex Junction to the airport for about $15.

AIR

A number of national carriers serve **Burlington International Airport** (BTV; ☑802-863-2874; www.btv.aero; 1200 Airport Dr, South Burlington), 3 miles east of the city center.

BOAT

Lake Champlain Ferries (☑802-864-9804; www.ferries.com; King St Dock) runs scenic, summer-only car ferries between Burlington and Port Kent, NY (one-way car and driver $30, additional adult/child $8/3.10, cyclist $9, 70 minutes, mid-June to September).

The company also operates ferries between Charlotte, VT (south of Burlington), and Essex, NY, for as long as the lake stays unfrozen; and 24-hour, year-round service from Grand Isle, VT (north of Burlington), to Plattsburgh, NY. See the website for fare and schedule details.

BUS

Greyhound (www.greyhound.com) runs multiple buses daily from Burlington International Airport to Montréal, Canada (from $18, 2½ hours) and Boston (from $28, 4½ to 5½ hours).

Megabus (☑877-462-6342; www.megabus.com; 119 Pearl St) also offers a once-daily bus service to Boston (from $25, four hours). Buses stop just around the corner from Burlington's **GMT Downtown Transit Center** (Green Mountain Transit; ☑802-864-2282; www.ridegmt.com; cnr St Paul & Cherry Sts; ☺6am-11pm Mon-Fri, 7am-5pm Sat).

Green Mountain Transit (www.ridegmt.com) operates a few long-distance buses to other cities in northwestern Vermont. See its website for fares and schedules.
Middlebury Routes 46 and 76
Montpelier Route 86

TRAIN

Amtrak's daily *Vermonter* train (www.amtrak.com/vermonter-train), which provides service as far south as New York City and Washington, DC, stops in Essex Junction, 5 miles from Burlington.

ⓘ Getting Around

Operating from the Downtown Transit Center, Green Mountain Transit runs a free College St shuttle bus (route 11) every 15 to 30 minutes between the UVM campus and Waterfront Park near the Burlington Boathouse, with a stop at Church Street Marketplace (p301).

Local fares on other GMT routes around Burlington are $1.25 for adults, 60¢ for children and seniors.

Burlington International Airport Route 1 to Route 12 (25 to 30 minutes, half-hourly, less frequent on Sunday).
Essex Junction Route 2 (30 to 40 minutes, every 15 minutes Monday to Friday, every 30 minutes Saturday, every 1¼ hours Sunday).
Shelburne Route 6.

Stowe & Smugglers Notch

In a cozy valley where the West Branch River flows into Little River and mountains rise in all directions, the quintessential Vermont village of Stowe (settled in 1794) bustles quietly. The town's longstanding reputation as one of the east's classiest mountain resorts draws well-heeled urbanites from Boston, New York and beyond. A bounty of inns and eateries lines the thoroughfares leading up to Smugglers Notch, an enchantingly narrow rock-walled pass through the Green Mountains just below Mt Mansfield (4393ft), the highest point in Vermont. More than 200 miles of cross-country ski trails, some of the finest mountain biking and downhill skiing in the east, and world-class rock- and ice-climbing lure adrenaline junkies and active families.

Waterbury, on the interstate highway 10 miles south, is Stowe's gateway. Its attractions include some standout restaurants and the world-famous Ben & Jerry's Ice Cream Factory (p315).

STOWE'S BEST HIKES

The Green Mountain Club (p316), 5 miles south of Stowe, was founded in 1910 to maintain the Long Trail. The club publishes some excellent hikers' materials, available here or by mail. Staff also lead guided hiking, biking, boating, skiing and snowshoeing day trips.

There are several excellent day hikes around Stowe, and in the Smugglers Notch area along VT 108. If you're here in peak summer season, the seasonal Barnes Camp Visitor Center (p316) along VT 108 can help you choose a route. Just outside the center you'll find a boardwalk (p312), granting wheelchair and stroller access to a montane wetland with lovely views of the notch.

Otherwise, here are our picks:

Stowe Recreation Path (p314): a fabulous four-season escape for all ages that rambles through woods, meadows and outdoor sculpture gardens.

Moss Glen Falls: an easy, delightful walk (1 mile, 30 minutes) leading to a deep cascade and waterfalls.

Kirchner Woods Trail (www.stowelandtrust.org; Taber Hill Rd): fine mountain views while roaming among hardwoods, maple trees and a working sugar house.

Smugglers Notch to Mt Mansfield: scenic, challenging climb (3.5 miles, five hours) – the highest peak in the state.

Nebraska Notch: moderately difficult trail (3.2 miles, 2½ hours) that eventually ascends past beaver dams and grand views.

Stowe Pinnacle: another moderately difficult hike (short but steep) to the rocky outcrop called Stowe Pinnacle (2651ft).

⊙ Sights

★Alchemist Brewery BREWERY
(www.alchemistbeer.com; 100 Cottage Club Rd; ⊙11am-7pm Tue-Sat) One of Vermont's most legendary beers, Heady Topper, was born at this microbrewery, which recently expanded operations into a spiffy new Stowe Visitors Center. Visitors to the state-of-the-art, solar-powered building with its silo-like tower can enjoy free tastes, observe the beer production process and purchase four-packs of Heady Topper, Focal Banger and other outstanding brews to bring home.

Stowe Cider WINERY
(☑802-253-2065; www.stowecider.com; 17 Town Farm Lane; ⊙noon-6pm Fri-Sun) At the sign of the winged apple, this warehouse-like facility houses the production facility and tasting room for Stowe's homegrown cider company, founded in 2013. Eighteen taps dispense pints ($6) and flights ($7 for four 3oz pours). Grab a minichalkboard as you enter, choose your flavors and bring it to the bar. Occasional live bands perform on Saturday afternoons.

Vermont Ski & Snowboard Museum MUSEUM
(☑802-253-9911; www.vtssm.com; 1 S Main St; suggested admission $5; ⊙noon-5pm Wed-Sun) Located in an 1818 meeting house that was rolled to its present spot by oxen in the 1860s, this museum is an inspired tribute to skiing and snowboarding history. It holds much more than an evolution of equipment (including 75 years of Vermont ski lifts) and a chance to chuckle at what was high slopeside fashion in the 1970s. A huge screen shows ski footage so crazy that you can hardly keep your footing.

The most moving exhibit tells the tale of the famous 10th Mountain Division of skiing troops from WWII – it inspires wonder at how they held out with the (then cutting-edge) canvas- and leather-based gear.

Helen Day Art Center ARTS CENTER
(☑802-253-8358; www.helenday.com; 90 Pond St; ⊙10am-5pm Tue-Sat) FREE In the heart of Stowe village, this gently provocative community art center has rotating exhibitions of traditional and avant-garde work. It also sponsors 'Exposed,' an annual

Stowe & Around

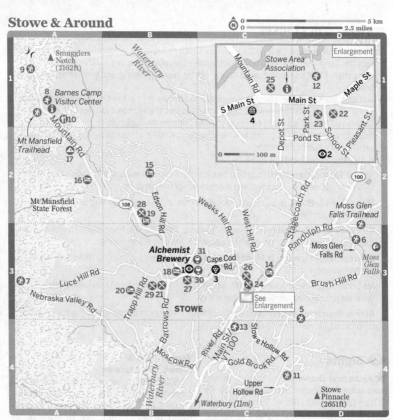

town-wide outdoor sculpture show that takes place from mid-July to mid-October.

West Branch Gallery & Sculpture Park
GALLERY

(☏ 802-253-8943; www.westbranchgallery.com; 17 Towne Farm Lane; ☉ 10am-5pm Tue-Sun) A captivating collection of contemporary sculpture, paintings, photography and fountains fills this gallery and sculpture park 1 mile up Mountain Rd from Stowe village. Don't miss the winding, sculpture-filled paths along the river's edge.

★ Activities

★ Smugglers Notch Boardwalk
OUTDOORS

This boardwalk represents a revolutionary improvement in accessibility to the Smugglers Notch area, allowing visitors in strollers or wheelchairs to follow a section of the Long Trail out through a montane wetland to a viewpoint with lovely perspectives on

the notch. Pull-offs along the way feature informational displays about the wetlands' ecology, flora, fauna and natural history.

★ Umiak Outdoor Outfitters
OUTDOORS

(☏ 802-253-2317; www.umiak.com; 849 S Main St; ☉ 9am-6pm) This place rents canoes and sport kayaks, gives kayak and stand-up paddleboard lessons, and offers a variety of guided and self-guided tours on local rivers, including the Lamoille and the Winooski. In winter, it also rents snowshoes, ice skates, sleds, tubes and telemark skis, books tours with local dog mushers and offers moonlit snowshoe tours.

Trapp Family Outdoor Center
SKIING

(☏ 802-253-5719, rentals & lessons 802-253-5755; www.trappfamily.com/skiing-snowshoeing.htm; 700 Trapp Hill Rd; trail pass adult/teen/child $25/15/10) America's oldest cross-country ski center, with 37 miles of groomed trails and 62 miles of backcountry trails. One of

Stowe & Around

◎ Top Sights
1 Alchemist Brewery...................................B3

◎ Sights
2 Helen Day Art Center...........................D2
3 Stowe Cider...C3
4 Vermont Ski & Snowboard
  Museum...C1
  West Branch Gallery
  & Sculpture Park.........................(see 3)

◎ Activities, Courses & Tours
5 Kirchner Woods Trail............................D3
6 Moss Glen Falls...................................D3
7 Nebraska Notch....................................A3
8 Smugglers Notch
  Boardwalk..A1
9 Smugglers Notch to Mt
  Mansfield..A1
10 Stowe Mountain Resort.......................A1
11 Stowe Pinnacle.....................................C4
12 Stowe Recreation Path........................D1
  Trapp Family Outdoor
  Center..(see 20)
13 Umiak Outdoor Outfitters....................C4

◎ Sleeping
14 Brass Lantern Inn B&B.........................C3
15 Edson Hill..B2
16 Fiddler's Green Inn...............................A2
  Green Mountain Inn.....................(see 4)
17 Smugglers' Notch State Park..............A2
18 Stowe Motel & Snowdrift......................B3
19 Topnotch at Stowe...............................B2
20 Trapp Family Lodge..............................B3

◎ Eating
21 Bistro at Ten Acres...............................B3
22 Black Cap Coffee & Beer.....................D1
23 Butler's Pantry.....................................D1
24 Doc Ponds...C3
25 Harrison's..C1
26 McCarthy's..C3
27 Pie-casso...B3
28 Trattoria La Festa.................................B2
29 Von Trapp Bierhall................................B3

◎ Drinking & Nightlife
30 Charlie B's...B3
31 Idletyme Brewing Co............................B3

the delights of skiing here is stopping to recharge your batteries with warm soup and hot chocolate by the fireplace at Slayton Pasture Cabin. In summer, these same trails become the domain of mountain bikers and hikers.

Stowe Mountain Resort
SKIING
(☑ 802-253-3000; www.stowe.com; 5781 Mountain Rd; lift ticket adult $85-115, child $72-98) This venerable resort encompasses two mountains: Mt Mansfield (which has a vertical drop of 2360ft) and Spruce Peak (1550ft). It offers 116 beautiful trails, two-thirds for beginners and intermediates, and the remainder for hard-core backcountry skiers – many of whom get their adrenaline rushes from the 'front four' runs: Starr, Goat, National and Liftline.

Smugglers' Notch Resort
SKIING
(☑ 802-332-6854; www.smuggs.com; 4323 VT 108; lift ticket adult/child $79/59; ⊛) This family-oriented resort on the west side of Smugglers' Notch is spread over Sterling (3010ft), Madonna (3640ft) and Morse (2250ft) mountains. It has incredible alpine skiing (78 trails ranging from beginner's runs at Morse to the triple black diamond Black Hole), plus 36 miles of cross-country ski and snowshoe trails, dogsled rides, a lit tubing hill and nightly family entertainment.

🛏 Sleeping

Smugglers' Notch State Park
CAMPGROUND $
(☑ 802-253-4014; www.vtstateparks.com/smugglers.html; 6443 Mountain Rd; tent sites $20-22, lean-tos $27-29; ⊘mid-May–mid-Oct) This 35-acre park, 8 miles northwest of Stowe, is perched up on the mountainside. It has 20 tent sites (mostly walk-in), and 14 lean-tos.

Fiddler's Green Inn
INN $
(☑ 802-253-8124; www.fiddlersgreeninn.com; 4865 Mountain Rd; r summer $79, fall & winter $99-149; ⊛) A throwback to simpler times, this homey yellow 1820s farmhouse is tucked off the main road a mile below the lifts, with rustic pine walls, spacious front porch, fieldstone fireplace and six unembellished guest rooms, the best overlooking the rushing creek out back. In winter, guests congregate around the wood-burning hearth. Long Trail hikers can phone for free pickup.

Stowe Motel & Snowdrift
MOTEL, APARTMENT $$
(☑ 802-253-7629; www.stowemotel.com; 2043 Mountain Rd; r $109-215, ste $195-265, apt $179-280; @ 🛜 🛝) In addition to motel-like rooms and suites – some with kitchenette and wood-burning fireplace – this sprawling 16-acre property midway between Stowe village and the slopes offers multibedroom

> **DON'T MISS**
>
> ## STOWE RECREATION PATH
>
> The flat to gently rolling 5.3-mile **Stowe Recreation Path** (www.stowerec.org/parks-facilities/rec-paths/stowe-recreation-path; 🚴🏃), which starts from the pointy-steepled Stowe Community Church in the village center, offers a fabulous four-season escape for all ages. It rambles through woods, meadows and outdoor sculpture gardens along the West Branch of Little River, with sweeping views of Mt Mansfield unfolding in the distance.
>
> Bike, walk, skate or ski – and swim in one of the swimming holes along the way.

houses and an apartment. Clinching the deal are countless amenities: a tennis court, two swimming pools, a hot tub, badminton, lawn games and free bicycles or snowshoes to use on the nearby recreation path.

Brass Lantern Inn B&B   B&B $$
(📞 802-253-2229; www.brasslanterninn.com; 717 Maple St/VT 100; r $130-295; 🛜) A cheerful welcome, friendly advice on local hikes and restaurants, and picture windows facing Mt Mansfield all contribute to the charm at this fully modernized 19th-century farmhouse just outside Stowe village. The nine rooms (six with fireplace and Jacuzzi) all come with handmade quilts, and other thoughtful touches abound, including a locked storage and washing station for mountain bikes.

Edson Hill   INN $$$
(📞 802-253-7371; www.edsonhill.com; 1500 Edson Hill Rd; r $285-485; 🛜♨) Secluded up a long dirt road, this charming inn with its own pond and cross-country ski center exudes blissful solitude. The central manor house has eight bedrooms, an inviting living room with log-burning fireplace and a restaurant. Rooms are even more spacious in the four newer buildings up the hill, where guests can ski right up to their own doorstep.

Trapp Family Lodge   LODGE $$$
(📞 802-253-8511; www.trappfamily.com; 700 Trapp Hill Rd; r $175-425, ste $275-750; @🛜♨🏊) This hilltop lodge 3km above town boasts Stowe's most dramatic setting. The Austrian-style chalet, built by Maria von Trapp of *Sound of Music* fame (note the family photos lining the walls), houses 96 traditional lodge

rooms, many renovated and most with balconies affording lovely mountain vistas. Alternatively, rent one of the cozy villas or guesthouses scattered across the property.

Green Mountain Inn   INN $$$
(📞 802-253-7301; www.greenmountaininn.com; 18 Main St; r/ste/apt from $169/239/259) The Stowe Recreation Path unfurls just a few steps from this 180-year-old redbrick inn, which sits in the heart of downtown Stowe. How best to relax? Settle into a rocking chair on the front porch, enjoy afternoon cookies and tea, then head to the spa. The 104 rooms are classically decorated and come in a variety of configurations.

Topnotch at Stowe   RESORT $$$
(📞 802-253-8585; www.topnotchresort.com; 4000 Mountain Rd; r $199-649; @🛜♨) Stowe's most lavish resort dazzles guests with amenities: indoor and outdoor pools, tennis courts, a legendary spa and the stylishly modern Roost pub, with cathedral windows overlooking Mt Mansfield. Accommodations range from comfortable standard rooms to immaculate two- and three-bedroom houses.

🍴 Eating

Black Cap Coffee & Beer   CAFE $
(📞 802-253-2123; www.facebook.com/blackcapcoffeeandbeer; 144 Main St, Stowe; sandwiches $7-9; ⏱7am-6pm Sun-Thu, to 7pm Fri & Sat; 🛜) Unwind over baked goods, sandwiches and coffee at this homey, refurbished cafe in the heart of the village, set in an inviting old house with armchairs, couches and a small but delightful front porch. The attached shop stocks an impressive collection of microbrews and hosts regular beer-tasting events.

★ Von Trapp Bierhall   AUSTRIAN $$
(📞 802-253-5750; www.vontrappbrewing.com/bierhall.htm; 1333 Luce Hill Rd; mains $13-31; ⏱11:30am-9pm) This grand post-and-beam structure with 30ft cathedral ceilings and views of mountains, meadows and birches has become an instant Stowe classic since its 2016 inauguration. Behind the semicircular blonde-wood bar, taps shaped like mountain-goat horns dispense the full lineup of pilsners and lagers brewed on-site, while the menu includes Austrian specialties like bratwurst, sauerkraut, spätzle and apple strudel.

Doc Ponds
AMERICAN $$

(☏802-760-6066; www.docponds.com; 294 Mountain Rd; mains $8-22; ⊙4pm-midnight Tue-Thu, from 11:30am Fri-Mon) Casual fare, from tacos to burgers to mac 'n' cheese and milkshakes, dominates the menu at this popular spot near the heart of Stowe village. Walls festooned with skateboards enhance the festive mood, as do the twin turntables spinning vintage vinyl at the entrance. Craft beer and cider specials go for $4 a pint every day.

Butler's Pantry
BREAKFAST $$

(☏802-253-2955; www.butlerhousestowe.com; 128 Main St; 8am-noon Mon-Fri, to 1pm Sat & Sun) At Stowe's newest breakfast hot spot, just off main street, friendly service and comfort food made from scratch are the name of the game. The biscuits and gravy here are legendary, as are the grit cakes, eggs Benedict and mimosas made with freshly squeezed orange juice. Prepare for long lines during ski season.

Harrison's
AMERICAN $$

(☏802-253-7773; www.harrisonsstowe.com; 25 Main St; sandwiches $13-15, mains $18-34; ⊙4:30-9:30pm Sun-Thu, to 10pm Fri & Sat) Ask Stowe locals for the best restaurant in town, and many will point you straight to Harrison's. The intimate subterranean space, with a brick fireplace at one end and a bar at the other, specializes in creative takes on American classics, from crab cakes and burgers to rib-eye steak and pecan-encrusted salmon, to carrot cake and hot fudge sundaes. Reserve ahead.

Pie-casso
PIZZA $$

(☏802-253-4411; www.piecasso.com; 1899 Mountain Rd; mains $9-24; ⊙11am-9pm Sun-Thu, to 10pm Fri & Sat) Best known for its ample pizzas, from the sausage-and-pepperoni-packed Heart Stopper to the veggie-laden Vienna, family-friendly Pie-casso also serves everything from eggplant Parmesan subs to fettuccine Alfredo and penne with pesto. Gluten-free crusts using flour from nearby West Meadow Farm are also available.

★Hen of the Wood
MODERN AMERICAN $$$

(☏802-244-7300; www.henofthewood.com; 92 Stowe St, Waterbury; small plates $12-15, mains $22-35; ⊙5-9pm Tue-Sat) 🖉 Arguably the finest dining in Northern Vermont, this chef-driven restaurant, set in a historic grist mill in Waterbury, gets rave reviews for its innovative farm-to-table cuisine. The ambience is as fine as the food, which features seasonal ingredients such as wild mushrooms and densely flavored dishes like smoked duck breast or sheep's-milk gnocchi.

Bistro at Ten Acres
FUSION $$$

(☏802-253-6838; www.tenacreslodge.com; 14 Barrows Rd; mains $14-34; ⊙5-10pm Wed-Sun) This immensely popular eatery in a plank-floored 1820s farmhouse blends cozy atmosphere with delicious food from New York–trained chef Gary Jacobson (think steak frites, slow-roasted duck, or lobster with bourbon-tarragon sauce and polenta). The attached bar serves a good selection of cocktails and draft beers, plus a cheaper burger-centric menu.

VERMONT STOWE & SMUGGLERS NOTCH

BEN & JERRY'S

In 1978 Ben Cohen and Jerry Greenfield took over an abandoned gas station in Burlington and, with a modicum of training, launched the outlandish flavors that forever changed the way ice cream would be made. While a tour of the **Ben & Jerry's Ice Cream Factory** (☏802-882-2047; www.benjerry.com/about-us/factory-tours; 1281 VT 100, Waterbury; adult/child under 13yr $4/free; ⊙9am-9pm Jul–mid-Aug, to 7pm mid-Aug–mid-Oct, 10am-6pm mid-Oct–late May, to 7pm late May–Jun; 🚼) is no over-the-top Willy Wonka experience, there is a campy video that follows the company's long, strange trip to corporate giant – albeit a very nice giant with an inspiring presence of community building and environmental leadership.

You'll head to a special glassed-in room where you glimpse the production line in action and a staff member explains how it is done. After chowing your (very teeny) free scoops, linger a while in the final hallway, which is festooned with mementos of how they've changed the world one scoop at a time. Behind the factory, a mock cemetery holds 'graves' of Cool Britannia, Holy Cannoli and other flavors that have been laid to rest. In summer, cows roam the pastures surrounding the factory. The factory is 1 mile north of I-89.

Michael's on the Hill
INTERNATIONAL $$$

(✆802-244-7476; www.michaelsonthehill.com; 4182 Waterbury-Stowe Rd, Waterbury Center; mains $28-43, tasting menus $46-68; ☺5:30-9pm Wed-Mon) ✦ A 10-minute drive south of Stowe, this is one of the area's standout eateries. A seasonally changing menu built on locally sourced ingredients is served in a pair of interior dining rooms and on an intimate wraparound porch.

Trattoria La Festa
ITALIAN $$$

(✆802-253-8480; www.trattoriastowe.com; 4080 Mountain Rd; mains $16-35; ☺5-9pm Tue-Sat) In business for over three decades, this Italian-owned trattoria in an old barn serves family-style Italian fare that makes ample use of veggies and herbs from the garden out back. It also has an award-winning (mainly Italian) wine list.

🍷 Drinking & Entertainment

Idletyme Brewing Co
MICROBREWERY

(✆802-253-4765; www.idletymebrewing.com; 1859 Mountain Rd; mains $13-34; ☺11:30am-9pm Sun-Thu, to 10pm Fri & Sat) Sip 5oz samples ($2.50 each) or go in for full pints at this microbrewery in a converted 19th-century blacksmith's shop between Stowe village and the slopes. The kitchen serves up burgers, bratwurst and cheese boards alongside dinner fare such as *steak frites*, grilled salmon or butternut-squash ravioli.

Charlie B's
PUB

(✆800-253-2232; www.stoweflake.com/charliepub.aspx; 1746 Mountain Rd; ☺7am-10pm) If you're searching for a standard après-ski scene with a bit of class, basic pub fare and occasional live music, head to this place.

ZenBarn
LIVE MUSIC

(✆802-244-8134; www.zenbarnvt.com; 179 Guptil Rd, Waterbury; ☺4:30pm-late Tue-Sun) Take a cavernous old Vermont barn, add a yoga studio, a restaurant and a bar serving cocktails and the state's best beers and ciders, plus a stage where local and national acts perform live a few nights per week. Since opening in late 2016, the ZenBarn has quickly become one of the area's most popular nightspots.

ⓘ Information

Barnes Camp Visitor Center (www.greenmountainclub.org; VT 108, 2 miles east of Smugglers Notch; ☺9am-5pm Fri-Sun mid-Jun–mid-Oct) This Green Mountain Club visitor center in a restored early-20th-century logging camp building sits strategically near the Long Trail's intersection with Smugglers Notch. Volunteer staff enlighten visitors about local recreation opportunities and the notch's natural history.

Green Mountain Club Visitors Center (✆802-244-7037; www.greenmountainclub.org; 4711 Waterbury-Stowe Rd/VT 100, Waterbury Center; ☺9am-5pm daily mid-May–mid-Oct, 10am-4pm Mon-Fri rest of year) The Green Mountain Club maintains the 270-mile Long Trail, which runs the length of Vermont from Massachusetts to the Canadian border. Visit its office (5 miles south of Stowe) or check the website for details about the Long Trail and shorter day hikes in the region.

Stowe Area Association (✆802-253-7321; www.gostowe.com; 51 Main St; ☺9am-6pm Mon-Sat, 11am-5pm Sun; 🛜) This well-organized association with comfy couches, free wi-fi and a fireplace in winter can help plan your trip, including making reservations for rental cars and local accommodations.

ⓘ Getting There & Away

To reach Stowe, take the Waterbury exit off I-89 and drive 10 miles north on VT 100 to the village center. From here, a left turn onto VT 108 continues northwest to the ski slopes.

GMTA (www.ridegmt.com) operates a couple of useful buses for those without a vehicle.

The Mountain Road Shuttle runs every half-hour daily during ski season from Stowe village up Mountain Rd to the ski slopes.

On weekdays, the Route 100 Commuter also offers limited service between Stowe and Waterbury, where you can connect to GMTA's Montpelier LINK Express bus to Montpelier or Burlington.

The Amtrak *Vermonter* train (www.amtrak.com/vermonter-train) stops daily at Waterbury (mornings southbound to Brattleboro and New York City, evenings northbound to Burlington). Some hotels and inns will arrange to pick up guests at the station. The Route 100 Commuter is the only bus service between Waterbury and Stowe, but it doesn't make good connections with Amtrak. Get a taxi from **Stowe Taxi** (✆802-253-9490; www.stowetaxi.com).

Montpelier

✆802 / POP 7480

Montpelier (mont-*peel*-yer) would qualify as nothing more than a large village in most places. But in sparsely populated Vermont it's the state capital – the smallest in the country (and the only one without a McDonald's, in case you were wondering). Remarkably cosmopolitan for a town of

7500 residents, its two main thoroughfares – State St and Main St – make for a pleasant wander, with some nice bookstores, boutiques and eateries.

Montpelier's smaller, distinctly working-class neighbor Barre (*bear*-ee), which touts itself as the 'granite capital of the world,' is a 15-minute drive southeast of the capital.

◎ Sights

Rock of Ages Quarries   MINE
(☑ 802-476-3119; www.rockofages.com; 558 Graniteville Rd, Graniteville; guided quarry tour adult/child $5/2.50, self-guided factory tour free; ◷ guided quarry tours 10am-4pm Mon-Sat late May–mid-Oct, self-guided factory tours 8:30am-3:30pm Mon-Fri Feb–mid-Dec) The world's largest granite quarries, 4 miles southeast of Barre off I-89 exit 6, cover 50 acres, tapping a granite vein that's a whopping 6 miles long, 4 miles wide and 10 miles deep. Most fascinating is the 35-minute guided minibus tour of the active quarry, where you can gaze down on seemingly ant-size workers in hard hats extracting massive granite blocks at the bottom of a 600ft-deep pit.

Hope Cemetery   CEMETERY
(☑ 802-476-6245; 201 Maple Ave, Barre; ◷ 7am-5pm) Barre's cemetery, 1 mile north of US 302 on VT 14, celebrates the artistic prowess of generations of local and immigrant stone carvers. The whimsical tombstones here include a man and his wife sitting up in bed holding hands, smiling for eternity; a precariously balanced granite cube; a giant soccer ball and a small airplane. If a cemetery can ever be a work of art, this one is. It's open to the living seven days a week.

State House   HISTORIC BUILDING
(☑ 802-828-1411; www.vtstatehousefriends.org; 115 State St; ◷ guided tours 10am-3:30pm Mon-Fri, 11am-2:30pm Sat Jul–mid-Oct, 9am-3pm Mon-Fri mid-Oct–Jun) FREE Montpelier's main landmark, the gold-domed capitol building, is open year-round for guided tours with volunteer guides; there are also self-guided audio tours in English, French, Spanish and German. The front doors are guarded by a massive statue of American Revolutionary hero Ethan Allen, and the base supporting the gold dome was built of granite quarried in nearby Barre in 1836. Don't miss the fossils embedded in the lobby's black-and-white checkerboard limestone floor.

Vermont History Museum   MUSEUM
(☑ 802-828-2291; www.vermonthistory.org/visit/vermont-history-museum; 109 State St; adult/child $7/5; ◷ 10am-4pm Tue-Sat) Near the Vermont State House, Montpelier's Pavilion Building houses an excellent museum that recounts Vermont's history with films, exhibits and re-creations of a Native American wigwam and the 18th-century tavern where Ethan Allen's Green Mountain Boys once convened.

🛏 Sleeping & Eating

Inn at Montpelier   INN $$
(☑ 802-223-2727; www.innatmontpelier.com; 147 Main St; r $170-300; ❉ 🖥) This first-rate inn made up of two refurbished Federal houses sits smack in the heart of town. All the rooms are luxuriously furnished, including some deluxe units with ornamental fireplaces. The wraparound veranda makes a delightful spot to enjoy the included homemade continental breakfast or a lazy afternoon of reading.

★ Three Penny Taproom   PUB FOOD $
(☑ 802-223-8277; www.threepennytaproom.com; 108 Main St; burgers $6-14, mains $9-16; ◷ kitchen 11am-9pm Mon-Thu, to 10pm Fri & Sat, to 4pm Sun, bar to midnight Mon-Thu, to 2am Fri & Sat, to 6pm Sun) Pouring two dozen microbrews from Vermont and beyond, this pub is a perennial late-night favorite. It's also popular for its pub grub: grilled cheese and soup, Greek quinoa salad, fish and chips and the budget-saving 'flatty,' a 2oz burger with Vermont cheddar and a half order of fries.

Hunger Mountain Co-op   HEALTH FOOD $
(☑ 802-223-8000; www.hungermountain.coop; 623 Stone Cutters Way; sandwiches $6-10, deli items per lb $8.99; ◷ 8am-8pm; 🖉) This terrific health-food store and deli has plenty of vegan and vegetarian options, with tables overlooking the Winooski River.

ℹ Information

Capitol Region Visitors Center (☑ 802-828-5981; www.informationcenter.vermont.gov; 134 State St; ◷ 6am-5pm Mon-Fri, from 9am Sat & Sun) Opposite the state capitol, helpful info center with free wi-fi and comfy seating.

ℹ Getting There & Away

Burlington (40 minutes, 39 miles) is an easy drive west on I-89.

On weekdays, you can also reach Burlington via the Montpelier LINK Express bus ($4, 1¼ hours, nine Monday to Friday) operated by Green Mountain Transit (www.ridegmt.com).

Amtrak's daily *Vermonter* train (www.amtrak. com/vermonter-train) runs from Montpelier to points northwest and southeast, including Brattleboro ($30, 2½ hours) and Burlington's Essex Junction station ($12, 45 minutes). The Amtrak station is 2 miles west of downtown Montpelier, on Junction Rd in the Montpelier Junction neighborhood.

Northeast Kingdom

When Senator George Aiken noted in 1949, 'this is such beautiful country up here. It ought to be called the Northeast Kingdom of Vermont,' locals were quick to take his advice. Today, the Northeast Kingdom connotes the large wedge between the Quebec and New Hampshire borders. Less spectacular than spectacularly unspoiled, the landscape is a sea of green hills dotted with farms and small villages.

Here, inconspicuous inns and dairy cows contrast with the slick resorts found elsewhere in the state; the white steeples are chipped, the barns in need of a fresh coat of paint. In a rural state known for its unpopulated setting (only Wyoming contains fewer people), the Kingdom is Vermont's equivalent to putting on its finest pastoral dress, with a few holes here and there. It's a region that doesn't put on any airs about attracting tourists, and locals speak wryly of its 'picturesque poverty.'

◉ Sights

★ Hill Farmstead Brewery
BREWERY

(☑ 802-533-7450; www.hillfarmstead.com; 403 Hill Rd, Greensboro; ⊘ noon-5pm Wed-Sat) The brainchild of Shaun Hill, known for his uncompromising adherence to creativity and quality, this unassuming-looking brewery down a remote dirt road – voted 'world's best' four consecutive years – has developed a cult following for its small-batch brews. Its eternal classic – hoppy Edward IPA – is complemented by a host of seasonal brews, available by the glass in the on-site taproom or in growlers and cans to go. Visit midweek if possible; long lines prevail in foliage season and on holiday weekends.

★ Lake Willoughby
LAKE

This stunning fjord-like lake, 30 miles north of St Johnsbury, sits sandwiched between Mt Hor and Mt Pisgah, whose cliffs plummet more than 1000ft to the glacial waters below. There's a beach at the north end for swimming.

Old Stone House Museum
MUSEUM

(☑ 802-754-2022; www.oldstonehousemuseum. org; 109 Old Stone House Rd, Brownington; adult/child $10/5; ⊘ 11am-5pm Wed-Sun mid-May–mid-Oct) This well-preserved but little-visited museum is just one of many lovely 19th-century buildings reposing under the shade of ancient maple trees in the historic village of Brownington. The museum pays tribute to educational trailblazer Alexander Twilight, the USA's first African American college graduate, who built Brownington's boarding school and ran it for decades. Self-guided visits and guided tours are both available.

Bread & Puppet Museum
MUSEUM

(☑ 802-525-3031; www.breadandpuppet.org/museum; 753 Heights Rd, Glover; donations welcome; ⊘ 10am-6pm Jun-Oct, self-serve access only Nov-May) **FREE** Formed in New York City by German artist Peter Shumann in 1963, the renowned Bread & Puppet theater collective presents carnivalesque pageants, circuses, and battles of Good and Evil with gaudy masks and gigantic puppets. This unique museum consists of a two-story barn crammed with puppets and masks from the company's past performances. The high-ceilinged top floor is especially arresting, with its collection of many-headed demons, menacing generals, priests, bankers, everyday people, animals and gods (some as large as 15ft).

St Johnsbury Athenaeum
GALLERY

(☑ 802-748-8291; www.stjathenaeum.org; 1171 Main St, St Johnsbury; $5 donation requested; ⊘ 10am-5:30pm Mon, Wed & Fri, noon-7pm Tue & Thu, 10am-3pm Sat) Home to one of America's oldest art galleries, this elegant public edifice was initially founded as a library by Horace Fairbanks in 1871. Comprising 9000 hand-bound classics of world literature, the library was soon complemented by a fine art collection, built around its crown jewel, Albert Bierstadt's 10ft-by-15ft painting, *Domes of the Yosemite*. The gallery also features landscapes by Bierstadt's fellow Hudson River School artists, including Asher B

WORTH A TRIP

DOG MOUNTAIN

Signposted 2 miles east of St Johnsbury, captivating **Dog Mountain** (☑ 802-748-2700; www.dogmt.com; 143 Parks Rd, St Johnsbury; ☺ gallery 10am-5pm Sat & Sun, 11am-4pm Mon, Thu & Fri, chapel dawn-dusk daily) celebrates the legacy of Vermont artist Stephen Huneck. There's an entire gallery devoted to Huneck's whimsical dog-themed artwork, but the real showstopper is the adjacent chapel, designed by Huneck to celebrate the enduring bond between humans and animals. Huneck's own contributions (a doggie weathervane, canine-themed doorknobs and stained-glass windows) are complemented by scores of photos and heartfelt notes plastered on the chapel's walls by visitors commemorating their own lost pets.

At least twice a year, Dog Mountain hosts its popular Dog Parties, where dogs are invited in for free dog biscuits, swimming, fun with Frisbees and good-natured canine competitions. Humans will appreciate the live music and superb views over the mountains of Vermont's Northeast Kingdom. See www.dogmt.com/events.html for details.

Durand, Worthington Whittredge and Jasper Cropsey.

Fairbanks Museum & Planetarium
MUSEUM

(☑ 802-748-2372; www.fairbanksmuseum.org; 1302 Main St, St Johnsbury; adult/child $9/7; ☺ 9am-5pm) In 1891, when Franklin Fairbanks' collection of stuffed animals and cultural artifacts from across the globe grew too large for his home, he built the Fairbanks Museum of Natural Science. This massive stone building with a 30ft-high barrel-vaulted ceiling still displays more than half of Franklin's original collection, including a 1200lb moose, a Bengal tiger and a bizarre collection of 'mosaics' made entirely from dead bugs. The attached planetarium offers shows ($6 per person) throughout the year.

🏃 Activities

Hiking

The stunning beauty of Lake Willoughby will leave even a jaded visitor in awe. The lake sits sandwiched between Mt Hor and Mt Pisgah, whose cliffs plummet more than 1000ft to the glacial waters below and create, in essence, a landlocked fjord.

The scenery is best appreciated on the hike to the summit of **Mt Pisgah** (three hours round trip). From West Burke, take VT 5A for 6 miles to a parking area on the left-hand side of the road, just south of Lake Willoughby. The 1.7-mile (one-way) **South Trail** begins across the highway. Alternatively, follow the dirt road north of the parking area 1.7 miles to the **Herbert Hawkes Trail**, and continue 1 mile on foot to the summit of

Mt Hor. The lake is about a 35-minute drive from St Johnsbury.

Biking

On VT 114 off I-91, East Burke is a terrific place to start a mountain-bike ride, with the vast Kingdom Trails network beckoning right at its doorstep.

★ Kingdom Trails
OUTDOORS

(☑ 802-626-0737; www.kingdomtrails.com; 478 VT 114, East Burke; day pass adult/child $15/7; ☺ 8am-5pm Sat-Thu, to 6pm Fri May-Oct; ⊕) ⌖ In 1997 a group of dedicated locals linked together 200-plus miles of single and double tracks and dirt roads to form this astounding, award-winning trail network. Passing through century-old farms and soft forest floors dusted with pine needles, it offers one of New England's best mountain-biking experiences. In winter, the trails are ideal for cross-country skiing, snowshoeing and fat biking.

Kingdom Cycling & Experiences
CYCLING

(☑ 802-427-3154; www.kingdomexperiences.com; guided tours from $70) This mountain-bike specialist on a bucolic hilltop 4 miles north of Lyndonville offers day rides, multiday tours, kids' mountain-bike camps and skills clinics for all ages and ability levels.

Village Sport Shop Trailside
CYCLING

(☑ 802-626-8444; www.villagesportshop.com; 2099 Darling Hill Rd, Lyndonville; bike rental per day $25-90; ☺ 9am-6pm Mon-Fri, from 8:30am Sat, to 5pm Sun May-Oct, 9am-5pm Mon-Sat, to 4pm Sun Nov-Apr) This excellent hilltop shop adjacent to the Kingdom Trails' main trailhead rents bikes for all ages and seasons, and sells day passes for the trail network.

East Burke Sports CYCLING
(☑ 802-626-3215; www.eastburkesports.com; 439 VT 114, East Burke; per day ski or snowboard package $30, bike rental $50-90; ⊙ 8am-6pm) Supplies maps and rents bikes, including top-of-the-line models for serious mountain bikers. In winter, it rents out skis (downhill and cross-country) and snowboards.

Skiing

⭐ **Craftsbury Outdoor Center** SKIING
(☑ 802-586-7767; www.craftsbury.com; 535 Lost Nation Rd, Craftsbury Common; trail pass adult/child $10/5, ski/bike rental per day $15/40; ⊙ 8:30am-5pm; ⊕) Cross-country skiers and fat bikers adore this full-service, low-key resort, complete with rentals, meals and accommodations, just outside Craftsbury Common (38 miles northwest of St Johnsbury). The 80 miles of trails roll over meadows and weave through forests of maples and firs, offering experiences for all levels. In summer, the center is also a mecca for runners and boaters.

Jay Peak SKIING
(☑ 802-988-2611; www.jaypeakresort.com; 830 Jay Peak Rd, off VT 242, Jay; lift ticket adult/child $89/69; ⊕) Even when Boston is balmy, you can still expect a blizzard at Vermont's northernmost ski resort. Only 10 miles south of the Quebec border, Jay gets more snow than any other New England ski area. Easy and intermediate runs are complemented by natural off-trail terrain that offers some of America's most challenging backcountry snowboarding and skiing.

Burke Mountain SKIING
(☑ 802-626-7300; www.skiburke.com; 223 Sherburne Lodge Rd, East Burke; lift ticket adult/child $73/52) Off US 5 in East Burke, Burke Mountain is relatively unknown to out-of-staters, even though nearby Burke Mountain Academy has been training Olympic skiers – such as 2018 giant slalom gold-medalist Mikaela Shiffrin – for decades. Locals enjoy its 52 trails, from beginner to double black diamond, and empty lift lines. In summer the mountain is also a mecca for mountain biking.

Kingdom Trails
Nordic Adventure Center SKIING
(2059 Darling Hill Rd, Lyndonville; day pass adult/child $15/7; ⊙ 8:30am-4pm Dec-Mar) In winter, buy passes for Kingdom Trails' cross-country ski and fat-biking trail network at this hilltop yurt.

🛏 Sleeping

Rodgers Country Inn INN $
(☑ 802-525-6677; www.rodgerscountryinn.com; 582 Rodgers Rd, West Glover; s/d $70/80, cabin per week $600) Not far from Shadow Lake's shores, Jim and Nancy Rodgers offer five guest rooms in their 1840s farmhouse, plus a secluded cabin sleeping up to six. Relax on the front porch and read, or take a stroll on this 350-acre former dairy farm. At this inn you can really feel what it's like to live in rural Vermont.

**Inn at Mountain
View Farm** INN $$
(☑ 802-626-9924; www.innmtnview.com; 3383 Darling Hill Rd, East Burke; r $215-245, ste $295-375; ❀ 🐾) Built in 1883, this spacious, elegant farmhouse is set on a hilltop with stunning views, surrounded by 440 acres that are ideal for mountain biking, cross-country skiing or simply taking a long stroll on the hillside. There's also an on-site animal sanctuary, which is a rescue center for large farm animals; guests are encouraged to visit.

Wildflower Inn INN $$
(☑ 802-626-8310; www.wildflowerinn.com; 2059 Darling Hill Rd, Lyndonville; r $157-249, ste $184-409, cottage $229-254; ⊙ Dec-Mar & May-Oct; 🐾 🏊) Gorgeously sited on a hilltop along a maple-lined dirt road, this smart inn with country furnishings and a wide variety of rooms (including a 19th-century schoolhouse cottage) is a favorite with families. Kingdom Trails' mountain-bike and skiing trails are right next door, and the game room, tennis courts, beer garden and heaps of other onsite activities keep everyone amused.

🍴 Eating

Kingdom Taproom PUB FOOD $
(☑ 802-424-1355; www.kingdomtaproom.com; 397 Railroad St, St Johnsbury; mains $8-16; ⊙ noon-10pm Tue-Thu, to midnight Fri & Sat, to 8pm Sun) You'll find the Northeast Kingdom's largest selection of microbrews on tap at this pub in the heart of St Johnsbury. A bevy of beers from Vermont and beyond, including selections from neighboring New Hampshire and Québec, come accompanied by mac 'n' cheese, soups, salads, flatbreads and sandwiches.

Miss Lyndonville Diner
DINER $

(☎ 802-626-9890; 686 Broad St/US 5, Lyndonville; mains $4-14.50; ⊗ 6am-8pm Mon-Sat, from 7am Sun) Five miles north of St Johnsbury and popular with locals, this place offers friendly, prompt service and a tantalizing display of pies. Large breakfasts are cheap, as are the sandwiches, but for a real steal try the tasty homemade dinners like roast turkey with all the fixings.

Anthony's Diner
DINER $

(☎ 802-748-3613; 50 Railroad St, St Johnsbury; mains breakfast & lunch $5-13, dinner $10-20; ⊗ 7am-4pm Mon, to 8pm Tue-Sat, to 3pm Sun) At this local institution with a large counter, the homemade soups, chowders and desserts are a deserved source of pride. Try the mountain-size Vermont woodsman burger made with local grass-fed beef.

Hardwick St Cafe
CAFE $$

(☎ 802-533-9399; www.highlandartsvt.org/cafe; 2875 Hardwick St, Greensboro; mains $9-22; ⊗ 9am-8pm Tue-Sat, 10:30am-2:30pm Sun) At Greensboro's Highland Center for the Arts, this bright, high-ceilinged cafe takes advantage of its proximity to some of Vermont's finest producers, serving Hillstead Farm Brewery beer on tap along with salads and sandwiches featuring local greens and stupendous cheeses from nearby Jasper Hill Farm. The daily lunch special (any two listed items for $9) is good value.

❶ Information

St Johnsbury Welcome Center (☎ 802-748-8575; www.discoverstjohnsbury.com; 51 Depot Sq; ⊗ 8:30am-5pm Mon-Fri) Atmospherically housed in St Johnsbury's historic railway station.

❶ Getting There & Away

Public transit in the Northeast Kingdom is very limited; the best way to get around is with your own wheels. St Johnsbury is the most convenient gateway, easily reached by I-91 from Brattleboro (two hours, 122 miles) or I-93 from Boston (three hours) and New Hampshire. To reach other destinations, use I-91 as your north–south thoroughfare, then branch off on smaller routes like VT 114, VT 5A or VT 14.

To get to St Johnsbury from Montpelier (55 minutes, 38 miles), take US 2 east; from Burlington, take I-89 to US 2 (1½ hours, 76 miles).

VERMONT NORTHEAST KINGDOM

New Hampshire

☑ 603 / POP 1.3 MILLION

Includes ➡

Portsmouth	324
Manchester	332
Hanover	338
Squam Lake	342
Wolfeboro	343
Franconia Notch State Park	351
Mt Washington Valley	354

Best Places to Eat

➡ Black Trumpet Bistro (p328)

➡ Thompson House Eatery (p358)

➡ Libby's Bistro & Saalt Pub (p363)

➡ Schilling Beer Co (p353)

➡ J-Town Deli & Country Store (p357)

Best Places to Stay

➡ Snowflake Inn (p357)

➡ Omni Mt Washington Hotel & Resort (p359)

➡ Centennial (p332)

➡ AMC Highland Center Lodge (p359)

➡ Notch Hostel (p349)

Why Go?

Jagged mountains, serene valleys and island-dotted lakes lurk in every corner of New Hampshire. The whole rugged state begs for exploration, whether kayaking the hidden coves of the Lakes Region or trekking the upper peaks surrounding Mt Washington. Each season yields a bounty of adrenaline and activity: skiing and snowshoeing in winter, with many slopes open into spring; magnificent walks and drives through fall's fiery colors; and swimming in crisp mountain streams and berry-picking in summer.

Jewel-box colonial settlements like Portsmouth set a sophisticated tone, while historical allure and small-town culture live on in pristine villages like Keene and Peterborough. Manchester and Concord are two urban strongholds sprucing up their main drags with indie shops and innovative eats. There's a relaxing whiff in the air, too – you're encouraged to gaze out at a loon-filled lake, recline on a scenic railway trip or chug across a waterway on a sunset cruise.

When to Go
Concord

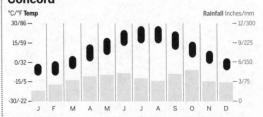

Dec High season for ski resorts; rugged touring vans climb to the Mt Washington tree line.	**Jul** Watch Exeter's American Independence Festival.	**Oct** Witness the technicolor brilliance of fall foliage in the White Mountains.

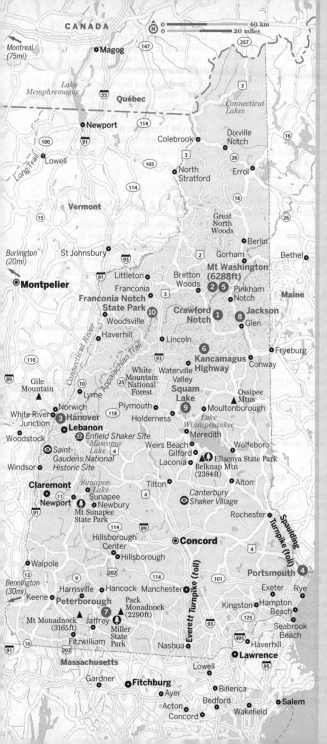

New Hampshire Highlights

❶ Crawford Notch (p358) Hiking the Appalachian Trail through the White Mountains.

❷ Mt Washington Cog Railway (p358) Trundling up the world's second-steepest railway track.

❸ Dartmouth College (p338) Wandering the campus and admiring José Clemente Orozco's mural.

❹ Portsmouth Black Heritage Trail (p327) Getting a new perspective on New England's history.

❺ Mt Washington Auto Road (p359) Driving to just below the 6288ft summit of Mt Washington.

❻ Kancamagus Hwy (p350) Camping by a rushing river beneath the White Mountains.

❼ Peterborough (p334) Experiencing daily life in a community where art and nature rule.

❽ Jackson XC (p357) Snowshoeing or skiing some of the state's best trails.

❾ Squam Lake (p342) Enjoying a boat-ride on this 'loony' lake.

❿ Franconia Notch State Park (p351) Exploring the Flume Gorge and riding the lofty tramway.

History

Named in 1629 after the English county of Hampshire, New Hampshire was one of the first American colonies to declare its independence from England in 1776. During the 19th-century industrialization boom the state's leading city, Manchester, became such a powerhouse that its textile mills were the world's largest.

New Hampshire played a high-profile role in 1944 when President Franklin D Roosevelt gathered leaders from 44 Allied nations to remote Bretton Woods for a conference to rebuild global capitalism. It was at the Bretton Woods Conference that the World Bank and the International Monetary Fund emerged.

In 1963 New Hampshire, long famed for its anti-tax sentiments, found another way to raise revenue – by becoming the first state in the USA to have a legal lottery.

State Parks & Wildlife

The feather in New Hampshire's cap is the White Mountain National Forest, which covers nearly 800,000 acres in New Hampshire and Maine. Hiking trails, skiing slopes, campgrounds, swimming beaches and a few carefully controlled auto roads provide access to this gigantic natural playground.

Aside from the White Mountain National Forest, New Hampshire has a small but exceedingly well-run network of state parks, including Franconia Notch, Crawford Notch and Echo Lake, along with the entire seacoast.

⊙ Getting There & Away

The Blue Star (or New Hampshire) Turnpike along the seacoast, Everett (or Central) Turnpike (I-93) and Spaulding Turnpike (NH 16) are toll roads.

AIR

Manchester-Boston Regional Airport (p334) is the state's largest airport and offers direct flights to a dozen North American cities. The smaller **Lebanon Municipal Airport** (https://lebanonnh. gov/150/Airport; 5 Airpark Rd) and **Portsmouth International Airport** (www.flyportsmouth airport.com; 36 Airline Ave) serve Hanover and Portsmouth, respectively. The nearby Portland International Jetport (p432), in Maine, is a major hub and offers additional flight options.

BUS

Concord Coach Lines (www.concordcoach lines.com) operates a bus route to and from Boston's South Station and Logan International Airport, with stops in Manchester, Concord, Meredith, Conway, North Conway, Jackson, Pinkham Notch, Gorham and Berlin. Another route runs through North Woodstock/Lincoln, Franconia and Littleton.

Dartmouth Coach (www.dartmouthcoach. com) provides services from Hanover, Lebanon and New London to Boston's South Station and Logan International Airport.

Vermont Translines (www.vttranslines.com) runs buses from Hanover to central Vermont, with stops in Woodstock, Killington and Rutland.

NEW HAMPSHIRE COAST

New Hampshire's coastline stretches for just 18 miles but provides access to the captivating coastal town of Portsmouth and a length of attractive beaches, sprinkled around rocky headlands and coves. The shore along these parts has substantial commercial development, but also includes well-regulated access to its state beaches and parks.

Portsmouth

📞 603 / POP 21,800

Perched on the edge of the Piscataqua River, Portsmouth is one of New Hampshire's most elegant towns, with a historical center set with tree-lined streets and 18th-century Colonial buildings. Despite its venerable history as an early hub of America's maritime industry, the town exudes a youthful energy, with tourists and locals filling its many restaurants and cafes. Numerous museums and historic houses allow visitors a glimpse into the town's multilayered past, while its proximity to the coast brings both lobster feasts and periodic days of fog that blanket the waterfront.

Still true to its name, Portsmouth remains a working port town, and its economic vitality has been boosted by the naval shipyard (actually located across the river in Maine) and by the influx of high-tech companies.

⊙ Sights

★**Strawbery Banke Museum**   MUSEUM
(📞 603-433-1100; www.strawberybanke.org; 14 Hancock St; adult/child 5-17yr $19.50/9; ⊙ 10am-5pm May-Oct, special events only Nov-Apr; 🅿 👪)
Spread across a 10-acre site, the Strawbery Banke Museum is an eclectic blend of period homes that date back to the 1690s. Costumed guides recount tales that took place

EXETER'S OWN INDEPENDENCE DAY

Founded in 1638, Exeter is utterly quiet on July 4. But on the second Saturday after the 4th, this small town celebrates Independence Day two weeks after the rest of the country. The spirited **American Independence Festival** (www.independencemuseum. org) brings out the whole town (seemingly) dressed up in Colonial garb. The procession, led by George Washington, and the reading of the Declaration of Independence take center stage. The unusual date of the festival pays homage to July 16, 1776, the date that the Declaration of Independence was read to the citizens of Exeter. Other events include Colonial cooking, militia drills, gunpowder races and, in a nod to modern times, fireworks.

The town's specially designated meetinghouse, unique in these parts, played a crucial role in 1774, when British governor John Wentworth dissolved the provincial assembly that met in Portsmouth in an attempt to prevent the election of a continental congress. The Revolutionary councils then began to gather at the meetinghouse in Exeter, which effectively became the seat of government.

Exeter's early history is best viewed at the **American Independence Museum** (☑603-772-2622; www.independencemuseum.org; 1 Governor's Lane; adult/child $6/3; ☺10am-4pm Tue-Sat May-Nov; P). Among the highlights of this National Landmark property are the furnishings and possessions of the Gilman family, who lived here from 1720 to 1820, along with a document archive, including two original drafts of the US Constitution and personal correspondence of George Washington. Exhibits on the 2nd floor spotlight the Society of the Cincinnati, which is headquartered here. President Washington visited **Folsom Tavern**, just down the hill, in 1789.

Downtown Exeter is packed with indie shops and casual eateries. The 1916 bandstand hosts concerts in summer. Swasey Pkwy beside the Squamscott River is a pretty place to stroll, especially with ice cream from **Stillwells Riverwalk Ice Cream** (☑603-777-5077; www.facebook.com/StillwellsRiverwalk; 190 Water St; 1 scoop $2.75; ☺noon-9pm). Bibliophiles, don't miss **Water Street Bookstore** (☑603-778-9731; www.waterstreetbooks.com; 125 Water St; ☺9am-8pm Mon-Sat, to 6pm Sun). The walk from downtown to **Philips Exeter Academy**, established in 1781, is less than a half mile. Grab dinner and a good night's sleep at the red-brick **Exeter Inn** (☑603-772-5901; www.theexeterinn.com; 90 Front St; r $199-239, ste $279; P ⊛ @ 🖤).

To reach Exeter, take I-95 to exit 2, then NH 101 west. Turn left on Portsmouth Ave/NH 10 and right on Water St. Amtrak's busy *Downeastern* train (www.amtrak.com) stops in Exeter five times daily on its run between Boston, Portland, ME, and Brunswick, ME. The train station (60 Lincoln St) is 0.7 miles from downtown.

among the 40 buildings (10 furnished). Strawbery Banke includes **Pitt Tavern** (1766), a hotbed of American revolutionary sentiment, **Goodwin Mansion** (a grand 19th-century house from Portsmouth's most prosperous time) and **Abbott's Little Corner Store** (1943). The admission ticket is good for two consecutive days.

Wentworth Gardner House HISTORIC SITE
(☑603-436-4406; www.wentworthlear.org; 50 Mechanic St; adult/child under 18yr $6/3; ☺11am-4pm Thu-Mon Jun-Oct) This 1760 structure is one of the finest Georgian houses in the US. Elizabeth and Mark Hunking Wentworth were among Portsmouth's wealthiest and most prominent citizens, so no expense was spared in building this home, which

was a wedding gift for their son. Access is by guided tour.

The adjacent Tobias Lear House (not open to the public) is a hip-roofed Colonial residence that was home to the family of George Washington's private secretary.

Moffatt-Ladd House HISTORIC SITE
(☑603-430-7968; www.moffattladd.org; 154 Market St; adult/child 6-12yr $8/2.50, gardens $2; ☺11am-5pm Mon-Sat, 1-5pm Sun Jun–mid-Oct) Originally built by an influential ship captain for his son, the Georgian Moffatt-Ladd House was later the home of General William Whipple, a signer of the Declaration of Independence. The 18th-century chestnut tree and the old-fashioned gardens behind the house are delightful.

Portsmouth

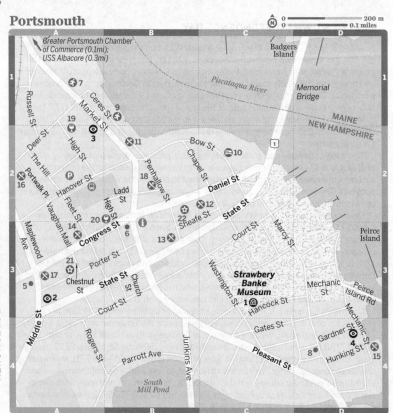

Children's Museum of New Hampshire
MUSEUM

(☎ 603-742-2002; www.childrens-museum.org; 6 Washington St, Dover; $10; ☺10am-5pm Mon-Sat, noon-5pm Sun, closed Mon Sep-May; ⊛) Just 12 miles north of Portsmouth, this children's museum teaches and entertains, with interactive exhibits like the Dino Detective (where kids can be a paleontologist for a day and excavate through mini digs) and the Yellow Submarine (a simulated deep dive). The focus is on having fun while learning.

John Paul Jones House
HISTORIC SITE

(☎ 603-436-8420; www.portsmouthhistory.org/john-paul-jones-house; 43 Middle St; adult/child under 13yr $6/free; ☺11am-5pm late May-early Oct) This former boardinghouse is where America's first great naval commander resided in Portsmouth. Jones, who uttered, 'I have not yet begun to fight!' during a particularly bloody engagement with the British, is believed to have lodged here during the outfitting of the *Ranger* (1777) and the *America* (1781). The marvelous Georgian mansion with gambrel roof is now the headquarters of the Portsmouth Historical Society.

USS Albacore
MUSEUM

(☎ 603-436-3680; www.ussalbacore.org; 600 Market St; adult/child under 18yr $8/3; ☺9:30am-5:30pm late May-mid-Oct; ℗) Like a fish out of water, this 205ft-long submarine is now a beached museum on a grassy lawn. Launched from Portsmouth Naval Shipyard in 1953, the *Albacore* was once the world's fastest submarine. It housed a crew of 55 and was piloted around the world for 19 years without firing a shot. A small maritime museum and gift shop sit beside the sub, which is located just north of the old town center.

Wentworth-Coolidge Mansion
HISTORIC SITE

(☎ 603-436-6607; www.nhstateparks.org; 375 Little Harbor Rd; guided tour adult/child 6-17yr $5/3;

Portsmouth

⊙ Top Sights
1 Strawbery Banke Museum..................C3

⊙ Sights
2 John Paul Jones House......................A3
3 Moffatt-Ladd House..........................A2
4 Wentworth Gardner House...............D4

⊕ Activities, Courses & Tours
5 Discover Portsmouth Walking
   Tour...A3
6 Harbour Trail Tours..........................B3
7 Isles of Shoals Steamship Co..............A1
8 Portsmouth Black Heritage Trail.......D4
9 Portsmouth Harbor Cruises...............B1

⊜ Sleeping
10 Ale House Inn.................................C2

⊗ Eating
11 Black Trumpet Bistro......................B2
12 Colby's..C2
13 Cure..B3
14 Friendly Toast................................A3
15 Geno's...D4
16 Green Elephant..............................A2
17 Jumpin' Jays Fish Cafe....................A3
18 Moxy...B2

⊖ Drinking & Nightlife
19 Earth Eagle Brewings.....................A2
20 Thirsty Moose Taphouse.................B2

⊛ Entertainment
21 Music Hall......................................A3
22 Press Room....................................B2

⊙10am-6pm Mon-Fri, 9am-6pm Sat & Sun early Jun-Aug, Sat & Sun only late May-early Jun & early Sep) This 42-room place south of the town center was home to New Hampshire's first royal governor and served as the colony's government center from 1741 to 1766. The lilacs on its grounds are descendants of the first lilacs planted in America, which were brought over from England by Governor Benning Wentworth.

🏃 Activities

Isles of Shoals Steamship Co CRUISE
(☑603-431-5500; www.islesofshoals.com; 315 Market St; adult/child from $28/18; ⊞) From mid-June to early October this company runs an excellent tour of the harbor and the historic Isles of Shoals aboard a replica 1900s ferry. It also offers walking tours of Star Island and party cruises featuring DJs or live bands.

Portsmouth Harbor Cruises CRUISE
(☑603-436-8084, 800-776-0915; www.ports mouthharbor.com; 64 Ceres St; adult $15-25, child $11-18; ⊙early May-late Oct) Daytime cruises on the *Heritage* explore Portsmouth harbor or the Isles of Shoals, a group of nine islands 6 miles offshore. Other options include wine and sunset cruises, and the Inland River Cruise, which heads inland through pretty tidal estuaries during the colorful fall foliage season.

Portsmouth Kayak Adventures KAYAKING
(☑603-559-1000; www.portsmouthkayak.com; 185 Wentworth Rd; tours $45-75, 3hr/half-day/full-day kayak rental $35/45/64; ⊙9am-5pm) This outfitter offers a range of peaceful kayaking tours out on the harbors near Portsmouth, including a naturalist-led ecotour of Great Bay (the East Coast's second-largest estuary), sunset and full-moon tours, and a combined kayaking/yoga-on-the-beach experience. It also rents out kayaks and stand up paddleboards.

🜚 Tours

Portsmouth Black Heritage Trail WALKING
(☑603-436-8433; www.portsmouthhistory.org/ portsmouth-black-heritage-trail/self-guided-tour; guided tour $20; ⊙tours 2pm most Sat mid-Apr–early Nov) Established by dedicated volunteers in 1995, this historic trail links a series of sites connected with the African American experience in Portsmouth. Bronze plaques commemorate nearly four centuries of Black history, from the arrival of the first enslaved people at Portsmouth's Prescott Park wharf in the 1680s to the formation of the local civil rights group Scorr in the 1960s.

Discover Portsmouth Walking Tour WALKING
(☑603-436-8433; www.portsmouthhistory.org/ take-a-tour; 10 Middle St; tour $15; ⊙10am May-Oct) Sponsored by the Portsmouth Historical Society, these daily 75-minute walking tours explore the history and architecture of downtown Portsmouth.

Harbour Trail Tours WALKING
(☑603-436-3988; www.goportsmouthnh.com; Market Sq; adult/child/teen $15/7/12; ⊙1pm Thu & Sat mid-May–early Oct) This guided walking tour of the historic downtown and waterfront takes you past 10 houses listed in the National Register of Historic Buildings and 10 National Historic Landmarks, including the Moffatt-Ladd House (p325), where a

signer of the Declaration of Independence lived, and the Warner House, one of the few remaining brick mansions in the downtown area.

New England Curiosities

WALKING

(☑ 603-343-7977; www.newenglandcuriosities.com; tours $21-32) New England Curiosities runs a variety of walking tours, including its trademark 'Legends, Ghosts & Graves' tour, visiting old graveyards, an abandoned prison, the 'haunted' pubs of Portsmouth, and other locales where history and mystery collide. Call or check the website for meeting places and times.

🎭 Festivals & Events

Prescott Park Arts Festival

PERFORMING ARTS

(www.prescottpark.org; ⊙ Jun-early Sep; 🐾) This summer arts festival, down by the waterfront in Portsmouth's Prescott Park, features a huge variety of family friendly music, theater, film and dance events with no fixed admission price.

🛌 Sleeping

Howard Johnson Portsmouth

HOTEL $$

(☑ 603-431-4400; www.wyndhamhotels.com; 383 Woodbury Ave; r $188; ⓟ🐾🐾) Orange remains a popular color at this outpost of the long-running HoJo's chain, but the company exudes a modern vibe at these happenin' digs. In fact, the decor has morphed from old school to hip, with rooms adorned with artsy mirrors and fanciful lamps. They also come with mini-refrigerators and microwaves. The only bummer is the loud-slamming doors. Breakfast included.

Port Inn

MOTEL $$$

(☑ 603-436-4378; www.portinnportsmouth.com; 505 US 1 Bypass; r $249-499, ste $499; ⓟ🐾@ 🐾🐾🐾) Wrapped neatly around a small courtyard, this welcoming and inviting motel is conveniently located off I-95, about 1.5 miles southwest of downtown. In the rooms, monochromatic pillows and throws add a dash of pizzazz to classic furnishings. Breakfast included. Pets are $25 per night.

Ale House Inn

INN $$$

(☑ 603-431-7760; www.alehouseinn.com; 121 Bow St; r $234-304; ⓟ🐾🐾) This former brick warehouse for the Portsmouth Brewing Company is Portsmouth's snazziest boutique inn, fusing contemporary design with comfort. Rooms are modern, with clean white lines, flat-screen TVs, and, in the suites,

plush tan sofas. All rooms feature an in-room iPad. Rates include use of Trek cruising bikes, but sadly, free beer is no longer included.

🍴 Eating

Moxy

TAPAS $

(☑ 603-319-8178; www.moxyrestaurant.com; 106 Penhallow St; tapas $7-15; ⊙ 5-9pm Sun-Thu, to 10pm Fri & Sat) Toto, I have a feeling we're not in Spain anymore! Yes, this cool little corner eatery specializes in tapas (small plates), but with a decidedly American twist. Expect anything from mini-burgers, chili-pepper cornbread and whoopie pie sliders to fried clams, oysters, calamari and scallops, accompanied by excellent martinis in a cozy candlelit interior enlivened with yellow-and-olive decor and green-brick walls.

Colby's

BREAKFAST $

(☑ 603-436-3033; 105 Daniel St; mains $4-11; ⊙ 7am-2pm) If you get to this 28-seat eatery after 8am on the weekend, there's going to be a wait, so give 'em your name and enjoy a cup of free coffee on the patio. Once in, egg lovers can choose from a multitude of Benedicts and omelets, along with French toast, pancakes, huevos rancheros and daily chalkboard specials.

Green Elephant

VEGETARIAN $

(☑ 603-427-8344; www.greenelephantnh.com; 35 Portwalk Pl; mains lunch $12-15, dinner $12-17; ⊙ 11:30am-9:30pm Sun-Wed, to 10pm Thu-Sat; 🐾) Vegetarians rejoice! The wildly popular Green Elephant bistro of Portland, ME, has opened its first New Hampshire franchise in Portsmouth. The Chinese-, Malaysian- and Thai-inspired menu of curries, noodles, rice dishes and stir-fries is 100% meat-free, with plenty of steamed veggies and a plethora of vegan and gluten-free options.

Friendly Toast

DINER $

(☑ 603-430-2154; www.thefriendlytoast.com; 113 Congress St; breakfast $7-20, lunch $10-20; ⊙ 7am-7pm Sun, to 8pm Mon-Thu, to 2am Fri & Sat; 🐾🐾) Fun, whimsical furnishings set the scene for filling sandwiches, omelets, Tex-Mex and vegetarian fare at this retro diner. The breakfast menu is huge and is served around the clock: a good thing since weekend morning waits can be long.

⭐ Black Trumpet Bistro

INTERNATIONAL $$

(☑ 603-431-0887; www.blacktrumpetbistro.com; 29 Ceres St; mains $19-32; ⊙ 5-9pm Sun-Thu, to 10pm Fri & Sat) This bistro, with brick walls and a sophisticated ambience, serves unique combinations – anything from housemade sausages infused with cocoa beans to seared haddock with yuzu (an Asian citrus fruit) and miso. The full menu is also available at its wine bar upstairs, which whips up equally inventive cocktails.

Cure
MODERN AMERICAN $$

(☑603-427-8258; www.curerestaurantportsmouth. com; 189 State St; mains $19-35; ⊗5-9pm Sun-Thu, to 10pm Fri & Sat) Constantly showered with accolades, chef Julie Cutting's refined but cozy brick-walled restaurant makes a romantic dinner spot. The menu revolves around New England cuisine 'revisited': pan-roasted duck breast, maple-glazed salmon, beef ribs slow-braised in red wine, horseradish-sour-cream mashed potatoes, crisp-skinned chicken and lobster bisque, all accompanied by seasonal vegetables and a superb cocktail list.

Geno's
SEAFOOD $$

(☑603-427-2070; www.genoschowder.com; 177 Mechanic St; mains $5-23; ⊗11am-4pm Mon-Sat mid-Mar–Oct) Not sure which chowder or stew you want with lunch? You can sample 'em before you decide at welcoming Geno's. For more than 40 years, this family owned no-frills place has been a local institution for homemade chowder and lobster rolls. Its outdoor deck overlooks Portsmouth Harbor – and your waiter might point out the boat that caught your lobster!

Jumpin' Jays Fish Cafe
SEAFOOD $$$

(☑603-766-3474; www.jumpinjays.com; 150 Congress St; mains $23-40; ⊗5-9pm Sun, to 9:30pm Mon-Thu, to 10pm Fri & Sat) This exceptional seafood cafe offers fresh catches of the day simply grilled or seared, plus unconventional twists like the haddock Piccata, with whitefish sliced and sautéed in butter, olive oil and white wine. Add a raw bar, a varied warm and cold appetizer menu, plus a buzzing modern space, and Jumpin' Jays wins on all counts.

🍷 Drinking & Entertainment

Earth Eagle Brewings
MICROBREWERY

(☑603-502-2244; www.eartheaglebrewings.com; 165 High St; ⊗11:30am-10pm Sun-Thu, to midnight Fri & Sat) Don't like the taste of hops? Then step into the rustic taproom at Earth Eagle, where the medieval-style 'gruit' beers rely on herbs and spices, not hops, for flavor. But don't worry, there are enough IPAs on the menu to keep hop-heads happy. Appetizers, hot dogs and a few sandwiches are served if you're hungry.

Thirsty Moose Taphouse
PUB

(☑603-427-8645; www.thirstymoosetaphouse. com; 21 Congress St; ⊗11:30am-1am) This convivial spot has more than 100 beers on tap – leaning heavily toward New England brews – and knowledgeable staff that can walk you through them. Bites include poutine (a Montreal fave: fries drenched in cheese and gravy), fish tacos, burgers and a handful of salads. Downstairs in the Moose Lounge you'll find live music on weekends plus Wednesday trivia nights.

★Music Hall
PERFORMING ARTS

(☑603-436-2400; www.themusichall.org; 28 Chestnut St) For a small-town theater, this venue hosts a surprising array of performances, including dance, theater, film, opera and other music. Musicians, comedians, authors and theater companies from around the country make appearances here.

Press Room
LIVE MUSIC

(☑603-431-5186; www.pressroomnh.com; 77 Daniel St; ⊗4pm-1am Sun-Thu, noon-1am Fri & Sat) Between the nightly live music (jazz to blues to folk, from 6pm to 9pm), the tasty pub fare and the wooden booths, this is one of Portsmouth's best watering holes. A year-long renovation a few years ago gave the place some much needed reconstructive surgery.

ⓘ Information

Greater Portsmouth Chamber of Commerce (☑603-610-5510; www.portsmouthchamber. org; 500 Market St; ⊗9am-5pm Mon-Fri year-round, plus 10am-5pm Sat & Sun late May–mid-Oct), on your way into town, has helpful staff and offers loads of information. Also operates an **information kiosk** (www.goports mouthnh.com; ⊗10am-5pm late May–mid-Oct) in the city center at Market Sq.

ⓘ Getting There & Away

Portsmouth is equidistant (about 57 miles) from Boston and Portland, ME. It takes roughly 1¼ hours to reach Portland and 1½ hours to Boston, both via I-95. Rush-hour and high-season traffic can easily double or triple this, however.

Greyhound (www.greyhound.com) runs one to two buses daily to Boston (from $15, 1¼ hours), Portland (from $17, one hour) and Bangor, ME (from $29, 4¼ hours). **Buses** (☑800-231-2222; www.greyhound.com) stop at 55 Hanover St.

C&J Trailways (☑ 603-430-1100; www.ridecj. com; 185 Grafton Dr) offers more frequent service to Boston from its office 5 miles west of downtown Portsmouth (off NH 33). Hourly buses run to Boston's South Station ($18, 1¾ hours) and Logan International Airport ($24, 1½ hours). C&J also runs two to three daily buses to New York City's Port Authority bus terminal ($79, five hours).

Rye & Hampton Beach

Littered with summer clam shacks, motels, fried-dough stands and arcades full of children, **Hampton Beach** (☑ 603-926-8990; www.nhstateparks.org; State Park Rd; per vehicle $15; P) isn't the classiest stretch of New England coastline, but it has New Hampshire's only sandy beach – a wide, inviting stretch of shore that gives pasty sunseekers their fix. To escape the beach crowds, head to the lower-key town of Hampton, 3 miles northwest of Hampton Beach.

As NH 1A enters Rye, parking along the road is restricted to vehicles with town parking stickers, but **Jenness State Beach** (☑ regional office 603-227-8722; www. nhstateparks.org; 2280 Ocean Blvd, Rye; P 🚻) has a small metered parking lot that's open to the general public. Come here to swim and watch the surfers. Further north near **Rye Harbor** you're allowed to park along the roadway. Climb over the seawall of rubble and rocks to get to the gravel beach. It lacks facilities but is much less crowded than anything further south. Continuing northward, **Wallis Sands State Beach** (☑ 603-436-9404, regional office 603-227-8722; www.nhstateparks. org; 1050 Ocean Blvd, Rye; per vehicle $15; ☉ 8am-4pm late May-late Jun, to 6pm late Jun-early Sep; P 🚻) has a wide sandy beach with views of the Isles of Shoals. Besides the bathhouses, there are grassy lawns for children's games, making this the top spot for families with smaller kids.

⊙ Sights & Activities

Odiorne Point State Park   STATE PARK
(☑ 603-436-7406; www.nhstateparks.org; 570 Ocean Blvd, Rye; adult/child 6-11yr $4/2; ☉ 8am-6pm; P) Walk the woodsy coastal trails, explore the **Seacoast Science Center** (☑ 603-436-8043; www.seacoastsciencecenter. org; 570 Ocean Blvd, Rye; adult/child 3-12yr $10/5; ☉ 10am-5pm mid-Feb–Oct, to 4pm Nov–mid-Feb; P 🚻) or simply sit by the rocky coast and enjoy the view and the breeze. Stop by the admissions desk at the science center for de-

tails about the *Sound of Footsteps in Time* 3-mile audio tour (available on a handheld wand or downloadable from iTunes). The tour covers local and natural history. For a pleasant stroll, try the 1-mile loop from the science center to Frost Point. Bird-watching is popular too.

Summer Sessions   SURFING
(☑ 603-319-8207;   www.newhampshiresurf.com; 2281 Ocean Blvd, Rye; 1hr surfing & SUP lessons $50-60, surfboard rentals half-/full day $25/35, paddleboard rentals half-/full day $35/45; ☉ 10am-7pm) Surfing and stand up paddleboarding lessons and rentals are available from Summer Sessions, located across the street from Jenness Beach State Park.

✦✦ Festivals & Events

**Hampton Beach
Seafood Festival**   FOOD & DRINK
(www.hamptonbeachseafoodfestival.com; Ocean Blvd; Fri/Sat/Sun $5/10/8; ☉ early Sep) Sixty regional restaurants serve lobster, fried clams, shrimp and other seafood dishes to large crowds beside the Atlantic Ocean. Live music and arts-and-crafts booths add to the fun. On Saturday afternoon there's a lobster-roll-eating contest. Unfortunately the admission fee does not include food.

🛏 Sleeping & Eating

Lamie's Inn & Tavern   INN $$
(☑ 603-926-0330; www.lamiesinn.com; 490 Lafayette Rd, Hampton; r $174-184; P ❄ @ 🛜) To escape the din of Hampton Beach, head to this colonial manor, built in 1740, in downtown Hampton. The graceful guest rooms have exposed brick walls, four-poster beds and lace curtains. Breakfast's included. For lunch or dinner, try the on-site Old Salt restaurant (mains $10 to $30), where you'll find a cozy dining room, a small bar and fresh seafood.

Lago's   ICE CREAM $
(☑ 603-964-9880; www.lagosicecream.com; 71 Lafayette Rd, Rye; ice cream $3-6.25; ☉ noon-9pm mid-Mar–May & mid-Aug–early Oct, to 10pm Jun–mid-Aug) Come summer, everyone flocks to Lago's, the New Hampshire coast's favorite spot for ice cream.

Galley Hatch   AMERICAN $$
(☑ 603-926-6152; www.galleyhatch.com; 325 Lafayette Rd/US 1, Hampton; burgers & sandwiches $11-15, mains $15-30; ☉ 11:30am-9pm Mon-Fri, to 10pm Sat & Sun; 🅟) Located in Hampton proper, Galley Hatch is a longtime favorite

for its wide menu of fresh fish, sandwiches, steaks, pastas, pizzas and veggie dishes. The owners also run the on-site Tino's Kitchen & Bar, serving Mediterranean fare, and Kay's Cafe, a coffee shop with a tempting array of pastries and desserts.

❶ Information

Hampton Beach Area Chamber of Commerce (☑603-926-8718; www.hamptonchamber.com; 47 Winnacunnet Rd, Hampton; ⊙9am-5pm Mon-Fri) Provides information about tourist attractions year-round. In summer you can also stop by the visitor information center at the beach (160 Ocean Blvd; open 9am to 9pm daily mid-June to early October).

❶ Getting There & Away

Hampton Beach is easily reached via I-95 from Portsmouth (15 miles), Boston (47 miles) and Portland, ME (66 miles). Take exit 1 if coming from the south, exit 2 if coming from the north. There is no public transportation to Hampton Beach.

MERRIMACK VALLEY

Although New Hampshire is noted more for mountains than for cities, Concord (the state's tidy capital) and Manchester (its largest city) are pleasant – if not overly exotic – places to spend a day. Both sit along the mighty Merrimack River.

Concord

☑603 / POP 43,000

New Hampshire's capital is a trim and tidy city with a wide Main St dominated by the striking State House, a granite-hewed 19th-century edifice topped with a glittering dome. The stone of choice in 'the Granite State' appears in other fine buildings about Concord's historical center, cut from the still-active quarries on Rattlesnake Hill, just north of town. Concord is worth an afternoon visit and also makes a good base for visiting the idyllic Canterbury Shaker Village.

⊙ Sights

New Hampshire Historical Society   MUSEUM
(☑603-228-6688; www.nhhistory.org; 30 Park St; adult/child $7/free; ⊙9:30am-5pm Tue-Sat) The *White Mountains in the Parlor* exhib-

WORTH A TRIP

CANTERBURY SHAKER VILLAGE

A traditional Shaker community from 1792, **Canterbury Shaker Village** (☑603-783-9511; www.shakers.org; 288 Shaker Rd, Canterbury; adult/child 6-17yr $19/9; ⊙10am-4pm Tue-Sat May-Aug, to 5pm daily Sep & Oct, 10am-4pm Sat & Sun Nov; ℗) maintains the Shaker heritage as a living-history museum. Interpreters demonstrate the Shakers' daily lives, artisans create Shaker crafts and walking trails invite pond-side strolls. The greening of America has deep roots here – for more than two centuries the Shakers' abundant gardens have been turning out vegetables, medicinal herbs and bountiful flowers the organic way.

The village is 15 miles north of Concord; take I-93 to exit 18 and follow the signs.

it is our favorite 'indoor space' in the entire Granite State. In this small gallery, vast 19th-century landscape paintings of the striking White Mountains inspire thoughts of adventure. Artifacts in the rest of the compact museum highlight key events in the state's history, with muskets, a voting ballot box used between 1850 and 1980, a 1972 Ski-Doo and more.

McAuliffe-Shepard Discovery Center   MUSEUM
(☑603-271-7827; www.starhop.com; 2 Institute Dr; adult/child 3-12yr $12/11; ⊙10:30am-4pm daily mid-Jun–early Sep, Fri-Sun rest of year; ℗) This science center is named after two New Hampshire astronauts. Christa McAuliffe was the schoolteacher chosen to be America's first teacher-astronaut – she and her fellow astronauts died in the tragic explosion of the *Challenger* spacecraft in 1986 – and Alan B Shepard was a member of NASA's elite *Mercury* corps and became America's first astronaut in 1961. Exhibits – some slightly tired – explore various aspects of space exploration but don't, unfortunately, spend much time on the lives of the two namesake astronauts.

State House   HISTORIC BUILDING
(☑603-271-2154; www.gencourt.state.nh.us; 107 N Main St; ⊙8am-4pm Mon-Fri) FREE The handsome 1819 New Hampshire state capitol

NEW HAMPSHIRE CONCORD

is the oldest such building in the US, and the state legislature still meets in the original chambers. Self-guided tour brochures point out the highlights of the building and its grounds, including the **Memorial Arch**, which commemorates those who served in the nation's wars. The capitol building's **Hall of Flags** holds 103 flags that New Hampshire military units carried into battle in various wars, including the Civil and Vietnam Wars.

🛏️ Sleeping & Eating

★ Centennial   HISTORIC HOTEL $$
(☑ 603-227-9000; www.thecentennialhotel.com; 96 Pleasant St; r $159-179, ste $209-249; P 🛜) This turn-of-the-20th-century turreted Victorian landmark has 32 luxurious rooms and suites. Stylish minimalism prevails, with subdued earth tones, deluxe bedding, trim furnishings, black-and-white artwork, and vessel-bowl sinks in the granite bathrooms. Several rooms are set in the turret, while the best have private outdoor porches. The hotel and its fine-dining, New American restaurant, the **Granite** (☑ 603-227-9005; www.graniterestaurant.com; mains lunch $11-18, dinner $15-25; ⏲ 7-10am, 11:30am-2:30pm & 5-9pm Mon-Thu, to 10pm Fri & Sat, 7am-2:30pm & 5-8pm Sun) are popular with business travelers.

Hotel Concord   BOUTIQUE HOTEL $$
(☑ 603-504-3500; www.hotelconcordnh.com; 11 S Main St; r $209; ❄️🛜) The bland corporate exterior is a bit soul-crushing, but the 38 rooms at this boutique hotel pop with fresh modern style. Spacious bathrooms are a plus, and each room has a mini-refrigerator; a few also have balconies. Located in the thick of the downtown action.

Crust & Crumb   BAKERY $
(☑ 603-219-0763; www.thecrustandcrumb.com; 125 N Main St; pastries $1-4; ⏲ 8am-6pm Tue-Fri, 8am-4pm Sat, 10am-2pm Sun) Get your whoopie pies here. And your scones, tarts, cookies and brownies. Did we mention it has coffee? It's a convenient downtown stop for a mid-afternoon snack and pick-me-up. Everything's homemade.

Barley House   GASTROPUB $$
(☑ 603-228-6363; www.concord.thebarleyhouse.com; 132 Main St; mains lunch $10-17, dinner $10-26; ⏲ 11am-1am) Solo travelers will do just fine at this welcoming downtown tavern's bar where burgers, classic Irish dishes, the lobster BLT and a few menu-crashers – we're looking at you beef brisket banh mi – pair well with the Jack's Abbey lager and other fine craft brews. Across the street from the State House.

ℹ️ Information

Greater Concord Chamber of Commerce
(☑ 603-224-2508; www.concordnhchamber.com; 49 S Main St, Suite 104; ⏲ 8:30am-5pm Mon-Fri) Provides tourist information.

ℹ️ Getting There & Away

Concord is 68 miles north of Boston on I-93.
Concord Coach Lines (☑ 603-228-3300, 800-639-3317; www.concordcoachlines.com; 30 Stickney Ave) operates frequent daily buses from the Concord Transportation Center to Boston's South Station ($17, 1½ hours) and Logan International Airport ($22, 1¾ hours).

Manchester

📞 603 / POP 111,200

Once home to the world's largest textile mill – at its peak, the Amoskeag Manufacturing Company employed 17,000 people (out of a city population of 70,000) – this riverside town retains, both historically and culturally, a bit of its blue-collar roots. Exploiting the abundant water power of the Merrimack River, and stretching along its east bank for over a mile, the mill made the city into a manufacturing and commercial powerhouse from 1838 until its bankruptcy in the 1930s.

Nowadays, attracted by low taxes and a diverse workforce, the high-tech and financial industries have moved in, bringing city culture with them. The former mill is a prime symbol of successful redevelopment: the redbrick swath of structures houses a museum, an arts center, a college, restaurants and a growing array of local businesses. Manchester has opera, several orchestras, a growing gallery and dining scene, and the state's most important art museum.

◎ Sights

Currier Museum of Art   MUSEUM
(☑ 603-669-6144; www.currier.org; 150 Ash St; adult/child $15/5, incl Zimmerman House tour $25/10; ⏲ 11am-5pm Sun, Mon & Wed-Fri, 10am-5pm Sat; P) Housing works by John Singer Sargent, Georgia O'Keeffe, Monet, Matisse and Picasso (among many others), this fine-arts museum is Manchester's greatest cultural gem. With advance reservation, mu-

LAKE SUNAPEE

Lake Sunapee is a worthwhile detour any time of year. In summer, head to the lake situated within **Mount Sunapee State Park** (☑603-763-5561; www.nhstateparks.org; 86 Beach Access Rd, Newbury; adult/child 6-11yr $5/2; ☉9am-6pm early Jun-early Sep, Sat & Sun mid-May–early Jun & mid-Sep; P), off NH 103, for hiking, picnicking, swimming and fishing. The wide sandy beach has a pleasant grassy sitting area. Canoes and kayaks are available for rental. From I-89 take exit 9, NH 103, to Newbury.

In winter, alpine skiing is the attraction at **Mt Sunapee Resort** (☑603-763-3500; www.mtsunapee.com; 1398 NH 103, Newbury; lift ticket adult/child 6-12yr $78/52; ☉skiing 9am-4pm Mon-Fri, 8am-4pm Sat & Sun late Dec-late Feb). Mt Sunapee has a vertical drop of 1510ft – the biggest in southern New Hampshire. It's not much to compete with Cannon or Loon Mountain, but it offers some challenging skiing all the same. Rentals, lessons and childcare are available. Coming from Hanover or Concord, take exit 12A off I-89 and turn right on Rte 11. In the town of Sunapee, turn left onto Rte 103B. Coming from the south, take exit 9 and follow NH 103 through Bradford and Newbury to Mt Sunapee.

seum guides also offer tours of the nearby **Zimmerman House**, the only Frank Lloyd Wright–designed house in New England that's open to the public.

Millyard Museum MUSEUM
(☑603-622-7531; www.manchesterhistory.org; 200 Bedford St; adult/child 12-18yr $8/4; ☉10am-4pm Tue-Sat) A highlight in the **Amoskeag Millyard Historic District** (P), this well-executed museum spotlights the various communities that have lived and worked near Amoskeag Falls from prehistoric times forward, with a focus on the city's years as a textile manufacturing center. Stories about the different immigrant enclaves during this time are particularly fascinating.

🛏 Sleeping

Ash Street Inn B&B $$
(☑603-668-9908; www.ashstreetinn.com; 118 Ash St; r $199-219; P❄🐾) Dating to 1885, this Victorian home has been thoughtfully renovated into a comfortable B&B. Rooms all come with top-of-the-line sheets and towels, plush robes, high-speed internet and good lighting for business travelers who need to get a little work done. It's just a one-minute walk from Manchester's Currier Museum of Art.

Manchester Downtown Hotel HOTEL $$
(☑603-625-1000; www.doubletree3.hilton.com; 700 Elm St; r $181-200, ste $430; P❄@🐾🏊) Now a Hilton Doubletree, this revamped hotel anchors Elm St and is within an easy walk of downtown's best restaurants, bars and shops. The hotel is large, with more than 200 rooms, but rooms are spacious,

fresh and modern. First-floor common areas were under construction during research. Rates drop by half on weekends.

🍴 Eating & Drinking

El Rincon Zacatecano Taqueria MEXICAN $
(☑603-232-4530; www.elrinconzt.com; 10 Lake Ave; mains $4-25; ☉11am-9pm Tue-Sat, to 6pm Sun) Why yes, I would like a margarita with my chicken enchilada, the one slathered in the specialty *molito* sauce (chilies, chocolate and spice). For a no-fuss but tasty Mexican meal, pop into this tiny taqueria around the corner from Veteran's Memorial Park downtown. Kids welcome.

Republic MEDITERRANEAN $$
(☑603-666-3723; www.republiccafe.com; 1069 Elm St; mains $7-24; ☉11am-9pm Mon-Thu, 11am-10pm Fri, 9am-10pm Sat & Sun) The first certified 'farm-to-restaurant' establishment in New Hampshire, Republic is still turning heads and impressing taste buds. Kudos you stylish thing! For lighter fare, check out the flatbreads, paninis and salads. For heartier eats, dive into one of the many Mediterranean dishes like Turkish chicken with spicy yogurt and couscous or Moroccan red-lentil stew. The atmosphere and service are upbeat.

Strange Brew CRAFT BEER
(☑603-666-4292; www.strangebrewtavern.net; 88 Market St; ☉4pm-1:30am) On a sunny Sunday afternoon the patio is the place to be at this long-running craft-beer bar with more than 80 beers on tap, from ales to shandies and lots in between. The interior? Dark with a low ceiling and small stage – and not quite as charming as the patio.

❶ Getting There & Away

Driving from Boston to Manchester via I-93 and the Everett Turnpike takes an hour. It's another 30 minutes from Manchester to Concord via I-93.

Concord Coach Lines (www.concordcoachlines.com) runs frequent daily buses to Logan International Airport ($19, 1¾ hours) and South Station ($15, 1½ hours) in Boston, as well as north to Concord ($6, 30 minutes). Buses depart from the Manchester Transportation Center.

Fast growing but still not too large, **Manchester-Boston Regional Airport** (☑603-624-6556; www.flymanchester.com; 1 Airport Rd; ☎), off US 3 south of Manchester, is a civilized alternative to Boston's Logan International Airport.

MONADNOCK REGION

In the southwestern corner of the state the pristine villages of Peterborough and Jaffrey Center anchor Mt Monadnock (moh-*nahd*-nock; 3165ft). 'Mountain That Stands Alone' in Algonquian, Monadnock is relatively isolated from other peaks, which means hikers to the summit are rewarded with fantastic views of the surrounding countryside. The trail, however, is anything but lonely. Monadnock is one of the most climbed mountains in the world.

Peterborough

☑603 / POP 6500

Picturesque Peterborough is a charming village of redbrick houses and tree-lined streets, with the idyllic Nubanusit River coursing through its historic center. Nestled between Temple Mountain and Mt Monadnock, Peterborough is a gateway to some captivating countryside, and its restaurants and B&Bs draw plenty of visitors in their own right.

Peterborough is also a thriving arts community, an impression left deeply by the nearby MacDowell Colony. Founded in the early 1900s, the country's oldest art colony has attracted a diverse and dynamic group of poets, composers, playwrights, architects, filmmakers, painters and photographers. Aaron Copland composed parts of *Appalachian Spring* at the colony; Virgil Thomson worked on *Mother of Us All*; Leonard Bernstein completed his Mass; and Thornton Wilder wrote *Our Town,* a play that was openly inspired by Peterborough. Milton Avery, James Baldwin, Barbara Tuchman and Alice Walker are among the luminaries that have passed this way.

◉ Sights

Miller State Park STATE PARK
(☑603-924-3672; www.nhstateparks.org; 13 Miller Park Rd; adult/child 6-11yr $4/2; ⊙8am-6pm Sun-Fri, to 8pm Sat late May-early Sep, hours vary rest of year; ℙ) New Hampshire's oldest state park, Miller revolves around Pack Monadnock, a 2290ft peak not to be confused with its better-known neighbor, Mt Monadnock. The park has three easy-to-moderate paths to the summit; you can also access the 21-mile Wapack Trail here. A 1.3-mile scenic auto road also ends at the summit, where you can climb the fire tower for magnificent views of surrounding peaks. Miller State Park is about 4.5 miles east of Peterborough along NH 101.

> **WORTH A TRIP**
>
> ### BURDICK'S OF WALPOLE
>
> Locals descend from surrounding villages to dine at this fabulous eatery. Originally a New York City chocolatier, Burdick relocated to this tiny gem of a New Hampshire village and opened a sophisticated cafe, simply known as **Burdick Chocolates** (☑603-756-2882; www.burdickchocolate.com/chocolateshop-cafe-walpole.aspx; 47 Main St, Walpole; pastries from $3; ⊙7am-5pm Mon, to 9pm Tue-Sat, 9am-5pm Sun), to showcase his desserts.
>
> Complementing these rich chocolaty indulgences, the adjacent **Restaurant at Burdick's** (☑603-756-9058; www.47mainwalpole.com/the-restaurant.html; 47 Main St, Walpole; mains lunch $17-27, dinner $17-33; ⊙11:30am-2:30pm Mon, 11:30am-3pm & 5:30-9pm Tue-Sat, 10am-2pm Sun) has a bistro-style menu of French-themed dishes like onion soup, steak frites and mussels *mariniere*, plus a few regional dishes like New England oysters plus artisanal cheeses and top-notch wines. Dress to feel special.

MACDOWELL COLONY

This century-old art colony (www.macdowellcolony.org) draws more than 250 poets, composers, writers, architects and playwrights to the Peterborough area each year. Playwright Thornton Wilder wrote *Our Town*, a play that drew its inspiration from Peterborough, while at the colony. The grounds are closed to the public, but on the first Friday of every month between March and November, MacDowell fellows share their work through the **MacDowell Downtown** program, a series of free performances and panel discussions held at various public venues in downtown Peterborough.

The grounds do open to the public on Medal Day, typically the second Sunday in August, when artists gather for a themed day of celebration.

Mariposa Museum MUSEUM
(✉ 603-924-4555; www.mariposamuseum.org; 26 Main St; adult/child $6/4; ⊙ 11am-5pm Tue-Sun; 🚼) This museum, which exhibits folk art and folklore from around the world, implores visitors to 'please touch.' It's a wonderful place for kids, who are invited to dive into the collections to try on costumes, experiment with musical instruments, play with toys and make their own art. For adults, permanent exhibits on display are somewhat limited, so consider visiting during one of the periodic interactive performances featuring musicians and storytellers, or when the temporary exhibits are of interest.

🛏 Sleeping & Eating

**Little River
Bed & Breakfast** B&B $
(✉ 603-924-3280; www.littleriverbedandbreakfast.com; 184 Union St; r $145-155; 🛜) One mile west of the village center on the gorgeous Nubanusit River, this 19th-century farmhouse once served as housing for artists at the nearby MacDowell Colony. Innkeepers Paula and Rob Fox have converted it into a cozy B&B with four immaculate guest rooms and tasty breakfasts featuring homemade granola and muffins.

Jack Daniels Motor Inn MOTEL $$
(✉ 603-924-7548; www.jackdanielsinn.com; 80 Concord St/US 202; r $159-179; 🅿 ❄ 🛜 🐾) With its flower-bedecked entrance and scenic perch beside the Contoocook River, the Jack Daniels is pretty darn lovely for a motel. Rooms, on two floors, come with microwaves and refrigerators. A few rooms are pet friendly; add $40 per stay if traveling with a pet.

Bakers Station BAKERY $
(✉ 693-784-5653; www.bakersstation.com; 18 Depot Sq; pastries $2-4, sandwiches $5-9; ⊙ 8am-2pm Tue-Sun) Need something sweet? Step into this bakery for cookies, muffins, pastries and other desserts. Also sells bagel sandwiches.

Nonie's CAFE $
(✉ 603-924-3451; www.facebook.com/noniespeterborough; 28 Grove St; mains breakfast $4-9, lunch $7-9; ⊙ 7am-2pm Mon-Sat, to 1pm Sun) A long-time Peterborough favorite, Nonie's serves excellent breakfasts as well as fresh bakery items. In the summer grab a table in the tiny front garden.

🍸 Drinking & Entertainment

Harlow's Pub PUB
(✉ 603-924-6365; www.harlowspub.com; 3 School St; ⊙ 4-10pm Mon, 11:30am-10pm Tue-Thu, to 1am Fri & Sat, to 9pm Sun) This local pub has a good selection of draft beers, including New England brews. It also serves pub fare until 9pm, but the real reason to come here is for the convivial wooden bar and to catch live music Thursday and Saturday nights.

Peterborough Players THEATER
(✉ 603-924-7585; www.peterboroughplayers.org; 55 Hadley Rd) This acclaimed community theatre group performs at a wonderful barn-style performance hall about 3.5 miles from Peterborough center. The group was founded in 1933, and today has a winter and a summer season.

**Peterborough Folk
Music Society** LIVE MUSIC
(✉ 603-827-2905; www.pfmsconcerts.org; 19 Grove St; tickets $20-28) This active group attracts nationally known folk musicians to perform in Bass Hall at the downtown Monadnock Center for History & Culture. Shows have included the Jonathan Edwards Trio and renowned New Hampshire singer-songwriter Tom Rush.

ℹ Information

Greater Peterborough Chamber of Commerce (☑ 603-924-7234; www.peterboroughchamber.com; 10 Wilton Rd/NH 101; ⊙ 9am-4pm Mon-Fri) Stop by for regional information.

ℹ Getting There & Away

Peterborough is at the intersection of US 202 and NH 101 (roughly one hour southwest of Concord and 15 minutes' drive northeast of Jaffrey Center). No public transportation is available.

Jaffrey Center

☑ 603 / POP 5260

The village of Jaffrey has an attractive downtown, but photographers and history buffs will want to head 2 miles west to Jaffrey Center, a tiny, picture-perfect snow globe of serene lanes, 18th-century homes and a dramatic white-steepled meetinghouse.

⊙ Sights

Jaffrey Meetinghouse   NOTABLE BUILDING
(www.townofjaffrey.com; Blackberry Lane; P) Built in 1775, this striking white building doubled as a church and a community meeting hall until the mid-1800s. It was later used for town business, until 1914. Although it's not open to the public during the day, you can check out the interior during lectures, concerts and the annual reading of the Declaration of Independence on July 4.

Old Burying Ground   CEMETERY
(Blackberry Lane; P) For a deeper look at Jaffrey history, wander the cemetery behind the meetinghouse. Willa Cather, a frequent area visitor who wrote portions of her novels in Jaffrey (including *My Ántonia* and *One of Ours*), is buried here (a quotation from *My Ántonia* graces her tombstone). Former slave Amos Fortune has also been laid to rest here. Fortune purchased his freedom and became a successful local tanner, later bequeathing money to the community.

Melville Academy Museum   MUSEUM
(www.townofjaffrey.com; 39 Thorndike Pond Rd; ⊙ 2-4pm Sat & Sun Jul & Aug) FREE Housed in Jaffrey's first high school, which opened in 1833, this museum spotlights local luminaries like novelist Willa Cather. You'll also find a mishmash of rural artifacts, including clothing from the 1880s, logging and farm tools, and decorative hatboxes, known as bandboxes, made out of spruce and pine in the early 1800s by Jaffrey native Hannah Davis.

🛏 Sleeping & Eating

Monadnock Inn   INN $
(☑ 603-532-7800; www.monadnockinn.com; 379 Main St; r $99-160; P🐾🛜🌀) Down the road from Mt Monadnock State Park, this 11-room family run inn has welcomed guests for more than 100 years. Rooms have a quirky, old-fashioned vibe, each with its own unique color scheme and decorative style. Beautifully maintained grounds and wide porches grace the exterior. A **restaurant and pub** (☑ 603-532-7800; mains restaurant $14-28, pub $10-13; ⊙ 5:30-8pm Tue-Thu, to 9pm Fri & Sat, 10am-2pm Sun) are on-site. Rates include breakfast.

Kimball Farm   ICE CREAM, SEAFOOD $$
(☑ 603-532-5765; www.kimballfarm.com/jaffrey; 158 Turnpike Rd/NH 124, Jaffrey; mains $7-32, small ice cream $5; ⊙ 10am-10pm mid-Apr–early

---

DON'T MISS

MT MONADNOCK STATE PARK

Visible from 50 miles in any direction, the commanding 3165ft peak of Mt Monadnock is southwestern New Hampshire's spiritual vortex. The surrounding **Mt Monadnock State Park** (☑ 603-532-8862; www.nhstateparks.org; 169 Poole Rd, Jaffrey; day use adult/child 6-11yr $5/2; P) is an outdoor wonderland, complete with a visitor center, a camp store, 12 miles of ungroomed cross-country ski trails and over 40 miles of hiking trails, about 10 miles of which reach the summit. The 3.9-mile **White Dot & White Cross** (www.nhstateparks.org; 169 Poole Rd, Mt Monadnock State Park, Jaffrey) loop is a popular hiking route to the top.

In summer there's camping on-site at **Gilson Pond Campground** (☑ info 603-532-2416, reservations 877-647-2757; www.nhstateparks.org; 585 Dublin Rd/NH 124, Jaffrey; tent sites $25; ⊙ early May-Oct; P). In winter, camping is available on a first-come, first-served basis at the Headquarters Campground near the park's main entrance. No pets.

Oct) This dairy has achieved more than local fame for its sinfully creamy ice cream, which comes in 40 flavors and unbelievable portion sizes; it's the perfect reward after a hike up nearby Mt Monadnock. It also serves excellent sandwiches and fried seafood – those in the know get the famous lobster rolls.

Sunflowers CAFE $$
(☑ 603-593-3303; www.sunflowerscatering.com; 21 Main St, Jaffrey; mains lunch $10-14, dinner $11-26; ⊙ 11am-2pm Mon-Fri, to 3pm Sat, 5-7:30pm Mon, Wed & Thu, to 8:30pm Fri & Sat, 9am-2pm Sun) In the heart of Jaffrey (2 miles east of Jaffrey Center), this cozy cafe with its cheerful blue and yellow facade is the perfect place to relax and enjoy the good life with creative salads and sandwiches at lunch and baked haddock and steaks for dinner. Burgers are always on the menu.

❶ Information

Jaffrey Chamber of Commerce (☑ 603-532-4549; www.jaffreychamber.com; 7 Main St, Jaffrey; ⊙ 10am-4pm Mon-Fri) Pick up a walking-tour brochure here.

❶ Getting There & Away

Jaffrey is at the intersection of US 202 and NH 124, while quaint Jaffrey Center is 2 miles west on NH 124. No public transportation is available.

Keene

☑ 603 / POP 23,000

This settlement of historic homes and manicured streets is a superb base for those wishing to explore the Monadnock region while staying in a classic New England town with a strong community feel. Although there aren't many noteworthy sights, you could easily spend an afternoon exploring the shops and restaurants along the photogenic Main St.

But be aware that the Norman Rockwell face of downtown has become a bit of a facade in recent years, hiding a community deeply affected by the opioid and heroin epidemic striking small towns across the US. Nearby I-93 has been dubbed the Heroin Highway. Evidence of the problem can be found in the increased number of transients and panhandlers on Main St. Their presence isn't overwhelming, and the bustling downtown feels very safe, but it's an unfortunate change.

◉ Sights

Thorne-Sagendorph Art Gallery GALLERY
(☑ 603-358-2720; www.keene.edu/tsag; Wyman Way; ⊙ noon-7pm Wed & Thu, to 5pm Fri-Sun) FREE Housed at **Keene State College** (☑ 603-358-2276; www.keene.edu; 229 Main St), the Thorne-Sagendorph Art Gallery plays a crucial role in supporting the arts in this rural region. Its spacious sky-lit halls showcase rotating exhibits of regional and national artists. Sagendorph also hosts regular exhibits focusing on New Hampshire native artists and promising art students at the college. The small permanent collection includes pieces by the many national artists that have been drawn to the Monadnock region since the 19th century.

⊨ Sleeping & Eating

**Fairfield Inn & Suites
Keene Downtown** HOTEL $$$
(☑ 603-357-7070; www.marriott.com; 30 Main St; r $249-279; ℗✸❋⊗) In a picture-perfect Main St location, this venerable century-old hotel (formerly known as the Lane Hotel) has 40 attractive rooms, each uniquely furnished in a classic style, ensuring you won't get the cookie-cutter experience. There are plenty of creature comforts (individual climate control, high-speed internet connections, on-site breakfast) and a good restaurant on the 1st floor.

Lindy's Diner DINER $
(☑ 603-352-4273; www.lindysdiner.com; 19 Gilbo Ave; mains $4-17; ⊙ 6am-8pm Sun-Thu, to 9pm Sat & Sun) During presidential primary season, Lindy's is the place to see and be seen by the leading candidates. Past presidential guests include Bill Clinton, George Bush, George W Bush and Barack Obama. The rest of the time, the easygoing staff at this 1961 prefab diner serve egg dishes, pancakes, burgers, sandwiches and house specialties like fried clams and Salisbury steak.

Stage AMERICAN $$
(☑ 603-357-8389; www.thestagerestaurant.com; 30 Central Sq; mains $11-24; ⊙ 11:30am-9pm Tue-Thu, to 10pm Fri, 8am-9pm Sat & Sun) Locals bump elbows at the bar and across the dining rooms at this lively spot on Central Sq, where you can tuck into hearty helpings of American fare. The Hell on Trottole, a spicy pasta dish with chicken, kielbasa and a kicky creole sauce, was one of our favorite dishes across the state.

NEW HAMPSHIRE KEENE

☆ Entertainment

Colonial Theater THEATER
(✆ 603-352-2033; www.thecolonial.org; 95 Main St) After 90 years, this classic Main St theater is still going strong. A diverse lineup of off-Broadway musicals, African and Eastern dance troupes, jazz ensembles, rock bands and stand-up comics graces its stage. Also screens movies.

❶ Getting There & Away

Keene is 20 miles west of Peterborough via NH 101 and 20 miles east of Brattleboro, VT, via NH 9.

UPPER CONNECTICUT RIVER VALLEY

The Connecticut River, New England's longest, is the boundary between New Hampshire and Vermont. The Upper Connecticut River Valley extends from Brattleboro, VT, in the south to Woodsville, NH, in the north, and includes towns on both banks. The river has long been an important byway for explorers and traders. Today it is an adventure destination for boaters, bird-watchers, canoeists and kayakers. The region's largest population center is Lebanon, while the cultural focal point is prestigious Dartmouth College in Hanover.

Hanover

✆ 603 / POP 11,400

Hanover is the quintessential New England college town. On warm days, students toss Frisbees on the wide college green fronting Georgian ivy-covered buildings, while locals and academics mingle at the laid-back cafes, restaurants and shops lining Main St. Dartmouth College has long been the town's focal point, giving the area a vibrant connection to the arts.

Dartmouth was chartered in 1769 primarily 'for the education and instruction of Youth of the Indian Tribes.' Back then, the school was located in the forests where its prospective students lived. Although teaching 'English Youth and others' was its secondary purpose, in fact, Dartmouth College graduated few Native Americans and was soon attended almost exclusively by colonists. The college's most illustrious alumnus is Daniel Webster (1782–1852), who graduated in 1801 and went on to be a prominent lawyer, US senator, secretary of state and perhaps the USA's most esteemed orator.

◉ Sights & Activities

Dartmouth College UNIVERSITY
(✆ 603-646-1110; www.dartmouth.edu) Hanover is all about Dartmouth College, so hit the campus. Join a free student-guided **campus walking tour** (✆ 603-646-2875; http://dartmouth.edu; 10 N Main St, 6016 McNutt Hall) FREE or just pick up a map at the admissions office and head off on your own.

Don't miss the **Baker-Berry Library** (✆ 603-646-2704; http://dartmouth.edu; 25 N Main St; ⊙ 8am-2am Mon-Fri, 10am-2am Sat & Sun), splashed with the grand *Epic of American Civilization,* painted by the outspoken Mexican muralist José Clemente Orozco (1883–1949), who taught at Dartmouth in the 1930s.

★ Dartmouth College Green SQUARE
The green is the focal point of the Dartmouth College campus, both physically and historically. Along the east side of the green, Dartmouth Row consists of four harmonious Georgian buildings: Wentworth, Dartmouth, Thornton and Reed. Dartmouth Hall was the original college building, constructed in 1791. Just north of Dartmouth Row, **Rollins Chapel** (College St) is a fine example of Richardsonian architecture and a peaceful place to collect your thoughts.

★ Hood Museum of Art MUSEUM
(✆ 603-646-2808; http://hoodmuseum.dartmouth.edu; 6 E Wheelock St; ⊙ 10am-5pm Tue & Thu-Sat, to 9pm Wed, noon-5pm Sun) FREE Shortly after the college's founding in 1769, Dartmouth began to acquire artifacts of artistic or historical interest. Since then the collection has expanded to include nearly 70,000 items, which are housed at the Hood Museum of Art. The collection is particularly strong in American pieces, including Native American art. One of the highlights is a set of Assyrian reliefs from the Palace of Ashurnasirpal that dates to the 9th century BCE. Special exhibitions often feature contemporary artists.

Sanborn Library NOTABLE BUILDING
(Dartmouth College; ⊙ 8am-midnight daily, teatime 4pm Mon-Fri) Named for Professor Edwin Sanborn, who taught for almost 50 years in Dartmouth's English department, the Sanborn Library features ornate woodwork, plush leather chairs, and books lining the

walls on two levels. One of Dartmouth's most endearing traditions is the afternoon tea served here on weekdays (when school is in session) between 4pm and 5pm – tea costs 10¢ and cookies 15¢; visitors are welcome but expected to maintain a respectful silence for the benefit of the diligently toiling students.

Enfield Shaker Museum
MUSEUM

(☎603-632-4346; www.shakermuseum.org; 447 NH 4A, Enfield; adult/child 6-10yr/youth 11-17yr $12/3/8; ⏰10am-5pm Mon-Sat, noon-5pm Sun; P) Set in a valley overlooking Mascoma Lake (11 miles southeast of Dartmouth), the Enfield Shaker site dates back to the late 18th century and grew into a small but prosperous community of Shaker farmers and craftspeople in the early 1800s. The museum centers on the Great Stone Dwelling, the largest Shaker dwelling house ever built.

Ledyard Canoe Club
KAYAKING, CANOEING

(☎603-643-6709; www.ledyardcanoeclub.org; Tuck Rd; canoe & kayak/stand up paddleboard rentals per hour $10/15; ⏰11am-7pm Mon-Fri, 10am-7pm Sat & Sun late Jun–mid-Aug, hours vary spring & fall) On the Connecticut River, this Dartmouth-run outfit rents canoes, kayaks and paddleboards to the general public. Cash or check only. See the website for directions; it's off W Wheelock St.

🛏 Sleeping

Storrs Pond Recreation Area
CAMPGROUND $

(☎603-643-2134; www.storrspond.org; 59 Oak Hill Dr/NH 10; tent/RV sites $32/40; ⏰mid-May–early Sep; P🐾) In addition to 21 woodsy sites next to a 15-acre pond, this private campground has tennis courts and two sandy beaches for swimming. From I-89 exit 13, take NH 10 north and look for signs.

Great Stone Dwelling
HOTEL $$

(☎603-632-4346; www.shakermuseum.org/stay withus.htm; 447 NH 4A, Enfield; s/d/tr $110/ 135/160; P🐾) This grand stone edifice – the centerpiece of the Enfield Shaker Museum – also doubles as an atmospheric lodging. On the 3rd and 4th floors are seven single rooms, 11 doubles and two triples. All are spacious and filled with natural light, with pretty wood floors, traditional Shaker furniture and wi-fi, but no air-conditioning or TV.

Hanover Inn
INN $$$

(☎603-643-4300; www.hanoverinn.com; 2 E Wheelock St; r $319-369, ste $369-569; ❄@🐾🏊) Owned by Dartmouth College and situated

Hanover

Hanover

◎ Top Sights
1 Baker-Berry Library A1
2 Dartmouth College Green A2
3 Hood Museum of Art B2

◎ Sights
4 Dartmouth College A2
5 Dartmouth Hall B2
6 Reed Hall B2
7 Rollins Chapel B1
8 Sanborn Library A1
9 Thornton Hall B2
10 Wentworth Hall B1

⊕ Activities, Courses & Tours
Dartmouth Campus
   Walking Tours .... (see 4)

🛏 Sleeping
11 Hanover Inn A2

✖ Eating
12 Candela Tapas Lounge B3
13 Lou's A2
14 Morano Gelato A3

directly opposite the college green, Hanover's loveliest guesthouse has nicely appointed rooms with elegant wood furnishings. It has a cocktail bar and a farm-to-table restaurant on-site.

✖ Eating

★ Morano Gelato
ICE CREAM $

(☑603-643-4233; www.facebook.com/Morano GelatoHanover; 57 S Main St; small gelato $3.75; ⊙noon-9:30pm Wed & Thu, noon-10pm Fri, 11am-10pm Sat, 11am-9:30pm Sun) Founder Morgan Morano fell head over heels for gelato while living in Florence. Next step? Import some genuine Italian equipment and launch this brilliant gelato shop in the heart of Hanover. With new batches made fresh every morning, complemented by cakes and espresso drinks, it's one of the best dessert spots in the state. Open on Tuesdays in warmer months.

Lou's
DINER $

(☑603-643-3321; www.lousrestaurant.net; 30 S Main St; mains $6-15; ⊙6am-3pm Mon-Fri, 7am-3pm Sat & Sun) A Dartmouth institution since 1947, this is Hanover's oldest establishment, always packed with students meeting for a coffee or perusing their books. From the retro tables or the Formica-topped counter, order typical diner food like eggs, sandwiches and burgers. Breakfast is served all day, and the bakery items are highly recommended (the bakery is open till 5pm, Monday to Saturday).

Candela Tapas Lounge
TAPAS $$

(☑603-277-9094; www.candelatapas.com; 15 Lebanon St; tapas $6-20; ⊙5-9pm Tue-Thu, to 10pm Fri & Sat) This chic spot serves classic Spanish-style tapas such as *gambas chorizo* (shrimp sautéed in garlic, white wine, butter and lemon with chorizo) and *albondigas* (meatballs), along with *tablas* (meat and cheese boards), empanadas, braised steak tacos, and Puerto Rican red beans and rice. Colorful cocktails and Mediterranean wines add to the romantic appeal.

❶ Information

Hanover Area Chamber of Commerce
(☑603-643-3115; www.hanoverchamber.org; 53 S Main St, Suite 208; ⊙9am-4pm Mon-Fri) Stop by the 2nd floor of the Nugget Building for maps and brochures. Appalachian Trail thru-hikers will find a helpful regional guide on the website.

Information Booth (Dartmouth Green; ⊙mid-Jun–mid-Sep) On the Dartmouth green, and only open between June commencement and student move-in day, this staffed booth has campus walking tour maps and can provide information about a wide range of topics, from hiking trails to kids' activities to local restaurants.

❶ Getting There & Around

From Boston to Hanover, it's a two- to three-hour drive depending on traffic; take I-93 to I-89 to I-91. From Hanover to Burlington, VT, it's an additional 1½ hours north via I-89.

Dartmouth Coach (www.dartmouthcoach. com) operates 10 daily shuttles from Hanover to Boston's South Station ($33, 2¾ hours) and Logan International Airport (adult/child under 15 years $38/free, three hours), plus twice-daily service to New York City (adult/child $80/40), with three trips on Sundays.

Vermont Translines (www.vttranslines.com) serves destinations in Vermont, including Woodstock ($5, 45 minutes), Killington ($10.50, 1¼ hours) and Rutland ($13, 1¾ hours).

Advance Transit (www.advancetransit.com) provides a free service to White River Junction and Norwich, both in Vermont, plus Lebanon and West Lebanon. Bus stops are indicated by a blue-and-yellow AT symbol.

MOOSILAUKE RAVINE LODGE

Set amid wooded hills and pristine countryside, **Moosilauke Ravine Lodge** (☑Dec-Apr 603-646-6543, May-Nov 603-764-5858; http://outdoors. dartmouth.edu/services/ravine_lodge; 1 Ravine Lodge Rd, Warren; dm adult/child $35/25, linen $8, breakfast/bag lunch/ dinner $9/8/16; ⊙mid-May–mid-Aug & mid-Sep–mid-Nov) is 50 miles north of Hanover and offers basic bunks, shared baths and family style meals. It's operated by the Dartmouth Outing Club (DOC) but open to the public. Thirty miles of hiking trails connect the lodge to the summit of Mt Moosilauke and other trailheads.

The lodge is actually closer to Lincoln, which is 12 miles to the northeast, than Hanover. Facilities here are closed to the public during DOC trips for first-year students between mid-August and mid-September.

LAKES REGION

The Lakes Region, with an odd mix of natural beauty and commercial tawdriness, is one of New Hampshire's most popular holiday destinations. Vast Lake Winnipesaukee, the region's centerpiece, has 183 miles of coastline, more than 300 islands and excellent salmon fishing. Catch the early morning mists off the lake and you'll understand

CASTLE IN THE CLOUDS

Perched on high like a king surveying his territory, the arts-and-crafts-style **Castle in the Clouds** (☎603-476-5900; www.castleintheclouds.org; 455 Old Mountain Rd/NH 171, Moultonborough; adult/child 5-17yr $17/10; ⊙10am-5:30pm daily late May–late Oct, Sat & Sun mid-May–late May; P) wows with its stone walls and exposed-timber beams, but it's the views of lakes and valleys that draw the crowds. In autumn the kaleidoscope of rust, red and yellow beats any postcard. The 5500-acre property features gardens, ponds and a path leading to a small waterfall. Admission includes a self-guided tour of the house, with stories about the eccentric millionaire Thomas Plant, who built it.

Paid at the front gate, the admission fee allows access to a 2-mile scenic road, which ends just below the house, originally known as the Lucknow Mansion. For an extra $15 you can take the Basement Tour, which explores the lives of the former servants. Last admission to the house is 4pm. From late June to late August, make reservations for sunset music performances and dinner on Monday and Thursday nights. Check the online calendar for other events, ranging from yoga on the lawn to star-gazing.

There is no admission fee to explore and hike the sprawling grounds, which can be reached via a public access road west of the main entrance (586 Ossipee Park Rd; open 10am to 6pm).

why the Native Americans named it 'Smile of the Great Spirit.' The prettiest stretches are in the southwest between Glendale and Alton (on the shoreline Belknap Point Rd), and in the northeast corner between Wolfeboro and Moultonborough (on NH 109). To the north lie the smaller Squam and Little Squam Lakes.

The roads skirting the shores and connecting the lakeside towns pass forested mountains and a riotous spread of small-town Americana: amusement arcades, go-kart tracks, clam shacks, junk-food outlets and boat docks. Even if you're just passing through, stop for a swim, a lakeside picnic or a cruise.

Meredith

☎603 / POP 6390

More upscale than Weirs Beach, Meredith is a lively lakeside town with a long commercial strip stretching along the shore. Its few backstreets are set with attractive colonial and Victorian homes. There are no sights per se, but it's a convenient base for exploring the Lakes Region and offers a slew of accommodations and dining options. US 3, NH 25 and NH 104 converge here.

🛏 Sleeping & Eating

**Long Island Bridge
Campground**   CAMPGROUND $

(☎603-253-6053; www.longislandbridgecampgroundnh.com; 29 Long Island Rd, Moultonborough; tent/RV sites from $32/41; ⊙mid-May–mid-Oct;

P) Thirteen miles northeast of Meredith, this camping area overlooking Lake Winnipesaukee has popular tent and RV sites and a private beach. Waterfront sites are more expensive; in July and August there's a one-week minimum stay for them. To get here, follow NH 25 east for 1.5 miles from Center Harbor, then go south on Moultonborough Neck Rd for 6.5 miles.

Meredith Inn B&B   INN $$

(☎603-279-0000; www.meredithinn.com; 2 Waukewan St; r $159-229; ❋🐾) This delightful Victorian inn has eight rooms outfitted with antique furnishings and luxurious bedding; several rooms also have Jacuzzis, gas fireplaces or walk-out bay windows. Breakfast included in the rates.

Lakeside Deli & Grille   SANDWICHES $

(☎603-677-7132; www.facebook.com/Lakeside DeliGrille; 2 Pleasant St; most sandwiches $6-11; ⊙11am-4pm Sun, Mon, Wed & Thu, to 8pm Fri & Sat) For a delicious lunch with prime Lake Winnipesaukee views, hit the front porch of this deli just east of downtown, beloved for its reasonably priced sandwiches, homemade soups, and fish tacos with fresh haddock and chipotle mayo.

Waterfall Cafe   CAFE $

(☎603-677-8631; www.millfalls.com/dine; Mill Falls Marketplace, 312 Daniel Webster Hwy/US 3; mains $6-10; ⊙6:30am-1pm Mon-Fri, 7am-1:30pm Sat, 7am-1pm Sun) A bright, friendly space on the top floor of the **Mill Falls Marketplace** (www.millfalls.com/shop; 312 Daniel Webster Hwy/ US 3; ⊙10am-5:30pm Mon-Thu, to 9pm Fri & Sat)

SWIMMING IN WHITE LAKE

Twenty-two miles northeast of Meredith off NH 16, you'll find some of New Hampshire's finest swimming in **White Lake State Park** (📞 603-323-7350; www.nhstateparks.org; 94 State Park Rd, Tamworth; adult/child 6-11yr $5/2). The pristine glacial lake's origins date back to the last ice age. The state park has 200 tent sites (available late May to mid-October; with/without water views $30/25) on over 600 acres, plus swimming and hiking trails.

(part of a former working mill), this cafe dishes up mainly breakfast food like omelets, buttermilk pancakes and eggs Benedict, with lunch items like salads and sandwiches. Country tables flank a spectacular wall mural depicting Lake Winnipesaukee and the surrounding rolling hills.

ℹ️ Information

Meredith Chamber of Commerce (📞 877-279-6121, 603-279-6121; www.meredithareachamber.com; 272 Daniel Webster Hwy/US 3; ⊙ 9am-4pm Mon-Fri Jun-Sep, Mon, Wed & Fri Oct-May) Provides information about local attractions for visitors.

ℹ️ Getting There & Away

Meredith is 40 miles north of Concord and 107 miles north of Boston. Take I-93 to exit 23, then follow NH 104 east into town.

Concord Coach Lines (www.concordcoachlines.com) passes through Meredith on its twice-daily run between Boston and North Conway. Buses stop near the Memorial parking sign in the public parking lot near the northeast corner of US 3 and NH 25. You cannot buy tickets at the stop. Destinations include Concord ($13, one hour), Boston's South Station ($25, 2½ hours) and Logan International Airport ($30, 2¾ hours).

Squam Lake

Northwest of Lake Winnipesaukee, Squam Lake is more tranquil, more tasteful and more pristine than its big sister. It is also less accessible, lacking any public beaches. Nonetheless, if you choose your lodging carefully, you can enjoy Squam Lake's natural wonders, just like Katharine Hepburn and Henry Fonda did in the 1981 film *On Golden Pond*. With 67 miles of shoreline and

67 islands, there are plenty of opportunities for fishing, kayaking and swimming.

Holderness is the area's main town, at the southwest corner of Squam Lake. Little Squam Lake is a much smaller branch further southwest.

⊙ Sights & Activities

Squam Lakes

Natural Science Center   SCIENCE CENTER
(📞 603-968-7194; www.nhnature.org; 23 Science Center Rd, off NH 113, Holderness; adult/child 3-15yr $20/15, boat tours $27/23; ⊙ 9:30am-5pm May-Oct; P 🚻) To get up close and personal with the wildlife in the Lakes Region, visit the Squam Lakes Natural Science Center. Four nature paths weave through the woods and around the marsh. The highlight is the **Gephart Trail**, leading past trailside enclosures that are home to various creatures, including bobcats, fishers (a kind of marten), mountain lions and a bald eagle. Note that last admission to the trail is at 3:30pm.

West Rattlesnake Mountain   WALKING
(🚻) One of New Hampshire's best family hikes, and a great sunset excursion, the gradual 1-mile climb of West Rattlesnake Mountain (1260ft) on the Old Bridle Path ends atop broad flat rocks overlooking the Lakes Region. Squam Lake is in the foreground, Lake Winnipesaukee in the distance. The trailhead is 4 miles north of Squam Lake (Holderness) on NH 113.

Experience Squam   BOATING
(📞 603-968-3990; www.experiencesquam.com; 859 US 3, Holderness; trips from $225; ⊙ Apr-Nov; 🚤) Take your pick of private boat excursions on Squam Lake, from *On Golden Pond* tours, with a member of the original film crew, to wildlife-spotting excursions, to sunset and moonlight cruises. Bring Fido on the Dog Lovers' trip. Owner Cynthia O'Leary has been running trips for more than 10 years.

🛏️ Sleeping & Eating

Squam Lake Inn   INN $$
(📞 800-839-6205, 603-968-4417; www.squamlakeinn.com; 28 Shepard Hill Rd, Holderness; r $219-319; P @ 🐾) This century-old Victorian farmhouse has eight rooms, all decorated in vintage New England style – quilts on the beds, antique furnishings and a local 'Lakes' theme – with modern touches like iPod docking stations. Higher-priced rooms in-

clude gas fireplaces and/or stoves. A mahogany deck and wraparound porch overlook woodsy grounds. Breakfast included.

Cottage Place on Squam Lake COTTAGE $$
(☑ 603-968-7116; www.cottageplaceonsquam.com; 1132 US 3, Holderness; 1-room cottages $129-135, 2-room cottages $160-189, ste $189-229; P 🛜 🐾) The cozy, comfortable Cottage Place fronts Squam Lake, offering a private beach, a swimming raft and docking space for boats. There is a wide variety of accommodations, including standard rooms and lakefront cottages; all come with a kitchen, many with wood-burning fireplaces. Weekly rentals are encouraged in summer. Pets cost $20 extra per night.

Squam Lake Marketplace SANDWICHES $
(☑ 603-968-8588; www.facebook.com/Squam LakeMarketplace; 863 US 3, Holderness; breakfast sandwiches $3-9, lunch sandwiches $8-10; ☉ 7am-7pm mid-Apr–Dec) This gourmet grocery store and bakery serves excellent breakfast and lunch sandwiches, local homemade fudge and other goodies. You'll also find beer, wines, sake, marinated meats and veggies (ready for grilling), pasta salads and marvelous scones. May close earlier in slower months.

Walter's Basin AMERICAN $$
(☑ 603-968-4412; www.waltersbasin.com; 859 US 3, Holderness; mains $10-26; ☉ 11:30am-9pm Sun-Thu, to 9:30pm Fri & Sat) Lake trippers are encouraged to dock their boats and come in for a meal at this casual waterfront spot. Located on Little Squam Lake near the bridge, the friendly restaurant features pan-fried haddock, elk meatloaf, grilled steak tip sandwiches, lobster macaroni and cheese, and other comfort fare. Sip a craft beer at the easygoing Basshole Lounge.

🛈 Getting There & Away

Holderness is 42 miles north of Concord and 109 miles north of Boston. Take I-93 to exit 24, then follow NH 25/US 3 into town, skirting the north shore of Little Squam Lake.

Concord Coach Lines (www.concordcoach lines.com) operates two daily buses from Boston to North Conway, stopping off in Center Harbor on the east side of Squam Lake. The bus stop is at Village Car Wash & Laundromat, on US 25 in Center Harbor. Destinations include Concord ($14, one hour), Boston's South Station ($26, 2¾ hours) and Logan International Airport ($31, three hours).

Wolfeboro

☑ 603 / POP 6285

On the eastern shore of Lake Winnipesaukee, Wolfeboro is an idyllic town where children still gather around the ice-cream stand on warm summer nights and a grassy lakeside park draws young and old to weekly concerts. Named for General Wolfe, who died vanquishing Montcalm on the Plains of Abraham in Quebec, Wolfeboro (founded in 1770) claims to be 'the oldest summer resort in America.' Whether that's true or not, it's certainly one of the most charming, with pretty lake beaches, intriguing museums, beautiful New England architecture (from Georgian through Federal, Greek Revival and Second Empire), cozy B&Bs and a worthwhile walking trail that runs along several lakes as it leads out of town.

◉ Sights

Wright Museum MUSEUM
(☑ 603-569-1212; www.wrightmuseum.org; 77 Center St; adult/child 5-17yr $10/6; ☉ 10am-4pm Mon-Sat, noon-4pm Sun May-Oct) For a Rosie-the-riveter and baked-apple-pie look at WWII, visit this museum's interactive exhibitions that feature music, documentary clips, posters and other American paraphernalia. There are also uniforms, equipment and military hardware (including a 42-ton Pershing tank), meticulously restored by the museum. The Tuesday-evening summer lecture series (June to mid-September) is a huge draw – speakers range from authors to war refugees.

Libby Museum MUSEUM
(☑ 603-569-1035; www.thelibbymuseum.org; 755 N Main St/NH 109, Winter Harbor; adult/child under 16yr $5/free; ☉ 10am-4pm Tue-Sat, noon-4pm Sun Jun–mid-Sep) At the age of 40, Dr Henry Forrest Libby, a local dentist, began collecting things. In 1912 he built a home for his collections, which later became the eccentric little Libby Museum. Starting with butterflies and moths, the amateur naturalist built up a private natural history collection. Other collections followed, including Abenaki relics and early American farm and home implements. It lies 3 miles north of Wolfeboro.

Clark House Museum Complex MUSEUM
(☑ 603-569-4997; www.wolfeborohistoricalsocie ty.org/clarkhouse.html; 233 S Main St; adult/student $4/2; ☉ 10am-4pm Wed-Fri, to 2pm Sat Jul & Aug) Wolfeboro's eclectic historical museum

comprises three historic buildings: the 1778 Clark family farmhouse, an 1805 one-room schoolhouse and a replica of an old firehouse. The buildings contain relevant artifacts (such as fire engines!), furniture and the like.

🏃 Activities

Cotton Valley Rail Trail
WALKING

(www.cottonvalleyrailtrail.org; Central Ave) This excellent multiuse rail trail starts at Wolfeboro's information office and runs for 12 miles along an old railway bed. It links the towns of Wolfeboro, Brookfield and Wakefield and passes two lakes, climbs through Cotton Valley, and winds through forests and fields around Brookfield. From Wolfeboro, the trail's first half mile is also known as the Bridge Falls Path.

Abenaki Ski Area
SKIING

(www.wolfeboronh.us/abenaki-ski-area; 390 Pine Hill Rd/NH 109A; lift ticket $20; ⊙ 4-7pm Wed-Fri, 11am-7pm Sat, 11am-6pm Sun late Dec-early Mar, closed Mon-Thu rest of Mar) An adorable anomaly in this age of corporate-run mega-resorts, America's oldest local ski hill (opened in 1936) charges a pittance for lift tickets but comes with unexpected amenities, like modern snowmaking equipment, night skiing and a new lodge. There are also 18 miles of cross-country ski trails. It's 3 miles north of town on NH 109A.

Dive Winnipesaukee
BOATING, DIVING

(☑ 603-569-8080; www.divewinnipesaukee.com; 4 N Main St; canoe or kayak rental per day $45; ⊙ 9am-6pm Jun-Oct, 9am-3pm Wed & Thu, 9am-5pm Fri, 7am-3pm Sat & Sun Nov-May) For adventures in the deep blue, visit this all-purpose water-sports outfitter by the lakeside in the heart of town. It rents canoes and kayaks and offers a range of diving courses in the frigid lake. Note that opening hours may vary slightly.

🛏 Sleeping & Eating

Suite Inn
APARTMENT $$

(☑ 603-569-9959; www.thesuiteinn.com; 7 Railroad Ave; apt $80-225; 🕾) Smack in the heart of town (a few steps from the tourist office), these four self-catering apartments are indeed a 'sweet' deal for anyone seeking the conveniences of home while on vacation. Each comes with two bedrooms, a living room and a kitchen, and the lakeshore is just a stone's throw away.

Wolfeboro Inn
INN $$$

(☑ 603-569-3016; www.wolfeboroinn.com; 90 N Main St; r $219-279, ste $319-359; P ❷ 🕾 🛎) The town's best-known lodging is right on the lake with a private beach. One of the region's most prestigious resorts since 1812, it has 44 rooms across a main inn and a modern annex. Rooms have modern touches like new beds and contemporary furnishings: it feels less historic but oh-so-luxurious. Facilities include a restaurant and pub, **Wolfe's Tavern** (www.wolfestavern.com; dinner mains $12-31; ⊙ 7am-9pm Sun-Thu, to 10pm Fri & Sat).

Downtown Grille Cafe
CAFE $

(☑ 603-569-4504; www.downtowngrillecafe.com; 33 S Main St; pastries $2-4, breakfast mains $4-9, lunch mains $8-14; ⊙ 7am-3pm) Order at the counter then head to the back patio for a great view of Lake Winn with your ham-and-pepper-jack panini, hot-pressed *cubano* or, our favorite, the kickin' buffalo chicken wrap with blue cheese and hot sauce. Stop by in the morning for pastries and breakfast sandwiches. Fancy coffees available, too.

Wolfetrap Grill & Rawbar
SEAFOOD $$

(☑ 603-569-1047; www.wolfetrapgrillandrawbar. com; 19 Bay St; mains $9-26; ⊙ 11am-9pm Tue-Sat May-late Nov) Nantucket meets New Hampshire at this airy eatery tucked away on Back Bay, an inlet of Lake Winnipesaukee. Inside tables are covered with parchment paper – ready for you to attack and get messy with shellfish (oysters, clams, shrimp, lobster) – while the deck has loungey chairs overlooking the water. The bar keeps going, as the bartenders say, 'till the wolf howls.'

Mise En Place
FRENCH, AMERICAN $$$

(☑ 603-569-5788; www.miseenplacenh.com; 96 Lehner St; mains $26-35; ⊙ 5-9pm Tue-Sat Jul & Aug, Wed-Sat late Jun, Thu-Sat Sep-late Jun) With its minimalist decoration and pleasant front patio, this is a wonderful place for dinner. Think filet mignon, roasted rack of lamb and a wide selection of seafood dishes, from lobster-and-crab risotto to seared sea scallops with sage butter and mushroom ravioli. Reservations advisable.

ℹ Information

Wolfeboro Chamber of Commerce Information Booth
(☑ 603-569-2200; www.wolfeboro chamber.com; 32 Central Ave; ⊙ 10am-3pm Mon-Sat, to noon Sun late May–mid-Oct, reduced hours rest of year) Located inside the old train station, this small office has the scoop on local activities.

ℹ Getting There & Away

Wolfeboro is on the east side of Lake Winnipesaukee, at the intersection of NH 28 with the lakeside NH 109. From I-93, take US 3 to its intersection with NH 11. Follow this road south as it skirts the lake. Pick up NH 28 in Alton and head north.

There is no public transportation to or from Wolfeboro.

Weirs Beach & Laconia

♪ 603

Called 'Aquedoctan' by its Native American settlers, Weirs Beach takes its English name from the weirs (enclosures for catching fish) that the first European settlers found along the small sand beach. Today Weirs Beach is the honky-tonk heart of Lake Winnipesaukee's childhood amusements, famous for video-game arcades and fried dough. The vacation scene is completed by a lakefront promenade, a public beach and a dock for small cruising ships. A water park and drive-in theater are also in the vicinity. Away from the din on the waterfront, you will notice evocative Victorian-era architecture – somewhat out of place in this capital of kitsch.

South of Weirs Beach lie Laconia, the largest town in the region but devoid of any real sights, and lake-hugging **Gilford**. Note that this side of the lake gets mobbed with bikers for nine days each June during Laconia Motorcycle Week (www.laconiamcweek.com), the world's oldest motorcycle rally.

🏃 Activities & Tours

Belknap Mountain   HIKING
(Belknap Carriage Rd) At 2384ft, Belknap Mountain is the highest peak in the Belknap range, with numerous hiking trails. The most direct route to the summit is from the Belknap Carriage Rd in Gilford. From NH 11A/Cherry Valley Rd, follow the signs for the Belknap Fire Tower. Three marked trails lead from the parking lot to Belknap summit, a one-hour trek.

Winnipesaukee Scenic Railroad   RAIL
(🗘 603-745-2135; www.hoborr.com; 211 Lakeside Ave; adult/child 3-11yr 1hr $18/14; 🚻) The touristy Scenic Railroad offers one- or two-hour lakeside rides aboard 1920s and '30s train cars departing from Weirs Beach and Meredith (154 Main St). The train travels to Lake Winnipesaukee's southern tip at Alton Bay before making a U-turn. Kids love the ice-

PUMPKIN MANIA

One of New Hampshire's quirkiest annual gatherings, the **New Hampshire Pumpkin Festival** (www.facebook.com/NHPumpkinFestival; Main St, Laconia; ⊙ Oct), on the third or fourth Saturday in October, draws thousands of visitors to downtown Laconia to admire the world's largest jack-o'-lantern tower. Started in 1991 by merchants in Keene, the event exploded over the years; the town's 2003 tally of nearly 29,000 pumpkins set a Guinness world record.

cream-parlor car; for $25 (per adult or child) you can ride in the caboose.

WOW Trail   WALKING, CYCLING
(www.wowtrail.org; 🚲) This ever-growing paved trail stretches south from Lakeport to downtown Laconia then continues to Belmont and the Winnisquam Scenic Trail. Currently 4.5-miles long, the WOW Trail is open to walkers, joggers and cyclists. You can access the trail behind the Laconia train station. The name is an acronym for the lakes on view: Winnipesaukee, Opechee and Winnisquam.

★ MV Sophie C   CRUISE
(🗘 603-366-5531; www.cruisenh.com/sophie.php; 211 Lakeside Ave; adult/child 5-12yr $28/14; ⊙ 11am & 2pm Mon-Sat mid-Jun–early Sep) The MV *Sophie C* is a veritable floating post office. Passengers are invited to accompany this US mail boat as it delivers packages and letters to quaint ports and otherwise inaccessible island residents across four to five islands. Between mid-June and early September, its two 1½-hour runs depart six days a week from Weirs Beach.

MS Mount Washington   CRUISE
(🗘 603-366-5531; www.cruisenh.com; 211 Lakeside Ave; adult/child 5-12yr regular cruises $32/16, Sun brunch cruises $52/26; ⊙ mid-May–late Oct) The classic MS *Mount Washington* steams out of Weirs Beach daily, making a relaxing 2½-hour scenic circuit around Lake Winnipesaukee, with regular stops in Wolfeboro and occasional visits to Alton Bay, Center Harbor and/or Meredith. Special events include Sunday champagne brunch cruises, and themed cruises (sunset dinner-and-dance, an Elvis Tribute, a Lobsterfest cruise) throughout summer and early fall.

NEW HAMPSHIRE WEIRS BEACH & LACONIA

🛏 Sleeping & Eating

Paugus Bay Campground CAMPGROUND $
(☑603-366-4757; www.paugusbaycampground.
com; 96 Hilliard Rd, Laconia; tent/RV sites $47/51;
☺mid-May–mid-Oct; 🅿🐾) Off US 3, Paugus
has wooded sites overlooking the lake. The
campground has a private beach as well
as other recreation facilities, and regularly
holds fun family friendly events like pancake breakfasts and ice-cream socials.

Proctor's
Lakehouse Cottages APARTMENT $$$
(☑603-366-5517; www.lakehousecottages.com;
1144 Weirs Blvd/US 3, Weirs Beach; cottages $250-
340, ste $315; ☺mid-May–early Oct; 🅿🐾🛜🐾)
This welcoming family-owned collection
of cottages and suites, all with kitchens, is
blissful. The more modern suites clustered
in the main structure feature porches, while
cottages exude old-school New England
with original wood walls and rustic (but
well-kept) furnishings. All have views of
the lake (there's a tiny beach and deck), and
every unit comes with its own lakeside grill.

NASWA Resort HOTEL $$$
(☑603-366-4341; www.naswa.com; 1086 Weirs
Blvd, Weirs Beach; r $289-349; ☺May-Oct;
🅿🛜🐾) If you like to be in the thick of
the action, pack your suntan lotion and
best sun-n-fun attire for this festive, multi-
building resort overlooking Lake Winnipesaukee. Rooms aren't posh, considering the
price point, but they are fresh and fairly
modern. Overall, the staff give a darn despite
the busyness. Private beach, a lakeside bar
and a restaurant on-site.

Union Diner DINER $
(☑603-524-6744; www.theuniondiner.com; 1331
Union Ave, Laconia; mains $5-14; ☺6am-3pm Mon-
Wed, to 8pm Thu-Sat, to 1pm Sun) Escape the
waterfront hubbub at this classic American
diner 3 miles south of Weirs Beach, housed
in a converted 1950s railway dining car with
oak-mahogany woodwork and decorative
floors. Grab a booth or a counterside stool
and treat yourself to early-bird breakfast
specials or a lunch of homemade meatloaf,
lobster stew, or roast turkey with stuffing
and cranberry sauce.

O Steaks & Seafood STEAK, SEAFOOD $$
(☑603-524-9373; www.magicfoodsrestaurant-
group.com/osteaks; 62 Doris Ray Ct, Lakeport;
mains lunch $10-20, dinner $16-56; ☺11:30am-
2:30pm Tue-Fri, dinner daily 5-10pm) At this styl-
ish spot with grand views of the lake, choose

from steaks, fish and the house specialty,
lobster mac-and-cheese. Salads, burgers and
fish and chips are served at lunchtime.

🍷 Drinking & Entertainment

NazBar & Grill BAR
(☑603-366-4341; www.naswa.com; 1086 Weirs
Blvd, Laconia; ☺from 11am late May-early Oct)
This colorful lakeside bar is recommended
because it's a scene. This is Weirs Beach, af-
ter all. Watch boats pull up to the dock as
you sip your cocktail beside – or in – the
lake. Bar fare includes nachos, salads, wraps
and burgers.

Weirs Drive-In CINEMA
(☑603-366-4723; www.weirsdrivein.com; 76
Endicott St/US 3; per car $28; ☺7-11pm mid-
May–early Sep; 📽) Opened in 1949 and in
continual operation since then, this drive-in
movie theater is a revered institution, show-
ing summertime double features on four
screens. The minimum charge per carload
is $28, which covers four people. Each addi-
tional person pays $6.

ℹ Information

Lakes Region Chamber of Commerce
(☑603-524-5531; www.lakesregionchamber.
org; 383 S Main St, Laconia; ☺9am-3pm Mon-
Fri) Supplies information year-round about the
Laconia/Weirs Beach area.

ℹ Getting There & Away

Weirs Beach is on the west side of Lake Winnipe-
saukee. From I-93 take exit 20 (from the south)
or 24 (from the north) to US 3. There is no bus
service or other public transportation to Laconia
or Weirs Beach.

WHITE MOUNTAINS

Covering one-quarter of New Hampshire
(and part of Maine), the vast White Moun-
tains area is a spectacular region of soaring
peaks and lush valleys, and contains New
England's most rugged mountains. There
are numerous activities on offer, including
hiking, camping, skiing and canoeing. Much
of the area – 786,000 acres – is protected
from overdevelopment as part of the White
Mountain National Forest (WMNF), which
celebrated its centennial in 2018. Note, how-
ever, that this wondrous place is popular: six
million visitors flock here annually to use its
1200 miles of hiking trails, 23 campgrounds
and eight Nordic and alpine ski areas.

WATERVILLE VALLEY

In winter the town of Waterville Valley shimmers like a snow globe come to life. Tucked in a valley in the shadow of Mt Tecumseh, just south of the White Mountains, the village was developed as a complete mountain resort community. Condominiums and golf courses are carefully set on picture-perfect Corcoran's Pond, surrounded by miles of downhill and cross-country ski trails, hiking trails, bike routes and in-line skating paths. The result is a harmonious – although a touch sterile – resort with lots of organized sports activities. The **Waterville Valley Ski Area** (☑800-468-2553; www.waterville.com; 1 Ski Area Rd; lift ticket adult/child 6-12yr/teen 13-17yr $93/73/83; ☺9am-3:45pm Mon-Fri, from 8am Sat & Sun) is accessible to non-resort visitors.

Connected by scenic drives and rugged trails, there are four popular areas in the White Mountains for recreation: Mt Washington Valley to the east, Crawford Notch and Bretton Woods along US 302 in the center, the Kancamagus Hwy along the southern fringe and the Franconia Range to the west and northwest.

ⓘ Getting There & Around

I-93, running north from Boston to St Johnsbury, VT, offers the most efficient access to the White Mountains. Take any of the exits between Waterville Valley in the south and Littleton in the north to explore smaller east–west roads that lead deeper into the mountains.

In Mt Washington Valley, Concord Coach Lines (www.concordcoachlines.com) offers service to Concord, Boston's South Station and Logan International Airport on its daily trip between Boston and Berlin, NH. Buses traveling this route stop in Gorham, Pinkham Notch, Jackson and North Conway.

In the western White Mountains, Greyhound (www.greyhound.com) and Concord Coach Lines stop at Irving Gas Station (p354) in Littleton. From here, Concord stops in Lincoln, Concord and Manchester on its way to Boston's South Station and Logan International Airport.

Every summer, the Appalachian Mountain Club (AMC) runs two convenient shuttle services (p360) ferrying hikers among the White Mountain National Forest's top trailheads. The western route links AMC's Highland Center at Crawford Notch (p360) with the Lincoln Woods Visitor Center (p351) on the Kancamagus Hwy, making intermediate stops at the Zealand, Gale River, Lafayette, Liberty Spring at Whitehouse and Old Bridle Path trailheads; the eastern route connects the AMC Highland Center with Pinkham Notch via the 19 Mile Brook and Ammonoosuc Ravine trailheads. Advance reservations are strongly recommended.

North Woodstock & Lincoln

North Woodstock and its neighboring settlement Lincoln gather a mix of adventure seekers and drive-by sightseers en route to the Kancamagus Hwy (NH 112). North Woodstock has a busy but small-town feel with weathered motels and diners lining the main street and a gurgling river running parallel to it. Nearby Lincoln has less charm, but serves as the starting point for the entertaining Hobo Railroad and other family friendly activities such as zipline tours and an aerial adventure park.

◉ Sights

Lost River Gorge & Boulder Caves CAVE, GORGE
(☑603-745-8031; www.lostrivergorge.com; 1712 Lost River Rd/NH 112, North Woodstock; adult/child 4-12yr $21/17, lantern tours per person $33; ☺9am-5pm early May–Jun & Sep–mid-Oct, to 6pm Jul & Aug; ⓟ👶) Adventurous kids will enjoy exploring this network of caverns and crevices formed by glaciers millions of years ago. Each cave has its own title and story, from the Bear Crawl to the Dungeon. Climbing, crawling and squeezing is required. On Saturday evenings throughout the season, plus Wednesdays and Fridays in July and August, there are guided two-hour lantern tours, which culminate with s'mores and roasted marshmallows around the firepit. It's 6 miles west of North Woodstock on NH 112.

Whale's Tale Waterpark AMUSEMENT PARK
(☑603-745-8810; www.whalestalewaterpark.net; 481 Daniel Webster Hwy, Lincoln; depending on season $30-40; ☺10am-4pm Jun, to 6pm Jul & Aug; ⓟ👶) This razzle-dazzle water park looks out of place in the staid White Mountains, but you know what? If the kids are cranky

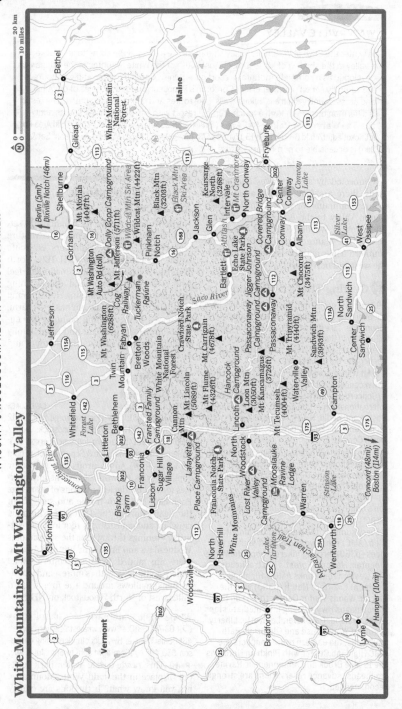

White Mountains & Mt Washington Valley

after all the hiking and scenic driving, the waterslides, lazy river and wave pool might be a fun – dare we say awesome – change of pace. And parents can enjoy a waterside beer while the kids do their thing.

🏃 Activities

Alpine Adventures
ADVENTURE SPORTS

(📞 603-745-9911; www.alpinezipline.com; 41 Main St, Lincoln; zipline tours from $39; ⊙ 9am-5pm; 🚸) Alpine Adventures offers a smorgasbord of adrenaline-charged activities: Thrillsville is an aerial park where you can clamber and fly (attached by a harness) over a hodge-podge of specially constructed bridges, cargo nets, rope ladders, ziplines, giant swings, tree houses and a free-fall device, or fly in a snow tube onto a giant airbag at the BigAir-Bag Stuntzone.

Café Lafayette
RAIL

(📞 603-745-3500; www.nhdinnertrain.com; 3 Crossing at River Place, North Woodstock; adult/child 6-11yr from $85/65; ⊙ mid-May–late Oct) Travel in the 1st-class dining car of the 1924 Pullman-Standard Victorian Coach while enjoying a four-course meal. The dining car has been completely and beautifully restored and decorated with dark wood, stained glass and brass fixtures. The train rides along a spur of the Boston and Maine railroad for two hours.

Hobo Railroad
RAIL

(📞 603-745-2135; www.hoborr.com; 64 Railroad St, Lincoln; adult/child 4-12yr $17/13; ⊙ daily mid-Jun–mid-Oct, reduced service Nov-early Jun; 🚸) The Hobo is a scenic 1½-hour train ride from Lincoln south to Woodstock. Seasonal themes include foliage trains and Santa trains that follow the same route, and summers feature Sunday storybook trips, where characters like Winnie-the-Pooh and Curious George hop aboard and entertain during the ride.

🛏 Sleeping & Eating

★ Notch Hostel
HOSTEL $

(📞 603-348-1483; www.notchhostel.com; 324 Lost River Rd, North Woodstock; dm $30, d $75-90; 🅿️@🛜🐾) Tibetan prayer flags mark your arrival at this gorgeous hostel, the brainchild of outdoor enthusiasts (and husband-and-wife team) Serena and Justin. A class act all round, it welcomes guests with outdoor decks, a spacious kitchen, a mountain-themed library, a sauna for chilly winter nights and a cozy vibe. Lots of info and support for Appalachian Trail thru-hikers.

Lost River Valley
Campground
CAMPGROUND $

(📞 800-370-5678, 603-745-8321; www.lostriver.com; 951 Lost River Rd/NH 112, North Woodstock; tent/RV sites from $22/36, 1-/2-room cabins $65/79; ⊙ mid-May–mid-Oct; 🅿️) This excellent 200-acre campground (which also contains rustic honest-to-goodness log cabins with ceiling fans) is on the site of a turn-of-the-century lumber mill, and the water wheel still churns. Many of the 139 sites are on the river, which also offers fishing and hiking possibilities. There's a three-night minimum stay late June to early September (two-night minimum at other times).

To get there, take exit 32 off I-93 and turn right onto NH 112.

Woodstock Inn
Station & Brewery
INN $$

(📞 603-745-3951; www.woodstockinnnh.com; 135 Main St/US 3, North Woodstock; r $96-257; ❋🛜) This Victorian country inn is North Woodstock's centerpiece. It has 39 individually appointed rooms across five separate buildings (three in a cluster, two across the street), each with modern amenities but in an old-fashioned style. The on-site upscale restaurant, **Woodstock Inn Station & Brewery** (mains $9-26; ⊙ 11:30am-9pm Sun-Thu, to 10pm Fri & Sat, bar open later), has outdoor seating on the lovely flower-filled patio. Breakfast included in rates.

Peg's Restaurant
AMERICAN $

(📞 603-745-2740; 97 Main St, North Woodstock; mains $4-11; ⊙ 5:30am-2:30pm Sat-Wed) Locals flock to this no-frills eatery for hearty early breakfasts and late-lunch sandwiches, such as roast turkey and meat loaf with gravy. Lunch specials, kids' specials and the infamous 'Hungry Man's Special' make everyone feel pretty special. Cash only, with ATM on-site.

ℹ Information

White Mountains Visitor Center (📞 National Forest info 603-745-3816, visitor info 603-745-8720; www.visitwhitemountains.com; 200 Kancamagus Hwy, off I-93, exit 32, North Woodstock; ⊙ visitor center 8:30am-5pm year-round, National Forest desk 9am-3:30pm mid-May–mid-Oct, Fri-Sun rest of year) A stuffed moose (not real) sets a mood for adventure while brochures and trail maps provide details

HIKING THE TRAILS & SKIING THE SLOPES

The White Mountains are a year-round playground for nature lovers with a good level of fitness. In the warmer months, Franconia Notch State Park has many trailheads as well as spectacular sights, such as the Flume Gorge and an aerial tramway from the park that goes up Cannon Mountain. Additionally, check out Moosilauke Ravine, Crawford Notch State Park (p358), Mt Washington and Pinkham Notch for additional hiking highlights.

The Kancamagus Hwy, a 34.5-mile scenic road set along a wandering river, is another popular place for hiking. For more info on short hikes, pick up the excellent AMC's *Best Day Hikes in the White Mountains*, a hiking guide published by the Appalachian Mountain Club. It's available online (https://amcstore.outdoors.org) and in some New Hampshire bookstores.

at this regional and National Forest visitor center. Get all the information you need about area trails and buy a White Mountain National Forest recreation pass, which is required for use of certain trails and other developed sites within the national forest.

ⓘ Getting There & Away

It's about 2¼ hours (140 miles) from Boston to North Woodstock/Lincoln via I-93.

Concord Coach Lines (www.concordcoach lines.com) stops in Lincoln at 7-Eleven (36 Main St) on its twice-daily run between Boston and Littleton. Destinations include Concord ($17.50, 1½ hours), Boston's South Station ($29, three hours) and Logan International Airport ($34, 3¼ hours).

Kancamagus Highway

One of New Hampshire's prettiest driving routes, the winding 34.5-mile Kancamagus Hwy (NH 112) between Lincoln and Conway runs right through the White Mountain National Forest (WMNF) and over Kancamagus Pass (2855ft). Paved only in 1964, and still unspoiled by commercial development, the 'Kanc' offers easy access to US Forest Service (USFS) campgrounds, hiking trails and fantastic scenery.

The route is named for Chief Kancamagus (The Fearless One), who assumed the powers of *sagamore* (leader) of the Penacook Native American tribe around 1684. He was the final *sagamore*, succeeding his grandfather, the great Passaconaway, and his uncle Wonalancet. Kancamagus tried to maintain peace between the indigenous peoples and European explorers and settlers, but the newcomers pushed his patience past breaking point. He finally resorted to battle

to rid the region of Europeans, but in 1691 he and his followers were forced to escape northward.

🏃 Activities

Sabbaday Falls WALKING
(NH 112/Kancamagus Hwy; day-use fee $5) A 0.3-mile one-way stroll on the popular Sabbaday Brook Trail ends at Sabbaday Falls, a gorge waterfall powering through narrow granite walls into lovely pools. Stairs lead to overlooks with mesmerizing views of the flume. The trailhead is about 15 miles west of the Saco Ranger District Office, and the trail is accessible for people with disabilities.

Loon Mountain SKIING
(✆800-229-5666; www.loonmtn.com; 60 Loon Mountain Rd, Lincoln) In winter, this popular ski mountain near the Kancamagus Hwy's western end offers 28 miles of trails crisscrossing the 3050ft peak. Skis and snowboards are available for rental. At night the trails open up for tubing. Summer activities include gondola rides to the summit, mountain-bike rentals ($35 per day), a climbing wall ($10), a zipline ($27) and more.

Lincoln Woods Trail HIKING
(✆603-630-5190; www.fs.usda.gov; NH 112/Kancamagus Hwy; day-use fee $5; ⊙visitor center 9am-3:30pm) Among the easiest and most popular trails in White Mountain National Forest, the 2.9-mile, 1157ft-elevation Lincoln Woods Trail follows an abandoned railway bed to the Pemigewasset Wilderness boundary (elevation 1450ft). To reach the trailhead, follow the Kancamagus Hwy 5 miles east of I-93 and park in the Lincoln Woods Visitor Center parking lot.

🛏 Sleeping & Eating

Camping is the name of the game along the Kancamagus. If you're looking for indoor accommodations, head to Lincoln or Conway, at the highway's western and eastern ends, respectively.

There are no services along the highway, but the surrounding wilderness is ideal for picnicking. Pick up supplies in Lincoln or Conway before hitting the road.

The heavily wooded US Forest Service (USFS) campgrounds east of Lincoln along the Kancamagus Hwy are primitive sites (mostly with pit toilets only) but are in high demand in the warm months: if you're up for camping, this is one of the best ways to experience the Kanc. It is not possible at every campground, but advance reservations are highly recommended. Otherwise, arrive early, especially on weekends.

Hancock Campground (☑ 603-745-3816; www.icampnh.com/kancamagus-east-west/hancock-campground; Kancamagus Hwy/NH 112; tent & RV sites $24; ⊙ year-round)

Passaconaway Campground (☑ 603-447-5448; www.icampnh.com/kancamagus-east-west/passaconaway; Kancamagus Hwy/NH 112; tent & RV sites $22; ⊙ mid-May–mid-Oct)

Jigger Johnson Campground (☑ 603-447-5448; www.icampnh.com/kancamagus-east-west/jigger-johnson; Kancamagus Hwy/NH 112; tent & RV sites $24; ⊙ mid-May–mid-Oct; P)

Covered Bridge Campground (☑ info 603-447-2166, reservations 877-444-6777; www.recreation.gov; Passaconaway Rd, Albany; tent sites $22; ⊙ mid-May–mid-Oct; P)

For more of life's creature comforts, the **Village of Loon Mountain** (☑ 800-228-2968, 603-745-3401; www.villageofloon.com; 72 Loon Village Rd, Lincoln; ste $109-244, town house $105-269; P ❄ 🔊 ≋) has lodge rooms that sleep four and ski in/out mountainside apartments, plus pools, hot tubs, tennis courts, horseback riding, hiking and biking.

ⓘ Information

Conway Village Chamber of Commerce Info Booth (☑ 603-447-2639; 205 E Main St/NH 16, Conway; ⊙ 9am-5pm late May–mid-Oct) The eastern gateway to the scenic highway.

Lincoln Woods Visitor Center (☑ 603-630-5190 visitor center, 603-536-6100 main office; www.fs.usda.gov/detail/whitemountain/about-forest/offices; Kancamagus Hwy/NH 112; ⊙ hours vary) Adjacent to the trailhead for the Lincoln Woods and Wilderness Trails, 5 miles east of Lincoln.

Saco Ranger District Office (☑ 603-447-5448; www.fs.usda.gov/detail/whitemountain/about-forest/offices; 33 Kancamagus Hwy, Conway; ⊙ 9am-4:30pm Mon, 8am-4:30pm Tue-Sun) At the eastern end of the Kancamagus Hwy near Conway.

White Mountains Visitor Center (p349) You can pick up detailed hiking brochures for area trails here. It's just east of I-93 (exit 32, between North Woodstock and Lincoln).

ⓘ Getting There & Away

To reach the Kancamagus Hwy's western starting point at Lincoln, take exit 32 off I-93 (130 miles north of Boston). For travelers coming from Maine, the highway's eastern entrance in Conway is more accessible; it's 60 miles (1½ hours) from Portland via ME 113 and US 302.

Franconia Notch State Park

Franconia Notch, a narrow gorge shaped over the eons by a wild stream cutting through craggy granite, is a dramatic mountain pass. This was long the residence of the beloved 'Old Man of the Mountain,' a rock formation geologists estimate had gazed out over Profile Lake for more than 12,000 years. That's why it was such a shock when, on May 3, 2003, he crumbled down the mountainside. Despite the Old Man's absence, the attractions of Franconia Notch are many, from the dramatic hike down the Flume Gorge to the fantastic views of the Presidential Range. Services are available in Lincoln and North Woodstock to the south and in Franconia and Littleton to the north.

◎ Sights

Cannon Mountain Aerial Tramway   CABLE CAR
(☑ 603-823-8800; www.cannonmt.com; 260 Tramway Dr; round trip adult/child 6-12yr $18/16; ⊙ 8:30am-5pm Jun–mid-Oct; P 🚠) This tram shoots up the side of Cannon Mountain, offering a breathtaking view of Franconia Notch. You can also hike up the mountain and take the tramway down (adult/child $13/10). At the summit, take the 1500ft walk along the **Rim Trail** to the observatory deck for gorgeous 360-degree views – on clear days you can see as far as Maine and Canada. There's a snack bar and picnic tables at the tram building. Located off I-93, exit 34B.

Old Man of the Mountain Museum
MUSEUM

(I-93, exit 34B; ☺10am-5pm late May–mid-Oct; **P**) **FREE** All New Hampshirites mourn the Old Man of the Mountain, a rock formation resembling a man's face in profile that remains the state symbol despite its collapse in May 2003. Adjacent to the parking lot for the Old Man of the Mountain Profile Plaza (I-93, exit 34B; **P**) is this museum, which displays forensically accurate diagrams of 'the Profile's' collapse, and other tributes to the beloved symbol. You'll also find exhibits in the Cannon Mountain Aerial Tramway (p351) base station.

🏃 Activities

⭐ Flume Gorge & the Basin
HIKING

(☎603-745-8391; www.flumegorge.com; I-93, exit 34A; adult/child 6-12yr $16/14; ☺8:30am-5pm early May-Jun & Sep–mid-Oct, to 5:30pm Jul & Aug) To see this natural wonder, take the 2-mile self-guided nature walk, which includes a 800ft boardwalk through the Flume, a natural 12ft- to 20ft-wide cleft in the granite bedrock. The granite walls tower 70ft to 90ft above you, with moss and plants growing from precarious niches and crevices. The Basin is a 15ft-deep granite pothole nearby.

Recreation Trail
CYCLING, WALKING

(I-93, exit 34A) For a casual walk or bike ride, you can't do better than head out to this 8-mile paved trail that wends its way along the Pemigewasset River and through the notch. Bikes are available for rental with Sport Thoma (www.sportthoma.com; half-/full day $35/50) at Cannon Mountain, with a shuttle drop-off if you're only up for a one-way trip.

Mt Pemigewasset Trail
HIKING

(I-93, exit 34A) This trail begins at the Franconia Notch State Park Visitor Center and climbs for 1.4 miles to the 2557ft summit of Mt Pemigewasset (Indian Head), offering excellent views. Return by the same trail or the Indian Head Trail, which joins US 3 after 1 mile. From there, it's a 1-mile walk north back to the visitor center.

Lonesome Lake Trail
HIKING

(I-93 btwn exit 34A & exit 34B) Departing from Lafayette Place and its campground, this trail climbs 1000ft in 1.6 miles to Lonesome Lake. Various spur trails lead further up to several summits on the Cannon Balls and Cannon Mountain (3700ft to 4180ft) and south to the Basin.

Kinsman Falls
HIKING

(I-93 btwn exit 34A & exit 34B) On the Cascade Brook, these falls are a short half-mile hike from the Basin via the Basin Cascade Trail.

Cannon Mountain Ski Area
SKIING

(☎603-823-8800, snow report 603-823-7771; www.cannonmt.com; 260 Tramway Dr; adult/child 6-12yr/teen 13-17yr $79/57/66) Thanks to its prime Franconia Notch location, Cannon Mountain receives 150in of snow annually. It has 97 runs, 25 miles of trails and New Hampshire's greatest vertical drop (2180ft). The slopes are equipped with an aerial tramway (p351), three triple and three quad chairlifts, one double chair, a rope tow and a wonder carpet (moving walkway). Located off I-93, exit 34B/34C.

🛏 Sleeping & Eating

Lafayette Place Campground (☑info 603-823-9513, reservations 877-647-2757; www.reserveamerica.com; I-93, btwn exit 34A & exit 34B; tent & RV sites $25; **P**) is located inside the state park. The best selection of motels is 5 miles south in Lincoln/North Woodstock. For inns and lodges in a more rural setting, Franconia (11 miles north of park headquarters) is your best bet.

The 1.6-mile Lonesome Lake Trail leads from Lafayette Place Campground to Lonesome Lake Hut. The AMC's Greenleaf Hut can be accessed from the state park on the 2.7-mile Greenleaf Trail or the 2.9-mile Old Bridle Path.

You'll find a good choice of restaurants near the park in Lincoln and North Woodstock (both 5 miles south of park headquarters). Snack bars serving light fare are located at the Franconia Notch State Park Visitor Center and the Cannon Mountain tram stations.

ℹ Information

Franconia Notch State Park Visitor Center
(☎603-745-8391; www.nhstateparks.org; I-93, exit 34A; ☺8:30am-mid-May–Jun & Sep-early Oct, to 5:30pm Jul & Aug, to 4:30pm mid-Oct–late Oct) Open seasonally, the state park visitor center at Flume Gorge has information about the park and surrounding area. There's also a cafeteria and gift shop.

ℹ Getting There & Away

I-93 runs right through the middle of the park. The visitor center is 135 miles north of Boston (2¼ hours without traffic). There is no public transportation to the park.

Littleton & Franconia

📍 603

A few miles north of Franconia Notch State Park via I-93, Franconia is a tranquil town with splendid mountain views and a poetic attraction: Robert Frost's farm. Other nearby communities include the tiny, picturesque village of Sugar Hill (a few miles west along tranquil NH 117), and the small towns of Bethlehem (north along NH 142) and Littleton (north on I-93).

Littleton is the largest of the bunch, and doubles as the economic hub for the northwestern fringe of the White Mountains region and the Great North Woods. With a bustling small-town Main St and a pretty perch beside the Ammonoosuc River, it's an inviting place to explore. In fact, the entire area is perfect for whiling away an afternoon driving down country roads, poking into antique shops, browsing farm stands and chatting with the locals at divey diners.

⊙ Sights

★ Frost Place   HISTORIC SITE
(📞 603-823-5510; www.frostplace.org; 158 Ridge Rd; adult/child $5/3; ⊙1-5pm Thu-Sun May & Jun, 1-5pm Wed-Mon Jul & Aug, 10am-5pm Wed-Mon Sep–mid-Oct; 🅿) Robert Frost (1874–1963) was America's most renowned and best-loved poet in the mid-20th century. For several years he lived with his family on a farm near Franconia, now known as Frost Place. Many of his best and most famous poems describe life on this farm and the scenery surrounding it, including 'The Road Not Taken' and 'Stopping by Woods on a Snowy Evening.' The years spent here were some of the most productive and inspired of his life.

Pollyanna Statue   STATUE
(www.golittleton.com/pollyanna.php; 92 Main St, Littleton Library; 🚻) Alright cynics, pessimists and grouches, give it up a minute for the joyous Pollyanna statue on the lawn of the library. The children's book character, an eternal optimist, stands with her arms flung wide, ready for your Instagram photo. The author of *Pollyanna,* published in 1913, was Eleanor H Porter, a Littleton native. Rub the statue's left shoe for good luck.

🛏 Sleeping & Eating

★ Sugar Hill Inn   INN $$
(📞 603-838-3229; www.sugarhillinn.com; 116 NH 117, Sugar Hill Village; r/ste from $210/350, cottage

COLONIAL THEATER

The classic **Colonial Theater** (📞 603-869-3422; www.bethlehemcolonial.org; 2050 Main St, Bethlehem; ⊙May-Oct) in downtown Bethlehem is a historic place to hear the jazz, blues and folk musicians that pass through this little town. The venue also serves as a cinema, showing independent and foreign films.

$525; 🅿 ❄ 🛜) This restored 1789 farmhouse sits atop a hill that has stunning panoramic views, especially in the fall, when the sugar maples lining the hill are ablaze. Sixteen acres of lawns and gardens and 15 romantic guest rooms (many with gas fireplaces and Jacuzzis), not to mention the delectable country breakfast (included in rates), make this a top choice.

Franconia Inn   INN $$
(📞 800-473-5299, 603-823-5542; www.franconiainn.com; 1172 Easton Rd/NH 116; r/ste from $129/189; ⊙closed Apr–mid-May; 🅿 🛜 ❄) This excellent 35-room inn, just 2 miles south of Franconia, is set on a broad, fertile, pine-fringed river valley. You'll find plenty of common space and well-maintained, traditional guest rooms. The 107-acre estate offers ice skating and prime cross-country skiing in winter, along with hiking and horseback riding in summer. Breakfast included.

★ Schilling Beer Co   PIZZA, PUB FOOD $
(📞 603-444-4800; www.schillingbeer.com; 18 Mill St, Littleton; pizzas $11-16; ⊙noon-10pm Mon-Thu, noon-11pm Fri, 11am-11pm Sat, 11am-10pm Sun) In a historic mill by the Ammonoosuc River, this bustling microbrewery serves delicious crunchy-crusted, wood-fired pizzas along with bratwurst and a nice selection of home brews, from Konundrum sour pale ale to Erastus Belgian abbey-style Tripel. The post-and-beam-style main room, looking out at a covered bridge, makes for a convivial setting, as does the riverside deck.

Polly's Pancake Parlor   AMERICAN $
(📞 603-823-5575; www.pollyspancakeparlor.com; 672 NH 117, Sugar Hill Village; mains $8-13; ⊙7am-3pm daily May-Columbus Day, Thu-Sun rest of year) Since 1938, when it began serving all-you-can-eat breakfast fare for 50¢, this local institution 2 miles west of Franconia has been cranking out pancakes, pancakes and more

NEW HAMPSHIRE LITTLETON & FRANCONIA

pancakes. They're excellent, made with home-ground flour and accompanied by the farm's own maple syrup, eggs, sausages and cob-smoked bacon. Sandwiches (made with homemade bread) and quiches are also available.

★ **Cold Mountain Cafe & Gallery**   INTERNATIONAL **$$**

(☎ 603-869-2500; www.coldmountaincafe.com; 2015 Main St, Bethlehem; sandwiches & salads $8.50-10, dinner mains $12-21; ⊙ 11am-3pm & 5-9pm Mon-Sat, closed Nov) Among the region's finest restaurants, this casual cafe and gallery has an eclectic, changing menu, featuring gourmet sandwiches, salads and quiches at lunchtime, and luscious dinner options, such as bouillabaisse, Indian-spiced lamb stew or its signature black bean cakes. There's occasional live music, from jazz to folk. Be prepared to wait for your table (outside, since the place is cozy).

🛈 Information

Pop into Thayer's Inn to get a walking tour map at the **Littleton Chamber of Commerce Welcome Center** (☎ 603-444-6561; www.littletonareachamber.com; 107 Main St, Thayer's Inn, Littleton; ⊙ hours vary). Beyond Littleton, stop by the **Bethlehem Visitors Center** (☎ 603-869-3409; www.bethlehemwhitemtns.com; 2182 Main St/NH 302, Bethlehem; ⊙ 10am-4pm Mon-Sat, 12.30-4pm Sun Jul & Aug, weekends only late May, Jun, Sep & Oct) or the **Franconia Notch Chamber of Commerce** (☎ 603-823-5661; www.franconianotch.org; 421 Main St, Franconia; ⊙ 10am-5pm Jun-early Oct; 🛜) for tourist information.

🛈 Getting There & Away

Greyhound (www.greyhound.com) and Concord Coach Lines (www.concordcoachlines.com) stop at **Irving Gas Station** (336 Cottage St, Littleton). Useful Concord Coach Lines routes include Boston's South Station (one way $33, 3½ hours) and Logan International Airport (one way $39, 3¾ hours).

Mt Washington Valley

Dramatic mountain scenery surrounds the tiny villages of this popular alpine destination, providing an abundance of outdoor adventures along the Presidential Range in all seasons. In summer, there's great hiking, skiing, kayaking and rafting, along with idyllic activities like swimming in local creeks,

overnighting in country farmhouses and simply exploring the countryside.

Mt Washington Valley stretches north from Conway, at the eastern end of the Kancamagus Hwy, and forms the eastern edge of the White Mountains. The valley's hub is North Conway, though any of the towns along NH 16/US 302 (also called the White Mountain Hwy) can serve as a White Mountain gateway. The five villages just north of North Conway are Intervale, Glen, Bartlett, Hart's Location and Jackson. The valley's namesake is – of course – Mt Washington, New England's highest peak (6288ft), which towers over the valley in the northwest.

🛈 Getting There & Away

From the western White Mountains, there are two main routes into the Mt Washington Valley: the Kancamagus Hwy (NH 112) from Lincoln/ North Woodstock, and US 302 from Littleton/ Bethlehem. To reach the valley from Portland, ME, take ME 113.

The US 302 and NH 16 are the two main thoroughfares running north–south through the valley. The two highways are one and the same in North Conway, forming that town's main street (also known as White Mountain Hwy). About 6 miles north of North Conway, the two highways split, with US 302 turning west toward Crawford Notch, and NH 16 continuing north toward Pinkham Notch.

A Concord Coach Lines (www.concordcoachlines.com) bus stops in North Conway at the Eastern Slope Inn (2760 Main St), offering service to Concord, Boston's South Station and Logan International Airport on its daily trip between Boston and Berlin, NH.

North Conway

POP 2360

A gateway to mountain adventure, North Conway is a bustling one-street town lined with motor inns, camping supply stores and other outfits designed with the traveler in mind. Although most people are just passing through, North Conway does have its charm, with a pleasant selection of restaurants, cozy cafes and nearby inns with historical allure. A popular and well-kept outlet mall also draws visitors.

⊙ Sights & Activities

Echo Lake State Park   STATE PARK

(☎ 603-356-2672; www.nhstateparks.org; 68 Echo Lake Rd; adult/child 6-11yr $4/2; ⊙ staffed 9am-7pm mid-May–mid-Oct; 🅿) Two miles west of North Conway via River Rd and West Side

MT WASHINGTON SUMMIT

The Sherman Adams Summit Building is the hub of Mt Washington State Park, which covers more than 63 acres atop its namesake mountain. Inside you'll find the private, non-profit **Mt Washington Observatory** (☑ ext 211 603-356-2137; www.mountwashington.org/visit-us; Mt Washington summit; observatory membership adult/child/family $50/30/75; ⊗ by arrangement; P), its observation tower and its museum (p359), which is one level down. The observation tower is open only by prearranged tour. Other occupants of the building include an information desk, a cafeteria, a gift shop and a tiny post office. Near the museum, a sobering list of fatalities on the mountain from 1849 through 2017 includes each person's cause of death – hypothermia, exposure and cardiac arrest are typical.

An open-air **observation deck** is perched atop the roof of the Sherman Adams building. Be aware that the summit is often cloudy and you may not see a darn thing beyond the observation deck's railing. On a clear day, however, you can see five states, Canada and the Atlantic Ocean. A photo-ready summit sign marking the 6288ft altitude is a few steps from the observation deck, as is the historic **Tip Top House**, which is open to the public. If you stroll the perimeter of the summit, take note of the boulders blanketing the slopes – you'll understand why this lofty place is nicknamed the Rock Pile.

The Mt Washington Cog Railway (p358) and the Mt Washington Auto Road (p359), which are separately owned, end at the summit. Each dropped off more than 100,000 visitors in 2017. Several hiking trails also reach the summit, adding more day-trippers to the mix. According to a recent study by the Mt Washington Commission, which oversees summit operations, visitors aren't yet put off by the crowds – but you may want to get there soon.

NEW HAMPSHIRE MT WASHINGTON VALLEY

Rd, this placid mountain lake lies at the foot of **White Horse Ledge**, a sheer rock wall. A scenic 1-mile trail circles the lake. There is also a mile-long auto road and hiking trail leading to the 700ft-high **Cathedral Ledge**, with panoramic White Mountains views. Both Cathedral Ledge and nearby White Horse Ledge are excellent for rock climbing. This is also a fine spot for swimming and picnicking.

★ **Conway Scenic Railroad**   RAIL
(☑ 603-356-5251; www.conwayscenic.com; 38 Norcross Circle; Notch Train coach/1st class/dome car $59/73/85; ⊗ Notch Train mid-Jun–Oct; 🚻 🚼) The Notch Train, dating to 1874, provides New England's most scenic rail journey, a slow but spectacular 5½-hour out-and-back trip from North Conway to Crawford Notch. Accompanying lively commentary recounts the railroad's history and folklore. Reservations are required. Dogs OK in coach class.

Mt Cranmore Resort   SKIING
(☑ 800-786-6754; www.cranmore.com; 1 Skimobile Rd; lift ticket adult/child/teen 13-18yr $83/49/62; ⊗ 8:30am-4pm Sun, 9am-4pm Mon-Fri, 8:30am-8pm Sat & holidays Jan-Mar, hours vary rest of year; 🚻) This ski resort on North Conway's outskirts has a vertical drop of 1200ft, 56 trails (28% beginner, 44% intermediate and 28%

expert), nine lifts and 98% snowmaking capability. There's also a terrain park, tubing and abundant facilities for nonskiers. In summer, the all-day play pass (54in-plus $74, 47-53in $64) includes the aerial adventure park, zipline, mountain coaster and more.

Eastern Mountain Sports Climbing School   CLIMBING
(☑ 800-310-4504, 603-356-5433; www.emsoutdoors.com/north-conway; 1498 White Mountain Hwy; lessons & climbs per day $150-315; ⊗ office 8:30am-5pm, store 8:30am-8pm Mon-Thu, to 9pm Fri & Sat, to 7pm Sun) This shop and climbing school sells maps and guides to the White Mountain National Forest and rents camping equipment, cross-country skis and snowshoes. Year-round, the school offers classes and tours, including one-day ascents of Mt Washington. Class rates depend on how many are in a group (two minimum).

🛏 Sleeping

White Mountains Hostel   HOSTEL $
(☑ 866-902-2521; www.wmhostel.com; 36 Washington St, Conway; dm $34, r $69-79; P 🞲) Set in an early-1900s farmhouse, this gem of a hostel is just off Main St/NH 16 in Conway. Environmentally conscientious and supremely welcoming, it has five bedrooms with bunk beds and four family size rooms,

LOCAL KNOWLEDGE

SWIMMING AT JACKSON FALLS

One of the best ways to spend a sun-drenched afternoon in Jackson is to take a swim in these falls on the Wildcat River just outside of town. You'll have marvelous mountain views as you splash about. To get to **Jackson Falls** (Carter Notch Rd/NH 16B; P), take the Carter Notch Rd/NH 16B half a mile north of town.

plus a communal lounge and kitchen. On Saturdays, friendly owners Tim and Samara host pay-what-you-like dinners of homemade lasagna, salad and fresh-baked bread and cookies.

Saco River Camping Area CAMPGROUND $
(✆603-356-3360; www.sacorivercampingarea.com; 1550 White Mountain Hwy/NH 16; tent/RV sites from $56/61; ◷mid-May–mid-Oct; P✿🐕🏊) This riverside campground away from the highway has 140 wooded and open sites and rustic lean-tos. Canoe and kayak rental with a shuttle ride is available ($39 to $59). Lots of kid-friendly activities and facilities, including playgrounds, volleyball, boccie and laser tag.

Golden Gables MOTEL $$
(✆603-356-2878; www.goldengablesinn.com; 1814 White Mountain Hwy; r $155-209, ste $209-429; P✿🐕🏊) The balconies with mountain views close the deal at this stylish motel. Mini-refrigerator and microwave in each room. There's a back lawn perfect for letting the kids run free.

Kearsarge Inn INN $$
(✆603-356-8700; www.kearsargeinn.com; 42 Seavey St; r $129-269, ste $239-319; ✿🐕🏊) Just off Main St in the heart of North Conway, this lovely inn is the perfect setting for an intimate experience near the center of town. The inn is a 'modern rendition' of the historic Kearsarge House, one of the region's first and grandest hotels. Each of the 15 rooms and one suite are spread across the main building.

✗ Eating & Drinking

Stairway Cafe BREAKFAST $
(✆603-356-5200; www.stairwaycafe.com; 2649 White Mountain Hwy; mains $4-15; ◷7am-3pm) The all-day breakfast treats are scrumptious at this brightly decorated, six-table upstairs cafe, from blackboard specials like homemade cinnamon muffins to lobster Benedict. Omelets come with grilled red Maine potatoes, veggie baked beans or homemade apple sauce, and there's a range of artisanal wild-game sausages (try the venison-merlot-blueberry or wild-boar-cranberry-shiraz varieties). Lunches include burgers, wraps and salads.

Delaney's Hole in the Wall AMERICAN, SUSHI $$
(✆603-356-7776; www.delaneys.com; 2966 White Mountain Hwy; most mains $9-23, sushi $6-27) Locals swear that the sushi at this quintessential mountain-town tavern is top-notch. Also serves pizza, sandwiches and burgers – all of it homemade. Catch the game, look at the sports memorabilia and just unwind like you live around here.

May Kelly's Cottage IRISH, AMERICAN $$
(✆603-356-7005; www.maykellys.com; 3002 White Mountain Hwy; mains $11-27; ◷4-9pm Wed, noon-9pm Thu, noon-10pm Fri & Sat, noon-8pm Sun) Irish conviviality and friendliness? May Kelly's is the real deal. Local-attic decor, helpful servers, mountain views, sandwiches and hearty mains like the Ploughman's Dinner (top sirloin steak, Irish potato cake, brown bread and baked beans) make it a local favorite.

★ Moat Mountain Smoke House & Brewing Co MICROBREWERY
(✆603-356-6381; www.moatmountain.com; 3378 White Mountain Hwy/NH 16; mains $11-28; ◷11:30am-11:45pm) The festive bar at this long-running brewpub is a popular local hangout, where you can choose from a dozen-plus brews made on-site. You'll find lots of hearty and tasty pub grub on the long menu: juicy burgers, BBQ brisket and pork sandwiches, luscious salads and wood-grilled pizzas. A good first stop after a day of adventuring.

❶ Information

Tourist information is available just south of the town center, at both the **Mt Washington Valley Chamber of Commerce** (✆info booth 603-356-5947, main office 603-356-5701; www.mtwashingtonvalley.org; 2617 White Mountain Hwy; ◷main office 9am-5pm Mon-Fri year-round, info booth 9am-6pm daily mid-May–mid-Oct, Fri & Sat rest of year) and its adjacent info booth.

❶ Getting There & Away

Concord Coach Lines (www.concordcoachlines. com) offers service to Concord ($20.50, 2¼ hours), Boston's South Station ($32, four hours) and Logan International Airport ($37, 4¼ hours) on its daily run between Boston and Berlin, NH. Buses stop in North Conway at the Eastern Slope Inn (2760 Main St).

Jackson & Glen

📞 603 / POP 820

A picturesque covered bridge welcomes guests to Jackson, a quintessential New England village and home to Mt Washington Valley's premier cross-country ski center. Packed tight with quaint but welcoming inns and several acclaimed restaurants, it's a recommended home base for exploring the White Mountains. And the aforementioned bridge? Dubbed the Honeymoon Bridge, it dates from 1876.

Glen, a hamlet located 3 miles south of Jackson, is a magnet for families as it's home to one of New Hampshire's most popular amusement parks, **Story Land** (📞 603-383-4186; www.storylandnh.com; 850 NH 16, Glen; $39; ⏲ 9:30am-6pm Jul & Aug, to 5pm mid-late Jun, to 5pm Sat & Sun late May–mid-Jun & Sep–mid-Oct; ▣ ⛹).

There are three ski resorts – **Attitash** (📞 800-223-7669; www.attitash.com; 775 US 302, Bartlett; lift ticket adult/child 7-17yr $89/67, weekdays $79/59), **Black Mountain** (📞 603-383-4490; www.blackmt.com; 373 Black Mountain Rd/NH 16B; lift ticket adult/child 6-17yr $59/45, weekdays $42/35; ⛷) and Wildcat Mountain (p361) – within 11 miles of Jackson village. The runs at **Tuckerman Ravine** (www.time fortuckerman.com; 361 NH 16, Pinkham Notch Visitor Center) at the base of Mt Washington are 9 miles north in Pinkham Notch. They are walk-up only.

You'll find some of the best cross-country skiing in the region at **Jackson XC** (Jackson Ski Touring Foundation; 📞 603-383-9355; www.jacksonxc.org; 153 Main St; day pass adult/child under 10yr/child 10-17yr $21/free/10, ski rentals per day adult/child under 10yr/under 49in $17/12/15; ⏲ typically mid-Dec–Mar), where there are more than 90 miles of trails, many of them accessible from trails that begin in the village. Snowshoers can take their pick from 18 snowshoe-only trails. You'll find even more cross-country and snowshoe trails at **Bear Notch Ski Touring** (www.bearnotchskitouring.com) in Bartlett, 10 miles south.

🛏 Sleeping & Eating

⭐ Snowflake Inn
INN $$

(📞 603-383-8259; www.thesnowflakeinn.com; 95 Main St, Jackson; ste incl breakfast $179-375; ▣ ❄ 🛜 🏊 🐾) All of the suites at this elegant inn are spacious and have fireplaces and two-person Jacuzzis. There are plenty of modern creature comforts, including 400-count triple sheets, flat-screen TVs and lavish sitting areas. An on-site spa adds to the charm. No children under 15 years.

There is one pet-friendly room with a pet fee of $30 per night.

Wentworth
INN $$

(📞 603-383-9700; www.thewentworth.com; 1 Carter Notch Rd/NH 16B; r/ste from $180/317; ▣ ❄ 🛜) This grand country inn is on the edge of Jackson village, beside a gorgeous public golf course. It's an elegant affair, with 61 spacious rooms, a gracious lobby and dining room, and facilities such as tennis courts. The best rooms have fireplaces, outdoor hot tubs and gorgeous antique furnishings. Packages include breakfast; some also include dinner and various local activities.

⭐ J-Town Deli & Country Store
BREAKFAST, SANDWICHES $

(📞 603-383-8064; www.jtowndeli.com; 174 Main St, Jackson; breakfast mains $5-9, sandwiches $9-10; ⏲ 7am-6pm) At this true-blue country store, the town's old salts gather in the morning to solve the world's problems – while enjoying some of the best breakfast sandwiches around. Trust us, the homemade sausage is delicious. Order at the counter, browse the sundries and gifts, then dig in at a table in back. Wraps, paninis and deli standards sold at lunch.

Cider Co Deli & Store
CAFE $

(📞 603-383-4414; www.ciderconh.com; 207 US 302, Glen; pies $5-7, sandwiches $7-9; ⏲ 7:30am-5pm) If you're packing a picnic for a day hike, stop at this country store and cafe. Besides jugs of cider, there's gourmet coffee, cider doughnuts, apple pie and a range of New England specialty products, including homemade hand pies. In winter, it serves cups of piping-hot cider; in summer, cider slushies cool things down. Closed Wednesdays in colder months.

Next door is the more formal **Cider Company Restaurant** (📞 603-383-9061; www.ciderconh.com; US 302, Glen; mains $12-32; ⏲ 5-9pm Sun-Thu, to 10pm Fri & Sat), serving expertly prepared cuisine (seared sea scallops,

WILDCAT TAVERN HOOTIN'

Everybody in town stops by **Wildcat Tavern Hoot Night** (☑ 603-383-4245; www.wildcattavern.com; 94 Main St, Jackson; ⊙ 8pm-midnight Tue) at some point for one of the state's longest-running open mike nights. Attracting acoustic acts from across the state and nearby Maine, the quality of the music is impressive.

pan-roasted duck breast, baked polenta, grilled hanger steak) in an elegant 1890s farmhouse.

★ **Thompson House Eatery**   AMERICAN $$$
(☑ 603-383-9341; www.thethompsonhouseeatery. com; 193 Main St, Jackson; mains $27-32; ⊙ 5-9pm Tue-Fri, to 10pm Sat Jul-Oct, closed Tue Nov-Jun) Housed in an early 1800s plank-and-timber farmhouse with a central chimney, this inviting place serves a thoughtfully curated menu of farm-to-table fare from chef Jeff Fournier. Local veggies accompany pan- and herb-roasted chicken, pork and beef dishes. Lighter options pair well with innovative cocktails at the bar. Hosts the weekly Jackson Farmers Market in summer (3:30pm to 6:30pm Tuesday).

❶ Information

Jackson Area Chamber of Commerce
(☑ 603-383-9356; www.jacksonnh.com; 18 Main St; ⊙ noon-5pm Mon, 9am-5pm Tue-Thu, 9am-noon Fri) The most helpful and knowledgeable chamber of commerce we came across in the entire state. Has loads of local insight; ask here about scenic walks in the area.

❶ Getting There & Away

Jackson is 7 miles north of North Conway. Take NH 16 and then cross the Ellis River via the historic red-covered bridge.

Concord Coach Lines (www.concordcoach lines.com) stops at the chamber of commerce information board on NH 16 beside the Honeymoon Bridge on its daily run between Boston and Berlin, NH. Destinations include Concord ($21.50, 2½ hours), Boston's South Station ($33, four hours) and Logan International Airport ($38, 4¼ hours).

Crawford Notch & Bretton Woods

This beautiful 1773ft mountain pass on the western slopes of Mt Washington is deeply rooted in New Hampshire lore. In 1826 tor-

rential rains here triggered massive mudslides, killing the Willey family in the valley below. The dramatic incident made the newspapers and fired the imaginations of painter Thomas Cole and author Nathaniel Hawthorne. Both men used the incident for inspiration, thus unwittingly putting Crawford Notch on tourist maps.

Even so, the area remained known mainly to locals and wealthy summer visitors who patronized the grand Mt Washington Hotel in Bretton Woods – until 1944, when President Roosevelt chose the hotel as the site of a conference to establish a post-WWII global economic order.

Today the hotel is as grand as ever, while a steady flow of visitors comes to hike the Presidential Range and climb Mt Washington – on foot, or aboard a steam-powered locomotive on the dramatic Mt Washington Cog Railway.

◉ Sights & Activities

For hikers, Crawford Notch is close to nirvana. Rugged, beautiful trails twist up through the forest, unfurling past rocky streams, commanding waterfalls, grand overlooks and windswept ridges; many of them also pass lonely alpine huts. The planning hub AMC Highland Center (p360) is a good place to begin your journey.

A morning hike to the 200ft-high **Arethusa Falls** (US 302, Hart's Location), New Hampshire's highest, is invigorating.

★ **Crawford Notch State Park**   STATE PARK
(☑ 603-374-2272; www.nhstateparks.org; 1464 US 302, Hart's Location; ⊙ visitor center 9:30am-5pm late May–mid-Oct, park year-round unless posted otherwise; ℗) **FREE** This pretty park maintains an extensive system of hiking trails. From the Willey House visitor center, you can walk the easy 0.5-mile Pond Loop Trail, the 1-mile Sam Willey Trail and the Ripley Falls Trail, a 1-mile round-trip hike from US 302 via the Ethan Pond Trail. The trailhead for Arethusa Falls, a 1.5-mile one-way hike, is 0.5 miles south of the Dry River Campground on US 302. Serious hikers can also tackle the much longer trek up Mt Washington.

★ **Mt Washington Cog Railway**   RAIL
(☑ 603-278-5404; www.thecog.com; 3168 Base Station Rd; adult $72-78, child 4-12yr $41; ⊙ daily Jun-Oct, Sat & Sun late Apr, May & Nov; ♿) Purists walk and the lazy drive, but the quaintest way to reach Mt Washington's summit is via this cog railway. Since 1869 coal-fired,

steam-powered locomotives have climbed a scenic 3.5-mile track up the mountainside (three hours round trip). Two of these old-fashioned trains run daily June to October. The steam trains are supplemented by faster, cleaner, biodiesel-fueled trains. Reservations recommended.

Instead of having drive wheels, a cog locomotive applies power to a cogwheel (gear wheel) on its undercarriage. The gears engage pins mounted between the rails to pull the locomotive and a single passenger car up the mountainside, burning a ton of coal and blowing a thousand gallons of water into steam along the way. Boilers are tilted to accommodate the grade. Up to seven trains (some of them now biodiesel) may be huffing and puffing at one time. The grade at the Jacob's ladder trestle is 37% – the second-steepest railway track in the world (the steepest is at Mt Pilatus, Switzerland). There's a small museum about the history of the railway at the base station.

The base station is 6 miles east of US 302. Turn east in Fabyan, just northwest of the Omni Mt Washington Hotel (between Bretton Woods and Twin Mountain). Also, remember that the average temperature at the summit is 40°F (4°C) in summer and the wind is always blowing, so bring a sweater and windbreaker.

Bretton Woods Ski Area SKIING
(☑603-278-3320; www.brettonwoods.com; 99 Ski Area Rd; lift tickets adult/child 5-12yr/teen 13-17yr weekends & holidays $99/57/77, Nordic day passes $21/14/19; ⛄) The region's largest ski area, Bretton Woods offers both downhill and cross-country winter skiing. The downhill area has a vertical drop of 1500ft, with 10 lifts serving 97 trails, most of which are intermediate. The resort also maintains a 45-mile network of Nordic (cross-country) ski trails (mid-November to early April), which traverse open fields, wooded paths and mountain streams.

🛏 Sleeping

You'll rarely find a 10-mile stretch of rural road with such a widely skewed range of accommodations. Take your pick: sleep cozily in a humble tent under the stars on the east side of Crawford Notch, live it up in five-star luxury just across the mountain at the **Omni Mt Washington Hotel & Resort** (☑603-278-1000; www.omnihotels.com; 310 Mt Washington Hotel Rd, Bretton Woods; r/ste from $449/619; P❄@🛜🏊) or go for one of the more moderately priced options in between.

Dry River Campground CAMPGROUND $
(☑info 603-374-2272, reservations 877-647-2757; www.reserveamerica.org; US 302, Hart's Location; campsites $25-29; ⊙peak season late May-early Oct, limited services early–mid-May & mid-Oct–Nov; P🐾) Near the southern end of Crawford Notch State Park, this quiet state-run campground has 36 tent sites with a clean bathhouse, flush toilets, showers and laundry facilities. Sites can be reserved in advance late May to early October. Limited pre- and post-season camping is also available on a first-come, first-served basis; dates vary annually – call the info number for details.

★ **AMC Highland Center Lodge** LODGE $$
(☑front desk 603-278-4453, reservations 603-466-2727; www.outdoors.org; NH 302, Bretton Woods; r incl breakfast & dinner per adult/child/teen $176/54/103, without bath $121/54/103; P🛜) This cozy Appalachian Mountain Club (AMC) lodge is set amid the splendor of Crawford Notch, an ideal base for hiking the trails crisscrossing the Presidential Range. The grounds are beautiful, rooms are

NEW HAMPSHIRE MT WASHINGTON VALLEY

DON'T MISS

MT WASHINGTON AUTO ROAD

One of New England's top adventures, the serpentine drive up the 7.6-mile **Mt Washington Auto Road** (☑603-466-3988; www.mountwashingtonautoroad.com; NH 16; car & driver $31, extra adult/child 5-12yr $9/7, guided tours adult/child $36/16; ⊙8am-6pm mid-Jun–Aug, shorter hours May–mid-Jun & Sep-late Oct) is not for the faint of heart. The Mt Washington Summit Rd Co operates this narrow, alpine toll road, which soars from the Pinkham Notch area to the parking lot just below the 6288ft summit. The price includes an audio-tour CD and entry to Mt Washington Observatory's **Extreme Weather Museum** (☑800-706-0432; www.mountwashington.org/visit-us; Mt Washington summit; $2, free with Auto Road ticket; ⊙hours vary depending on weather; P). 'This car climbed Mt Washington' bumper stickers are sold in the summit gift shop.

basic but comfortable, meals are hearty and guests are outdoor enthusiasts. Discounts for AMC members. The information center, open to the public, has loads of information about regional hiking.

Eating

In addition to offering lavish accommodations, the Omni Mt Washington Hotel & Resort (p359) has an extensive breakfast buffet and dress-up dinners, plus several restaurants. Meals are also served at the **Bretton Arms Inn** (☑ 603-278-3000; www.omnihotels. com; 173 Mt Washington Rd, Bretton Woods; r/ste $389/449; P✳️🛜) and the AMC Highland Center Lodge (p359).

❶ Information

AMC Highland Center at Crawford Notch (☑ 603-466-2727; www.outdoors.org; NH 302; ⊗24hr) Complete information about hiking, biking and camping in the area, including maps and trail guides. Daily activities and guided hikes are offered.

Crawford Depot & Visitor Center (www. outdoors.org; NH 302; ⊗9am-2pm Mon-Fri, to 4pm Sat & Sun Jun-Sep) AMC's summer visitor center in Crawford Notch is housed in a historic railway depot.

Crawford Notch State Park Visitor Center (☑ 603-374-2272; www.nhstateparks.org; ⊗9:30am-5pm late May–mid-Oct) State park visitor center, on the historic Willey home site.

Twin Mountain-Bretton Woods Chamber of Commerce (☑ 800-245-8946; www.twin mountain.org; cnr US 302 & US 3; ⊗info booth staffed 9am-5pm Fri-Sun late May–mid-Oct, daily Jul & Aug, self-serve rest of year) Year-round info board and seasonally staffed kiosk.

❶ Getting There & Around

From North Conway, NH, it's an easy 25-mile drive up US 302 to Crawford Notch (or 29 miles to Bretton Woods). The notch is also easily reachable from I-93. If traveling northbound on I-93, take exit 35 and continue north on US 3 to eastbound US 302. If coming south down I-93, take exit 40 and follow signs for US 302 east. There is no public transportation to the notch.

In summer, the helpful **AMC hiker shuttle** (☑ reservations 603-466-2727; www.outdoors. org/lodging/lodging-shuttle.cfm; 1-way trip AMC members/nonmembers $20/24; ⊗daily Jun–mid-Sep, Sat & Sun mid-Sep–mid-Oct) loops between various trailheads in Crawford Notch and the western White Mountains. Reservations recommended.

Pinkham Notch

Pinkham Notch (2032ft) is a mountain-pass area known for its wild beauty, and its useful facilities for campers and hikers make it one of the most popular and crowded activity centers in the White Mountains. Wildcat Mountain and Tuckerman Ravine offer good skiing, and an excellent system of trails provides access to the natural beauties of Mt Washington and the Presidential Range, which stretches north from Crawford Notch to Mt Washington and then on to Mt Madison. For the less athletically inclined, the Mt Washington Auto Road provides easy – if white-knuckled – access to the summit, where you'll find a weather museum, a historic inn and sweeping views on clear days.

🏃 Activities

For a hike that works well for the whole family, pull over for the **Glen Ellis Falls Trail** (NH 16; day-use pass $5; 🅿️), a 0.6-mile round-trip walk, which ends at the 64ft-high falls. There are a few steep sections as you follow the scenic Ellis River, so watch younger kids. The trailhead is on the highway's west side about 0.7 miles south of the AMC Pinkham Notch Visitor Center.

But for those of you who can hack it, the strenuous 8.4 mile **Tuckerman Ravine Trail** (361 NH 16, Pinkham Notch Visitor Center) is a bucket-list hike that powers to the summit of New Hampshire's highest mountain, traversing a glacial cirque, an alpine plateau and a giant's marble yard of boulders. The hike begins at the Pinkham Notch Visitor Center and ends at the Mt Washington State Park observation deck atop the mountain, from where views can stretch 130 miles.

🛏️ Sleeping & Eating

Guests and the general public can eat meals at the dining hall at Joe Dodge Lodge or order a sandwich to go from the deli. There's also a cafe at the **Great Glen Trails Outdoor Center** (☑ 603-466-2333; www.greatglen trails.com; 1 Mt Washington Auto Rd; SnowCoach adult/child 5-12yr $55/30; ⊗8:30am-4:30pm). The closest alternatives are the cafeteria and pub at Wildcat Mountain ski area, 2 miles north toward Gorham.

Joe Dodge Lodge　　　　　　　　　　LODGE $
(☑ 603-466-2727;　www.outdoors.org/lodging/ lodges/pinkham; 361 NH 16; r per person adult/ child 3-12yr/teen 13-17yr incl breakfast & dinner

from $86/39/74; P✱☎) The AMC complex at Pinkham Notch incorporates this lodge, with dorms holding 100-plus beds. Rooms come in a variety of configurations and the price is per person. With the Tuckerman Ravine trailhead a few steps away, this cozy facility is a great place to overnight before hiking to the summit of Mt Washington. Reservations recommended. Discounts available for AMC members.

Glen House Hotel   HOTEL $$$
(☎603-466-3420; www.glenhousehotel.com; 979 NH 16; r $249-369; P✱☎☀☀) This classy number will surely go gangbusters due to its fresh rustic style and its location beside the Mt Washington Auto Road (p359). The fifth hotel on the sight since 1852, this incarnation embraces its location with big-windowed views of Mt Washington, clean-lined Shaker-style furniture and whimsical touches like a mounted moosehead made from colorful cloth.

ℹ Information

The nerve center for hiking in the Whites is the **Pinkham Notch Visitor Center** (☎603-466-2721; www.facebook.com/pg/JoeDodgeLodge; 361 NH 16; ⊗6:30am-10pm Jun-Oct, to 9pm Nov-May). You'll find hiking guidebooks here, a diorama of the trails, a daily weather update and very helpful staff.

ℹ Getting There & Away

NH 16 runs north 11 miles from North Conway and Jackson to Pinkham Notch, then past the Wildcat Mountain ski area and Tuckerman Ravine, through the small settlement of Glen House and past the Dolly Copp Campground to Gorham and Berlin.

Concord Coach Lines (www.concordcoachlines.com) stops at Pinkham Notch on its daily run between Boston and Berlin, NH. Destinations include Concord ($23.50, 2¾ hours), Boston's South Station ($35, 4¼ hours) and Logan International Airport ($40, 4½ hours). The bus stop is at the Pinkham Notch Visitor Center.

Great North Woods

Not too many people make it all the way up to the North Country, but New Hampshire offers three scenic routes north of the Notches and Bretton Woods. Nothing beats US 2 from the Vermont–New Hampshire state line to the Maine–New Hampshire line: the expansive but looming mountain views are unparalleled. Alternatively, if you're heading to the outposts of Maine, take NH 16 north

WILDCAT ZIPRIDER

For spectacular summertime views of Mt Washington, **Wildcat Mountain** (☎603-466-3326; www.skiwildcat.com; 542 NH 16) resort offers a high-altitude experience. The **Ziprider** (☎888-754-9453; www.skiwildcat.com/ziprider; tickets $20; ⊗10am-5pm daily mid-Jun–early Sep, Sat & Sun mid-Sep–mid-Oct), like a zipline, but you're suspended from the steel cables, whizzes 70ft above the treetops, descending 2100ft at a 12% grade. The view is spectacular, though when you're flying by at 45mph, it's secondary to the adrenaline rush.

from Gorham to Errol. This route runs parallel to the birch-lined Androscoggin River.

To really get remote, follow US 3 through the Connecticut Lakes region up to New Hampshire's extreme northern tip, just below the Quebec border. This is the heart of New Hampshire's moose country. Take it slow and heed the ubiquitous signs warning of 'hundreds of collisions' – they're not joking! For a better chance of spotting a moose 'in the flesh,' consider the moose tours sponsored by the town of Gorham.

◉ Sights

Milan Hill State Park   STATE PARK
(☎603-449-2429; www.nhstateparks.org; 72 Fire Tower Rd, Milan; day-use adult/child 6-11yr $4/2; ⊗year-round; P✱) How often do you get to spend the night in a purple yurt? Yep, that's an option at this park, also known for its cross-country skiing and snowshoe trails. The 45ft fire tower provides expansive views of New Hampshire's mountains, as well as mountain ranges in Vermont, Maine and Canada. The park is pet-friendly, so bring Fido for a walk or picnic. The park is open year-round but only staffed seasonally. No day-use fee is collected in the low season.

Weeks State Park   STATE PARK
(☎603-788-4004; www.nhstateparks.org; 200 Weeks State Park Rd, off US 3, Lancaster; adult/child 6-17yr $5/3; ⊗10am-5pm late May-early Oct; P✱) Sitting atop Mt Prospect, this park is named for US senator John Weeks, a Lancaster native who introduced legislation in 1909 that helped to stem the degradation of local lands caused by unregulated logging. Weeks' legislation became known as the

GOOSE IS TO GEESE AS MOOSE IS TO...?

If you don't know the answer to that question, you can find the answer and most likely spot a real, live one (or more) on these evening **moose tours** (☑877-986-6673, 603-466-3103; www.gorhammoosetours.org; 69 Main St; adult/child 5-12yr $30/20; ☺late May-Sep) sponsored by the town of Gorham. These three-hour, 21-passenger van tours are led by naturalist guides, who claim a 93% to 97% success rate at spotting moose (if the moose are no-shows, you'll get a voucher for another tour). Tours leave five to six days a week at 7pm. Call or see its website for the latest schedule.

Weeks Act, a precursor to the national forest system. The park encompasses the 420-acre Weeks estate, where you can drive the 1.5-mile scenic auto road, explore the Weeks home and enjoy 360-degree mountain views from the property's stone fire tower.

Santa's Village AMUSEMENT PARK
(☑603-586-4445; www.santasvillage.com; 528 Presidential Hwy/US 2, Jefferson; $33; ☺9:30am-6pm daily Jul & Aug, to 5pm late Jun, 9:30am-5pm Sat & Sun late May, early Jun & Sep–early Oct; ℗♿) Just west of mountain-ringed Jefferson is this theme park. Look for Santa's 26 elves as you enjoy the kiddie-focused rides, a Ferris wheel and the Jingle Bell Express train. Kids can even visit Santa himself, usually found relaxing at home. The attached splash park, Ho Ho H20, is open on warm days. The park also opens on some weekend days in late October through December for Halloween, Thanksgiving, Christmas and New Year's events; see the website for details.

🛏 Sleeping & Eating

Jefferson Inn B&B $
(☑603-586-7998; www.jeffersoninn.com; 6 Renaissance Lane/US 2, Jefferson; r $125-145, ste $175; ℗♿🐾) Eleven homespun rooms – with quilts, old brooms and washboards on the wall – fill this attractive Victorian house perched on a hill above the Presidential Hwy. Four rooms have air-con and two rooms are pet friendly. Breakfast included in rates.

Evergreen Motel MOTEL $
(☑603-586-4449; www.evergreenmotelnh.com; 537 Presidential Hwy/US 2, Jefferson; r $105; ℗♿🐾) This 18-room mom-and-pop establishment is across the street from Santa's Village. There's also a complimentary 18-hole miniature golf course on-site. Snowmobilers can ride to their doors from the Corridor 5 route. Breakfast included in rates.

Water Wheel AMERICAN $
(☑603-586-4313; www.waterwheelnh.com; 1955 Presidential Hwy/US 2, Jefferson; mains $3-9; ☺6am-2pm Jun-Aug, Thu-Mon Sep-May) A red water wheel marks the spot at this down-home eatery where decorative bears hang from the wooden rafters. Portions are hearty, service can be a tad slow and breakfast is served all day.

ℹ Information

Great North Woods Welcome Center (☑603-788-3212; www.northerngatewaychamber.org; 25 Park St, Lancaster; ☺10am-4pm Mon-Sat) Photo op! Substitute your face for Paul Bunyan's, then head inside to pick up maps and brochures before wandering past the boutiques and antique stores lining nearby Main St.

ℹ Getting There & Away

Gorham sits on US 2 just east of its junction with NH 16. From here, it's 18 miles to Jefferson or 25 miles to Lancaster via US 2 west, or 14 miles to Milan via NH 16 north.

Concord Coach Lines (www.concordcoachlines.com) stops in Gorham daily on its route connecting Berlin, NH, Boston's South Station and Logan International Airport. Greyhound (www.greyhound.com) buses also stop in Gorham (350 Main St).

Gorham
☑603 / POP 2630

Established in 1836, Gorham is a four-season adventure town in the Androscoggin Valley at the northern edge of the Presidential Range. A little less picturesque than Jackson to the south but still home to a handful of inviting restaurants and motels, Gorham has a certain hanging-in-there charm. It's also a good base camp for exploring the Presidential Range and the Great North Woods. The entrance to the Mt Washington Auto Road is 8 miles south. And hey, this is the only town we know of that runs its own moose tours!

🛏 Sleeping & Eating

Top Notch Inn   MOTEL $
(📞 603-466-5496, 800-228-5496; www.topnotch
inn.com; 265 Main St; r $119-127, house $199;
🅿 ❄ @ 🛜 🛇 🐾) A brown moose stands guard
outside the welcoming Top Notch. In addition to standard but stylish motel rooms, the
inn offers the three-room Pinkham House,
a restored farmhouse, which sleeps up to
eight people. A heated pool and laundry facilities are available. The pet fee is $10 per
pet per night.

★ Libby's Bistro
& Saalt Pub   INTERNATIONAL $$
(📞 603-466-5330; www.libbysbistro.org; 111 Main
St/NH 16; mains $12-23; ⊙ bistro 5-9pm Fri & Sat,
pub 5-9pm Wed-Sun) A labor of love for acclaimed chef Liz Jackson, this 20-year-old
spot serves a seasonally changing, globally
inspired menu that draws heavily on locally
sourced ingredients; offerings run from Latin American to Middle Eastern, Vietnamese
to Mediterranean. You'll also find creative
burgers, a Thai fried chicken salad and four-
cheese baked penne. The bistro and pub
have the same menu.

ℹ Information

Androscoggin Ranger District (📞 603-466-
2713; www.fs.usda.gov; NH 16; ⊙ 8am-4:30pm
late May–mid-Oct, closed Sat & Sun rest of
year) Provides information on camping in White
Mountain National Forest. Located 3 miles
south of Gorham.

ℹ Getting There & Away

Thirty miles north of North Conway, Gorham sits
at the junction of Hwy 16 and US 2. The Maine
border is 9 miles east.

Concord Coach Lines (www.concordcoach
lines.com) stops at Irving Oil/Circle K (350
Main St) on its daily run between Berlin, NH, and
Boston. Destinations include Concord ($25.50,
three hours), Boston's South Station ($37, 4½
hours) and Logan International Airport ($42,
4¾ hours).

NEW HAMPSHIRE MT WASHINGTON VALLEY

Maine

📄 207 / POP 1.3 MILLION

Includes ➜

Ogunquit	369
The Kennebunks	370
Portland	373
Brunswick	380
Rockland	386
Camden	387
Mount Desert Island	395
Bar Harbor	395
Acadia National Park	397
Baxter State Park	404

Best Places to Eat

➜ Fore Street (p378)

➜ Aragosta (p395)

➜ Helen's Restaurant (p402)

➜ Chase's Daily (p389)

➜ Thurston's Lobster Pound (p368)

Best Places to Stay

➜ Danforth Inn (p377)

➜ NEOC Twin Pines Camp (p405)

➜ Bass Cottage Inn (p397)

➜ Pentagöet Inn (p401)

➜ Squire Tarbox Inn (p384)

Why Go?

With more lobsters, lighthouses and charming resort villages than you can shake a selfie stick at, Maine is New England at its most iconic. The sea looms large here, with mile upon mile of jagged sea cliffs, peaceful harbors and pebbly beaches. Eat and drink your way through food- and beer-crazed Portland, one of America's coolest small cities. Explore the historic shipbuilding villages of the Midcoast. Hike through Acadia National Park, a spectacular island of mountains and fjord-like estuaries. Let the coastal wind whip through those cobwebs and inhale the salty air. Venture into the state's inland region, a vast wilderness of pine forest and snowy peaks.

Outdoor adventurers can race white-water rapids, cycle the winding shore roads or kayak beside playful seals. For slower-paced fun, there are plenty of antique shops, cozy lobster shacks, charming inns and locally brewed beer.

When to Go
Portland

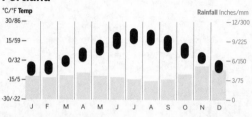

Jun–Sep Coastal towns fill up with travelers hungry for fresh lobster.

Oct Leaf-peepers descend upon villages with cameras at the ready.

Nov–Mar Skiers and snowmobiles ride the mountain trails.

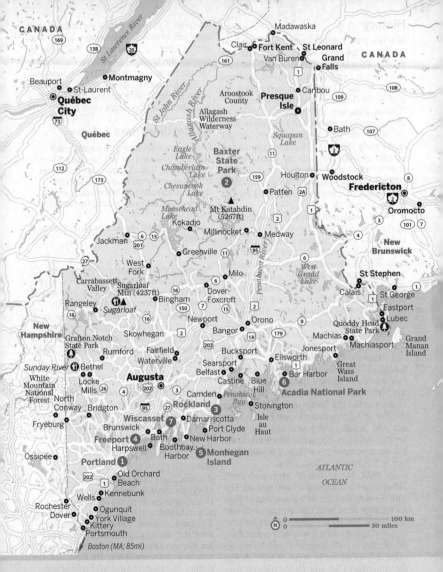

Maine Highlights

1 **Portland Museum of Art** (p373) Appreciating this impressive collection of American Art.

2 **Baxter State Park** (p405) Bagging the end point of the 2190-mile-long Appalachian Trail at Mt Katahdin.

3 **Farnsworth Art Museum** (p386) Exploring iconic American art in Rockland.

4 **LL Bean** (p382) Picking up a cozy new fleece at the flagship store in Freeport.

5 **Monhegan Island** (p385) Painting or photographing the windswept rocks of this solitary isle.

6 **Acadia National Park** (p397) Hiking up Cadillac Mountain, then taking a (chilly) dip in Echo Lake.

7 **Red's Eats** (p384) Cracking a freshly steamed crustacean at Maine's best-known lobster shack, in Wiscasset.

History

Maine's past reaches back to the earliest Paleo-Indians known as the Wabanaki: the People of the Dawn. They were part of a vast Algonquian Confederation stretching from Maine to the Great Lakes and relied on diverse food sources throughout the year – fishing, foraging and tending to crops in the summer; trapping and hunting in winter. When the first English settlers arrived in the early 1600s, the Wabanaki numbered around 20,000, but over the course of the 17th century, it is estimated that 80% to 90% of that population died during mass contagions of diseases transmitted by the European colonizers.

The Massachusetts Bay Colony established by the British in 1630 served as a launchpad to search for new regions for settlement. By the 1640s, a number of new colonies had been set up in southern Maine, including York, Saco, Kittery, Falmouth and Wells, but the rugged, glacier-carved wilderness proved ultimately too challenging, and the region has remained lightly populated to this day.

Tensions flared regularly between the British and the local tribes, but the French, who developed diplomatic ties with the Wabanaki and established friendly trade for lumber and furs, had better luck. Trouble between the two colonizers erupted into full-scale war in the 18th century, with the Wabanaki caught in the middle. The Treaty of Paris (1763) gave the British victors control over French Canada and Acadia, but peace was shortlived. Tensions re-ignited between colonists and the British government, escalating to inevitable war in the American Revolution.

In 1820 Maine finally separated from Massachusetts and gained its statehood. The 19th century was one of tremendous growth for the new state, with the emergence of new industries, but by the 20th century, as sawmills collapsed and the seas were overfished, population growth stagnated and Maine became a backwater. In spite of this, during the American Civil war (1861–5) more than 70,000 Mainers joined the cause, an astonishing figure considering the state's population was a little over 600,000 at the time. It was the highest figure in proportion to its population of any state in the north.

Maine's rustic, undeveloped landscape was later to be seen at the heart of its appeal. In the late 1800s high-end summer colonies sprang up in places like Bar Harbor, Scarborough and Isleboro, catering to wealthy urbanites from Boston, New York and Philadelphia, and the slogan 'Vacationland' (still seen on Maine license plates today) was coined. Later, as travel became attainable for the middle class, Maine's tourism boomed, though it was (and remains) highly seasonal.

Today, tourists spend about $6 billion per year, supporting around 106,000 jobs – roughly 16% of the state's work force.

ⓘ Getting There & Away

While the two most common ways to reach Maine are by air and car, you can also get here by train and bus. Maine's airports are quite small, and it's generally more expensive to fly into them. You can often get better deals by flying into Boston (two hours south of Portland) and driving up from there.

Flights, cars and tours can be booked online at lonelyplanet.com/bookings.

AIR

The main gateway to Maine is Portland International Jetport (p379), about 4 miles west of Portland's city center. A number of airlines also serve Bangor International Airport (p391).

Aside from the big national carriers, the small regional Cape Air (www.flycapeair.com) has daily flights connecting Boston with Augusta (65 minutes), Bar Harbor (80 minutes) and Rockland (65 minutes).

BOAT

In summer, Bay Ferries (www.ferries.ca/thecat) operates the CAT service, sailing daily between Portland and Yarmouth, Nova Scotia (Canada; six hours). Discussions are underway to end the service in Portland and open a ferry line between Bar Harbor and Yarmouth instead.

BUS

Concord Coach Lines (www.concordcoachlines. com) operates daily buses between Boston (including Logan Airport) and Portland, continuing on to Midcoast Maine towns (Bath, Belfast, Brunswick, Camden, Damariscotta, Lincolnville, Rockland, Searsport and Waldoboro). There are also services connecting Boston, Portland and the inland towns of Augusta, Waterville and Bangor. Two services a day link Portland with New York City.

Greyhound (www.greyhound.com) stops in Bangor, Portland, Bath, Rockland and various other towns.

CAR & MOTORCYCLE

Except for the Maine Turnpike (I-95 and I-495) and part of I-295, Maine has no fast, limited-access highways. Roads along the coast flood with traffic during the summer tourist season. As a result, you must plan for more driving time when traveling in Maine.

TRAIN

The *Downeaster,* run by Amtrak (www.amtrak.com), makes five trips daily between Boston and Portland (2½ hours). A couple of these services extend to Freeport and Brunswick, too.

❶ Getting Around

Maine has limited public transportation; hiring a car is the best way to get around the state. The highways are generally in good shape, with decent road signage, and driving here is fairly straightforward.

Car The most convenient option for seeing rural Maine, exploring small towns and partaking in outdoor adventure.

Train The Amtrak *Downeaster* has limited service but does connect five towns in the south of the state. The line, which starts/ends at Boston North Station, has stops in Wells, Saco, Freeport, Portland and Brunswick.

Bus Concord Coach Lines connects Bangor with bigger towns (Belfast, Bath and Portland) along the southern coast. There's also a line that runs from Bangor to Augusta and Portland.

SOUTHERN MAINE COAST

Maine's southern coast embodies the state slogan 'Vacationland,' with busy commercial strips, sandy beaches and resort towns that get packed in the summer months. Despite the crowds, there are some charming features to be found. While Kittery is a long, commercial strip mall, Ogunquit has a lovely beach and is Maine's gay mecca. Between the two lie quaint York Village and busy, populist York Beach. Beyond, the Kennebunks are small historic settlements with lavish mansions (some of which are now B&Bs) near pretty beaches and rugged coastline.

Although you'll have to use your imagination, the southern coast is deeply associated with the works of American artist Winslow Homer, who spent his summers in Prouts Neck (just south of Portland), which has some magnificent scenery.

The Yorks

Four communities – **York Village**, **York Harbor**, **York Beach** and **Cape Neddick** – collectively make up 'the Yorks,' which all like to think of themselves as the gateway to Maine.

York Village is the one most commonly referred to as simply 'York.' It feels like a living history museum, with a small downtown filled with impeccably maintained historic buildings – this was the first English city chartered in North America. York Harbor was developed more than a century ago as a posh summer resort and many of its grand Victorian mansions and hotels remain. York Beach, with its RV parks, candy shops and arcades galore, feels a socioeconomic world away. Cape Neddick, a small, mostly residential peninsula jutting out into the sea, is home to the famous Nubble Light.

Note that off-the-highway areas in between these communities are often just (confusingly) labeled 'York.'

❍ Sights & Activities

Museums of Old York   MUSEUM

(☏207-363-1756; www.oldyork.org; visitor center 3 Lindsay Rd, York Village; 1 bldg/all bldgs adult $8/15, child $5/10; ⊙10am-5pm Tue-Sat, 1-5pm Sun Jun-Aug, 10am-5pm Thu-Sat, 1-5pm Sun Sep–mid-Oct) York, called Agamenticus by its original Native American inhabitants, was settled by the British in 1624 and granted a charter by King Charles I in 1642. One of its best-preserved buildings are now cared for by the Old York Historical Society, which has turned them into individual museums. Highlights include the cells and stockades of the Old Gaol; the Emerson-Wilcox House, now a museum of decorative arts; and John Hancock Wharf, a warehouse with displays commemorating the area's maritime history.

Wiggly Bridge & Steedman Woods   BRIDGE

(off Mill Dam Rd, York Village; ☒) FREE Who knows how many generations of New Englanders have childhood memories of balancing their way across this wibbly-wobbly suspension bridge, which spans a 75ft estuary between the York River and artificial Barrel Mill Pond. The bridge is adjacent to Steedman Woods, a small parcel of preserved forest where people often walk their dogs.

Nubble Light   LIGHTHOUSE

(Sohier Park Rd, off Nubble Rd, Cape Neddick) Perched on Nubble Island, just off the tip of Cape Neddick, this white lighthouse and Victorian lighthouse-keeper's cottage provide one of Maine's best photo ops. A busy parking lot is guarded by a souvenir store and a casual lobster restaurant.

MAINE'S BEST LOBSTER POUNDS

Once considered a food fit only for prisoners and indentured servants, the American lobster has come a long way in the last 200 years. The tasty crustacean is now the most iconic of Maine foods; around 5000 Mainers still make their living hauling lobster traps out of the sea.

Every self-respecting coastal town from Kittery north to Calais has a lobster pound or shack not far from the local dock: these are great places to slurp thick seafood chowder and savor warm lobster rolls, or go the whole hog – tie on a bib and get cracking. They're usually low on frills but high on rustic charm, with waterfront views enjoyed from outdoor picnic tables (there is often no indoor seating; BYOB is a common policy). The term 'pound' usually implies that the establishment has a saltwater holding pen keeping lobsters alive for sale.

From south to north, here are some of our favorites (but there are dozens more):

Chauncey Creek Lobster Pier (☏207-439-1030; www.chaunceycreek.com; 16 Chauncey Creek Rd, Kittery Point; mains $9-25; ⊙11am-8pm early May-Aug, to 7pm Tue-Sun Sep–mid-Oct; 🛜) Just out of Kittery.

Cape Neddick Lobster Pound In Cape Neddick, near York.

Nunan's Lobster Hut (p371) In Cape Porpoise, near Kennebunkport.

Harraseeket Lunch & Lobster Co (☏207-865-4888; www.harraseeketlunchandlobster. com; 36 Main St, South Freeport; mains $7-34; ⊙11am-7:45pm May-Oct, to 8:45pm Jul & Aug) In Freeport.

Five Islands Lobster Company (☏207-371-2990; www.fiveislandslobster.com; 1447 Five Islands Rd; mains $6-30; ⊙11:30am-7pm Sat & Sun May–mid-Oct, daily mid-Jun–early Sep) In Georgetown, near Bath.

Young's Lobster Pound (☏207-338-1160; www.facebook.com/youngslobsterpound; 2 Fairview St; mains $10-28; ⊙7:30am-8pm Jun–mid-Sep, 8am-4pm mid-Sep–May) Just out of Belfast.

Thurston's Lobster Pound (☏207-244-7600; www.thurstonslobster.com; 9 Thurston Rd, Bernard; mains $12-30; ⊙11am-8pm late May–mid-Oct) In Bass Harbor on Mount Desert Island.

For step-by-step instructions on how to crack and eat the spiny little beasts, visit the useful website of the Gulf of Maine Research Institute (www.gma.org/lobsters) or check out the 'How to Eat' page at www.lobsterfrommaine.com.

If you want to get closer to the lobstering process, join a lobster boat tour; they operate out of numerous coastal towns.

Cliff Walk WALKING
(off York St, York Harbor; ⊙sunrise-sunset) Cliff walks are pretty common across Maine, but York Harbor's deserves credit for being a little more old school than its siblings. In places the 1-mile path is level and paved, but much of it is a rough, rocky scrabble that feels dangerously slippery after rain (watch your step!). That said, the raw oceanside scenery is simply outstanding.

There's no dedicated parking for this walk, but there is street parking on York St. You can access the walk via the **Hartley Mason Reserve** (481 York St, York Harbor; ⊙sunrise-sunset) FREE.

Fisherman's Walk WALKING
(Barrell Lane Rd, York Harbor) This pleasant trail, which runs about 1.7 miles, meanders along the York River. Strollers can enjoy the very new England sights of working boats, pretty yachts and stately old homes. Fisherman's Walk links the Wiggly Bridge & Steedman Woods (to the west) and the Cliff Walk (to the east).

🛏 Sleeping & Eating

Inn at Tanglewood Hall B&B $$
(☏207-351-1075; www.tanglewoodhall.com; 611 York St, York Harbor; r $135-175; ❄🛜) This lovely B&B has six sweetly furnished rooms with feather beds and abundant country charm.

Several rooms have gas fireplaces and private porches. The wraparound veranda of the 1880s inn provides a peaceful vantage point overlooking the gardens.

Harbor Cliffs Inn
B&B $$$

(☑ 207-363-5119; www.yorkharborinn.com/lodging/harbor-cliffs; 480 York St, York Harbor; r $249-299) You'll find seven uniquely appointed rooms at this upscale B&B; five of them come with grand ocean views, four have fireplaces and some have decks or on-site hot tubs. Rooms have a more minimalist, hip aesthetic than the thousand identikit chintzy B&Bs found elsewhere in the region. Located adjacent to and operated by the same owners as **York Harbor Inn** (☑ reservations 800-343-3869; www.yorkharborinn.com; r $159-219, ste $299; P ❋ 🖙).

Flo's Hot Dogs
HOT DOGS $

(www.floshotdogs.com; 1359 US 1, Cape Neddick; hot dogs $2.75; ⊙ 11am-3pm Thu-Tue) Flo's is a local institution: a little roadside shack doling out steamed hot dogs a few hours a day around lunchtime. What brings the crowds is the star ingredient: the secret-recipe relish (so popular it's also available in jars). The hot dogs themselves are fine, if nothing too special, a sentiment that may get us banned from Maine. Cash only.

Cape Neddick Lobster Pound
SEAFOOD $$

(☑ 207-363-5471; www.capeneddick.com; 60 Shore Rd, Cape Neddick; mains $13-38; ⊙ noon-9pm Jun-Sep, shorter hours rest of year) In a tranquil spot overlooking the Cape Neddick River, this sunny, open dining room is popular with locals and in-the-know summer regulars. Ignore the fancy-sounding appetizers and stick with the classics – fresh-steamed lobster dripping with melted butter, washed down with local beer.

ℹ Information

Greater York Chamber of Commerce (☑ 207-363-4422; www.gatewaytomaine.org/visitor; 1 Stonewall Lane; ⊙ 9am-4pm Mon-Fri, to 1pm Sat) For visitor information, stop by the helpful visitors center at the Greater York Chamber of Commerce, just off US 1 between York Village and York Harbor.

ℹ Getting There & Away

From Kittery, it's another 6 miles up US 1 or I-95 to York Village. York Harbor is about 1 mile east of York Village via US 1A; York Beach is 3 miles north of York Village via US 1A. Cape Neddick is just north of York Beach. The nearest major bus station is 10 miles away in Portsmouth, NH.

Ogunquit

POP 920

The Abenaki came up with the lovely name Ogunquit, which apparently means 'the beautiful place by the sea.' After a few minutes strolling around town, we were inclined to believe it meant, 'Family-friendly resort town with a thriving arts and LGBTIQ+ scene,' but our eastern woodland linguistic skills admittedly aren't up to snuff.

Seriously though: Ogunquit is simply a wonderful little arts colony/LGBTIQ+ vacation escape/spot where your kids can experience the American seaside holiday in all its quaint glory. Wide stretches of pounding surf front the Atlantic, while warm back-cove waters make an idyllic setting for a swim. In summer, the 3-mile beach draws hordes of visitors from near and far, increasing the town's population exponentially.

Before its resort status, Ogunquit was a shipbuilding center in the 17th century. Later it became an important arts center when the Ogunquit art colony was founded in 1898.

◎ Sights & Activities

Perkins Cove
WATERFRONT

(access from Shore Rd) This picturesque inlet is dotted with sailboats and fishing boats; a narrow pedestrian bridge spans the harbor. The cove is home to a handful of attractive restaurants, art galleries and boutiques. It's a good spot come dinnertime, but it's also popular with ice-cream-toting day-trippers.

Ogunquit Beach
BEACH

(access from Beach St) A sublime stretch of family-friendly coastline, Ogunquit Beach is only a five-minute walk along Beach St, east of US 1. Walking to the beach is a good idea in summer as the parking lot fills up early (and it costs $4 per hour to park!). The 3-mile beach fronts Ogunquit Bay to the south; on the west side of the beach are the warmer waters of the tidal Ogunquit River.

★ Marginal Way
WALKING

(access from Shore Rd) Tracing the 'margin' of the sea, Ogunquit's famed mile-long footpath winds above the crashing gray waves, taking in grand sea vistas and rocky coves, and allowing for some excellent real-estate admiring. The neatly paved path, fine for children and slow walkers, is dotted with restful benches. It starts south of Beach St at Shore Rd and ends near Perkins Cove.

WORTH A TRIP

OGUNQUIT PLAYHOUSE

The beloved 1933 **Ogunquit Playhouse** (📞 207-646-5511; www.ogunquit playhouse.org; 10 Main St/US 1; tickets $52-92; �) May-Oct; ♿) wears the tag 'America's foremost summer theater.' It hosts Broadway musicals each season. Well-known performers occasionally appear in the cast, although the productions are high quality even without them.

🛏 Sleeping

⭐ Gazebo Inn   B&B $$
(📞 207-646-3733; www.gazeboinnogt.com; 572 Main St/US 1; r $149-289, ste $259-379; ❄ 🤖 🏊) This stately 1847 farmhouse and converted barn feature 14 rooms and suites – the space feels more like a boutique lodge. Rustic-chic touches abound and there's ample common space, including an inviting lounge-bar with beamed ceilings. There's a lovely pool area, and a calm, mature feel (it's kid-free).

Bourne Bed & Breakfast   B&B $$
(📞 207-646-3891; http://b3ogt.com; 13 Bourne Lane; r $129-229; 🅿 ❄ 🤖) This refreshing B&B has pleasantly modern furnishings; some rooms feel more like comfortably appointed contemporary apartments than traditional lacy B&B accommodations. Management is helpful but very relaxed (in a good way), and this spot is supported by a crew of faithful returning customers.

Ogunquit Beach Inn   B&B $$
(📞 207-646-1112; www.ogunquitbeachinn.com; 67 School St; r $169-199, ste $189-229; ☉ May-Oct; ❄ 🤖) In a tidy little arts-and-crafts-style bungalow, this gay-and-lesbian-friendly B&B has five colorful, homey rooms and chatty owners who know all about the best new bistros and bars in town. The central location makes walking to dinner a breeze.

🍴 Eating

Northern Union   AMERICAN $$
(📞 207-216-9639; www.northern-union.me; 261 Shore Rd; mains $20-28; ☉ 5-9pm Mon & Thu, to 10pm Fri & Sat) Warm, inviting Northern Union emphasizes wine pairings, although its food is pretty fantastic with or without *vino*. To wit: try mushrooms with black garlic

aioli, or Maine duck with parsnip custard. There are dozens of bottles of wine on offer, as well as a huge selection of beers and a very fine cocktail menu.

That Place   FUSION $$$
(📞 207-646-8600; www.thatplaceinogunquit.com; 331 Shore Rd; mains $22-34; ☉ 4-11:15pm Thu-Mon) Hip, smart and a cut above the usual high-end dining options on the south coast, That Place mixes up new American vibe, Asia Pacific influences and Ogunquit's artsy, accommodating attitude: try buttermilk fried chicken with honey-thyme glaze, or crispy pork belly served alongside mango slaw. The menu changes often based on seasonal availability. Reservations are a good idea.

ℹ Information

Ogunquit Chamber of Commerce (📞 207-646-2939; www.ogunquit.org; 36 Main St/US 1; ☉ 9am-5pm Mon-Sat, 10am-4pm Sun late May-early Oct, 10am-4pm Mon-Fri rest of year) Located on US 1, near the Ogunquit Playhouse and just south of the town's center.

ℹ Getting There & Around

There's no direct bus service to Ogunquit; the nearest Greyhound (www.greyhound.com) stop is in Portsmouth, NH, 16 miles south.

Amtrak's *Downeaster* (www.amtrakdowneaster.com) train service stops in Wells on its Portland–Boston loop.

Driving around Ogunquit during high tourist season is a congested nightmare. Opt instead to move around town via the **Ogunquit Trolley** (www.ogunquittrolley.com; adult/child $2/1.50; ☉ 8am-11pm late Jun-early Sep, 9am-8pm Mon-Sat, 9am-5pm Sun mid-Sep–early Oct).

The Kennebunks

A longtime escape for moneyed East Coasters, the Kennebunks comprise the towns of **Kennebunk** and **Kennebunkport**.

Kennebunk is a modest town largely centered on US 1, with few tourist attractions beyond its lovely beaches. Just across the river, adjacent to Kennebunk's shop-lined Lower Village, is chic Kennebunkport. To call Kennebunkport preppy would be like calling Antarctica 'cold'; preppiness is the zeitgeist, the very soul of this town, which always has a scarf tied around its neck. Don't get us wrong: people here are nice and accommodating and gracious hosts. It's just unabashedly blue-blood wasp-y (white, Anglo-Saxon Protestant).

The epicenter of activity is Dock Sq, lined with cafes, art galleries and upscale boutiques. Drive down Ocean Ave to gawk at the grand mansions and hotels overlooking the surf, including the massive compound that belongs to the family of George HW Bush, set on a protected spit of land called Walker's Point.

⊙ Sights & Activities

Madelyn Marx Preserve　　NATURE RESERVE
(http://kennebunklandtrust.org; ME 9; P) FREE
This 24-acre nature preserve protects a gorgeous sweep of local salt marsh ecosystem, cut through with flat forest trails that are perfect for a leisurely nature walk. The best access point is located off ME 9, where that road crosses the Mousam River; there's a small parking lot on-site.

Maine Art Hill　　GALLERY
(207-967-2803; www.maine-art.com; 14 Western Ave, Kennebunk; ⊙10am-5pm) This complex of galleries and studios, noticeable thanks to its outside rotating wind sculptures, attracts crowds of art lovers and those who just want a quiet respite from the masses. Dozens of local artists are showcased here, and there are regular special events.

Walker's Point　　HOUSE
(Ocean Ave, Kennebunkport) Most visitors to Kennebunkport want to check out Walker's Point, the summer compound of the Bush family. To view the estate, which sits on a small promontory, take Ocean Ave from Dock Sq for about 2 miles. It's a great drive: mansions on one side, Atlantic on the other. You'll spy a handy little overlook on the roadside, with a reasonable view of the property...and that's the closest you'll get.

Parson's Way　　WALKING
(Ocean Ave) This 2-mile coastal trail takes you past a series of rocky beaches and the summer cottages – read enormous mansions – of the bluest of New England blue bloods; you'll also be able to see Walker's Point, the compound of the Bush political dynasty. The way is marked by benches, and follows Ocean Ave.

🛏 Sleeping

Captain Fairfield Inn　　B&B $$$
(207-967-4454; www.captainfairfield.com; 8 Pleasant St, Kennebunkport; r $159-499; ❄🤖) A

bold, boutique mix of modern and traditional has breathed new life into this 1813 Federal mansion. No two rooms are the same, but each boasts fine linens and fireplaces. An honesty-system bar, iPads for guests and creative small-plates breakfasts add a distinctively up-to-date flair.

Cabot Cove Cottages　　COTTAGE $$$
(207-967-5424; www.cabotcovecottages.com; 7 S Maine St, Kennebunkport; cottages $250-460; ⊙early May–mid-Oct; ❄🤖) Set in a semi-circle in a forest glade, these 16 miniature cottages look almost like fairy houses. Decor is airy and peaceful, all whitewashed walls and vintage botanical prints. Cottages range in size; all have full kitchens, though breakfast is dropped off on your doorstep each morning. Bikes, kayaks and rowboats are available for guest use.

Cape Arundel Inn　　INN $$$
(855-346-5700; www.capearundelinn.com; 208 Ocean Ave, Kennebunkport; r $200-220, ste $270-550; P❄🤖) Perched high above the sea on Kennebunkport's famed Ocean Ave, this shingled 19th-century beach mansion has some of the most dramatic views in town. The sunny guest rooms, most of which qualify as suites, are done up in pale blues and whites for an elegant, summery feel. This is a fancy spot, and has the clientele to match.

🍴 Eating

★Nunan's Lobster Hut　　SEAFOOD $$
(207-967-4362; www.nunanslobsterhut.com; 9 Mills Rd, Cape Porpoise; mains $7-25; ⊙5-10pm May–mid-Oct; �foot) Just 2.3 miles east of Kennebunkport, Nunan's is *the* place to roll up your sleeves and flex your lobster-cracking muscles. Owners Richard and Keith Nunan still trap and cook the lobsters just like their grandfather did when he opened the restaurant in 1953. Decor is 'haute Maine fishing shack,' with wooden walls hung with ancient nets and buoys.

★Clam Shack　　SEAFOOD $$
(207-967-3321; www.theclamshack.net; 2 Western Ave, Kennebunk; mains $5-31; ⊙11am-8pm May-Oct) Standing in line at this teeny gray hut perched on stilts above the river is a time-honored Kennebunks summer tradition. Order a box of fat, succulent, fried whole-belly clams or a one-pound lobster roll ($19), which is served with your choice of mayo or melted butter. Outdoor seating only.

MAINE THE KENNEBUNKS

SHOPPING IN KITTERY

Founded in 1623, Kittery is one of Maine's oldest settlements, and today its proud little downtown boasts historic homes, manicured parks and an energetic food scene, with plenty of off-the-boat lobster to be found a few miles along ME103 to Kittery Point.

Today, the main reason travelers come to Kittery is to shop. The busy roads leading from New Hampshire are lined with shopping malls and vast parking lots. For that low-cost, big-name, holiday shopping spree you just had to have...head to **Kittery Outlets** (📞888-548-8379; www.thekitteryoutlets.com; US 1; ⊙9am-9pm Mon-Sat, 10am-6pm Sun). From Portsmouth, NH, it's a mere 3 miles to Kittery via US 1 or I-95 across the Piscataqua River.

White Barn Inn Restaurant MODERN AMERICAN **$$$**
(📞207-967-2321; www.gracehotels.com/white barninn; 37 Beach Ave, Kennebunk; 4-course dinner $109, 9-course tasting menu $165; ⊙5-10pm) One of Maine's most renowned high-end restaurants, the White Barn boasts country-elegant decor and a menu that changes weekly. Expect top-quality local seafood, meat and produce, such as Kennebunkport lobster on homemade fettuccine with cognac butter sauce, or foie-gras-crusted tenderloin of beef. Reservations are essential, as is smart attire.

❶ Information

Kennebunk-Kennebunkport Chamber of Commerce (📞207-967-0857; www.visitthe kennebunks.com; 16 Water St, Kennebunk; ⊙9am-4pm Mon-Fri year-round, plus 9am-3pm Sat & Sun Jun-Sep) Has a year-round visitor center in Kennebunk town.

Kennebunkport Visitor Center (📞207-967-0857; www.visitthekennebunks.com; 1 Chase Hill, Lower Village) A summertime information kiosk on Western Ave in the Lower Village, just across the bridge from Dock Sq.

❶ Getting There & Away

The Kennebunks lie halfway (28 miles from each city) between Portsmouth, NH, and Portland, ME, just off I-95 on ME 9.

There's no direct bus service to Kennebunkport; Greyhound (www.greyhound.com) stops in both Portland and Portsmouth.

Amtrak's *Downeaster* (www.amtrakdown easter.com) train service stops in Wells, about 9 miles to the south, on its Boston–Portland loop.

❶ Getting Around

Cycling is a good idea for getting around. In summer, the streets are congested and parking is pricey. There's a free parking lot in Kennebunkport at 30 North St, 0.4 miles north of Dock Sq (about an eight-minute walk). If you want to avoid driving, you could also try the **Intown Trolley** (📞207-967-3686; www.intowntrolley. com; 21 Ocean Ave; adult/child $16/6; ⊙last tour 4pm Jul & Aug, 3pm Sep-Jun).

Saco Bay & Old Orchard Beach

Just south of Portland, this area encompasses beaches, marshes, nature preserves and small towns. The most interesting of the latter are Biddeford and the adjacent Saco. Biddeford is an interior town aiming for livability that doesn't involve blatant commercial tourism development, which ironically makes it an interesting place to visit. At its center is Pepperell Mill Campus, a former 35-acre textile mill district filled with businesses and residences.

Old Orchard Beach is a quintessential beach playground, where fun-loving sun worshippers make the rounds of candy shops, mechanical amusements and neon-lit trinket emporiums. The atmosphere isn't as Americana-esque as you might think – many tourists speak French, as Old Orchard has long been a preferred summer destination for Quebecois families.

◉ Sights & Activities

Biddeford Pool VILLAGE
(off ME 208, Biddeford) Biddeford Pool refers to many things: a large tidal pool, a small, well-kept town that surrounds said pool, and a quiet beach cove that feels a world away from the crowds at Old Orchard Beach. Parking is difficult to find, but any walk you take to the beach area will run past quaint residential side streets and local nature trails.

Ferry Beach State Park STATE PARK
(📞207-283-0067; www.maine.gov/ferrybeach; 95 Bayview Rd, Saco; adult/child $7/1; ⊙9am-sunset Jun-Sep; 🅿) A pretty stretch of beach, inland walking areas, a small nature center,

picnic spots and a rare (for this far north) grove of tupelo trees can all be found at this 117-acre park, as well as nice views of the sandy shore stretching in either direction. The park can get crowded, but nonetheless is one of the more pleasant beaches in the area.

🛏 Sleeping & Eating

Edgewater Motel   MOTEL **$$**
(☑ 207-934-2221; http://theedgewatermotorinn. com; 57 W Grand Ave, Old Orchard Beach; r high season $150-300, low season $89-145; P 🅿 📶 🏊) 🖋 There are a thousand beachside (or beachside-ish) motels in Old Orchard Beach offering more or less the same lodging experience. We like the Edgewater for its clean, blue-and-white rooms with wooden floors, genuine commitment to sustainability (it uses solar power) and tradition of family ownership.

★ Palace Diner   DINER **$**
(☑ 207-284-0015; www.palacedinerme.com; 18 Franklin St, Biddeford; mains $8-16; ⊗ 8am-2pm) This 15-seat diner is the oldest in Maine, and it's lasted so long for a reason: the breakfast and lunch dishes are totally on point. Buttermilk pancakes, corned beef hash, tuna salad melts and fried chicken – the menu might be simple, but everything is executed with skill and craftsmanship.

ℹ Information

Get information at the **Old Orchard Beach Chamber of Commerce** (☑ 207-934-2500; https://oldorchardbeachmaine.com; 11 1st St, Old Orchard Beach; ⊗ 8:30am-4:30pm Mon-Fri). If you're in Biddeford or Saco, or just like '+' signs, head to the **Biddeford+Saco Chamber of Commerce+Industry** (☑ 207-282-1567; 28 Water St, Biddeford; ⊗ 8am-4pm Mon-Fri).

ℹ Getting There & Away

Biddeford is about 18 miles south of Portland along US 1; Old Orchard Beach is just a few miles further away on the coast (of course). Beachfront ME 9 is the heart of the action at Old Orchard.

No buses run here, but Amtrak's *Downeaster* runs to the **Saco Transportation Center** (http://amtrakdowneaster.com/stations/ saco; 138 Main St, Saco) between Biddeford and Saco. Trains come through five times a day on their way to Portland ($8 to $18, 25 minutes) or Brunswick ($12 to $22, 70 minutes).

PORTLAND

POP 66,900

Seagulls scream, the smell of beer and fish fry flows through the streets like the fog off Casco Bay, and everywhere the salt wind licks your skin. Maine's largest city has capitalized on the gifts of its port history – the redbrick warehouse buildings, the narrow cobblestone streets – to become one of the hippest, most vibrant small cities in the Americas. You'll find excellent museums and galleries, abundant green space, and both a food culture and a brewing scene worthy of a town many times its size.

Set on a peninsula, Portland's always been a city of the sea. Today, the Old Port district is the town's historic heart, with handsomely restored brick buildings filled with cafes, shops and bars. There are more hipsters than fishmongers living here these days, but there's also genuine ethnic diversity – Portland boasts a large African population – generally lacking in the rest of Maine.

◎ Sights & Activities

★ Portland Head Light   LIGHTHOUSE
(☑ 207-799-2661; https://portlandheadlight.com; 1000 Shore Rd, Cape Elizabeth; museum adult/child $2/1; ⊗ Fort Williams Park sunrise-sunset, museum 10am-4pm Jun-Oct, Sat & Sun only Apr, May & Nov) Fort Williams Park, on Cape Elizabeth, has rolling lawns dotted with bunkers and gun emplacements. Within the park stands the beloved, and much-photographed, Portland Head Light, the oldest of Maine's 52 functioning lighthouses. It was commissioned by President George Washington in 1791 and staffed until 1989, when machines took over. The keeper's house is now a museum, which traces the maritime and military history of the region.

★ Portland Museum of Art   MUSEUM
(☑ 207-775-6148; www.portlandmuseum.org; 7 Congress Sq; adult/child $15/free, 4-8pm Fri free; ⊗ 10am-6pm Sat-Wed, to 8pm Thu & Fri, shorter hours Oct-May) Founded in 1882, this well-respected museum houses an outstanding collection of American artists. Maine artists, including Winslow Homer, Edward Hopper, Louise Nevelson and Andrew Wyeth, are particularly well represented. You'll also find a few works by European masters, including Monet, Degas, Picasso and Renoir.

Central Portland

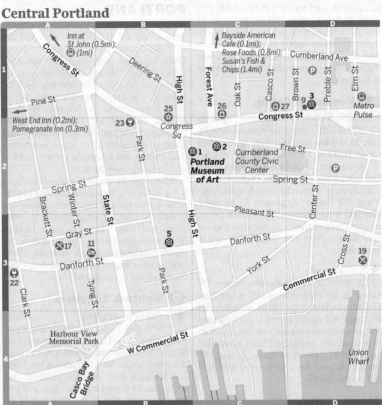

Central Portland

◎ Top Sights
1 Portland Museum of Art C2

◎ Sights
2 Children's Museum & Theatre
   of Maine C2
3 Longfellow House D1
4 Portland Observatory H1
5 Victoria Mansion B3

✪ Activities, Courses & Tours
6 Casco Bay Lines F4
7 Lucky Catch Lobstering E3
8 Maine Brew Bus F3
9 Maine Historical Society D1

🛏 Sleeping
10 Black Elephant Hostel F2
11 Danforth Inn A3
12 Press Hotel E2

✖ Eating
13 Central Provisions E3
14 DuckFat F2
15 Fore Street F3
16 Holy Donut E3
17 OhNo Cafe A3
18 Terlingua G1
19 Veranda Noodle Bar D3

🍷 Drinking & Nightlife
20 Hunt + Alpine Club E2
21 Novare Res Bier Cafe E2
22 Ruski's A3
23 Sagamore Hill B2

✪ Entertainment
24 Portland Symphony Orchestra E1
25 State Theatre B1

🛍 Shopping
26 Flea-for-All C1
27 Maine Craft C1

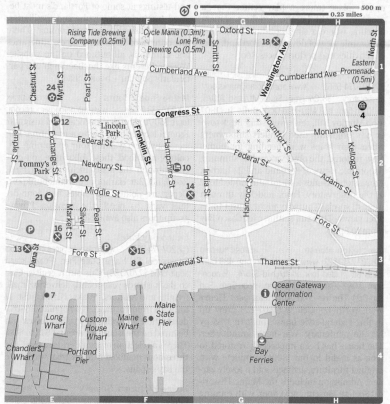

Tate House Museum
MUSEUM

(☎ 207-774-6177; www.tatehouse.org; 1267 Westbrook St; adult/child $15/7; ⊙ 10am-4pm Wed-Sat, from 1pm Sun; P) This home preserves the Colonial residence of George Tate, Maine's last British 'mast agent' (mast agents procured New England white pine trees as construction material for the British navy). Tate's elegant home is the only one in Portland that dates from pre-Revolutionary times that's open to the public. Besides getting a glimpse of upper-class 18th-century life, tours (departing on the hour) provide a grounding in the mast trade and general history of Colonial New England.

Victoria Mansion
HISTORIC BUILDING

(☎ 207-772-4841; www.victoriamansion.org; 109 Danforth St; adult/child $15/5; ⊙ 10am-3:45pm Mon-Sat, 1:15-4:45pm Sun May-Oct) This Italianate palace, whose exterior would work well in a Tim Burton movie, dates back to 1860. Inside it's sumptuously decorated with rich furniture, frescoes, paintings, carpets, gilt, exotic woods and stone. The former owner of the house was a hotelier in New Orleans, and many details, like a stained-glass window displaying Louisiana's and Maine's respective state seals, hint at a split identity between the far north and Deep South.

The mansion gets decked out in holiday decorations come December, when it is open to the public from 10am to 3:45pm Tuesday to Sunday, and until 6pm Monday.

Children's Museum & Theatre of Maine
MUSEUM

(☎ 207-828-1234; www.kitetails.org; 142 Free St; $11.50; ⊙ 10am-5pm late May-early Sep, closed Mon rest of year; ⚐) Kids aged zero to 10 shriek and squeal as they haul traps aboard a replica lobster boat, milk a fake cow on a model farm, operate a sound studio, or monkey around on an indoor rock-climbing wall. The highlight of this ultra-interactive, upbeat place (more a play center than a museum) might be the 3rd-floor camera obscura, where a single pinhole projects a panoramic view of downtown Portland. Lots of activities and performances, too.

Portland Observatory
HISTORIC BUILDING

(☑207-774-5561; www.portlandlandmarks.org/observatory; 138 Congress St; adult/child $10/5; ⊙10am-5pm late May–mid-Oct) Built in 1807 atop Munjoy Hill, this seven-story brick tower was originally used to alert shipowners when their ships were heading for home. Now restored, the observatory has stunning panoramic views of Portland and its harbor. Admission includes a 45-minute guided tour of the observatory. From mid-July through August, special Thursday-night sunset tours offer views of the sun setting over Casco Bay (5pm to 8pm).

Longfellow House
HISTORIC BUILDING

(☑207-774-1822; www.mainehistory.org; 489 Congress St; guided tour adult/child $15/4; ⊙noon-5pm May, 10am-5pm Mon-Sat, noon-5pm Sun Jun-Oct) The revered American poet Henry Wadsworth Longfellow (1807–82) grew up in this Federal-style house, built in 1785 by his Revolutionary War–hero grandfather. The house has been impeccably restored to look as it did in the 1800s, complete with original furniture, artifacts and a lovely garden. Admission includes the Maine Historical Society Museum next door, with rotating exhibits about life in Maine over the past few centuries. Ask about historical walking tours, offered by the society from June to mid-October.

★ Eastern Promenade
WALKING

(http://trails.org/our-trails/eastern-prom-trail; Eastern Promenade) Don't leave town without having a walk or bicycle ride along this 2.1-mile trail, which offers superb, sweeping views of Casco Bay, all speckled with sailboats and rocky islets. The well-paved path has two small rises, but is otherwise flat and accessible to all levels of physical fitness. The promenade can be easily accessed throughout Portland's East End.

⟲ Tours

★ Maine Brew Bus
BUS

(☑207-200-9111; https://themainebrewbus.com; 79 Commercial St; tours $45-85) Want to drink your way around Portland? We know the feeling. Hop aboard the green bus for tours and tastings at some of Portland's most beloved breweries, brewpubs and distilleries, from established to up-and-coming. There are dozens of departure times, itineraries and durations, all outlined on the website. Weekend events like the 'Beerunch' are particularly popular – book ahead.

Maine Foodie Tours
FOOD & DRINK

(☑207-233-7485; www.mainefoodietours.com; tours $50-70) Hungry for local food insights? From a lobster boat trip to a lunchtime lobster crawl or a walking tour combining art, culture and food, these folks have you covered around the state, including Portland, Rockland, Bar Harbor and Kennebunkport. Departure points, timetables and tour details vary, so check the website. Private group tours also available.

Casco Bay Lines
CRUISE

(☑207-774-7871; www.cascobaylines.com; 56 Commercial St, Maine State Pier; Peaks Island adult/child $7.70/3.85) This outfit cruises Casco Bay's islands year-round, delivering mail, freight and visitors. Peaks Island, just 17 minutes from Portland, is a popular day-trip destination for walks or cycling; bikes can be hired on the island for around $15 to $20. There's a selection of scenic cruises, too – the three-hour mailboat run is a great way to see the bay's sights.

Maine Historical Society
WALKING

(☑207-774-1822; www.mainehistory.org; 489 Congress St; tours $15; ⊙1:30pm Mon-Fri mid-Jun–mid-Oct) Weather permitting, these guided walking tours leave from the Maine Historical Society (beside Longfellow House) each afternoon, and last about one to 1¼ hours. The focus is on Portland's waterfront, highlighting history and maritime heritage. Tours are limited to 12 guests and are first-come, first-served. You can get a combination ticket to the Longfellow House for $25.

✷ Festivals & Events

Harvest on the Harbor
FOOD & DRINK

(www.harvestontheharbor.com; 100 W Commercial St; ⊙early Nov) A five-day feast for all the senses (but especially taste), this is Maine's premier food and wine festival. Buy tickets in advance for events such as the Lobster Chef of the Year competition, a five-course moonlight gala, or a celebration of local suds and cider.

MAINE PORTLAND

🛏 Sleeping

★ Black Elephant Hostel
HOSTEL $

(📞 207-712-7062; www.blackelephanthostel.com; 33 Hampshire St; dm $40-60, d $65-150; 🛜) The Black Elephant is Portland's first dedicated hostel, and it's an exceptionally good one, with funky interior art, exterior murals, a central location and a range of clean and comfortable rooms. The lobby and kitchen spaces are super-colorful and inviting, and there's even a 'vampire' themed bathroom.

West End Inn
B&B $$

(📞 207-772-1377; www.westendbb.com; 146 Pine St; r $149-249; 🅿 ❄ 🛜) In a redbrick town house in Portland's tony Western Promenade district, this recommended six-room B&B is arty and elegant. Rooms are sunny and unfussy, with bright decor ranging from sweet florals to crisp nautical prints. The multicourse breakfast and sunny patio add appeal.

★ Press Hotel
HOTEL $$$

(📞 207-573-2425; www.thepresshotel.com; 119 Exchange St; r $220-413; 🅿 ❄ 🛜) Opened in mid-2015, the Press Hotel, a creative conversion of the building that once housed the offices and printing plant of Maine's largest newspaper, has since become something of a Portland institution. The press theme shines in unique details – a wall of vintage typewriters, and old headlines on hallway wallpapers. Smart, navy-toned rooms are sexy and local art adorns walls.

★ Danforth Inn
BOUTIQUE HOTEL $$$

(📞 207-879-8755; www.danforthinn.com; 163 Danforth St; r $199-359, ste $699; 🅿 ❄ 🛜) Staying at this ivy-shrouded West End boutique hotel feels like being a guest at an eccentric millionaire's mansion. Shoot pool in the wood-paneled games room (a former speakeasy) or climb into the rooftop cupola for views across Portland Harbor. The nine rooms are decorated with flair, in a sophisticated mix of antique and modern.

Be sure to stop by the bar-lounge, which is a thing of beauty (check out the moss-covered light fitting).

★ Pomegranate Inn
B&B $$$

(📞 207-772-1006; www.pomegranateinn.com; 49 Neal St; r $189-409; ❄ 🛜) Whimsy prevails at this eight-room inn, a historic home transformed into a showcase for antiques and contemporary art: life-size classical statues, leopard rugs, Corinthian columns and ab-stract sketches. Common spaces are a riot of colors and patterns; guest rooms come with hand-painted, oversized flower patterns and a wild mix of antique and contemporary furniture. Somehow everything fits together beautifully.

🍴 Eating

★ Bayside American Cafe
AMERICAN $

(📞 207-774-0005; www.baysideamericancafe.com; 98 Portland St; mains $9-17; ⊘ 7am-2pm; 👶) This charming brunch and lunch spot is great for a rib-sticking meal to start your day. It uses steak in its corned beef and one of its eggs Benedict dishes; to go meatless, try the huevos rancheros. Staff are friendly and ingredients are often locally sourced. Reservations are accepted, otherwise expect a line.

★ Rose Foods
JEWISH $

(📞 207-835-0991; www.rosefoods.me; 428 Forest Ave; mains $8-15; ⊘ 7am-2pm) Life doesn't get much better than a good bagel, and the best bagels in Portland are served at Rose. There are about nine bagel sandwich options – we love the classic with salmon, onions, cream cheese, cucumber and capers, but you may prefer some chopped liver, pickles and gribenes (chicken cracklin'). Kosher sandwiches are also served, on rye, of course.

★ Holy Donut
SWEETS $

(📞 207-775-7776; www.theholydonut.com; 7 Exchange St; doughnuts $2.50; ⊘ 7am-4pm Mon-Thu, to 5pm Fri-Sun) Doughnuts made from *potato*? Yep, and they're awesome. Local Maine potatoes and sweet potatoes go into the recipe for these doughnuts, creating a moist, cakey texture. Flavors range from fabulous (maple bacon) to more fabulous (dark-chocolate sea salt). There's a second branch at 194 Park Ave, north of the center. Both outlets close when they sell out of the goods.

Gluten-free and vegan options are also available.

★ OhNo Cafe
SANDWICHES $

(📞 208-774-0773; http://ohnocafe.com; 87 Brackett St; sandwiches $4.50-7.50; ⊘ 6:30am-8:30pm Tue-Fri, 8am-8pm Sat, 8am-3pm Sun) Actually, oh yes. This bare-bones operation looks like a corner store with a kitchen, because that's more or less what it is. The sandwiches here are simply fantastic. You've got breakfast variations, say, maple-glazed prosciutto, cheddar, hot sauce and egg on a bagel, and lunch stuff, like a perfect veggie burger with avocado, tomato and spinach.

LGBTIQ+ PORTLAND

Portland is very LGBTIQ+ friendly, while nearby towns like Ogunquit are veritable gay travel destinations. For years, Portland has consistently been in the top 10 cities in the USA for same-sex married couples. Every business we list in Portland is LGBTIQ+ friendly, some outspokenly so. Check out www.gayportlandme.com for more information.

Explicitly gay bars are rare, but many businesses attract LGBTIQ+ clientele, including the Black Elephant Hostel (p377), **Inn at St John** (☑207-773-6481; www.innatstjohn.com; 939 Congress St; r $109-289; **P❋🛜**) and Press Hotel (p377), and drinking venues such as **Novare Res Bier Cafe** (☑207-761-2437; www.novareresbiercafe.com; 4 Canal Plaza; ⊙4pm-1am Mon-Thu, 3pm-1am Fri, noon-1am Sat & Sun), Sagamore Hill, **Lone Pine Brewing Co** (☑207-536-4952; 219 Anderson St; ⊙2-8pm Mon-Wed, noon-9pm Thu-Sat, noon-8pm Sun) and **Hunt + Alpine Club** (☑207-747-4754; www.huntandalpineclub.com; 75 Market St; ⊙3pm-1am Mon-Thu, from 1pm Fri-Sun).

MAINE PORTLAND

Veranda Noodle Bar
VIETNAMESE $

(☑207-874-9090; www.verandanoodlebar.com; 245 Commercial St; mains $11-15; ⊙11am-9:30pm Sun-Thu, to 10:30pm Fri & Sat) Cheap and cheerful Vietnamese is the name of the game at this lovely spot, where friendly staff crank out very solid bowls of *pho*, duck noodle soup, and rice noodle and meatball soup. It's an old-school family restaurant, and deserves all of its well-earned popularity.

Susan's Fish & Chips
SEAFOOD $

(☑207-878-3240; http://susansfishnchips.com; 1135 Forest Ave; mains $10-20; ⊙11am-8pm; 🚸) Pop in for fish-and-chips and plenty of deep-fried seafood at this no-fuss, family-friendly eatery on US 302. It's low on pretension, high on good cheer and set up in a former garage with under-the-sea decor.

DuckFat
FAST FOOD $

(☑207-774-8080; http://duckfat.com; 43 Middle St; small fries $5.50, panini $10-14; ⊙11am-10pm) DuckFat is famous for its fries cooked in (yes) duck fat. On the right night, they're shatteringly crisp, with fluffy centers. Dipping sauces (truffle ketchup, horseradish mayo etc) are good but unnecessary. The fancy panini are also excellent, and people flock to the poutine. Decor is 'hipster fast-food joint,' with a blackboard menu and a handful of bistro tables.

★ Central Provisions
MODERN AMERICAN $$

(☑207-805-1085; www.central-provisions.com; 414 Fore St; lunch plates $4-18, dinner plates $5-30; ⊙11am-2pm & 5-10pm Sun-Thu, to 10:30pm Fri & Sat) Snug, redbrick Central Provisions is a consistent winner in the Portland haute cuisine stakes. Angle for a seat at the bar, overlooking the line chefs in action, and choose from a masterful small-plates menu

that swings from tuna crudo to suckling pig. Local oysters, fish and cheese are staples.

Terlingua
BARBECUE $$

(☑207-808-8502; www.terlingua.me; 52 Washington Ave; mains $14-21; ⊙11:30am-9pm Mon-Sat, from 10am Sun) This fascinating gem serves up small-batch barbecue dinners starting at 5pm, and a menu inspired by the Southwest and the Caribbean at all other times. The ever-shifting menu might feature pork belly lettuce wraps, red chili with brisket, adobo pork or mushroom empanadas. On Sunday nights, a 'neighborhood dinner' provides a reduced menu with lower prices.

★ Fore Street
MODERN AMERICAN $$$

(☑207-775-2717; www.forestreet.biz; 288 Fore St; small plates $12-16, mains $26-42; ⊙5:30-10pm Sun-Thu, to 10:30pm Fri & Sat) 🍽 Fore Street is the lauded, long-running restaurant many consider to be the originator of today's food obsession in Portland. Chef-owner Sam Hayward has turned roasting into a high art: chickens turn on spits in the open kitchen as chefs slide iron kettles of mussels into the wood-burning oven. Local, seasonal eating is taken very seriously and the menu changes daily.

🍷 Drinking & Nightlife

★ Sagamore Hill
BAR

(☑207-808-8622; www.sagamorehillmaine.com; 150 Park St; ⊙4pm-1am) Early-20th-century elegance meets a 21st-century cocktail menu, plus lots of Teddy Roosevelt memorabilia and a ton of taxidermy at this excellent bar. The interior has an art-deco appeal that's tough not to love, especially after a Louisiana Purchase (rye, vermouth, bitters, charred thyme). Serves seasonal drinks, plus nonalcoholic mocktails.

★**Rising Tide**
Brewing Company   BREWERY
(📞207-370-2337; www.risingtidebrewing.com; 103 Fox St; ⊙tastings noon-7pm Mon-Sat, to 5pm Sun) In a pocket of town growing in stature (and with a neighboring distillery), Rising Tide is well worth investigating. Locals congregate in the car park, and food trucks visit in summer, from Wednesday to Sunday. Check the website for events (live music etc). Tours are held daily at 3pm; also on Saturday at 1pm and 5pm, on Sunday at 1pm.

★**Ruski's**   BAR
(📞207-774-7604; 212 Danforth St; ⊙7am-1am Mon-Sat, from 9am Sun) Portland's drinking scene is suffused with microbreweries and craft cocktail spots, and these are all very nice, but this old port also deserves a down-and-dirty dive where the whiskey and attitude aren't watered down. Along comes Ruski's, a simple neighborhood bar where you can get drunk with no judgment; bless it forever.

☆ **Entertainment**

State Theatre   LIVE PERFORMANCE
(📞207-956-6000; www.statetheatreportland.com; 609 Congress St) This gorgeous old gem is the kind of old-school performance hall every great city deserves. The State is accented with art-deco and Moorish influences, and it's enjoyable even without seeing a show. That said, a lot of musical acts and comedy performances grace this main stage; check the online calendar before you get to Portland.

Portland Symphony
Orchestra   CLASSICAL MUSIC
(📞207-773-6128; https://portlandsymphony.org; 20 Myrtle St, Merrill Auditorium) The Portland Symphony Orchestra has a solid reputation in these parts; it's been around since 1923 and continues to perform popular classical and pop concerts. Events are held at the 2000-seat Merrill Auditorium. The season runs from September to June.

🔒 **Shopping**

★**Maine Craft**   ARTS & CRAFTS
(📞207-808-8184; https://mainecrafts.org/center-formaine-craft/portland; 521 Congress St; ⊙10am-6pm Sun-Wed, to 7pm Thu, to 8pm Fri & Sat) Past the clever title of this shop is an excellent retail and arts space, showcasing the best of the state's contemporary crafts and maker movement. You'll find handmade jewelry, objets d'art and general captivating creativity. Even the setting – Mechanic's Hall, a handsome 19th-century gem on the National Register of Historic Places – is superb.

Flea-for-All   VINTAGE
(📞207-370-7570; http://portlandfleaforall.com; 585 Congress St; ⊙noon-6pm Fri, 10am-6pm Sat, 10am-5pm Sun) Besides having an excellent name, Portland's Flea-for-All is a fantastic secondhand market, full of everything from centuries-old silk kimonos and hand-painted furniture to ancient records and dusty books.

ℹ️ **Information**

Ocean Gateway Information Center (📞20 7-772-5800; www.visitportland.com; 14 Ocean Gateway Pier; ⊙9am-5pm Mon-Fri, to 4pm Sat & Sun Jun-Oct, shorter hours rest of year) Visitor information, down at the waterfront.

ℹ️ **Getting There & Away**

AIR
Portland International Jetport (PWM; 📞207-874-8877; www.portlandjetport.org; 1001 Westbrook St) is Maine's largest air terminal. It's served by domestic airlines, with nonstop flights to cities in the eastern USA. Metro bus 5 takes you to the center of town for $1.50. Taxis are about $20 to downtown.

BOAT
There are passenger ferries between Portland and the islands of Casco Bay, operated by Casco Bay Lines (p376).

In summer, **Bay Ferries** (📞877-762-7245; www.ferries.ca/thecat; Ocean Gateway Pier; ⊙mid-Jun–Sep) operates a fast ferry CAT service between Portland and Yarmouth, Nova Scotia (Canada), daily from mid-June to September. Journey time is six hours. Adult one-way/round-trip fares are $107/194; car passage is from $199 one way. Arrival and departure is from the Ocean Gateway Pier.

BUS
Greyhound (📞207-772-6588; www.greyhound.com; 950 Congress St) offers direct daily trips to Bangor and Boston, with connections on to the rest of the USA.

Concord Coach Lines (📞800-639-3317; https://concordcoachlines.com; 100 Thompson's Point Rd) operates daily buses between Boston (including Logan Airport; $30, two hours) and Portland, continuing on to mid-coast Maine towns. There are also services connecting Portland and the towns of Augusta ($16, one hour), Waterville ($18, 1¾ hours) and Bangor ($28, 2½ hours). Two services a day link Portland with New York City ($75, six hours).

CAR & MOTORCYCLE

Coming from the south, take I-95 to I-295, then exit 7 onto Franklin St, which leads down to the Old Port. To bypass Portland, simply stay on I-95.

TRAIN

The *Downeaster*, run by Amtrak (www.amtrak. com), makes five trips daily between Boston and Portland ($29 to $39, 2½ hours) from **Portland Transportation Center** (100 Thompson's Point Rd). Services extend up the midcoast all the way to Brunswick.

ⓘ Getting Around

Cycling is a popular way to get around Portland. Rent bikes from **Cycle Mania** (☑ 207-774-2933; www.cyclemania1.com; 65 Cove St; bike rental per day/week from $30/140; ☺ 10am-6pm Mon-Fri, to 5pm Sat). At the time of research, Portland was very close to launching a bike-share program.

Portland's city bus company is the Metro. The main terminal is the **Metro Pulse** (☑ 20 7-774-0351; http://gpmetrobus.net; Elm St; fare $1.50), near Monument Sq. Routes serve Old Port, the Jetport, the Maine Mall, Cape Elizabeth and Falmouth, among other locations.

MIDCOAST MAINE

On a map, rocky 'fingers' claw at Penobscot Bay, each peninsula clad in ancient forests, studded with lonely, windswept fishing villages and fog-wreathed paths through the woods. This is midcoast Maine. But it's also resort towns that cater to wealthy vacationers from the northeast and Canada, cheap lobster rolls, organic farm-to-table restaurants, writing retreats and tall masts creaking in harbors icebound in winter, and sun-kissed in summer. Imagine Maine, a hybrid of mountains, ocean, forests and villages, and this, too, is the midcoast.

The English first settled this region in 1607, which coincided with the Jamestown settlement in Virginia. Unlike their southerly compatriots, though, these early settlers returned to England within a year. British colonization resumed in 1620. After suffering through the long years of the French and Indian War, the area became home to a thriving shipbuilding industry, which continues today.

Brunswick

POP 20,620

On the banks of the Androscoggin River, Brunswick (settled in 1628) is a handsome, well-kept town with a pretty village green and historic homes tucked along tree-lined streets. It's home to the respected Bowdoin College (founded 1794), which infuses the town with a lively intellectual and artistic culture.

A short drive through the city center reveals stately Federal and Greek mansions built by wealthy sea captains. Harriet Beecher Stowe wrote *Uncle Tom's Cabin* at 63 Federal St. This story of a runaway slave, published in 1852, was hugely popular among people in the northern states, and became one of the nation's primary literary indictments of slavery.

Brunswick's green, called the Town Mall, is along Maine St. Farmers markets are set up Tuesday and Friday mornings, with free concerts Wednesday evenings in summer.

⊙ Sights

Bowdoin College COLLEGE
(☑ 207-725-3000; www.bowdoin.edu; 255 Maine St) Bowdoin, established in 1794, is one of the oldest colleges in the US and the alma mater of Henry Wadsworth Longfellow, Nathaniel Hawthorne and US president Franklin Pierce. For a tour of the handsome campus, follow the signs from Maine St to Moulton Union. Smith Union is the student center; there's an information desk on the mezzanine, as well as a cafe, pub, lounge and small art gallery.

**Peary-MacMillan
Arctic Museum** MUSEUM
(☑ 207-725-3416; www.bowdoin.edu/arctic-muse um; 9500 College Station, Bowdoin College campus, Hubbard Hall; ☺ 10am-5pm Tue-Sat, 2-5pm Sun) FREE This small but fascinating campus museum holds memorabilia from the expeditions of Robert Peary and Donald MacMillan, Bowdoin alumni who were among the first explorers to reach the North Pole. Particularly notable are MacMillan's massive collection of Arctic photographs; an oak-and-rawhide sledge used to carry the expedition to the pole; and stuffed polar bears.

🛏 Sleeping & Eating

Daniel BOUTIQUE HOTEL $$
(☑ 207-373-1824; www.thedanielhotel.com; 10 Water St; r $144-169; P ❄ 🛜) This smart

Midcoast Maine

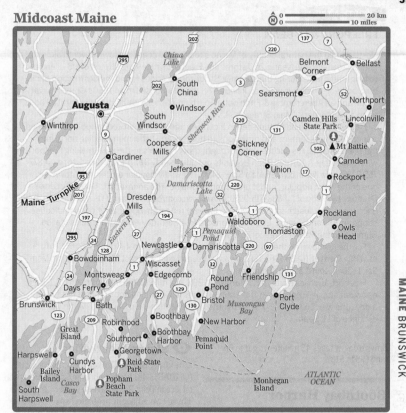

hotel, popular with Bowdoin families, may be located in a huge, c 1809 building, but it's suffused with elegant, modern touches like flat-screen TVs, simple, stately design and K-cup coffee makers. As midrange choices go, this is a solid base for exploring the area.

★ Frontier Cafe

BAR

(207-725-5222; www.explorefrontier.com; 14 Maine St; mains $13-23; ⊙ 8am-10pm Tue-Fri, from 9am Sat & Sun) On the 2nd floor of the colossal Fort Andross mill complex overlooking the Androscoggin, this raw, loft-like space is part cafe, part bar, part theater and part gallery. Arty student and professor types recline on vintage couches, sipping coffee or wine and eating antipasto platters or paella. The theater features an ever-changing schedule of art-house films, live theater and music performances.

❶ Information

Visitor Center (207-721-0999; https:// brunswickdowntown.org/about/visitor-center; 16 Station Ave; ⊙ 9:30am-6pm) This friendly visitor center is also the bus stop for buses coming in and out of Brunswick.

❶ Getting There & Away

Brunswick, off I-295 exit 28 or 31, is the point at which I-295 heads north and inland toward Augusta, Waterville and Bangor, and US 1 heads northeast along the coast. It's about 9 miles from Freeport and 8 miles from Bath.

Concord Coach Lines (www.concordcoach lines.com) offers bus services to Bangor ($26, four hours), Portland ($15, 45 minutes), Boston ($30, three hours) and a handful of midcoast towns, departing from the visitor center that's west of Maine St and close to the train station.

The Amtrak *Downeaster* line terminates at Brunswick, and departs for points south five

FREEPORT & LL BEAN

Nestled amid the natural beauty of Maine's rockbound coast is a town devoted almost entirely to shopping. Nearly 200 stores line Freeport's mile-long stretch of US 1, leading to long traffic jams during the summer. Strict zoning codes forbid the destruction of historic buildings, which is why you'll find a McDonald's housed in an 1850s Greek Revival home and an Abercrombie & Fitch outlet in a turn-of-the-20th-century library. It all adds up to a slightly eerie 'Main Street, USA' vibe.

Freeport's fame and fortune began a century ago when Leon Leonwood Bean opened a shop to sell equipment and provisions to hunters and fishermen heading north into the Maine woods. His success later brought other retailers to the area, making Freeport what it is today. A 10ft-tall Bean Boot sits outside the **LL Bean Flagship Store** (☑877-755-2326; www.llbean.com; 95 Main St; ☺24hr), the wildly popular epicenter of town and one of the most popular tourist attractions in Maine. The annexed **LL Bean Outdoor Discovery School** (☑888-615-9979; www.llbean.com/ods; 95 Main St) is more like an outdoor-themed amusement park, with an archery range, an indoor trout pond and coffee shops. In July and August, LL Bean sponsors free Saturday-evening concerts (called Summer in the Park) in Freeport's Discovery Park.

For the lowdown on the otherwise largely uninspiring town, hit the **Freeport Information Center** (☑207-865-1212; www.visitfreeport.com; 23 Depot St; ☺7am-6:45pm Mon-Sat, 11:30am-1pm & 5:30-6:45pm Sun).

Freeport, 15 miles north of Portland via I-295, is a mile off the interstate on US 1. Buses do not stop in Freeport. Amtrak train services link Portland and Freeport five times a day (one way $6 to $16, 30 to 40 minutes). The station is on Depot St, within walking distance of LL Bean.

times a day; it takes 45 minutes to get to Portland ($8 to $18).

Boothbay Harbor

POP 2200

Once a beautiful little seafarers' village on a wide blue harbor, Boothbay Harbor is now an extremely popular tourist resort in the summer, when its narrow and winding streets are packed with visitors. Still, there's good reason to join the holiday masses in this picturesque place. Overlooking a pretty waterfront, large, well-kept Victorian houses crown the town's many knolls, and a wooden footbridge ambles across the harbor. From May to October, whale-watching is a major draw.

After you've strolled the waterfront along Commercial St and the business district along Todd and Townsend Aves, walk along McKown St to the top of **McKown Hill** for a fine view. Then, take the footbridge across the harbor to the town's East Side, where there are several huge dockside seafood restaurants.

Boothbay and **East Boothbay** are separate from Boothbay Harbor, the largest, busiest and prettiest of the three towns.

◉ Sights & Activities

Linekin & Burley Preserves   NATURE RESERVE
(☑207-633-4818; www.bbrlt.org/linekin-preserve; off Ocean Point Rd; ☺sunrise-sunset; ℗) FREE
These two adjacent protected spaces encompass some 140 acres of forested Maine prettiness, situated on a windy stretch of lovely, gravel-studded waterfront. There are 3 miles of trails to explore, plus forest ponds, rocky ledges and a general sense of quiet just minutes from the bustle of Boothbay.

Boothbay Railway Village   MUSEUM
(☑207-633-4727; www.railwayvillage.org; 586 Wiscasset Rd/ME 27; adult/child $14/7; ☺10am-5pm late May–mid-Oct; ℗🎠) Ride the narrow-gauge steam train through this endearing village, a historic replica of an old-fashioned New England town. The 28 buildings house more than 60 antique steam- and gas-powered vehicles, as well as exhibits on turn-of-the-20th-century Maine culture. Frequent special events include craft fairs, auto shows and visits from Thomas the Tank Engine.

Boothbay Region Land Trust   HIKING
(☑207-633-4818; www.bbrlt.org; 60 Samoset Rd) This land trust manages over 30 miles of year-round hiking trails traversing tidal coves, shoreline forest, flower meadows and

salt marshes. Bird-watchers should keep their eyes peeled for great blue herons, eider ducks, herring gulls and migratory birds. Stop by the office (call ahead to see if it's open) or go online for maps and schedules of guided hikes.

🛏 Sleeping & Eating

★ Topside Inn
B&B $$$

(☑ 207-633-5404; www.topsideinn.com; 60 McKown St; r $239-389; ☺ May–mid-Oct; P❄🛜) Atop McKown Hill, this grand gray mansion has Boothbay's best harbor views. Rooms are elegantly turned out in crisp nautical prints and beachy shades. Main-house rooms have more historic charm, but rooms in the two adjacent modern guesthouses are sunny and lovely too. Enjoy the sunset from an Adirondack chair on the inn's sloping, manicured lawn.

★ Shannon's Unshelled
SEAFOOD $

(☑ 207-446-4921; www.shannonsunshelled.biz; 11 Granary Way; mains $7-15; ☺ from 10:30am; 🐾) If you like your lobster rolls simple, with no accoutrements but melted butter on the side, Shannon's is ideal. The meat is fresh and there's lots of it, and it comes on thick, nicely toasted bread. Shannon's closes when it runs out of lobster – sometimes late afternoon, sometimes much earlier.

Cabbage Island Clambakes
SEAFOOD $$$

(☑ 207-633-7200; www.cabbageislandclambakes. com; 22 Commercial St, Pier 6; clambake incl boat tour $70; ☺ Jul–mid-Sep) A prized Maine tradition: a scenic cruise from Boothbay Harbor to the small, family owned Cabbage Island, where a traditional clambake provides a fabulously memorable feast for diners, who can explore the island in between courses. Chow down on chowder, steamed clams, lobster and all the fixings, plus delicious blueberry cake. Lunch cruise daily, plus additional departure on weekends. Book ahead.

❶ Information

Boothbay Harbor Region Chamber of Commerce (☑ 207-633-2353; www.boothbay harbor.com; 192 Townsend Ave; ☺ 8am-5pm Mon-Fri, 9am-4pm Sat Jun-Sep) offers good info on its website; it also operates a downtown **information center** (17 Commercial St; ☺ 9am-6pm late May-early Oct) in summer.

❶ Getting There & Around

From Wiscasset, continue on US 1 for 1.5 miles and then head south on ME 27 for 11 miles through Boothbay to Boothbay Harbor.

There's no direct bus service to Boothbay Harbor. Concord Coach Lines (www.concordcoach lines.com) stops in Wiscasset; you can then take a taxi. Try **Twin Village Taxi** (☑ 207-380-0050).

Damariscotta

POP 2140

So many towns on the midcoast make the most of their seaside geography; Damariscotta bucks the trend with a riverside setting that is still unspeakably beautiful. The town's estuarine identity isn't just distinctive in terms of physical location – the river Damariscotta is named for produces some 80% of Maine's annual oyster harvest. As a result, if you're going to pop a raw one in Maine, do so here: the oysters do not get fresher.

Other attractions include a glut of good bookstores, a nice local theater, and a general friendliness and warm embrace of life's good things – seafood, beer and good company – that's easy to fall in love with.

◉ Sights & Activities

Dodge Point Preserve
NATURE RESERVE

(www.damariscottariver.org; off River Rd, Newcastle; ☺ sunrise-sunset; P) 🚶 FREE Some 500 acres of land, once managed as a tree farm, now constitute a lovely slice of preserved red pine woods and breezy riparian shorescapes. Four easy trails web throughout the reserve, taking visitors past pebbly river shores, old stone walls, still ponds, curious raccoons and the occasional fox (and even moose!).

Damariscotta River Cruises
CRUISE

(☑ 207-315-5544; https://damariscottarivercruis es.com; 47 Main St; adult/child $31/16, tasting cruise $55-65) Get on board the 49-passenger *River Tripper* and take a two-hour cruise up and down the Damariscotta River, spotting commercial oyster boats and pods of seals along the way. Oyster-tasting cruises pair your voyage (and shellfish) with wine, beer, champagne and sake.

🛏 Sleeping & Eating

Oak Gables B&B
B&B $

(☑ 207-563-1476; https://oakgablesbb.com; 36 Pleasant St; r $120; P❄🛜🏊) This B&B, located in a large, comfortable home situated on 9 secluded acres, is nonetheless within walking distance of 'downtown' Damariscotta. Rooms have a quilted, antique–New England vibe, and are understated but

DON'T MISS

WISCASSET: RED'S EATS' FAMOUS LOBSTER ROLLS

Wiscasset's history as a major shipbuilding port in the 19th century has left it with a legacy of exceptionally beautiful houses, all perched near the Sheepscot River. The tidy streets are dotted with antique shops, galleries, restaurants and a few old-fashioned inns. Back in the day, folks stopped here for boats and the goods they carried. Today, they line up for **Red's Eats** (☑207-882-6128; www.redseatsmaine.com; cnr Water St & US 1; mains $5-25; ☺11:30am-5pm Mon-Thu, to 8pm Fri-Sun), a seafood shack on US 1 that slows down summer traffic to such a degree that the local government has for decades been searching for a solution, including re-routing roads (no joke)!

Incredible lobster rolls, overflowing with unadorned chunks of fresh meat (and a side of either drawn butter or mayo), are what pulls 'em in. Order at the counter and take a seat at one of the plastic tables overlooking the river. But remember expectation often leads to disappointment...and traffic jams!

While you're here, why not stay at the charmingly rustic yet elegantly modern-country **Squire Tarbox Inn** (☑207-882-7693; www.squiretarboxinn.com; 1181 Main Rd; r $165-225; ☺Apr-Dec; ⊛), on nearby Westport Island. The dozen guest rooms in the 1763 farmhouse are sunny and old-fashioned and the pastoral setting is achingly lovely.

Wiscasset is 10 miles northeast of Bath, 13 miles north of Boothbay Harbor and 23 miles south of Augusta.

comfortably appointed. There's a swimming pool on-site and lots of land for just soaking up nature.

Damariscotta River Grill   SEAFOOD $$
(☑207-563-2992; http://damariscottarivergrill.com; 155 Main St; mains $8-24; ☺11am-3pm Tue-Sat, 5:30-8:30pm Tue-Thu & Sun, to 9pm Fri & Sat) Seared tuna, lobster cakes and potato pancakes are all on the menu at this upscale but casual seafood restaurant, but the main draw, as you might guess, are platters of glistening Pemaquid oysters, as cold and fresh as the river they were just plucked from. Vegetarians should try the 'Plank,' a mixed platter of hummus, nuts, chutney, cheddar and figs.

❶ Information

Damariscotta Region Chamber of Commerce (☑207-563-8340; http://damariscottaregion.com; 67 Main St; ☺10am-noon Mon & Wed, noon-2pm Fri) Offers some generalized tourism information on the region.

❶ Getting There & Away

Damariscotta lies just off US 1, about 8 miles east of Wiscasset and 26 miles west of Rockland. You can get here via Concord Coach Lines (https://concordcoachlines.com), which connects Damariscotta to Portland ($19, 1½ hours), Bangor ($25, three hours) and many towns on the midcoast via a Main St **bus stop** (167 Main St).

Pemaquid Point

Along a 3500-mile coastline famed for its natural beauty, Pemaquid Point stands out for its twisted rock formations pounded by the restless seas. A major destination for its natural beauty, artists and nature lovers from across the globe come here to record the memorable seascape in drawings, paintings and photographs. ME 130 goes from Damariscotta (northeast of Wiscasset) through the heart of the Pemaquid Peninsula (the longest on the coast of Maine) to Pemaquid Point.

⊙ Sights

★**La Verna Preserve**   NATURE RESERVE
(☑207-563-2196; www.pemaquidwatershed.org/land-2/preserves-trails/laverna; off ME 32, Round Pond; ☺sunrise-sunset; ℗) **FREE** This forested nature reserve is pretty compact, but within its confines there are 2.5 miles of trails and some 3600ft of shoreline. This waterfront is particularly arresting, all slabbed teeth of layered rock jawing into the waves of the Atlantic; a little way inland, those rocks are studded with small opalescent tide pools.

Colonial Pemaquid
State Historic Site   HISTORIC SITE
(☑207-677-2423; www.maine.gov/colonialpemaquid; Colonial Pemaquid Dr, New Harbor; adult/child $4/free; ☺9am-5pm Jun-Sep, reduced hours rest of year; ℗) If you or your kids are into history, make sure to pop by this state park,

where experts have rebuilt the c 1692 Fort William Henry, and an on-site museum exhibits a trove of archaeological treasures: coins, pottery, musket balls and the like. There's also a diorama of an indigenous Pemaquid village and gravestones that date from the early 1700s. It's a quiet, windblown spot that's great to poke around and soak up some history.

Sleeping & Eating

Hotel Pemaquid   HOTEL $$
(207-677-2312; www.hotelpemaquid.com; 3098 Bristol Rd, New Harbor; r $99-225, cottage $275; P) The Pemaquid's been hosting guests since July 4, 1888, so staff here have a decent idea of how to cater to tourists. There are 31 rooms, running the gamut from family rooms with multiple beds to an old potting shed perfect for those seeking privacy. A three-bedroom guesthouse can be rented by the weekend/week ($750/1050).

Bradley Inn   INN $$
(207-677-2105; www.bradleyinn.com; 3063 Bristol Rd, New Harbor; r $180-285, ste $300-475; P❋🛜) This old-school inn with helpful staff has individually decorated rooms, with themes ranging from classic nautical to rustic, rough-hewn chic. Depending on your room, you may find four-poster beds, classic tubs or views over Johns Bay. Being end-of-road Maine, it's a great spot for those seeking peace and quiet.

Pemaquid Seafood   SEAFOOD $$
(207-677-2642; https://pemaquidseafood.com; 32 Co-Op Rd, Pemaquid; mains $10-26; ☉noon-8pm; P) Once a lobsterman co-op, this quintessentially midcoast seafood spot serves up the sea's fresh bounty and good views of the water. Order some fried clams, a cup of chowder or a straight up freshly boiled lobster and enjoy life.

❶ Getting There & Away

From Damariscotta, on US 1 between Wiscasset and Waldoboro, follow ME 129 then ME 130 south for 15 miles to reach the Lighthouse Park. There is no public transportation to the area.

Monhegan Island

207 / POP 68

Monhegan Island is not for the faint-hearted or the easily bored. There are no TVs, no cars, no bars and no shopping, save for a few small convenience stores. The weather is unpredictable and often foggy. The 1½-hour mail-boat ride from the mainland can be bumpy. Cell-phone coverage is spotty. The sole village remains small and limited in its services, with almost no cars. The few unpaved roads are lined with stacks of lobster traps. Do you smoke? You can't outside of the village.

But for a world that's almost completely removed from the bustle of the 21st century, this rock is a refuge. With dramatic granite cliffs, gnarled maritime forest and lush floral meadows, the island's isolated vistas have been attracting artists since the 19th century. To this day, Monhegan residents and visitors are drawn to plain living, traditional village life and peaceful contemplation.

Sleeping & Eating

★ Shining Sails   B&B $$
(207-596-0041; www.shiningsails.com; r $125-240; 🛜) Run by a friendly lobsterman and his wife, this year-round B&B has seven comfy, basic rooms, some with kitchenettes; stay upstairs for the best ocean views. The fresh blueberry muffins at breakfast are a treat. The owners also rent out various rooms and cottages throughout the island. The B&B is easy walking distance from the ferry dock.

Fish House Fish Market   SEAFOOD $
(207-594-9342; www.facebook.com/fishhouse monhegan; mains $7-18; ☉11:30am-7pm late May-Sep) On Fish Beach, this fresh seafood market sells lobster rolls and chowder. Relax and eat at the nearby picnic tables.

❶ Getting There & Away

You can reach Monhegan Island on passenger boats from Port Clyde, New Harbor and

MAINE MONHEGAN ISLAND

MAINE'S MOST ISOLATED BREWERY

That settles it: you can be in the most isolated, off-the-radar corner of a basically medieval-tech-level island in the middle of the damn ocean, and Maine will still give you a brewery. **Monhegan Brewing Company** (207-596-0011; www.monheganbrewing.com; tap room 1 Boody Lane, Monhegan; ☉11am-6pm Sun-Thu, to 7pm Fri & Sat Jun-Aug, noon-6pm daily Sep & Oct) is a great one, too: enjoy a citrus-y kölsch, a light milk stout or a malty, hoppy double IPA.

Boothbay Harbor. In peak summer a day trip is possible using these services.

During high season, **Monhegan Boat Line** (📞 207-372-8848; www.monheganboat.com; Port Clyde; round-trip adult/child $38/25) runs two or three daily trips to Monhegan Island from Port Clyde, while **Hardy Boat Cruise** (📞 20 7-677-2026; www.hardyboat.com; 132 ME 32, New Harbor; round-trip adult/child $38/20; ⊙ late May–mid-Oct) departs for Monhegan from New Harbor twice daily in summer (mid-June to September), and less frequently in spring and fall.

You can also visit Monhegan on a day excursion from Boothbay Harbor via **Balmy Days Cruises** (📞 207-633-2284; www.balmydays cruises.com; 42 Commercial St, Pier 8; one-way passage to Monhegan adult/child $20/10), which operates a schedule that allows 3¾ hours on the island.

Rockland

POP 7200

This thriving port boasts a large fishing fleet and a proud year-round population that gives Rockland a vibrancy lacking in some other midcoast towns. Main St is a window into the city's sociocultural diversity, with a jumble of working-class diners, bohemian cafes and high-end restaurants alongside galleries, old-fashioned storefronts and one of the state's best art museums, the Center for Maine Contemporary Art (CMCA). Rockland is developing a reputation as an art center, partly thanks to the CMCA's relocation here in 2016.

Settled in 1769, Rockland was once an important shipbuilding center and a transportation hub for goods moving up and down the coast. Today, tall-masted sailing ships still fill the harbor, as Rockland is a center for Maine's busy windjammer cruises (along with Camden).

Rockland is also the birthplace of poet Edna St Vincent Millay (1892–1950), who grew up in neighboring Camden.

⊙ Sights

★Rockland Breakwater Lighthouse   LIGHTHOUSE
(📞 207-542-7574; www.rocklandharborlights. org; Samoset Rd; ⊙ 10am-5pm Sat & Sun late May–mid-Oct) FREE Tackle the rugged stone breakwater that stretches almost 1 mile into Rockland Harbor from Jameson Point at the harbor's northern shore. Made of granite blocks, this 'walkway' – which took 18 years to build – ends at the Rockland Breakwater Lighthouse, a sweet light sitting atop a brick house, with a sweeping view of town.

While on the breakwater, watch for slippery rocks and ankle-twisting gaps between stones. Bring a sweater, and don't hike if a storm is on the horizon.

★Farnsworth Art Museum   MUSEUM
(📞 207-596-6457; www.farnsworthmuseum.org; 16 Museum St; adult/child $15/free; ⊙ 10am-5pm Jun-Oct, to 8pm Wed Jul-Sep, closed Mon Nov, Dec, Apr & May, 10am-4pm Wed-Sun Jan-Mar) One of the country's best small regional museums, the Farnsworth houses a collection spanning 200 years of American art. Artists who have lived or worked in Maine are the museum's definite strength – look for works by the Wyeth family (Andrew, NC and Jamie), Edward Hopper, Louise Nevelson, Rockwell Kent and Robert Indiana. Exhibits on the Wyeth family continue in the Wyeth Center, in a renovated church across the garden from the main museum (open in summer).

Center for Maine Contemporary Art   GALLERY
(CMCA; 📞 207-701-5005; www.cmcanow.org; 21 Winter St; adult/child $8/free; ⊙ 10am-5pm Wed-Sat, from noon Sun) The CMCA's fabulous home is a clever, glass-enclosed space with a sawtooth roofline, designed by Toshiko Mori. The digs are perfect for featuring exhibitions of work by artists (both established and emerging) connected with the state of Maine, such as Alex Katz and Jonathan Borofsky. Arts events – lectures, lessons etc – kick off on a regular basis.

🛏 Sleeping & Eating

★Captain Lindsey Hotel   BOUTIQUE HOTEL $$
(📞 207-596-7950; www.lindseyhotel.com; 5 Lindsey St; r $215; ❄🐾) There's a sophisticated seafaring theme at this nine-room boutique hotel on a side street just steps from Main St. The building started as a sea-captain's home, but has had other incarnations; check out the 'snack vault' and the handsome oak-paneled breakfast room, or get cozy by the fire in your guest room or in the hotel library.

Lobster Shack   SEAFOOD $
(📞 207-390-0102; 346 Main St; mains $6-19; ⊙ 11am-4pm Mon-Fri, to 7pm Sat & Sun) This spot truly lives up to its name: it's a shack and

it serves lobster rolls (and hot dogs, clam chowder, pulled pork and a few other goodies). Sometimes someone plays a guitar out front; sometimes people take their food to go for a picnic. As lunches go, this one is hard to beat.

★ **Fog Bar & Cafe** AMERICAN $$
(☑207-593-9371; www.facebook.com/Fogbarcafe; 328 Main St; mains $16-23; ☺4:30-10pm Thu-Mon) Industrial-chic aesthetic meets an experimental theater, and everything gets overlaid with maritime Maine ingredients and flourishes. The menu changes according to what's fresh and seasonal – in fall you might try saag pumpkin curry, pork belly and roasted apples or pot pies you'd fight your family for. Cocktails are great too, and served until around midnight when the restaurant's open.

★ **Primo** ITALIAN $$$
(☑207-596-0770; www.primorestaurant.com; 2 Main St/ME 73; mains $32-48; ☺5-10pm Wed-Sun mid-May–Oct) 🍴 In a sprawling Victorian house a mile from downtown sits Primo, widely considered to be one of Maine's best restaurants. Awarded chef Melissa Kelly has reached celebrity status for her creative ways with New England ingredients. Try the scallops atop local wild leek and fiddlehead ferns, or farm-raised chicken with ricotta *gnudi* (dumplings). The menu, truly a farm-to-table ode, changes daily.

ℹ️ **Information**

Penobscot Bay Regional Chamber of Commerce (☑207-596-0376; www.camdenrockland.com; 1 Park Dr; ☺9am-5pm Jun-Oct, to 4pm Mon-Fri Nov-May) Visitor center just off Main St (in the same building as the Maine Lighthouse Museum).

ℹ️ **Getting There & Away**

Cape Air (www.capeair.com) connects Rockland's **Knox County Regional Airport** (☑207-594-4131; www.knoxcountymaine.gov/airport; 19 Airport Rd, Owls Head), 3.5 miles south of town, and Boston's Logan International Airport. Fares are around $80 to $100 one way.

Concord Coach Lines (www.concordcoachlines.com) runs buses to and from Boston ($35, 4½ hours), Portland ($23, two hours) and various other midcoast towns, departing from the **Maine State Ferry Terminal** (517a Main St).

Camden

POP 4850

With its picture-perfect harbor, framed against the mountains of Camden Hills State Park, Camden is one of the prettiest sites in Maine. Home to the state's large and justly famed fleet of windjammers, Camden continues its historic intimacy with the sea, but these days more power yachts and pleasure boats pack the docks. This is one of the more upscale towns on the coast, and during summer this town is as preppy as it is pretty. But hey – it's *very* pretty, and there are loads of art galleries, fine restaurants and backstreets that are ideal for exploring. Pick up a walking-tour guide to the town's historic buildings at the chamber of commerce.

Like many communities along the Maine coast, Camden has a long history of shipbuilding. The mammoth six-masted schooner *George W Wells* was built here in 1900, setting the world record for the most masts on a sailing ship.

⊙ **Sights**

★ **Camden Hills State Park** STATE PARK
(☑207-236-3109; www.maine.gov/camdenhills; 280 Belfast Rd/US 1; adult/child $6/1; ☺9am-sunset) With more than 30 miles of trails, this densely forested park is a choice place to take in the midcoast's magic. A favorite hike is the 45-minute (half-mile) climb up 780ft **Mt Battie**, which offers exquisite views over island-dotted Penobscot Bay. Short on time or energy? You can also drive to the summit via the Mt Battie Auto Road.

Camden Public Library LIBRARY
(☑207-236-3440; www.librarycamden.org; 55 Main St; ☺9am-6pm Mon-Sat, to 9pm Thu, 1-5pm Sun; 👶) This gorgeous example of stately redbrick New England architecture is on the National Register of Historic Places. A library has

occupied this building since 1928, although there's been a library in Camden since at least 1796. The airy reading room looks out onto a spacious lawn landscaped with an amphitheater, and the entire effect is one of bucolic intellectual contentment. In addition to being a library, the building is a family-friendly lynchpin for local community events.

🛏 Sleeping

Camden Hills State Park CAMPGROUND $
(📞 Feb-Apr 207-236-0849, May-Oct 207-236-3109; www.campwithme.com; 280 Belfast Rd/US 1; tent sites $35, RV sites with/without hookups $45/35; ⊙ mid-May–mid-Oct; 🛜) The park's appealing campground has hot showers and wooded sites, some with electric hookups. There's also wi-fi. Reserve online through Maine's government reservations portal.

★ Whitehall INN $$
(📞 207-236-3391; www.whitehallmaine.com; 52 High St; r $129-209, ste $219-269; ⊙ May-Oct; 🛜) Whitehall was once the summer home for Camden's elite visitors (poet Edna St Vincent Millay got her start reciting verse here in 1912). New owners have breathed new life into the inn, making it a fun and fashionable destination once more. Check out the on-trend rooms (some have a loft!), rambling porches and stylish restaurant and you'll understand the appeal.

★ Norumbega B&B $$$
(📞 207-236-4646; www.norumbegainn.com; 63 High St; r $289-389, ste $449-539; 🛜) Looking like something out of a slightly creepy fairy

MAINE MEDIA WORKSHOPS

One of the world's leading instructional centers in photography, film, book design, writing and digital media, **Maine Media Workshops** (📞 207-236-8581; www.mainemedia.edu; 70 Camden St, Rockport) offers hundreds of workshops and master classes throughout the year, from beginner to professional level. Changing exhibitions of student and faculty work are displayed in a gallery in Rockport (18 Central St; opens 10:30am Wednesday to Saturday, flexible closing time).

Class prices vary: a four-day photography composition course may run to $995, while a one-week writing workshop might cost $1100.

tale, this 1886 turreted stone mansion was built to incorporate elements of the owner's favorite European castles. Today, it's Camden's poshest and most dramatically situated B&B, perched on a hill above the bay, with 11 distinctive rooms and suites.

ℹ Information

Penobscot Bay Regional Chamber of Commerce (📞 207-236-4404; www.camdenrockland.com; 2 Public Landing; ⊙ 9am-5pm Mon-Fri, 10am-4pm Sat & Sun late May–mid-Oct, 9am-4pm Mon-Fri rest of year) has an information office on the waterfront at the public landing in Camden.

ℹ Getting There & Away

South of Bangor (53 miles) on US 1, Camden is 81 miles north of Portland and 77 miles southwest of Bar Harbor. Camden shares a Concord Coach Lines (www.concordcoachlines.com) **bus stop**, and fares, with Rockport; among the available destinations are Portland ($25, 2½ hours), Bangor ($19, two hours) and many midcoast towns.

Rockport
POP 3330

The sleepy seaside town of Rockport is an affluent community primarily known for its gorgeous harbor and the world-renowned Maine Media Workshops, which offer courses on everything from creative writing to filmmaking. This is basically a one-street town, but it's a pretty street, and you can lose a day strolling up and down it and watching the boats bobbing in the harbor.

👁 Sights

Rockport Marine Park PARK
(🅿) FREE Tiny Rockport's harbor is justifiably famous across the region as one of the most beautiful in New England. The all-encompassing park space area includes the ruins of a historic lime kiln furnace, walkways that wend past the docks, and picnic tables, benches and boat launches.

🛏 Sleeping & Eating

Island View Inn MOTEL $$
(📞 207-596-0040; www.islandviewinnmaine.com; 908 Commercial St/US 1; r $159-279; ⊙ May-Oct; 🅿 ❄ 🛜 🏊) Each room comes with a pair of binoculars at this inviting motel – scanning Penobscot Bay for wildlife from your balcony is a nice way to start the day. Rooms are

bright, crisp and spacious, with modern but comfy decor. It's on US 1 between Rockland and Rockport. A solid midrange option.

★ **Seafolk** CAFE $
(22 Central St; mains $3-11; ☻8am-5pm Wed-Sun; ☏) This beautiful little cafe has great views of the harbor, strong, excellent coffee, and a stellar lineup of egg sandwiches, blueberry pie, delightful little cakes and general community good vibes. A great space to load up on both caffeine and the bohemian-posh vibe of Rockport.

❶ Getting There & Away

Rockport is only 2 miles south of Camden, and about 80 miles northeast of Portland via US 1.

Belfast
POP 6750

Belfast is really nice. We know that sounds a little trite, but sometimes simplicity is the best descriptive tool at our fingertips, and Belfast is just, well...it's the kind of town you get to and start checking the local real estate listings. There's a handsome 19th-century Main St, a pleasant seaside park, lively farmers markets (more than one!), good restaurants, cool bookstores, a sweet theater and a general sense of passionate community.

On top of all this, there's a welcome shortage of tourists, which gives Belfast a lived-in feeling of realness that is sometimes lacking in more resort-y midcoast towns. Come to think of it, maybe you shouldn't come here... No, just kidding: Belfast is lovely, and decidedly worth some exploration.

◉ Sights & Activities

★ **United Farmers Market of Maine** MARKET
(☏207-218-7005; www.belfastmarket.com; 18 Spring St; ☻9am-2pm Sat) This excellent, year-round farmers market features lots of prepared foods and a ton of craftspeople, artisans, artists and entertainment. It's basically a weekly community carnival for the region, and you'd be remiss not to stop by on a Saturday.

Harbor Walk WALKING
(☻) FREE Access Belfast's pretty shoreline via this pedestrian pathway, which winds through parks, meanders by boat launches and leads to the pedestrian-only **Armistice**

Bridge (cnr Water & Pierce Sts). On a nice day, it's a pleasant little break from reality. Live music performances and similar events are held on the green spaces that surround the walkway.

🛏 Sleeping & Eating

Belfast Bay Inn INN $$$
(☏207-338-5600; www.belfastbayinn.com; 72 Main St; r $259-439; ❋☏) In downtown Belfast, this very polished, elegant inn has eight luxe suites with exposed brick walls and preppy New England prints. Breakfast is delivered to your door.

★ **Chase's Daily** VEGETARIAN $
(☏207-338-0555; www.chasesdaily.me; 96 Main St; dishes $6-14; ☻7am-5pm Tue-Sat, 8am-1pm Sun, plus 5:30-8pm Wed-Fri; ☑) A true farm-to-table experience, this cafe/bakery/farmers market presents fabulous, all-vegetarian fare – plus wicked-good baked treats, from cauliflower and Gruyère tarts to custard buns. The lunch menu (creative salads, soups, pasta, sandwiches) kicks in from 11am. All food utilizes produce from the Chase family farm, and in summer the store sells its farm produce, too.

★ **Laan Xang** LAOTIAN $
(☏207-338-6338; www.laanxangcafe.com; 19 Main St; mains $11-14; ☻11:30am-3pm & 5-7pm Mon-Sat) Oh, of course: 'Laan Xang,' named for the medieval Lao kingdom of a 'Million Elephants and White Parasols' – totally expecting a restaurant to bear that namesake in...Belfast? Yep, and it serves seriously good Lao and northern Thai cuisine. Try steamed fish with lemongrass, curried Cornish hen cooked in coconut milk, or real-deal sticky rice, and marvel at the world's smallness.

🍷 Drinking & Entertainment

Marshall Wharf Brewing Company BREWERY
(☏207-338-1707; www.marshallwharf.com; 40 Marshall Wharf; ☻11am-4pm Tue-Sun) The tasting room for this dockside brewpub stays true to its maritime roots, serving, for example, a Scotch ale brewed with Maine kelp, and more conventionally, a nice range of ales, stouts and porters.

Colonial Theatre CINEMA
(☏207-338-1930; www.colonialtheatre.com; 163 High St; adult/child $8.50/5.50) This art-deco gem has been showing movies since before WWI (1912, to be exact – the Colonial

WORTH A DETOUR: SEARSPORT

The relatively sleepy air in Searsport belies what a major center of commerce and maritime activity this town once was. Possessing the second-largest deepwater port in Maine, during the 19th century Searsport boasted 17 shipyards and produced an enormous number of the nation's deepwater merchant marine captains. Today the town retains a handsome facade via 19th-century mansions built by these masters of the sea.

It's appropriate, then, that the superb **Penobscot Marine Museum** (☑207-548-0334; www.penobscotmarinemuseum.org; 2 Church St/US 1; adult/child $15/10; ◎10am-5pm Mon-Sat, noon-5pm Sun late May–mid-Oct; P) houses Maine's biggest collection of mariner art and artifacts, which is spread through a number of historic buildings. You'll find dozens of small craft, souvenirs collected by Maine sea captains and a terrific collection of folk art. There's some wonderfully evocative photography collections, and fun kid-friendly activities, too.

If you want to make a day of it, head to **Sears Island** (https://friendsofsearsisland.org), an uninhabited, 940-acre conservation area is connected by causeway to the mainland, north of town. You can drive to the end of the causeway, but you'll have to walk across from there, and access the trails. Follow Jetty Rd (1.5 miles, most of which is paved) for a lovely view of the bay.

In the evening, dine at **Me Lon Togo** (☑207-872-9146; www.melontogo.com; 375 E Main St; prix-fixe 4-course meal $40; ◎5-11pm Fri-Sun), which belongs on your 'Didn't expect that in small-town Maine' list, right alongside unseasonably warm winters. Meaning 'I love Togo' in Ewe, the restaurant was opened by a Togolese drumming instructor at Colby College. High-end European dishes like monkfish osso buco and grilled duck appear alongside chicken in peanut sauce, palm butter and fufu (cassava dough), and are served in a romantic setting. Reservations recommended.

Continue the romance with oceanfront camping at **Searsport Shores Camping Resort** (☑207-548-6059; https://maineoceancamping.com; 216 W Main St/US 1; campsites $30-94, cottages $82-190; ◎May-Oct; P), or Captain AV Nickels' 1874 **inn** (☑207-548-1104; www.captainnickelsinn.com; 127 E Main St; r $135-185, ste $250; P), listed on the National Register of Historic Places. Searsport is about 7 miles east of Belfast.

opened the day the *Titanic* set sail). This spot lures moviegoers with a neon sign, a rooftop elephant and, these days, a sense of warm nostalgia for a classic beauty of a movie house.

ⓘ Getting There & Away

Belfast is 18 miles north of Camden via US 1. Concord Coach Lines (https://concordcoachlines.com) stops on its route along the coast linking to Portland ($27, three hours) and other coastal towns. Buses pick up from the **Circle K** (22 Belmont Ave) convenience store.

INLAND MAINE

This inland corridor offers some fascinating areas to explore.

The former lumbering boomtown of Bangor has a pleasantly old-fashioned main street, architectural intrigue (including Stephen King's spooky mansion) and riverside walks, plus a giant lumberjack statue welcoming you into town.

Further west lies Maine's state capital, Augusta. It has one of the state's best history museums, as well as America's oldest wooden fort, strategically perched over the Kennebec River. The sleepy main street is undergoing a culinary burst of revitalization, and there are some excellent eating and drinking options in nearby Hallowell.

Inland Maine is also home to colleges, in which you'll find some excellent museums and pretty parks. There aren't many tourists in these parts, so you'll be something of a pioneer if you make your way here.

Bangor

☑207 / POP 31,900

Once the lumber capital of the world, Bangor is inland Maine's commercial and cultural capital. Main St is lined with sleepy antique shops and wood-paneled taverns, while the elegant Victorians along West Broadway attest to its former timber wealth. Only a handful of tourists make it to this largely working-class town, which may be reason enough to visit if you're coming from Bar Harbor.

Among the attractions: a giant statue of Paul Bunyan (reputedly a native son), a few curious museums, and periodic ghostly walking tours (hosted by the Bangor Historical Society) – an appropriate activity for the hometown of novelist Stephen King.

◉ Sights

Maine Discovery Museum
MUSEUM

(☑207-262-7200; www.mainediscoverymuseum. org; 74 Main St; $12.50; ☉10am-5pm Mon-Sat, noon-5pm Sun Jul & Aug, closed Mon Sep-Jun; 👪) Conveniently located in the heart of downtown Bangor, the Maine Discovery Museum has fun, hands-on activities for the under-12 crowd. You can go for a dinosaur-bone dig, draw and build in the Artscape, and learn about your insides on the Body Journey and Maine's animal life in the nature section.

Bangor Historical Society
HISTORIC BUILDING

(☑207-942-1900; www.bangorhistoricalsociety. org; 159 Union St; ☉10am-4pm Mon-Fri, noon-4pm Sat) For a primer on Bangor's fascinating history, stop by this Greek Revival house two blocks northwest of Main St. Staff offer guided tours of the 1836 home, which has period furnishings and striking architectural details. You'll learn about some of Bangor's illustrious and not-so-illustrious native sons as well as pivotal events in Bangor's past, such as the Great Fire of 1911 that destroyed a huge swath of downtown.

Stephen King's House
NOTABLE BUILDING

(West Broadway) The mega-best-selling author of horror novels like *Carrie* and *The Shining* resides in an appropriately Gothic red Victorian house on West Broadway (not to be confused with Broadway), off Hammond St. No, you can't go inside. But you can snap a photo of his splendidly creepy wrought-iron front fence and gate, adorned with spiderwebs and bats. Note that this is a private home in a residential neighborhood, so please act accordingly.

🛏 Sleeping & Eating

Charles Inn
HOTEL $$

(☑207-992-2820; www.thecharlesinn.com; 20 Broad St; r $125-180) This pleasant inn is the best place to stay in Bangor. It's in a great location within walking distance of restaurants and bars, and set in an 1873 building with an eclectic and old-fashioned flair (gilded mirrors and wallpaper in some rooms, nautical implements in others).

Fiddlehead
AMERICAN $$

(☑207-942-3336; www.thefiddleheadrestaurant. com; 84 Hammond St; mains $18-29; ☉4-9pm Tue-Fri, 5-10pm Sat, 5-9pm Sun) 🍃 The young chef at this downtown place has been earning raves (and a packed dining room) for her international spin on local, seasonal ingredients. Think *okonomiyaki* (Japanese pancake) with Maine shrimp, seared halibut with *char siu* pork, and rose-petal crème brûlée. Exposed brick walls, cool cocktails and a bar crowded with hipsters make this a definite hot spot.

❶ Information

Greater Bangor Convention & Visitors Bureau (☑207-947-5205; www.visitbangormaine. com; 330 Harlow St; ☉9am-5pm Mon-Fri) A good source of local info.

❶ Getting There & Away

Bangor is the last city on the map before the North Woods. It's 75 miles northeast of Augusta and 130 miles northeast of Portland.

The small **Bangor International Airport** (☑866-359-2264; www.flybangor.com; 287 Godfrey Blvd) is a few miles northwest of downtown and serviced by regional carriers.

Concord Coach Lines (www.concordcoach lines.com) runs regular services between Boston, Portland, Augusta and Bangor, as well as services to towns in Midcoast Maine. Greyhound (www.greyhound.com) buses run here from Boston. Arrivals and departures for both are at **Bangor Transportation Center** (☑800-639-3317; 1039 Union St). It's out by the airport, about 2.5 miles northwest of downtown.

Augusta

☑207 / POP 18,600

Although not the smallest state capital in the USA (an honor reserved for Montpelier, Vermont), Augusta sure feels like it. On a peaceful stretch of the Kennebec River, boaters cast for dinner while the glittering

MAINE AUGUSTA

dome of the State House looms just over the treeline.

While there isn't much reason to venture here, there are several fine historic sites (a good history museum and an old wooden fort) and some antique shops and cafes in the more charming nearby town of **Hallowell**. Also in the area is **Gardiner**, another sleepy town with a few galleries and a good restaurant.

Augusta's traditional commercial district sits on the eastern bank of the Kennebec River. Water St (US 201/ME 27) runs south from Memorial Circle and past the capitol to Hallowell (2 miles) and Gardiner (7 miles).

⊙ Sights

Maine State Museum
MUSEUM

(☑ 207-287-2301; www.mainestatemuseum.org; 230 State St; adult/child $3/2; ⊙ 9am-5pm Tue-Fri, 10am-4pm Sat) What happens when a moose and his rival lock horns in mortal combat? Their interlocked racks end up in the Cabinet of Curiosities at the Maine State Museum. The museum, an engaging, four-story ode to all things Maine, is situated around a multifloor mill that churns on water power. The newest permanent exhibit, At Home in Maine, looks at homes throughout the years; in the mod 1970s house you can watch a family filmstrip and dial a rotary phone.

Old Fort Western
FORT

(16 Cony St; adult/child $10/6; ⊙ 10am-4pm) Just across the river from Augusta's main drag (Water St) stands this 1754 landmark, America's oldest wooden fort. It was built by a Boston-based outfit called the Kennebec Proprietors with support from the Province of Massachusetts, in the hope of expanding Britain's colonial reach in North America. Tensions were high here during the British-French conflict later known as the French and Indian War, but the fort was never attacked directly.

State House
HISTORIC BUILDING

(☑ 207-287-2301; www.legislature.maine.gov/lio; cnr State & Capitol Sts; ⊙ 8am-5pm Mon-Fri) **FREE** Built in 1832 and enlarged in 1909, this stately, granite-domed edifice was designed by Charles Bulfinch (the Boston architect behind the nation's Capitol building in Washington, DC). Walk-in visitors are welcome; you can pick up a leaflet for a self-guided tour or join a free guided tour (hourly from 9am to noon).

Eating

Lisa's Legit Burritos
MEXICAN $

(☑ 207-620-1040; 185 Water St; mains $7-11; ⊙ 11am-4pm Mon-Fri; ☑) On Augusta's restaurant-lined main drag, Lisa's serves up outstanding burritos as well as tacos, quesadillas and tortilla-free bowls. The build-your-own burritos feature classic ingredients like slow-cooked pork, beef or chicken, as well as vegan-friendly sweet potato or butternut squash. Our favorite: the 'veggie grilled,' served in a black-bean tortilla.

Cushnoc
PIZZA $$

(☑ 207-213-6332; www.cushnocbrewing.com; 243 Water St; pizzas $15-17; ⊙ 11am-10pm; ☑) Pizzas and craft beers make a winning combination at this handsomely designed new space on Water St. Wood-fired pizzas come topped with delicious ingredients such as IPA caramelized onions, shaved brussels sprouts or crispy pancetta. The 10 beers on draft (six from Cushnoc's own microbrewery) offer some nice variety, from the refreshing (Water Street Wit) to the full-bodied (All Souls).

ⓘ Getting There & Away

Augusta is 23 miles north of Wiscasset, 75 miles southwest of Bangor and 55 miles northeast of Portland.

Cape Air (www.capeair.com) connects **Augusta State Airport** (☑ 706-798-3236; www.augustaairport.org; Airport Rd) with Boston four times daily.

Concord Coach Lines (www.concordcoachlines.com) has regular services that connect with Boston, Portland, Augusta and Bangor. Arrivals and departures are from the **Augusta Transportation Center** (9 Industrial Dr). Greyhound (www.greyhound.com) buses also stop here on similar routes.

Sabbathday Lake & Poland Spring

If you've got some free time in Portland and a hankering for an excursion that doesn't skirt the coast, pretty Rte 26 is worth considering for its array of under-the-radar attractions. The best reason to venture out this way is a cool wildlife park, a fascinating (and still active) Shaker village and a photogenic former resort tucked into the woods that serves as a remarkable time capsule of early-20th-century vacationing for Maine rusticators.

⊙ Sights

★ Maine Wildlife Park   WILDLIFE RESERVE
(📞207-657-4977; www.mainewildlifepark.com; 56 Game Farm Rd, Gray; adult/child $7.50/5.50; ⊙9:30am-4:30pm mid-Apr–early Nov) Not quite a zoo but a great place to view native Maine wildlife, this park is a bucolic reserve with picnic tables, short walking trails and animal enclosures. Residing here are various animals (30 species, including bears, moose, lynx, eagles, cougars and a beaver) that can't be released back into the wild because they were injured, orphaned, or raised in captivity.

Sabbathday Lake Shaker Village   VILLAGE
(📞207-926-4597; www.maineshakers.com; 707 Shaker Rd, New Gloucester; guided tour adult/child $10/2; ⊙10am-4:30pm Mon-Sat late May-early Oct) The Shakers, a Protestant religious sect named for their habit of ecstatic spiritual dancing, once inhabited communities up and down the East Coast. They believed in simple living, prayer, egalitarianism and hard work – as well as celibacy, which is likely why their numbers have dwindled over time to precisely two members at Sabbathday Lake, the last active Shaker community in the world (established in 1783). Many non-Shaker volunteers and workers help out around the farm and in the village.

Poland Spring   HISTORIC SITE
(📞207-998-4142; www.polandspringps.org; 37 Preservation Way, Poland Spring) The settlement of Poland Spring is famous for its mineral water, which is now sold throughout the USA. From the mid-19th century, Poland Spring was a destination for its curative waters and picturesque setting, so in the early 1900s a bottling facility was built – plus, eventually, a resort. Surrounding the resort is a golf course and a pretty, trailed-filled park. There are also various historical buildings you can visit, including the **Maine State Building** (⊙9am-4pm Mon & Thu-Sat, to 1pm Sun Jul & Aug, 9am-4pm Fri & Sat, to 11am Sun mid-May–Jun & Sep-mid-Oct) **FREE**, a bottling museum and a chapel.

🛏 Sleeping & Eating

Poland Spring Resort   RESORT $$
(📞207-998-4351; www.polandspringinns.com; 640 Maine St; r $110-220; ⊙May-Oct; P ❄ 🎧 ⛱) This resort offers various lodging options, spread among the large, colonial-style Maine Inn (overlooking the golf course), the Presidential Inn, various cottages and the more budget-friendly Lodge (a quarter-mile past the main property entrance off Rte 26, and the only accommodations open year-round). Rooms are pleasantly equipped, and the service is friendly and laid-back.

Cyndi's Dockside   AMERICAN $$
(📞207-998-5008; www.dockside.me; 723 Maine St; mains $10-20; ⊙11:30am-8pm daily May-Oct, 11:30am-8pm Thu-Sun Nov-Apr) Run by the same family behind the Poland Spring Resort, Cyndi's is the best place to eat in the area. The wood-paneled restaurant and bar have an easygoing vibe, and draw locals and out-of-towners who come for satisfying haddock sandwiches, fried clams, burgers and good crispy-crust pizzas.

ⓘ Getting There & Away

Sabbathday Lake Shaker Village is around 28 miles north of Portland (around a 40-minute drive). Take take I-95 to exit 63, then follow Rte 26 north; look for the small white sign announcing 'Shaker Village next right.' Poland Spring is a further 3 miles north along Rte 26. Watch for the green sign 'Poland Spring Inn & Resort' on the right.

DOWN EAST

Without question, this is quintessential Maine: as you head further up the coast toward Canada, the peninsulas seem to narrow, jutting further into the sea. The fishing villages get smaller; the lobster pounds are closer to the water. If you make time to drive to the edge of the shore, south off US 1, let it be here.

The star of the Midcoast is Mount Desert Island, home to the spectacular Acadia National Park, where the mountains meet the sea. It offers some of the best hiking in coastal Maine. Island destinations worth visiting include the vibrant summer resort town of Bar Harbor, the elegant village of Northeast Harbor and heart-of-gold Southwest Harbor.

For quiet walks and traditional coastal villages away from the tourist throngs, continue further up the coast from Bar Harbor all the way to the rugged sea cliffs near Lubec, the last town before the Canadian border.

Down East

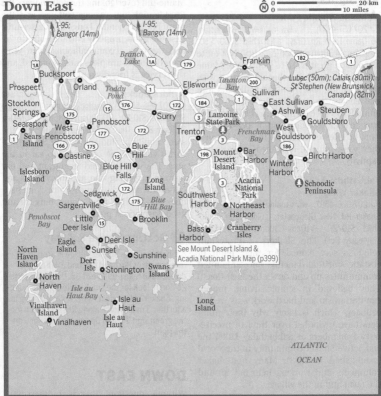

Deer Isle & Stonington

POP 1940

Traveling south along ME 15, the forest opens up to reveal tranquil harbors framed by distant hilly islands. This is Deer Isle – actually a collection of islands joined by causeways and connected to the mainland by a picturesque suspension bridge near Sargentville. There are few actual sights, but the area is worth a drive for its idyllic views.

Deer Island's main town, Stonington, is a quaint settlement where lobstermen and artists live side by side. A few galleries and restaurants draw the odd traveler or two. In peak summer, it's worth investigating boat cruises and kayaking tours to take in the beauty of this island-dotted coastline.

Boats depart from Stonington for the enchanting Isle au Haut.

⊙ Sights

★ Nervous Nellie's
Jams & Jellies   LANDMARK

(📞 800-777-6845; www.nervousnellies.com; 598 Sunshine Rd; ⊙ 9am-5pm May-Oct, by appointment Nov-Apr; 🚺) Nervous Nellie's cooks up delicious jams and chutneys the old-fashioned way from its base on Deer Isle. It's well worth making the trip to load up on jars of sweetness made from Maine blueberries, strawberries and raspberries. But Nervous Nellie's is also a sprawling fantasyland where the artist Peter Beerits has taken old buildings and transformed them into vivid installations using found and repurposed objects. Afterward, visit the shop and cafe for hot drinks and jam-topped scones.

Sand Beach   BEACH

(Sand Beach Rd) About 1.5 miles west of Stonington, a short path leads to a lovely cove overlooking a serene coastline. True to its name, this beach is sandy: a rarity on Maine's rocky coastline. Short forested paths lead from the shoreline past large boulders to pretty viewpoints.

Courses & Tours

Haystack Mountain
School of Crafts   ARTS & CRAFTS
(☎207-348-2306; www.haystack-mtn.org; 89 Haystack School Dr; ⊙early Jun-early Sep) In a gorgeous setting on the eastern end of Deer Isle, Haystack offers summer courses for artists and craft-makers. The nonprofit school is famous in these parts and its two-week-long sessions working with clay, wood, glass, fiber and metals attract adult learners from across the globe. Visiting artists (musicians, writers, poets and occasionally a scientist) lecture and perform.

Sleeping & Eating

★ Pilgrim's Inn   INN $$
(☎207-348-6615; www.pilgrimsinn.com; 20 Main St, Deer Isle village; r $119-219, cottages $199-259; ⊙mid-May–mid-Oct; @🖘) Overlooking the Northwest Harbor, this handsome post-and-beam inn was built in 1793 and offers refined country charm in its 10 rooms and three cottages. Pine floors and solid-wood furnishings are common throughout; some rooms have gas fireplaces and pretty views over the millpond.

★ Aragosta   AMERICAN $$$
(☎207-367-5500; www.aragostamaine.com; 27 Main St, Stonington; mains $21-38; ⊙5-9pm Thu-Mon late May–mid-Oct) 🍽 The best restaurant for miles around, Aragosta serves delicious, painstakingly prepared dishes sourced locally from farm and sea. The seasonal menu is small (around seven main courses and an equal number of appetizers), ensuring there are no bad choices, whether you opt for roasted Long Cove oysters, Common Wealth Farm duck breast or the outstanding Stonington lobster *casoncelli* (stuffed pasta).

❶ Information

Deer Isle–Stonington Chamber of Commerce (☎207-348-6124; www.deerislemaine. com; 114 Little Deer Isle Rd; ⊙10am-4pm late May-early Oct) The Deer Isle–Stonington Chamber of Commerce maintains an information booth 0.25 miles south of the suspension bridge.

❶ Getting There & Away

From Blue Hill, take ME 15 southwest for 4 miles and then head south on ME 15/176 for 9 miles to Little Deer Isle. Follow ME 15 further south to reach Deer Isle village (6 miles) and Stonington (6 miles beyond Deer Isle village).

MOUNT DESERT ISLAND

Formed by glaciers some 18,000 years ago, Mount Desert Island (MDI) is the jewel of the Down East region. It offers vast geographical variety, from freshwater lakes to dense forests, and from stark granite cliffs to voluptuous river valleys. There are many ways to experience the 108-sq-mile island's natural beauty, whether hiking the forested mountains, swimming in the secluded lakes or kayaking along the rocky coast. About two-thirds of Mount Desert Island belongs to Acadia National Park, one of New England's biggest draws.

While the coastal vistas and spruce forests are impressive, Acadia draws enormous crowds, particularly in July and August. Be prepared for long lines and heavily congested roads, or plan your visit for the off-season. You could also opt to stay on the 'Quietside,' an affectionate and apt nickname given to the area west of the Somes Sound.

Bar Harbor

☎207 / POP 5430

The agreeable hub for Acadia visits, Bar Harbor is crowded for the warmer months of the year with vacationers and cruise-ship passengers. Downtown is packed with souvenir stores, ice-cream shops, cafes and bars, each advertising bigger and better happy hours, early-bird specials or two-for-one deals. The quieter residential back-streets seem to have almost as many B&Bs as private homes.

Although Bar Harbor's hustle and bustle is not for everybody, it has by far the most amenities of any town around here. Even if you stay elsewhere, you'll probably wind up here to eat dinner, grab a drink or schedule a kayaking, sailing or rock-climbing tour.

Bar Harbor's busiest season is late June through August. There's a short lull just after Labor Day (early September); it gets busy again during foliage season, which lasts through mid-October. The season ends

ISLE AU HAUT

Much of Isle au Haut, a rocky island 6 miles long, is under the auspices of Acadia National Park. Accessed by boat and more remote than the parklands near Bar Harbor, it escapes the big summer crowds. If you're looking for an unspoiled, untouristed, unhyped outpost of Acadia...well, you've found it.

The island's main draw is the superb hiking along the coastal trails near Duck Harbor on the southwest side, where you'll find the **Duck Harbor Campground** (www.nps.gov/acad; tent sites $20; ☉mid-May–mid-Oct). Thick forests, wave-battered sea cliffs, trickling brooks and misty ponds are all part of its allure. On the island's northwest side lies the main settlement, also called Isle au Haut, with a tiny year-round population of about 70 residents, which triples during the warm summer months. Grab your supplies at the **Isle au Haut General Store** (☑207-335-5211; www.theislandstore.net; 3 Main St; ☉8am-6pm Mon-Sat, 11:30am-2:30pm Sun Jul-early Sep, shorter hours rest of year), 400m from the ferry dock, next to the **Maine Lobster Lady** (www.mainelobsterlady.com; 3 Main St; mains $14-20; ☉11am-6pm Tue-Sat Jul-early Sep): so good.

Isle au Haut Boat Services (☑207-367-5193; www.isleauhautferryservice.com; 37 Seabreeze Ave, Stonington; round-trip adult/child $40/20) operates a year-round mail-boat service, ferrying people and freight between Stonington and the village settlement on the island. In July and August, a couple of services also stop at the Duck Harbor Boat Landing, near the campground and trailheads. Note that bikes aren't allowed at this stop.

To park your car in Stonington while visiting Isle au Haut costs $12 per day.

the weekend following Columbus Day with the Mount Desert Island Marathon (www.runmdi.org).

◉ Sights & Activities

Abbe Museum
MUSEUM

(☑207-288-3519; www.abbemuseum.org; 26 Mount Desert St; adult/child $8/4; ☉10am-5pm May-Oct, to 4pm Thu-Sat Nov-Apr, closed Jan) This downtown museum contains a fascinating collection of cultural artifacts related to Maine's Native American heritage – particularly the Wabanaki people, who inhabited Mount Desert Island for thousands of years before the Europeans arrived. More than 50,000 objects are in the collection, including pottery, tools, combs and fishing implements spanning the last 2000 years. Contemporary pieces include finely wrought wood carvings, birch-bark containers and baskets.

Bar Island Trail
WALKING

(access from Bridge St) The 157-acre island that lies directly offshore, north of Bar Harbor, can be reached on foot at low tide. For two hours either side of low tide, a gravel bar is exposed, connecting the town to Bar Island. A trail continues to the summit of the island, allowing great views. It's just under 2 miles, out and back.

♥ Tours

Maine Foodie Tours
FOOD & DRINK

(☑207-233-7485; www.mainefoodietours.com; tours $70; ☉May-Oct) Join a three-hour lunchtime stroll around Bar Harbor, which involves lots of local flavor, from mini lobster rolls to blueberry crumb cake. Culinary tours depart from the Village Green (the corner of Main St and Firefly Lane) most days at 10:30am. Bookings are essential (and possible online).

Lulu Lobster Boat
CRUISE

(☑207-288-3136; www.lululobsterboat.com; 55 West St; adult/child from $35/20; ☉May-late Oct) Brush up on your lobster knowledge aboard a lobster boat, while combining sightseeing and seal-watching. This two-hour tour involves raising traps and getting a fascinating look at Maine's iconic sea critter. No kids under six permitted.

☰ Sleeping & Eating

Moseley Cottage Inn & Town Motel
B&B, MOTEL $$

(☑207-288-5548; http://moseleycottage.net; 12 Atlantic Ave; r $165-305, motel r $97-200; ❈ 🛜) This elegant option is down a quiet street just steps from Main St, and covers its bases very well. There are nine large, charming, antique-filled B&B rooms in a traditional 1884 inn (some with a fireplace and a private porch), plus a small collection of more affordable motel-style units next door. All are of a consistently high standard.

★ **Bass Cottage Inn** INN $$$
(☑ 207-288-1234; www.basscottage.com; 14 The Field; r $280-460; ⊗ mid-May–Oct; ❄ ☎) If most Bar Harbor B&Bs rate about a '5' in terms of stylishness, this Gilded Age mansion deserves an '11.' The 10 light-drenched guest rooms have an elegant summer-cottage chic, all crisp white linens and understated botanical prints. Tinkle the ivories at the parlor's grand piano or read a novel beneath the Tiffany stained-glass ceiling of the wood-paneled sitting room.

★ **Mount Desert Island Ice Cream** ICE CREAM $
(☑ 207-801-4006; www.mdiic.com; 325 Main St; ice cream $4-7; ⊗ 11am-11pm Jul & Aug, shorter hours May, Jun & Oct) A cult hit for innovative flavors such as stout beer with fudge, chocolate with wasabi, and blueberry-basil sorbet, this ice-cream counter is a post-dinner must. The smaller original outlet is at 7 Firefly Lane, by the Village Green.

Jeannie's Great Maine Breakfast BREAKFAST $
(☑ 207-288-4166; www.jeanniesbreakfast.com; 15 Cottage St; breakfast $8-15; ⊗ sunrise-1pm early May–mid-Oct) Looking to warm up after watching the sunrise from Cadillac Mountain (p398)? Here's your spot. Jeannie's serves hearty breakfasts of eggs, pancakes and omelets to early risers. The Great Maine Breakfast has heft: three eggs any style, baked beans, grilled ham, home fries, toast and a buttermilk pancake.

★ **Havana** LATIN AMERICAN $$$
(☑ 207-288-2822; www.havanamaine.com; 318 Main St; mains $30-42; ⊗ 4:30-9pm Tue-Sat May-Oct & 9:30am-2pm Sun Jul & Aug) First things first: order a refreshing mojito or caipirinha. Then you can take your time with the menu and the epic global wine list. Havana puts a Latin spin on dishes that highlight local produce, and the kitchen output is accomplished. Signature dishes include seafood paella, braised lamb shank and a deliciously light lobster *moqueca* (Brazilian-style stew with coconut milk).

ℹ Information

There is a number of options for visitor information. Best for park info is the NPS-run Hulls Cove Visitor Center (p399) inside Acadia National Park.

The **Bar Harbor Chamber of Commerce** (Acadia Welcome Center; ☑ 207-288-5103; www.visitbarharbor.com; 2 Cottage St; ⊗ 8am-4pm) maintains a central year-round information office in downtown Bar Harbor.

ℹ Getting There & Away

Cape Air (www.capeair.com) connects Bar Harbor and Boston with flights year-round. The **Hancock County–Bar Harbor Airport** (☑ 207-667-7329; www.bhbairport.com; ME 3, Trenton) is just north of the Trenton Bridge.

Getting to Bar Harbor by public transport is not easy. The only bus route to Bar Harbor is from Ellsworth, via Downeast Transportation (www.downeasttrans.org), but it is geared to local commuters rather than travelers.

Drivers need to take ME 3 off US 1 at Ellsworth. It's about 20 miles from Ellsworth to Bar Harbor; en route you'll pass the turnoff to the Hulls Cove Visitor Center (p399) in Acadia National Park.

Acadia National Park

The only national park in all of New England, **Acadia** (☑ 207-288-3338; www.nps.gov/acad; 7-day admission per car/motorcycle $30/25, walk-ins & cyclists $15) offers unrivaled coastal beauty and activities for both leisurely hikers and adrenaline junkies. Most people spend about three days here, which is just enough to take in the park highlights. But you could easily spend a week, taking in mountaintop hikes, bike rides, scenic drives and shoreline strolls, as well as leaving time to relax on the shores of Echo Lake or Sand Beach.

The park, which incorporates both coastline and mountains, protects a remarkably diverse landscape. You can spend the morning checking out tidal pools and watching the sea crash against the cliffs down by the waterfront, then head into the interior for a walk through dense forest up past a boulder-filled ridgeline with osprey and the occasional bald eagle soaring overhead. There are scenic lakes and ponds to discover too, plus plenty of fine picnic spots.

⊙ Sights

★ **Sand Beach** BEACH
(Park Loop Rd) One of Acadia's most surprising features is this beautiful stretch of sandy shoreline tucked between mountains on the east side of Mount Desert Island. The beach

is around 300m long and attracts sunbathers, strollers and a few intrepid souls willing to brave the 55°F/12.7°C (summertime) water temperatures for a dip. A beautiful hiking trail starts from here.

★Cadillac Mountain   MOUNTAIN
Don't leave the park without driving – or hiking – to the 1530ft summit of Cadillac Mountain. For panoramic views of Frenchman Bay, walk the paved 0.5-mile Cadillac Mountain Summit loop. The summit is a popular place in the early morning because it's touted as the first spot in the USA to see the sunrise. Not an early riser? The sunset is always a good bet.

★Jordan Pond   LAKE
On clear days, the glassy waters of this 176-acre pond reflect the image of Penobscot Mountain like a mirror. A stroll around the pond and its surrounding forests and flower meadows is one of Acadia's most popular and family-friendly activities. (Sorry, no swimming allowed.) Follow the 3-mile self-guided nature trail around the pond before stopping for a cuppa at the Jordan Pond House.

Thunder Hole   NATURAL FEATURE
(Park Loop Rd) Waves rushing into a natural opening carved into the rocks create a thunderous splash, with waves reaching high into the air when conditions are right. Steps from the road (and a parking area above) lead down to this natural attraction, which can get mobbed with visitors on fine days. Aside from the delightful play of water on rocks, the viewing platform offers fine views across to Sand Beach and the Otter Cliffs.

Echo Lake   LAKE
(Echo Lake Beach Rd) Ringed with lush forests and nestled between the slopes of two mountains, Echo Lake makes for a lovely escape from the crowds on the busier eastern side of the island. The lake is also one of the park's only non-ocean swimming holes, with slightly warmer waters than at Sand Beach. It's a favorite local spot on warm summer days.

Somes Sound   NATURAL FEATURE
(Off Sargent Dr) This fjord-like embayment is one of the most striking natural features in Acadia. It was formed by glaciers and makes for a picturesque backdrop to a scenic drive along Sargent Dr or a cruise – Sea Princess (⏏207-276-5332; www.barharborcruises.com; Northeast Harbor ferry dock, 26 Sea St; cruise adult

$26-31, child $16-18) sails there. If you prefer to hoof it, head up Acadia or St Sauveur mountains, which both offer majestic views over the waterway.

🏃 Activities

★Great Head   HIKING
(Off Park Loop Rd) Jutting out to sea on the eastern side of Sand Beach is the forested headland known as Great Head. A trail loops around the headland, providing spectacular views of the craggy coastline and the pounding surf hitting against the rocks below.

Park Loop Road   SCENIC DRIVE
This fabulous 27-mile one-way loop road takes you past some of Acadia's great natural treasures, including Sand Beach, Thunder Hole and Jordan Pond. Countless trails start just off this road and you could easily spend days exploring all the highlights found here. Go early in the morning to avoid large crowds.

Precipice Trail   HIKING
(Off Park Loop Rd) A tough, much-loved hike in the park, the Precipice Trail feels a bit like a via ferrata, with its iron rungs hammered into the cliff face. Definitely not recommended for anyone afraid of heights (nor for inexperienced hikers), this scenic ascent up Champlain Mountain takes you along narrow ledges, up granite stairs and straight up cliff faces.

Beehive Loop   HIKING
(Off Park Loop Rd) Though short in length (about 1.6 miles), the Beehive is one of the park's more challenging hikes. Starting at the trailhead just north of Sand Beach, you'll soon be climbing up steep sections along narrow exposed cliffs. At times, you'll have to scramble up iron-rung ladders along the mountain. The views at the top are outstanding – well worth the effort!

Acadia Mountain   HIKING
(Off Hwy 102) If you want to escape the crowds in Acadia, head to the trails on the eastern side of the island. Acadia Mountain is one of the best of the bunch, as you'll have excellent views over the Somes Sound from its 681ft peak. It's a moderate 1-mile (one way) hike to the top from the trailhead off Highway 102.

🛏 Sleeping & Eating
Most of the hotels, B&Bs and private campgrounds are in Bar Harbor (p396). There are

Map labels:
Ellsworth (4.5mi) · 184 · East Lamoine · Lamoine State Park · Trenton · Lamoine Beach · Sand Point · Frenchman Bay · Bayside · Mount Desert Narrows · Hancock County–Bar Harbor Airport · Hadley Point · Salisbury Cove · Parker Point · Ferry to Winter Harbor (May–Oct) · Trenton Bridge · Eden · Hamilton Pond · Hulls Cove · Lookout Pt · Burnt Porcupine Island · The Hop · Crooked Rd · Hulls Cove Visitor Center & Entrance · Bar Island · Sheep Porcupine Island · Long Porcupine Island · Bayside Rd · Alley Island · Lake Wood · Witch Hole Pond · Bar Harbor · Bald Porcupine Island · Western Bay · Green Island · Town Hill · Norway Dr · Breakneck Ponds · Mount Desert Island · Black Island · Cadillac Mtn Entrance · Wild Gardens of Acadia · Sieur de Monts Entrance · Bartlett Island · Somes Pond · Somesville · Park Headquarters · Eagle Lake · Champlain Mtn · Precipice Trail · Acadia National Park · Cadillac Mtn (1530ft) · The Beehive (520ft) · Overlook Entrance · Pretty Marsh · Northern Neck · Hall Quarry · Echo Lake · Penobscot Mtn · Bubble Pond · The Beehive Trailhead · Sand Beach · Southern Neck · Long Pond · Acadia Mtn (681ft) · Jordan Pond Trailhead · Jordan Pond · Thunder Hole · Echo Lake Beach · Valley Cove · Jordan Pond House · Otter Creek · Otter Cliffs · Seal Cove Pond · Fernald Point Rd · Northeast Harbor · Long Pond · Seal Harbor · Blackwoods Campground · Stanley Brook Entrance · Seal Cove · Western Mountain Rd · Seal Cove Rd · Southwest Harbor · Greening Island · Bear Island · Seal Harbor · Moose Island · Sutton Island · Blue Hill Bay · Goose Cove · Tremont · Manset · Hio Rd · Little Cranberry Island (Islesford) · Trumpet Island · Duck Cove · Bernard · Bass Harbor · Seawall Campground · Great Cranberry Island · Baker Island · Ship Island · Bass Harbor · Bass Harbor Head · Ship Harbor · ATLANTIC OCEAN · Bass Harbor Head

two great rustic campgrounds in the Mount Desert Island section of the park, with around 500 tent sites between them. Both are densely wooded but only a few minutes' walk from the ocean.

Note that reservations for the park campgrounds are handled by **Recreation.gov** (☎877-444-6777; www.recreation.gov), not the park itself.

Blackwoods Campground (ME 3; tent & RV sites $30; ☉year-round) has 12 accessible sites. **Seawall Campground** (668 Seawall Rd, Southwest Harbor; tent sites $22-30, RV sites $30; ☉late May–mid-Oct) has five accessible drive-in sites and five accessible walk-in sites.

Both campgrounds also have RV sites (electricity not available).

The only eating option inside the park is **Jordan Pond House** (☎207-276-3316; https://jordanpondhouse.com; Park Loop Rd; tea & popovers $11, mains $13-29; ☉11am-7pm mid-May–mid-Oct). Picnickers will find plenty of areas to enjoy alfresco dining – bring supplies from Bar Harbor.

ℹ Information

Hulls Cove Visitor Center (☎207-288-3338; www.nps.gov/acad; ME 3; ☉8:30am-4:30pm mid-Apr–Jun, Sep & Oct, 8am-6pm Jul & Aug) This informative center anchors the park's main Hulls Cove entrance, 3 miles northwest of Bar Harbor via ME 3. Buy your park pass and pick up maps and info here. The 27-mile-long Park Loop Road, which circumnavigates the eastern section of Mount Desert Island, starts near here.

When the visitor center is closed (November to mid-April), head to the Bar Harbor Chamber of Commerce (p397). National park staff provide information there during winter and spring.

Be sure to purchase your park pass before entering the park. Passes can be purchased on the Acadia National Park website: www.nps.gov/acad/planyourvisit/fees.htm. If you're purchasing a pass online, you'll need to print it out and display it in your vehicle window (or carry it with you if you're arriving by bike or on foot).

❶ Getting There & Away

There are various access points to Acadia National Park. If you're coming by car, go south along ME 3 when you reach Ellsworth (located along US 1). It's about 17 miles from Ellsworth to Hulls Cove Visitor Center.

By plane, you can fly into the Hancock County–Bar Harbor Airport (p397) in Trenton. Cape Air (www.capeair.com) connects Bar Harbor and Boston with flights year-round.

Getting to Mount Desert Island by public transport is not easy. The only bus route to Bar Harbor is from Ellsworth, via Downeast Transportation (www.downeasttrans.org), but it's geared to local commuters rather than travelers. West Bus Service (www.westbusservice.com) connects Ellsworth with Bangor and bigger towns to the east along US 1.

❶ Getting Around

Hiring a bike in nearby Bar Harbor is a breeze, and a good way to avoid traffic snarls and parking problems. All Island Explorer (www.exploreacadia.com) buses accommodate bikes (from four to six per bus), though if you want speedy transport to the carriage roads, take the free **Bicycle Express** (www.exploreacadia.com/bikeexpress.htm; ⊗ late Jun-Sep). This takes cyclists and their wheels from Bar Harbor's Village Green to Eagle Lake.

Cranberry Isles

South of Mount Desert Island and accessible only by ferry, the Cranberry Isles (www.cranberryisles.com) are an off-the-beaten-path delight and a sweet spot for a summer day trip.

The 400-acre Little Cranberry, home to the village of Islesford, is about 20 minutes offshore from Southwest Harbor. Diversions include a few galleries, a couple of summer rental cottages, the very popular Islesford Dock restaurant, and some pretty stretches of coastline. Great Cranberry Island is even more low-key, but has a tiny historical museum (like Little Cranberry) and short paths through woods to untouched coastline.

⊙ Sights

Islesford Historical Museum MUSEUM
(☑ 207-288-3338; Main St, Little Cranberry Island; ⊗ 9am-3pm Mon-Sat, noon-4pm Sun) **FREE** Run by the National Park Service, this appealing little museum gives the lowdown on all things Cranberry Isles–related. Exhibits cover everything from lobstering life to the island's impressive number of artisans and poets. Several ranger talks happen daily – call a park office for times.

**Great Cranberry Island
Historical Society** MUSEUM
(☑ 207-244-7800; www.gcihs.org; 163 Cranberry Rd, Great Cranberry Island; ⊗ 10am-4pm late May-early Oct) **FREE** Less than half a mile up the road from the town dock, the Historical Society runs a small but intriguing museum with changing exhibitions covering island themes – from schoolhouse life in the 19th century to Cranberry's sailing culture. You can also access several trails from here that lead to serene stretches of coastline, including a 1-mile round-trip walk to Whistler Cove through lush, mossy forest.

✕ Eating

Little Cranberry Lobster SEAFOOD $
(Islesford, Little Cranberry Island; ⊗ 10am-3:30pm Mon-Sat) This tiny food truck near the dock whips up tasty lobster rolls as well as hot dogs. There's a small convenience store next door for drinks and snacks.

★**Islesford Dock Restaurant** AMERICAN $$
(☑ 207-244-7494; www.islesforddock.com; 1 Main St, Islesford, Little Cranberry Island; mains lunch $15-21, dinner $19-32; ⊗ 11am-3pm & 5-9pm Wed-Sat, 10am-2pm & 5-9pm Sun mid-Jun–Sep; ☑) This beautifully sited spot on Little Cranberry Island makes an impressive pledge: 'Dock's commitment to our customers is to serve lobster taken from the water and cooked the day you eat it.' There's impressive variety here beyond lobster, including mussels in white wine, Glidden Point oysters, fish and chips, and spaghetti (squash) with vegan meatballs, plus great desserts.

BLUE HILL PENINSULA

If you're looking for the soul of coastal Maine, the Blue Hill Peninsula is well worth exploring. You'll find charming seaside villages, pretty walks through forest and along shoreline, and a vibrant locavore scene (a coffee roaster, a microbrewer, a chocolate maker and an artisanal bakery are among its many food and drink producers).

This region has far fewer crowds than nearby Mount Desert Island, but you'll still need to plan accommodations ahead. The main towns here:

Castine One of Maine's prettiest villages. Its picturesque **town common** (Court St) is ringed with historic buildings and its pleasant waterfront overlooks the magnificent island-dotted Penobscot Bay. The **Pentagöet Inn** (☑ 207-326-8616; www.pentagoet.com; 26 Main St; r $160-295; 🛜) is a standout for the Peninsula's best accommodations and dining.

Blue Hill Elegant houses are backed by the forested Blue Hill Mountain. Artists and writers have long been drawn to the area, and Blue Hill has a surprising number of cultural offerings, including the **Kneisel Hall Chamber Music Festival** (☑ office 207-374-2811, tickets 207-374-2203; www.kneisel.org; 36 Main St; admission $25-35) and **Word** (Blue Hill Literary Arts Festival; www.wordfestival.org; ⊘ Oct) literary festival.

Brooklin A sleepy settlement with a few artisan stores and an inn. Brooklin is also home to the renowned **WoodenBoat School** (☑ 207-359-4651; www.thewoodenboatschool.com; Great Cove Dr), which draws craftspeople and aspiring boatbuilders from across the globe.

The peninsula is just south of well-traveled US 1, located between Searsport and Ellsworth. If you're coming from the west, you'll see the turnoff for Blue Hill after the Penobscot Narrows. Take ME 175 south to reach Castine, and ME 15 south to reach the town of Blue Hill. The bridge to Little Deer Isle extends off the south side of the peninsula.

Be sure to reserve ahead. If you're dining by night, be aware that Beal & Bunker runs a night service from June to early October on Friday and Saturday nights (and from Tuesday to Sunday in July and August). Call to confirm times. If you miss the boat back, you'll have to phone **Delight Water Taxi** (☑ 207-244-5724; 2hr tour from $50 per person) for a private lift (upwards of $130).

❶ Getting There & Around

Cranberry Cove Ferry (☑ 207-244-5882; www.cranberrycoveferry.com; round-trip adult/child $30/22; ⊘ late May–mid-Oct) carries passengers to and from Great Cranberry and Little Cranberry, departing from Southwest Harbor (and Manset, located about 2 miles south of there). Trips run four times daily in summer. The **Beal & Bunker Mailboat** (☑ 207-244-3575; round-trip adult/child $32/16) offers year-round service between Northeast Harbor and the Cranberry Isles.

On Great Cranberry Island, the Historical Society runs the **Cranberry Explorer** (☑ 207-812-6712) – a seven-person golf cart that takes visitors from the dock to a stop anywhere on Cranberry Rd. The service is free but donations are appreciated.

Machias Bay Area

The Machias Bay area is home to some gorgeous stretches of coastline. The fact that it's so little known by out-of-towners is just fine with the locals, who enjoy spectacular hikes and boat rides far from the madding crowd of nearby Mount Desert Island. The bay's towns are quite modest: Machias is best known for a tiny historical site (an 18th-century tavern that played a minor role in the Revolutionary War), magnificent blueberry pie and its wild blueberry festival – not surprising since this is the heart of wild blueberry country. Just south of Machias is Jasper Beach, which is covered with wave-clattering, polished jasper stones.

Nearby Cutler Harbor is the departure point for very popular tours to see the largest puffin colony in the USA.

◉ Sights

★ **Cutler Coast
Public Lands**   NATURE RESERVE
(www.discoverboldcoast.com/hiking;   ME 191)
FREE This little-known reserve a few miles northeast of Cutler has hiking trails amid

MACHIAS SEAL ISLAND

Around 10 miles off the coast, the barren rocks of Machias Seal Island are home to a colony of so-awkward-they're-cute Atlantic puffins, plus plenty more seabirds. The tiny, foggy and entirely uninhabitable island is also the subject of the sole remaining land dispute between the USA and Canada – both countries claim ownership of Machias Seal Island and the nearby outcropping of North Rock.

During peak season, **Bold Coast Charter** (☑207-259-4484; www.bold-coast.com; Off Cutler Rd/ME 191, Cutler Harbor; tours $150; ☉late May–mid-Aug) runs very popular tours. Five-hour tours depart from Cutler Harbor, and they are extremely popular. Bold Coast begins accepting reservations around January 1, and the entire season typically sells out within a few days.

spectacular coastal scenery. If you've visited Acadia National Park and wondered what the shoreline trails would be like without the crowds, this is the place to come. This 12,000-acre expanse encompasses lush forests thick with moss and ferns, blueberry barrens, and jagged headlands overlooking hidden coves and rocky beaches.

Jasper Beach BEACH
(Jasper Beach Rd, off Port Rd) Jasper Beach is a bizarre, mile-long beach consisting entirely of polished, red-hued jasper stones. As the waves wash in, the rocks slide against one another, creating a rather haunting song. It's one of two such beaches in the world (the other is in Japan).

🍴 Sleeping & Eating

Machias River Inn MOTEL $$
(☑207-255-4861; www.machiasriverinn.com; 103 Main St/US 1, Machias; r $84-144, ste $110-160, apt $120-175; ❄🔊🐾) Next to Helen's Restaurant, this roadside lodge exceeds expectations with its clean, comfortable rooms and more spacious suites and apartments. All have mini-fridges, microwaves and coffee makers; pricier rooms have great views of the Machias River out back. Bikes are available for hire.

⭐**Helen's Restaurant** AMERICAN $
(☑207-255-8423; www.helensrestaurantmachias.com; 111 Main St/US 1, Machias; mains $8-30; ☉6am-8pm Mon-Sat, 7am-2pm Sun; 🐾) Helen's is the kind of friendly locals' joint where waitresses call you 'hon,' but their food makes your standard American diner fare look like mud in comparison. Fresh haddock is moist and flakey, salads are made with local goat's cheese, the hot roast-beef sandwich comes on homemade bread, and the blueberry pie is the envy of restaurants across the state.

ℹ Information

Machias Bay Area Chamber of Commerce
(☑207-255-4402; www.machiaschamber.org; Station 1898, 2 Kilton Lane, Machias; ☉10am-3pm Wed-Fri) The local chamber of commerce is based at the old train station across the road from Helen's Restaurant.

ℹ Getting There & Away

From Ellsworth (the gateway to Bar Harbor), Machias is 60 miles northeast via US 1. East Machias is 4 miles further north on US 1; Machiasport is 4 miles east of Machias on ME 92.

WESTERN MAINE

Western Maine receives far fewer visitors than the coast, which thrills the outdoorsy types who love its dense forests and solitary peaks just the way they are. While much of the land is still wilderness, there are some notable settlements. The fine old town of Bethel and the mountain setting of Rangeley are relatively accessible to city dwellers in the northeast, while Bridgton's quirky offerings make it a cool weekend retreat.

In the fall, leaf-peepers make their way inland with cameras and picnic baskets. In winter, skiers and snowmobilers turn the mountains into their playground. In the warmer months, the lakes, rivers, campgrounds and hiking trails draw lovers of the great outdoors. This is rural America at its most rustic. So bring a map and don't expect to rely on your cell phone – signals can be few and far between in these parts.

Bethel

☑207 / POP 2700
A 90-minute drive northwest of Portland, Bethel is surprisingly lively and refined for a town surrounded on all sides by deep, dark

woods. Summer visitors have been coming here to escape the coastal humidity since the 1800s, and many of its fine old cottages and lodges are still operating. It's a prime spot to be during Maine's colorful fall-foliage months and during the winter ski season.

If you head west on US 2 toward New Hampshire, be sure to admire the **Shelburne birches**, a high concentration of the white-barked trees that grow between Gilead and Shelburne.

⊙ Sights & Activities

Grafton Notch State Park   STATE PARK
(☎207-824-2912; www.maine.gov/graftonnotch; 1941 Bear River Rd/ME 26; adult/child $4/1; ☺9am-sunset) Sitting astride the Grafton Notch Scenic Byway within the Mahoosuc Range, this rugged park is a stunner. Carved by a glacier that retreated 12,000 years ago, the Notch is a four-season playground, chock-full of waterfalls, gorges, lofty viewpoints and hiking trails, including over 20 miles of the Appalachian Trail (www.appalachiantrail.org).

Peregrine falcons build nests in the cliffs, helping the park earn its spot on the **Maine Birding Trail** (www.mainebirdingtrail.com); the best viewing is May to October.

Bethel Outdoor Adventure
& Campground   KAYAKING, OUTDOORS
(☎207-824-4224; www.betheloutdooradventure. com; 121 Mayville Rd/US 2; canoe/kayak per day with shuttle $65/45, without shuttle $40/35; ☺8am-6pm mid-May–late Oct) Based at a bucolic riverside campground, this reputable outfitter rents out canoes, kayaks and stand-up paddleboards. It shuttles you upriver to the drop-off point, and you paddle back downstream. It also offers tubing, guided trips, fishing excursions and sluicing (sorting through a bucket of materials in search of tourmalines, quartz crystals, garnets and other stones).

Carter's X-C Ski Center   SKIING
(☎207-824-3880; www.cartersxcski.com; 786 Intervale Rd; day pass adult/child $15/10; ☺9am-4pm mid-Dec–Mar) In the winter, you'll find some outstanding spots for cross-country skiing and snowshoeing in the area. One of the best places for wintertime fun is the family-run Carter's X-C Ski Center, with over 30 miles of well-groomed field and forest trails. You can also hire gear at this spot (around $15 for the day), located 5 miles north of Bethel.

🍴 Sleeping & Eating

Bethel Village Motel   MOTEL $
(☎207-824-2989; www.bethelvillagemotel.com; 88 Main St; r $65-95; ❄🐾🐕) Sitting pretty on Main St, with a blue exterior and a rainbow of flowers and hanging plants, this simple, spotless, old-school motel offers great-value rooms. It's run by a sparkling hostess, Ruthie, who has a clothing boutique downstairs.

Cho Sun   ASIAN $$
(☎207-824-7370; www.chosunrestaurant.com; 141 Main St; mains $18-27; ☺5-9pm Wed-Sun) Korea meets rural Maine at this unassuming Victorian house, whose interior has been transformed into an Asian oasis of bamboo and paper lanterns. Try flavor-filled dishes from the owner's native South Korea, like *bibimbap* (rice pot with steamed veggies and chicken, shrimp, calamari or tofu) or *bulkalbi* (barbecue beef short ribs). There's also a high-quality sushi bar and a (booze) bar.

ℹ Information

Bethel Area Chamber of Commerce (☎800-
442-5826, 207-824-2282; www.bethelmaine. com; 8 Station Pl; ☺9am-5pm Mon-Fri year-round, weekend hours vary in high season; 🐕) This helpful organization maintains an information office in the Bethel Station building, with loads of handouts on various sights, trails and activities.

ℹ Getting There & Away

Bethel lies 73 miles north of Portland, via ME 26. If you're heading into the White Mountains of New Hampshire, take US 2 west from Bethel toward Gorham, NH (22 miles) and head south to North Conway.

Rangeley Lake

POP 1200

Surrounded by mountains and thick hardwood forests, the Rangeley Lake region is a marvelous year-round destination for adventurers. The gateway to the alpine scenery is the laid-back town of **Rangeley**, whose tidy inns and down-home restaurants make a useful base for skiing, hiking, white-water rafting and mountain biking in the nearby hills.

During the early 20th century, the lakes in this region were dotted with vast frame hotels and peopled with vacationers from Boston, New York and Philadelphia. Though most of the great hotels are gone, the reasons for coming here remain.

⊙ Sights & Activities

★ Height of Land   VIEWPOINT
(ME 17) The expansive view of island-dotted
Mooselookmeguntic Lake (the largest of the
Rangeley Lakes) as it sweeps north toward
distant mountains is astounding. Vistas of
undeveloped forest stretch for up to 100
miles; you can even see the White Mountains
in New Hampshire. The dogged Appalachian
Trail runs alongside the viewpoint, and an interpretive sign shares a few details about the
2190-mile hiking trail. The overlook is on ME
17, around 18 miles southwest of Rangeley.

Rangeley Lakes
National Scenic Byway   SCENIC DRIVE
(ME 17) For a fabulous drive, head out of
Rangeley on ME 4 and turn left (south) onto
ME 17. From here there's some magnificent
scenery, with the pull-off at Height of Land
providing one of the best panoramic views
anywhere in New England. Keep going
south until you reach Coos Canyon (about
30 miles from Rangeley) – a fine picnic spot
near a gorge.

Rangeley Lakes Trails Center   SKIING, HIKING
(☑ 207-864-4309; www.rangeleylakestrailscenter.
com; 524 Saddleback Mountain Rd; day pass $10-
20) A green yurt marks your arrival at Rangeley Lakes Trails Center, a four-season trail
system covering gorgeous woodland terrain
beside Saddleback Lake, which offers more
than 40 miles of trails for cross-country skiing and snowshoeing during snow season.
(Rental equipment is available, along with
hot soup!) In summer, cross-country routes
double as hiking trails, and snowshoe trails
allow single-track biking.

Sugarloaf   SKIING
(☑ 800-843-5623, 207-237-2000; www.sugarloaf.
com; 5092 Access Rd, Carrabassett Valley; full-day
lift ticket adult $99, child $69-79) This popular
ski resort has a vertical drop of 2820ft, with
162 trails and glades, and 13 lifts, all set on
Maine's second-highest peak (4237ft). It's
accessed from ME 27 between the towns
of Kingfield and Stratton (both have sleeping and eating options), or by ME 16 from
Rangeley. The resort village complex also
has lots of hospitality options.

🛏 Sleeping & Eating

Rangeley Inn & Tavern   INN $$
(☑ 207-864-3341; www.therangeleyinn.com; 2443
Main St, Rangeley; r $135-295; ❄ 🐾) Behind the
inn's pretty powder-blue facade, you can

relax by the fire and admire the mounted
bear and moose head in the lobby. Rooms
are simple and old-fashioned in this creaky,
turn-of-the-20th-century lodge, and come
with floral wallpaper and brass beds. There's
also a motel-style lodge on the property.

ⓘ Information

Rangeley Lakes Chamber of Commerce
(☑ 207-864-5571; www.rangeleymaine.com;
6 Park Rd, Rangeley; ⊙10am-4pm Mon-Fri, to
2pm Sat) Offers info about restaurants, lodging
options, local trails and moose watching.

ⓘ Getting There & Away
Rangeley is about 2½ hours (120 miles) north of
Portland by car, on the northeast side of Range-
ley Lake. From I-95, take ME 4 N.

NORTH MAINE WOODS
If you were to fly over Maine's Great North
Woods at night, you'd see barely a twinkle
of light below. This is one of America's truly impressive wildernesses, a vast expanse
of dark forest, raging rivers and herds of
moose. Human settlements feel almost inci-
dental here.

Not surprisingly, outdoor activities are
unrivaled in the region. You could spend
days hiking, canoeing and camping in Baxter
State Park, or head off on moose-watching
safaris, scenic flights and lake cruses across
the aptly named Moosehead Lake.

The North Woods is logging country. In
the 19th century, Maine's legendary lumber-
jacks floated logs down the rivers in massive 'log drives,' until the practice polluted
the water and the drives were replaced by
trucks. The woods here are crisscrossed by
rough logging roads, which are often used
by hunters and outdoor adventurers with
4WDs.

Baxter State Park

Baxter State Park (☑ 207-723-5140; www.
baxterstatepark.org; Baxter Park Rd; entry per day
$15, season pass $40; ⊙main gates usually 6am-
10pm mid-May–mid-Oct) is Maine at its most
primeval: the wind whips around dozens of
mountain peaks, black bears root through
the underbrush and hikers go for miles
without seeing another soul. Visitors can
walk hundreds of miles of trails through
the park, climb the sheer cliffs (this is a

rock-climber's paradise), fly-fish the ponds and rivers, and spot wild animals, such as bald eagles, moose and fox-like martens. The park is most popular in the warmer months, but it's also open for winter sports like snowmobiling.

Baxter's 5267ft **Mt Katahdin** – the park's crowning glory – is Maine's tallest mountain and the northern end of the 2190-mile-long Appalachian Trail.

🛏 Sleeping & Eating

Restaurants, fast-food joints, supermarkets and other pre-park amenities are in Millinocket.

Within the park, there are only primitive facilities: no paved roads and no electricity. BYO, and pack in and pack out everything.

There are no treated water sources in the park, so bring your own water or carry a means of purification.

Appalachian Trail Lodge   HOSTEL $
(☑207-723-4321; www.appalachiantraillodge. com; 33 Penobscot Ave, Millinocket; dm/d with shared bathroom $25/55, ste for 2/3/4 people $95/105/115; ☺May–mid-Oct; 🛜) A favorite stop for Appalachian Trail hikers in the area is this well-equipped lodge in downtown Millinocket. It has a hostel-style bunkroom as well as a few pleasantly furnished private rooms (these share bathrooms and a kitchenette), and one spacious suite (more like a one-bedroom apartment) with a full kitchen and a living room with pull-out futons.

Baxter State Park
Campgrounds   CAMPGROUND $
(☑207-723-5140; www.baxterstatepark.org; tent sites $32, dm $12, cabins $57-135) Baxter State Park has 11 campgrounds, a handful of bunkhouses and basic cabins sleeping from two to six, and numerous backcountry sites ($21), including some sites with lean-tos and bunkhouses. Locations, facilities and opening dates are outlined on the park website. Summer season is generally mid-May to mid-October; winter season is from December to March. Make reservations well in advance.

★ NEOC Twin Pines Camp   CABIN $$$
(☑800-634-7238, 207-723-5438; www.neoc.com; 30 Twin Pines Rd, Millinocket Lake, Millinocket; cabin $296-750; 🛜🐾) En route to Baxter State Park, the New England Outdoor Center (NEOC) offers a delectable slice of rural Maine, with creature comforts in abundance

in a glorious lakeside setting. Spread over the property are 22 comfy cabins and stylish lodges with all mod cons (including full kitchen); some can sleep up to 14.

River Drivers
Restaurant & Pub   PUB FOOD $$
(☑207-723-8475; www.neoc.com/river-drivers-res taurant-maine; 30 Twin Pines Rd, Millinocket Lake, Millinocket; mains $14-28; ☺7am-9pm; 🛜📶🐾) At this handsomely designed restaurant at the NEOC Twin Pines Camp, enjoy upscale comfort fare (blackened haddock tacos, vegetarian lasagna, pork with pineapple-mango salsa) in a laid-back setting with a great view of Mt Katahdin. It's open year-round, but it's worth checking the latest opening hours online (or on the restaurant's Facebook page). It's signed off the road to Baxter State Park.

ℹ Getting There & Away

North of Bangor, traffic levels drop considerably on I-95. This is your gateway to the North Woods: take ME 157 off I-95. With more time up your sleeve, consider the slower-paced ME 11.

Moosehead Lake

Glassy-silver and dotted with islands, 120-sq-mile Moosehead Lake sprawls through the North Woods wilderness. Named, some say, after its shape from the air, it's one of the state's most glorious – and underrated – places. **Greenville** (population 1620), on the south side of the lake, is the region's main settlement. This is lumber and backwoods country, which is why Greenville has the region's largest seaplane station. Pontoon planes will take you even deeper into the Maine woods for fishing or hiking trips. Though once a bustling summer resort, Greenville is now a sleepy tourist town with a few grand lodges.

◎ Sights & Activities

Lily Bay State Park   STATE PARK
(☑207-695-2700; www.maine.gov/lilybay; 13 Myrle's Way, Greenville; adult/child $6/1) At this lovely, 925-acre park you can relax on the sandy beach, bird-watch and stroll the 2-mile shoreline trail. The park is a good base for other area hikes. To camp here on the shores of Moosehead Lake, pitch your tent (per site $33) at one of the 90 campsites. Note that while the park is open year-round, the office is staffed only from late May to early October.

Moosehead Marine Museum
MUSEUM

(☑207-695-2716; www.katahdincruises.com/museum; 12 Lily Bay Rd, Greenville; entry by donation; ⊙9am-5pm Tue-Sat, 10am-4pm Sun & Mon mid-Jun–mid-Oct) Moosehead Lake's colorful history is preserved in the Moosehead Marine Museum, next to the dock that shelters the SS *Katahdin*. The museum also operates **cruises** (3hr cruise adult/child $35/5; ⊙Jun–mid-Oct) on the steamboat.

Northwoods Outfitters
WILDLIFE

(☑207-695-3288; www.maineoutfitter.com; 5 Lily Bay Rd, Greenville; ⊙8am-7pm) For moose-spotting safaris, white-water rafting, ATV tours, fishing and canoe trips, stop by this outfitters in the center of Greenville. Staff are super-knowledgeable and friendly, equipment can be hired, and the store also sells outdoor gear and hot coffee. The popular moose-spotting safaris (from $50) run from April to December (on land and water, conditions permitting).

🛏 Sleeping & Eating

★Blair Hill Inn
B&B $$$

(☑207-695-0224; www.blairhill.com; 351 Lily Bay Rd, Greenville; r $329-499; ⊙late May–mid-Oct; 🕸) The Chicago socialite who commissioned this dreamy hilltop cottage in the late 1800s had it cleverly built atop a 20ft-high stone foundation, thus providing views of Moosehead Lake from almost every window. Today it's a 10-room B&B, whose smallest detail whispers good taste: plush, white down comforters, fluffy robes, in-room fireplaces and a sleek wooden bar. There's also a spa.

Stress Free Moose
AMERICAN $$

(☑207-695-3100; www.stressfreemoose.com; 65 Pritham Ave, Greenville; mains $10-25; ⊙11am-9pm; 🅟) The liveliest dining spot in town, the Stress Free Moose serves up fish tacos, pastrami reuben sandwiches, NY strip steak, smoked trout and other comfort fare. There's a good beer selection (over a dozen craft beers on tap), a friendly crowd and regular evening amusement (Tuesday trivia nights, football-game screenings and live music some weekends).

ℹ Information

Moosehead Lake Region Chamber of Commerce (☑207-695-2702; www.destinationmooseheadlake.com; 480 Moosehead Lake Rd/ME 15; ⊙10am-4pm) Runs a helpful visitor center south of Greenville's town center, with regional information, including on local accommodations.

ℹ Getting There & Away

From Bangor, take ME 15 north for about 70 miles to Greenville, the gateway to Moosehead Lake.

Understand
New England

HISTORY 408

The history of New England is the history of America: 400 years of political, philosophical, industrial and technological revolution.

NEW ENGLAND LITERATURE..... 417

The region's rich literary tradition runs the gamut from groundbreaking philosophy to thought-provoking poetry to spine-tingling horror.

UNIVERSITIES &
COLLEGES..................... 421

Hundreds of colleges and universities provide New England with an annual influx of energy and an ever-active incubator for ideas.

Harvard Yard (p67), Harvard University

History

When the Pilgrims landed in Plymouth back in 1620, they started something big. In the four centuries since, New England has been at the forefront of American history, instigating the War of Independence, inspiring the transcendentalist thinkers and writers, embracing technological innovation and spurring on social change.

James Mavor and Byron Dix provide detailed, illustrated descriptions of Native American archaeological sites around New England in *Manitou: The Sacred Landscape of New England's Native Civilization*.

Culture Clash & Colonization

When the first European settlers arrived in the New World, they found about 100,000 Native American inhabitants, mostly Algonquians, organized into small regional tribes. The northern tribes were solely hunter-gatherers, while the southern tribes hunted and practiced slash-and-burn agriculture, growing corn, squash and beans.

Before the English Pilgrims, the Native Americans were already acquainted with Portuguese fishermen, French fur traders, English explorers, Dutch merchants and Jesuit missionaries. The Europeans were welcomed as a source of valued manufactured goods, but they were also feared, and for good reason – in the Great Sadness of 1617, a smallpox epidemic had devastated the Native American population in the southeast. The Pilgrims were notable as the first Europeans to make a successful settlement in New England. Chief Massasoit of the Wampanoag tribe did not view this scrawny band of settlers as a threat and even hoped that they might be useful allies against his tribal rivals.

But the clash of cultures soon proved fatal to the Native American way of life. English coastal encampments spread as lands were claimed for the king and commodity export – John Winthrop, the first governor of the Massachusetts Bay Colony, declared 'God hath hereby cleared our title to this place.' In less than 100 years, the indigenous population was reduced by 90% due to disease, war and forced migration.

Brave New World

Seventeenth-century England was torn by religious strife. Protestants were assailed by the Catholic-leaning King James I, who vowed to 'harry them out of the country.'

TIMELINE	c 400–1000	1497	1606–07
	During the late Woodland period, Native Americans – mainly Algonquian tribes – built semipermanent, seasonal settlements throughout the region.	The Italian explorer John Cabot lands in Newfoundland and explores the coast of New England, claiming the territory for his patron, King Henry VII of England.	King James I issues a charter for the Plymouth Company to establish a settlement in the New World. The resulting Popham Colony (in present-day Maine) was abandoned after one year.

Plymouth Colony

In 1620 the Pilgrims – led by Separatist devotee William Bradford – crossed the Atlantic to establish a community dedicated to religious austerity.

Trouble arose when the badly off-course *Mayflower* weighed anchor in Cape Cod Bay. A group of nonreligious passengers had booked their fares expecting to strike out on their own in Virginia; they threatened a mutiny when they realized they would have to spend the winter with the Separatists. The resulting Mayflower Compact brokered a deal in which both parties would have an equal say in matters of governance. Under Bradford's capable leadership, Plymouth Colony maintained a religious focus and grew modestly over the next decade. Today, you can visit a historically accurate re-creation of this first settlement at Plimoth Patuxet Museums.

Massachusetts Bay Colony

In 1630 the merchant vessel *Arabella* delivered another group of Protestant Separatists, the Puritans, 50 miles north of Plymouth. The Puritans were better prepared: they were well financed, well equipped and 1000 strong, and included those of high social rank. At the head of their party, John Winthrop stood atop the Shawmut peninsula of present-day Boston and proclaimed the founding of 'a shining city on a hill.'

The Massachusetts Bay Colony was a product of the Puritan gentry's ambition to build a Christian community of personal virtue and industriousness – a community purified of pompous ceremony and official corruption, and disdainful of tyranny. Theirs was a kind of legalistic Calvinism, enforced Old Testament style. Anyone who missed church without good cause was apt to catch a whipping. Governor Winthrop constructed centralized institutions to maintain unity among the settlers, who dispersed to choice locations around the harbor and along the rivers. The General Court, an assembly of propertied men, became the principal mechanism of government. Church membership was a prerequisite for political and property rights.

Dissension & Expansion

The Puritan theocracy did not go unchallenged. In Boston, Anne Hutchinson started a women's Bible circle in the mid-1630s, promoting the idea of salvation through personal revelation. The popularity of this individualist-inspired view was threatening to the colony's patriarchal elders, who arrested the heretic Hutchinson and banished her to an island in 1637. One of Hutchinson's arch defenders was her brother-in-law, the Reverend John Wheelwright, who led a group to resettle in New Hampshire in 1638.

Colonial History

Pilgrim Monument
(Provincetown, MA)

Plimoth Patuxet Museums
(Plymouth, MA)

Mayflower II
(Plymouth, MA)

Witch House
(Salem, MA)

College Hill
(Providence, RI)

1614	1614–17	1620	1630
At the behest of future King Charles I, Captain John Smith braves the frigid North Atlantic, travels from Maine to Cape Cod, maps the coastline and dubs the region 'New England.'	Massachusett Indians living around Boston Bay were among the first to encounter Europeans. Over the course of three years, three different epidemics wipe out 75% of the indigenous population.	A group of English religious dissidents known as Pilgrims sail from their self-imposed exile in Holland and establish Plymouth Colony, the second successful European settlement in the New World.	Led by Governor John Winthrop, Puritan settlers flee the repressive Church of England and establish the theocratic Massachusetts Bay Colony.

FIRST COLONY TO DECLARE INDEPENDENCE

Everyone wants to be first. Both Rhode Island and New Hampshire make claims about being the first colony to declare independence from Great Britain. But there is only one 'first.' So whose claim is legit?

The New Hampshire Provincial Government was kicked out of Portsmouth in 1774, so it moved up the road to Exeter, thus establishing the *first* independent government in the colonies. In January 1776, this local body ratified a constitution, the *first* colony to do so. But the document was explicit in 'declaring that we never sought to throw off our dependence upon Great Britain, but felt ourselves happy under Her protection while we could enjoy our constitutional rights and privileges, and that we shall rejoice if such a reconciliation between us and our parent state can be affected.' The local governance was a temporary provision, put in place until the dispute with Britain could be resolved. Not exactly a declaration of independence.

In May of that same year, still two months before the unveiling of *the* Declaration of Independence, Rhode Island issued its formal statement. With none of the stipulations and explanations of New Hampshire's constitution, Rhode Island was the first to declare outright independence.

New Hampshire finally came around six weeks later resolving 'to join with the other Colonies in declaring the 13 United Colonies a free and independent State.'

Around the Massachusetts Bay Colony, independent folk exasperated by encroachments on individual liberty began to found their own settlements including Providence, along Narragansett Bay, and Hartford, in Connecticut.

Over time, the Puritan gentry were less effective in compelling others to embrace their vision of an ideal Christian community. The incessant pull of individual interests and the rise of a secular commercial culture proved to be the undoing of Winthrop's vision.

> Everyone knows that March 17 is St Patrick's Day, but not everyone knows it is also Evacuation Day in the greater Boston area, commemorating the day in 1776 that British troops relinquished the city of Boston after 11 months of occupation.

Cradle of Liberty

In the late 18th century, New England and the British throne clashed over the issue of taxation, igniting sparks that culminated in the American Revolution and the United States' independence.

No Taxation Without Representation

In 1765 the British Parliament passed the Stamp Act to finance colonial defense. Massachusetts colonists were the first to object. To safeguard colonial autonomy, local businessman Sam Adams formed the Sons of Liberty, which incited a mob to ransack the royal stamp office. The actions were defended in a treatise written by a local lawyer, Sam's cousin John Adams, who cited the Magna Carta's principle of no taxation with-

---

1636	1655	1675–78	1686–89
Freethinking theologian Roger Williams founds the colony of Rhode Island and Providence Plantations. His radical ideas include freedom of religion and separation of church and state.	Wampanoag Caleb Cheeshahteaumuck becomes the first Native American to graduate from Harvard.	Wampanoag chief King Philip leads a rebellion against the colonists. Twenty-five towns are destroyed and thousands are killed before he is shot, ending King Philip's War.	After the colonies openly flout trade restrictions such as the Navigation Acts, King James II establishes the Dominion of New England, instituting more rigorous controls over the colonies.

out representation. Eastern Connecticut and Rhode Island joined the protest. When New England merchants threatened a boycott of British imports, the measure was repealed.

The British government devised new revenue-raising schemes. Again, they were met with hostile noncompliance, and Boston emerged as the center of conflict. Parliament closed the Massachusetts General Assembly and dispatched two armed regiments to the city, which only inflamed local passions.

Forced underground, the Sons of Liberty set up a covert correspondence system to agitate public sentiment and coordinate strategy with sympathizers. In December 1773, the Sons of Liberty disguised themselves as Mohawks and dumped a cargo of taxable tea into the harbor. The Boston Tea Party enraged King George, whose retribution was swift and vengeful. The port was blockaded and the city placed under direct military rule.

Join or Die

The conflict tested the region's political loyalties. Tory sympathizers included influential merchants, manufacturers and financiers, while the rebels tended to be drawn from lesser merchants, artisans and yeoman farmers. The colonial cause was strongly supported in Rhode Island, Hartford and New Hampshire, where local assemblies voted to provide economic assistance to Boston. Acts of resistance increased region-wide. In 1772, agitated Providence residents set fire to the British warship *Gaspee* when it ran aground in Narragansett Bay while chasing suspected smugglers, and in 1774 New Hampshire instigators seized Fort William and Mary after the panicky loyalist governor attempted to enlist more British reinforcements.

War of Independence

In April 1775 the British again attempted to break colonial resistance, this time arresting rebel ringleaders Sam Adams and John Hancock and seizing a secret store of gunpowder and arms. As the troops assembled, Paul Revere slipped across the river into Charlestown, where he mounted his famous steed Brown Beauty and galloped off into the night to spread the alarm. By next morning, armed local militias began converging on the area. The incident sparked a skirmish between British troops and local farmers on the Old North Bridge in Concord and the Lexington Green, leaving over 100 dead. The inevitable had arrived: the American War of Independence.

Other colonies soon joined ranks, heeding the advice of Boston-born Benjamin Franklin, who said, 'if we do not hang together, we will surely hang separately.' New Hampshire, Connecticut and Maine (then part of

Revolutionary History

Freedom Trail
(Boston, MA)

Minute Man National Historic Park (Lexington, MA)

Old North Bridge (Concord, MA)

Fort Griswold Battlefield (Groton, CT)

Bennington Battlefield (Bennington, VT)

1692–93	1775	1776	1777
Witch hysteria in Salem sends 14 women and five men to the gallows. One man is crushed to death when he refuses to confess his guilt.	British troops respond to reports that colonists are stockpiling weapons. Warned by Paul Revere and William Dawes, the Minutemen confront the Redcoats in Lexington and Concord, starting the War of Independence.	Colonial leaders from 13 colonies – including Connecticut, Massachusetts, New Hampshire and Rhode Island – sign the Declaration of Independence, asserting that they are no longer a part of the British Empire.	The Republic of Vermont declares its independence, not only from Britain but also from New York. The state constitution is the first to abolish slavery and advocate universal male suffrage.

Massachusetts) wholeheartedly supported the revolutionary cause. The Green Mountain Boys, led by Ethan Allen, were a bandit gang in present-day Vermont who resisted the advances of British soldiers from the New York colony into northwest New England.

The war did not go well at first for the feisty but ill-prepared colonists, but the tide turned when the French were finally persuaded to ally with the rebellion. In 1781, the American army and French navy cornered the main British army on the Yorktown peninsula in Virginia and forced their surrender. British rule had come to an end in the American colonies.

Of Sails & Whales

New England port cities flourished during the Age of Sail. In the 17th century, the infamous 'triangular trade route' was developed, involving West Indian sugar, New England rum and West African slaves. Merchants who chose not to traffic in human cargo could still make large profits by illicitly undercutting European trade monopolies. In the late 17th century, Rhode Island provided a safe haven for pirates.

In the 18th century, Britain's stricter enforcement of trade monopolies and imposition of higher tariffs squeezed the merchants' profits. But after the American Revolution, New England merchants amassed fortunes by opening up trade routes to the Far East. Shipbuilding thrived in Massachusetts, Maine and Connecticut, and cities such as Salem, Newburyport and Portsmouth were among the richest trading cities in the world.

The whaling industry also thrived. Even today, the rich feeding grounds of Stellwagen Bank off Cape Cod attract whales to the region. In the preindustrial period, whales provided commodities, such as oil for lamps, teeth and bone for decorative scrimshaw, and other material for hoop skirts, umbrellas and perfume.

The whalers in New England were strategically placed to pursue the highly sought-after sperm whales along Atlantic migratory routes. Buzzards Bay, Nantucket Island and New Bedford were all prominent whaling centers. In the mid-19th century, New Bedford hosted a whaling fleet of over 300 ships, employing more than 10,000 people directly and indirectly, and cashing in over $12 million in profits.

Industrial Revolution

New England's industrial revolution began in Rhode Island in 1793 when Quaker merchant Moses Brown contracted English mechanic Samuel Slater to construct a water-powered cotton-spinning factory. The Brown–Slater partnership was a brilliant success. Their mills sprouted up along the Blackstone River, driving a vibrant Rhode Island textile industry.

Maritime History

Salem Maritime NHS (Salem, MA)

Essex Shipbuilding Museum (Essex, MA)

New Bedford Whaling Museum (New Bedford, MA)

Nantucket Whaling Museum (Nantucket, MA)

Mystic Seaport Museum (Mystic, CT)

1787	1788	1791	1793
The Beverly Cotton Manufactory – the country's first cotton mill – is constructed in Beverly, MA, kicking off the industrial revolution. The era's largest mill operates for more than 40 years.	New Hampshire ratifies the US Constitution, providing the ninth and final vote needed to execute it. The new government begins operations the following year.	After 14 years as a sovereign entity (complete with currency, a postal service and diplomats), Vermont becomes the first new state to join the Union after the original 13.	Samuel Slater constructs one of the country's first commercially viable, water-powered cotton spinning mills on the banks of the Blackstone River in Pawtucket, RI.

THE FIRST THANKSGIVING

The 'first' Thanksgiving was held in the fall of 1621 in Plymouth Colony. The Pilgrims were thankful, but not for a bountiful harvest; they were thankful simply to be alive. (Of the 100 passengers aboard the *Mayflower*, only half survived the first year in the wilderness.)

True to legend, Native Americans were on hand for the feast. Chief Massasoit of the Wampanoags had no problems with the pathetic Pilgrims, since they inhabited the land of a rival tribe, the Patuxet, which had been wiped out by smallpox. The Wampanoag, in fact, provided most of the food. There may have been a wild turkey on the table, but the plates more likely featured venison, lobster and squirrel. There was no pumpkin pie; alas, the Pilgrims did not have any ovens.

Although there were no Lions or Cowboys, games were played that weekend. The Pilgrim menfolk competed against the Native Americans in shooting, archery and a crude colonial version of croquet.

Thanksgiving with the Pilgrims pretty much ended there, as the fall festival was not repeated in subsequent years. The Pilgrims were pious, not party people. For their part, the Wampanoag came to reconsider their stance on the newcomers. Over the years, a fall harvest feast was a common occurrence in some colonies, especially in New England. In 1789 George Washington called for a national day of Thanksgiving to honor the new constitution, but again this did not become an annual event.

The modern Thanksgiving holiday has more to do with 19th-century nationalism than with 17th-century settlers. In 1863, in the midst of civil war, Abraham Lincoln proclaimed the last Thursday in November as a national Thanksgiving holiday. Popular depictions of the Pilgrims in harmony with natives and nature served to emphasize the common heritage of a people at war with itself. The Thanksgiving tradition is the celebration of a myth – albeit one with the intent to unify.

Today, the perception of Thanksgiving is shifting as the devastation that colonization brought to Native Americans is more widely recognized and acknowledged.

In the 1820s, 30 miles northwest of Boston along the Merrimack River, a group of wealthy merchants built one of the wonders of the industrial age: a planned city of five-story redbrick factories, lining the river for nearly a mile, driven by a network of power canals. Named for the project's deceased visionary, Francis Cabot Lowell, the city counted over 40 mills and employed over 10,000 workers; machines hummed 12 hours a day, six days a week.

This was not the grimy squalor of Manchester, England. Lowell was an orderly city. The workforce at first was drawn from the region's young farm women, who lived in dormitories under paternalistic supervision. The 'mill girls' were gradually replaced by cheaper Irish immigrant labor.

Sarah Messer's youth in the historic Hatch house in Marshfield, MA, inspired her to write *Red House: Being a Mostly Accurate Account of New England's Oldest Continuously Lived-in House* (2004).

1820	1831	1836	1863
Maine gains independence from Massachusetts, becoming the 23rd state to enter the Union.	Abolitionist agitator William Lloyd Garrison first publishes the *Liberator*. The first issue includes an open letter, which advocates 'immediate and complete emancipation of all slaves' in the United States.	With the publication of his essay *Nature*, Ralph Waldo Emerson introduces the philosophy of transcendentalism, which elevates intuition over doctrine and spirituality over empiricism.	Massachusetts native Robert Gould Shaw leads the 54th Regiment of Black troops into battle in the Civil War. Colonel Shaw is killed in action and buried in a common grave next to the fallen Black soldiers.

By the mid-19th century, steam power and metal machines had transformed New England. Railroads crisscrossed the region, hastening industrialization and urbanization. Textile mills arose along rivers in Lawrence, Nashua, Concord and Fall River. Leather works and shoemaking factories appeared near Boston. Springfield and Worcester became centers for tool- and dye-making, southern Connecticut manufactured machinery, and the Maine woods furnished paper mills. Even Paul Revere, the famed Boston silversmith and early American patriot, abandoned his shop in the North End and set up a rolling copper mill and foundry 15 miles southwest along the Neponset River.

New England Melting Pot

The rapid rise of industry led to social as well as economic changes. The second half of the 19th century brought a wave of immigrant laborers to New England, throwing the world of English-descended Whig Protestants into turmoil.

The first Irish immigrants arrived to work in the mills in the 1820s. Disparaged by native New Englanders, the Irish were considered an inferior race of delinquents, whose spoken brogue suggested that one had a 'shoe in one's mouth.' They undercut local workers in the job market and, worse yet, brought the dreaded papist religion from which the Puritans had fled. Tensions ran high, occasionally erupting in violence. In 1834, rumors of licentiousness and kidnapping led a Boston mob to torch the Ursuline Convent in present-day Somerville, MA.

A potato famine back home spurred an upsurge in Irish immigration to Boston. Between 1846 and 1856, more than 1000 new immigrants stepped off the boat per month, a human flood tide that the city was not prepared to absorb. Anti-immigrant and anti-Catholic sentiments were shrill. As a political expression of this rabid reaction, the Know Nothing Party swept into office in Massachusetts, Rhode Island and Connecticut, promising to reverse the flow of immigration, deny the newcomers political rights and mandate readings from the Protestant Bible in public school.

Subsequent groups of Italian, Portuguese, French Canadian and East European Jewish immigrants suffered similar prejudices and indignities. By the end of the 19th century, the urban landscape of New England resembled a mosaic of clannish ethnic enclaves. Sticking together became an immigrant survival strategy for finding work, housing and companionship. Neighborhoods took on the feel of the old country with familiar language, cuisine and customs. The New England melting pot was more like a stew than a puree.

In the early 20th century, when new southern and Eastern European immigrants began preaching class solidarity, they were met with renewed fury from New England's ruling elite. Labor unrest in the factories mobilized a harsh political reaction against foreigners and socialism.

At just 22 years old, enslaved woman Ona Judge ran away from Philadelphia to freedom in New Hampshire – an especially brave act given that her owner was president George Washington. The full story of Judge's intrepid escape and Washington's dogged pursuit is told in Erica Armstrong Dunbar's *Never Caught* (2017).

1895	1925	1945	1954
WEB Du Bois becomes the first African American to earn a PhD from Harvard University. The Massachusetts-born historian becomes a tireless advocate for civil rights for blacks.	The New Bedford–based *John R Manta* returns home for the last time, bringing New England whaling to an end, overtaken by industrial technology and changes in social attitudes.	Maine scientist Percy Spencer accidentally melts a chocolate bar in his pocket while standing in front of a magnetron. From this observation, he invents the microwave oven.	General Dynamics Shipyard in Groton, CT, launches the *Nautilus*, the world's first nuclear-powered submarine. Nuclear power means that the sub can remain submerged for much longer periods of time.

Reform & Racism

The legacy of race relations in New England is marred by contradictions. Abolitionists and segregationists, reformers and racists have all left their mark.

The first enslaved people were delivered to Massachusetts Bay Colony from the West Indies in 1638. By 1700, roughly 400 people were enslaved in Boston. In the 18th century, Rhode Island merchants played a leading role in the Atlantic slave trade, financing over 1000 slave ventures and transporting more than 100,000 Africans to lives spent in bondage.

A number of New England's enslaved people earned their freedom by fighting against the British in the Revolution. Crispus Attucks, a runaway slave of African and Native American descent, became a martyr by falling victim in the Boston Massacre. Salem Poor, who bought his freedom, was distinguished for heroism in the Battle of Bunker Hill.

In the early 19th century, New England became a center of the abolition movement. In Boston, newspaper publisher William Lloyd Garrison, Unitarian minister Theodore Parker and aristocratic lawyer Wendell Phillips launched the Anti-Slavery Society to engage public sentiment – Frederick Douglass, then living in Massachusetts, became a prominent member. New England provided numerous stops along the Underground Railroad, a network of safe houses that helped runaway slaves reach freedom in Canada.

The New England states still maintained their own informal patterns of racial segregation, however, with African Americans as an underclass. Although Massachusetts was the first state to elect an African American to the US Senate by popular vote in 1966, race relations remained fraught.

In 1974, Judge W Arthur Garrity determined that separate was not equal in the Boston public school system – meaning that schools segregated by race did not provide equal educational opportunity for non-white students. Garrity's court order to integrate the schools through redistricting and busing exposed underlying racial tensions, and resulted in the same protests and violence as desegregation efforts in the South. Busing was eventually abandoned, and wounds remain.

African American History

Black Heritage Trail
(Boston, MA)

African Meeting House
(Nantucket, MA)

Oak Bluffs
(Martha's Vineyard, MA)

Harriet Beecher-Stowe Center
(Hartford, CT)

Black Heritage Trail
(Portsmouth, NH)

20th- & 21st-Century Trends

The fears of the Yankee old guard were finally realized in the early 20th century when ethnic-based political machines gained control of city governments in Massachusetts, Rhode Island and Connecticut.

While the Democratic Party was originally associated with rural and radical interests, it became the political instrument of the recently arrived working poor in urban areas. Flamboyant city bosses pursued a

1960	1966	1970s	1980s
Massachusetts native John F Kennedy is elected president, ushering in the era of Camelot. He is the first Irish American president and the first Catholic president.	Republican Edward Brooke of Massachusetts is the first African American popularly elected to the US Senate. During two terms, Brooke is a relentless advocate for affordable housing.	Boston tries to racially integrate schools by busing students between neighborhoods, inciting violent reactions. School attendance declines dramatically, and several people are killed.	Massachusetts experiences a period of economic growth. Known as the Massachusetts Miracle, the economic turnaround is fueled by the technology industry.

populist and activist approach to city politics. Their administrations were steeped in public works and patronage. According to Providence boss Charlie Brayton, 'an honest voter is one who stays bought.'

The Republican Party in New England was cobbled together in the mid-19th century from the Whigs, the Know Nothings and the antislavery movement. In the 20th century, it became the political vehicle for the old English-descended elite, who envisioned a paternalistic and frugal government and preached self-help and sobriety.

Economically, New England experienced its share of booms and busts. The good times of the early 20th century crashed down in the Great Depression. After a brief recovery, the region began to lose its textile industry and manufacturing base to the South. With the mills shut down and the seaports quieted, the regional economy languished and its cities fell into disrepair.

But entrepreneurial spirit and technological imagination combined to revive the region, sustained by science, medicine and higher education. Boston, Providence and Hartford were buoyed by banking, finance and insurance. The biggest boost came from the technological revolution, which enabled local high-tech companies to make the Massachusetts Miracle, an economic boom in the 1980s. Even with stock-market corrections and bubble bursts, technological developments continue to reinvigorate New England.

In the first two decades of the 21st century, New England has emerged as a leader in US social trends. In 2000, Vermont legalized same-sex civil unions, and in 2004 Massachusetts became the first state to legalize same-sex marriage. Both Massachusetts (2006) and Connecticut (2009) passed universal health-care legislation prior to the 2010 passage of the federal Affordable Care Act, and four New England states (Massachusetts, Maine, Vermont and Connecticut) legalized marijuana between 2016 and 2021.

On November 26, 1970 – Thanksgiving Day – Native Americans gathered on Cole's Hill, Plymouth, to counter the traditional Thanksgiving narrative in a 'National Day of Mourning.' It became an annual march and rally, allowing indigenous peoples to mourn the loss of sovereignty that began with these early encounters with European colonists.

2004	2004	2013	2020
The Boston Red Sox win the World Series for the first time in 86 years, officially ending the Curse of the Bambino and ushering in a winning era.	Massachusetts becomes the first state in the Union to legalize same-sex marriage. The city of Cambridge becomes the first municipality to issue marriage licenses to gay and lesbian couples.	Two bombs explode at the Boston Marathon, killing three and injuring hundreds. In response to the terrorist attack, the city embraces the motto 'Boston Strong.'	The 400th anniversary of the Pilgrim landing at Plymouth. In light of racial strife around the country, celebrations emphasize the experiences of the indigenous Wampanoag and the complicated legacy of the Pilgrims.

New England Literature

New England's reverence for the written word arrived with the Puritans and was nurtured over the centuries by the area's universities and literary societies. Indeed, the region was the nucleus of the Golden Age of American Literature, with the nation's formative writers coming out of Boston, Concord, MA, and Hartford, CT. This literary tradition thrives today, as writers and scholars continue to congregate in New England's university classrooms and crowded cafes.

Colonial Literature

The literary tradition in New England dates to the days of Puritan settlement. As early as 1631, Anne Bradstreet was writing poetry and meditations. Shortly thereafter, Harvard College was founded (1636) and the first printing press was set up (1638), thus establishing Boston/Cambridge as an important literary center that would attract writers and scholars for generations to come.

Early colonial writings were either spiritual or historical in nature. Governor John Winthrop chronicled the foundation of Boston in his journals. Governor William Bradford, the second governor of Plymouth Colony, was the author of the primary historical reference about the Pilgrims, *Of Plimouth Plantation*. The most prolific writer was Reverend Cotton Mather (1663–1728), who wrote more than 400 books on issues of spirituality – most notably the Salem witch trials.

The Golden Age

It was during the 19th century that New England became a region renowned for its intellect. The universities had become a magnet for writers, poets and philosophers, as well as publishers and bookstores. The local literati were expounding on social issues such as slavery, women's rights and religious reawakening. Boston, Cambridge and Concord, MA, were fertile breeding grounds for ideas, nurturing the seeds of America's literary and philosophical flowering. This was the Golden Age of American literature, and New England was its nucleus.

Ralph Waldo Emerson (1803–82) promulgated his teachings from his home in Concord, MA. He and Henry David Thoreau (1817–62) wrote compelling essays about their beliefs and their attempts to live in accordance with the mystical unity of all creation. Thoreau's notable writings included *Walden; or, Life in the Woods* (1854), which advocated a life of simplicity and living in harmony with nature, and *Civil Disobedience* (1849), a treatise well before its time.

Nathaniel Hawthorne (1804–64) traveled in this Concordian literary circle. America's first great short-story writer, Hawthorne was the author of *The Scarlet Letter* (1850) and *The House of the Seven Gables* (1851), both offering insightful commentary on Colonial culture. Louisa May Alcott (1832–88) grew up at Orchard House, also in Concord, where she wrote her much-loved and largely autobiographical novel *Little Women* (1868).

New England Literary Sites

The Mount
(Lenox, MA)

Mark Twain House
& Museum
(Hartford, CT)

Providence
Athenaeum
(Providence, RI)

Frost Place
(Franconia, NH)

Harriet
Beecher-Stowe
Center
(Hartford, CT)

Around this time, poet Henry Wadsworth Longfellow (1807–82) was the most illustrious resident of Cambridge, MA, where he taught at Harvard. Longfellow often hosted his contemporaries from Concord for philosophical discussions at his home on Brattle St (now the Longfellow National Historic Site). Here he wrote poems such as 'Song of Hiawatha' and 'Paul Revere's Ride,' both cherished accounts of American lore.

Concord Literary Sites

Ralph Waldo Emerson Memorial House

Orchard House

Walden Pond

Old Manse

Meanwhile, some of these luminaries would travel one Saturday a month to Boston to congregate with their contemporaries at the old Parker House (now the Omni Parker House hotel). Presided over by Oliver Wendell Holmes, the Saturday Club was known for its jovial atmosphere and stimulating discourse, attracting such renowned visitors as Charles Dickens. Out of these meetings was born the *Atlantic Monthly*, a literary institution that continues to showcase innovative authors and ideas.

Down the street, the Old Corner Bookstore (now a stop on the Freedom Trail) was the site of Ticknor & Fields, the first publishing house to offer author royalties. Apparently Mr Fields had a special gift for discovering new local talent; by all accounts, his bookstore was a lively meeting place for writers and readers.

All around the region, progressive writers fueled the abolitionist movement with fiery writings. William Lloyd Garrison founded the radical newspaper *The Abolitionist* on Boston's Beacon Hill. Social activist Lydia Maria Child had her privileges at the Boston Athenaeum revoked for her provocative antislavery pamphlets. Harriet Beecher Stowe (1811–96), whose influential book *Uncle Tom's Cabin* recruited thousands to the antislavery cause, was born in Litchfield, CT, and lived in Brunswick, ME, before she eventually moved to Hartford, CT.

In 1895 WEB Du Bois (1868–1963) became the first Black man to receive a PhD from Harvard University. A few years later, he wrote his seminal tract *The Souls of Black Folk,* in which he sought to influence the way blacks dealt with segregation, urging pride in African heritage.

LITERARY LIGHTS

Ralph Waldo Emerson (1803–82) Essayist with a worldwide following and believer in the mystical beauty of all creation; founder of transcendentalism.

Henry David Thoreau (1817–62) Best remembered for *Walden; or, Life in the Woods,* his journal of observations written during his solitary sojourn from 1845 to 1847 in a log cabin at Walden Pond.

Emily Dickinson (1830–86) This reclusive 'Belle of Amherst' crafted beautiful poems, mostly published after her death.

Edith Wharton (1862–1937) The Pulitzer Prize–winning novelist's *Ethan Frome* paints a grim portrayal of emotional attachments on a New England farm.

WEB DuBois (1868–1963) Best known for his illuminating essay collection, *The Souls of Black Folk*, Massachusetts-born DuBois was among the founders of the National Association for the Advancement of Colored People (NAACP).

Robert Frost (1874–1963) The region's signature poet used New England imagery to explore the depths of human experience.

Sylvia Plath (1932–1963) Born in Boston and a graduate of Smith College; known for her searing novel, *The Bell Jar*, and ferocious poetry.

John Irving (b 1942) New Hampshire native writes novels set in New England, including *The World According to Garp* and *A Prayer for Owen Meany.*

Anita Shreve (1946–2018) Boston-born writer of thoughtful, emotional novels, most of which are set in New England. *The Pilot's Wife* (1998) was an Oprah Book Club pick.

Stephen King (b 1947) Maine horror novelist; wrote *Carrie* and *The Shining.*

Banned in Boston

In the 20th century, New England continued to attract authors, poets and playwrights, but the Golden Age was over. This region was no longer the center of progressive thought and social activism that had so inspired American literature.

This shift in cultural geography was due in part to a shift in consciousness in the late 19th century. Moral crusaders and local officials promoted stringent censorship of books, films and plays that they deemed offensive or obscene. Many writers were 'banned in Boston' – a trend that contributed to that city's image as a provincial outpost instead of cultural capital. Eugene O'Neill (1888–1953) is the most celebrated example. O'Neill attended Harvard, he was a key participant in the Provincetown Players on Cape Cod and he spent the last two years of his life in Back Bay, but his experimental play *Strange Interlude* was prohibited from showing on Boston stages.

Henry James (1843–1916) grew up in Cambridge. Although he was undoubtedly influenced by his New World upbringing, he eventually emigrated to England. A prolific writer, he often commented on American society in his novels, which include *Daisy Miller* and *The Bostonians*.

The revolutionary poet ee cummings (1894–1962) was also born in Cambridge, although it was his experiences in Europe that inspired his most famous novel, *The Enormous Room*. Descended from an old New England family, TS Eliot (1888–1965) taught at Harvard for a spell, but he wrote his best work in England.

Robert Lowell (1917–77) was another Boston native who was restless in his hometown. He spent many years living in Back Bay and teaching at Boston University, where he wrote *Life Studies* and *For the Union Dead*. Encouraged by his interactions with Beat Generation poet Allen Ginsberg, Lowell became the seminal 'confessional poet.' At BU, he counted Sylvia Plath (1932–63) and Anne Sexton (1928–74) among the students he inspired before he finally moved to Manhattan.

One of the Beat Generation's defining authors, Jack Kerouac was born in Lowell, MA. His hometown features prominently in many of his novels, but he too eventually decamped to the new cultural capital to the south.

America's favorite poet, Robert Frost (1874–1963), was an exception to this trend. He moved from California and spent most of his life in New England, doing stints at Dartmouth and Harvard, teaching for four decades at Middlebury College's Bread Loaf School of English, and living on farms in Shaftsbury, VT, and Franconia, NH, where he wrote poems including 'Nothing Gold Can Stay' and 'The Road Not Taken.'

New England Bookstores

Montague Bookmill
(Montague, MA)

Harvard Bookstore
(Cambridge, MA)

Northshire Bookstore
(Manchester, VT)

Mainely Murders
(Kennebunk, ME)

Where the Sidewalk Ends
(Chatham, MA)

Gibson's Bookstore
(Concord, NH)

Contemporary Literature

Boston never regained its status as the hub of the literary solar system. But its rich legacy and ever-influential universities ensure that the region continues to contribute to American literature. Many of New England's most prominent writers are transplants from other cities or countries, drawn to its academic and creative institutions. John Updike (1932–2009), author of the Pulitzer Prize–winning Rabbit series, moved to Massachusetts to attend Harvard (where he was president of *Harvard Lampoon*), before settling in Ipswich, which is where he died.

Born in Ithaca, NY, David Foster Wallace (1962–2008) studied philosophy at Harvard. Although he abandoned the course and moved out of the city, his Boston-based novel, *Infinite Jest,* earned him a MacArthur Genius Award. Jhumpa Lahiri (b 1967) is a Bengali Indian American writer who studied creative writing at Boston University. Her debut collection of short stories, *Interpreter of Maladies,* won a Pulitzer Prize for Fiction

LOWELL: THE TOWN & THE CITY

'Follow along to the center of town, the Square, where at noon everybody knows everybody else.' So Beat Generation author Jack Kerouac described his hometown of Lowell, MA, in his 1950 novel *The Town & The City*.

One of the most influential American authors of the 20th century, Jack Kerouac (1922–69) was born in Lowell at the mill town's industrial peak. He inhabited Lowell's neighborhoods, he graduated from Lowell High School and he wrote for the *Lowell Sun*. It is not surprising, then, that the author used Lowell as the setting for five of his novels that draw on his youth.

Kerouac is remembered annually during the Lowell Celebrates Kerouac (LCK) festival (p109). Aside from the festival, there are walking tours and films based on places that Kerouac wrote about and experienced.

Of course, Kerouac is most famous for his classic novel *On the Road* (1957). With it, he became a symbol of the spirit of the open road. He eventually went to New York, where he, Allen Ginsberg and William Burroughs formed the core of the Beat Generation of writers. Nonetheless, Kerouac always maintained ties to Lowell, and he is buried in Edson Cemetery, a pilgrimage site for devotees who were inspired by his free spirit.

in 2000. Set in Boston and surrounding neighborhoods, her works address the challenges and triumphs in the lives of her Indian American characters. Geraldine Brooks (b 1955) is an Australian-born writer who resides part-time on Martha's Vineyard. Several of her novels are set in New England, including *March*, which earned her a Pulitzer Prize.

Of course, New England has also fostered some homegrown contemporary talent. John Cheever (1912–82) was born in Quincy and lived in Boston. His novel, *The Wapshot Chronicle*, takes place in a Massachusetts fishing village. Born and raised in Dorchester, Dennis Lehane (b 1965) wrote *Mystic River* and *Gone, Baby Gone*, compelling tales set in working-class Boston 'hoods, both of which were made into excellent films.

Stephen King (b 1947), author of horror novels such as *Carrie* and *The Shining*, lives and sets his novels in Maine. King is a well-known Boston Red Sox fan, and is often sighted at home games.

John Irving (b 1942) was born and raised in Exeter, NH, which serves as the setting for many of his stories, including *The World According to Garp, A Prayer for Owen Meany* and *A Widow for a Year*. In 1999 Irving won an Academy Award for his adapted screenplay of *The Cider House Rules*, which takes place in rural Maine.

Novelist Annie Proulx (b 1935), author of *The Shipping News* and *Brokeback Mountain*, was born in Connecticut and grew up in Maine. Although she lived for more than 30 years in Vermont, most of her stories are not set in New England.

Elizabeth Strout (b 1956) was born and raised in Portland, ME, and has set several of her novels in fictional New England towns, including her wonderfully quirky Pulitzer Prize–winning *Olive Kitteridge* (2008). Strout's works regularly appear on national bestseller lists and continue to garner critical acclaim – most recently *Anything Is Possible*, winner of the 2017 Story Prize.

Mary Oliver (1935–2019), one of America's most beloved contemporary poets, drew much of her inspiration from the natural landscapes surrounding her adopted home of Provincetown, MA. Winner of the Pulitzer Prize and the National Book Award, Oliver passed away in early 2019.

It seems incongruous, but Rudyard Kipling actually penned his famous *Jungle Book* in the not-so-jungly woods of southern Vermont, during a four-year sojourn near Brattleboro. Want to host your own literary retreat in Kipling's former home? The house – which sleeps up to eight – is available for short-term holiday rentals (www.landmarktrustusa.org/properties/rudyard-kiplings-naulakha).

Universities & Colleges

No single element has influenced the region as profoundly as its educational institutions. New England's colleges and universities attract scholars, scientists, philosophers and writers who thrive off and contribute to the region's evolving culture. This renewable source of cultural energy supports poetry slams, film festivals, music scenes, art galleries, coffee shops, hip clubs and Irish pubs. Take your pick from the eminent Ivies, the urban campuses, the liberal arts colleges or the edgier art and music schools.

Ivy League

New England is home to four of the eight Ivy League universities, all of which were founded before the American Revolution. They are known for academic excellence, selective admissions and Yankee elitism.

Yale University

Yale University is the centerpiece of the gritty city of New Haven, CT. Founded in 1701 as the Collegiate School, the university was renamed in 1718 to honor a gift from rich merchant Elihu Yale. In the 1930s Yale instituted a system of residential colleges, whereby students eat, sleep, study and play in a smaller community within the larger university. There are now 14 residential, Oxford-style colleges, each with its own distinctive style of architecture. The school is also home to the enigmatic 'Skull and Bones,' an elitist secret society of aspiring kleptomaniacs. So-called 'Bonesmen' try to outdo each other by 'crooking' valuable artifacts and objets d'art from around the university. Its alumni include presidents, senators, Supreme Court justices and other upstanding citizens.

Brown University

Brown University has lent its progressive viewpoints to Providence, RI, since 1764 (though prior to American independence, it was known as the College in the English Colony of Rhode Island and Providence Plantations). The university charter specified that religion would not be a criterion for admission – the first institution in the New World to do so.

Brown has earned a reputation for refined radical-chic academics. In 1969 the university adopted the New Curriculum, which eliminated distribution requirements and allowed students to take courses without grades. In 1981 the university opened a research center devoted to sexuality and gender. The previous university president, Ruth J Simmons, was the first African American president of an Ivy League institution.

Today, the Georgian-era campus on College Hill enrolls about 6700 undergraduate students and 2500 graduate students. It is unique for its program that allows students to design their own course of study.

Dartmouth College

Dartmouth College dominates Hanover, NH, making it the quintessential New England college town. Dartmouth is unique among the Ivies for its small size, its rural setting and its emphasis on undergraduate education. Dartmouth also employs a year-round quarter system, known as the

In the 1980s Yale University became known as the 'gay ivy,' after the *Wall Street Journal* published an article about homosexuality on campus. The active community at Yale originated the LGBTIQ+ rallying cry 'One in Four, Maybe More.'

Brown University's most esteemed faculty member is Josiah Stinkney Carberry, professor of psychoceramics (the study of cracked pots). Every Friday the 13th is known as Carberry Day, when students donate their loose change to a fund for books.

A WALK ACROSS THE HARVARD BRIDGE

The Harvard Bridge – from Back Bay in Boston to Massachusetts Institute of Technology (MIT) in Cambridge – is the longest bridge across the Charles River. It is not too long to walk, but it is long enough to do some wondering while you walk. You might wonder, for example, why the bridge that leads into the heart of MIT is named the Harvard Bridge.

According to legend, the state offered to name the bridge after Cambridge's second university. But the brainiac engineers at MIT analyzed the plans for construction and found the bridge was structurally unsound. Not wanting the MIT moniker associated with a faulty feat of engineering, it was suggested that the bridge better be named for the neighboring university up the river. That the bridge subsequently needed to be rebuilt validated the superior brainpower of MIT.

That is only a legend, however (one invented by an MIT student, no doubt). The fact is that the Harvard Bridge was first constructed in 1891 and MIT only moved to its current location in 1916. The bridge was rebuilt in the 1980s to modernize and expand it, but the original name has stuck, at least officially. Most Bostonians actually refer to this bridge as the 'Mass Ave bridge' because, frankly, it makes more sense.

By now, walking across the bridge, perhaps you have reached the halfway point: 'Halfway to Hell' reads the scrawled graffiti here. Elsewhere along the bridge, other graffiti make reference to 'smoots.' Huh?! What the heck is a 'smoot'?

A smoot is an obscure unit of measurement that was used to measure the distance of the Harvard Bridge, first in 1958 and every year since. One smoot is approximately 5ft, 7in, the height of Oliver R Smoot, who was a pledge of the MIT fraternity Lambda Chi Alpha in 1958. He was the shortest pledge that year. And, yes, his physical person was actually used for all the measurements that year.

And now that you have reached the other side of the river, surely you are wondering exactly how long this bridge is. We can't speak for Harvard students, but certainly every MIT student knows that the Harvard Bridge is 364.4 smoots plus one ear.

D-Plan. The school is famed for its spirited student body and the cult-like loyalty of its alumni. To get a sense of campus culture, think William F Buckley in Birkenstocks.

Dartmouth's 270-acre Georgian-era campus is centered on a picturesque green. The university also owns huge tracts of land in the White Mountains region and in Northern New Hampshire. No surprise, then, that the university has an active outdoors club (which incidentally maintains portions of the Appalachian Trail).

Harvard University

A slew of superlatives accompanies the name of this venerable institution in Cambridge, MA. It is America's oldest university, founded in 1636. It has by far the largest endowment, measuring $39.2 billion in 2018. It is often first in the list of national universities, according to US News & World Report. Harvard is actually comprised of 11 independent graduate schools dedicated to the study of business, medicine, dentistry, law, engineering, divinity, design, education, public health, arts and science, and public policy, in addition to the original undergraduate institution, Harvard College.

Harvard Yard is the heart and soul of the university campus, with buildings dating back to its founding. But the university continues to expand in all directions. In 2021, Harvard opened its newest campus, across the Charles River in Allston, featuring a state-of-the-art, environmentally sustainable science center, sporting facilities and more.

In 2003 a couple of Harvard computer-science students hacked into university computers to copy students' photographs and publish them online. Although their site was shut down by Harvard officials, the students were inspired to found Facebook. See how the story unfolds in the film The Social Network.

Boston & Cambridge Institutions

More than 50 institutions of higher education are located in Boston (too many to mention here). About a dozen smaller schools are located in the Fenway, while the residential areas west of the center (Brighton and Allston) have been dubbed the 'student ghetto.'

Massachusetts Institute of Technology

On the north bank of the Charles River, the Massachusetts Institute of Technology (MIT) offers a completely novel perspective on Cambridge academia: proudly nerdy and not so tweedy as Harvard. It excels in science, design and engineering. MIT seems to pride itself on being offbeat. Wander into a courtyard and you might find it is graced with a sculpture by Henry Moore or Alexander Calder; or you might just as well find a Ping-Pong table or a trampoline. MIT's campus is home to some of the most architecturally unusual and intriguing structures you'll find on either side of the river, including the Ray and Maria Stata Center (Frank Gehry's whimsical complex of classrooms and research facilities), and Simmons Hall, a high-rise student residence pockmarked with multi-colored windows – the brainchild of architect Steven Holl.

Boston University

Boston University (BU) is a massive urban campus sprawling west of Kenmore Sq. BU enrolls more than 33,000 undergraduate and graduate students in all fields of study. The special collections of BU's Mugar Memorial Library include 20th-century archives that balance pop culture and scholarly appeal. Peruse the rotating exhibits and you might find papers from Arthur Fiedler's collection, the archives of Douglas Fairbanks, Jr, or the correspondence of BU alumnus Dr Martin Luther King, Jr.

Boston College

Not to be confused with BU, Boston College (BC) could not be more different. BC is situated between Brighton in Boston and Chestnut Hill in the tony suburb of Newton; the attractive campus is recognizable by its neo-Gothic towers. It is home to the nation's largest Jesuit community. Its Catholic influence makes it more socially conservative and more social-service oriented than other universities. It also has one of the nation's highest graduation rates for student athletes. Visitors to the campus will find a good art museum and excellent Irish and Catholic ephemera collections in the library. Aside from the vibrant undergraduate population, it has a strong education program and an excellent law school.

Liberal Arts Colleges

The small, private liberal arts college is a New England social institution. Dedicated to a well-rounded traditional curriculum, these schools are known for first-rate instruction, pricey tuition and upper-class pretension. The schools place an emphasis on the undergraduate classroom, where corduroy-clad professors are more likely to be inspiring teachers than prolific researchers. Their cozy campuses are nestled amid white steeples and red barns in the rolling New England countryside. Mandatory for all first-year students: Plato's *Republic,* a rugby shirt and a lacrosse stick – or a quidditch broom!

Little Ivies

The 'Little Ivies' are a self-anointed collection of a dozen elite liberal arts colleges, 10 of which are found in New England: Amherst, Williams and Tufts in Massachusetts; Connecticut College, Trinity and Wesleyan in Connecticut; Middlebury in Vermont; and Bowdoin, Bates and Colby in Maine. From this select cohort, Williams and Amherst annually battle it out for top spot on the *US News & World Report* ranking of Best Liberal Arts Colleges (currently numbered one and two, respectively).

If you think mortarboards and moguls don't mix, you haven't seen Middlebury College's winter graduation ceremony. Every February, dozens of mid-year graduates (known as 'Febs') slalom down the slopes in full valedictory regalia. See it for yourself at the Middlebury College Snow Bowl – or check out the videos on YouTube!

Rhode Island School of Design (RISD) was founded when a local women's group had $1675 left over in their fund for Rhode Island's exhibit at the 1876 Centennial Exhibition in Philadelphia. Some sources claim the competing proposal for the funds was for a drinking fountain in the local park.

Seven Sisters

Massachusetts is also home to four of the Seven Sisters, elite undergraduate women's colleges, founded in the days when the Ivy League was still a boys-only club. Mount Holyoke and Smith College are situated in the state's hippie-chic central Pioneer Valley; Wellesley is found in a posh Boston suburb of the same name; and Radcliffe is in Cambridge next to Harvard, to which it now officially belongs.

Art & Music Schools

Some of America's finest musicians, visual artists and stage performers got their start in New England. The region's stellar lineup of educational institutions includes the nation's preeminent design school and a host of top-ranked music, art and theater programs.

Rhode Island School of Design

In a league of its own, the Rhode Island School of Design (RISD) boasts many famous graduates who have become pop-culture trailblazers, such as musicians David Byrne, Tina Weymouth and fellow members of Talking Heads, graffiti artist and designer Shepard Fairey, painter and silhouettist Kara Walker and animation expert Seth MacFarlane. The concentration of creativity at RISD makes this Providence neighborhood among the edgiest and artiest in all New England.

MassArt

More formally known as the Massachusetts College of Art and Design, this is the country's first and only four-year independent public art college. In 1873 state leaders decided the new textile mills in Lowell and Lawrence needed a steady stream of designers, so they established MassArt in Boston to educate some. With thousands of square feet of exhibition space on campus, there's always some thought-provoking or sense-stimulating exhibits to see.

Berklee College of Music

Housed in and around the Back Bay in Boston, Berklee is an internationally renowned school for contemporary music, especially jazz. The school was founded in 1945 by Lawrence Berk (the Lee came from his son's first name). Created as an alternative to the classical agenda and stuffy attitude of traditional music schools, Berk taught courses in composition and arrangement for popular music. Not big on musical theory, Berk emphasized learning by playing. His system was a big success and the school flourished. Among Berklee's Grammy-laden alumni are jazz musicians Gary Burton, Esperanza Spalding, Al Di Meola, Keith Jarrett and Diana Krall; pop and rock artists Quincy Jones, Donald Fagen and John Mayer; singer-songwriters St Vincent and Aimee Mann; and film composer Howard Shore.

Emerson College

Founded in 1880, Emerson is a liberal arts college that specializes in communications and the performing arts. Located in Boston's theater district, the college operates the Cutler Majestic Theater and the Paramount Theater, and its students run Boston's coolest radio station, WERS. Emerson celebs include Norman Lear, Jay Leno and 'the Fonz' (Henry Winkler).

University Art Collections

Hood Museum of Art (Hanover, NH)

Museum of Art, RISD (Providence, RI)

Yale Center for British Art (New Haven, CT)

Harvard Art Museum (Cambridge, MA)

MICHAEL MOLONEY/SHUTTERSTOCK ©

Survival Guide

DIRECTORY A–Z . . . 426

Accessible Travel 426
Accommodations 426
Children 426
Electricity 427
Food 427
Health 427
Insurance 427
Internet Access 427
Legal Matters 428
LGBTIQ+ Travelers 428
Money 428
Opening Hours 428
Post 428

Public Holidays 428
Responsible Travel 429
Safe Travel 429
Telephone 429
Time 430
Toilets 430
Tourist Information 430
Visas 430

TRANSPORTATION . . 431

**Getting
There & Away 431**
Entering the
Country/Region 431

Air 431
Land 432
Sea 433
Getting Around 433
Air 433
Bicycle 433
Boat 434
Bus 434
Car & Motorcycle 434
Local Transportation 435
Train 435

Blue Bikes for hire (p98)

Directory A–Z

Accessible Travel

Travel within New England is gradually becoming less difficult for people with disabilities. Public buildings are now required by law to be wheelchair accessible and also to have appropriate restroom facilities. Public transportation services must be made accessible to all, and telephone companies are required to provide relay operators for the hearing impaired.

Many banks provide ATM instructions in Braille, curb ramps are common, many busy intersections have audible crossing signals, and most chain hotels have suites for guests with disabilities.

Mobility International USA (www.miusa.org) advises travelers with disabilities on mobility issues and runs educational international exchange programs.

Download Lonely Planet's free Accessible Travel guides from https://shop.lonely planet.com/categories/accessible-travel.com.

Accommodations

For the lowdown on accommodations in New England, see p26.

Children

Traveling within New England with children presents no destination-specific problems. Parents will find that New England offers a great variety of educational and entertaining ways to keep their kiddies busy. Most facilities – including hotels and restaurants – welcome families with children.

Look for the family-friendly icon in the listings for particularly welcoming spots. Lonely Planet's *Travel with Children* (available at https://shop.lonelyplanet.com) is a helpful resource.

Practicalities

Many restaurants have children's menus with significantly lower prices. High chairs are usually available, but it pays to inquire ahead of time. Roadside stands pepper rural New England, offering kid-friendly fare like fish sticks, burgers, fries, chicken fingers and soft-serve ice cream.

Children are not welcome at many smaller B&Bs and inns (even if they do not say so outright); make sure you inquire before booking. In motels and hotels, children under 17 or 18 years are usually free when sharing a room with their parents.

Cots and roll-away beds are often available (sometimes for an additional fee) in hotels and resorts. Campgrounds are fantastic choices for families with kids – many are situated on waterways or lakes and offer family activities (tube rental, swimming, kayaking etc). For those who don't want to rough it, many campgrounds also offer simple cabins to rent.

Most car-rental companies lease child safety seats, but they don't always have them on hand; reserve in advance if you can. Rest stops generally have changing stations for parents' convenience. Most public transportation (bus, train etc) offers half-price tickets or reduced fares for children.

PRACTICALITIES

Boston Discounts City Pass (www.citypass.com) and Smart Destinations (www.smartdestinations.com)

Smoking All six New England states have banned smoking in restaurants and bars. Hotel rooms in Vermont and dozens of Massachusetts municipalities – including Boston – must also be 100% smoke-free.

Electricity

Type A
120V/60Hz

Type B
120V/60Hz

Food

Eating in New England is a treat, whether feasting on fresh seafood, munching berries from the bush or dining at one of the region's top, chef-driven restaurants.

The finest dining and most innovative cooking takes place in New England's cities, especially Boston, Portland, Providence and Burlington. At high-end restaurants, reservations for dinner are usually recommended, especially during peak tourist seasons and on weekends. Reservations are not usually needed for lunch.

Except in the most rural areas or the smallest towns, vegetarians will have no problem finding animal-free eats. Other dietary restrictions are also usually accommodated.

Health
Before You Go

Given the high cost of health care in the US, it's advisable to have health insurance that covers emergency room visits here and/or repatriation to your home country. Unlike many other developed countries, the United States does not have a socialized medicine system, and you will be expected to pay in full for any services that your insurance does not cover. Health insurance brokers such as www.visitorscoverage.com and www.insubuy.com specialize in health insurance for foreign visitors to the US and can be helpful if your home country insurance does not provide adequate coverage.

COVID-19 vaccination is required for travel to New England or elsewhere in the United States. For an up-to-date list of disease outbreaks worldwide, see www.cdc.gov/outbreaks.

In New England

Health care in the United States is widely available and of excellent quality, but extremely expensive by world standards. Prices are especially high for emergency room care, which costs on average about $2000 per visit if it's not covered by your health insurance. For non-life-threatening emergencies, 'urgent care' facilities offer a less expensive alternative to the emergency room. Check with your insurance provider before traveling to determine what expenses it will cover in the United States.

Insurance

Travelers should protect themselves in case of theft, illness or car accidents. Your regular home owners' insurance, auto insurance and health insurance may offer certain coverage while traveling but be sure to check your policies.

Internet Access

Many hotels, restaurants and cafes offer wireless access for free or for a small fee. Most public libraries also offer free online computer access, and some cities and towns have free public wi-fi hotspots. If you bring a laptop with you from outside the US, it's worth investing in a universal AC and plug adapter.

EATING PRICE RANGES

The following price ranges refer to a standard main course at dinner. Unless otherwise stated, a service charge and taxes are not included.

$ less than $15

$$ $15–25

$$$ more than $25

Legal Matters

The minimum age for drinking alcoholic beverages is 21. You'll need a government-issued photo ID (such as a passport or a US driver's license). Stiff fines, jail time and penalties can be incurred if you are caught driving under the influence of alcohol or providing alcohol to minors.

LGBTIQ+ Travelers

Out and active gay communities are visible across New England, especially in cities such as Boston and New Haven, CT, which have substantial LGBTIQ+ populations. Several smaller cities also have well-established queer communities, including Portland, ME, Northampton, MA, and Burlington, VT.

Provincetown, MA, and Ogunquit, ME, are gay meccas, especially in summer when both towns have a lively beach scene. Provincetown's annual **Carnival** (www.ptown.org/provincetown-carnival), replete with drag queens and flowery floats, is the region's most boisterous LGBTIQ+ party, drawing tens of thousands of revelers every August.

Cities throughout the region also stage well-attended pride festivals, with Boston Pride (www.bostonpride.org), Rhode Island PrideFest (www.prideri.org), Pride Portland! (www.prideportland.org) and Northampton's NoHo Pride (www.nohopride.org) being among the biggest.

The Rainbow Times (www.therainbowtimesmass.com) is a great New England–wide resource for news and entertainment listings with an LGBTIQ+ focus.

Money

ATMs

ATMs are ubiquitous in towns throughout New England. Most banks in New England charge at least $2 per withdrawal. The Cirrus and Plus systems both have extensive ATM networks that will give cash advances on major credit cards and allow cash withdrawals with affiliated ATM cards.

If you're carrying foreign currency, it can be exchanged for US dollars at Logan International Airport in Boston. Many banks do not change currency, so stock up on dollars when there's an opportunity to do so.

Credit Cards

Major credit cards are widely accepted throughout New England, including at car-rental agencies and at most hotels, restaurants, gas stations, grocery stores and tour operators. However, some restaurants and B&Bs do not accept credit cards. We have noted in our reviews when this is the case.

Visa and MasterCard are the most common credit cards. American Express and Discover are less widely accepted.

Exchange Rates

Australia	A$1	$0.72
Canada	C$1	$0.78
Euro zone	€1	$1.12
Japan	¥100	$0.87
New Zealand	NZ$1	$0.67
UK	UK£1	$1.34

For current exchange rates see www.xe.com.

Tipping

Many service providers depend on tips for their livelihoods, so tip generously for good service.

Baggage carriers $1 per bag

Housekeeping $2 to $5 per day, $5 to $10 per week

Servers and bartenders 15% to 20%

Taxi drivers 15%

Tour guides $5 to $10 for a one-hour tour

Opening Hours

The following is a general guideline for opening hours. Shorter hours may apply during low seasons, when some venues close completely. Seasonal variations are noted in the listings.

Banks and offices 9am to 5pm or 6pm Monday to Friday; sometimes 9am to noon Saturday

Bars and pubs 5pm to midnight, some until 2am

Restaurants Breakfast 6am to 10am, lunch 11:30am to 2:30pm, dinner 5pm to 10pm daily

Shops 9am to 7pm Monday to Saturday; some open noon to 5pm Sunday, or until evening in tourist areas

Post

No matter how much people like to complain, the US postal service (www.usps.com) is extremely reliable for the price. If you have the correct postage, drop your mail into any blue mailbox. To send a package weighing 16oz or more, you must bring it to a post office or a shipping company such as UPS or FedEx.

Post offices are generally open from 8am to 5pm weekdays, with shorter hours on a Saturday; exact hours vary by branch.

Public Holidays

New Year's Day January 1

Martin Luther King Jr Day Third Monday of January

Presidents' Day Third Monday of February

Easter In March or April

Patriots' Day Third Monday of April (Maine and Massachusetts only)

Memorial Day Last Monday of May

Independence Day July 4

Labor Day First Monday of September

Columbus Day Second Monday of October

Veterans Day November 11

Thanksgiving Fourth Thursday of November

Christmas Day December 25

Responsible Travel

Cycle Cities

Travel around cities by public transportation or local bike-share programs:

➡ Blue Bikes (www.bluebikes.com) in Boston.

➡ GreenRide (www.greenridebikeshare.com) in Burlington.

➡ ValleyBike (www.valleybike.org) in the Pioneer Valley.

➡ A so-far-unnamed program coming to Portland in 2022.

Support Local

➡ Support local farms by buying directly from the growers at farms or farmers' markets.

➡ Stay at locally owned lodgings.

➡ Visit the many state parks and nature preserves that are protecting the region's natural resources.

Reduce, Reuse, Recycle

➡ Carry a tote bag to reduce use of plastic and avoid a surcharge for store bags.

➡ Don't forget your reusable water bottle and/or coffee mug.

Safe Travel

You're unlikely to come across any major problems while traveling in New England. Most of the region enjoys high standards of living, and tourists are usually well taken care of.

COVID-19 Requirements

➡ There are no state-wide mask mandates in place in New England, but many municipalities require face masks in public indoor settings.

➡ In Boston, individuals are required to show proof of vaccination at all indoor restaurants, gyms and entertainment venues. See www.boston.gov for the latest information about the 'B Together' vaccine mandate.

➡ Elsewhere in the region, individual venues may require proof of vaccination to enter.

➡ Get up-to-date information about US COVID-19 travel requirements at www.travel.state.gov.

Driving Hazards

New England driving can be tricky, particularly in big cities, where narrow streets, clogged traffic and illogical street layouts can make unfamiliar drivers miserable. New England's urban drivers are notoriously impatient. Beware the 'Boston left,' where the first left-turning vehicle jumps out in front of oncoming traffic.

Ice and snow pose hazards during New England's long winter, when snow tires or all-season tires are a must – especially in rural areas where roads are plowed less frequently.

In the northern wilds of Maine, New Hampshire and Vermont, watch for moose; as the signs warn, collisions with these massive animals can be fatal.

Outdoor Hazards

Outdoor activities, from beach-going to mountain-hiking, can be dangerous anywhere in the world. Pay attention to weather and water conditions before setting out on any sort of adventure.

➡ The White Mountains are notorious for strong winds and wild weather, but conditions can be dangerous on any of the New England mountain trails. Hypothermia is a key concern in chilly, windy or damp weather; carry adequate clothing for changing conditions.

➡ Always stay on marked trails and do not disturb wildlife while hiking.

➡ In recent years, shark sightings have not been uncommon off Cape Cod, and beaches may close for that reason. In 2018, the region saw its first fatal shark attack in nearly a century. Not all public beaches are guarded, so inquire about riptides and other dangers before swimming at area beaches.

Weather

It snows a lot in New England. If you're visiting between December and March, there's a good chance you'll experience a major snowstorm, possibly impeding your progress until roads are plowed.

Telephone

All phone numbers in the US consist of a three-digit area code followed by a seven-digit local number. You must dial 1 plus all 10 digits for local and long-distance calls in most areas, particularly in Eastern Massachusetts.

Always dial '1' before toll-free (800, 888 etc) and domestic long-distance numbers. Remember that some toll-free numbers may only work within the region or from the US mainland.

To make direct international calls, dial 011 plus the country code plus the area code plus the number. (An exception is calls made to Canada, where you dial 1 plus the area code, plus the number. International rates apply to Canada.) For international operator assistance, dial 0.

If you're calling New England from abroad, the international country code for the US is 1. All calls to New England are then followed by the area code and the seven-digit local number.

Time

New England is on US Eastern Standard Time (GMT-5). From spring through mid-autumn, the region switches over to daylight saving time (GMT-4), which involves setting clocks ahead one hour on the second Sunday in March and back one hour on the first Sunday in November.

Toilets

Most parks, beaches and other public places offer public toilets, although they are not common in big cities. There is no public mandate stating that restaurants, hotels or public sites must open their doors to those in need, but you can usually find relief at information centers, libraries, museums and larger hotels.

Americans have many names for public toilet facilities, but the most common are 'restroom,' 'bathroom' or 'ladies'/men's room.' Of course, you can just ask for the 'toilet.'

Tourist Information

Connecticut Office of Tourism (www.ctvisit.com)

Greater Boston Convention & Visitors Bureau (www.bostonusa.com)

Maine Office of Tourism (www.visitmaine.com)

Massachusetts Office of Travel & Tourism (www.massvacation.com)

New Hampshire Division of Travel & Tourism (www.visitnh.gov)

Rhode Island Tourism Division (www.visitrhodeisland.com)

Vermont Division of Tourism (www.vermontvacation.com)

Visas

Citizens of many countries are eligible for the Visa Waiver Program, which requires prior approval via Electronic System for Travel Authorization (ESTA).

Electronic System for Travel Authorization

Since January 2009 the US has had the Electronic System for Travel Authorization (ESTA), a system that was implemented to mitigate security risks concerning those who travel to the US by air or sea (travelers entering by land, such as via Canada, do not need to file an ESTA application). This pre-authorization system applies to citizens of approximately three dozen countries that fall under the Visa Waiver Program.

This process requires that you register specific information online, prior to entering the US. Information required

includes details such as your name, current address and passport information, including the number and expiration date, and details about any communicable diseases you may carry (including HIV). It is recommended that you fill out the online form as early as possible, and at least 72 hours prior to departure.

You will receive one of three responses:

➡ 'Authorization Approved' usually comes within minutes; most applicants can expect to receive this response.

➡ 'Authorization Pending' means you should go back online to check the status within roughly 72 hours.

➡ 'Travel not Authorized' indicates that your application is not approved and you will need to apply for a visa.

Once approved, registration is valid for two years, but note that if you renew your passport or change your name, you will need to re-register. The cost is $14. The entire process is stored electronically and linked to your passport, but it is recommended that you bring a printout of the ESTA approval just to be safe. If you don't have access to the internet, a travel agent can apply on your behalf.

Visa Applications

Citizens of non-Visa Waiver Program countries must generally apply for a non-immigrant visa using Form DS-160 (ceac.state.gov/genniv), pay a nonrefundable application fee ($160) and schedule an interview at a US embassy or consulate.

Transportation

GETTING THERE & AWAY

While the two most common ways to reach New England are by air and car, you can also get here easily by train and bus. Boston is the region's hub for air travel, but some international travelers fly into New York City to do some sightseeing before heading up to New England.

Entering the Country/Region

If you're flying to the US, the first airport that you land in is where you must go through immigration and customs, even if you're flying to another destination. Upon arrival, all international visitors must register with the Department of Homeland Security's Office of Biometric Identity Management program, which entails having your fingerprints scanned and a digital photo taken.

Once you go through immigration, you collect your baggage and pass through customs. If you have nothing to declare, you'll probably clear customs without a baggage search, but don't assume this. If you're continuing on the same plane or connecting to another flight, your checked baggage must be rechecked. There are usually airline representatives just outside the customs area who can help you.

If you're a single parent, grandparent or guardian traveling with anyone under 18 years of age, carry proof of legal custody or a notarized letter from the non-accompanying parent(s) authorizing the trip. This isn't required, but the USA is concerned with thwarting child abduction, and not having authorizing papers could cause delays or even result in being denied admittance to the country.

Passport

No particular passport (or stamps in your passport) will automatically disqualify you from entry into the US, but many countries – including Iran, Libya, Somalia, Syria, Yemen, North Korea, Venezuela, Chad, Iraq and Sudan – are 'red flags' which may invite greater scrutiny and interrogation by immigration officials. Note that immigration officials reserve the right to grant or deny admission into the USA, so there is no guarantee until you have actually crossed the border.

Air

Because of New England's location on the densely populated US Atlantic seaboard between New York and eastern Canada, air travelers have a number of ways to approach the region.

Airports & Airlines

The major gateway to the region is Boston's **Logan International Airport** (BOS; ☏800-235-6426; www.massport.com/logan), which offers many direct, nonstop flights from major airports in the US and abroad.

Depending on where you will be doing the bulk of your exploring, several other airports in the region receive national and international flights. It's also feasible to fly into one of New York City's major airports.

Bangor International Airport (☏866-359-2264; www.flybangor.com; 287 Godfrey Blvd) Bangor International Airport in Maine is served by regional carriers associated with American Airlines, Delta and United.

Bradley International Airport (BDL; ☏860-292-2000; www.bradleyairport.com; Schoephoester Rd, Windsor Locks) New England's second largest airport, 12 miles north of Hartford, CT, in Windsor Locks (I-91 exit 40), is served by American Airlines, Delta, JetBlue, Southwest Airlines and United.

DEPARTURE TAX

Departure tax is included in the ticket price for all flights leaving the United States.

CLIMATE CHANGE & TRAVEL

Every form of transport that relies on carbon-based fuel generates CO_2, the main cause of human-induced climate change. Modern travel is dependent on airplanes, which might use less fuel per mile per person than most cars but travel much greater distances. The altitude at which aircraft emit gases (including CO_2) and particles also contributes to their climate change impact. Many websites offer 'carbon calculators' that allow people to estimate the carbon emissions generated by their journey and, for those who wish to do so, to offset the impact of the greenhouse gases emitted with contributions to portfolios of climate-friendly initiatives throughout the world. Lonely Planet offsets the carbon footprint of all staff and author travel.

Burlington International Airport (BTV; ☑802-863-2874; www.btv.aero; 1200 Airport Dr, South Burlington) Vermont's major airport.

Green Airport (☑888-268-7222; www.pvdairport.com; 2000 Post Rd, Warwick) Located 20 minutes south of Providence, RI.

Manchester-Boston Regional Airport (☑603-624-6556; www.flymanchester.com; 1 Airport Rd; 🛜) A quiet alternative to Logan, Manchester Airport is just 55 miles north of Boston in New Hampshire.

Portland International Jetport (PWM; ☑207-874-8877; www.portlandjetport.org; 1001 Westbrook St) Serves coastal Maine.

Worcester Regional Airport (ORH; www.massport.com; 375 Airport Dr) Serves central Massachusetts.

Land

Border Crossings

Sharing a border with Canada, Vermont has 15 places to cross, while New Hampshire has one and Maine has 25. Generally, crossing the US–Canadian border is straightforward, though the length of the lines can be a hassle at main crossings. American and Canadian citizens entering the USA from Canada must present a valid passport, enhanced driver's license or trusted traveler card (NEXUS, FAST or SENTRI); citizens of all other countries are required to carry passports.

Bus

You can get to New England by bus from all parts of the US and Canada, but the trip will be long and may not be much less expensive than a discounted flight. Bus companies usually offer special promotional fares.

Greyhound (www.greyhound.com) The national bus line, serving all major cities in the USA.

Peter Pan Bus (www.peterpanbus.com) Regional bus company serving over 50 destinations in Massachusetts, Connecticut and Rhode Island, with connections as far south as Washington, DC.

Several other bus companies offer service from New York City to New England, including Go Bus (www.gobuses.com), Lucky Star Bus (www.luckystarbus.com), Megabus (www.megabus.com) and Dartmouth Coach (www.dartmouthcoach.com).

Car & Motorcycle

Interstate highways crisscross New England and offer forest, farm and mountain scenery, once you are clear of urban areas and the I-95 corridor between Boston and New York. These interstate highways connect the region to New York; Washington, DC; Montréal; and points west. Major interstate highways in New England include the following:

I-95 along the Atlantic seaboard from New York City through Providence, Boston and Portland to the Canadian border.

I-91 up the Connecticut River valley from New Haven through Hartford and central Massachusetts, then along the Vermont–New Hampshire line to Canada.

I-90 (Mass Pike) spanning Massachusetts east–west from Albany, NY, to Boston.

I-89 northwest from Concord, NH, through New Hampshire and Vermont to the Canadian border (near Montréal).

I-93 north from Boston through New Hampshire into Vermont.

Hitchhiking

Hitchhiking is never entirely safe, and we don't recommend it. Travelers who hitchhike should understand that they are taking a small but potentially serious risk.

Crossing the US–Canadian border can be a challenge for hitchhikers. Most drivers will not want to take the risk or endure the hassle of transporting a stranger across the border. It is possible to cross the border on foot, although border guards are likely to be suspicious: expect extensive interrogation. Non-US citizens will likely be asked to prove their means (ie access to money) and plan to exit the country (ie return ticket).

Hitchhiking is legal in all six New England states, as well as in neighboring New York, as long as you stay off the traveled part of the road or on the shoulder. On interstate highways, hitchhiking is restricted to on-ramps.

According to Hitchwiki (www.hitchwiki.org), all six states rank as 'easy' on the Ease of Hitchhiking map, with Vermont cited as the easiest place to thumb a ride in the entire country.

Train

Amtrak (www.amtrak.com) is the main rail passenger service in the US. Services along the Northeast Corridor (connecting Boston, Providence, RI, and New Haven, CT, with New York and Washington, DC) are some of the most frequent in Amtrak's system, running several times daily in each direction. Amtrak's high-speed *Acela Express* makes the trip from New York City to Boston in 3¾ hours.

Amtrak also offers the following once-daily services to New England:

➡ The *Ethan Allen Express* travels from New York City north to Rutland, VT (5½ hours), via Albany, NY.

➡ The *Vermonter* runs north to St Albans, VT, from Washington, DC (12¾ hours), and New York City (9¼ hours), passing en route through New Haven and Hartford, CT, Springfield and Amherst, MA, and several towns in Vermont.

➡ The *Lake Shore Limited* runs from Chicago to Boston (22 hours), passing through Cleveland, OH, Buffalo, NY, and Albany, NY, then continuing east through Massachusetts, with stops in Pittsfield, Springfield and Worcester.

Connecticut is also served by commuter trains from New York City, operated by Metro-North (www.mta.info) and Shore Line East (www.shorelineeast.com).

Sea

Seastreak (www.seastreak.com) High-speed weekend ferry service from New York City to Martha's Vineyard (5¼ hours)

and Nantucket (6½ hours) between late May and early September.

Bridgeport & Port Jefferson Steamboat Company (✆ in Connecticut 888-443-3779, in Long Island 631-473-0286; www.88844ferry.com; 1 Ferry Access Rd, Bridgeport) Year-round ferry from Port Jefferson (Long Island), NY, to Bridgeport, CT (1¼ hours).

Cross Sound Ferry (✆860-443-5281; www.longislandferry.com; 2 Ferry St) Year-round car ferry (80 minutes) and seasonal high-speed passenger ferry (40 minutes) from Orient Point (Long Island), NY, to New London, CT.

Fishers Island Ferry (✆860-442-0165; www.fiferry.com; 5 Waterfront Park; adult/senior & child/car mid-May–mid-Sep $25/18/58, mid-Sep–mid-May $19/14/40) Year-round ferry between Fishers Island, NY, and New London, CT (45 minutes).

Bay Ferries (✆877-762-7245; www.ferries.ca/thecat; Ocean Gateway Pier; ☺mid-Jun–Sep) Operates the summertime CAT service, sailing daily between Portland, ME, and Yarmouth, Nova Scotia (5½ hours).

Lake Champlain Ferries (✆802-864-9804; www.ferries.com; King St Dock) Runs three routes across Lake Champlain between Vermont and New York state (15 minutes to one hour).

Fort Ti Ferry (www.forttiferry.com) Makes regular crossings from Shoreham, VT, to Ticonderoga Landing, NY (seven minutes), between May and October.

GETTING AROUND

Simply put, the best way to get around New England is by car. The region is relatively small, the highways are good and public transportation is not as frequent or as widespread as it could be.

Bus Regional bus lines connect bigger towns throughout New England. While less comfortable and scenic than trains, buses

serve more destinations and are almost always the most economical form of public transportation.

Car The most convenient option for seeing rural New England, exploring small towns and partaking of outdoor adventure. Driving and parking can be a challenge in Boston.

Train Amtrak's main line travels up and down the Northeast Corridor, connecting Boston to Portland, ME, Providence, RI, New Haven, CT, and other coastal destinations. Two other inland routes serve Connecticut, Massachusetts and Vermont.

Air

Flying can be an efficient way to reach the islands and other more distant corners of New England. Flights are short, airplanes are small, and weather is a critical factor in the safety and reliability of flights. Buy tickets directly from the airlines for the cheapest fares.

Airlines in New England

Regional and commuter airlines connect New England's cities and resorts with Boston and New York City.

There are several regional airlines, especially serving Cape Cod and the islands:

Cape Air (www.flycapeair.com) Flights to several New England destinations, including Cape Cod, Martha's Vineyard, Nantucket, Bar Harbor, ME, Lebanon, NH, and Rutland, VT.

Nantucket Air (www.nantucketairlines.com) Flights between Nantucket and Hyannis, MA.

New England Airlines (www.block-island.com/nea) Very short flights to Block Island from mainland Rhode Island.

Bicycle

Cycling is a popular New England sport and means of transportation on both city streets and country roads.

Several of the larger cities have systems of bike paths that make bike travel easier and more pleasant. Disused railroad rights-of-way have also been turned into bike trails that are perfect for bicycle touring (p41).

Several cities have low-cost bike-share programs, including New Haven and Mystic, CT, Portland, ME, Burlington, VT, and Boston. Bicycle rentals are also available in most New England cities, towns and resorts at reasonable prices (typically $20 to $35 per day).

Boat

Regular ferries serve islands and other destinations up and down New England's Atlantic shoreline.

Bay State Cruise Company (617-748-1428; www.baystatecruisecompany.com; Commonwealth Pier, Seaport Blvd; round-trip adult/child from $89/66; SL1, SL2, South Station) Boston to Provincetown, MA.

Block Island Express (860-444-4624; www.goblockisland.com; 2 Ferry St; adult/child/bike $26/13/10; May-Sep) From New London, CT, to Block Island, RI.

Block Island Ferry (401-783-7996; www.blockislandferry.com) From Newport and Point Judith, RI.

Falmouth–Edgartown Ferry (www.falmouthedgartownferry.com) Shuttles between Falmouth, MA (Cape Cod), and Edgartown (Martha's Vineyard).

Hy-Line Cruises (www.hylinecruises.com) From Hyannis, MA, to Nantucket and Martha's Vineyard.

Island Queen (www.islandqueen.com) Between Falmouth, MA (Cape Cod), and Oak Bluffs (Martha's Vineyard).

Maine State Ferry Service (www.maine.gov/mdot/ferry) Runs ferries around Penobscot Bay from terminals at Rockland, Bass Harbor and Lincolnville, ME.

Provincetown Ferry (Map p52; 617-227-4320; www.bostonharborcruises.com/water-taxi; 1 Long Wharf; water taxi one-way adult/child $15/3, Provincetown round-trip adult/child $93/68, Salem round-trip adult/child $45/35; taxi 6:30am-10pm Mon-Sat, to 8pm Sun; Aquarium) From Boston.

Salem Ferry (Map p52; 617-227-4320; www.bostonharborcruises.com/water-taxi; 1 Long Wharf; water taxi one-way adult/child $15/3, Provincetown round-trip adult/child $93/68, Salem round-trip adult/child $45/35; taxi 6:30am-10pm Mon-Sat, to 8pm Sun; Aquarium) From Boston.

Seastreak (www.seastreak.com) Operates from New Bedford, MA, to Martha's Vineyard and Nantucket.

Steamship Authority (www.steamshipauthority.com) Hyannis, MA, to Nantucket; Woods Hole, MA, to Martha's Vineyard.

Bus

Buses go to more places and generally cost less than airplanes or trains, but the routes still bypass some prime destinations, especially in rural areas.

America's national bus company, **Greyhound** (www.greyhound.com), together with regional carrier **Peter Pan** (www.peterpanbus.com), provides service within New England. Other regional bus companies that ply routes within New England include the following:

Concord Coach Lines (www.concordcoachlines.com) Service from Boston to New Hampshire (Concord, Manchester, Plymouth, Littleton, Conway and Berlin) and Maine (Portland, Mid-Coast, Bangor, Augusta, Lewiston and Auburn).

C&J Trailways (www.ridecj.com) Provides daily service between Boston and Newburyport, MA, as well as Portsmouth and Dover, NH.

Dartmouth Coach (www.dartmouthcoach.com) Servicing Hanover, Lebanon and New London, NH, from Boston.

Plymouth & Brockton Street Railway Co (www.p-b.com) Provides frequent bus service to the South Shore and to most towns on Cape Cod, including Hyannis and Provincetown.

Car & Motorcycle

Yes, driving is really the best way to see New England. But heads-up: around Boston and other urban areas, traffic jams are common, and drivers can be aggressive, speedy and unpredictable. Outside the cities, driving is a lot more serene, though twisty mountain roads and coastal traffic jams can make the going slower than you might expect.

Municipalities control parking by signs on the street, stating explicitly where you may or may not park. A yellow line or yellow-painted curb means that no parking is allowed there.

Automobile Associations

The American Automobile Association (www.aaa.com) provides members with maps and other information. Members get discounts on car rentals, air tickets, hotels and attractions, as well as emergency road service and towing. The AAA has reciprocal agreements with automobile associations in other countries. Bring your membership card from your country of origin.

Driver's License

An International Driving Permit (IDP), obtained before you leave home, is only necessary if your regular license is not in English.

Fuel

Gas stations are ubiquitous and many are open 24 hours a day. Small-town stations may be open only from 7am to 8pm or 9pm. Gas prices in New England ranged between

$2.25 and $2.55 per US gallon at the time of research.

At some stations, you must pay before you pump; at others, you may pump before you pay. More modern pumps have credit-/debit-card terminals built into them, so you can pay with plastic right at the pump. At 'full service' stations, an attendant will pump your gas for you; no tip is expected.

Car Rental

Rental cars are readily available. With advance reservations for a small car, the daily rate with unlimited mileage starts around $50, while typical weekly rates run $200 and up. Rates for mid-size cars are often only a tad higher. Dropping off the car at a different location from where you picked it up usually incurs an additional fee. It always pays to shop around between rental companies on sites such as www.kayak. com and www.expedia.com.

Having a major credit card greatly simplifies the rental process. Without one, some agencies simply will not rent vehicles, while others require prepayment, a deposit higher than the cost of your rental, pay stubs, proof of round-trip airfare and more.

The following companies operate in New England:

Alamo (www.alamo.com)

Avis (www.avis.com)

Budget (www.budget.com)

Dollar (www.dollar.com)

Enterprise (www.enterprise.com)

Hertz (www.hertz.com)

National (www.nationalcar.com)

Rent-A-Wreck (www.rentawreck. com) Rents out cars that may have more wear and tear than your typical rental vehicle, but are actually far from wrecks.

Thrifty (www.thrifty.com)

Insurance

Should you have an accident, liability insurance covers the people and property that you have hit. For damage to the actual rental vehicle, a collision damage waiver (CDW) starts at around $10 a day. If you have collision coverage on your vehicle at home, it might cover damages to car rentals; inquire before departing. Additionally, some credit cards offer reimbursement coverage for collision damages if you rent the car with that credit card; again, check before departing. Most credit-card coverage isn't valid for rentals of more than 15 days or for 'exotic' models, such as 4WD Jeeps and vans.

Road Conditions & Hazards

Roads are very good – even the hard-packed dirt roads that crisscross much of interior northern New England. Some roads across mountain passes in Vermont, New Hampshire and Maine are closed during the winter, but good signage gives you plenty of warning.

Road Rules

Driving laws are different in each of the New England states, but most require the use of safety belts. In every state, children under four years of age must be placed in a child safety seat secured by a seat belt. Most states require motorcycle riders to wear helmets whenever they ride.

The maximum speed limit on New England interstate highways ranges from 55mph to 70mph. On undivided highways, the limit varies from 30mph to 55mph. Police enforce speed limits by patrolling in police cruisers and in unmarked cars. Fines start around $50 and can increase to several hundred dollars, depending on the severity of the infraction.

Local Transportation

City buses and the T (Boston's subway/underground system) provide useful transportation within the larger cities and to some suburbs. Resort areas also tend to have regional bus lines.

Taxis and Uber are common in the largest cities, but in smaller cities and towns you will probably have to telephone a cab to pick you up. Shuttles may take travelers from their hotel to the airport.

Train

Rail service in New England is generally more limited and expensive than bus service, but you'll find dependable commuter trains along the region's urban coastal corridor, along with a few scenic routes in more rural areas. Amtrak's *Downeaster* (www.amtrakdowneaster. com) runs from Boston's North Station to Brunswick, ME, via Exeter, Portland, Freeport and other stops in New Hampshire and Maine. Amtrak's *Northeast Regional* (www.amtrak.com/northeast-regional-train), *Lakeshore Limited* (www. amtrak.com/lake-shore-limited-train) and *Vermonter* (www.amtrak.com/vermonter-train) serve several other destinations in Massachusetts, Rhode Island, Connecticut and Vermont.

Other regional train services:

Shore Line East (www.shore lineeast.com) Service between New Haven and New London on Connecticut's Long Island Sound.

MBTA Commuter Rail (www. mbta.com) Boston's commuter rail travels west to Concord, Lowell and Worcester, north to Salem, Rockport, Gloucester and Newburyport, and south to Plymouth and Providence.

Behind the Scenes

SEND US YOUR FEEDBACK

We love to hear from travelers – your comments keep us on our toes and help make our books better. Our well-traveled team reads every word on what you loved or loathed about this book. Although we cannot reply individually to your submissions, we always guarantee that your feedback goes straight to the appropriate authors, in time for the next edition. Each person who sends us information is thanked in the next edition.

Visit **lonelyplanet.com/contact** to submit your updates and suggestions or to ask for help. Our award-winning website also features inspirational travel stories and news.

Note: We may edit, reproduce and incorporate your comments in Lonely Planet products such as guidebooks, websites and digital products, so let us know if you are happy to have your name acknowledged. For a copy of our privacy policy visit lonelyplanet.com/legal.

WRITER THANKS

Benedict Walker

A special thanks to Cheryl Cowie and Keri Berthelot for their guidance, support and Reiki II's on the road. As always, to Trish Walker for countless hours in the prayer chair, and a big shout-out to family; Andy, Sally and P for making sure I didn't overdo the lobster! In memory of Kevin Hennessy, Ainsley Crabbe and Ben Carey, my fellow adventurers who passed away in other lands while I was researching this title. A little part of you remains in Rhode Island for me, always. You'll like it there!

Isabel Albiston

Thanks to everyone in Massachusetts who answered my questions so patiently and treated me so kindly, especially to all the museum guides who showed me around along the way. Thanks also to Leah, Julie and Andrea for your warm hospitality and to Trisha for commissioning me for such a great project. Lastly, huge thanks to Ellie, Alan and Liz for traveling out to join me at the end of my trip.

Amy C Balfour

Thank you Amy Scannell and Michael Billings for your hospitality and NH expertise. Eleanor Barnes and Whit Andrews, endless gratitude for climbing

THIS BOOK

This 10th edition of Lonely Planet's *New England* guidebook was researched and written by Benedict Walker, Isabel Albiston, Amy C Balfour, Robert Balkovich, Gregor Clark, Adam Karlin, Brian Kluepfel, Regis St Louis and Mara Vorhees. The previous edition was also written by this team if writers. This guidebook was produced by the following:

Destination Editor Trisha Ping

Senior Product Editors Martine Power, Kirsten Rawlings, Vicky Smith

Regional Senior Cartographers Mark Griffiths, Alison Lyall

Product Editors Carolyn Boicos, Katie Connolly

Book Designers Gwen Cotter, Mazzy Prinsep

Cartographer Rachel Imeson

Assisting Editors Imogen Bannister, Michelle Bennett, Nigel Chin, Samantha Cook, Lucy Cowie, Michelle Coxall, Peter Cruttenden, Carly Hall, Clare Healy, Kellie Langdon, Kristin Odijk, Mani Ramaswamy, Monica Woods

Cover Researcher Brendan Dempsey-Spencer

Thanks to Bruce Evans, Jay Farihi, Evan Godt, Shona Gray, David Grumett, Donna Harshman, Karen Henderson, Andi Jones, Sonia Kapoor, Brigitte Mortier, Claire Naylor, Angela Tinson, Gillian Weale

Mt Washington with me. Peaches and Genienne Hockensmith, thanks for sharing the best of Keene! Cheers to the crew atop New England at Mt Washington Observatory: Adam, Ian, Brian, Zach, Tessa, Bruce and Priscilla. Your passion for weather and your regional recs are much appreciated. Thanks for key assistance Lynn Neumann and Randy Propster. Duby Thompson, thanks for lunch in Littleton!

Robert Balkovich

Thank you to my family – my mother, father and sister – and friends for their love and support. Special thanks to Michael, Raghnild, Elizabeth and Ming for their hospitality and wealth of tips, and to Matthew for your friendship on the road. And thank you to Trisha Ping for this opportunity, and many others.

Gregor Clark

Thanks to the many fellow Vermonters who shared their favorite spots in the Green Mountain State with me this edition – especially Shawn O'Neil, Margo Whitcomb, Victoria St John, Jim Lockridge and Joy Cohen – and to Gaen, Meigan and Chloe for a lifetime of companionship on our family adventures in this gorgeous place we call home.

Adam Karlin

Thanks to: Trisha Ping for letting me poke around the Pine Tree State, the Barclays for hosting us, friends and family and kind strangers met along the way, and Rachel and Sanda, my two favorite partners for climbing up rocks and swimming in the cold ocean.

Brian Kluepfel

First and always, to my wife Paula, my co-pilot in life. Secondly, to all my kinfolk who helped on this journey: June and Alan Kluepfel (formerly

of Noank), Neil Kluepfel and his wife Irene Koenig of Stonington, and Jim and Eileen Flynn of Mystic. Thirdly (and crucially), to Trisha Ping at Lonely Planet who gave me such a delightful assignment.

Regis St Louis

I am grateful to countless innkeepers, park rangers, baristas, shop owners and folks 'from away' who provided shared Maine insight. Special thanks to Brother Arnold for a fabulous meal at Sabbathday Shaker Village, Scott Cowger for the tips and barn tour in Hallowell, Jack Burke and Julie Van De Graaf for their kindness in Castine, and Gregor Clark and Diane Plauche for general Maine suggestions. Special thanks to my family, who make coming home the best part of travel.

Mara Vorhees

To the server at a Gloucester restaurant, who recommended that I spend my afternoon at a certain delightful beach (which is not in this book). Thanks for sharing your secret spot. I won't tell.

ACKNOWLEDGEMENTS

Climate map data adapted from Peel MC, Finlayson BL & McMahon TA (2007) 'Updated World Map of the Köppen-Geiger Climate Classification', *Hydrology and Earth System Sciences*, 11, 1633–44.

Cover photograph: Lobster buoys in autumn, Maine (p364); Leena Robinson/ Shutterstock ©

Index

A

Acadia National Park 19, 397-400, **399**, **6-7**
accessible travel 426
accommodations 26-7, *see also individual locations*
activities 28-31, 40-3, *see also individual activities*
resources 42
safety 429
Adams, John 124
Adams, John Quincy 124
African American history 173, 415
air travel
to/from New England 431-2
within New England 433
Alcott, Bronson 105
Alcott, Louisa May 106
American Independence Festival 325
American Revolution 410-11
Amherst 190-1
amusement parks
Santa's Village 362
Story Land 357
Whale's Tale Waterpark 347, 349
antiques 145, 182
Appalachian Mountains 14-15
Appalachian Trail 15, 41, 207, 403, 404, **4**, **14-15**
aquariums
Echo Leahy Center for Lake Champlain 302
Mystic Aquarium & Institute for Exploration 256-7
New England Aquarium 55
Sea Pocket Aquarium 115
Aquinnah 176-7
Aquinnah cliffs 20, 176-7, **20**
area codes 430
art galleries
Aldrich Contemporary Art Museum 269

Center for Maine Contemporary Art 386
Clark Art Institute 204
Currier Museum of Art 332-3
DeCordova Sculpture Park & Museum 104
Farnsworth Art Museum 386
Florence Griswold Museum 252
Harvard Art Museums 67
Hood Museum of Art 338
HyArts District 138
Hygienic Art 253
Institute of Contemporary Art 59
Isabella Stewart Gardner Museum 65
List Visual Arts Center 70
Martha's Vineyard Glassworks 176
MASS MoCA 205
Mead Art Museum 190
Museum of Fine Arts (Boston) 65
Museum of Fine Arts (Springfield) 184
New Britain Museum of American Art 247
Newport Museum of Art 227
North Adams Art Walk 206
North Shore Arts Association 116
Portland Museum of Art 373
Provincetown Art Association & Museum 154
Punto Urban Art Museum 110
RISD Museum of Art 212
Rocky Neck Art Colony 115
Sculpturedale 274
Smith Art Museum 184
Smith College Museum of Art 187
Southern Vermont Arts Center 286
SoWa Artists Guild 61
St Johnsbury Athenaeum 318-19
Thorne-Sagendorph Art Gallery 337
Underground at Ink Block 61

West Branch Gallery & Sculpture Park 312
Whistler House Museum of Art 108
Williams College Museum of Art 204
Worcester Art Museum 180
Yale Center for British Art 262
Yale University Art Gallery 262
ATMs 428
Augusta 391-2

B

Bangor 390-1
Bantam 272
Bar Harbor 395-7
Bartholomew's Cobble 194
baseball 65
bathrooms 430
Battleship Cove 130
beaches 20
Acadia National Park 397, **6-7**
Block Island 237
Boston 72
Cape Cod National Seashore 150
Chatham 146
Dennis 142
Eastham 149-50
Edgartown 174
Falmouth 135
Gloucester 116
Hammonasset Beach State Park 250
Hampton Beach 330
Hyannis 138
Ipswich 121
Machias Bay 402
Misquamicut 234
Nantucket 168
Narragansett 233
New London 254
Newport 224
Oak Bluffs 172
Ogunquit 369
Old Orchard Beach 372
Orleans 148-9

Plum Island 123
Provincetown 155
Rockport (Massachusetts) 119
Rye 330
Siasconset 167
Stonington (Maine) 394
Truro 153
Wellfleet 151
Yarmouth 141
Beecher-Stowe, Harriet 245-6
beer 13, 188, 271, **13**, *see also breweries*
Belfast 389-90
Ben & Jerry's Ice Cream Factory 315, **36**
Bennington 282-5
Berkshires 45, 178, 193-208, **179**, **195**
accommodations 178
climate 178
food 178
highlights 179, **179**
travel seasons 178
Bethel 402-3
Bethlehem 353
bicycling, *see* cycling
Biddeford 372
bird-watching
Barn Island Wildlife Management Area 259
Eagle Landing State Park 250
Felix Neck Wildlife Sanctuary 174
Grafton Notch State Park 403
Grassland Bird Conservation Center 261
Long Point Wildlife Refuge 176
Old Lyme 253
Parker River National Wildlife Refuge 122
VINS Nature Center 290
Wellfleet Bay Wildlife Sanctuary 151
Blackstone River Valley 219-21
Block Island 235-9, **236**
Blue Hill Peninsula 401

blueberries 297
boat travel 433, 434
boat trips 18, 42-3, **18**
 Boston 70-1, 72-3
 Lake Champlain 303-4
 Newport 228-9
 Penobscot Bay 18, **18**
 Plymouth 127
 Portsmouth 327
 Squam Lake 342
 Wolfeboro 344
books
 history 408, 413, 414
 literature 417-20
Boothbay Harbor 382-3
border crossings 432
Boston 44, 48-99, **49**, **52-3**, **57**, **62-3**, **66**, **76**
 accommodations 48, 75-81, **76**
 activities 70-2
 Back Bay 61, 64-5, 80, 85-6, 95, **62-3**
 Beacon Hill 50-1, 75, 81, 87-8, 93, **52-3**
 Boston Common 50-1, 75, 81, 87-8, 93, **52-3**
 Boston Harbor Islands 69-70
 Cambridge 65-9, 80-1, 87, 89, 95-6, **66**
 Charlestown 58-9, 78
 Chinatown 61, 79-80, 84-5, 88-9, 94-5, **62-3**
 children, travel with 50
 climate 48
 Downtown 51, 54-6, 75, 78, 81-2, 88, 93-4, **52-3**
 drinking & nightlife 87-9
 emergency services 96
 entertainment 89-93
 Fenway 65, 80, 86-7, 89, **62-3**
 festivals & events 74-5
 food 48, 81-7
 highlights 49, **49**
 history 50
 internet access 96
 internet resources 96
 Kenmore Square 65, 80, 86-7, 89, **62-3**
 LGBTIQ+ 73
 medical services 96
 North End 56, 58, 78, 82-3, 94
 Seaport District 59-60, 79, 83-4, 88, 94
 shopping 93-6
 sights 50-70
 South Boston 59-60, 79, 83-4, 88, 94
 South End 61, 79-80, 84-5, 88-9, 94-5, **62-3**
 tourist offices 96

tours 72-4
travel seasons 48
travel to/from 96-7
travel within 97-9
walks 57, 74, **57**
Waterfront 51, 54-6, 75, 78, 81-2, 88, 93-4, **52-3**
West End 56-8, 78, 82-3, 94
Boston Calling 28
Boston Light 70
Boston Red Sox 92
Boston Symphony Orchestra 91
bowling 72, 111
Brattleboro 278-81, **279**
Bread & Puppet 21, 318
Breakers, the 224, **17**
Bretton Woods 358-60
breweries
 Abandoned Building Brewery 189
 Alchemist Brewery 311
 Cisco Brewers 168
 Fort Hill Brewery 189
 Hill Farmstead Brewery 318
 Magic Hat Brewery 301-2
 Monhegan Brewing Company 385
 New City Brewery 189
 Tree House Brewing Company 183
Brewster 144-5
Brimfield Antique Show 182
Bristol 221-2
Brooklin 401
Brown University 213, 421, **39**
Browningtown 306
Brunswick 380-2
budget 25, 26, 427
Burlington 301-10, **302**
bus travel
 to/from New England 432
 within New England 434
business hours 25, 428

C

cable cars 351
Cadillac Mountain 19, 398, **19**
Camden 387-8
camping 26, 27
Candlewood Lake 270
Cannon Mountain 351, 352
canoeing, see kayaking & canoeing
Canterbury Shaker Village 331
Cape Cod 44, 132, 133, 134-60, **133**, **136-7**
Cape Cod National Seashore 20, 150, **20**
Cape Cod Potato Chip Factory 140
Cape Cod Rail Trail 142

car travel 429, 432, 434-5
casinos 186
Castine 401
castles
 Castle in the Clouds 341
 Gillette Castle 250
cell phones 24
cemeteries
 Copp's Hill Burying Ground 56
 Edson Cemetery 109
 Forest Hills 60
 Granary Burying Ground 51
 Grove Street Cemetery 262
 Hancock Cemetery 125
 Hope Cemetery 317
 King's Chapel & Burying Ground 56
 Mt Auburn Cemetery 67
 Tyler Point Cemetery 221
 West Cemetery 190
central Massachusetts 45, 178, 180-3, **179**
 accommodations 178
 climate 178
 food 178
 highlights 179, **179**
 travel seasons 178
Chappaquiddick 174
Chatham 146-8
cheese 282, 286
Chester 251
Chester-Hadlyme Ferry 251
children, travel with 27, 50, 60, 426
Chilmark 172
churches
 First Congregational Church 163
 King's Chapel & Burying Ground 56
 Old First Church 283
 Old North Church 56
 Park St Church 57
 Seamen's Bethel 130
 Trinity Church (Boston) 61, 64
 Trinity Church (Newport) 228
Citgo Sign 65
Cliff Walk 17, 229
climate 24, 28, 30, 31, see also individual regions
climbing 355
colleges & universities 22, 421-4
 Amherst College 190
 Berklee College of Music 424
 Boston College 423
 Boston University 423
 Bowdoin College 380
 Brown University 213, 421, **39**

Dartmouth College 338, 421-2
Emerson College 424
Harvard University 22, 67, 422, **4**, **22**, **407**
Massachusetts College of Art and Design 424
Massachusetts Institute of Technology 70, 423
Middlebury College 423
Mount Holyoke College 22, 188, **22**
Rhode Island School of Design 213, 423, 424
Smith College 187
Williams College 204
Yale University 22, 261-2, 421, **22**
Conanicut Island 232-3
Concord (Massachusetts) 104-8, **106**
Concord (New Hampshire) 331-2
Connecticut 45, 240-75, **242-3**
 accommodations 240
 climate 240
 food 240
 highlights 242-3, **242-3**
 history 241
 travel seasons 240
Connecticut Beer Trail 271
Connecticut River Valley 249-53, **249**
Connecticut Wine Trail 271
Cornwall 274
costs 25, 26, 427
covered bridges 274, **11**
COVID-19 5, 429
craft beer 13, **13**, see also beer, breweries
Cranberry Isles 400-1
Crawford Notch 358-60
credit cards 428
cruises, see boat trips
currency 24
Cutler Coast Public Lands 401-2
cycling 41-2, 433-4, see also mountain biking
 Blackstone River Bikeway 220
 Boston 71
 Brattleboro 279
 Burlington 304
 Cape Cod Rail Trail 142
 Falmouth 136
 Grafton 286
 Minuteman Bikeway 71
 Minuteman Commuter Bikeway 103
 Northampton 187-8
 Woodstock 290

D

Damariscotta 383-4
dangers, see safety
Dartmouth College 338, 421-2
Deer Isle 394-5
Deerfield 193
Dennis 142-4
Dickinson, Emily 190
disabilities, travelers with 426
distilleries 153, 168, 272
diving 344
Dog Mountain 319
Dogtown 117
Dorset 289
Dr Seuss 184, 185
driving 429, 432, 434-5

E

eagles 250, 290, 342, 397
East Bay 221-3
East Haddam 249-50
Eastham 149-51
Echo Lake 398
economy 416
Edgartown 174-5
electricity 427
Elms, the 224
Emerald Necklace 59
emergencies 25
Emerson, Ralph Waldo 106-7, 417
Essex (Connecticut) 251-2
Essex (Massachusetts) 120-2
events 28-31, see also individual events
exchange rates 25, 428
Exeter 325

F

fall foliage 10-11, 31, 294, 10, 11, 15
Falmouth 135-8
farmers markets
  Belfast 389
  Boston 94, 95
  Brattleboro 279
  Bristol 221
  Burlington 309
  Chester 251
  West Tisbury 175, 176
farms 13, 13
  Allenholm Orchards 308
  Appleton Farms 121
  Billings Farm & Museum 290
  Champlain Orchards 296
  Coogan Farm 255-6
  Grace Farms 269
  Hyland Orchard 182
  Intervale Center 301
  Merck Forest & Farmland Center 287
  Mount Hope Farm 221
  Retreat Farm 279
  Robb Family Farm 279
  Shelburne Farms 301
  Sugarbush Farm 290
  University of Vermont Morgan Horse Farm 296
  Watson Farm 232
  Windy Hill Farm 194
  Woodstock Orchards 261
fat biking 41-2, see also cycling, mountain biking
Fenway Park 65
ferry travel 251, 433, 434
festivals 21, 28-31, 21, see also individual festivals
  music 21, 28, 30, 201, 228
fishing 238, 274
food 12-13, 427, see also individual locations
  cheese 282, 286
  costs 427
  flatbreads 298
  jam 394
  lobster 12, 30, 258, 368, 387, 2, 12-13
Fort Adams State Park 225
forts 69, 392
Franconia 353-4
Franconia Notch State Park 15, 351-2, 15
Freedom Trail 17, 57, 74, 57, 2, 17
Freeport 382
Frost, Robert 283, 353

G

galleries, see art galleries
gardens, see parks & gardens
Gardiner 392
Gay Head Cliffs 20, 176-7, 20
gay travelers, see LGBTIQ+ travelers
Geisel, Theodor Seuss 184, 185
Georges Island 69
Gilford 345
Gillette Castle 250
Glass Float Project 238
Glass House 269
Glen 357-8
gliding 299
Gloucester 115-19
Gold Coast 267-70
Gorey, Edward 141-2
Gorham 362-3
Grafton 286, 294

graveyards, see cemeteries
Great Barrington 194-6
Great North Woods 361-2
Greenville 405
Griswold, Florence 252

H

Hadley 188
Hallowell 392
Hampton Beach 330-1
Hanover 338-41, 339
Hartford 241-9, 244
Harvard Bridge 422
Harvard Square 22, 95, 22
Harvard University 22, 67, 422, 4, 22, 407
Harvard Yard 67, 407
Harvest on the Harbor 31
Harwich 145-6
health 427
Height of Land 404
hiking 40-1, see also walks
  Acadia National Park 398
  Appalachian Trail 15, 41, 207, 403, 404, 4, 14-15
  Atlantic White Cedar Swamp Trail 151
  Bartholomew's Cobble 194
  Belknap Mountain 345
  Block Island 237
  Boothbay Harbor 383
  Crawford Notch State Park 358
  Dune Shacks Trail 155
  Equinox Preserve 286
  Fort Hill 150
  Franconia Notch State Park 15, 351-2, 15
  Hoosac Range Trail 206
  Lincoln Woods Trail 350
  Long Trail 296
  Lover's Leap State Park 270
  Monument Mountain 194
  Mt Greylock 207
  Mt Monadnock State Park 336
  Northeast Kingdom 319
  Pinkham Notch 360, 36-7
  Rangeley Lake 404
  Stowe 311
  West Rattlesnake Mountain 342
  White Mountains 350
historic buildings & sites
  1667 Jabez Howland House 126
  1677 Harlow Old Fort House 127
  1749 Spooner House 127
  1809 Hedge House 127
  Abbott Hall 110
  Adams National Historic Park 125
  Battle Green 103
  Beauport 115
  Bennington Battlefield Historic Site 283
  Bennington Battle Monument 283
  Breakers, the 224, 17
  Charlestown Navy Yard 59
  Colonial Pemaquid State Historic Site 384-5
  Elms, the 224
  Ethan Allen Homestead 302
  Faneuil Hall 55-6
  Flying Horses Carousel 173
  Frost Place 353
  Hancock-Clarke House 103
  Highfield Hall 135
  Hildene 286
  Historic Deerfield Village 193
  House of the Seven Gables 110
  Kingscote 227
  Longfellow House (Boston) 69
  Longfellow House (Portland) 376
  Lowell National Historic Park 108
  Massachusetts Hall 69
  Mission House 197
  Mount 199
  Munroe Tavern 103
  Nantucket Atheneum 162
  Narrowest House 58
  Old Manse 107
  Old North Bridge 105
  Old South Meeting House 54-5
  Old State House 54, 17
  Orchard House 106
  Paul Revere House 56, 58
  President Calvin Coolidge State Historic Site 306
  Ralph Waldo Emerson Memorial House 106
  Richard Sparrow House 126
  Rosecliff 225, 227
  Rough Point 224
  Salem Maritime National Historic Site 110
  Springfield Armory National Historic Site 184
  Thoreau Farm 107
  Witch House 110-11
historic sites, see historic buildings & sites
history 16-17, 408-16
  20th & 21st century 415-16
  African American history 173, 415
  American Revolution 410-11
  books 408, 413, 414

Boston Tea Party 31, 54-5, 60, 75
colonization 408
independence 410
industrial revolution 220, 412-13
maritime history 412
Native American history 30, 241, 408
Pilgrims 125-6, 409
Puritans 409
race relations 415
slavery 414, 415
Thanksgiving 413, 416
War of Independence 411-12
witch trials 111
hitchhiking 432-3
holidays 428-9
horseback riding 273, 299
hostels 26
hotels 27
Housatonic Valley 270-5
Hyannis 138-41

I
ice skating 214
immigration 431
inns 26-7
insurance
car 435
travel 427
internet access 427
internet resources 25, 78, 81
Ipswich 120-2
Isle au Haut 396
itineraries 32-9, **32**, **34**, **37**, **38**

J
Jackson 357-8
Jaffrey 336-7
Jamaica Pond 59
Jamestown 232-3
John Hancock Tower 65
John Harvard Statue 69
Jordan Pond 398
Jordan Pond House 19

K
Kancamagus Highway 11, 350-1, **11**
kayaking & canoeing
Dennis 143
Hanover 339
Plum Island 123
Portsmouth 327
Rockport (Massachusetts) 119
Keene 337-8
Kennebunks 370-2

Kennedy family sites 58
Kent 273
Kerouac, Jack 420
Killington Mountain 293-5
King, Stephen 391, 418, 420
Kingdom Trails 319, 320
Kingscote 227
Kipling, Rudyard 420
Kittery 372

L
Laconia 345-7
Lake Champlain 23, 303-4, 308
Lake Sunapee 333
Lake Waramaug 271-2
Lake Willoughby 294
Lake Winnipesaukee 23, 340-1, 345, **23**
language 24
leaf-peeping season 10-11, 31, 294, **10**, **11**, **15**
Lee 198-9
legal matters 428
Lenox 199-202
Leverett Peace Pagoda 190
Lexington 103-4
LGBTIQ+ travelers 428
Boston 73
Portland 378
Providence 218
Provincetown 158
libraries
Beinecke Rare Book & Manuscript Library 262
Boston Public Library 61
Camden Public Library 387-8
John F Kennedy Presidential Library & Museum 60
Mary Baker Eddy Library & Mapparium 65
Providence Athenaeum 212
Provincetown Public Library 155
Redwood Athenaeum 224
lighthouses
Beavertail Lighthouse Museum 232
Boston Light 70
Brant Point Light 162
Cape Cod Highland Light 153
Chatham Light 147
Edgartown Lighthouse 174-5
Gay Head Lighthouse 177
Nauset Light 150
North Lighthouse 237
Nubble Light 367
Portland Head Light 373, **32-3**
Rear Range Lighthouse 124

Rockland Breakwater Lighthouse 386
Sankaty Head Light 167
Southeast Light 237
Lincoln 347-50
Litchfield 272-3
Litchfield Hills 15, 271-5, **15**
literature 417-20, see also books
Little Brewster Island 70
Little Compton 223-4
Little Pink House 254
Littleton 353-4
LL Bean 382
lobster 12, 30, 258, 368, 387, **2**, **12-13**
Longfellow, Henry Wadsworth 376
Lost River Gorge & Boulder Caves 347
Louisburg Square 51
Lovells Island 70
Lowell 108-9
Ludlow 284

M
MacDowell Colony 335
Machias Bay 401-2
Machias Seal Island 402
Mad River Glen 294, 298-9
Mad River Valley 298-300
Maine 46, 364-406, **365**, **381**, **394**
accommodations 364
climate 364
food 364
highlights 365, **365**
history 366
travel seasons 364
Maine Lobster Festival 30, 387
Maine Media Workshops 388
Manchester (New Hampshire) 332-4
Manchester (Vermont) 285-9
maple sugaring 285
Marblehead 115
maritime museums
Battleship Cove 130
Cape Cod Maritime Museum 138
Chatham Marconi Maritime Center 147
Custom House Maritime Museum (New London) 254
Custom House Maritime Museum (Newburyport) 122-3
Essex Shipbuilding Museum 121
Herreshoff Marine Museum 222
Maritime Gloucester 115

Moosehead Marine Museum 406
Mystic Seaport Museum 255
Nantucket Whaling Museum 161-2
New Bedford Whaling Museum 130
Penobscot Marine Museum 390
Whydah Pirate Museum 141
markets, see farmers markets
Martha's Vineyard 20, 132, 133, 169-77, **133**, **170**, **20**
Mashpee Wampanoag people 134
Massachusetts Institute of Technology 70, 423
Massachusetts State House 51
Mayflower II 126
medical services 427
memorials, see monuments & memorials
Menemsha 172
Merck Forest & Farmland Center 287
Meredith 341-2
Merrimack Valley 331-4
merry-go-rounds 234, 245
Middlebury 295-8
Minute Man National Historic Park 103
Misquamicut State Beach 234
mobile phones 24
Moby-Dick 130, 131
Mohawk Trail 11, **11**
Monadnock Region 334-8
money 24, 25, 426, 428
Monhegan Island 385-6
Monomoy National Wildlife Refuge 146-7
Montague Bookmill 191
Montpelier 316-18
Monument Mountain 194
monuments & memorials
Boston Massacre Site 54
Bunker Hill Monument 58
New England Holocaust Memorial 55
Pilgrim Monument 155
Plymouth Rock 127
Sacrifice Rock 127
Witch Trials Memorial 111
moose spotting 362
Moosehead Lake 405
motorcycle travel 429, 432, 434-5
Mount Desert Island 395-402, **399**
Mount Holyoke College 22, 188, **22**

mountain biking 41-2, *see also* cycling
Killington Mountain 293
Mt Snow 281
Northeast Kingdom 319-20
Mt Equinox Skyline Drive 287
Mt Greylock State Reservation 207-8
Mt Holyoke 188
Mt Katahdin 405
Mt Mansfield 294, **10**
Mt Monadnock State Park 336
Mt Snow 281
Mt Washington Auto Road 359
Mt Washington Valley 354-63
museums, *see also* art galleries, maritime museums
Abbe Museum 396
Amazing World of Dr Seuss 184
American Independence Museum 325
American Museum of Fly Fishing 286
Beneski Museum of Natural History 190
Bennington Museum 282-3
Berkshire Museum 202
Berkshire Scenic Railway Museum 200
Boothbay Railway Village 382
Boott Cotton Mills Museum 108
Boston Tea Party Ships & Museum 60
Bread & Puppet Museum 21, 318
Brewster Historical Society Museum 144
Buckman Tavern 103
Bunker Hill Museum 58
Cape Ann Museum 116
Cape Cod Museum of Natural History 144
Chatham Railroad Museum 147
Chatham Shark Center 146
Chesterwood 197
Children's Museum 245
Concord Museum 105
Connecticut Industrial Museum 274
Connecticut River Museum 252
Connecticut Science Center 244
Design Museum Boston 56

Discovery Museum & Discovery Woods 105
EcoTarium 180
Edward Gorey House 141-2
Edward M Kennedy Institute for the United States Senate 60
Emily Dickinson Museum 190
Enfield Shaker Museum 339
Eric Carle Museum of Picture Book Art 190
Fairbanks Museum & Planetarium 319
Falmouth Museums on the Green 135-6
French Cable Station Museum 149
Fruitlands Museums 105
Green Briar Nature Center & Jam Kitchen 134
Hammond Castle Museum 116
Hancock Shaker Village 202
Harriet Beecher-Stowe Center 245-6
Harvard Museum of Natural History 68-9
Heritage Museums & Gardens 134
Historic Deerfield Village 193
Ipswich Museum 121
John Brown House Museum 213
John F Kennedy Hyannis Museum 138
John F Kennedy Presidential Library & Museum 60
Maine Discovery Museum 391
Maine State Museum 392
Mark Twain House & Museum 244
Martha's Vineyard Museum 171
Mashpee Wampanoag Museum 134
Mayflower Society Museum 127
MIT Museum 70
Museum of African American History (Boston) 51
Museum of African American History (Nantucket) 163
Museum of Connecticut History 244-5
Museum of Newport History at Brick Market 227
Museum of Science 56
Museum of Springfield History 184

Museums of Old York 367
Naismith Memorial Basketball Hall of Fame 183-4
Nantucket Lightship Basket Museum 163
National Museum of American Illustration 225
New England Quilt Museum 108
Newport Car Museum 224-5
Norman Rockwell Museum 197
Park-McCullough House Museum 283
Peabody Essex Museum 110
Peabody Museum of Archaeology & Ethnology 69
Peabody Museum of Natural History 262, 264
PEZ Visitor Center & Museum 262
Pilgrim Hall Museum 126
Plimoth Grist Mill 126
Plimoth Patuxet Museums 16, 126, **16**
Providence Children's Museum 213
Provincetown Museum 155
Robert Frost Stone House Museum 283
Roseland Cottage 260-1
Russian Icon Exhibit 182
Sandwich Glass Museum 135
Shelburne Museum 301
Shore Line Trolley Museum 262
Springfield Science Museum 184
Strawbery Banke Museum 324-5
Sugar Shack & Norman Rockwell Exhibition 283
University of Vermont Fleming Museum 303
Vermont Ski & Snowboard Museum 311
Wadsworth Atheneum 241, 244, **38-9**
West End Museum 58
Wethersfield Museum at the Keeney Memorial Cultural Center 245
Whitehorne House Museum 228
WHOI Ocean Science Exhibit Center 139
Wilbor House Museum 223
Witch Dungeon Museum 111
music festivals 28, 30, 201, 228
Mystic 255-8, **256**

N
Nantucket 44, 132, 133, 160-8, **133, 162-3**
Nantucket Town 161-7, **164**
Narragansett 233-4
national & state parks, *see also* nature & wildlife reserves
Acadia National Park 19, 397-400, **399, 6-7**
Baxter State Park 404-5
Beartown State Forest 194
Beavertail State Park 232
Burton Island State Park 291
Camden Hills State Park 387
Colt State Park 221
Crawford Notch State Park 358
Eagle Landing State Park 250
Echo Lake State Park 354-5
Ferry Beach State Park 372-3
Fort Adams State Park 225
Franconia Notch State Park 15, 351-2, **15**
Grafton Notch State Park 403
Grand Isle State Park 308
Green Mountain National Forest 296
Halibut Point State Park & Reservation 119
Hammonasset Beach State Park 250
Jamaica State Park 291
Kent Falls State Park 274
Lily Bay State Park 405
Lover's Leap State Park 270
Lowell National Historic Park 108
Marsh-Billings-Rockefeller National Historical Park 290
Milan Hill State Park 361
Miller State Park 334
Minute Man National Historic Park 103
Mount Sunapee State Park 333
Mt Greylock State Reservation 207-8
Mt Monadnock State Park 336
Mt Washington State Park 355
Myles Standish State Forest 126
Nickerson State Park 144
October Mountain State Forest 198
Odiorne Point State Park 330

Seyon Lodge State Park 291
Skinner State Park 188
Squantz Pond State
 Park 270
Underhill State Park 291
Weeks State Park 361-2
White Lake State Park 342
Native American history, 30,
 241, 408
nature & wildlife reserves,
 see also national & state
 parks
Barn Island Wildlife
 Management Area 259
Cape Poge Wildlife
 Refuge 174
Cedar Tree Neck
 Sanctuary 176
Denison Pequotsepos
 Nature Center 256
Dodge Point Preserve 383
Felix Neck Wildlife
 Sanctuary 174
Grassland Bird
 Conservation Center 261
La Verna Preserve 384
Linekin & Burley
 Preserves 382
Long Point Wildlife
 Refuge 176
Maine Wildlife Park 393
Monomoy National Wildlife
 Refuge 146-7
Napatree Point
 Conservation Area 234
Parker River National
 Wildlife Refuge 122
Pleasant Valley Wilderness
 Sanctuary 200
Polly Hill Arboretum 175-6
Stellwagen Bank National
 Marine Sanctuary
 116, 155
VINS Nature Center 290
Wellfleet Bay Wildlife
 Sanctuary 151
New Bedford 130-1
New Britain 247
New Canaan 269
New Hampshire 46,
 322-63, **323**
 accommodations 322
 climate 322
 food 322
 highlights 323, **323**
 history 324
 travel seasons 322
New Haven 261-7, **263**
New London 253-5
Newburyport 122-4
Newfane 280
Newport 223-32, **225, 226**
Newport Folk Festival 30
Newport Jazz Festival 228, **21**
Noank 258

North Adams 205-6
North Conway 354-7, **35**
North Woodstock 347-50
Northampton 187-90
Northeast Kingdom 318-21
Norwalk 268

O
Oak Bluffs 172-4
Ogunquit 369-70, **20**
Okemo Valley 284
Old King's Highway 145
Old Lyme 252-3
Old Orchard Beach 372
opening hours 25, 428
Orleans 148-9

P
parks & gardens
 Arnold Arboretum 56
 Back Bay Fens 65
 Beebe Woods 135
 Boston Common 51
 Bushnell Park 245
 Castle Island & Fort
  Independence 60
 Charles River Esplanade 61
 Connecticut College
  Arboretum 253-4
 Elizabeth Park Rose
  Gardens 244
 Essex Park 251-2
 Franklin Park 59
 Heritage Museums &
  Gardens 134
 Lighthouse Point Park 262
 Lyman Conservatory 187
 Olmsted Park 59
 Prospect Terrace Park
  212-13
 Public Garden (Boston) 51
 Rose Kennedy Greenway
  51, 54
 Waterplace Park 213
 World's End 70
passports 431
Patriots' Day 104
Pawtucket 220
Pawtucket Arts Festival 217
Peacham 306
Pemaquid Point 384-5
Penobscot Bay 18, 380, **18**
Peterborough 334-6
Pilgrims 125-6, 409
Pinkham Notch 36, 360-1,
 36-7
Pioneer Valley 183-93
Pittsfield 202-3
planning
 accommodations 26-7
 activities 40-3
 budgeting 25, 26

calendar of events 28-31
 internet resources 25
 itineraries 32-9, **32, 34,
  37, 38**
 New England basics 24-5
 New England's regions 44-6
 travel seasons 24, 28,
  30, 31
Plimoth Patuxet Museums
 16, 126, **16**
Plum Island 122-3
Plymouth 125-30, **128**
Plymouth Notch 306
Plymouth Rock 127
Point Judith 234
Poland Spring 393
politics 415-16
Pomfret 260, 261
Portland 373-80, **374-5**
Portsmouth 324-30, **326,
 2-3**
postal services 428
Preservation Society of
 Newport County 227
Prospect Mountain 283
Providence 212-19, **214**
Provincetown 154-61, **156**
Prudence Island 222
Prudential Center Skywalk
 Observatory 64-5
public holidays 428-9
puffins 402
Puritans 409

Q
Quechee Gorge 289-90
Quechee Village 289-93
Quiet Corner 260-1
Quincy 124-5

R
rafting 192
Rangeley Lake 23, 403-4
Ray & Maria Stata Center 70
responsible travel 429
Revere 114
Revere, Paul 58
Rhode Island 45, 209-39, **210**
 accommodations 209
 climate 209
 food 209
 highlights 210, **210**
 history 211
 travel seasons 209
Rhode Island School of
 Design 423, 424
Ridgefield 269-70
Rock of Ages Quarries 317
Rockland 386-7
Rockport (Maine) 388-9
Rockport (Massachusetts)
 119-20

Rockwell, Norman 197, 283
Rosecliff 225, 227
Rough Point 224
Rye 330

S
Sabbathday Lake 392-3
Saco Bay 372-3
safety 429
 activities 429
 driving 429, 435
 hitchhiking 432
 weather 429
sailing, see boat trips
Salem 110-15, **112**
Sandwich 134-5
scenic drives
 Acadia National Park 398
 Mt Equinox Skyline
  Drive 287
 Mt Washington Auto
  Road 359
 Rangeley Lakes National
  Scenic Byway 404
 Vermont Rte 100 11, 294
seafood, see lobster
Sears Island 390
Searsport 390
Shaker communities 331, 393
Shelburne Falls 192-3
ships
 Mayflower II 126
 USS Albacore 326
 USS Constitution 58-9, **17**
 USS Massachusetts 130
shopping, see also individual
 locations
 antiques 145, 182
Siasconset 167-8
skating 71
skiing 43, **43**
 Bethel 402
 Bretton Woods 359
 Bromley Mountain 287
 Franconia Notch State
  Park 352
 Grafton 286
 Jackson 357
 Jiminy Peak Mountain
  Resort 203
 Killington Mountain 293
 Loon Mountain 350
 Ludlow 284
 Mad River Glen 298-9
 Middlebury 296
 Mohawk Mountain Ski
  Area 275
 Mt Snow 281
 Mt Sunapee Resort 333
 North Conway 355
 Northeast Kingdom 320
 Prospect Mountain 283

skiing *continued*
Rangeley Lake 404
Smugglers Notch 313
Stowe 312-13
Stratton Mountain 287
Sugarbush 299
Sugarloaf 404
Suicide Six 290
Waterville Valley 347
Wolfeboro 344
Woodstock (Vermont) 290
Skull & Bones Club 264
Slater Mill 220
Smith College 187
smoking 426
Smugglers Notch 310-16
snowboarding 43
Somes Sound 398
South Deerfield 193
South Hadley 188
Spectacle Island 70
Springfield 183-7, **186**
Squam Lake 342-3
state parks, *see* national & state parks
Stellwagen Bank National Marine Sanctuary 116, 155
Stockbridge 197-8
Stonington (Connecticut) 259-60
Stonington (Maine) 394-5
Stowe 310-16, **312**, **11**
Sturbridge 181-3
Sugar Hill 353
surfing 168, 330
swimming 42, 72
synagogues 227

T
Tanglewood Music Festival 201, **21**
telephone services 24, 429-30
Thanksgiving 413, 416
Thoreau, Henry David 107, 108
Thunder Hole 398
time 24, 430

tipping 428
Tiverton 222-3
toilets 430
Tomb, the 264
tourist information 430
Touro Synagogue National Historic Site 227-8
train travel
to/from New England 433
within New England 435
train trips
Mt Washington 358-9
North Conway 355
North Woodstock 349
Weirs Beach 345
travel to/from New England 431-3
travel within New England 25, 433-5
trekking, *see* hiking
trolley tours 74-5
Truro 153-4
Twain, Mark 244

U
universities, *see* colleges & universities
Upper Connecticut River Valley 338-40

V
vacations 429-30
vegetarian & vegan travelers 82
Vermont 45, 276-321, **277**
accommodations 276
climate 276
food 276
highlights 277, **277**
history 278
travel seasons 276
Vermont Rte 100 11, 294
Vineyard Haven 169-72
vineyards
Carolyn's Sakonnet Vineyard 223
Hopkins Vineyard 271
Saltwater Farm Vineyard 259

Sharpe Hill 261
Shelburne Vineyard 301
Snow Farm Winery 308
Stowe Cider 311
Truro 153
White Silo Farm 270
visas 24, 430

W
Wadsworth Atheneum 241, 244, **38-9**
Walden Pond 108
walks, *see also* hiking
Bar Island 396
Boston 57, 74, **57**
Brattleboro 279
Burlington Greenway 303
Cliff Walk 229
Freedom Trail 17, 57, 74, **57**, **2**, **17**
Housatonic River Walk 194
Kennebunks 371
Laconia 345
Litchfield 273
Portland 376
Smugglers Notch Boardwalk 312
Stowe Recreation Path 314
Wolfeboro 344
Yorks, the 368
Walpole 334
Wampanoag people 126
War of Independence 411-12
Watch Hill 234
waterfalls
Bartlett Falls 299
Bash Bish Falls 196
Glacial Potholes 192
Jackson Falls 356
Kent Falls 274
Otter Creek Falls 295
Sabbaday Falls 350
WaterFire 216
Waterville Valley 347
weather 24, 28, 30, 31, 429, *see also* individual regions
websites, *see* internet resources

Weirs Beach 345-6
Wellfleet 151-3
West Tisbury 175-6
Westerly 234-5
Weston 284
Westport 268-9
whale watching 18, **18**
Boston 72
Gloucester 115, 116
Plymouth 128
Provincetown 155, 156
Stellwagen Bank National Marine Sanctuary 18, 116, 155, **18**
White Mountains 15, 346-63, **348**
Wildcat Mountain 361
wildlife reserves, *see* nature & wildlife reserves
Williamstown 203-5, **34-5**
Wilmington 281-2
windjammers 18, **18**
windsurfing 171
wine 271, *see also* vineyards
Winnipesaukee Scenic Railroad 345
Wiscasset 384
witch trials 111
Wolfeboro 343-5
Woods Hole 139
Woodstock (Vermont) 289-93
Woonsocket 219-20
Worcester 180-1

Y
Yale University 22, 261-2, 421, **22**
Yarmouth 141-2
yoga 200
Yorks, the 367-9

Z
zip lining 134, 192
zipriding 361
zoos 59

Map Legend

Sights

- Beach
- Bird Sanctuary
- Buddhist
- Castle/Palace
- Christian
- Confucian
- Hindu
- Islamic
- Jain
- Jewish
- Monument
- Museum/Gallery/Historic Building
- Ruin
- Shinto
- Sikh
- Taoist
- Winery/Vineyard
- Zoo/Wildlife Sanctuary
- Other Sight

Activities, Courses & Tours

- Bodysurfing
- Diving
- Canoeing/Kayaking
- Course/Tour
- Sento Hot Baths/Onsen
- Skiing
- Snorkeling
- Surfing
- Swimming/Pool
- Walking
- Windsurfing
- Other Activity

Sleeping

- Sleeping
- Camping
- Hut/Shelter

Eating

- Eating

Drinking & Nightlife

- Drinking & Nightlife
- Cafe

Entertainment

- Entertainment

Shopping

- Shopping

Information

- Bank
- Embassy/Consulate
- Hospital/Medical
- Internet
- Police
- Post Office
- Telephone
- Toilet
- Tourist Information
- Other Information

Geographic

- Beach
- Gate
- Hut/Shelter
- Lighthouse
- Lookout
- Mountain/Volcano
- Oasis
- Park
- Pass
- Picnic Area
- Waterfall

Population

- Capital (National)
- Capital (State/Province)
- City/Large Town
- Town/Village

Transport

- Airport
- BART station
- Border crossing
- Boston T station
- Bus
- Cable car/Funicular
- Cycling
- Ferry
- Metro/Muni station
- Monorail
- Parking
- Petrol station
- Subway/SkyTrain station
- Taxi
- Train station/Railway
- Tram
- Underground station
- Other Transport

Routes

- Tollway
- Freeway
- Primary
- Secondary
- Tertiary
- Lane
- Unsealed road
- Road under construction
- Plaza/Mall
- Steps
- Tunnel
- Pedestrian overpass
- Walking Tour
- Walking Tour detour
- Path/Walking Trail

Boundaries

- International
- State/Province
- Disputed
- Regional/Suburb
- Marine Park
- Cliff
- Wall

Hydrography

- River, Creek
- Intermittent River
- Canal
- Water
- Dry/Salt/Intermittent Lake
- Reef

Areas

- Airport/Runway
- Beach/Desert
- Cemetery (Christian)
- Cemetery (Other)
- Glacier
- Mudflat
- Park/Forest
- Sight (Building)
- Sportsground
- Swamp/Mangrove

Note: Not all symbols displayed above appear on the maps in this book

Gregor Clark

Vermont Gregor is a US-based writer whose love of foreign languages and curiosity about what's around the next bend have taken him to dozens of countries on five continents. Chronic wanderlust has also led him to visit all 50 states and most Canadian provinces on countless road trips through his native North America. Since 2000, Gregor has regularly contributed to Lonely Planet guides, with a focus on Europe and the Americas. Gregor earned his degree in Romance Languages at Stanford University and has remained an avid linguist throughout careers in publishing, teaching, translation and tour leadership. Gregor also wrote the Plan Your Trip, Understand New England and Survival Guide chapters.

Adam Karlin

Maine Adam has contributed to dozens of Lonely Planet guidebooks, covering an alphabetical spread that ranges from the Andaman Islands to the Zimbabwe border. As a journalist, he has written on travel, crime, politics, archaeology and the Sri Lankan Civil War, among other topics. He has sent dispatches from every continent barring Antarctica (one day!) and his essays and articles have featured in the BBC, NPR and multiple nonfiction anthologies. Adam is based out of New Orleans, which helps explain his love of wetlands, food and good music. Learn more at http://walkonfine.com or follow on Instagram @adamwalkonfine.

Brian Kluepfel

Connecticut Brian lived in three states and seven different residences by the time he was nine, and just kept moving, making stops in Berkeley, Bolivia, the Bronx and the 'burbs further down the line. His journalistic work across the Americas has ranged from the Copa America soccer tournament in Paraguay to an accordion festival in Quebec. His titles for Lonely Planet include *Venezuela, Costa Rica, Belize & Guatemala, Bolivia* and *Ecuador*. He's an avid birder and musician and dabbles in both on the road.

Regis St Louis

Maine Regis grew up in a small town in the American Midwest – the kind of place that fuels big dreams of travel – and he developed an early fascination with foreign dialects and world cultures. He spent his formative years learning Russian and a handful of Romance languages, which served him well on journeys across much of the globe. Regis has contributed to more than 50 Lonely Planet titles, covering destinations across six continents. His travels have taken him from the mountains of Kamchatka to remote island villages in Melanesia, and to many grand urban landscapes. When not on the road, he lives in New Orleans.

Mara Vorhees

Boston, Massachusetts Mara writes about food, travel and family fun around the world. Her work has been published by *BBC Travel, Boston Globe, Delta Sky,* the *Vancouver Sun* and more. For Lonely Planet, she regularly writes about destinations in Central America and Eastern Europe, as well as New England, where she lives. She often travels with her twin boys in tow, earning her expertise in family travel. Follow their adventures and misadventures at www.havetwinswilltravel.com.

OUR STORY

A beat-up old car, a few dollars in the pocket and a sense of adventure. In 1972 that's all Tony and Maureen Wheeler needed for the trip of a lifetime – across Europe and Asia overland to Australia. It took several months, and at the end – broke but inspired – they sat at their kitchen table writing and stapling together their first travel guide, *Across Asia on the Cheap*. Within a week they'd sold 1500 copies. Lonely Planet was born.

Today, Lonely Planet has offices in the US, Ireland and China, with a network of over 2000 contributors in every corner of the globe. We share Tony's belief that 'a great guidebook should do three things: inform, educate and amuse'.

OUR WRITERS

Benedict Walker

Rhode Island Born in Newcastle, Australia, Ben holds notions of the beach core to his idea of self, though he's traveled thousands of miles from the sandy shores of home to live in Leipzig, Germany. Ben was given his first Lonely Planet guide when he was 12. Two decades later, he'd write chapters for the same publication: a dream come true. A communications graduate and travel agent by trade, Ben whittled away his twenties gallivanting around the globe. He thinks the best thing about travel isn't as much where you go as who you meet: living vicariously through the stories of kind strangers enriches one's own experience. Come along for the ride on Instagram @wordsandjourneys.

Isabel Albiston

Massachusetts After six years working for the *Daily Telegraph* in London, Isabel left to spend more time on the road. A job as a writer for a magazine in Sydney, Australia, was followed by a four-month overland trip across Asia and five years living and working in Buenos Aires, Argentina. Isabel started writing for Lonely Planet in 2014 and has contributed to 12 guidebooks. She's currently based in Ireland.

Amy C Balfour

New Hampshire Amy practiced law in Virginia before moving to Los Angeles to try to break in as a screenwriter. After a stint as a writer's assistant on *Law & Order,* she jumped into freelance writing, focusing on travel, food and the outdoors. She has hiked, biked and paddled across Southern California and the Southwest. Books authored or co-authored include Lonely Planet's *Pocket Los Angeles, Los Angeles & Southern California, Caribbean Islands, California, California's Best Trips, USA, USA's Best Trips* and *Arizona*.

Robert Balkovich

Massachusetts Robert was born and raised in Oregon, but has called New York City home for almost a decade. When he was a child and other families were going to theme parks and grandma's house, he went to Mexico City and toured Eastern Europe by train. He's now a writer and travel enthusiast seeking experiences that are ever so slightly out of the ordinary to report back on. Follow on Instagram @oh_balky.

OVER PAGE / MORE WRITERS

Published by Lonely Planet Global Limited
CRN 554153
10th edition – Aug 2022
ISBN 978 1 78868 457 6
© Lonely Planet 2022   Photographs © as indicated 2022
10 9 8 7 6 5 4 3 2 1
Printed in Singapore